Blackstone's Statutes on

COMPANY LAW

Blackstone's Statutes on
COMPANY LAW

Edited by

Derek French

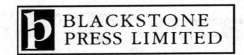

BLACKSTONE
PRESS LIMITED

First published in Great Britain 1997 by Blackstone Press Limited,
Aldine Place, London W12 8AA. Telephone 0181-740 2277

© Derek French, 1997
Second edition, 1998

ISBN: 1 85431 799 7

British Library Cataloguing in Publication Data.
A CIP catalogue record for this book is available from the British Library

Typeset by Montage Studios Limited, Tonbridge, Kent
Printed by Livesey Limited, Shrewsbury, Shropshire

CONTENTS

EDITOR'S PREFACE

This book provides the text of the main statutes and statutory instruments concerning company law in England and Wales. The selection should provide all the legislation that is required for degree-level courses in company law, including courses that cover company insolvency. To keep the book to a handy size, provisions relating only to banking, insurance and oversea companies have been omitted, and there is only a representative sample from the detailed schedule on accounting requirements.

The text of all legislation incorporates all amendments and repeals in force on 29 July 1998. At the end of the book there is a list of sources of amendments so that the legislative history of any provision can be investigated if necessary.

Enactments which had not been brought into force by 29 July 1998 are printed in italics. Where a provision is subject to an amendment or repeal that has not been brought into force (or is only in force for certain purposes), the text of the provision currently in force is printed, accompanied by a note of relevant amendments and repeals. The Department of Trade and Industry has indicated that several amendments made by the Companies Act 1989 will not be brought into force. The text of those amendments is set out under the heading 'Companies Act 1989'.

The legislation on companies has been attacked for its length and complexity. One of the tasks of the long review of company law announced by the Department of Trade and Industry in March 1998 is to consider the structure and drafting of this legislation. However, that review is not expected to result in a new Companies Act until 2002 at the earliest. It is easy to be impatient with the tedious length of the present companies legislation, but my own view is that nearly all of it is clearly and accurately expressed, within the style of legislative drafting generally used in this country. There are, though, occasional lapses into unintelligibility through excessive compression, such as the second sentence of the Companies Act 1985, s. 44(5), and note 10 to the balance sheet formats in sch. 4 to that Act. There are also some minor drafting anomalies, which are indicated in notes at appropriate points in this book and have been communicated to the Department of Trade and Industry.

The significant problem with the drafting of this, and all UK legislation is the insistence on using only masculine pronouns. In legislation, though not in real life, all company directors, auditors, liquidators, official receivers and so on are 'he'. It is to be hoped that this country will join Australia in abandoning this drafting convention.

In this edition I have incorporated all legislative amendments made since the previous edition, and, in response to requests from users, I have included more of the Financial Services Act 1986.

If there are any errors in this edition, I must take the blame for not noticing them, but the praise for the accuracy of the text must go to the marvellous typesetting of Linda Murdoch and the meticulous proof reading of the first edition by Debbie Butler.

Derek French
29 July 1998

PART I STATUTES

PARTNERSHIP ACT 1890
(53 & 54 Vict., c. 39)

An Act to declare and amend the Law of Partnership.   [14 August 1890]

Nature of Partnership

1. Definition of partnership.
(1) Partnership is the relation which subsists between persons carrying on a business in common with a view of profit.

(2) But the relation between members of any company or association which is—

(a) Registered as a company under the Companies Act 1862, or any other Act of Parliament for the time being in force and relating to the registration of joint stock companies; or

(b) Formed or incorporated by or in pursuance of any other Act of Parliament or letters patent, or Royal Charter; or

(c) A company engaged in working mines within and subject to the jurisdiction of the Stannaries;

is not a partnership within the meaning of this Act.

2. Rules for determining existence of partnership.
In determining whether a partnership does or does not exist, regard shall be had to the following rules:

(1) Joint tenancy, tenancy in common, joint property, common property, or part ownership does not of itself create a partnership as to anything so held or owned, whether the tenants or owners do or do not share any profits made by the use thereof.

(2) The sharing of gross returns does not of itself create a partnership, whether the persons sharing such returns have or have not a joint or common right or interest in any property from which or from the use of which the returns are derived.

(3) The receipt by a person of a share of the profits of a business is prima facie evidence that he is a partner in the business, but the receipt of such a share, or of a payment contingent on or varying with the profits of a business, does not of itself make him a partner in the business; and in particular—

(a) The receipt by a person of a debt or other liquidated amount by instalments or otherwise out of the accruing profits of a business does not of itself make him a partner in the business or liable as such:

(b) A contract for the remuneration of a servant or agent of a person engaged in a business by a share of the profits of the business does not of itself make the servant or agent a partner in the business or liable as such:

(c) A person being the widow or child of a deceased partner, and receiving by way of annuity a portion of the profits made in the business in which the deceased person was a partner, is not by reason only of such receipt a partner in the business or liable as such:

(d) The advance of money by way of loan to a person engaged or about to engage in any business on a contract with that person that the lender shall receive a rate of interest varying with the profits, or shall receive a share of the profits arising from carrying on the business, does not of itself make the lender a partner with the person or persons carrying on the business or liable as such. Provided that the contract is in writing, and signed by or on behalf of all the parties thereto:

(e) A person receiving by way of annuity or otherwise a portion of the profits of a business in consideration of the sale by him of the goodwill of the business is not by reason only of such receipt a partner in the business or liable as such.

3. Postponement of rights of person lending or selling in consideration of share of profits in case of insolvency.
In the event of any person to whom money has been advanced by way of loan upon such a contract as is mentioned in the last foregoing section, or of any buyer of a goodwill in consideration of a share of the profits of the business, being adjudged a bankrupt, entering into an arrangement to pay his creditors less than [100p] in the pound, or dying in insolvent circumstances, the lender of the loan shall not be entitled to recover anything in respect of his loan, and the seller of the goodwill shall not be entitled to recover anything in respect of the share of profits contracted for, until the claims of the other creditors of the borrower or buyer for valuable consideration in money or money's worth have been satisfied.

4. Meaning of firm.
(1) Persons who have entered into partnership with one another are for the purposes of this Act called collectively a firm, and the name under which their business is carried on is called the firm-name.

(2) In Scotland a firm is a legal person distinct from the partners of whom it is composed, but an individual partner may be charged on a decree or diligence directed against the firm, and on payment of the debts is entitled to relief pro rata from the firm and its other members.

Relations of Partners to persons dealing with them

5. Power of partner to bind the firm.
Every partner is an agent of the firm and his other partners for the purpose of the business of the partnership; and the acts of every partner who does any act for carrying on in the usual way business of the kind carried on by the firm of which he is a member bind the firm and his partners, unless the partner so acting has in fact no authority to act for the firm in the particular matter, and the person with whom he is dealing either knows that he has no authority, or does not know or believe him to be a partner.

6. Partners bound by acts on behalf of firm.
An act or instrument relating to the business of the firm and done or executed in the firm-name, or in any other manner showing an intention to bind the firm, by any person thereto authorised, whether a partner or not, is binding on the firm and all the partners.

Provided that this section shall not affect any general rule of law relating to the execution of deeds or negotiable instruments.

7. Partner using credit of firm for private purposes.
Where one partner pledges the credit of the firm for a purpose apparently not connected with the firm's ordinary course of business, the firm is not bound, unless he is in fact specially authorised by the other partners; but this section does not affect any personal liability incurred by an individual partner.

8. Effect of notice that firm will not be bound by acts of partner.
If it has been agreed between the partners that any restriction shall be placed on the power of any one or more of them to bind the firm, no act done in contravention of the agreement is binding on the firm with respect to persons having notice of the agreement.

9.   Liability of partners.

Every partner in a firm is liable jointly with the other partners, and in Scotland severally also, for all debts and obligations of the firm incurred while he is a partner; and after his death his estate is also severally liable in a due course of administration for such debts and obligations, so far as they remain unsatisfied, but subject in England or [Northern Ireland] to the prior payment of his separate debts.

10.   Liability of the firm for wrongs.

Where, by any wrongful act or omission of any partner acting in the ordinary course of the business of the firm, or with the authority of his co-partners, loss or injury is caused to any person not being a partner in the firm, or any penalty is incurred, the firm is liable therefor to the same extent as the partner so acting or omitting to act.

11.   Misapplication of money or property received for or in custody of the firm.

In the following cases; namely—

(a)   Where one partner acting within the scope of his apparent authority receives the money or property of a third person and misapplies it; and

(b)   Where a firm in the course of its business receives money or property of a third person, and the money or property so received is misapplied by one or more of the partners while it is in the custody of the firm;

the firm is liable to make good the loss.

12.   Liability for wrongs joint and several.

Every partner is liable jointly with his co-partners and also severally for everything for which the firm while he is a partner therein becomes liable under either of the two last preceding sections.

13.   Improper employment of trust-property for partnership purposes.

If a partner, being a trustee, improperly employs trust-property in the business or on the account of the partnership, no other partner is liable for the trust-property to the persons beneficially interested therein.

Provided as follows:—

(1)   This section shall not affect any liability incurred by any partner by reason of his having notice of a breach of trust; and

(2)   Nothing in this section shall prevent trust money from being followed and recovered from the firm if still in its possession or under its control.

14.   Persons liable by 'holding out'.

(1)   Every one who by words spoken or written or by conduct represents himself, or who knowingly suffers himself to be represented, as a partner in a particular firm, is liable as a partner to any one who has on the faith of any such representation given credit to the firm, whether the representation has or has not been made or communicated to the person so giving credit by or with the knowledge of the apparent partner making the representation or suffering it to be made.

(2)   Provided that where after a partner's death the partnership business is continued in the old firm-name, the continued use of that name or of the deceased partner's name as part thereof shall not of itself make his executors or administrators estate or effects liable for any partnership debts contracted after his death.

15.   Admissions and representations of partners.

An admission or representation made by any partner concerning the partnership affairs, and in the ordinary course of its business, is evidence against the firm.

16. Notice to acting partner to be notice to the firm.
Notice to any partner who habitually acts in the partnership business of any matter relating to partnership affairs operates as notice to the firm, except in the case of a fraud on the firm committed by or with the consent of that partner.

17. Liabilities of incoming and outgoing partners.
(1) A person who is admitted as a partner into an existing firm does not thereby become liable to the creditors of the firm for anything done before he became a partner.

(2) A partner who retires from a firm does not thereby cease to be liable for partnership debts or obligations incurred before his retirement.

(3) A retiring partner may be discharged from any existing liabilities, by an agreement to that effect between himself and the members of the firm as newly constituted and the creditors, and this agreement may be either express or inferred as a fact from the course of dealing between the creditors and the firm as newly constituted.

18. Revocation of continuing guaranty by change in firm.
A continuing guaranty or cautionary obligation given either to a firm or to a third person in respect of the transactions of a firm is, in the absence of agreement to the contrary, revoked as to future transactions by any change in the constitution of the firm to which, or of the firm in respect of the transactions of which, the guaranty or obligation was given.

Relations of Partners to one another

19. Variation by consent of terms of partnership.
The mutual rights and duties of partners, whether ascertained by agreement or defined by this Act, may be varied by the consent of all the partners, and such consent may be either express or inferred from a course of dealing.

20. Partnership property.
(1) All property and rights and interests in property originally brought into the partnership stock or acquired, whether by purchase or otherwise, on account of the firm, or for the purposes and in the course of the partnership business, are called in this Act partnership property, and must be held and applied by the partners exclusively for the purposes of the partnership and in accordance with the partnership agreement.

(2) Provided that the legal estate or interest in any land, or in Scotland the title to and interest in any heritable estate, which belongs to the partnership shall devolve according to the nature and tenure thereof, and the general rules of law thereto applicable, but in trust, so far as necessary, for the persons beneficially interested in the land under this section.

(3) Where co-owners of an estate or interest in any land, or in Scotland of any heritable estate, not being itself partnership property, are partners as to profits made by the use of that land or estate, and purchase other land or estate out of the profits to be used in like manner, the land or estate so purchased belongs to them, in the absence of an agreement to the contrary, not as partners, but as co-owners for the same respective estates and interests as are held by them in the land or estate first mentioned at the date of the purchase.

21. Property bought with partnership money.
Unless the contrary intention appears, property bought with money belonging to the firm is deemed to have been bought on account of the firm.

23. Procedure against partnership property for a partner's separate judgment debt.
(1) A writ of execution shall not issue against any partnership property except on a judgment against the firm.

(2)   The High Court, or a judge thereof, or a county court, may, on the application by summons of any judgment creditor of a partner, make an order charging that partner's interest in the partnership property and profits with payment of the amount of the judgment debt and interest thereon, and may by the same or a subsequent order appoint a receiver of that partner's share of profits (whether already declared or accruing), and of any other money which may be coming to him in respect of the partnership, and direct all accounts and inquiries, and give all other orders and directions which might have been directed or given if the charge had been made in favour of the judgment creditor by the partner, or which the circumstances of the case may require.

(3)   The other partner or partners shall be at liberty at any time to redeem the interest charged, or in case of a sale being directed, to purchase the same.

(4)   This section shall apply in the case of a cost-book company as if the company were a partnership within the meaning of this Act.

(5)   This section shall not apply to Scotland.

24.   Rules as to interests and duties of partners subject to special agreement.

The interests of partners in the partnership property and their rights and duties in relation to the partnership shall be determined, subject to any agreement express or implied between the partners, by the following rules:

(1)   All the partners are entitled to share equally in the capital and profits of the business, and must contribute equally towards the losses whether of capital or otherwise sustained by the firm.

(2)   The firm must indemnify every partner in respect of payments made and personal liabilities incurred by him—

(a)   In the ordinary and proper conduct of the business of the firm; or,

(b)   In or about anything necessarily done for the preservation of the business or property of the firm.

(3)   A partner making, for the purpose of the partnership, any actual payment or advance beyond the amount of capital which he has agreed to subscribe, is entitled to interest at the rate of five per cent per annum from the date of the payment or advance.

(4)   A partner is not entitled, before the ascertainment of profits, to interest on the capital subscribed by him.

(5)   Every partner may take part in the management of the partnership business.

(6)   No partner shall be entitled to remuneration for acting in the partnership business.

(7)   No person may be introduced as a partner without the consent of all existing partners.

(8)   Any difference arising as to ordinary matters connected with the partnership business may be decided by a majority of the partners, but no change may be made in the nature of the partnership business without the consent of all existing partners.

(9)   The partnership books are to be kept at the place of business of the partnership (or the principal place, if there is more than one), and every partner may, when he thinks fit, have access to and inspect and copy any of them.

25.   Expulsion of partner.

No majority of the partners can expel any partner unless a power to do so has been conferred by express agreement between the partners.

26.   Retirement from partnership at will.

(1)   Where no fixed term has been agreed upon for the duration of the partnership, any partner may determine the partnership at any time on giving notice of his intention so to do to all the other partners.

(2)   Where the partnership has originally been constituted by deed, a notice in writing, signed by the partner giving it, shall be sufficient for this purpose.

27. Where partnership for term is continued over, continuance on old terms presumed.

(1) Where a partnership entered into for a fixed term is continued after the term has expired, and without any express new agreement, the rights and duties of the partners remain the same as they were at the expiration of the term, so far as is consistent with the incidents of a partnership at will.

(2) A continuance of the business by the partners or such of them as habitually acted therein during the term, without any settlement or liquidation of the partnership affairs, is presumed to be a continuance of the partnership.

28. Duty of partners to render accounts, &c.

Partners are bound to render true accounts and full information of all things affecting the partnership to any partner or his legal representatives.

29. Accountability of partners for private profits.

(1) Every partner must account to the firm for any benefit derived by him without the consent of the other partners from any transaction concerning the partnership, or from any use by him of the partnership property name or business connection.

(2) This section applies also to transactions undertaken after a partnership has been dissolved by the death of a partner, and before the affairs thereof have been completely wound up, either by any surviving partner or by the representatives of the deceased partner.

30. Duty of partner not to compete with firm.

If a partner, without the consent of the other partners, carries on any business of the same nature as and competing with that of the firm, he must account for and pay over to the firm all profits made by him in that business.

31. Rights of assignee of share in partnership.

(1) An assignment by any partner of his share in the partnership, either absolute or by way of mortgage or redeemable charge, does not, as against the other partners, entitle the assignee, during the continuance of the partnership, to interfere in the management or administration of the partnership business or affairs, or to require any accounts of the partnership transactions, or to inspect the partnership books, but entitles the assignee only to receive the share of profits to which the assigning partner would otherwise be entitled, and the assignee must accept the account of profits agreed to by the partners.

(2) In case of a dissolution of the partnership, whether as respects all the partners or as respects the assigning partner, the assignee is entitled to receive the share of the partnership assets to which the assigning partner is entitled as between himself and the other partners, and, for the purpose of ascertaining that share, to an account as from the date of the dissolution.

Dissolution of Partnership, and its consequences

32. Dissolution by expiration or notice.

Subject to any agreement between the partners, a partnership is dissolved—

(a) If entered into for a fixed term, by the expiration of that term:

(b) If entered into for a single adventure or undertaking, by the termination of that adventure or undertaking:

(c) If entered into for an undefined time, by any partner giving notice to the other or others of his intention to dissolve the partnership.

In the last-mentioned case the partnership is dissolved as from the date mentioned in the notice as the date of dissolution, or, if no date is so mentioned, as from the date of the communication of the notice.

33. Dissolution by bankruptcy, death, or charge.

(1) Subject to any agreement between the partners, every partnership is dissolved as regards all the partners by the death or bankruptcy of any partner.

(2) A partnership may, at the option of the other partners, be dissolved if any partner suffers his share of the partnership property to be charged under this Act for his separate debt.

34. Dissolution by illegality of partnership.

A partnership is in every case dissolved by the happening of any event which makes it unlawful for the business of the firm to be carried on or for the members of the firm to carry it on in partnership.

35. Dissolution by the Court.

On application by a partner the Court may decree a dissolution of the partnership in any of the following cases:

(b) When a partner, other than the partner suing, becomes in any other way permanently incapable of performing his part of the partnership contract:

(c) When a partner, other than the partner suing, has been guilty of such conduct as, in the opinion of the Court, regard being had to the nature of the business, is calculated to prejudicially affect the carrying on of the business:

(d) When a partner, other than the partner suing, wilfully or persistently commits a breach of the partnership agreement, or otherwise so conducts himself in matters relating to the partnership business that it is not reasonably practicable for the other partner or partners to carry on the business in partnership with him:

(e) When the business of the partnership can only be carried on at a loss:

(f) Whenever in any case circumstances have arisen which, in the opinion of the Court, render it just and equitable that the partnership be dissolved.

36. Rights of persons dealing with firm against apparent members of firm.

(1) Where a person deals with a firm after a change in its constitution he is entitled to treat all apparent members of the old firm as still being members of the firm until he has notice of the change.

(2) An advertisement in the London Gazette as to a firm whose principal place of business is in England or Wales, in the Edinburgh Gazette as to a firm whose principal place of business is in Scotland, and in the [Belfast Gazette] as to a firm whose principal place of business is in [Northern Ireland], shall be notice as to persons who had not dealings with the firm before the date of the dissolution or change so advertised.

(3) The estate of a partner who dies, or who becomes bankrupt, or of a partner who, not having been known to the person dealing with the firm to be a partner, retires from the firm, is not liable for partnership debts contracted after the date of the death, bankruptcy, or retirement respectively.

37. Right of partners to notify dissolution.

On the dissolution of a partnership or retirement of a partner any partner may publicly notify the same, and may require the other partner or partners to concur for that purpose in all necessary or proper acts, if any, which cannot be done without his or their concurrence.

38. Continuing authority of partners for purposes of winding up.

After the dissolution of a partnership the authority of each partner to bind the firm, and the other rights and obligations of the partners, continue notwithstanding the dissolution so far as may be necessary to wind up the affairs of the partnership, and to complete transactions begun but unfinished at the time of the dissolution, but not otherwise.

Provided that the firm is in no case bound by the acts of a partner who has become bankrupt; but this proviso does not affect the liability of any person who has after the bankruptcy represented himself or knowingly suffered himself to be represented as a partner of the bankrupt.

39. Rights of partners as to application of partnership property.

On the dissolution of a partnership every partner is entitled, as against the other partners in the firm, and all persons claiming through them in respect of their interests as partners, to have the property of the partnership applied in payment of the debts and liabilities of the firm, and to have the surplus assets after such payment applied in payment of what may be due to the partners respectively after deducting what may be due from them as partners to the firm; and for that purpose any partner or his representatives may on the termination of the partnership apply to the Court to wind up the business and affairs of the firm.

40. Apportionment of premium where partnership prematurely dissolved.

Where one partner has paid a premium to another on entering into a partnership for a fixed term, and the partnership is dissolved before the expiration of that term otherwise than by the death of a partner, the Court may order the repayment of the premium, or of such part thereof as it thinks just, having regard to the terms of the partnership contract and to the length of time during which the partnership has continued; unless

(a) the dissolution is, in the judgment of the Court, wholly or chiefly due to the misconduct of the partner who paid the premium, or

(b) the partnership has been dissolved by an agreement containing no provision for a return of any part of the premium.

41. Rights where partnership dissolved for fraud or misrepresentation.

Where a partnership contract is rescinded on the ground of the fraud or misrepresentation of one of the parties thereto, the party entitled to rescind is, without prejudice to any other right, entitled—

(a) to a lien on, or right of retention of, the surplus of the partnership assets, after satisfying the partnership liabilities, for any sum of money paid by him for the purchase of a share in the partnership and for any capital contributed by him, and is

(b) to stand in the place of the creditors of the firm for any payments made by him in respect of the partnership liabilities, and

(c) to be indemnified by the person guilty of the fraud or making the representation against all the debts and liabilities of the firm.

42. Right of outgoing partner in certain cases to share profits made after dissolution.

(1) Where any member of a firm has died or otherwise ceased to be a partner, and the surviving or continuing partners carry on the business of the firm with its capital or assets without any final settlement of accounts as between the firm and the outgoing partner or his estate, then, in the absence of any agreement to the contrary, the outgoing partner or his estate is entitled at the option of himself or his representatives to such share of the profits made since the dissolution as the Court may find to be attributable to the use of his share of the partnership assets, or to interest at the rate of five per cent per annum on the amount of his share of the partnership assets.

(2) Provided that where by the partnership contract an option is given to surviving or continuing partners to purchase the interest of a deceased or outgoing partner, and that option is duly exercised, the estate of the deceased partner, or the outgoing partner or his estate, as the case may be, is not entitled to any further or other share of profits; but if any partner assuming to act in exercise of the option does not in all material respects comply with the terms thereof, he is liable to account under the foregoing provisions of this section.

43. Retiring or deceased partner's share to be a debt.

Subject to any agreement between the partners, the amount due from surviving or continuing partners to an outgoing partner or the representatives of a deceased partner in respect of the outgoing or deceased partner's share is a debt accruing at the date of the dissolution or death.

44. Rule for distribution of assets on final settlement of accounts.

In settling accounts between the partners after a dissolution of partnership, the following rules shall, subject to any agreement, be observed:

(a) Losses, including losses and deficiencies of capital, shall be paid first out of profits, next out of capital, and lastly, if necessary, by the partners individually in the proportion in which they were entitled to share profits:

(b) The assets of the firm including the sums, if any, contributed by the partners to make up losses or deficiencies of capital, shall be applied in the following manner and order:

1. In paying the debts and liabilities of the firm to persons who are not partners therein:

2. In paying to each partner rateably what is due from the firm to him for advances as distinguished from capital:

3. In paying to each partner rateably what is due from the firm to him in respect of capital:

4. The ultimate residue, if any, shall be divided among the partners in the proportion in which profits are divisible.

Supplemental

45. Definitions of 'court' and 'business'.

In this Act, unless the contrary intention appears,—

The expression 'court' includes every court and judge having jurisdiction in the case;

The expression 'business' includes every trade, occupation, or profession.

46. Saving for rules of equity and common law.

The rules of equity and of common law applicable to partnership shall continue in force except so far as they are inconsistent with the express provisions of this Act.

50. Short title.

This Act may be cited as the Partnership Act 1890.

STOCK TRANSFER ACT 1963
(1963, c. 18)

An Act to amend the law with respect to the transfer of securities.   [10 July 1963]

1. Simplified transfer of securities.

(1) Registered securities to which this section applies may be transferred by means of an instrument under hand in the form set out in Schedule 1 to this Act (in this Act referred to as a stock transfer), executed by the transferor only and specifying (in addition to the particulars of the consideration, of the description and number or amount of the securities, and of the person by whom the transfer is made) the full name and address of the transferee.

(2) The execution of a stock transfer need not be attested; and where such a transfer has been executed for the purpose of a stock exchange transaction, the particulars of the consideration and of the transferee may either be inserted in that transfer or, as the case may require, supplied by means of separate instruments in the form set out in Schedule 2 to this Act (in this Act referred to as brokers transfers), identifying the stock transfer and specifying the securities to which each such instrument relates and the consideration paid for those securities.

(3)   Nothing in this section shall be construed as affecting the validity of any instrument which would be effective to transfer securities apart from this section; and any instrument purporting to be made in any form which was common or usual before the commencement of this Act, or in any other form authorised or required for that purpose apart from this section, shall be sufficient, whether or not it is completed in accordance with the form, if it complies with the requirements as to execution and contents which apply to a stock transfer.

(4)   This section applies to fully paid up registered securities of any description, being—

(a)   securities issued by any company within the meaning of the Companies Act 1985 except a company limited by guarantee or an unlimited company;

. . .

2.   Supplementary provisions as to simplified transfer.

(1)   Section 1 of this Act shall have effect in relation to the transfer of any securities to which that section applies notwithstanding anything to the contrary in any enactment or instrument relating to the transfer of those securities; but nothing in that section affects—

(a)   any right to refuse to register a person as the holder of any securities on any ground other than the form in which those securities purport to be transferred to him: or

(b)   any enactment or rule of law regulating the execution of documents by companies or other bodies corporate, or any articles of association or other instrument regulating the execution of documents by any particular company or body corporate.

(2)   Subject to the provisions of this section, any enactment or instrument relating to the transfer of securities to which section 1 of this Act applies shall, with any necessary modifications, apply in relation to an instrument of transfer authorised by that section as it applies in relation to an instrument of transfer to which it applies apart from this subsection; and without prejudice to the generality of the foregoing provision, the reference in section 184 of the Companies Act 1985 (certification of transfers) to any instrument of transfer shall be construed as including a reference to a brokers transfer.

(3)   In relation to the transfer of securities by means of a stock transfer and a brokers transfer—

(a)   any reference in any enactment or instrument (including in particular section 183(1) and (2) of the Companies Act 1985 *and section 56(4) of the Finance Act 1946*) to the delivery or lodging of an instrument (or proper instrument) of transfer shall be construed as a reference to the delivery or lodging of the stock transfer and the brokers transfer;

(b)   any such reference to the date on which an instrument of transfer is delivered or lodged shall be construed as a reference to the date by which the later of those transfers to be delivered or lodged has been delivered or lodged; *and*

(c)   subject to the foregoing provisions of this subsection, the brokers transfer (and not the stock transfer) shall be deemed to be the conveyance or transfer for the purposes of the enactments relating to stamp duty.

. . .

[*The words in italics will be repealed when the relevant provisions of the Finance Act 1990, sch. 19, part VI, are brought into force.*]

3.   Additional provisions as to transfer forms.

(1)   References in this Act to the forms set out in Schedule 1 and Schedule 2 include references to forms substantially corresponding to those forms respectively.

(2)   The Treasury may by order amend the said Schedules either by altering the forms set out therein or by substituting different forms for those forms or by the addition of forms for use as alternatives to those forms; and references in this Act to the forms set out in those Schedules (including references in this section) shall be construed accordingly.

(3) Any order under subsection (2) of this section which substitutes a different form for a form set out in Schedule 1 to this Act may direct that subsection (3) of section 1 of this Act shall apply, with any necessary modifications, in relation to the form for which that form is substituted as it applies to any form which was common or usual before the commencement of this Act.

(4) Any order of the Treasury under this section shall be made by statutory instrument, and may be varied or revoked by a subsequent order; and any statutory instrument made by virtue of this section shall be subject to annulment in pursuance of a resolution of either House of Parliament.

(5) An order under subsection (2) of this section may—

(a) provide for forms on which some of the particulars mentioned in subsection (1) of section 1 of this Act are not required to be specified;

(b) provide for that section to have effect, in relation to such forms as are mentioned in the preceding paragraph or other forms specified in the order, subject to such amendments as are so specified (which may include an amendment of the reference in subsection (1) of that section to an instrument under hand);

(c) provide for all or any of the provisions of the order to have effect in such cases only as are specified in the order.

4. Interpretation.

(1) In this Act the following expressions have the meanings hereby respectively assigned to them, that is to say—

. . .

'registered securities' means transferable securities the holders of which are entered in a register (whether maintained in Great Britain or not);

'securities' means shares, stock, debentures, debenture stock, loan stock, bonds, units of a collective investment scheme within the meaning of the Financial Services Act 1986, and other securities of any description;

'stock exchange transaction' means a sale and purchase of securities in which each of the parties is a member of a stock exchange acting in the ordinary course of his business as such or is acting through the agency of such a member;

'stock exchange' means the Stock Exchange, London, and any other stock exchange (whether in Great Britain or not) which is declared by order of the Treasury to be a recognised stock exchange for the purposes of this Act.

(2) Any order of the Treasury under this section shall be made by statutory instrument, and may be varied or revoked by a subsequent order.

6. Short title and commencement.

(1) This Act may be cited as the Stock Transfer Act 1963.

. . .

COMPANIES ACT 1985
(1985, c. 6)

An Act to consolidate the greater part of the Companies Acts   [11 March 1985]

PART I
FORMATION AND REGISTRATION OF COMPANIES; JURIDICAL STATUS AND MEMBERSHIP
CHAPTER I
COMPANY FORMATION

Memorandum of association

1. Mode of forming incorporated company.

(1) Any two or more persons associated for a lawful purpose may, by subscribing their names to a memorandum of association and otherwise complying with the

requirements of this Act in respect of registration, form an incorporated company, with or without limited liability.

(2)   A company so formed may be either—

    (a)   a company having the liability of its members limited by the memorandum to the amount, if any, unpaid on the shares respectively held by them ('a company limited by shares');

    (b)   a company having the liability of its members limited by the memorandum to such amount as the members may respectively thereby undertake to contribute to the assets of the company in the event of its being wound up ('a company limited by guarantee'); or

    (c)   a company not having any limit on the liability of its members ('an unlimited company').

(3)   A 'public company' is a company limited by shares or limited by guarantee and having a share capital, being a company—

    (a)   the memorandum of which states that it is to be a public company, and

    (b)   in relation to which the provisions of this Act or the former Companies Acts as to the registration or re-registration of a company as a public company have been complied with on or after 22 December 1980;

and a 'private company' is a company that is not a public company.

(3A)   Notwithstanding subsection (1), one person may, for a lawful purpose, by subscribing his name to a memorandum of association and otherwise complying with the requirements of this Act in respect of registration, form an incorporated company being a private company limited by shares or by guarantee.

(4)   With effect from 22 December 1980, a company cannot be formed as, or become, a company limited by guarantee with a share capital.

2.   Requirements with respect to memorandum.

(1)   The memorandum of every company must state—

    (a)   the name of the company;

    (b)   whether the registered office of the company is to be situated in England and Wales, or in Scotland;

    (c)   the objects of the company.

(2)   Alternatively to subsection (1)(b), the memorandum may contain a statement that the company's registered office is to be situated in Wales; and a company whose registered office is situated in Wales may by special resolution alter its memorandum so as to provide that its registered office is to be so situated.

(3)   The memorandum of a company limited by shares or by guarantee must also state that the liability of its members is limited.

(4)   The memorandum of a company limited by guarantee must also state that each member undertakes to contribute to the assets of the company if it should be wound up while he is a member, or within one year after he ceases to be a member, for payment of the debts and liabilities of the company contracted before he ceases to be a member, and of the costs, charges and expenses of winding up, and for adjustment of the rights of the contributories among themselves, such amount as may be required, not exceeding a specified amount.

(5)   In the case of a company having a share capital—

    (a)   the memorandum must also (unless it is an unlimited company) state the amount of the share capital with which the company proposes to be registered and the division of the share capital into shares of a fixed amount;

    (b)   no subscriber of the memorandum may take less than one share; and

    (c)   there must be shown in the memorandum against the name of each subscriber the number of shares he takes.

(6)   The memorandum must be signed by each subscriber in the presence of at least one witness, who must attest the signature. . . .

(7)   A company may not alter the conditions contained in its memorandum except in the cases, in the mode and to the extent, for which express provision is made by this Act.

3.   Forms of memorandum.

(1)   Subject to the provisions of sections 1 and 2, the form of the memorandum of association of—

    (a)   a public company, being a company limited by shares,

    (b)   a public company, being a company limited by guarantee and having a share capital,

    (c)   a private company limited by shares,

    (d)   a private company limited by guarantee and not having a share capital,

    (e)   a private company limited by guarantee and having a share capital, and

    (f)   an unlimited company having a share capital,

shall be as specified respectively for such companies by regulations made by the Secretary of State, or as near to that form as circumstances admit.

(2)   Regulations under this section shall be made by statutory instrument subject to annulment in pursuance of a resolution of either House of Parliament.

3A.   Statement of company's objects: general commercial company.

Where the company's memorandum states that the object of the company is to carry on business as a general commercial company—

    (a)   the object of the company is to carry on any trade or business whatsoever, and

    (b)   the company has power to do all such things as are incidental or conducive to the carrying on of any trade or business by it.

4.   Resolution to alter objects.

(1)   A company may by special resolution alter its memorandum with respect to the statement of the company's objects.

(2)   If an application is made under the following section, an alteration does not have effect except in so far as it is confirmed by the court.

5.   Procedure for objecting to alteration.

(1)   Where a company's memorandum has been altered by special resolution under section 4, application may be made to the court for the alteration to be cancelled.

(2)   Such an application may be made—

    (a)   by the holders of not less in the aggregate than 15 per cent in nominal value of the company's issued share capital or any class of it or, if the company is not limited by shares, not less than 15 per cent of the company's members; or

    (b)   by the holders of not less than 15 per cent of the company's debentures entitling the holders to object to an alteration of its objects;

but an application shall not be made by any person who has consented to or voted in favour of the alteration.

(3)   The application must be made within 21 days after the date on which the resolution altering the company's objects was passed, and may be made on behalf of the persons entitled to make the application by such one or more of their number as they may appoint in writing for the purpose.

(4)   The court may on such an application make an order confirming the alteration either wholly or in part and on such terms and conditions as it thinks fit, and may—

    (a)   if it thinks fit, adjourn the proceedings in order that an arrangement may be made to its satisfaction for the purchase of the interests of dissentient members, and

    (b)   give such directions and make such orders as it thinks expedient for facilitating or carrying into effect any such arrangement.

(5)   The court's order may (if the court thinks fit) provide for the purchase by the company of the shares of any members of the company, and for the reduction

accordingly of its capital, and may make such alterations in the company's memorandum and articles as may be required in consequence of that provision.

(6) If the court's order requires the company not to make any, or any specified, alteration in its memorandum or articles, the company does not then have power without the leave of the court to make any such alteration in breach of that requirement.

(7) An alteration in the memorandum or articles of a company made by virtue of an order under this section, other than one made by resolution of the company, is of the same effect as if duly made by resolution; and this Act applies accordingly to the memorandum or articles as so altered.

(8) The debentures entitling the holders to object to an alteration of a company's objects are any debentures secured by a floating charge which were issued or first issued before 1 December 1947 or form part of the same series as any debentures so issued; and a special resolution altering a company's objects requires the same notice to the holders of any such debentures as to members of the company.

In the absence of provisions regulating the giving of notice to any such debenture holders, the provisions of the company's articles regulating the giving of notice to members apply.

6. Provisions supplementing ss. 4, 5.

(1) Where a company passes a resolution altering its objects, then—

   (a) if with respect to the resolution no application is made under section 5, the company shall within 15 days from the end of the period for making such an application deliver to the registrar of companies a printed copy of its memorandum as altered; and

   (b) if such an application is made, the company shall—

      (i) forthwith give notice (in the prescribed form) of that fact to the registrar, and

      (ii) within 15 days from the date of any order cancelling or confirming the alteration, deliver to the registrar an office copy of the order and, in the case of an order confirming the alteration, a printed copy of the memorandum as altered.

(2) The court may by order at any time extend the time for the delivery of documents to the registrar under subsection (1)(b) for such period as the court may think proper.

(3) If a company makes default in giving notice or delivering any document to the registrar of companies as required by subsection (1), the company and every officer of it who is in default is liable to a fine and, for continued contravention, to a daily default fine.

(4) The validity of an alteration of a company's memorandum with respect to the objects of the company shall not be questioned on the ground that it was not authorised by section 4, except in proceedings taken for the purpose (whether under section 5 or otherwise) before the expiration of 21 days after the date of the resolution in that behalf.

(5) Where such proceedings are taken otherwise than under section 5, subsections (1) to (3) above apply in relation to the proceedings as if they had been taken under that section, and as if an order declaring the alteration invalid were an order cancelling it, and as if an order dismissing the proceedings were an order confirming the alteration.

Articles of association

7. Articles prescribing regulations for companies.

(1) There may in the case of a company limited by shares, and there shall in the case of a company limited by guarantee or unlimited, be registered with the memorandum articles of association signed by the subscribers to the memorandum and prescribing regulations for the company.

(2) In the case of an unlimited company having a share capital, the articles must state the amount of share capital with which the company proposes to be registered.

(3)   Articles must—
   (a)   be printed,
   (b)   be divided into paragraphs numbered consecutively, and
   (c)   be signed by each subscriber of the memorandum in the presence of at least one witness who must attest the signature. . . .

8.   Tables A, C, D and E.

(1)   Table A is as prescribed by regulations made by the Secretary of State; and a company may for its articles adopt the whole or any part of that Table.

(2)   In the case of a company limited by shares, if articles are not registered or, if articles are registered, in so far as they do not exclude or modify Table A, that Table (so far as applicable, and as in force at the date of the company's registration) constitutes the company's articles, in the same manner and to the same extent as if articles in the form of that Table had been duly registered.

(3)   If in consequence of regulations under this section Table A is altered, the alteration does not affect a company registered before the alteration takes effect, or repeal as respects that company any portion of the Table.

(4)   The form of the articles of association of—
   (a)   a company limited by guarantee and not having a share capital,
   (b)   a company limited by guarantee and having a share capital, and
   (c)   an unlimited company having a share capital,
shall be respectively in accordance with Table C, D or E prescribed by regulations made by the Secretary of State, or as near to that form as circumstances admit.

(5)   Regulations under this section shall be made by statutory instrument subject to annulment in pursuance of a resolution of either House of Parliament.

8A.   Table G.

(1)   The Secretary of State may by regulations prescribe a Table G containing articles of association appropriate for a partnership company, that is, a company limited by shares whose shares are intended to be held to a substantial extent by or on behalf of its employees.

(2)   A company limited by shares may for its articles adopt the whole or any part of that Table.

(3)   If in consequence of regulations under this section Table G is altered, the alteration does not affect a company registered before the alteration takes effect, or repeal as respects that company any portion of the Table.

(4)   Regulations under this section shall be made by statutory instrument which shall be subject to annulment in pursuance of a resolution of either House of Parliament.

[*Section 8A will be inserted when the Companies Act 1989, s. 128, is brought into force.*]

9.   Alteration of articles by special resolution.

(1)   Subject to the provisions of this Act and to the conditions contained in its memorandum, a company may by special resolution alter its articles.

(2)   Alterations so made in the articles are (subject to this Act) as valid as if originally contained in them, and are subject in like manner to alteration by special resolution.

Registration and its consequences

10.   Documents to be sent to registrar.

(1)   The company's memorandum and articles (if any) shall be delivered—
   (a)   to the registrar of companies for England and Wales, if the memorandum states that the registered office of the company is to be situated in England and Wales, or that it is to be situated in Wales; and
   (b)   to the registrar of companies for Scotland, if the memorandum states that the registered office of the company is to be situated in Scotland.

(2)   With the memorandum there shall be delivered a statement in the prescribed form containing the names and requisite particulars of—

(a)   the person who is, or the persons who are, to be the first director or directors of the company; and

(b)   the person who is, or the persons who are, to be the first secretary or joint secretaries of the company;

and the requisite particulars in each case are those set out in Schedule 1.

(3)   The statement shall be signed by or on behalf of the subscribers of the memorandum and shall contain a consent signed by each of the persons named in it as a director, as secretary or as one of joint secretaries, to act in the relevant capacity.

(4)   Where a memorandum is delivered by a person as agent for the subscribers, the statement shall specify that fact and the person's name and address.

(5)   An appointment by any articles delivered with the memorandum of a person as director or secretary of the company is void unless he is named as a director or secretary in the statement.

(6)   There shall in the statement be specified the intended situation of the company's registered office on incorporation.

11.   Minimum authorised capital (public companies).

When a memorandum delivered to the registrar of companies under section 10 states that the association to be registered is to be a public company, the amount of the share capital stated in the memorandum to be that with which the company proposes to be registered must not be less than the authorised minimum (defined in section 118).

12.   Duty of registrar.

(1)   The registrar of companies shall not register a company's memorandum delivered under section 10 unless he is satisfied that all the requirements of this Act in respect of registration and of matters precedent and incidental to it have been complied with.

(2)   Subject to this, the registrar shall retain and register the memorandum and articles (if any) delivered to him under that section.

(3)   A statutory declaration in the prescribed form by—

(a)   a solicitor engaged in the formation of a company, or

(b)   a person named as a director or secretary of the company in the statement delivered under section 10(2),

that those requirements have been complied with shall be delivered to the registrar of companies, and the registrar may accept such a declaration as sufficient evidence of compliance.

13.   Effect of registration.

(1)   On the registration of a company's memorandum, the registrar of companies shall give a certificate that the company is incorporated and, in the case of a limited company, that it is limited.

(2)   The certificate may be signed by the registrar, or authenticated by his official seal.

(3)   From the date of incorporation mentioned in the certificate, the subscribers of the memorandum, together with such other persons as may from time to time become members of the company, shall be a body corporate by the name contained in the memorandum.

(4)   That body corporate is then capable forthwith of exercising all the functions of an incorporated company, but with such liability on the part of its members to contribute to its assets in the event of its being wound up as is provided by this Act and the Insolvency Act.

This is subject, in the case of a public company, to section 117 (additional certificate as to amount of allotted share capital).

(5)   The persons named in the statement under section 10 as directors, secretary or joint secretaries are, on the company's incorporation, deemed to have been respectively appointed as its first directors, secretary or joint secretaries.

(6)   Where the registrar registers an association's memorandum which states that the association is to be a public company, the certificate of incorporation shall contain a statement that the company is a public company.

(7)   A certificate of incorporation given in respect of an association is conclusive evidence—

(a)   that the requirements of this Act in respect of registration and of matters precedent and incidental to it have been complied with, and that the association is a company authorised to be registered, and is duly registered, under this Act, and

(b)   if the certificate contains a statement that the company is a public company, that the company is such a company.

14.   Effect of memorandum and articles.

(1)   Subject to the provisions of this Act, the memorandum and articles, when registered, bind the company and its members to the same extent as if they respectively had been signed and sealed by each member, and contained covenants on the part of each member to observe all the provisions of the memorandum and of the articles.

(2)   Money payable by a member to the company under the memorandum or articles is a debt due from him to the company, and in England and Wales is of the nature of a specialty debt.

15.   Memorandum and articles of company limited by guarantee.

(1)   In the case of a company limited by guarantee and not having a share capital, every provision in the memorandum or articles, or in any resolution of the company purporting to give any person a right to participate in the divisible profits of the company otherwise than as a member, is void.

(2)   For purposes of provisions of this Act relating to the memorandum of a company limited by guarantee, and for those of section 1(4) and this section, every provision in the memorandum or articles, or in any resolution, of a company so limited purporting to divide the company's undertaking into shares or interests is to be treated as a provision for a share capital, notwithstanding that the nominal amount or number of the shares or interests is not specified by the provision.

16.   Effect of alteration on company's members.

(1)   A member of a company is not bound by an alteration made in the memorandum or articles after the date on which he became a member, if and so far as the alteration—

(a)   requires him to take or subscribe for more shares than the number held by him at the date on which the alteration is made; or

(b)   in any way increases his liability as at that date to contribute to the company's share capital or otherwise to pay money to the company.

(2)   Subsection (1) operates notwithstanding anything in the memorandum or articles; but it does not apply in a case where the member agrees in writing, either before or after the alteration is made, to be bound by the alteration.

17.   Conditions in memorandum which could have been in articles.

(1)   A condition contained in a company's memorandum which could lawfully have been contained in articles of association instead of in the memorandum may be altered by the company by special resolution; but if an application is made to the court for the alteration to be cancelled, the alteration does not have effect except in so far as it is confirmed by the court.

(2)   This section—

(a)   is subject to section 16, and also to Part XVII (court order protecting minority), and

(b)   does not apply where the memorandum itself provides for or prohibits the alteration of all or any of the conditions above referred to, and does not authorise any variation or abrogation of the special rights of any class of members.

(3)   Section 5 (except subsections (2)(b) and (8)) and section 6(1) to (3) apply in relation to any alteration and to any application made under this section as they apply in relation to alterations and applications under sections 4 to 6.

18.   Amendments of memorandum or articles to be registered.

(1)   Where an alteration is made in a company's memorandum or articles by any statutory provision, whether contained in an Act of Parliament or in an instrument made under an Act, a printed copy of the Act or instrument shall, not later than 15 days after that provision comes into force, be forwarded to the registrar of companies and recorded by him.

(2)   Where a company is required (by this section or otherwise) to send to the registrar any document making or evidencing an alteration in the company's memorandum or articles (other than a special resolution under section 4), the company shall send with it a printed copy of the memorandum or articles as altered.

(3)   If a company fails to comply with this section, the company and any officer of it who is in default is liable to a fine and, for continued contravention, to a daily default fine.

19.   Copies of memorandum and articles to be given to members.

(1)   A company shall, on being so required by any member, send to him a copy of the memorandum and of the articles (if any), and a copy of any Act of Parliament which alters the memorandum, subject to payment—

(a)   in the case of a copy of the memorandum and of the articles, of 5 pence or such less sum as the company may prescribe, and

(b)   in the case of a copy of an Act, of such sum not exceeding its published price as the company may require.

(2)   If a company makes default in complying with this section, the company and every officer of it who is in default is liable for each offence to a fine.

20.   Issued copy of memorandum to embody alterations.

(1)   Where an alteration is made in a company's memorandum, every copy of the memorandum issued after the date of the alteration shall be in accordance with the alteration.

(2)   If, where any such alteration has been made, the company at any time after the date of the alteration issues any copies of the memorandum which are not in accordance with the alteration, it is liable to a fine, and so too is every officer of the company who is in default.

A company's membership

22.   Definition of 'member'.

(1)   The subscribers of a company's memorandum are deemed to have agreed to become members of the company, and on its registration shall be entered as such in its register of members.

(2)   Every other person who agrees to become a member of a company, and whose name is entered in its register of members, is a member of the company.

23.   Membership of holding company.

(1)   Except as mentioned in this section, a body corporate cannot be a member of a company which is its holding company and any allotment or transfer of shares in a company to its subsidiary is void.

(2)   The prohibition does not apply where the subsidiary is concerned only as personal representative or trustee unless, in the latter case, the holding company or a subsidiary of it is beneficially interested under the trust.

For the purpose of ascertaining whether the holding company or a subsidiary is so interested, there shall be disregarded—

(a) any interest held only by way of security for the purposes of a transaction entered into by the holding company or subsidiary in the ordinary course of a business which includes the lending of money;

(b) any such interest as is mentioned in Part I of Schedule 2.

(3) The prohibition does not apply where shares in the holding company are held by the subsidiary in the ordinary course of its business as an intermediary.

For this purpose a person is an intermediary if that person—

(a) carries on a bona fide business of dealing in securities;

(b) is a member of an EEA exchange (and satisfies any requirements for recognition as a dealer in securities laid down by that exchange) or is otherwise approved or supervised as a dealer in securities under the laws of an EEA State; and

(c) does not carry on an excluded business.

(3A) The excluded businesses are the following—

(a) any business which consists wholly or mainly in the making or managing of investments;

(b) any business which consists wholly or mainly in, or is carried on wholly or mainly for the purpose of, providing services to persons who are connected with the person carrying on the business;

(c) any business which consists in insurance business;

(d) any business which consists in managing or acting as trustee in relation to a pension scheme or which is carried on by the manager or trustee of such a scheme in connection with or for the purposes of the scheme;

(e) any business which consists in operating or acting as trustee in relation to a collective investment scheme or is carried on by the operator or trustee of such a scheme in connection with or for the purposes of the scheme.

(3B) For the purposes of subsections (3) and (3A)—

(a) the question whether a person is connected with another shall be determined in accordance with the provisions of section 839 of the Income and Corporation Taxes Act 1988;

(b) 'collective investment scheme' has the meaning given in section 75 of the Financial Services Act 1986;

(c) 'EEA exchange' means a market which appears on the list drawn up by an EEA State pursuant to Article 16 of Council Directive 93/22/EEC on investment services in the securities field;

(d) 'insurance business' means long term business or general business as defined in section 1 of the Insurance Companies Act 1982;

(e) 'securities' include investments falling within paragraphs 7, 8 and 9 of Schedule 1 to the Financial Services Act 1986 and, so far as relevant to any of those paragraphs, paragraph 11 of that Schedule;

(f) 'trustee' and 'the operator' shall, in relation to a collective investment scheme, be construed in accordance with section 75(8) of the Financial Services Act 1986.

(3C) Where—

(a) a subsidiary which is a dealer in securities has purportedly acquired shares in its holding company in contravention of the prohibition in subsection (1); and

(b) a person acting in good faith has agreed, for value and without notice of that contravention, to acquire shares in the holding company from the subsidiary or from someone who has purportedly acquired the shares after their disposal by the subsidiary, any transfer to that person of the shares mentioned in paragraph (a) shall have the same effect as it would have had if their original acquisition by the subsidiary had not been in contravention of the prohibition.

(4) Where a body corporate became a holder of shares in a company—

    (a)   before 1 July 1948, or

    (b)   on or after that date and before 20 October 1997, in circumstances in which this section as it then had effect did not apply,

but at any time on or after 20 October 1997 falls within the prohibition in subsection (1) above in respect of those shares, it may continue to be a member of that company; but for so long as that prohibition would apply, apart from this subsection, it has no right to vote in respect of those shares at meetings of the company or of any class of its members.

    (5)   Where a body corporate becomes a holder of shares in a company on or after 20 October 1997 in circumstances in which the prohibition in subsection (1) does not apply, but subsequently falls within that prohibition in respect of those shares, it may continue to be a member of that company; but for so long as that prohibition would apply, apart from this subsection, it has no right to vote in respect of those shares at meetings of the company or of any class of its members.

    (6)   Where a body corporate is permitted to continue as a member of a company by virtue of subsection (4) or (5), an allotment to it of fully paid shares in the company may be validly made by way of capitalisation of reserves of the company; but for so long as the prohibition in subsection (1) would apply, apart from subsection (4) or (5), it has no right to vote in respect of those shares at meetings of the company or of any class of its members.

    (7)   The provisions of this section apply to a nominee acting on behalf of a subsidiary as to the subsidiary itself.

    (8)   In relation to a company other than a company limited by shares, the references in this section to shares shall be construed as references to the interest of its members as such, whatever the form of that interest.

24. Minimum membership for carrying on business.

If a company, other than a private company limited by shares or by guarantee, carries on business without having at least two members and does so for more than 6 months, a person who, for the whole or any part of the period that it so carries on business after those 6 months—

    (a)   is a member of the company, and

    (b)   knows that it is carrying on business with only one member,

is liable (jointly and severally with the company) for the payment of the company's debts contracted during the period or, as the case may be, that part of it.

CHAPTER II
COMPANY NAMES

25. Name as stated in memorandum.

    (1)   The name of a public company must end with the words 'public limited company' or, if the memorandum states that the company's registered office is to be situated in Wales, those words or their equivalent in Welsh ('cwmni cyfyngedig cyhoeddus'); and those words or that equivalent may not be preceded by the word 'limited' or its equivalent in Welsh ('cyfyngedig').

    (2)   In the case of a company limited by shares or by guarantee (not being a public company), the name must have 'limited' as its last word, except that—

    (a)   this is subject to section 30 (exempting, in certain circumstances, a company from the requirement to have 'limited' as part of the name), and

    (b)   if the company is to be registered with a memorandum stating that its registered office is to be situated in Wales, the name may have 'cyfyngedig' as its last word.

26. Prohibition on registration of certain names.

    (1)   A company shall not be registered under this Act by a name—

(a)   which includes, otherwise than at the end of the name, any of the following words or expressions, that is to say, 'limited', 'unlimited' or 'public limited company' or their Welsh equivalents ('cyfyngedig', 'anghyfyngedig' and 'cwmni cyfyngedig cyhoeddus' respectively);

(b)   which includes, otherwise than at the end of the name, an abbreviation of any of those words or expressions;

(bb)   which includes, at any place in the name, the expression 'investment company with variable capital' or its Welsh equivalent ('cwmni buddsoddi â chyfalaf newidiol');

(c)   which is the same as a name appearing in the registrar's index of company names;

(d)   the use of which by the company would in the opinion of the Secretary of State constitute a criminal offence; or

(e)   which in the opinion of the Secretary of State is offensive.

(2)   Except with the approval of the Secretary of State, a company shall not be registered under this Act by a name which—

(a)   in the opinion of the Secretary of State would be likely to give the impression that the company is connected in any way with Her Majesty's Government or with any local authority; or

(b)   includes any word or expression for the time being specified in regulations under section 29.

'Local authority' means any local authority within the meaning of the Local Government Act 1972 or the Local Government (Scotland) Act 1973, the Common Council of the City of London or the Council of the Isles of Scilly.

(3)   In determining for purposes of subsection (1)(c) whether one name is the same as another, there are to be disregarded—

(a)   the definite article, where it is the first word of the name;

(b)   the following words and expressions where they appear at the end of the name, that is to say—

'company' or its Welsh equivalent ('cwmni'),

'and company' or its Welsh equivalent ('a'r cwmni'),

'company limited' or its Welsh equivalent ('cwmni cyfyngedig'),

'and company limited' or its Welsh equivalent ('a'r cwmni cyfyngedig'),

'limited' or its Welsh equivalent ('cyfyngedig'),

'unlimited' or its Welsh equivalent ('anghyfyngedig'),

'public limited company' or its Welsh equivalent ('cwmni cyfyngedig cyhoeddus'), and

'investment company with variable capital' or its Welsh equivalent ('cwmni buddsoddi â chyfalaf newidiol');

(c)   abbreviations of any of those words or expressions where they appear at the end of the name; and

(d)   type and case of letters, accents, spaces between letters and punctuation marks;

and 'and' and '&' are to be taken as the same.

27.   Alternatives of statutory designations.

(1)   A company which by any provision of this Act is either required or entitled to include in its name, as its last part, any of the words specified in subsection (4) below may, instead of those words, include as the last part of the name the abbreviations there specified as alternatives in relation to those words.

(2)   A reference in this Act to the name of a company or to the inclusion of any of those words in a company's name includes a reference to the name including (in place

of any of the words so specified) the appropriate alternative, or to the inclusion of the appropriate alternative, as the case may be.

(3)   A provision of this Act requiring a company not to include any of those words in its name also requires it not to include the abbreviated alternative specified in subsection (4).

(4)   For the purposes of this section—

(a)   the alternative of 'limited' is 'ltd.';

(b)   the alternative of 'public limited company' is 'p.l.c.';

(c)   the alternative of 'cyfyngedig' is 'cyf.'; and

(d)   the alternative of 'cwmni cyfyngedig cyhoeddus' is 'c.c.c.'.

28.   Change of name.

(1)   A company may by special resolution change its name (but subject to section 31 in the case of a company which has received a direction under subsection (2) of that section from the Secretary of State).

(2)   Where a company has been registered by a name which—

(a)   is the same as or, in the opinion of the Secretary of State, too like a name appearing at the time of the registration in the registrar's index of company names, or

(b)   is the same as or, in the opinion of the Secretary of State, too like a name which should have appeared in that index at that time,

the Secretary of State may within 12 months of that time, in writing, direct the company to change its name within such period as he may specify.

Section 26(3) applies in determining under this subsection whether a name is the same as or too like another.

(3)   If it appears to the Secretary of State that misleading information has been given for the purpose of a company's registration with a particular name, or that undertakings or assurances have been given for that purpose and have not been fulfilled, he may within 5 years of the date of its registration with that name in writing direct the company to change its name within such period as he may specify.

(4)   Where a direction has been given under subsection (2) or (3), the Secretary of State may by a further direction in writing extend the period within which the company is to change its name, at any time before the end of that period.

(5)   A company which fails to comply with a direction under this section, and any officer of it who is in default, is liable to a fine and, for continued contravention, to a daily default fine.

(6)   Where a company changes its name under this section, the registrar of companies shall (subject to section 26) enter the new name on the register in place of the former name, and shall issue a certificate of incorporation altered to meet the circumstances of the case; and the change of name has effect from the date on which the altered certificate is issued.

(7)   A change of name by a company under this section does not affect any rights or obligations of the company or render defective any legal proceedings by or against it; and any legal proceedings that might have been continued or commenced against it by its former name may be continued or commenced against it by its new name.

29.   Regulations about names.

(1)   The Secretary of State may by regulations—

(a)   specify words or expressions for the registration of which as or as part of a company's corporate name his approval is required under section 26(2)(b), and

(b)   in relation to any such word or expression, specify a Government department or other body as the relevant body for purposes of the following subsection.

(2)   Where a company proposes to have as, or as part of, its corporate name any such word or expression and a Government department or other body is specified under subsection (1)(b) in relation to that word or expression, a request shall be made (in

writing) to the relevant body to indicate whether (and if so why) it has any objections to the proposal; and the person to make the request is—

    (a)   in the case of a company seeking to be registered under this Part, the person making the statutory declaration required by section 12(3),

    (b)   in the case of a company seeking to be registered under section 680, the persons making the statutory declaration required by section 686(2), and

    (c)   in any other case, a director or secretary of the company concerned.

    (3)   The person who has made that request to the relevant body shall submit to the registrar of companies a statement that it has been made and a copy of any response received from that body, together with—

    (a)   the requisite statutory declaration, or

    (b)   a copy of the special resolution changing the company's name,

according as the case is one or other of those mentioned in subsection (2).

    (4)   Sections 709 and 710 (public rights of inspection of documents kept by registrar of companies) do not apply to documents sent under subsection (3) of this section.

    (5)   Regulations under this section may contain such transitional provisions and savings as the Secretary of State thinks appropriate and may make different provision for different cases or classes of case.

    (6)   The regulations shall be made by statutory instrument, to be laid before Parliament after it is made; and the regulations shall cease to have effect at the end of 28 days beginning with the day on which the regulations were made (but without prejudice to anything previously done by virtue of them or to the making of new regulations), unless during that period they are approved by resolution of each House. In reckoning that period, no account is to be taken of any time during which Parliament is dissolved or prorogued or during which both Houses are adjourned for more than 4 days.

30.   Exemption from requirement of 'limited' as part of the name.

    (1)   Certain companies are exempt from requirements of this Act relating to the use of 'limited' as part of the company name.

    (2)   A private company limited by guarantee is exempt from those requirements, and so too is a company which on 25 February 1982 was a private company limited by shares with a name which, by virtue of a licence under section 19 of the Companies Act 1948, did not include 'limited'; but in either case the company must, to have the exemption, comply with the requirements of the following subsection.

    (3)   Those requirements are that—

    (a)   the objects of the company are (or, in the case of a company about to be registered, are to be) the promotion of commerce, art, science, education, religion, charity or any profession, and anything incidental or conducive to any of those objects; and

    (b)   the company's memorandum or articles—

        (i)   require its profits (if any) or other income to be applied in promoting its objects,

        (ii)   prohibit the payment of dividends to its members, and

        (iii)   require all the assets which would otherwise be available to its members generally to be transferred on its winding up either to another body with objects similar to its own or to another body the objects of which are the promotion of charity and anything incidental or conducive thereto (whether or not the body is a member of the company).

    (4)   A statutory declaration that a company complies with the requirements of subsection (3) may be delivered to the registrar of companies, who may accept the declaration as sufficient evidence of the matters stated in it; and the registrar may refuse to register a company by a name which does not include the word 'limited' unless such a declaration has been delivered to him.

(5)   The statutory declaration must be in the prescribed form and be made—

(a)   in the case of a company to be formed, by a solicitor engaged in its formation or by a person named as director or secretary in the statement delivered under section 10(2);

(b)   in the case of a company to be registered in pursuance of section 680, by two or more directors or other principal officers of the company; and

(c)   in the case of a company proposing to change its name so that it ceases to have the word 'limited' as part of its name, by a director or secretary of the company.

(6)   References in this section to the word 'limited' include (in an appropriate case) its Welsh equivalent ('cyfyngedig'), and the appropriate alternative ('ltd.' or 'cyf.', as the case may be).

(7)   A company which is exempt from requirements relating to the use of 'limited' and does not include that word as part of its name, is also exempt from the requirements of this Act relating to the publication of its name and the sending of lists of members to the registrar of companies.

31.   Provisions applying to company exempt under s. 30.

(1)   A company which is exempt under section 30 and whose name does not include 'limited' shall not alter its memorandum or articles of association so that it ceases to comply with the requirements of subsection (3) of that section.

(2)   If it appears to the Secretary of State that such a company—

(a)   has carried on any business other than the promotion of any of the objects mentioned in that subsection, or

(b)   has applied any of its profits or other income otherwise than in promoting such objects, or

(c)   has paid a dividend to any of its members,

he may, in writing, direct the company to change its name by resolution of the directors within such period as may be specified in the direction, so that its name ends with 'limited'.

A resolution passed by the directors in compliance with a direction under this subsection is subject to section 380 of this Act (copy to be forwarded to the registrar of companies within 15 days).

(3)   A company which has received a direction under subsection (2) shall not thereafter be registered by a name which does not include 'limited', without the approval of the Secretary of State.

(4)   References in this section to the word 'limited' include (in an appropriate case) its Welsh equivalent ('cyfyngedig'), and the appropriate alternative ('ltd.' or 'cyf.', as the case may be).

(5)   A company which contravenes subsection (1), and any officer of it who is in default, is liable to a fine and, for continued contravention, to a daily default fine.

(6)   A company which fails to comply with a direction by the Secretary of State under subsection (2), and any officer of the company who is in default, is liable to a fine and, for continued contravention, to a daily default fine.

32.   Power to require company to abandon misleading name.

(1)   If in the Secretary of State's opinion the name by which a company is registered gives so misleading an indication of the nature of its activities as to be likely to cause harm to the public, he may direct it to change its name.

(2)   The direction must, if not duly made the subject of an application to the court under the following subsection, be complied with within a period of 6 weeks from the date of the direction or such longer period as the Secretary of State may think fit to allow.

(3)   The company may, within a period of 3 weeks from the date of the direction, apply to the court to set it aside; and the court may set the direction aside or confirm it

and, if it confirms the direction, shall specify a period within which it must be complied with.

(4)   If a company makes default in complying with a direction under this section, it is liable to a fine and, for continued contravention, to a daily default fine.

(5)   Where a company changes its name under this section, the registrar shall (subject to section 26) enter the new name on the register in place of the former name, and shall issue a certificate of incorporation altered to meet the circumstances of the case; and the change of name has effect from the date on which the altered certificate is issued.

(6)   A change of name by a company under this section does not affect any of the rights or obligations of the company, or render defective any legal proceedings by or against it; and any legal proceedings that might have been continued or commenced against it by its former name may be continued or commenced against it by its new name.

33.   Prohibition on trading under misleading name.

(1)   A person who is not a public company is guilty of an offence if he carries on any trade, profession or business under a name which includes, as its last part, the words 'public limited company' or their equivalent in Welsh ('cwmni cyfyngedig cyhoeddus').

(2)   A public company is guilty of an offence if, in circumstances in which the fact that it is a public company is likely to be material to any person, it uses a name which may reasonably be expected to give the impression that it is a private company.

(3)   A person guilty of an offence under subsection (1) or (2) and, if that person is a company, any officer of the company who is in default, is liable to a fine and, for continued contravention, to a daily default fine.

34.   Penalty for improper use of 'limited' or 'cyfyngedig'.

If any person trades or carries on business under a name or title of which 'limited' or 'cyfyngedig', or any contraction or imitation of either of those words, is the last word, that person, unless duly incorporated with limited liability, is liable to a fine and, for continued contravention, to a daily default fine.

35.   A company's capacity not limited by its memorandum.

(1)   The validity of an act done by a company shall not be called into question on the ground of lack of capacity by reason of anything in the company's memorandum.

(2)   A member of a company may bring proceedings to restrain the doing of an act which but for subsection (1) would be beyond the company's capacity; but no such proceedings shall lie in respect of an act to be done in fulfilment of a legal obligation arising from a previous act of the company.

(3)   It remains the duty of the directors to observe any limitations on their powers flowing from the company's memorandum; and action by the directors which but for subsection (1) would be beyond the company's capacity may only be ratified by the company by special resolution.

A resolution ratifying such action shall not affect any liability incurred by the directors or any other person; relief from any such liability must be agreed to separately by special resolution.

(4)   The operation of this section is restricted by section 65(1) of the Charities Act 1993 and section 112(3) of the Companies Act 1989 in relation to companies which are charities; and section 322A below (invalidity of certain transactions to which directors or their associates are parties) has effect notwithstanding this section.

35A.   Power of directors to bind the company.

(1)   In favour of a person dealing with a company in good faith, the power of the board of directors to bind the company, or authorise others to do so, shall be deemed to be free of any limitation under the company's constitution.

(2) For this purpose—

(a) a person 'deals with' a company if he is a party to any transaction or other act to which the company is a party;

(b) a person shall not be regarded as acting in bad faith by reason only of his knowing that an act is beyond the powers of the directors under the company's constitution; and

(c) a person shall be presumed to have acted in good faith unless the contrary is proved.

(3) The references above to limitations on the directors' powers under the company's constitution include limitations deriving—

(a) from a resolution of the company in general meeting or a meeting of any class of shareholders, or

(b) from any agreement between the members of the company or of any class of shareholders.

(4) Subsection (1) does not affect any right of a member of the company to bring proceedings to restrain the doing of an act which is beyond the powers of the directors; but no such proceedings shall lie in respect of an act to be done in fulfilment of a legal obligation arising from a previous act of the company.

(5) Nor does that subsection affect any liability incurred by the directors, or any other person, by reason of the directors' exceeding their powers.

(6) The operation of this section is restricted by section 65(1) of the Charities Act 1993 and section 112(3) of the Companies Act 1989 in relation to companies which are charities; and section 322A below (invalidity of certain transactions to which directors or their associates are parties) has effect notwithstanding this section.

35B. No duty to enquire as to capacity of company or authority of directors.

A party to a transaction with a company is not bound to enquire as to whether it is permitted by the company's memorandum or as to any limitation on the powers of the board of directors to bind the company or authorise others to do so.

36. Company contracts: England and Wales.

Under the law of England and Wales a contract may be made—

(a) by a company, by writing under its common seal, or

(b) on behalf of a company, by any person acting under its authority, express or implied;

and any formalities required by law in the case of a contract made by an individual also apply, unless a contrary intention appears, to a contract made by or on behalf of a company.

36A. Execution of documents: England and Wales.

(1) Under the law of England and Wales the following provisions have effect with respect to the execution of documents by a company.

(2) A document is executed by a company by the affixing of its common seal.

(3) A company need not have a common seal, however, and the following subsections apply whether it does or not.

(4) A document signed by a director and the secretary of a company, or by two directors of a company, and expressed (in whatever form of words) to be executed by the company has the same effect as if executed under the common seal of the company.

(5) A document executed by a company which makes it clear on its face that it is intended by the person or persons making it to be a deed has effect, upon delivery, as a deed; and it shall be presumed, unless a contrary intention is proved, to be delivered upon its being so executed.

(6) In favour of a purchaser a document shall be deemed to have been duly executed by a company if it purports to be signed by a director and the secretary of the company,

or by two directors of the company, and where it makes it clear on its face that it is intended by the person or persons making it to be a deed, to have been delivered upon its being executed.

A 'purchaser' means a purchaser in good faith for valuable consideration and includes a lessee, mortgagee or other person who for valuable consideration acquires an interest in property.

36C. Pre-incorporation contracts, deeds and obligations.

(1) A contract which purports to be made by or on behalf of a company at a time when the company has not been formed has effect, subject to any agreement to the contrary, as one made with the person purporting to act for the company or as agent for it, and he is personally liable on the contract accordingly.

(2) Subsection (1) applies—
  (a) to the making of a deed under the law of England and Wales, and
  (b) to the undertaking of an obligation under the law of Scotland,
as it applies to the making of a contract.

37. Bills of exchange and promissory notes.

A bill of exchange or promissory note is deemed to have been made, accepted or endorsed on behalf of a company if made, accepted or endorsed in the name of, or by or on behalf or on account of, the company by a person acting under its authority.

38. Execution of deeds abroad.

(1) A company may, by writing under its common seal, empower any person, either generally or in respect of any specified matters, as its attorney, to execute deeds on its behalf in any place elsewhere than in the United Kingdom.

(2) A deed executed by such an attorney on behalf of the company has the same effect as if it were executed under the company's common seal.

39. Power of company to have official seal for use abroad.

(1) A company which has a common seal whose objects require or comprise the transaction of business in foreign countries may, if authorised by its articles, have for use in any territory, district or place elsewhere than in the United Kingdom, an official seal, which shall be a facsimile of its common seal, with the addition on its face of the name of every territory, district or place where it is to be used.

(2) The official seal when duly affixed to a document has the same effect as the company's common seal.

(3) A company having an official seal for use in any such territory, district or place may, by writing under its common seal, authorise any person appointed for the purpose in that territory, district or place to affix the official seal to any deed or other document to which the company is party in that territory, district or place.

(4) As between the company and a person dealing with such an agent, the agent's authority continues during the period (if any) mentioned in the instrument conferring the authority, or if no period is there mentioned, then until notice of the revocation or determination of the agent's authority has been given to the person dealing with him.

(5) The person affixing the official seal shall certify in writing on the deed or other instrument to which the seal is affixed the date on which and the place at which it is affixed.

40. Official seal for share certificates, etc.

A company which has a common seal may have, for use for sealing securities issued by the company and for sealing documents creating or evidencing securities so issued, an official seal which is a facsimile of its common seal with the addition on its face of the word 'Securities'.

The official seal when duly affixed to a document has the same effect as the company's common seal.

41.   Authentication of documents.

A document or proceeding requiring authentication by a company is sufficiently authenticated for the purposes of the law of England and Wales by the signature of a director, secretary or other authorised officer of the company.

42.   Events affecting a company's status.

(1)   A company is not entitled to rely against other persons on the happening of any of the following events—

(a)   the making of a winding-up order in respect of the company, or the appointment of a liquidator in a voluntary winding up of the company, or

(b)   any alteration of the company's memorandum or articles, or

(c)   any change among the company's directors, or

(d)   (as regards service of any document on the company) any change in the situation of the company's registered office,

if the event had not been officially notified at the material time and is not shown by the company to have been known at that time to the person concerned, or if the material time fell on or before the 15th day after the date of official notification (or, where the 15th day was a non-business day, on or before the next day that was not) and it is shown that the person concerned was unavoidably prevented from knowing of the event at that time.

(2)   In subsection (1)—

(a)   'official notification' and 'officially notified' have the meanings given by section 711(2) (registrar of companies to give public notice of the issue or receipt by him of certain documents), and

(b)   'non-business day' means a Saturday or Sunday, Christmas Day, Good Friday and any other day which is a bank holiday in the part of Great Britain where the company is registered.

PART II
RE-REGISTRATION AS A MEANS OF ALTERING A COMPANY'S STATUS

Private company becoming public

43.   Re-registration of private company as public.

(1)   Subject to this and the following five sections, a private company (other than a company not having a share capital) may be re-registered as a public company if—

(a)   a special resolution that it should be so re-registered is passed; and

(b)   an application for re-registration is delivered to the registrar of companies, together with the necessary documents.

A company cannot be re-registered under this section if it has previously been re-registered as unlimited.

(2)   The special resolution must—

(a)   alter the company's memorandum so that it states that the company is to be a public company; and

(b)   make such other alterations in the memorandum as are necessary to bring it (in substance and in form) into conformity with the requirements of this Act with respect to the memorandum of a public company (the alterations to include compliance with section 25(1) as regards the company's name); and

(c)   make such alterations in the company's articles as are requisite in the circumstances.

(3)   The application must be in the prescribed form and be signed by a director or secretary of the company; and the documents to be delivered with it are the following—

(a)   a printed copy of the memorandum and articles as altered in pursuance of the resolution;

(b) a copy of a written statement by the company's auditors that in their opinion the relevant balance sheet shows that at the balance sheet date the amount of the company's net assets (within the meaning given to that expression by section 264(2)) was not less than the aggregate of its called-up share capital and undistributable reserves;

(c) a copy of the relevant balance sheet, together with a copy of an unqualified report (defined in section 46) by the company's auditors in relation to that balance sheet;

(d) if section 44 applies, a copy of the valuation report under subsection (2)(b) of that section; and

(e) a statutory declaration in the prescribed form by a director or secretary of the company—

(i) that the special resolution required by this section has been passed and that the conditions of the following two sections (so far as applicable) have been satisfied, and

(ii) that, between the balance sheet date and the application for re-registration, there has been no change in the company's financial position that has resulted in the amount of its net assets becoming less than the aggregate of its called-up share capital and undistributable reserves.

(4) 'Relevant balance sheet' means a balance sheet prepared as at a date not more than 7 months before the company's application under this section.

(5) A resolution that a company be re-registered as a public company may change the company name by deleting the word 'company' or the words 'and company', or its or their equivalent in Welsh ('cwmni', 'a'r cwmni'), including any abbreviation of them.

44. Consideration for shares recently allotted to be valued.

(1) The following applies if shares have been allotted by the company between the date as at which the relevant balance sheet was prepared and the passing of the special resolution under section 43, and those shares were allotted as fully or partly paid up as to their nominal value or any premium on them otherwise than in cash.

(2) Subject to the following provisions, the registrar of companies shall not entertain an application by the company under section 43 unless beforehand—

(a) the consideration for the allotment has been valued in accordance with section 108, and

(b) a report with respect to the value of the consideration has been made to the company (in accordance with that section) during the 6 months immediately preceding the allotment of the shares.

(3) Where an amount standing to the credit of any of the company's reserve accounts, or of its profit and loss account, has been applied in paying up (to any extent) any of the shares allotted or any premium on those shares, the amount applied does not count as consideration for the allotment, and accordingly subsection (2) does not apply to it.

(4) Subsection (2) does not apply if the allotment is in connection with an arrangement providing for it to be on terms that the whole or part of the consideration for the shares allotted is to be provided by the transfer to the company or the cancellation of all or some of the shares, or of all or some of the shares of a particular class, in another company (with or without the issue to the company applying under section 43 of shares, or of shares of any particular class, in that other company).

(5) But subsection (4) does not exclude the application of subsection (2), unless under the arrangement it is open to all the holders of the shares of the other company in question (or, where the arrangement applies only to shares of a particular class, all the holders of the other company's shares of that class) to take part in the arrangement.

In determining whether that is the case, shares held by or by a nominee of the company allotting shares in connection with the arrangement, or by or by a nominee of a company which is that company's holding company or subsidiary or a company which is a subsidiary of its holding company, are to be disregarded.

(6)   Subsection (2) does not apply to preclude an application under section 43, if the allotment of the company's shares is in connection with its proposed merger with another company; that is, where one of the companies concerned proposes to acquire all the assets and liabilities of the other in exchange for the issue of shares or other securities of that one to shareholders of the other, with or without any cash payment to shareholders.

(7)   In this section—

(a)   'arrangement' means any agreement, scheme or arrangement, including an arrangement sanctioned in accordance with section 425 (company compromise with creditors and members) or section 110 of the Insolvency Act (liquidator in winding up accepting shares as consideration for sale of company's property), and

(b)   'another company' includes any body corporate and any body to which letters patent have been issued under the Chartered Companies Act 1837.

45.   Additional requirements relating to share capital.

(1)   For a private company to be re-registered under section 43 as a public company, the following conditions with respect to its share capital must be satisfied at the time the special resolution under that section is passed.

(2)   Subject to subsections (5) to (7) below—

(a)   the nominal value of the company's allotted share capital must be not less than the authorised minimum, and

(b)   each of the company's allotted shares must be paid up at least as to one-quarter of the nominal value of that share and the whole of any premium on it.

(3)   Subject to subsection (5), if any shares in the company or any premium on them have been fully or partly paid up by an undertaking given by any person that he or another should do work or perform services (whether for the company or any other person), the undertaking must have been performed or otherwise discharged.

(4)   Subject to subsection (5), if shares have been allotted as fully or partly paid up as to their nominal value or any premium on them otherwise than in cash, and the consideration for the allotment consists of or includes an undertaking to the company (other than one to which subsection (3) applies), then either—

(a)   the undertaking must have been performed or otherwise discharged, or

(b)   there must be a contract between the company and some person pursuant to which the undertaking is to be performed within 5 years from the time the resolution under section 43 is passed.

(5)   For the purpose of determining whether subsections (2)(b), (3) and (4) are complied with, certain shares in the company may be disregarded; and these are—

(a)   subject to the next subsection, any share which was allotted before 22 June 1982, and

(b)   any share which was allotted in pursuance of an employees' share scheme and by reason of which the company would, but for this subsection, be precluded under subsection (2)(b) (but not otherwise) from being re-registered as a public company.

(6)   A share is not to be disregarded under subsection (5)(a) if the aggregate in nominal value of that share and other shares proposed to be so disregarded is more than one-tenth of the nominal value of the company's allotted share capital; but for this purpose the allotted share capital is treated as not including any shares disregarded under subsection (5)(b).

(7)   Any shares disregarded under subsection (5) are treated as not forming part of the allotted share capital for the purposes of subsection (2)(a).

46.   Meaning of 'unqualified report' in s. 43(3).

(1)   The following subsections explain the reference in section 43(3)(c) to an unqualified report of the company's auditors on the relevant balance sheet.

(2)   If the balance sheet was prepared for a financial year of.the company, the reference is to an auditors' report stating without material qualification the auditors' opinion that the balance sheet has been properly prepared in accordance with this Act.

(3)   If the balance sheet was not prepared for a financial year of the company, the reference is to an auditors' report stating without material qualification the auditors' opinion that the balance sheet has been properly prepared in accordance with the provisions of this Act which would have applied if it had been so prepared.

For the purposes of an auditors' report under this subsection the provisions of this Act shall be deemed to apply with such modifications as are necessary by reason of the fact that the balance sheet is not prepared for a financial year of the company.

(4)   A qualification shall be regarded as material unless the auditors state in their report that the matter giving rise to the qualification is not material for the purpose of determining (by reference to the company's balance sheet) whether at the balance sheet date the amount of the company's net assets was not less than the aggregate of its called up share capital and undistributable reserves.

In this subsection 'net assets' and 'undistributable reserves' have the meaning given by section 264(2) and (3).

47.   Certificate of re-registration under s. 43.

(1)   If the registrar of companies is satisfied, on an application under section 43, that a company may be re-registered under that section as a public company, he shall—

(a)   retain the application and other documents delivered to him under the section; and

(b)   issue the company with a certificate of incorporation stating that the company is a public company.

(2)   The registrar may accept a declaration under section 43(3)(e) as sufficient evidence that the special resolution required by that section has been passed and the other conditions of re-registration satisfied.

(3)   The registrar shall not issue the certificate if it appears to him that the court has made an order confirming a reduction of the company's capital which has the effect of bringing the nominal value of the company's allotted share capital below the authorised minimum.

(4)   Upon the issue to a company of a certificate of incorporation under this section—

(a)   the company by virtue of the issue of that certificate becomes a public company; and

(b)   any alteration in the memorandum and articles set out in the resolution take effect accordingly.

(5)   The certificate is conclusive evidence—

(a)   that the requirements of this Act in respect of re-registration and of matters precedent and incidental thereto have been complied with; and

(b)   that the company is a public company.

48.   Modification for unlimited company re-registering.

(1)   In their application to unlimited companies, sections 43 to 47 are modified as follows.

(2)   The special resolution required by section 43(1) must, in addition to the matters mentioned in subsection (2) of that section—

(a)   state that the liability of the members is to be limited by shares, and what the company's share capital is to be; and

(b)   make such alterations in the company's memorandum as are necessary to bring it in substance and in form into conformity with the requirements of this Act with respect to the memorandum of a company limited by shares.

(3)   The certificate of incorporation issued under section 47(1) shall, in addition to containing the statement required by paragraph (b) of that subsection, state that the company has been incorporated as a company limited by shares; and—

(a)   the company by virtue of the issue of the certificate becomes a public company so limited; and

(b)   the certificate is conclusive evidence of the fact that it is such a company.

Limited company becoming unlimited

49.   Re-registration of limited company as unlimited.

(1)   Subject as follows, a company which is registered as limited may be re-registered as unlimited in pursuance of an application in that behalf complying with the requirements of this section.

(2)   A company is excluded from re-registering under this section if it is limited by virtue of re-registration under section 44 of the Companies Act 1967 or section 51 of this Act.

(3)   A public company cannot be re-registered under this section; nor can a company which has previously been re-registered as unlimited.

(4)   An application under this section must be in the prescribed form and be signed by a director or the secretary of the company, and be lodged with the registrar of companies, together with the documents specified in subsection (8) below.

(5)   The application must set out such alterations in the company's memorandum as—

(a)   if it is to have a share capital, are requisite to bring it (in substance and in form) into conformity with the requirements of this Act with respect to the memorandum of a company to be formed as an unlimited company having a share capital; or

(b)   if it is not to have a share capital, are requisite in the circumstances.

(6)   If articles have been registered, the application must set out such alterations in them as—

(a)   if the company is to have a share capital, are requisite to bring the articles (in substance and in form) into conformity with the requirements of this Act with respect to the articles of a company to be formed as an unlimited company having a share capital; or

(b)   if the company is not to have a share capital, are requisite in the circumstances.

(7) · If articles have not been registered, the application must have annexed to it, and request the registration of, printed articles; and these must, if the company is to have a share capital, comply with the requirements mentioned in subsection (6)(a) and, if not, be articles appropriate to the circumstances.

(8)   The documents to be lodged with the registrar are—

(a)   the prescribed form of assent to the company's being registered as unlimited, subscribed by or on behalf of all the members of the company;

(b)   a statutory declaration made by the directors of the company—

(i)   that the persons by whom or on whose behalf the form of assent is subscribed constitute the whole membership of the company, and

(ii)   if any of the members have not subscribed that form themselves, that the directors have taken all reasonable steps to satisfy themselves that each person who subscribed it on behalf of a member was lawfully empowered to do so;

(c)   a printed copy of the memorandum incorporating the alterations in it set out in the application; and

(d)   if articles have been registered, a printed copy of them incorporating the alterations set out in the application.

(9)   For purposes of this section—

(a)   subscription to a form of assent by the legal personal representative of a deceased member of a company is deemed subscription by him; and

(b)   a trustee in bankruptcy of a member of a company is, to the exclusion of the latter, deemed a member of the company.

50.   Certificate of re-registration under s. 49.

(1)   The registrar of companies shall retain the application and other documents lodged with him under section 49 and shall—

(a)   if articles are annexed to the application, register them; and

(b)   issue to the company a certificate of incorporation appropriate to the status to be assumed by it by virtue of that section.

(2)   On the issue of the certificate—

(a)   the status of the company, by virtue of the issue, is changed from limited to unlimited; and

(b)   the alterations in the memorandum set out in the application and (if articles have been previously registered) any alterations to the articles so set out take effect as if duly made by resolution of the company; and

(c)   the provisions of this Act apply accordingly to the memorandum and articles as altered.

(3)   The certificate is conclusive evidence that the requirements of section 49 in respect of re-registration and of matters precedent and incidental to it have been complied with, and that the company was authorised to be re-registered under this Act in pursuance of that section and was duly so re-registered.

Unlimited company becoming limited

51.   Re-registration of unlimited company as limited.

(1)   Subject as follows, a company which is registered as unlimited may be re-registered as limited if a special resolution that it should be so re-registered is passed, and the requirements of this section are complied with in respect of the resolution and otherwise.

(2)   A company cannot under this section be re-registered as a public company; and a company is excluded from re-registering under it if it is unlimited by virtue of re-registration under section 43 of the Companies Act 1967 or section 49 of this Act.

(3)   The special resolution must state whether the company is to be limited by shares or by guarantee and—

(a)   if it is to be limited by shares, must state what the share capital is to be and provide for the making of such alterations in the memorandum as are necessary to bring it (in substance and in form) into conformity with the requirements of this Act with respect to the memorandum of a company so limited, and such alterations in the articles as are requisite in the circumstances;

(b)   if it is to be limited by guarantee, must provide for the making of such alterations in its memorandum and articles as are necessary to bring them (in substance and in form) into conformity with the requirements of this Act with respect to the memorandum and articles of a company so limited.

(4)   The special resolution is subject to section 380 of this Act (copy to be forwarded to registrar within 15 days); and an application for the company to be re-registered as limited, framed in the prescribed form and signed by a director or by the secretary of the company, must be lodged with the registrar of companies, together with the necessary documents, not earlier than the day on which the copy of the resolution forwarded under section 380 is received by him.

(5)   The documents to be lodged with the registrar are—

(a)   a printed copy of the memorandum as altered in pursuance of the resolution; and

(b)   a printed copy of the articles as so altered.

(6)   This section does not apply in relation to the re-registration of an unlimited company as a public company under section 43.

52.   Certification of re-registration under s. 51.

(1)   The registrar shall retain the application and other documents lodged with him under section 51, and shall issue to the company a certificate of incorporation appropriate to the status to be assumed by the company by virtue of that section.

(2)   On the issue of the certificate—

(a)   the status of the company is, by virtue of the issue, changed from unlimited to limited; and

(b)   the alterations in the memorandum specified in the resolution and the alterations in, and additions to, the articles so specified take effect.

(3)   The certificate is conclusive evidence that the requirements of section 51 in respect of re-registration and of matters precedent and incidental to it have been complied with, and that the company was authorised to be re-registered in pursuance of that section and was duly so re-registered.

Public company becoming private

53.   Re-registration of public company as private.

(1)   A public company may be re-registered as a private company if—

(a)   a special resolution complying with subsection (2) below that it should be so re-registered is passed and has not been cancelled by the court under the following section;

(b)   an application for the purpose in the prescribed form and signed by a director or the secretary of the company is delivered to the registrar of companies, together with a printed copy of the memorandum and articles of the company as altered by the resolution; and

(c)   the period during which an application for the cancellation of the resolution under the following section may be made has expired without any such application having been made; or

(d)   where such an application has been made, the application has been withdrawn or an order has been made under section 54(5) confirming the resolution and a copy of that order has been delivered to the registrar.

(2)   The special resolution must alter the company's memorandum so that it no longer states that the company is to be a public company and must make such other alterations in the company's memorandum and articles as are requisite in the circumstances.

(3)   A company cannot under this section be re-registered otherwise than as a company limited by shares or by guarantee.

54.   Litigated objection to resolution under s. 53.

(1)   Where a special resolution by a public company to be re-registered under section 53 as a private company has been passed, an application may be made to the court for the cancellation of that resolution.

(2)   The application may be made—

(a)   by the holders of not less in the aggregate than 5 per cent in nominal value of the company's issued share capital or any class thereof;

(b)   if the company is not limited by shares, by not less than 5 per cent of its members; or

(c)   by not less than 50 of the company's members;

but not by a person who has consented to or voted in favour of the resolution.

(3)   The application must be made within 28 days after the passing of the resolution and may be made on behalf of the persons entitled to make the application by such one or more of their number as they may appoint in writing for the purpose.

(4)   If such an application is made, the company shall forthwith give notice in the prescribed form of that fact to the registrar of companies.

(5)   On the hearing of the application, the court shall make an order either cancelling or confirming the resolution and—

(a)   may make that order on such terms and conditions as it thinks fit, and may (if it thinks fit) adjourn the proceedings in order that an arrangement may be made to the satisfaction of the court for the purchase of the interests of dissentient members; and

(b)   may give such directions and make such orders as it thinks expedient for facilitating or carrying into effect any such arrangement.

(6)   The court's order may, if the court thinks fit, provide for the purchase by the company of the shares of any of its members and for the reduction accordingly of the company's capital, and may make such alterations in the company's memorandum and articles as may be required in consequence of that provision.

(7)   The company shall, within 15 days from the making of the court's order, or within such longer period as the court may at any time by order direct, deliver to the registrar of companies an office copy of the order.

(8)   If the court's order requires the company not to make any, or any specified, alteration in its memorandum or articles, the company has not then power without the leave of the court to make any such alteration in breach of the requirement.

(9)   An alteration in the memorandum or articles made by virtue of an order under this section, if not made by resolution of the company, is of the same effect as if duly made by resolution; and this Act applies accordingly to the memorandum or articles as so altered.

(10)   A company which fails to comply with subsection (4) or subsection (7), and any officer of it who is in default, is liable to a fine and, for continued contravention, to a daily default fine.

55.   Certificate of re-registration under s. 53.

(1)   If the registrar of companies is satisfied that a company may be re-registered under section 53, he shall—

(a)   retain the application and other documents delivered to him under that section; and

(b)   issue the company with a certificate of incorporation appropriate to a private company.

(2)   On the issue of the certificate—

(a)   the company by virtue of the issue becomes a private company; and

(b)   the alterations in the memorandum and articles set out in the resolution under section 53 take effect accordingly.

(3)   The certificate is conclusive evidence—

(a)   that the requirements of section 53 in respect of re-registration and of matters precedent and incidental to it have been complied with; and

(b)   that the company is a private company.

PART III
CAPITAL ISSUES

CHAPTER I
ISSUES BY COMPANIES REGISTERED, OR TO BE REGISTERED, IN GREAT BRITAIN

The prospectus

58.   Document offering shares etc. for sale deemed a prospectus.

(1)   If a company allots or agrees to allot its shares or debentures with a view to all or any of them being offered for sale to the public, any document by which the offer for sale to the public is made is deemed for all purposes a prospectus issued by the company.

(2) All enactments and rules of law as to the contents of prospectuses, and to liability in respect of statements in and omissions from prospectuses, or otherwise relating to prospectuses, apply and have effect accordingly, as if the shares or debentures had been offered to the public for subscription and as if persons accepting the offer in respect of any shares or debentures were subscribers for those shares or debentures.

This is without prejudice to the liability (if any) of the persons by whom the offer is made, in respect of misstatements in the document or otherwise in respect of it.

(3) For purposes of this Act it is evidence (unless the contrary is proved) that an allotment of, or an agreement to allot, shares or debentures was made with a view to their being offered for sale to the public if it is shown—

(a)   that an offer of the shares or debentures (or of any of them) for sale to the public was made within 6 months after the allotment or agreement to allot, or

(b)   that at the date when the offer was made the whole consideration to be received by the compapny in respect of the shares or debentures had not been so received.

(4) Section 56 as applied by this section has effect as if it required a prospectus to state, in addition to the matters required by that section—

(a)   the net amount of the consideration received or to be received by the company in respect of the shares or debentures to which the offer relates, and

(b)   the place and time at which the contract under which those shares or debentures have been or are to be allotted may be inspected.

[The Financial Services Act 1986, sch. 17, part I, has repealed the Companies Act 1985, ss. 58 to 60, except so far as those sections are necessary for the purposes of ss. 81, 83, 246, 248 and 744 (Financial Services Act 1986 (Commencement) (No. 13) Order 1995 (SI 1995/ 1538), art. 2(a)(i)).]

59.   Rule governing what is an 'offer to the public'.

(1) Subject to the next section, any reference in this Act to offering shares or debentures to the public is to be read (subject to any provision to the contrary) as including a reference to offering them to any section of the public, whether selected as members or debenture holders of the company concerned, or as clients of the person issuing the prospectus, or in any other manner.

(2) The same applies to any reference in this Act, or in a company's articles, to an invitation to the public to subscribe for shares or debentures.

[See note after s. 58.]

60.   Exceptions from rule in s. 59.

(1) Section 59 does not require an offer or invitation to be treated as made to the public if it can properly be regarded, in all the circumstances, as not being calculated to result, directly or indirectly, in the shares or debentures becoming available for subscription or purchase by persons other than those receiving the offer or invitation, or otherwise as being a domestic concern of the persons receiving and making it.

(2) In particular, a provision in a company's articles prohibiting invitations to the public to subscribe for shares or debentures is not to be taken as prohibiting the making to members or debenture holders of an invitation which can properly be regarded as falling within the preceding subsection.

(3) For purposes of that subsection, an offer of shares in or debentures of a private company, or an invitation to subscribe for such shares or debentures, is to be regarded (unless the contrary is proved) as being a domestic concern of the persons making and receiving the offer or invitation if it falls within any of the following descriptions.

(4) It is to be so regarded if it is made to—

(a)   an existing member of the company making the offer or invitation.

(b)   an existing employee of that company,

(c)   a member of the family of such a member or employee, or

(d)   an existing debenture holder.

(5) For purposes of subsection (4) (c), the members of a person's family are—

(a) the person's husband or wife, widow or widower and children (including step-children) and their descendants, and

(b) any trustee (acting in his capacity as such) of a trust the principal beneficiary of which is the person him or herself, or any of those relatives.

(6) The offer or invitation is also to be so regarded if it is to subscribe for shares or debentures to be held under an employees' share scheme.

(7) The offer or invitation is also to be so regarded if it falls within subsection (4) or (6) and it is made on terms which permit the person to whom it is made to renounce his right to the allotment of shares or issue of debentures, but only in favour—

(a) of such a person as is mentioned in any of the paragraphs of subsection (4), or

(b) where there is an employees' share scheme, of a person entitled to hold shares or debentures under the scheme.

(8) Where application has been made to the competent authority for the purposes of Part IV of the Financial Services Act 1986 for admission of any securities to the Official List of the Stock Exchange, then an offer of those securities for subscription or sale to a person whose ordinary business it is to buy or sell shares or debentures (whether as principal or agent) is not deemed an offer to the public for purposes of this Part.

[See note after s. 58.]

62. Meaning of 'expert'.

The expression 'expert', in both Chapters of this Part, includes engineer, valuer, accountant and any other person whose profession gives authority to a statement made by him.

[The Financial Services Act 1986, sch. 17, part I, has repealed the Companies Act 1985, s. 62, except so far as it is necessary for the purposes of s. 744 (Financial Services Act 1986 (Commencement) (No. 13) Order 1995 (SI 1995/1538), art. 2(a)(iii)).]

PART IV
ALLOTMENT OF SHARES AND DEBENTURES

General provisions as to allotment

80. Authority of company required for certain allotments.

(1) The directors of a company shall not exercise any power of the company to allot relevant securities, unless they are, in accordance with this section or section 80A, authorised to do so by—

    (a) the company in general meeting; or

    (b) the company's articles.

(2) In this section 'relevant securities' means—

    (a) shares in the company other than shares shown in the memorandum to have been taken by the subscribers to it or shares allotted in pursuance of an employees' share scheme, and

    (b) any right to subscribe for, or to convert any security into, shares in the company (other than shares so allotted);

and a reference to the allotment of relevant securities includes the grant of such a right but (subject to subsection (6) below), not the allotment of shares pursuant to such a right.

(3) Authority under this section may be given for a particular exercise of the power or for its exercise generally, and may be unconditional or subject to conditions.

(4) The authority must state the maximum amount of relevant securities that may be allotted under it and the date on which it will expire, which must be not more than 5 years from whichever is relevant of the following dates—

    (a) in the case of an authority contained in the company's articles at the time of its original incorporation, the date of that incorporation; and

    (b) in any other case, the date on which the resolution is passed by virtue of which the authority is given;

but such an authority (including an authority contained in the articles) may be previously revoked or varied by the company in general meeting.

(5)   The authority may be renewed or further renewed by the company in general meeting for a further period not exceeding 5 years; but the resolution must state (or restate) the amount of relevant securities which may be allotted under the authority or, as the case may be, the amount remaining to be allotted under it, and must specify the date on which the renewed authority will expire.

(6)   In relation to authority under this section for the grant of such rights as are mentioned in subsection (2)(b), the reference in subsection (4) (as also the corresponding reference in subsection (5)) to the maximum amount of relevant securities that may be allotted under the authority is to the maximum amount of shares which may be allotted pursuant to the rights.

(7)   The directors may allot relevant securities, notwithstanding that authority under this section has expired, if they are allotted in pursuance of an offer or agreement made by the company before the authority expired and the authority allowed it to make an offer or agreement which would or might require relevant securities to be allotted after the authority expired.

(8)   A resolution of a company to give, vary, revoke or renew such an authority may, notwithstanding that it alters the company's articles, be an ordinary resolution; but it is in any case subject to section 380 of this Act (copy to be forwarded to registrar within 15 days).

(9)   A director who knowingly and wilfully contravenes, or permits or authorises a contravention of, this section is liable to a fine.

(10)   Nothing in this section affects the validity of any allotment.

(11)   This section does not apply to any allotment of relevant securities by a company, other than a public company registered as such on its original incorporation, if it is made in pursuance of an offer or agreement made before the earlier of the following two dates—

(a)   the date of the holding of the first general meeting of the company after its registration or re-registration as a public company, and

(b)   22 June 1982;

but any resolution to give, vary or revoke an authority for the purposes of section 14 of the Companies Act 1980 or this section has effect for those purposes if passed at any time after the end of April 1980.

80A.   Election by private company as to duration of authority.

(1)   A private company may elect (by elective resolution in accordance with section 379A) that the provisions of this section shall apply, instead of the provisions of section 80(4) and (5), in relation to the giving or renewal, after the election, of an authority under that section.

(2)   The authority must state the maximum amount of relevant securities that may be allotted under it and may be given—

(a)   for an indefinite period, or

(b)   for a fixed period, in which case it must state the date on which it will expire.

(3)   In either case an authority (including an authority contained in the articles) may be revoked or varied by the company in general meeting.

(4)   An authority given for a fixed period may be renewed or further renewed by the company in general meeting.

(5)   A resolution renewing an authority—

(a)   must state, or restate, the amount of relevant securities which may be allotted under the authority or, as the case may be, as the amount remaining to be allotted under it, and

(b)   must state whether the authority is renewed for an indefinite period or for a fixed period, in which case it must state the date on which the renewed authority will expire.

(6)   The references in this section to the maximum amount of relevant securities that may be allotted shall be construed in accordance with section 80(6).

(7)   If an election under this section ceases to have effect, an authority then in force which was given for an indefinite period or for a fixed period of more than five years—

(a)   if given five years or more before the election ceases to have effect, shall expire forthwith, and

(b)   otherwise, shall have effect as if it had been given for a fixed period of five years.

81.   Restriction on public offers by private company.

(1)   A private limited company (other than a company limited by guarantee and not having a share capital) commits an offence if it—

(a)   offers to the public (whether for cash or otherwise) any shares in or debentures of the company; or

(b)   allots or agrees to allot (whether for cash or otherwise) any shares in or debentures of the company with a view to all or any of those shares or debentures being offered for sale to the public (within the meaning given to that expression by sections 58 to 60).

(2)   A company guilty of an offence under this section, and any officer of it who is in default, is liable to a fine.

(3)   Nothing in this section affects the validity of any allotment or sale of shares or debentures, or of any agreement to allot or sell shares or debentures.

[*The Financial Services Act 1986, sch. 17, part I, has repealed the Companies Act 1985, ss. 81 to 83, 86 and 87, and the words in italics in ss. 84, 85 and 97, to the extent to which they would apply in relation to: (a) any investment which is listed or the subject of an application for listing in accordance with part IV of the Financial Services Act 1986 (Financial Services Act 1986 (Commencement No. 3) Order 1986 (SI 1986/2246), art. 5 and sch. 4); (b) a prospectus offering for subscription, or any form of application for, units in a body corporate which is a recognised scheme (Financial Services Act 1986 (Commencement) (No. 8) Order 1988 (SI 1988/740), art. 2 and sch.).*]

82.   Application for, and allotment of, shares and debentures.

(1)   No allotment shall be made of a company's shares or debentures in pursuance of a prospectus issued generally, and no proceedings shall be taken on applications made in pursuance of a prospectus so issued, until the beginning of the third day after that on which the prospectus is first so issued or such later time (if any) as may be specified in the prospectus.

(2)   The beginning of that third day, or that later time, is 'the time of the opening of the subscription lists'.

(3)   In subsection (1), the reference to the day on which the prospectus is first issued generally is to the day when it is first so issued as a newspaper advertisement; and if it is not so issued as a newspaper advertisement before the third day after that on which it is first so issued in any other manner, the reference is to the day on which it is first so issued in any manner.

(4)   In reckoning for this purpose the third day after another day—

(a)   any intervening day which is a Saturday or Sunday, or is a bank holiday in any part of Great Britain, is to be disregarded; and

(b)   if the third day (as so reckoned) is itself a Saturday or Sunday, or a bank holiday, there is to be substituted the first day after that which is none of them.

(5)   The validity of an allotment is not affected by any contravention of subsections (1) to (4); but in the event of contravention, the company and every officer of it who is in default is liable to a fine.

(6)   As applying to a prospectus offering shares or debentures for sale, the above provisions are modified as follows—

(a)   for references to allotment, substitute references to sale; and

(b)   for the reference to the company and every officer of it who is in default, substitute a reference to any person by or through whom the offer is made and who knowingly and wilfully authorises or permits the contravention.

(7)   An application for shares in or debentures of a company which is made in pursuance of a prospectus issued generally is not revocable until after the expiration of the third day after the time of the opening of the subscription lists, or the giving before the expiration of that day of the appropriate public notice; and that notice is one given by some person responsible under sections 67 to 69 for the prospectus and having the effect under those sections of excluding or limiting the responsibility of the giver.
[*See note after s. 81.*]

83.   No allotment unless minimum subscription received.

(1)   No allotment shall be made of any share capital of a company offered to the public for subscription unless—

(a)   there has been subscribed the amount stated in the prospectus as the minimum amount which, in the opinion of the directors, must be raised by the issue of share capital in order to provide for the matters specified in paragraph 2 of Schedule 3 (preliminary expenses, purchase of property, working capital, etc.); and

(b)   the sum payable on application for the amount so stated has been paid to and received by the company.

(2)   For purposes of subsection (1) (b), a sum is deemed paid to the company, and received by it, if a cheque for that sum has been received in good faith by the company and the directors have no reason for suspecting that the cheque will not be paid.

(3)   The amount so stated in the prospectus is to be reckoned exclusively of any amount payable otherwise than in cash and is known as 'the minimum subscription'.

(4)   If the above conditions have not been complied with on the expiration of 40 days after the first issue of the prospectus, all money received from applicants for shares shall be forthwith repaid to them without interest.

(5)   If any of the money is not repaid within 48 days after the issue of the prospectus, the directors of the company are jointly and severally liable to repay it with interest at the rate of 5 per cent per annum from the expiration of the 48th day; except that a director is not so liable if he proves that the default in the repayment of the money was not due to any misconduct or negligence on his part.

(6)   Any condition requiring or binding an applicant for shares to waive compliance with any requirement of this section is void.

(7)   This section does not apply to an allotment of shares subsequent to the first allotment of shares offered to the public for subscription.
[*See note after s. 81.*]

84.   Allotment where issue not fully subscribed.

(1)   No allotment shall be made of any share capital of a public company offered for subscription unless—

(a)   that capital is subscribed for in full; or

(b)   the offer states that, even if the capital is not subscribed for in full, the amount of that capital subscribed for may be allotted in any event or in the event of the conditions specified in the offer being satisfied;

and, where conditions are so specified, no allotment of the capital shall be made by virtue of paragraph (b) unless those conditions are satisfied.

This is without prejudice to section 83.

(2)   If shares are prohibited from being allotted by subsection (1) and 40 days have elapsed after the first issue of the prospectus, all money received from applicants for shares shall be forthwith repaid to them without interest.

(3)   If any of the money is not repaid within 48 days after the issue of the prospectus, the directors of the company are jointly and severally liable to repay it with interest at the rate of 5 per cent per annum from the expiration of the 48th day; except that a director is not so liable if he proves that the default in repayment was not due to any misconduct or negligence on his part.

(4)   This section applies in the case of shares offered as wholly or partly payable otherwise than in cash as it applies in the case of shares offered for subscription (the word 'subscribed' in subsection (1) being construed accordingly).

(5)   In subsections (2) and (3) as they apply to the case of shares offered as wholly or partly payable otherwise than in cash, references to the repayment of money received from applicants for shares include—

(a)   the return of any other consideration so received (including, if the case so requires, the release of the applicant from any undertaking), or

(b)   if it is not reasonably practicable to return the consideration, the payment of money equal to its value at the time it was so received,

and references to interest apply accordingly.

(6)   Any condition requiring or binding an applicant for shares to waive compliance with any requirement of this section is void.

[*See note after s. 81.*]

85.   Effect of irregular allotment.

(1)   An allotment made by a company to an applicant in contravention of section *83 or* 84 is voidable at the instance of the applicant within one month after the date of the allotment, and not later, and is so voidable notwithstanding that the company is in the course of being wound up.

(2)   If a director of a company knowingly contravenes, or permits or authorises the contravention of, any provision of either of those sections with respect to allotment, he is liable to compensate the company and the allottee respectively for any loss, damages or costs which the company or the allottee may have sustained or incurred by the contravention.

(3)   But proceedings to recover any such loss, damages or costs shall not be commenced after the expiration of 2 years from the date of the allotment.

[*See note after s. 81.*]

86.   Allotment of shares etc. to be dealt in on stock exchange.

(1)   The following applies where a prospectus, whether issued generally or not, states that application has been or will be made for permission for the shares or debentures offered by it to be listed on any stock exchange.

(2)   An allotment made on an application in pursuance of the prospectus is, whenever made, void if the permission has not been applied for before the third day after the first issue of the prospectus or if the permission has been refused before the expiration of 3 weeks from the date of the closing of the subscription lists or such longer period (not exceeding 6 weeks) as may, within those 3 weeks, be notified to the applicant for permission by or on behalf of the stock exchange.

(3)   In reckoning for this purpose the third day after another day—

(a)   any intervening day which is a Saturday or Sunday, or is a bank holiday in any part of Great Britain, is to be disregarded; and

(b)   if the third day (as so reckoned) is itself a Saturday or Sunday, or a bank holiday, there is to be substituted the first day after that which is none of them.

(4)   Where permission has not been applied for as above, or has been refused as above, the company shall forthwith repay (without interest) all money received from applicants in pursuance of the prospectus.

(5)   If any of the money is not repaid within 8 days after the company becomes liable to repay it, the directors of the company are jointly and severally liable to repay the money with interest at the rate of 5 per cent per annum from the expiration of the 8th day, except that a director is not liable if he proves that the default in the repayment of the money was not due to any misconduct or negligence on his part.

(6)   All money received from applicants in pursuance of the prospectus shall be kept in a separate bank account so long as the company may become liable to repay it under subsection

(4); and if default is made in complying with this subsection, the company and every officer of it who is in default is liable to a fine.

(7)   Any condition requiring or binding an applicant for shares or debentures to waive compliance with any requirement of this section is void.

(8)   For purposes of this section, permission is not deemed to be refused if it is intimated that the application for it, though not at present granted, will be given further consideration.

(9)   This section has effect in relation to shares or debentures agreed to be taken by a person underwriting an offer of them by a prospectus as if he had applied for them in pursuance of the prospectus.

[See note after s. 81.]

87.   Operation of s. 86 where prospectus offers shares for sale.

(1)   The following has effect as regards the operation of section 86 in relation to a prospectus offering shares for sale.

(2)   Subsections (1) and (2) of that section apply, but with the substitution for the reference in subsection (2) to allotment of a reference to sale.

(3)   Subsections (4) and (5) of that section do not apply; but—

(a)   if the permission referred to in section 86(2) has not been applied for as there mentioned, or has been refused as there mentioned, the offeror of the shares shall forthwith repay (without interest) all money received from applicants in pursuance of the prospectus, and

(b)   if any such money is not repaid within 8 days after the offeror becomes liable to repay it, he becomes liable to pay interest on the money due, at the rate of 5 per cent per annum from the end of the 8th day.

(4)   Subsections (6) to (9) apply, except that in subsection (6)—

(a)   for the first reference to the company there is substituted a reference to the offeror, and

(b)   for the reference to the company and every officer of the company who is in default there is substituted a reference to any person by or through whom the offer is made and who knowingly and wilfully authorises or permits the default.

[See note after s. 81.]

88.   Return as to allotments, etc.

(1)   This section applies to a company limited by shares and to a company limited by guarantee and having a share capital.

(2)   When such a company makes an allotment of its shares, the company shall within one month thereafter deliver to the registrar of companies for registration—

(a)   a return of the allotments (in the prescribed form) stating the number and nominal amount of the shares comprised in the allotment, the names and addresses of the allottees, and the amount (if any) paid or due and payable on each share, whether on account of the nominal value of the share or by way of premium; and

(b)   in the case of shares allotted as fully or partly paid up otherwise than in cash—

(i)   a contract in writing constituting the title of the allottee to the allotment together with any contract of sale, or for services or other consideration in respect of which that allotment was made (such contracts being duly stamped), and

(ii)   a return stating the number and nominal amount of shares so allotted, the extent to which they are to be treated as paid up, and the consideration for which they have been allotted.

(3)   Where such a contract as above mentioned is not reduced to writing, the company shall within one month after the allotment deliver to the registrar of companies for registration the prescribed particulars of the contract stamped with the same stamp duty as would have been payable if the contract had been reduced to writing.

(4)   Those particulars are deemed an instrument within the meaning of the Stamp Act 1891; and the registrar may, as a condition of filing the particulars, require that the duty payable on them be adjudicated under section 12 of that Act.

(5)   If default is made in complying with this section, every officer of the company who is in default is liable to a fine and, for continued contravention, to a daily default fine, but subject as follows.

(6)   In the case of default in delivering to the registrar within one month after the allotment any document required by this section to be delivered, the company, or any officer liable for the default, may apply to the court for relief; and the court, if satisfied that the omission to deliver the document was accidental or due to inadvertence, or that it is just and equitable to grant relief, may make an order extending the time for the delivery of the document for such period as the court thinks proper.

Pre-emption rights

89.   Offers to shareholders to be on pre-emptive basis.

(1)   Subject to the provisions of this section and the seven sections next following, a company proposing to allot equity securities (defined in section 94)—

(a)   shall not allot any of them on any terms to a person unless it has made an offer to each person who holds relevant shares or relevant employee shares to allot to him on the same or more favourable terms a proportion of those securities which is as nearly as practicable equal to the proportion in nominal value held by him of the aggregate of relevant shares and relevant employee shares, and

(b)   shall not allot any of those securities to a person unless the period during which any such offer may be accepted has expired or the company has received notice of the acceptance or refusal of every offer so made.

(2)   Subsection (3) below applies to any provision of a company's memorandum or articles which requires the company, when proposing to allot equity securities consisting of relevant shares of any particular class, not to allot those securities on any terms unless it has complied with the condition that it makes such an offer as is described in subsection (1) to each person who holds relevant shares or relevant employee shares of that class.

(3)   If in accordance with a provision to which this subsection applies—

(a)   a company makes an offer to allot securities to such a holder, and

(b)   he or anyone in whose favour he has renounced his right to their allotment

accepts the offer,

subsection (1) does not appy to the allotment of those securities, and the company may allot them accordingly; but this is without prejudice to the application of subsection (1) in any other case.

(4)   Subsection (1) does not apply to a particular allotment of equity securities if these are, or are to be, wholly or partly paid up otherwise than in cash; and securities which a company has offered to allot to a holder of relevant shares or relevant employee shares may be allotted to him, or anyone in whose favour he has renounced his right to their allotment, without contravening subsection (1)(b).

(5)   Subsection (1) does not apply to the allotment of securities which would, apart from a renunciation or assignment of the right to their allotment, be held under an employees' share scheme.

90.   Communication of pre-emption offers to shareholders.

(1)   This section has effect as to the manner in which offers required by section 89(1), or by a provision to which section 89(3) applies, are to be made to holders of a company's shares.

(2)   Subject to the following subsections, an offer shall be in writing and shall be made to a holder of shares either personally or by sending it by post (that is to say prepaying and posting a letter containing the offer) to him or to his registered address or, if he has no registered address in the United Kingdom, to the address in the United Kingdom supplied by him to the company for the giving of notice to him.

If sent by post, the offer is deemed to be made at the time at which the letter would be delivered in the ordinary course of post.

(3) Where shares are held by two or more persons jointly, the offer may be made to the joint holder first named in the register of members in respect of the shares.

(4) In the case of a holder's death or bankruptcy, the offer may be made—

(a) by sending it by post in a prepaid letter addressed to the persons claiming to be entitled to the shares in consequence of the death or bankruptcy by name, or by the title of representatives of the deceased, or trustee of the bankrupt, or by any like description, at the address in the United Kingdom supplied for the purpose by those so claiming, or

(b) (until such an address has been so supplied) by giving the notice in any manner in which it might have been given if the death or bankruptcy had not occurred.

(5) If the holder—

(a) has no registered address in the United Kingdom and has not given to the company an address in the United Kingdom for the service of notices on him, or

(b) is the holder of a share warrant,

the offer may be made by causing it, or a notice specifying where a copy of it can be obtained or inspected, to be published in the Gazette.

(6) The offer must state a period of not less than 21 days during which it may be accepted; and the offer shall not be withdrawn before the end of that period.

(7) This section does not invalidate a provision to which section 89(3) applies by reason that that provision requires or authorises an offer under it to be made in contravention of any of subsections (1) to (6) above; but, to the extent that the provision requires or authorises such an offer to be so made, it is of no effect.

91. Exclusion of ss. 89, 90 by private company.

(1) Section 89(1), section 90(1) to (5) or section 90(6) may, as applying to allotments by a private company of equity securities or to such allotments of a particular description, be excluded by a provision contained in the memorandum or articles of that company.

(2) A requirement or authority contained in the memorandum or articles of a private company, if it is inconsistent with any of those subsections, has effect as a provision excluding that subsection; but a provision to which section 89(3) applies is not to be treated as inconsistent with section 89(1).

92. Consequences of contravening ss. 89, 90.

(1) If there is a contravention of section 89(1), or of section 90(1) to (5) or section 90(6), or of a provision to which section 89(3) applies, the company, and every officer of it who knowingly authorised or permitted the contravention, are jointly and severally liable to compensate any person to whom an offer should have been made under the subsection or provision contravened for any loss, damage, costs or expenses which the person has sustained or incurred by reason of the contravention.

(2) However, no proceedings to recover any such loss, damage, costs or expenses shall be commenced after the expiration of 2 years from the delivery to the registrar of companies of the return of allotments in question or, where equity securities other than shares are granted, from the date of the grant.

93. Savings for other restrictions as to offers.

(1) Sections 89 to 92 are without prejudice to any enactment by virtue of which a company is prohibited (whether generally or in specified circumstances) from offering or allotting equity securities to any person.

(2) Where a company cannot by virtue of such an enactment offer or allot equity securities to a holder of relevant shares or relevant employee shares, those sections have effect as if the shares held by that holder were not relevant shares or relevant employee shares.

94. Definitions for ss. 89–96.

(1)   The following subsections apply for the interpretation of sections 89 to 96.

(2)   'Equity security', in relation to a company, means a relevant share in the company (other than a share shown in the memorandum to have been taken by a subscriber to the memorandum or a bonus share), or a right to subscribe for, or to convert securities into, relevant shares in the company.

(3)   A reference to the allotment of equity securities or of equity securities consisting of relevant shares of a particular class includes the grant of a right to subscribe for, or to convert any securities into, relevant shares in the company or (as the case may be) relevant shares of a particular class; but such a reference does not include the allotment of any relevant shares pursuant to such a right.

(4)   'Relevant employee shares', in relation to a company, means shares of the company which would be relevant shares in it but for the fact that they are held by a person who acquired them in pursuance of an employees' share scheme.

(5)   'Relevant shares', in relation to a company, means shares in the company other than—

(a)   shares which as respects dividends and capital carry a right to participate only up to a specified amount in a distribution, and

(b)   shares which are held by a person who acquired them in pursuance of an employees' share scheme or, in the case of shares which have not been allotted, are to be allotted in pursuance of such a scheme.

(6)   A reference to a class of shares is to shares to which the same rights are attached as to voting and as to participation, both as respects dividends and as respects capital, in a distribution.

(7)   In relation to an offer to allot securities required by section 89(1) or by any provision to which section 89(3) applies, a reference in sections 89 to 94 (however expressed) to the holder of shares of any description is to whoever was at the close of business on a date, to be specified in the offer and to fall in the period of 28 days immediately before the date of the offer, the holder of shares of that description.

95. Disapplication of pre-emption rights.

(1)   Where the directors of a company are generally authorised for purposes of section 80, they may be given power by the articles, or by a special resolution of the company, to allot equity securities pursuant to that authority as if—

(a)   section 89(1) did not apply to the allotment, or

(b)   that subsection applied to the allotment with such modifications as the directors may determine;
and where the directors make an allotment under this subsection, sections 89 to 94 have effect accordingly.

(2)   Where the directors of a company are authorised for purposes of section 80 (whether generally or otherwise), the company may by special resolution resolve either—

(a)   that section 89(1) shall not apply to a specified allotment of equity securities to be made pursuant to that authority, or

(b)   that that subsection shall apply to the allotment with such modifications as may be specified in the resolution;
and where such a resolution is passed, sections 89 to 94 have effect accordingly.

(3)   The power conferred by subsection (1) or a special resolution under subsection (2) ceases to have effect when the authority to which it relates is revoked or would (if not renewed) expire; but if the authority is renewed, the power or (as the case may be) the resolution may also be renewed, for a period not longer than that for which the authority is renewed, by a special resolution of the company.

(4)   Notwithstanding that any such power or resolution has expired, the directors may allot equity securities in pursuance of an offer or agreement previously made by the

company, if the power or resolution enabled the company to make an offer or agreement which would or might require equity securities to be allotted after it expired.

(5)   A special resolution under subsection (2), or a special resolution to renew such a resolution, shall not be proposed unless it is recommended by the directors and there has been circulated, with the notice of the meeting at which the resolution is proposed, to the members entitled to have that notice a written statement by the directors setting out—

(a)   their reasons for making the recommendation,

(b)   the amount to be paid to the company in respect of the equity securities to be allotted, and

(c)   the directors' justification of that amount.

(6)   A person who knowingly or recklessly authorises or permits the inclusion in a statement circulated under subsection (5) of any matter which is misleading, false or deceptive in a material particular is liable to imprisonment or a fine, or both.

96.   Saving for company's pre-emption procedure operative before 1982.

(1)   Where a company which is re-registered or registered as a public company is or, but for the provisions of the Companies Act 1980 and the enactments replacing it, would be subject at the time of re-registration or (as the case may be) registration to a pre-1982 pre-emption requirement, sections 89 to 95 do not apply to an allotment of the equity securities which are subject to that requirement.

(2)   A 'pre-1982 pre-emption requirement' is a requirement imposed (whether by the company's memorandum or articles, or otherwise) before the relevant date in 1982 by virtue of which the company must, when making an allotment of equity securities, make an offer to allot those securities or some of them in a manner which (otherwise than because involving a contravention of section 90(1) to (5) or 90(6)) is inconsistent with sections 89 to 94; and 'the relevant date in 1982' is—

(a)   except in a case falling within the following paragraph, 22 June in that year, and

(b)   in the case of a company which was re-registered or registered as a public company on an application made before that date, the date on which the application was made.

(3)   A requirement which—

(a)   is imposed on a private company (having been so imposed before the relevant date in 1982) otherwise than by the company's memorandum or articles, and

(b)   if contained in the company's memorandum or articles, would have effect under section 91 to the exclusion of any provisions of sections 89 to 94.

has effect, so long as the company remains a private company, as if it were contained in the memorandum or articles.

(4)   If on the relevant date in 1982 a company, other than a public company registered as such on its original incorporation, was subject to such a requirement as is mentioned in section 89(2) imposed otherwise than by the memorandum or articles, the requirement is to be treated for purposes of sections 89 to 94 as if it were contained in the memorandum or articles.

Commissions and discounts

97.   Power of company to pay commissions.

(1)   It is lawful for a company to pay a commission to any person in consideration of his subscribing or agreeing to subscribe (whether absolutely or conditionally) for any shares in the company, or procuring or agreeing to procure subscriptions (whether absolute or conditional) for any shares in the company, if the following conditions are satisfied.

(2)   The payment of the commission must be authorised by the company's articles; and—

(a) the commission paid or agreed to be paid must not exceed 10 per cent of the price at which the shares are issued or the amount or rate authorised by the articles, whichever is the less; *and*

(b) *the amount or rate per cent of commission paid or agreed to be paid, and the number of shares which persons have agreed for a commission to subscribe absolutely, must be disclosed in the manner required by the following subsection.*

(3) *Those matters must, in the case of shares offered to the public for subscription, be disclosed in the prospectus; and in the case of shares not so offered—*

(a) *they must be disclosed in a statement in the prescribed form signed by every director of the company or by his agent authorised in writing, and delivered (before payment of the commission) to the registrar of companies for registration; and*

(b) *where a circular or notice (not being a prospectus) inviting subscription for the shares is issued, they must also be disclosed in that circular or notice.*

(4) *If default is made in complying with subsection (3)(a) as regards delivery to the registrar of the statement in prescribed form, the company and every officer of it who is in default is liable to a fine.*

[*See note after s. 81.*]

98. Apart from s. 97, commissions and discounts barred.

(1) Except as permitted by section 97, no company shall apply any of its shares or capital money, either directly or indirectly in payment of any commission, discount or allowance to any person in consideration of his subscribing or agreeing to subscribe (whether absolutely or conditionally) for any shares in the company, or procuring or agreeing to procure subscriptions (whether absolute or conditional) for any shares in the company.

(2) This applies whether the shares or money be so applied by being added to the purchase money of any property acquired by the company or to the contract price of any work to be executed for the company, or the money be paid out of the nominal purchase money or contract price, or otherwise.

(3) Nothing in section 97 or this section affects the power of a company to pay such brokerage as has previously been lawful.

(4) A vendor to, or promoter of, or other person who receives payment in money or shares from, a company has, and is deemed always to have had, power to apply any part of the money or shares so received in payment of any commission, the payment of which, if made directly by the company, would have been lawful under section 97 and this section.

Amount to be paid for shares; the means of payment

99. General rules as to payment for shares on allotment.

(1) Subject to the following provisions of this Part, shares allotted by a company, and any premium on them, may be paid up in money or money's worth (including goodwill and know-how).

(2) A public company shall not accept at any time, in payment up of its shares or any premium on them, an undertaking given by any person that he or another should do work or perform services for the company or any other person.

(3) If a public company accepts such an undertaking in payment up of its shares or any premium on them, the holder of the shares when they or the premium are treated as paid up (in whole or in part) by the undertaking is liable—

(a) to pay the company in respect of those shares an amount equal to their nominal value, together with the whole of any premium or, if the case so requires, such proportion of that amount as is treated as paid up by the undertaking; and

(b) to pay interest at the appropriate rate on the amount payable under paragraph (a) above.

(4)   This section does not prevent a company from allotting bonus shares to its members or from paying up, with sums available for the purpose, any amounts for the time being unpaid on any of its shares (whether on account of the nominal value of the shares or by way of premium).

(5)   The reference in subsection (3) to the holder of shares includes any person who has an unconditional right to be included in the company's register of members in respect of those shares or to have an instrument of transfer of them executed in his favour.

100.   Prohibition on allotment of shares at a discount.

(1)   A company's shares shall not be allotted at a discount.

(2)   If shares are allotted in contravention of this section, the allottee is liable to pay the company an amount equal to the amount of the discount, with interest at the appropriate rate.

101.   Shares to be allotted as at least one-quarter paid-up.

(1)   A public company shall not allot a share except as paid up at least as to one-quarter of its nominal value and the whole of any premium on it.

(2)   Subsection (1) does not apply to shares allotted in pursuance of an employees' share scheme.

(3)   If a company allots a share in contravention of subsection (1), the share is to be treated as if one-quarter of its nominal value, together with the whole of any premium on it, had been received.

(4)   But the allottee is liable to pay the company the minimum amount which should have been received in respect of the share under subsection (1) (less the value of any consideration actually applied in payment up, to any extent, of the share and any premium on it), with interest at the appropriate rate.

(5)   Subsections (3) and (4) do not apply to the allotment of bonus shares, unless the allottee knew or ought to have known the shares were allotted in contravention of subsection (1).

102.   Restriction on payment by long-term undertaking.

(1)   A public company shall not allot shares as fully or partly paid up (as to their nominal value or any premium on them) otherwise than in cash if the consideration for the allotment is or includes an undertaking which is to be, or may be, performed more than 5 years after the date of the allotment.

(2)   If a company allots shares in contravention of subsection (1), the allottee is liable to pay the company an amount equal to the aggregate of their nominal value and the whole of any premium (or, if the case so requires, so much of that aggregate as is treated as paid up by the undertaking), with interest at the appropriate rate.

(3)   Where a contract for the allotment of shares does not contravene subsection (1), any variation of the contract which has the effect that the contract would have contravened the subsection, if the terms of the contract as varied had been its original terms, is void.

(4)   Subsection (3) applies also to the variation by a public company of the terms of a contract entered into before the company was re-registered as a public company.

(5)   The following subsection applies where a public company allots shares for a consideration which consists of or includes (in accordance with subsection (1)) an undertaking which is to be performed within 5 years of the allotment, but the undertaking is not performed within the period allowed by the contract for the allotment of the shares.

(6)   The allottee is then liable to pay the company, at the end of the period so allowed, an amount equal to the aggregate of the nominal value of the shares and the

whole of any premium (or, if the case so requires, so much of that aggregate as is treated as paid up by the undertaking), with interest at the appropriate rate.

(7)   A reference in this section to a contract for the allotment of shares includes an ancillary contract relating to payment in respect of them.

103.   Non-cash consideration to be valued before allotment.

(1)   A public company shall not allot shares as fully or partly paid up (as to their nominal value or any premium on them) otherwise than in cash unless—

(a)   the consideration for the allotment has been independently valued under section 108; and

(b)   a report with respect to its value has been made to the company by a person appointed by the company (in accordance with that section) during the 6 months immediately preceding the allotment of the shares; and

(c)   a copy of the report has been sent to the proposed allottee.

(2)   Where an amount standing to the credit of any of a company's reserve accounts, or of its profit and loss account, is applied in paying up (to any extent) any shares allotted to members of the company or any premiums on shares so allotted, the amount applied does not count as consideration for the allotment, and accordingly subsection (1) does not apply in that case.

(3)   Subsection (1) does not apply to the allotment of shares by a company in connection with an arrangement providing for the allotment of shares in that company on terms that the whole or part of the consideration for the shares allotted is to be provided by the transfer to that company (or the cancellation) of all or some of the shares, or of all or some of the shares of a particular class, in another company (with or without the issue to that company of shares, or of shares of any particular class, in that other company).

(4)   But subsection (3) does not exclude the application of subsection (1) unless under the arrangement it is open to all the holders of the shares in the other company in question (or, where the arrangement applies only to shares of a particular class, to all the holders of shares in that other company, being holders of shares of that class) to take part in the arrangement.

In determining whether that is the case, shares held by or by a nominee of the company proposing to allot the shares in connection with the arrangement, or by a nominee of a company which is that company's holding company or subsidiary or a company which is a subsidiary of its holding company, shall be disregarded.

(5)   Subsection (1) also does not apply to the allotment of shares by a company in connection with its proposed merger with another company; that is, where one of the companies proposes to acquire all the assets and liabilities of the other in exchange for the issue of shares or other securities of that one to shareholders of the other, with or without any cash payment to shareholders.

(6)   If a company allots shares in contravention of subsection (1) and either—

(a)   the allottee has not received the valuer's report required by that subsection to be sent to him; or

(b)   there has been some other contravention of this section or section 108 which the allottee knew or ought to have known amounted to a contravention,

the allottee is liable to pay the company an amount equal to the aggregate of the nominal value of the shares and the whole of any premium (or, if the case so requires, so much of that aggregate as is treated as paid up by the consideration), with interest at the appropriate rate.

(7)   In this section—

(a)   'arrangement' means any agreement, scheme or arrangement (including an arrangement sanctioned in accordance with section 425 (company compromise with creditors and members) or section 110 of the Insolvency Act (liquidator in winding up accepting shares as consideration for sale of company property)), and

(b)   any reference to a company, except where it is or is to be construed as a reference to a public company, includes any body corporate and any body to which letters patent have been issued under the Chartered Companies Act 1837.

104.   Transfer to public company of non-cash asset in initial period.

(1)   A public company formed as such shall not, unless the conditions of this section have been complied with, enter into an agreement with a person for the transfer by him during the initial period of one or more non-cash assets to the company or another, if—

(a)   that person is a subscriber to the company's memorandum, and

(b)   the consideration for the transfer to be given by the company is equal in value at the time of the agreement to one-tenth or more of the company's nominal share capital issued at that time.

(2)   The 'initial period' for this purpose is 2 years beginning with the date of the company being issued with a certificate under section 117 (or the previous corresponding provision) that it was entitled to do business.

(3)   This section applies also to a company re-registered as a public company (except one re-registered under section 8 of the Companies Act 1980 or section 2 of the Consequential Provisions Act), or registered under section 685 (joint stock company) or the previous corresponding provision; but in that case—

(a)   there is substituted a reference in subsection (1)(a) to a person who is a member of the company on the date of registration or re-registration, and

(b)   the initial period is then 2 years beginning with that date.

In this subsection the reference to a company re-registered as a public company includes a private company so re-registered which was a public company before it was a private company.

(4)   The conditions of this section are as follows—

(a)   the consideration to be received by the company, and any consideration other than cash to be given by the company, must have been independently valued under section 109;

(b)   a report with respect to the consideration to be so received and given must have been made to the company in accordance with that section during the 6 months immediately preceding the date of the agreement;

(c)   the terms of the agreement must have been approved by an ordinary resolution of the company; and

(d)   not later than the giving of the notice of the meeting at which the resolution is proposed, copies of the resolution and report must have been circulated to the members of the company entitled to receive the notice and, if the person with whom the agreement in question is proposed to be made is not then a member of the company so entitled, to that person.

(5)   In subsection (4)(a)—

(a)   the reference to the consideration to be received by the company is to the asset to be transferred to it or the advantage to the company of the asset's transfer to another person; and

(b)   the specified condition is without prejudice to any requirement to value any consideration for purposes of section 103.

(6)   In the case of the following agreements, this section does not apply—

(a)   where it is part of the company's ordinary business to acquire, or arrange for other persons to acquire, assets of a particular description, an agreement entered into by the company in the ordinary course of its business for the transfer of an asset of that description to it or to such a person, as the case may be;

(b)   an agreement entered into by the company under the supervision of the court, or of an officer authorised by the court for the purpose, for the transfer of an asset to the company or to another.

105. Agreements contravening s. 104.

(1)   The following subsection applies if a public company enters into an agreement contravening section 104, the agreement being made with the person referred to in subsection (1)(a) or (as the case may be) subsection (3) of that section, and either—

(a)   that person has not received the valuer's report required for compliance with the conditions of the section, or

(b)   there has been some other contravention of the section or of section 108(1), (2) or (5) or section 109, which he knew or ought to have known amounted to a contravention.

(2)   The company is then entitled to recover from that person any consideration given by it under the agreement, or an amount equal to the value of the consideration at the time of the agreement; and the agreement, so far as not carried out, is void.

(3)   However, if the agreement is or includes an agreement for the allotment of shares in the company, then—

(a)   whether or not the agreement also contravenes section 103, subsection (2) above does not apply to it in so far as it is for the allotment of shares; and

(b)   the allottee is liable to pay the company an amount equal to the aggregate of the nominal value of the shares and the whole of any premium (or, if the case so requires, so much of that aggregate as is treated as paid up by the consideration), with interest at the appropriate rate.

106. Shares issued to subscribers of memorandum.

Shares taken by a subscriber to the memorandum of a public company in pursuance of an undertaking of his in the memorandum, and any premium on the shares, shall be paid up in cash.

107. Meaning of 'the appropriate rate'.

In sections 99 to 105 'the appropriate rate', in relation to interest, means 5 per cent per annum or such other rate as may be specified by order made by the Secretary of State by statutory instrument subject to annulment in pursuance of a resolution of either House of Parliament.

Valuation provisions

108. Valuation and report (s. 103).

(1)   The valuation and report required by section 103 (or, where applicable, section 44) shall be made by an independent person, that is to say a person qualified at the time of the report to be appointed, or continue to be, an auditor of the company.

(2)   However, where it appears to the independent person (from here on referred to as 'the valuer') to be reasonable for the valuation of the consideration, or part of it, to be made (or for him to accept such a valuation) by another person who—

(a)   appears to him to have the requisite knowledge and experience to value the consideration or that part of it; and

(b)   is not an officer or servant of the company or any other body corporate which is that company's subsidiary or holding company or a subsidiary of that company's holding company or a partner or employee of such an officer or servant,

he may arrange for or accept such a valuation, together with a report which will enable him to make his own report under this section and provide the note required by subsection (6) below.

(3)   The reference in subsection (2)(b) to an officer or servant does not include an auditor.

(4)   The valuer's report shall state—

(a)   the nominal value of the shares to be wholly or partly paid for by the consideration in question;

(b)   the amount of any premium payable on the shares;

(c)   the description of the consideration and, as respects so much of the consideration as he himself has valued, a description of that part of the consideration, the method used to value it and the date of the valuation;

(d)   the extent to which the nominal value of the shares and any premium are to be treated as paid up—

    (i)   by the consideration;

    (ii)   in cash

(5)   Where the consideration or part of it is valued by a person other than the valuer himself, the latter's report shall state that fact and shall also—

(a)   state the former's name and what knowledge and experience he has to carry out the valuation, and

(b)   describe so much of the consideration as was valued by the other person, and the method used to value it, and specify the date of the valuation.

(6)   The valuer's report shall contain or be accompanied by a note by him—

(a)   in the case of a valuation made by a person other than himself, that it appeared to himself reasonable to arrange for it to be so made or to accept a valuation so made;

(b)   whoever made the valuation, that the method of valuation was reasonable in all the circumstances;

(c)   that it appears to the valuer that there has been no material change in the value of the consideration in question since the valuation; and

(d)   that on the basis of the valuation the value of the consideration, together with any cash by which the nominal value of the shares or any premium payable on them is to be paid up, is not less than so much of the aggregate of the nominal value and the whole of any such premium as is treated as paid up by the consideration and any such cash.

(7)   Where the consideration to be valued is accepted partly in payment up of the nominal value of the shares and any premium and partly for some other consideration given by the company, section 103 (and, where applicable, section 44) and the foregoing provisions of this section apply as if references to the consideration accepted by the company included the proportion of that consideration which is properly attributable to the payment up of that value and any premium; and—

(a)   the valuer shall carry out, or arrange for, such other valuations as will enable him to determine that proportion; and

(b)   his report shall state what valuations have been made under this subsection and also the reason for, and method and date of, any such valuation and any other matters which may be relevant to the determination.

109.   Valuation and report (s. 104).

(1)   Subsections (1) to (3) and (5) of section 108 apply also as respects the valuation and report for the purposes of section 104.

(2)   The valuer's report for those purposes shall—

(a)   state the consideration to be received by the company, describing the asset in question (specifying the amount to be received in cash) and the consideration to be given by the company (specifying the amount to be given in cash);

(b)   state the method and date of valuation;

(c)   contain or be accompanied by a note as to the matters mentioned in section 108(6)(a) to (c); and

(d)   contain or be accompanied by a note that on the basis of the valuation the value of the consideration to be received by the company is not less than the value of the consideration to be given by it.

(3)   A reference in section 104 or this section to consideration given for the transfer of an asset includes consideration given partly for its transfer; but—

(a)   the value of any consideration partly so given is to be taken as the proportion of the consideration properly attributable to its transfer;

(b)   the valuer shall carry out or arrange for such valuations of anything else as will enable him to determine that proportion; and

(c)   his report for purposes of section 104 shall state what valuation has been made under this subsection and also the reason for and method and date of any such valuation and any other matters which may be relevant to that determination.

110.   Entitlement of valuer to full disclosure.

(1)   A person carrying out a valuation or making a report under section 103 or 104, with respect to any consideration proposed to be accepted or given by a company, is entitled to require from the officers of the company such information and explanation as he thinks necessary to enable him to carry out the valuation or make the report and provide a note under section 108(6) or (as the case may be) section 109(2)(c).

(2)   A person who knowingly or recklessly makes a statement which—

(a)   is misleading, false or deceptive in a material particular, and

(b)   is a statement to which this subsection applies,

is guilty of an offence and liable to imprisonment or a fine, or both.

(3)   Subsection (2) applies to any statement made (whether orally or in writing) to a person carrying out a valuation or making a report under section 108 or 109, being a statement which conveys or purports to convey any information or explanation which that person requires, or is entitled to require, under subsection (1) of this section.

111.   Matters to be communicated to registrar.

(1)   A company to which a report is made under section 108 as to the value of any consideration for which, or partly for which, it proposes to allot shares shall deliver a copy of the report to the registrar of companies for registration at the same time that it files the return of the allotments of those shares under section 88.

(2)   A company which has passed a resolution under section 104 with respect to the transfer of an asset shall, within 15 days of so doing, deliver to the registrar of companies a copy of the resolution together with the valuer's report required by that section.

(3)   If default is made in complying with subsection (1), every officer of the company who is in default is liable to a fine and, for continued contravention, to a daily default fine; but this is subject to the same exception as is made by section 88(6) (relief on application to the court) in the case of default in complying with that section.

(4)   If a company fails to comply with subsection (2), it and every officer of it who is in default is liable to a fine and, for continued contravention, to a daily default fine.

Other matters arising out of allotment &c.

111A.   Right to damages, &c. not affected.

A person is not debarred from obtaining damages or other compensation from a company by reason only of his holding or having held shares in the company or any right to apply or subscribe for shares or to be included in the company's register in respect of shares.

112.   Liability of subsequent holders of shares allotted.

(1)   If a person becomes a holder of shares in respect of which—

(a)   there has been a contravention of section 99, 100, 101 or 103; and

(b)   by virtue of that contravention, another is liable to pay any amount under the section contravened,

that person is also liable to pay that amount (jointly and severally with any other person so liable), unless he is exempted from liability by subsection (3) below.

(2)   If a company enters into an agreement in contravention of section 104 and—

(a)   the agreement is or includes an agreement for the allotment of shares in the company; and

(b)   a person becomes a holder of shares allotted under the agreement; and

(c)   by virtue of the agreement and allotment under it, another person is liable to pay any amount under section 105,
the person who becomes the holder of the shares is also liable to pay that amount (jointly and severally with any other person so liable), unless he is exempted from liability by the following subsection; and this applies whether or not the agreement also contravenes section 103.

(3)   A person otherwise liable under subsection (1) or (2) is exempted from that liability if either—

(a)   he is a purchaser for value and, at the time of the purchase, he did not have actual notice of the contravention concerned; or

(b)   he derived title to the shares (directly or indirectly) from a person who became a holder of them after the contravention and was not liable under subsection (1) or (as the case may be) subsection (2).

(4)   References in this section to a holder, in relation to shares in a company, include any person who has an unconditional right to be included in the company's register of members in respect of those shares or to have an instrument of transfer of the shares executed in his favour.

(5)   As subsection (1) and (3) apply in relation to the contraventions there mentioned, they also apply—

(a)   to a contravention of section 102; and

(b)   to a failure to carry out a term of a contract as mentioned in subsections (5) and (6) of that section.

113.   Relief in respect of certain liabilities under ss. 99 ff.

(1)   Where a person is liable to a company under—

(a)   section 99, 102, 103 or 105;

(b)   section 112(1) by reference to a contravention of section 99 or 103; or

(c)   section 112(2) or (5),

in relation to payment in respect of any shares in the company, or is liable by virtue of an undertaking given to it in, or in connection with, payment for any such shares, the person so liable may make an application to the court to be exempted in whole or in part from the liability.

(2)   If the liability mentioned in subsection (1) arises in relation to payment in respect of any shares, the court may, on an application under that subsection, exempt the applicant from the liability only—

(a)   if and to the extent that it appears to the court just and equitable to do so having regard to the matters mentioned in the following subsection,

(b)   if and to the extent that it appears to the court just and equitable to do so in respect of any interest which he is liable to pay the company under any of the relevant sections.

(3)   The matters to be taken into account by the court under subsection (2)(a) are—

(a)   whether the applicant has paid, or is liable to pay, any amount in respect of any other liability arising in relation to those shares under any of the relevant sections, or of any liability arising by virtue of any undertaking given in or in connection with payment for those shares;

(b)   whether any person other than the applicant has paid or is likely to pay (whether in pursuance of an order of the court or otherwise) any such amount; and

(c)   whether the applicant or any other person has performed in whole or in part, or is likely so to perform, any such undertaking, or has done or is likely to do any other thing in payment or part payment for the shares.

(4)   Where the liability arises by virtue of an undertaking given to the company in, or in connection with, payment for shares in it, the court may, on an application under subsection (1), exempt the applicant from the liability only if and to the extent that it appears to the court just and equitable to do so having regard to—

(a)   whether the applicant has paid or is liable to pay any amount in respect of liability arising in relation to the shares under any of the provisions mentioned in that subsection; and

(b)   whether any person other than the applicant has paid or is likely to pay (whether in pursuance of an order of the court or otherwise) any such amount.

(5)   In determining whether it should exempt the applicant in whole or in part from any liability, the court shall have regard to the following overriding principles, namely—

(a)   that a company which has allotted shares should receive money or money's worth at least equal in value to the aggregate of the nominal value of those shares and the whole of any premium or, if the case so requires, so much of that aggregate as is treated as paid up; and

(b)   subject to this, that where such a company would, if the court did not grant the exemption, have more than one remedy against a particular person, it should be for the company to decide which remedy it should remain entitled to pursue.

(6)   If a person brings proceedings against another ('the contributor') for a contribution in respect of liability to a company arising under any of sections 99 to 105 or 112, and it appears to the court that the contributor is liable to make such a contribution, the court may exercise the powers of the following subsection.

(7)   The court may, if and to the extent that it appears to it, having regard to the respective culpability (in respect of the liability to the company) of the contributor and the person bringing the proceedings, that it is just and equitable to do so—

(a)   exempt the contributor in whole or in part from his liability to make such a contribution; or

(b)   order the contributor to make a larger contribution than, but for this subsection, he would be liable to make.

(8)   Where a person is liable to a company under section 105(2), the court may, on application, exempt him in whole or in part from that liability if and to the extent that it appears to the court just and equitable to do so having regard to any benefit accruing to the company by virtue of anything done by him towards the carrying out of the agreement mentioned in that subsection.

114.   Penalty for contravention.

If a company contravenes any of the provisions of sections 99 to 104 and 106 the company and any officer of it who is in default is liable to a fine.

115.   Undertakings to do work, etc.

(1)   Subject to section 113, an undertaking given by any person, in or in connection with payment for shares in a company, to do work or perform services or to do any other thing, if it is enforceable by the company apart from this Act, is so enforceable notwithstanding that there has been a contravention in relation to it of , 102 or 103.

(2)   Where such an undertaking is given in contravention of section 104 in respect of the allotment of shares, it is so enforceable notwithstanding the contravention.

116.   Application of ss. 99 ff to special cases.

Except as provided by section 9 of the Consequential Provisions Act (transitional cases dealt with by section 31 of the Companies Act 1980), sections 99, 101 to 103, 106, 108, 110, 111 and 112 to 115 apply—

(a)   to a company which has passed and not revoked a resolution to be re-registered under section 43 as a public company, and

(b)   to a joint stock company which has passed, and not revoked, a resolution that the company be a public company,

as those sections apply to a public company.

PART V
SHARE CAPITAL, ITS INCREASE, MAINTENANCE AND REDUCTION

CHAPTER I
GENERAL PROVISIONS ABOUT SHARE CAPITAL

117. Public company share capital requirements.

(1)   A company registered as a public company on its original incorporation shall not do business or exercise any borrowing powers unless the registrar of companies has issued it with a certificate under this section or the company is re-registered as a private company.

(2)   The registrar shall issue a company with such a certificate if, on an application made to him by the company in the prescribed form, he is satisfied that the nominal value of the company's allotted share capital is not less than the authorised minimum, and there is delivered to him a statutory declaration complying with the following subsection.

(3)   The statutory declaration must be in the prescribed form and be signed by a director or secretary of the company; and it must—

(a)   state that the nominal value of the company's allotted share capital is not less than the authorised minimum;

(b)   specify the amount paid up, at the time of the application, on the allotted share capital of the company;

(c)   specify the amount, or estimated amount, of the company's preliminary expenses and the persons by whom any of those expenses have been paid or are payable; and

(d)   specify any amount or benefit paid or given, or intended to be paid or given, to any promoter of the company, and the consideration for the payment or benefit.

(4)   For the purposes of subsection (2), a share allotted in pursuance of an employees' share scheme may not be taken into account in determining the nominal value of the company's allotted share capital unless it is paid up at least as to one-quarter of the nominal value of the share and the whole of any premium on the share.

(5)   The registrar may accept a statutory declaration delivered to him under this section as sufficient evidence of the matters stated in it.

(6)   A certificate under this section in respect of a company is conclusive evidence that the company is entitled to do business and exercise any borrowing powers.

(7)   If a company does business or exercises borrowing powers in contravention of this section, the company and any officer of it who is in default is liable to a fine.

(8)   Nothing in this section affects the validity of any transaction entered into by a company; but, if a company enters into a transaction in contravention of this section and fails to comply with its obligations in that connection within 21 days from being called upon to do so, the directors of the company are jointly and severally liable to indemnify the other party to the transaction in respect of any loss or damage suffered by him by reason of the company's failure to comply with those obligations.

118. The authorised minimum.

(1)   In this Act, 'the authorised minimum' means £50,000, or such other sum as the Secretary of State may by order made by statutory instrument specify instead.

(2)   An order under this section which increases the authorised minimum may—

(a)   require any public company having an allotted share capital of which the nominal value is less than the amount specified in the order as the authorised minimum to increase that value to not less than that amount or make application to be re-registered as a private company;

(b)   make, in connection with any such requirement, provision for any of the matters for which provision is made by this Act relating to a company's registration, re-registration or change of name, to payment for any share comprised in a company's capital and to offers of shares in or debentures of a company to the public, including provision as to the consequences (whether in criminal law or otherwise) of a failure to comply with any requirement of the order; and

(c)   contain such supplemental and transitional provisions as the Secretary of State thinks appropriate, make different provision for different cases and, in particular, provide for any provision of the order to come into operation on different days for different purposes.

(3)   An order shall not be made under this section unless a draft of it has been laid before Parliament and approved by resolution of each House.

119.   Provision for different amounts to be paid on shares.

A company, if so authorised by its articles, may do any one or more of the following things—

(a)   make arrangements on the issue of shares for a difference between the shareholders in the amounts and times of payment of calls on their shares;

(b)   accept from any member the whole or a part of the amount remaining unpaid on any shares held by him, although no part of that amount has been called up;

(c)   pay dividend in proportion to the amount paid up on each share where a larger amount is paid up on some shares than on others.

120.   Reserve liability of limited company.

A limited company may by special resolution determine that any portion of its share capital which has not been already called up shall not be capable of being called up except in the event and for the purposes of the company being wound up; and that portion of its share capital is then not capable of being called up except in that event and for those purposes.

121.   Alteration of share capital (limited companies).

(1)   A company limited by shares or a company limited by guarantee and having a share capital, if so authorised by its articles, may alter the conditions of its memorandum in any of the following ways.

(2)   The company may—

(a)   increase its share capital by new shares of such amount as it thinks expedient;

(b)   consolidate and divide all or any of its share capital into shares of larger amount than its existing shares;

(c)   convert all or any of its paid-up shares into stock, and reconvert that stock into paid-up shares of any denomination;

(d)   subdivide its shares, or any of them, into shares of smaller amount than is fixed by the memorandum (but subject to the following subsection);

(e)   cancel shares which, at the date of the passing of the resolution to cancel them, have not been taken or agreed to be taken by any person, and diminish the amount of the company's share capital by the amount of the shares so cancelled.

(3)   In any subdivision under subsection (2)(d) the proportion between the amount paid and the amount, if any, unpaid on each reduced share must be the same as it was in the case of the share from which the reduced share is derived.

(4)   The powers conferred by this section must be exercised by the company in general meeting.

(5)   A cancellation of shares under this section does not for purposes of this Act constitute a reduction of share capital.

122.   Notice to registrar of alteration.

(1)   If a company having a share capital has—

(a)   consolidated and divided its share capital into shares of larger amount than its existing shares; or

(b)   converted any shares into stock; or
(c)   reconverted stock into shares; or
(d)   subdivided its shares or any of them; or
(e)   redeemed any redeemable shares; or
(f)   cancelled any shares (otherwise than in connection with a reduction of share capital under section 135),

it shall within one month after so doing give notice in the prescribed form to the registrar of companies, specifying (as the case may be) the shares consolidated, divided, converted, subdivided, redeemed or cancelled, or the stock reconverted.

(2)   If default is made in complying with this section, the company and every officer of it who is in default is liable to a fine and, for continued contravention, to a daily default fine.

123.   Notice to registrar of increased share capital.

(1)   If a company having a share capital (whether or not its shares have been converted into stock) increases its share capital beyond the registered capital, it shall within 15 days after the passing of the resolution authorising the increase, give to the registrar of companies notice of the increase, and the registrar shall record the increase.

(2)   The notice must include such particulars as may be prescribed with respect to the classes of shares affected and the conditions subject to which the new shares have been or are to be issued.

(3)   There shall be fowarded to the registrar together with the notice a printed copy of the resolution authorising the increase, or a copy of the resolution in some other form approved by the registrar.

(4)   If default is made in complying with this section, the company and every officer of it who is in default is liable to a fine and, for continued contravention, to a daily default fine.

124.   Reserve capital of unlimited company.

An unlimited company having a share capital may by its resolution for re-registration as a public company under section 43, or as a limited company under section 51—

(a)   increase the nominal amount of its share capital by increasing the nominal amount of each of its shares (but subject to the condition that no part of the increased capital is to be capable of being called up except in the event and for the purpose of the company being wound up), and

(b)   alternatively or in addition, provide that a specified portion of its uncalled share capital is not to be capable of being called up except in that event and for that purpose.

CHAPTER II
CLASS RIGHTS

125.   Variation of class rights.

(1)   This section is concerned with the variation of the rights attached to any class of shares in a company whose share capital is divided into shares of different classes.

(2)   Where the rights are attached to a class of shares otherwise than by the company's memorandum, and the company's articles do not contain provision with respect to the variation of the rights, those rights may be varied if, but only if—

(a)   the holders of three-quarters in nominal value of the issued shares of that class consent in writing to the variation; or

(b)   an extraordinary resolution passed at a separate general meeting of the holders of that class sanctions the variation;

and any requirement (howsoever imposed) in relation to the variation of those rights is complied with to the extent that it is not comprised in paragraphs (a) and (b) above.

(3)   Where—

(a)   the rights are attached to a class of shares by the memorandum or otherwise;

(b)   the memorandum or articles contain provision for the variation of those rights; and

(c)   the variation of those rights is connected with the giving, variation, revocation or renewal of an authority for allotment under section 80 or with a reduction of the company's share capital under section 135;

those rights shall not be varied unless—

(i)   the condition mentioned in subsection (2)(a) or (b) above is satisfied; and

(ii)   any requirement of the memorandum or articles in relation to the variation of rights of that class is complied with to the extent that it is not comprised in that condition.

(4)   If the rights are attached to a class of shares in the company by the memorandum or otherwise and—

(a)   where they are so attached by the memorandum, the articles contain provision with respect to their variation which had been included in the articles at the time of the company's original incorporation; or

(b)   where they are so attached otherwise, the articles contain such provision (whenever first so included),

and in either case the variation is not connected as mentioned in subsection (3)(c), those rights may only be varied in accordance with that provision of the articles.

(5)   If the rights are attached to a class of shares by the memorandum, and the memorandum and articles do not contain provision with respect to the variation of those rights, those rights may be varied if all the members of the company agree to the variation.

(6)   The provisions of section 369 (length of notice for calling company meetings), section 370 (general provisions as to meetings and votes), and sections 376 and 377 (circulation of members' resolutions) and the provisions of the articles relating to general meetings shall, so far as applicable, apply in relation to any meeting of shareholders required by this section or otherwise to take place in connection with the variation of the rights attached to a class of shares, and shall so apply with the necessary modifications and subject to the following provisions, namely—

(a)   the necessary quorum at any such meeting other than an adjourned meeting shall be two persons holding or representing by proxy at least one-third in nominal value of the issued shares of the class in question and at an adjourned meeting one person holding shares of the class in question or his proxy;

(b)   any holder of shares of the class in question present in person or by proxy may demand a poll.

(7)   Any alteration of a provision contained in a company's articles for the variation of the rights attached to a class of shares, or the insertion of any such provision into the articles, is itself to be treated as a variation of those rights.

(8)   In this section and (except where the context otherwise requires) in any provision for the variation of the rights attached to a class of shares contained in a company's memorandum or articles, references to the variation of those rights are to be read as including references to their abrogation.

126.   Saving for court's powers under other provisions.

Nothing in subsections (2) to (5) of section 125 derogates from the powers of the court under the following sections of this Act, namely—

sections 4 to 6 (company resolution to alter objects),

section 54 (litigated objection to public company becoming private by re-registration),

section 425 (court control of company compromising with members and creditors),

section 427 (company reconstruction or amalgamation),

sections 459 to 461 (protection of minorities).

127.   Shareholders' right to object to variation.

(1)´   This section applies if, in the case of a company whose share capital is divided into different classes of shares—

(a)   provision is made by the memorandum or articles for authorising the variation of the rights attached to any class of shares in the company, subject to—

(i)   the consent of any specified proportion of the holders of the issued shares of that class, or

(ii)   the sanction of a resolution passed at a separate meeting of the holders of those shares,

and in pursuance of that provision the rights attached to any such class of shares are at any time varied; or

(b)   the rights attached to any class of shares in the company are varied under section 125(2).

(2)   The holders of not less in the aggregate than 15 per cent of the issued shares of the class in question (being persons who did not consent to or vote in favour of the resolution for the variation), may apply to the court to have the variation cancelled; and if such an application is made, the variation has no effect unless and until it is confirmed by the court.

(3)   Application to the court must be made within 21 days after the date on which the consent was given or the resolution was passed (as the case may be), and may be made on behalf of the shareholders entitled to make the application by such one or more of their number as they may appoint in writing for the purpose.

(4)   The court, after hearing the applicant and any other persons who apply to the court to be heard and appear to the court to be interested in the application, may, if satisfied having regard to all the circumstances of the case, that the variation would unfairly prejudice the shareholders of the class represented by the applicant, disallow the variation and shall, if not so satisfied, confirm it.

The decision of the court on any such application is final.

(5)   The company shall within 15 days after the making of an order by the court on such an application forward a copy of the order to the registrar of companies; and, if default is made in complying with this provision, the company and every officer of it who is in default is liable to a fine and, for continued contravention, to a daily default fine.

(6)   'Variation', in this section, includes abrogation; and 'varied' is to be construed accordingly.

128.   Registration of particulars of special rights.

(1)   If a company allots shares with rights which are not stated in its memorandum or articles, or in any resolution or agreement which is required by section 380 to be sent to the registrar of companies, the company shall deliver to the registrar of companies, within one month from allotting the shares, a statement in the prescribed form containing particulars of those rights.

(2)   This does not apply if the shares are in all respects uniform with shares previously allotted; and shares are not for this purpose to be treated as different from shares previously allotted by reason only that the former do not carry the same rights to dividends as the latter during the 12 months immediately following the former's allotment.

(3)   Where the rights attached to any shares of a company are varied otherwise than by an amendment of the company's memorandum or articles or by a resolution or agreement subject to section 380, the company shall within one month from the date on which the variation is made deliver to the registrar of companies a statement in the prescribed form containing particulars of the variation.

(4)   Where a company (otherwise than by any such amendment, resolution or agreement as is mentioned above) assigns a name or other designation, or a new name

or other designation, to any class of its shares, it shall within one month from doing so deliver to the registrar of companies a notice in the prescribed form giving particulars of the name or designation so assigned.

(5)   If a company fails to comply with this section, the company and every officer of it who is in default is liable to a fine and, for continued contravention, to a daily default fine.

129.   Registration of newly created class rights.

(1)   If a company not having a share capital creates a class of members with rights which are not stated in its memorandum or articles or in a resolution or agreement to which section 380 applies, the company shall deliver to the registrar of companies within one month from the date on which the new class is created a statement in the prescribed form containing particulars of the rights attached to that class.

(2)   If the rights of any class of members of the company are varied otherwise than by an amendment of the memorandum or articles or by a resolution or agreement subject to section 380, the company shall within one month from the date on which the variation is made deliver to the registrar a statement in the prescribed form containing particulars of the variation.

(3)   If a company (otherwise than by such an amendment, resolution or agreement as is mentioned above) assigns a name or other designation, or a new name or other designation, to any class of its members, it shall within one month from doing so deliver to the registrar a notice in the prescribed form giving particulars of the name or designation so assigned.

(4)   If a company fails to comply with this section, the company and every officer of it who is in default is liable to a fine and, for continued contravention, to a daily default fine.

CHAPTER III
SHARE PREMIUMS

130.   Application of share premiums.

(1)   If a company issues shares at a premium, whether for cash or otherwise, a sum equal to the aggregate amount or value of the premiums on those shares shall be transferred to an account called 'the share premium account'.

(2)   The share premium account may be applied by the company in paying up unissued shares to be allotted to members as fully paid bonus shares, or in writing off—

(a)   the company's preliminary expenses; or

(b)   the expenses of, or the commission paid or discount allowed on, any issue of shares or debentures of the company,

or in providing for the premium payable on redemption of debentures of the company.

(3)   Subject to this, the provisions of this Act relating to the reduction of a company's share capital apply as if the share premium account were part of its paid-up share capital.

(4)   Sections 131 and 132 below give relief from the requirements of this section, and in those sections references to the issuing company are to the company issuing shares as above mentioned.

131.   Merger relief.

(1)   With the exception made by section 132(8) (group reconstruction) this section applies where the issuing company has secured at least a 90 per cent equity holding in another company in pursuance of an arrangement providing for the allotment of equity shares in the issuing company on terms that the consideration for the shares allotted is to be provided—

(a)   by the issue or transfer to the issuing company of equity shares in the other company, or

(b)   by the cancellation of any such shares not held by the issuing company.

(2)   If the equity shares in the issuing company allotted in pursuance of the arrangement in consideration for the acquisition or cancellation of equity shares in the other company are issued at a premium, section 130 does not apply to the premiums on those shares.

(3)   Where the arrangement also provides for the allotment of any shares in the issuing company on terms that the consideration for those shares is to be provided by the issue or transfer to the issuing company of non-equity shares in the other company or by the cancellation of any such shares in that company not held by the issuing company, relief under subsection (2) extends to any shares in the issuing company allotted on those terms in pursuance of the arrangement.

(4)   Subject to the next subsection, the issuing company is to be regarded for purposes of this section as having secured at least a 90 per cent equity holding in another company in pursuance of such an arrangement as is mentioned in subsection (1) if in consequence of an acquisition or cancellation of equity shares in that company (in pursuance of that arrangement) it holds equity shares in that company (whether all or any of those shares were acquired in pursuance of that arrangement, or not) of an aggregate nominal value equal to 90 per cent or more of the nominal value of that company's equity share capital.

(5)   Where the equity share capital of the other company is divided into different classes of shares, this section does not apply unless the requirements of subsection (1) are satisfied in relation to each of those classes of shares taken separately.

(6)   Shares held by a company which is the issuing company's holding company or subsidiary, or a subsidiary of the issuing company's holding company, or by its or their nominees, are to be regarded for purposes of this section as held by the issuing company.

(7)   In relation to a company and its shares and capital, the following definitions apply for purposes of this section—

(a)   'equity shares' means shares comprised in the company's equity share capital; and

(b)   'non-equity shares' means shares (of any class) not so comprised; and 'arrangement' means any agreement, scheme or arrangement (including an arrangement sanctioned under section 425 (company compromise with members and creditors) or section 110 of the Insolvency Act (liquidator accepting shares etc. as consideration for sale of company property)).

(8)   The relief allowed by this section does not apply if the issue of shares took place before 4 February 1981.

132.   Relief in respect of group reconstructions.

(1)   This section applies where the issuing company—

(a)   is a wholly-owned subsidiary of another company ('the holding company'), and

(b)   allots shares to the holding company or to another wholly-owned subsidiary of the holding company in consideration for the transfer to the issuing company of assets other than cash, being assets of any company ('the transferor company') which is a member of the group of companies which comprises the holding company and all its wholly-owned subsidiaries.

(2)   Where the shares in the issuing company allotted in consideration for the transfer are issued at a premium, the issuing company is not required by section 130 to transfer any amount in excess of the minimum premium value to the share premium account.

(3)   In subsection (2), 'the minimum premium value' means the amount (if any) by which the base value of the consideration for the shares allotted exceeds the aggregate nominal value of those shares.

(4)   For the purposes of subsection (3), the base value of the consideration for the shares allotted is the amount by which the base value of the assets transferred exceeds the base value of any liabilities of the transferor company assumed by the issuing company as part of the consideration for the assets transferred.

(5)   For the purposes of subsection (4)—

(a)   the base value of the assets transferred is to be taken as—

(i)   the cost of those assets to the transferor company, or

(ii)   the amount at which those assets are stated in the transferor company's accounting records immediately before the transfer,
whichever is the less; and

(b)   the base value of the liabilities assumed is to be taken as the amount at which they are stated in the transferor company's accounting records immediately before the transfer.

(6)   The relief allowed by this section does not apply (subject to the next subsection) if the issue of shares took place before the date of the coming into force of the Companies (Share Premium Account) Regulations 1984 (which were made on 21 December 1984).

(7)   To the extent that the relief allowed by this section would have been allowed by section 38 of the Companies Act 1981 as originally enacted (the text of which section is set out in Schedule 25 to this Act), the relief applies where the issue of shares took place before the date of the coming into force of those Regulations, but not if the issue took place before 4 February 1981.

(8)   Section 131 does not apply in a case falling within this section.

133.   Provisions supplementing ss. 131, 132.

(1)   An amount corresponding to one representing the premiums or part of the premiums on shares issued by a company which by virtue of sections 131 or 132 of this Act, or section 12 of the Consequential Provisions Act, is not included in the company's share premium account may also be disregarded in determining the amount at which any shares or other consideration provided for the shares issued is to be included in the company's balance sheet.

(2)   References in this Chapter (however expressed) to—

(a)   the acquisition by a company of shares in another company; and

(b)   the issue or allotment of shares to, or the transfer of shares to or by, a company, include (respectively) the acquisition of any of those shares by, and the issue or allotment or (as the case may be) the transfer of any of those shares to or by, nominees of that company; and the reference in section 132 to the company transferring the shares is to be construed accordingly.

(3)   References in this Chapter to the transfer of shares in a company include the transfer of a right to be included in the company's register of members in respect of those shares.

(4)   In sections 131 to 133 'company', except in references to the issuing company, includes any body corporate.

134.   Provision for extending or restricting relief from s. 130.

(1)   The Secretary of State may by regulations in a statutory instrument make such provision as appears to him to be appropriate—

(a)   for relieving companies from the requirements of section 130 in relation to premiums other than cash premiums, or

(b)   for restricting or otherwise modifying any relief from those requirements provided by this Chapter.

(2)   Regulations under this section may make different provision for different cases or classes of case and may contain such incidental and supplementary provisions as the Secretary of State thinks fit.

(3)   No such regulations shall be made unless a draft of the instrument containing them has been laid before Parliament and approved by a resolution of each House.

CHAPTER IV
REDUCTION OF SHARE CAPITAL

135.   Special resolution for reduction of share capital.

(1)   Subject to confirmation by the court, a company limited by shares or a company limited by guarantee and having a share capital may, if so authorised by its articles, by special resolution reduce its share capital in any way.

(2)   In particular, and without prejudice to subsection (1), the company may—

(a)   extinguish or reduce the liability on any of its shares in respect of share capital not paid up; or

(b)   either with or without extinguishing or reducing liability on any of its shares, cancel any paid-up share capital which is lost or unrepresented by available assets; or

(c)   either with or without extinguishing or reducing liability on any of its shares, pay off any paid-up share capital which is in excess of the company's wants;

and the company may, if and so far as is necessary, alter its memorandum by reducing the amount of its share capital and of its shares accordingly.

(3)   A special resolution under this section is in this Act referred to as 'a resolution for reducing share capital'.

136.   Application to court for order of confirmation.

(1)   Where a company has passed a resolution for reducing share capital, it may apply to the court for an order confirming the reduction.

(2)   If the proposed reduction of share capital involves either—

(a)   diminution of liability in respect of unpaid share capital; or

(b)   the payment to a shareholder of any paid-up share capital,

and in any other case if the court so directs, the next three subsections have effect, but subject throughout to subsection (6).

(3)   Every creditor of the company who at the date fixed by the court is entitled to any debt or claim which, if that date were the commencement of the winding up of the company, would be admissible in proof against the company is entitled to object to the reduction of capital.

(4)   The court shall settle a list of creditors entitled to object, and for that purpose—

(a)   shall ascertain, as far as possible without requiring an application from any creditor, the names of those creditors and the nature and amount of their debts or claims; and

(b)   may publish notices fixing a day or days within which creditors not entered on the list are to claim to be so entered or are to be excluded from the right of objecting to the reduction of capital.

(5)   If a creditor entered on the list whose debt or claim is not discharged or has not determined does not consent to the reduction, the court may, if it thinks fit, dispense with the consent of that creditor, on the company securing payment of his debt or claim by appropriating (as the court may direct) the following amount—

(a)   if the company admits the full amount of the debt or claim or, though not admitting it, is willing to provide for it, then the full amount of the debt or claim;

(b)   if the company does not admit, and is not willing to provide for, the full amount of the debt or claim, or if the amount is contingent or not ascertained, then an amount fixed by the court after the like enquiry and adjudication as if the company were being wound up by the court.

(6)   If a proposed reduction of share capital involves either the diminution of any liability in respect of unpaid share capital or the payment to any shareholder of any paid-up share capital, the court may, if having regard to any special circumstances of the

case it thinks proper to do so, direct that subsections (3) to (5) of this section shall not apply as regards any class or any classes of creditors.

137. Court order confirming reduction.

(1)   The court, if satisfied with respect to every creditor of the company who under section 136 is entitled to object to the reduction of capital that either—

(a)   his consent to the reduction has been obtained; or

(b)   his debt or claim has been discharged or has determined, or has been secured,

may make an order confirming the reduction on such terms and conditions as it thinks fit.

(2)   Where the court so orders, it may also—

(a)   if for any special reason it thinks proper to do so, make an order directing that the company shall, during such period (commencing on or at any time after the date of the order) as is specified in the order, add to its name as its last words the words 'and reduced'; and

(b)   make an order requiring the company to publish (as the court directs) the reasons for reduction of capital or such other information in regard to it as the court thinks expedient with a view to giving proper information to the public and (if the court thinks fit) the causes which led to the reduction.

(3)   Where a company is ordered to add to its name the words 'and reduced', those words are, until the expiration of the period specified in the order, deemed to be part of the company's name.

138. Registration of order and minute of reduction.

(1)   The registrar of companies, on production to him of an order of the court confirming the reduction of a company's share capital, and the delivery to him of a copy of the order and of a minute (approved by the court) showing, with respect to the company's share capital as altered by the order—

(a)   the amount of the share capital;

(b)   the number of shares into which it is to be divided, and the amount of each share; and

(c)   the amount (if any) at the date of the registration deemed to be paid up on each share,

shall register the order and minute (but subject to section 139).

(2)   On the registration of the order and minute, and not before, the resolution for reducing share capital as confirmed by the order so registered takes effect.

(3)   Notice of the registration shall be published in such manner as the court may direct.

(4)   The registrar shall certify the registration of the order and minute; and the certificate—

(a)   may be either signed by the registrar, or authenticated by his official seal;

(b)   is conclusive evidence that all the requirements of this Act with respect to the reduction of share capital have been complied with, and that the company's share capital is as stated in the minute.

(5)   The minute when registered is deemed to be substituted for the corresponding part of the company's memorandum, and is valid and alterable as if it had been originally contained therein.

(6)   The substitution of such a minute for part of the company's memorandum is deemed an alteration of the memorandum for purposes of section 20.

139. Public company reducing capital below authorised minimum.

(1)   This section applies where the court makes an order confirming a reduction of a public company's capital which has the effect of bringing the nominal value of its allotted share capital below the authorised minimum.

(2)   The registrar of companies shall not register the order under section 138 unless the court otherwise directs, or the company is first re-registered as a private company.

(3)   The court may authorise the company to be so re-registered without its having passed the special resolution required by section 53; and where that authority is given, the court shall specify in the order the alterations in the company's memorandum and articles to be made in connection with that re-registration.

(4)   The company may then be re-registered as a private company, if an application in the prescribed form and signed by a director or secretary of the company is delivered to the registrar, together with a printed copy of the memorandum and articles as altered by the court's order.

(5)   On receipt of such an application, the registrar shall retain it and the other documents delivered with it and issue the company with a certificate of incorporation appropriate to a company that is not a public company; and—

(a)   the company by virtue of the issue of the certificate becomes a private company, and the alterations in the memorandum and articles set out in the court's order take effect; and

(b)   the certificate is conclusive evidence that the requirements of this section in respect of re-registration and of matters precedent and incidental thereto have been complied with, and that the company is a private company.

140.   Liability of members on reduced shares.

(1)   Where a company's share capital is reduced, a member of the company (past or present) is not liable in respect of any share to any call or contribution exceeding in amount the difference (if any) between the amount of the share as fixed by the minute and the amount paid on the share or the reduced amount (if any), which is deemed to have been paid on it, as the case may be.

(2)   But the following two subsections apply if—

(a)   a creditor, entitled in respect of a debt or claim to object to the reduction of share capital, by reason of his ignorance of the proceedings for reduction of share capital, or of their nature and effect with respect to his claim, is not entered on the list of creditors; and

(b)   after the reduction of capital, the company is unable (within the meaning of section 123 of the Insolvency Act) to pay the amount of his debt or claim.

(3)   Every person who was a member of the company at the date of the registration of the order for reduction and minute is then liable to contribute for the payment of the debt or claim in question an amount not exceeding that which he would have been liable to contribute if the company had commenced to be wound up on the day before that date.

(4)   If the company is wound up, the court, on the application of the creditor in question and proof of ignorance referred to in subsection (2)(a), may (if it thinks fit) settle accordingly a list of persons so liable to contribute, and make and enforce calls and orders on the contributories settled on the list, as if they were ordinary contributories in a winding up.

(5)   Nothing in this section affects the rights of the contributories among themselves.

141.   Penalty for concealing name of creditor, etc.

If an officer of the company—

(a)   wilfully conceals the name of a creditor entitled to object to the reduction of capital; or

(b)   wilfully misrepresents the nature or amount of the debt or claim of any creditor; or

(c)   aids, abets or is privy to any such concealment or misrepresentation as is mentioned above,

he is guilty of an offence and liable to a fine.

CHAPTER V
MAINTENANCE OF CAPITAL

142. Duty of directors on serious loss of capital.

(1)   Where the net assets of a public company are half or less of its called-up share capital, the directors shall, not later than 28 days from the earliest day on which that fact is known to a director of the company, duly convene an extraordinary general meeting of the company for a date not later than 56 days from that day for the purpose of considering whether any, and if so what, steps should be taken to deal with the situation.

(2)   If there is a failure to convene an extraordinary general meeting as required by subsection (1), each of the directors of the company who—

(a)   knowingly and wilfully authorises or permits the failure, or

(b)   after the expiry of the period during which that meeting should have been convened, knowingly and wilfully authorises or permits the failure to continue,

is liable to a fine.

(3)   Nothing in this section authorises the consideration, at a meeting convened in pursuance of subsection (1), of any matter which could not have been considered at that meeting apart from this section.

143. General rule against company acquiring own shares.

(1)   Subject to the following provisions, a company limited by shares or limited by guarantee and having a share capital shall not acquire its own shares, whether by purchase, subscription or otherwise.

(2)   If a company purports to act in contravention of this section, the company is liable to a fine, and every officer of the company who is in default is liable to imprisonment or a fine, or both; and the purported acquisition is void.

(3)   A company limited by shares may acquire any of its own fully paid shares otherwise than for valuable consideration; and subsection (1) does not apply in relation to—

(a)   the redemption or purchase of shares in accordance with Chapter VII of this Part,

(b)   the acquisition of shares in a reduction of capital duly made,

(c)   the purchase of shares in pursuance of an order of the court under section 5 (alteration of objects), section 54 (litigated objection to resolution for company to be re-registered as private) or Part XVII (relief to members unfairly prejudiced), or

(d)   the forfeiture of shares, or the acceptance of shares surrendered in lieu, in pursuance of the articles, for failure to pay any sum payable in respect of the shares.

144. Acquisition of shares by company's nominee.

(1)   Subject to section 145, where shares are issued to a nominee of a company mentioned in section 143(1), or are acquired by a nominee of such a company from a third person as partly paid up, then, for all purposes—

(a)   the shares are to be treated as held by the nominee on his own account; and

(b)   the company is to be regarded as having no beneficial interest in them.

(2)   Subject to that section, if a person is called on to pay any amount for the purpose of paying up, or paying any premium on, any shares in such a company which were issued to him, or which he otherwise acquired, as the company's nominee and he fails to pay that amount within 21 days from being called on to do so, then—

(a)   if the shares were issued to him as subscriber to the memorandum by virtue of an undertaking of his in the memorandum, the other subscribers to the memorandum, or

(b)   if the shares were otherwise issued to or acquired by him, the directors of the company at the time of the issue or acquisition,

are jointly and severally liable with him to pay that amount.

(3)   If in proceedings for the recovery of any such amount from any such subscriber or director under this section it appears to the court—

(a)   that he is or may be liable to pay that amount, but

(b)   that he has acted honestly and reasonably and, having regard to all the circumstances of the case, he ought fairly to be excused from liability,

the court may relieve him, either wholly or partly, from his liability on such terms as the court thinks fit.

(4)   Where any such subscriber or director has reason to apprehend that a claim will or might be made for the recovery of any such amount from him, he may apply to the court for relief; and the court has the same power to relieve him as it would have had in proceedings for the recovery of that amount.

145.   Exceptions from s. 144.

(1)   Section 144(1) does not apply to shares acquired otherwise than by subscription by a nominee of a public company, where a person acquires shares in the company with financial assistance given to him directly or indirectly by the company for the purpose of or in connection with the acquisition, and the company has a beneficial interest in the shares.

(2)   Section 144(1) and (2) do not apply—

(a)   to shares acquired by a nominee of a company when the company has no beneficial interest in those shares, or

(b)   to shares issued in consequence of an application made before 22 December 1980, or transferred in pursuance of an agreement to acquire them made before that date.

(3)   Schedule 2 to this Act has effect for the interpretation of references in this section to a company having, or not having, a beneficial interest in shares.

146.   Treatment of shares held by or for public company.

(1)   Except as provided by section 148, the following applies to a public company—

(a)   where shares in the company are forfeited, or surrendered to the company in lieu, in pursuance of the articles, for failure to pay any sum payable in respect of the shares;

(b)   where shares in the company are acquired by it (otherwise than by any of the methods mentioned in section 143(3)(a) to (d)) and the company has a beneficial interest in the shares;

(c)   where the nominee of the company acquires shares in the company from a third person without financial assistance being given directly or indirectly by the company and the company has a beneficial interest in the shares; or

(d)   where a person acquires shares in the company with financial assistance given to him directly or indirectly by the company for the purpose of or in connection with the acquisition, and the company has a beneficial interest in the shares.

Schedule 2 to this Act has effect for the interpretation of references in this subsection to the company having a beneficial interest in shares.

(2)   Unless the shares or any interest of the company in them are previously disposed of, the company must, not later than the end of the relevant period from their forfeiture or surrender or, in a case within subsection (1)(b), (c) or (d), their acquisition—

(a)   cancel them and diminish the amount of the share capital by the nominal value of the shares cancelled, and

(b)   where the effect of cancelling the shares will be that the nominal value of the company's allotted share capital is brought below the authorised minimum, apply for re-registration as a private company, stating the effect of the cancellation.

(3)   For this purpose 'the relevant period' is—

(a)   3 years in the case of shares forfeited or surrendered to the company in lieu of forfeiture, or acquired as mentioned in subsection (1)(b) or (c);

(b)   one year in the case of shares acquired as mentioned in subsection (1)(d).

(4)   The company and, in a case within subsection (1)(c) or (d), the company's nominee or (as the case may be) the other shareholder must not exercise any voting rights in respect of the shares; and any purported exercise of those rights is void.

147.   Matters arising out of compliance with s. 146(2).

(1)   The directors may take such steps as are requisite to enable the company to carry out its obligations under section 146(2) without complying with sections 135 and 136 (resolution to reduce share capital; application to court for approval).

(2)   The steps taken may include the passing of a resolution to alter the company's memorandum so that it no longer states that the company is to be a public company; and the resolution may make such other alterations in the memorandum as are requisite in the circumstances.

Such a resolution is subject to section 380 (copy to be forwarded to registrar within 15 days).

(3)   The application for re-registration required by section 146(2)(b) must be in the prescribed form and be signed by a director or secretary of the company, and must be delivered to the registrar of companies together with a printed copy of the memorandum and articles of the company as altered by the resolution.

(4)   If the registrar is satisfied that the company may be re-registered under section 146, he shall retain the application and other documents delivered with it and issue the company with a certificate of incorporation appropriate to a company that is not a public company; and—

(a)   the company by virtue of the issue of the certificate becomes a private company, and the alterations in the memorandum and articles set out in the resolution take effect accordingly, and

(b)   the certificate is conclusive evidence that the requirements of sections 146 to 148 in respect of re-registration and of matters precedent and incidental to it have been complied with, and that the company is a private company.

148.   Further provisions supplementing ss. 146, 147.

(1)   Where, after shares in a private company—

(a)   are forfeited in pursuance of the company's articles or are surrendered to the company in lieu of forfeiture, or

(b)   are acquired by the company (otherwise than by such surrender or forfeiture, and otherwise than by any of the methods mentioned in section 143(3)), the company having a beneficial interest in the shares, or

(c)   are acquired by the nominee of a company in the circumstances mentioned in section 146(1)(c), or

(d)   are acquired by any person in the circumstances mentioned in section 146(1)(d),

the company is re-registered as a public company, sections 146 and 147, and also section 149, apply to the company as if it had been a public company at the time of the forfeiture, surrender or acquisition, but with the modification required by the following subsection.

(2)   That modification is to treat any reference to the relevant period from the forfeiture, surrender or acquisition as referring to the relevant period from the re-registration of the company as a public company.

(3)   Schedule 2 to this Act has effect for the interpretation of the reference in subsection (1)(b) to the company having a beneficial interest in shares.

(4)   Where a public company or a nominee of a public company acquires shares in the company or an interest in such shares, and those shares are (or that interest is) shown in a balance sheet of the company as an asset, an amount equal to the value of the shares or (as the case may be) the value to the company of its interest in them shall

be transferred out of profits available for dividend to a reserve fund and are not then available for distribution.

149. Sanctions for non-compliance.

(1) If a public company required by section 146(2) to apply to be re-registered as a private company fails to do so before the end of the relevant period referred to in that subsection, section 81 (restriction on public offers) applies to it as if it were a private company such as is mentioned in that section; but, subject to this, the company continues to be treated for the purpose of this Act as a public company until it is so re-registered.

(2) If a company when required to do so by section 146(2) (including that subsection as applied by section 148(1)) fails to cancel any shares in accordance with paragraph (a) of that subsection or to make an application for re-registration in accordance with paragraph (b) of it, the company and every officer of it who is in default is liable to a fine and, for continued contravention, to a daily default fine.

150. Charges of public companies on own shares.

(1) A lien or other charge of a public company on its own shares (whether taken expressly or otherwise), except a charge permitted by any of the following subsections, is void.

This is subject to section 6 of the Consequential Provisions Act (saving for charges of old public companies on their own shares).

(2) In the case of any description of company, a charge on its own shares is permitted if the shares are not fully paid and the charge is for any amount payable in respect of the shares.

(3) In the case of a company whose ordinary business—

   (a)   includes the lending of money, or

   (b)   consists of the provision of credit or the bailment (in Scotland, hiring) of goods under a hire-purchase agreement, or both,

a charge of the company on its own shares is permitted (whether the shares are fully paid or not) if it arises in connection with a transaction entered into by the company in the ordinary course of its business.

(4) In the case of a company which is re-registered or is registered under section 680 as a public company, a charge on its own shares is permitted if the charge was in existence immediately before the company's application for re-registration or (as the case may be) registration.

This subsection does not apply in the case of such a company as is referred to in section 6(3) of the Consequential Provisions Act (old public company remaining such after 22 March 1982, not having applied to be re-registered as public company).

CHAPTER VI
FINANCIAL ASSISTANCE BY A COMPANY FOR ACQUISITION OF ITS OWN SHARES

Provisions applying to both public and private companies

151. Financial assistance generally prohibited.

(1) Subject to the following provisions of this Chapter, where a person is acquiring or is proposing to acquire shares in a company, it is not lawful for the company or any of its subsidiaries to give financial assistance directly or indirectly for the purpose of that acquisition before or at the same time as the acquisition takes place.

(2) Subject to those provisions, where a person has acquired shares in a company and any liability has been incurred (by that or any other person), for the purpose of that acquisition, it is not lawful for the company or any of its subsidiaries to give financial assistance directly or indirectly for the purpose of reducing or discharging the liability so incurred.

(3) If a company acts in contravention of this section, it is liable to a fine, and every officer of it who is in default is liable to imprisonment or a fine, or both.

152. Definitions for this Chapter.

(1) In this Chapter—

(a) 'financial assistance' means—

(i) financial assistance given by way of gift,

(ii) financial assistance given by way of guarantee, security or indemnity, other than an indemnity in respect of the indemnifier's own neglect or default, or by way of release or waiver,

(iii) financial assistance given by way of a loan or any other agreement under which any of the obligations of the person giving the assistance are to be fulfilled at a time when in accordance with the agreement any obligation of another party to the agreement remains unfulfilled, or by way of the novation of, or the assignment of rights arising under, a loan or such other agreement, or

(iv) any other financial assistance given by a company the net assets of which are thereby reduced to a material extent or which has no net assets;

(b) 'distributable profits', in relation to the giving of any financial assistance—

(i) means those profits out of which the company could lawfully make a distribution equal in value to that assistance, and

(ii) includes, in a case where the financial assistance is or includes a non-cash asset, any profit which, if the company were to make a distribution of that asset, would under section 276 (distributions in kind) be available for that purpose,

and

(c) 'distribution' has the meaning given by section 263(2).

(2) In subsection (1)(a)(iv), 'net assets' means the aggregate of the company's assets, less the aggregate of its liabilities ('liabilities' to include any provision for liabilities or charges within paragraph 89 of Schedule 4).

(3) In this Chapter—

(a) a reference to a person incurring a liability includes his changing his financial position by making an agreement or arrangement (whether enforceable or unenforceable, and whether made on his own account or with any other person) or by any other means, and

(b) a reference to a company giving financial assistance for the purpose of reducing or discharging a liability incurred by a person for the purpose of the acquisition of shares includes its giving such assistance for the purpose of wholly or partly restoring his financial position to what it was before the acquisition took place.

153. Transactions not prohibited by s. 151.

(1) Section 151(1) does not prohibit a company from giving financial assistance for the purpose of an acquisition of shares in it or its holding company if—

(a) the company's principal purpose in giving that assistance is not to give it for the purpose of any such acquisition, or the giving of the assistance for that purpose is but an incidental part of some larger purpose of the company, and

(b) the assistance is given in good faith in the interests of the company.

(2) Section 151(2) does not prohibit a company from giving financial assistance if—

(a) the company's principal purpose in giving the assistance is not to reduce or discharge any liability incurred by a person for the purpose of the acquisition of shares in the company or its holding company, or the reduction or discharge of any such liability is but an incidental part of some larger purpose of the company, and

(b) the assistance is given in good faith in the interests of the company.

(3) Section 151 does not prohibit—

(a) a distribution of a company's assets by way of dividend lawfully made or a distribution made in the course of the company's winding up,

(b)   the allotment of bonus shares,

(c)   a reduction of capital confirmed by order of the court under section 137,

(d)   a redemption or purchase of shares made in accordance with Chapter VII of this part,

(e)   anything done in pursuance of an order of the court under section 425 (compromises and arrangements with creditors and members),

(f)   anything done under an arrangement made in pursuance of section 110 of the Insolvency Act (acceptance of shares by liquidator in winding up as consideration for sale of property), or

(g)   anything done under an arrangement made between a company and its creditors which is binding on the creditors by virtue of Part I of the Insolvency Act.

(4)   Section 151 does not prohibit—

(a)   where the lending of money is part of the ordinary business of the company, the lending of money by the company in the ordinary course of its business,

(b)   the provision by a company, in good faith in the interests of the company, of financial assistance for the purposes of an employees' share scheme,

(bb)   without prejudice to paragraph (b), the provision of financial assistance by a company or any of its subsidiaries for the purposes of or in connection with anything done by the company (or a company in the same group) for the purpose of enabling or facilitating transactions in shares in the first-mentioned company between, and involving the acquisition of beneficial ownership of those shares by, any of the following persons—

(i)   the bona fide employees or former employees of that company or of another company in the same group; or

(ii)   the wives, husbands, widows, widowers, children or stepchildren under the age of eighteen of any such employees or former employees,

(c)   the making by a company of loans to persons (other than directors) employed in good faith by the company with a view to enabling those persons to acquire fully paid shares in the company or its holding company to be held by them by way of beneficial ownership.

(5)   For the purposes of subsection (4)(bb) a company is in the same group as another company if it is a holding company or subsidiary of that company, or a subsidiary of a holding company of that company.

154.   Special restriction for public companies.

(1)   In the case of a public company, section 153(4) authorises the giving of financial assistance only if the company has net assets which are not thereby reduced or, to the extent that those assets are thereby reduced, if the assistance is provided out of distributable profits.

(2)   For this purpose the following definitions apply—

(a)   'net assets' means the amount by which the aggregate of the company's assets exceeds the aggregate of its liabilities (taking the amount of both assets and liabilities to be as stated in the company's accounting records immediately before the financial assistance is given);

(b)   'liabilities' includes any amount retained as reasonable necessary for the purpose of providing for any liability or loss which is either likely to be incurred, or certain to be incurred but uncertain as to amount or as to the date on which it will arise.

Private companies

155.   Relaxation of s. 151 for private companies.

(1)   Section 151 does not prohibit a private company from giving financial assistance in a case where the acquisition of shares in question is or was an acquisition of shares in the company or, if it is a subsidiary of another private company, in that other company

if the following provisions of this section, and sections 156 to 158, are complied with as respects the giving of that assistance.

(2)   The financial assistance may only be given if the company has net assets which are not thereby reduced or, to the extent that they are reduced, if the assistance is provided out of distributable profits.

Section 154(2) applies for the interpretation of this subsection.

(3)   This section does not permit financial assistance to be given by a subsidiary, in a case where the acquisition of shares in question is or was an acquisition of shares in its holding company, if it is also a subsidiary of a public company which is itself a subsidiary of that holding company.

(4)   Unless the company proposing to give the financial assistance is a wholly-owned subsidiary, the giving of assistance under this section must be approved by special resolution of the company in general meeting.

(5)   Where the financial assistance is to be given by the company in a case where the acquisition of shares in question is or was an acquisition of shares in its holding company, that holding company and any other company which is both the company's holding company and a subsidiary of that other holding company (except, in any case, a company which is a wholly-owned subsidiary) shall also approve by special resolution in general meeting the giving of the financial assistance.

(6)   The directors of the company proposing to give the financial assistance and, where the shares acquired or to be acquired are shares in its holding company, the directors of that company and of any other company which is both the company's holding company and a subsidiary of that other holding company shall before the financial assistance is given make a statutory declaration in the prescribed form complying with the section next following.

156.   Statutory declaration under s. 155.

(1)   A statutory declaration made by a company's directors under section 155(6) shall contain such particulars of the financial assistance to be given, and of the business of the company of which they are directors, as may be prescribed, and shall identify the person to whom the assistance is to be given.

(2)   The declaration shall state that the directors have formed the opinion, as regards the company's initial situation immediately following the date on which the assistance is proposed to be given, that there will be no ground on which it could then be found to be unable to pay its debts; and either—

(a)   if it is intended to commence the winding up of the company within 12 months of that date, that the company will be able to pay it debts in full within 12 months of the commencement of the winding up, or

(b)   in any other case, that the company will be able to pay its debts as they fall due during the year immediately following that date.

(3)   In forming their opinion for purposes of subsection (2), the directors shall take into account the same liabilities (including contingent and prospective liabilities) as would be relevant under section 122 of the Insolvency Act (winding up by the court) to the question whether the company is unable to pay its debts.

(4)   The directors' statutory declaration shall have annexed to it a report addressed to them by their company's auditors stating that—

(a)   they have enquired into the state of affairs of the company, and

(b)   they are not aware of anything to indicate that the opinion expressed by the directors in the declaration as to any of the matters mentioned in subsection (2) of this section is unreasonable in all the circumstances.

(5)   The statutory declaration and auditors' report shall be delivered to the registrar of companies—

(a)   together with a copy of any special resolution passed by the company under section 155 and delivered to the registrar in compliance with section 380, or

(b) where no such resolution is required to be passed, within 15 days after the making of the declaration.

(6) If a company fails to comply with subsection (5), the company and every officer of it who is in default is liable to a fine and, for continued contravention, to a daily default fine.

(7) A director of a company who makes a statutory declaration under section 155 without having reasonable grounds for the opinion expressed in it is liable to imprisonment or a fine, or both.

157. Special resolution under s. 155.

(1) A special resolution required by section 155 to be passed by a company approving the giving of financial assistance must be passed on the date on which the directors of that company make the statutory declaration required by that section in connection with the giving of that assistance, or within the week immediately following that date.

(2) Where such a resolution has been passed, an application may be made to the court for the cancellation of the resolution—

(a) by the holders of not less in the aggregate than 10 per cent in nominal value of the company's issued share capital or any class of it, or

(b) if the company is not limited by shares, by not less than 10 per cent of the company's members;
but the application shall not be made by a person who has consented to or voted in favour of the resolution.

(3) Subsections (3) to (10) of section 54 (litigation to cancel resolution under section 53) apply to applications under this section as to applications under section 54.

(4) A special resolution passed by a company is not effective for purposes of section 155—

(a) unless the declaration made in compliance with subsection (6) of that section by the directors of the company, together with the auditors' report annexed to it, is available for inspection by members of the company at the meeting at which the resolution is passed,

(b) if it is cancelled by the court on an application under this section.

158. Time for giving financial assistance under s. 155.

(1) This section applies as to the time before and after which financial assistance may not be given by a company in pursuance of section 155.

(2) Where a special resolution is required by that section to be passed approving the giving of the assistance, the assistance shall not be given before the expiry of the period of 4 weeks beginning with—

(a) the date on which the special resolution is passed, or

(b) where more than one such resolution is passed, the date on which the last of them is passed,
unless, as respects that resolution (or, if more than one, each of them), every member of the company which passed the resolution who is entitled to vote at general meetings of the company voted in favour of the resolution.

(3) If application for the cancellation of any such resolution is made under section 157, the financial assistance shall not be given before the final determination of the application unless the court otherwise orders.

(4) The assistance shall not be given after the expiry of the period of 8 weeks beginning with—

(a) the date on which the directors of the company proposing to give the assistance made their statutory declaration under section 155, or

(b)   where that company is a subsidiary and both its directors and the directors of any of its holding companies made such a declaration, the date on which the earliest of the declarations is made,
unless the court, on an application under section 157, otherwise orders.

CHAPTER VII
REDEEMABLE SHARES: PURCHASE BY A COMPANY OF ITS OWN SHARES

Redemption and purchase generally

159.   Power to issue redeemable shares.

(1)   Subject to the provisions of this Chapter, a company limited by shares or limited by guarantee and having a share capital may, if authorised to do so by its articles, issue shares which are to be redeemed or are liable to be redeemed at the option of the company or the shareholder.

(2)   No redeemable shares may be issued at a time when there are no issued shares of the company which are not redeemable.

(3)   Redeemable shares may not be redeemed unless they are fully paid; and the terms of redemption must provide for payment on redemption.

[*A new s. 159A would be inserted if s. 133 of the Companies Act 1989 were brought into force.*]

160.   Financing etc. of redemption.

(1)   Subject to the next subsection and to sections 171 (private companies redeeming or purchasing own shares out of capital) and 178(4) (terms of redemption or purchase enforceable in a winding up)—

(a)   redeemable shares may only be redeemed out of distributable profits of the company or out of the proceeds of a fresh issue of shares made for the purposes of the redemption; and

(b)   any premium payable on redemption must be paid out of distributable profits of the company.

(2)   If the redeemable shares were issued at a premium, any premium payable on their redemption may be paid out of the proceeds of a fresh issue of shares made for the purposes of the redemption, up to an amount equal to—

(a)   the aggregate of the premiums received by the company on the issue of the shares redeemed, or

(b)   the current amount of the company's share premium account (including any sum transferred to that account in respect of premiums on the new shares),
whichever is the less; and in that case the amount of the company's share premium account shall be reduced by a sum corresponding (or by sums in the aggregate corresponding) to the amount of any payment made by virtue of this subsection out of the proceeds of the issue of the new shares.

(3)   Subject to the following provisions of this Chapter, redemption of shares may be effected on such terms and in such manner as may be provided by the company's articles.

(4)   Shares redeemed under this section shall be treated as cancelled on redemption, and the amount of the company's issued share capital shall be diminished by the nominal value of those shares accordingly; but the redemption of shares by a company is not to be taken as reducing the amount of the company's authorised share capital.

(5)   Without prejudice to subsection (4), where a company is about to redeem shares, it has power to issue shares up to the nominal value of the shares to be redeemed as if those shares had never been issued.

[*Section 160(3) would be repealed and s. 160(4) amended if s. 133 of the Companies Act 1989 were brought into force.*]

162.   Power of company to purchase own shares.

(1)   Subject to the following provisions of this Chapter, a company limited by shares or limited by guarantee and having a share capital may, if authorised to do so by its articles, purchase its own shares (including any redeemable shares).

(2)   Sections 159 to 161 apply to the purchase by a company under this section of its own shares as they apply to the redemption of redeemable shares, save that the terms and manner of purchase need not be determined by the articles as required by section 160(3).

(3)   A company may not under this section purchase its shares if as a result of the purchase there would no longer be any member of the company holding shares other than redeemable shares.

[*Section 162(2) would be replaced by a new subsection if s. 133 of the Companies Act 1989 were brought into force.*]

163.   Definitions of 'off-market' and 'market' purchase.

(1)   A purchase by a company of its own shares is 'off-market' if the shares either—

(a)   are purchased otherwise than on a recognised investment exchange, or

(b)   are purchased on a recognised investment exchange but are not subject to a marketing arrangement on that investment exchange.

(2)   For this purpose, a company's shares are subject to a marketing arrangement on a recognised investment exchange if either—

(a)   they are listed under Part IV of the Financial Services Act 1986; or

(b)   the company has been afforded facilities for dealings in those shares to take place on that investment exchange without prior permission for individual transactions from the authority governing that investment exchange and without limit as to the time during which those facilities are to be available.

(3)   A purchase by a company of its own shares is a 'market purchase' if it is a purchase made on a recognised investment exchange, other than a purchase which is an off-market purchase by virtue of subsection (1)(b).

(4)   In this section 'recognised investment exchange' means a recognised investment exchange other than an overseas investment exchange within the meaning of the Financial Services Act 1986.

164.   Authority for off-market purchase.

(1)   A company may only make an off-market purchase of its own shares in pursuance of a contract approved in advance in accordance with this section or under section 165 below.

(2)   The terms of the proposed contract must be authorised by a special resolution of the company before the contract is entered into; and the following subsections apply with respect to that authority and to resolutions conferring it.

(3)   Subject to the next subsection, the authority may be varied, revoked or from time to time renewed by special resolution of the company.

(4)   In the case of a public company, the authority conferred by the resolution must specify a date on which the authority is to expire; and in a resolution conferring or renewing authority that date must not be later than 18 months after that on which the resolution is passed.

(5)   A special resolution to confer, vary, revoke or renew authority is not effective if any member of the company holding shares to which the resolution relates exercises the voting rights carried by any of those shares in voting on the resolution and the resolution would not have been passed if he had not done so.

For this purpose—

(a)   a member who holds shares to which the resolution relates is regarded as exercising the voting rights carried by those shares not only if he votes in respect of them

on a poll on the question whether the resolution shall be passed, but also if he votes on
the resolution otherwise than on a poll;

(b) notwithstanding anything in the company's articles, any member of the
company may demand a poll on that question; and

(c) a vote and a demand for a poll by a person as proxy for a member are the same
respectively as a vote and a demand by the member.

(6) Such a resolution is not effective for the purposes of this section unless (if the
proposed contract is in writing) a copy of the contract or (if not) a written memorandum
of its terms is available for inspection by members of the company both—

(a) at the company's registered office for not less than 15 days ending with the
date of the meeting at which the resolution is passed, and

(b) at the meeting itself.

A memorandum of contract terms so made available must include the names of any
members holding shares to which the contract relates; and a copy of the contract so
made available must have annexed to it a written memorandum specifying any such
names which do not appear in the contract itself.

(7) A company may agree to a variation of an existing contract so approved, but
only if the variation is authorised by a special resolution of the company before it is
agreed to; and subsections (3) to (6) above apply to the authority for a proposed
variation as they apply to the authority for a proposed contract, save that a copy of the
original contract or (as the case may require) a memorandum of its terms, together with
any variations previously made, must also be available for inspection in accordance with
subsection (6).

165. Authority for contingent purchase contract.

(1) A contingent purchase contract is a contract entered into by a company and
relating to any of its shares—

(a) which does not amount to a contract to purchase those shares, but

(b) under which the company may (subject to any conditions) become entitled or
obliged to purchase those shares.

(2) A company may only make a purchase of its own shares in pursuance of a
contingent purchase contract if the contract is approved in advance by a special
resolution of the company before the contract is entered into; and subsections (3) to (7)
of section 164 apply to the contract and its terms.

166. Authority for market purchase.

(1) A company shall not make a market purchase of its own shares unless the
purchase has first been authorised by the company in general meeting.

(2) That authority—

(a) may be general for that purpose, or limited to the purchase of shares of any
particular class or description, and

(b) may be unconditional or subject to conditions.

(3) The authority must—

(a) specify the maximum number of shares authorised to be acquired,

(b) determine both the maximum and the minimum prices which may be paid for
the shares, and

(c) specify a date on which it is to expire.

(4) The authority may be varied, revoked or from time to time renewed by the
company in general meeting, but this is subject to subsection (3) above; and in a
resolution to confer or renew authority, the date on which the authority is to expire must
not be later than 18 months after that on which the resolution is passed.

(5) A company may under this section make a purchase of its own shares after the
expiry of the time limit imposed to comply with subsection (3)(c), if the contract of
purchase was concluded before the authority expired and the terms of the authority

permitted the company to make a contract of purchase which would or might be executed wholly or partly after its expiration.

(6)   A resolution to confer or vary authority under this section may determine either or both the maximum and minimum prices for purchase by—

(a)   specifying a particular sum, or

(b)   providing a basis or formula for calculating the amount of the price in question without reference to any person's discretion or opinion.

(7)   A resolution of a company conferring, varying, revoking or renewing authority under this section is subject to section 380 (resolution to be sent to registrar of companies within 15 days).

167.   Assignment or release of company's right to purchase own shares.

(1)   The rights of a company under a contract approved under section 164 or 165, or under a contract for a purchase authorised under section 166, are not capable of being assigned.

(2)   An agreement by a company to release its rights under a contract approved under section 164 or 165 is void unless the terms of the release agreement are approved in advance by a special resolution of the company before the agreement is entered into; and subsections (3) to (7) of section 164 apply to approval for a proposed release agreement as to authority for a proposed variation of an existing contract.

168.   Payments apart from purchase price to be made out of distributable profits.

(1)   A payment made by a company in consideration of—

(a)   acquiring any right with respect to the purchase of its own shares in pursuance of a contract approved under section 165, or

(b)   the variation of a contract approved under section 164 or 165, or

(c)   the release of any of the company's obligations with respect to the purchase of any of its own shares under a contract approved under section 164 or 165 or under a contract for a purchase authorised under section 166,

must be made out of the company's distributable profits.

(2)   If the requirements of subsection (1) are not satisfied in relation to a contract—

(a)   in a case within paragraph (a) of the subsection, no purchase by the company of its own shares in pursuance of that contract is lawful under this Chapter,

(b)   in a case within paragraph (b), no such purchase following the variation is lawful under this Chapter, and

(c)   in a case within paragraph (c), the purported release is void.

169.   Disclosure by company of purchase of own shares.

(1)   Within the period of 28 days beginning with the date on which any shares purchased by a company under this Chapter are delivered to it, the company shall deliver to the registrar of companies for registration a return in the prescribed form stating with respect to shares of each class purchased the number and nominal value of those shares and the date on which they were delivered to the company.

(2)   In the case of a public company, the return shall also state—

(a)   the aggregate amount paid by the company for the shares; and

(b)   the maximum and minimum prices paid in respect of shares of each class purchased.

(3)   Particulars of shares delivered to the company on different dates and under different contracts may be included in a single return to the registrar; and in such a case the amount required to be stated under subsection (2)(a) is the aggregate amount paid by the company for all the shares to which the return relates.

(4)   Where a company enters into a contract approved under section 164 or 165, or a contract for a purchase authorised under section 166, the company shall keep at its registered office—

(a)   if the contract is in writing, a copy of it; and

(b)   if not, a memorandum of its terms,

from the conclusion of the contract until the end of the period of 10 years beginning with the date on which the purchase of all the shares in pursuance of the contract is completed or (as the case may be) the date on which the contract otherwise determines.

(5)   Every copy and memorandum so required to be kept shall be open to inspection without charge—

(a)   by any member of the company, and

(b)   if it is a public company, by any other person.

(6)   If default is made in delivering to the registrar any return required by this section, every officer of the company who is in default is liable to a fine and, for continued contravention, to a daily default fine.

(7)   If default is made in complying with subsection (4), or if an inspection required under subsection (5) is refused, the company and every officer of it who is in default is liable to a fine and, for continued contravention, to a daily default fine.

(8)   In the case of a refusal of an inspection required under subsection (5) of a copy or memorandum, the court may by order compel an immediate inspection of it.

(9)   The obligation of a company under subsection (4) to keep a copy of any contract or (as the case may be) a memorandum of its terms applies to any variation of the contract so long as it applies to the contract.

170.   The capital redemption reserve.

(1)   Where under this Chapter shares of a company are redeemed or purchased wholly out of the company's profits, the amount by which the company's issued share capital is diminished in accordance with section 160(4) on cancellation of the shares redeemed or purchased shall be transferred to a reserve, called 'the capital redemption reserve'.

(2)   If the shares are redeemed or purchased wholly or partly out of the proceeds of a fresh issue and the aggregate amount of those proceeds is less than the aggregate nominal value of the shares redeemed or purchased, the amount of the difference shall be transferred to the capital redemption reserve.

(3)   But subsection (2) does not apply if the proceeds of the fresh issue are applied by the company in making a redemption or purchase of its own shares in addition to a payment out of capital under section 171;

(4)   The provisions of this Act relating to the reduction of a company's share capital apply as if the capital redemption reserve were paid-up share capital of the company, except that the reserve may be applied by the company in paying up its unissued shares to be allotted to members of the company as fully paid bonus shares.

Redemption or purchase of own shares out of capital (private companies only)

171.   Power of private companies to redeem or purchase own shares out of capital.

(1)   Subject to the following provisions of this Chapter, a private company limited by shares or limited by guarantee and having a share capital may, if so authorised by its articles, make a payment in respect of the redemption or purchase under section 160 or (as the case may be) section 162, of its own shares otherwise than out of its distributable profits or the proceeds of a fresh issue of shares.

(2)   References below in this Chapter to payment out of capital are (subject to subsection (6)) to any payment so made, whether or not it would be regarded apart from this section as a payment out of capital.

(3)   The payment which may (if authorised in accordance with the following provisions of this Chapter) be made by a company out of capital in respect of the redemption or purchase of its own shares is such an amount as, taken together with—

(a)   any available profits of the company, and

(b)   the proceeds of any fresh issue of shares made for the purposes of the redemption or purchase,

is equal to the price of redemption or purchase; and the payment permissible under this subsection is referred to below in this Chapter as the permissible capital payment for the shares.

(4)   Subject to subsection (6), if the permissible capital payment for shares redeemed or purchased is less than their nominal amount, the amount of the difference shall be transferred to the company's capital redemption reserve.

(5)   Subject to subsection (6), if the permissible capital payment is greater than the nominal amount of the shares redeemed or purchased—

(a)   the amount of any capital redemption reserve, share premium account or fully paid share capital of the company, and

(b)   any amount representing unrealised profits of the company for the time being standing to the credit of any reserve maintained by the company in accordance with paragraph 34 of Schedule 4 or paragraph 34 of Schedule 8 (revaluation reserve),

may be reduced by a sum not exceeding (or by sums not in the aggregate exceeding) the amount by which the permissible capital payment exceeds the nominal amount of the shares.

(6)   Where the proceeds of a fresh issue are applied by a company in making any redemption or purchase of its own shares in addition to a payment out of capital under this section, the references in subsections (4) and (5) to the permissible capital payment are to be read as referring to the aggregate of that payment and those proceeds.

172.   Availability of profits for purposes of s. 171.

(1)   The reference in section 171(3)(a) to available profits of the company is to the company's profits which are available for distribution (within the meaning of Part VIII); but the question whether a company has any profits so available and the amount of any such profits are to be determined for purposes of that section in accordance with the following subsections, instead of sections 270 to 275 in that Part.

(2)   Subject to the next subsection, that question is to be determined by reference to—

(a)   profits, losses, assets and liabilities,

(b)   provisions of any of the kinds mentioned in paragraphs 88 and 89 of Schedule 4 (depreciation, diminution in value of assets, retentions to meet liabilities, etc.), and

(c)   share capital and reserves (including undistributable reserves),

as stated in the relevant accounts for determining the permissible capital payment of shares.

(3)   The relevant accounts for this purpose are such accounts, prepared as at any date within the period for determining the amount of the permissible capital payment, as are necessary to enable a reasonable judgment to be made as to the amounts of any of the items mentioned in subsection (2)(a) to (c) above.

(4)   For purposes of determining the amount of the permissible capital payment for shares, the amount of the company's available profits (if any) determined in accordance with subsections (2) and (3) is treated as reduced by the amount of any distributions lawfully made by the company after the date of the relevant accounts and before the end of the period for determining the amount of that payment.

(5)   The reference in subsection (4) to distributions lawfully made by the company includes—

(a)   financial assistance lawfully given out of distributable profits in a case falling within section 154 or 155,

(b)   any payment lawfully made by the company in respect of the purchase by it of any shares in the company (except a payment lawfully made otherwise than out of distributable profits), and

(c)   a payment of any description specified in section 168(1) lawfully made by the company.

(6)   References in this section to the period for determining the amount of the permissible capital payment for shares are to the period of 3 months ending with the date on which the statutory declaration of the directors purporting to specify the amount of that payment is made in accordance with subsection (3) of the section next following.

173.   Conditions for payment out of capital.

(1)   Subject to any order of the court under section 177, a payment out of capital by a private company for the redemption or purchase of its own shares is not lawful unless the requirements of this and the next two sections are satisfied.

(2)   The payment out of capital must be approved by a special resolution of the company.

(3)   The company's directors must make a statutory declaration specifying the amount of the permissible capital payment for the shares in question and stating that, having made full inquiry into the affairs and prospects of the company, they have formed the opinion—

(a)   as regards its initial situation immediately following the date on which the payment out of capital is proposed to be made, that there will be no grounds on which the company could then be found unable to pay its debts, and

(b)   as regards its prospects for the year immediately following that date, that, having regard to their intentions with respect to the management of the company's business during that year and to the amount and character of the financial resources which will in their view be available to the company during that year, the company will be able to continue to carry on business as a going concern (and will accordingly be able to pay its debts as they fall due) throughout that year.

(4)   In forming their opinion for purposes of subsection (3)(a), the directors shall take into account the same liabilities (including prospective and contingent liabilities) as would be relevant under section 122 of the Insolvency Act (winding up by the court) to the question whether a company is unable to pay its debts.

(5)   The directors' statutory declaration must be in the prescribed form and contain such information with respect to the nature of the company's business as may be prescribed, and must in addition have annexed to it a report addressed to the directors by the company's auditors stating that—

(a)   they have inquired into the company's state of affairs; and

(b)   the amount specified in the declaration as the permissible capital payment for the shares in question is in their view properly determined in accordance with sections 171 and 172; and

(c)   they are not aware of anything to indicate that the opinion expressed by the directors in the declaration as to any of the matters mentioned in subsection (3) is unreasonable in all the circumstances.

(6)   A director who makes a declaration under this section without having reasonable grounds for the opinion expressed in the declaration is liable to imprisonment or a fine, or both.

174.   Procedure for special resolution under s. 173.

(1)   The resolution required by section 173 must be passed on, or within the week immediately following, the date on which the directors make the statutory declaration required by that section; and the payment out of capital must be made no earlier than 5 nor more than 7 weeks after the date of the resolution.

(2)   The resolution is ineffective if any member of the company holding shares to which the resolution relates exercises the voting rights carried by any of those shares in voting on the resolution and the resolution would not have been passed if he had not done so.

(3)   For purposes of subsection (2), a member who holds such shares is to be regarded as exercising the voting rights carried by them in voting on the resolution not only if he votes in respect of them on a poll on the question whether the resolution shall be passed, but also if he votes on the resolution otherwise than on a poll; and, notwithstanding anything in a company's articles, any member of the company may demand a poll on that question.

(4)   The resolution is ineffective unless the statutory declaration and auditors' report required by the section are available for inspection by members of the company at the meeting at which the resolution is passed.

(5)   For purposes of this section a vote and a demand for a poll by a person as proxy for a member are the same (respectively) as a vote and demand by the member.

175.   Publicity for proposed payment out of capital.

(1)   Within the week immediately following the date of the resolution for payment out of capital the company must cause to be published in the Gazette a notice—

(a)   stating that the company has approved a payment out of capital for the purpose of acquiring its own shares by redemption or purchase or both (as the case may be);

(b)   specifying the amount of the permissible capital payment for the shares in question and the date of the resolution under section 173;

(c)   stating that the statutory declaration of the directors and the auditors' report required by that section are available for inspection at the company's registered office; and

(d)   stating that any creditor of the company may at any time within the 5 weeks immediately following the date of the resolution for payment out of capital apply to the court under section 176 for an order prohibiting the payment.

(2)   Within the week immediately following the date of the resolution the company must also either cause a notice to the same effect as that required by subsection (1) to be published in an appropriate national newspaper or give notice in writing to that effect to each of its creditors.

(3)   'An appropriate national newspaper' means a newspaper circulating throughout England and Wales (in the case of a company registered in England and Wales), and a newspaper circulating throughout Scotland (in the case of a company registered in Scotland).

(4)   References below in this section to the first notice date are to the day on which the company first publishes the notice required by subsection (1) or first publishes or gives the notice required by subsection (2) (whichever is the earlier).

(5)   Not later than the first notice date the company must deliver to the registrar of companies a copy of the statutory declaration of the directors and of the auditors' report required by section 173.

(6)   The statutory declaration and auditors' report—

(a)   shall be kept at the company's registered office throughout the period beginning with the first notice date and ending 5 weeks after the date of the resolution for payment out of capital, and

(b)   shall be open to the inspection of any member or creditor of the company without charge.

(7)   If an inspection required under subsection (6) is refused, the company and every officer of it who is in default is liable to a fine and, for continued contravention, to a daily default fine.

(8)   In the case of refusal of an inspection required under subsection (6) of a declaration or report, the court may by order compel an immediate inspection of that declaration or report.

176. Objections by company's members or creditors.

(1)   Where a private company passes a special resolution approving for purposes of this Chapter any payment out of capital for the redemption or purchase of any of its shares—

    (a)   any member of the company other than one who consented to or voted in favour of the resolution; and

·   (b)   any creditor of the company,

may within 5 weeks of the date on which the resolution was passed apply to the court for cancellation of the resolution.

(2)   The application may be made on behalf of the persons entitled to make it by such one or more of their number as they may appoint in writing for the purpose.

(3)   If an application is made, the company shall—

    (a)   forthwith give notice in the prescribed form of that fact to the registrar of companies; and

    (b)   within 15 days from the making of any order of the court on the hearing of the application, or such longer period as the court may by order direct, deliver an office copy of the order to the registrar.

(4)   A company which fails to comply with subsection (3), and any officer of it who is in default, is liable to a fine and for continued contravention, to a daily default fine.

177. Powers of court on application under s. 176.

(1)   On the hearing of an application under section 176 the court may, if it thinks fit, adjourn the proceedings in order that an arrangement may be made to the court's satisfaction for the purchase of the interests of dissentient members or for the protection of dissentient creditors (as the case may be); and the court may give such directions and make such orders as it thinks expedient for facilitating or carrying into effect any such arrangement.

(2)   Without prejudice to its powers under subsection (1), the court shall make an order on such terms and conditions as it thinks fit either confirming or cancelling the resolution; and, if the court confirms the resolution, it may in particular by order alter or extend any date or period of time specified in the resolution or in any provision in this Chapter which applies to the redemption or purchase of shares to which the resolution refers.

(3)   The court's order may, if the court thinks fit, provide for the purchase by the company of the shares of any of its members and for the reduction accordingly of the company's capital, and may make such alterations in the company's memorandum and articles as may be required in consequence of that provision.

(4)   If the court's order requires the company not to make any, or any specified, alteration in its memorandum or articles, the company has not then power without leave of the court to make any such alteration in breach of the requirement.

(5)   An alteration in the memorandum or articles made by virtue of an order under this section, if not made by resolution of the company, is of the same effect as if duly made by resolution; and this Act applies accordingly to the memorandum or articles as so altered.

Supplementary

178. Effect of company's failure to redeem or purchase.

(1)   This section has effect where a company has, on or after 15 June 1982,—

    (a)   issued shares on terms that they are or are liable to be redeemed, or

    (b)   agreed to purchase any of its own shares.

(2)   The company is not liable in damages in respect of any failure on its part to redeem or purchase any of the shares.

(3)   Subsection (2) is without prejudice to any right of the holder of the shares other than his right to sue the company for damages in respect of its failure; but the court shall not grant an order for specific performance of the terms of redemption or purchase if the company shows that it is unable to meet the costs of redeeming or purchasing the shares in question out of distributable profits.

(4)   If the company is wound up and at the commencement of the winding up any of the shares have not been redeemed or purchased, the terms of redemption or purchase may be enforced against the company; and when shares are redeemed or purchased under this subsection, they are treated as cancelled.

(5)   However, subsection (4) does not apply if—

(a)   the terms provided for the redemption or purchase to take place at a date later than that of the commencement of the winding up, or

(b)   during the period beginning with the date on which the redemption or purchase was to have taken place and ending with the commencement of the winding up the company could not at any time have lawfully made a distribution equal in value to the price at which the shares were to have been redeemed or purchased.

(6)   There shall be paid in priority to any amount which the company is liable under subsection (4) to pay in respect of any shares—

(a)   all other debts and liabilities of the company (other than any due to members in their character as such),

(b)   if other shares carry rights (whether as to capital or as to income) which are preferred to the rights as to capital attaching to the first-mentioned shares, any amount due in satisfaction of those preferred rights;

but, subject to that, any such amount shall be paid in priority to any amounts due to members in satisfaction of their rights (whether as to capital or income) as members.

179.   Power for Secretary of State to modify this Chapter.

(1)   The Secretary of State may by regulations made by statutory instrument modify the provisions of this Chapter with respect to any of the following matters—

(a)   the authority required for a purchase by a company of its own shares,

(b)   the authority required for the release by a company of its rights under a contract for the purchase of its own shares or a contract under which the company may (subject to any conditions) become entitled or obliged to purchase its own shares,

(c)   the information to be included in a return delivered by a company to the registrar of companies in accordance with section 169(1),

(d)   the matters to be dealt with in the statutory declaration of the directors under section 173 with a view to indicating their opinion of their company's ability to make a proposed payment out of capital with due regard to its financial situation and prospects, and

(e)   the contents of the auditors' report required by that section to be annexed to that declaration.

(2)   The Secretary of State may also by regulations so made make such provision (including modification of the provisions of this Chapter) as appears to him to be appropriate—

(a)   for wholly or partly relieving companies from the requirement of section 171(3)(a) that any available profits must be taken into account in determining the amount of the permissible capital payment for shares under that section, or

(b)   for permitting a company's share premium account to be applied, to an extent appearing to the Secretary of State to be appropriate, in providing for the premiums payable on the redemption or purchase by the company of any of its own shares.

(3)   Regulations under this section—

(a)   may make such further modification of any provisions of this Chapter as appears to the Secretary of State to be reasonably necessary in consequence of any provision made under such regulations by virtue of subsection (1) or (2),

(b)   may make different provision for different cases or classes of case, and

(c)   may contain such further consequential provisions, and such incidental and supplementary provisions, as the Secretary of State thinks fit.

(4)   No regulations shall be made under this section unless a draft of the instrument containing them has been laid before Parliament and approved by resolution of each House.

180.   Transitional cases arising under this Chapter; and savings.

(1)   Any preference shares issued by a company before 15 June 1982 which could but for the repeal by the Companies Act 1981 of section 58 of the Companies Act 1948 (power to issue redeemable preference shares) have been redeemed under that section are subject to redemption in accordance with the provisions of this Chapter.

(2)   In a case to which sections 159 and 160 apply by virtue of this section, any premium payable on redemption may, notwithstanding the repeal by the 1981 Act of any provision of the 1948 Act, be paid out of the share premium account instead of out of profits, or partly out of that account and partly out of profits (but subject to the provisions of this Chapter so far as payment is out of profits).

(3)   Any capital redemption reserve fund established before 15 June 1982 by a company for the purposes of section 58 of the Act of 1948 is to be known as the company's capital redemption reserve and be treated as if it had been established for the purposes of section 170 of this Act; and accordingly, a reference in any enactment or in the articles of any company, or in any other instrument, to a company's capital redemption reserve fund is to be construed as a reference to the company's capital redemption reserve.

181.   Definitions for Chapter VII.

In this Chapter—

(a)   'distributable profits', in relation to the making of any payment by a company, means those profits out of which it could lawfully make a distribution (within the meaning given by section 263(2)) equal in value to the payment, and

(b)   'permissible capital payment' means the payment permitted by section 171; and references to payment out of capital are to be construed in accordance with section 171.

CHAPTER VIII
MISCELLANEOUS PROVISIONS ABOUT SHARES AND DEBENTURES

Share and debenture certificates, transfers and warrants

182.   Nature, transfer and numbering of shares.

(1)   The shares or other interest of any member in a company—

(a)   are personal estate or, in Scotland, movable property and are not in the nature of real estate or heritage,

(b)   are transferable in manner provided by the company's articles, but subject to the Stock Transfer Act 1963 (which enables securities of certain descriptions to be transferred by a simplified process) and to regulations made under section 207 of the Companies Act 1989 (which enable title to securities to be evidenced and transferred without a written instrument).

(2)   Each share in a company having a share capital shall be distinguished by its appropriate number; except that, if at any time all the issued shares in a company, or all the issued shares in it of a particular class, are fully paid up and rank *pari passu* for all purposes, none of those shares need thereafter have a distinguishing number so long as it remains fully paid up and ranks *pari passu* for all purposes with all shares of the same class for the time being issued and fully paid up.

183. Transfer and registration.

(1)   It is not lawful for a company to register a transfer of shares in or debentures of the company unless a proper instrument of transfer has been delivered to it, or the transfer is an exempt transfer within the Stock Transfer Act 1982 or is in accordance with regulations made under section 207 of the Companies Act 1989.

This applies notwithstanding anything in the company's articles.

(2)   Subsection (1) does not prejudice any power of the company to register as shareholder or debenture holder a person to whom the right to any shares in or debentures of the company has been transmitted by operation of law.

(3)   A transfer of the share or other interest of a deceased member of a company made by his personal representative, although the personal representative is not himself a member of the company, is as valid as if he had been such a member at the time of the execution of the instrument of transfer.

(4)   On the application of the transferor of any share or interest in a company, the company shall enter in its register of members the name of the transferee in the same manner and subject to the same conditions as if the application for the entry were made by the transferee.

(5)   If a company refuses to register a transfer of shares or debentures, the company shall, within 2 months after the date on which the transfer was lodged with it, send to the transferee notice of the refusal.

(6)   If default is made in complying with subsection (5), the company and every officer of it who is in default is liable to a fine and, for continued contravention, to a daily default fine.

184. Certification of transfers.

(1)   The certification by a company of any instrument of transfer of any shares in, or debentures of, the company is to be taken as a representation by the company to any person acting on the faith of the certification that there have been produced to the company such documents as on their face show a prima facie title to the shares or debentures in the transferor named in the instrument.

However, the certification is not to be taken as a representation that the transferor has any title to the shares or debentures.

(2)   Where a person acts on the faith of a false certification by a company made negligently, the company is under the same liability to him as if the certification had been made fraudulently.

(3)   For purposes of this section—

(a)   an instrument of transfer is deemed certificated if it bears the words 'certificate lodged' (or words to the like effect);

(b)   the certification of an instrument of transfer is deemed made by a company if—

(i)   the person issuing the instrument is a person authorised to issue certificated instruments of transfer on the company's behalf, and

(ii)   the certification is signed by a person authorised to certificate transfers on the company's behalf or by an officer or servant either of the company or of a body corporate so authorised;

(c)   a certification is deemed signed by a person if—

(i)   it purports to be authenticated by his signature or initials (whether handwritten or not), and

(ii)   it is not shown that the signature or initials was or were placed there neither by himself nor by a person authorised to use the signature or initials for the purpose of certificating transfers on the company's behalf.

185. Duty of company as to issue of certificates.

(1)   Subject to the following provisions, every company shall—

(a)   within 2 months after the allotment of any of its shares, debentures or debenture stock, and

(b)   within 2 months after the date on which a transfer of any such shares, debentures or debenture stock is lodged with the company,

complete and have ready for delivery the certificates of all shares, the debentures and the certificates of all debenture stock allotted or transferred (unless the conditions of issue of the shares, debentures or debenture stock otherwise provide).

(2)   For this purpose, 'transfer' means a transfer duly stamped and otherwise valid, or an exempt transfer within the Stock Transfer Act 1982, and does not include such a transfer as the company is for any reason entitled to refuse to register and does not register.

(3)   Subsection (1) does not apply in the case of a transfer to any person where, by virtue of regulations under section 3 of the Stock Transfer Act 1982, he is not entitled to a certificate or other document of or evidencing title in respect of the securities transferred; but if in such a case the transferee—

(a)   subsequently becomes entitled to such a certificate or other document by virtue of any provision of those regulations, and

(b)   gives notice in writing of that fact to the company,

this section has effect as if the reference in subsection (1)(b) to the date of the lodging of the transfer were a reference to the date of the notice.

(4)   A company of which shares or debentures are allotted or debenture stock is allotted to a recognised clearing house or a nominee of a recognised clearing house or of a recognised investment exchange, or with which a transfer is lodged for transferring any shares, debentures or debenture stock of the company to such a clearing house or nominee, is not required, in consequence of the allotment or the lodging of the transfer, to comply with subsection (1); but no person shall be a nominee for the purposes of this section unless he is a person designated for the purposes of this section in the rules of the recognised investment exchange in question.

'Recognised clearing house' means a recognised clearing house within the meaning of the Financial Services Act 1986 acting in relation to a recognised investment exchange and 'recognised investment exchange' has the same meaning as in that Act.

(5)   If default is made in complying with subsection (1), the company and every officer of it who is in default is liable to a fine and, for continued contravention, to a daily default fine.

(6)   If a company on which a notice has been served requiring it to make good any default in complying with subsection (1) fails to make good the default within 10 days after service of the notice, the court may, on the application of the person entitled to have the certificates or the debentures delivered to him, exercise the power of the following subsection.

(7)   The court may make an order directing the company and any officer of it to make good the default within such time as may be specified in the order; and the order may provide that all costs of and incidental to the application shall be borne by the company or by an officer of it responsible for the default.

186.   Certificate to be evidence of title.

A certificate under the common seal of the company specifying any shares held by a member is—

(a)   in England and Wales, prima facie evidence, and

(b)   in Scotland, sufficient evidence unless the contrary is shown,

of his title to the shares.

187.   Evidence of grant of probate or confirmation as executor.

The production to a company of any document which is by law sufficient evidence of probate of the will, or letters of administration of the estate, or confirmation as executor, of a deceased person having been granted to some person shall be accepted by the company as sufficient evidence of the grant.

This has effect notwithstanding anything in the company's articles.

188.   Issue and effect of share warrant to bearer.

(1)   A company limited by shares may, if so authorised by its articles, issue with respect to any fully paid shares a warrant (a 'share warrant') stating that the bearer of the warrant is entitled to the shares specified in it.

(2)   A share warrant issued under the company's common seal entitles the bearer to the shares specified in it; and the shares may be transferred by delivery of the warrant.

(3)   A company which issues a share warrant may, if so authorised by its articles, provide (by coupons or otherwise) for the payment of the future dividends on the shares included in the warrant.

Debentures

190.   Register of debenture holders.

(1)   A company registered in England and Wales shall not keep in Scotland any register of holders of debentures of the company or any duplicate of any such register or part of any such register which is kept outside Great Britain.

(2)   A company registered in Scotland shall not keep in England and Wales any such register or duplicate as above-mentioned.

(3)   Neither a register of holders of debentures of a company nor a duplicate of any such register or part of any such register which is kept outside Great Britain shall be kept in England and Wales (in the case of a company registered in England and Wales) or in Scotland (in the case of a company registered in Scotland) elsewhere than—

(a)   at the company's registered office; or

(b)   at any office of the company at which the work of making it up is done; or

(c)   if the company arranges with some other person for the making up of the register or duplicate to be undertaken on its behalf by that other person, at the office of that other person at which the work is done.

(4)   Where a company keeps (in England and Wales or in Scotland, as the case may be) both such a register and such a duplicate, it shall keep them at the same place.

(5)   Every company which keeps any such register or duplicate in England and Wales or Scotland shall send to the registrar of companies notice (in the prescribed form) of the place where the register or duplicate is kept and of any change in that place.

(6)   But a company is not bound to send notice under subsection (5) where the register or duplicate has, at all times since it came into existence, been kept at the company's registered office.

191.   Right to inspect register.

(1)   Every register of holders of debentures of a company shall, except when duly closed, be open to the inspection—

(a)   of the registered holder of any such debentures or any holder of shares in the company without fee; and

(b)   of any other person on payment of such fee as may be prescribed.

(2)   Any such registered holder of debentures or holder of shares, or any other person, may require a copy of the register of the holders of debentures of the company or any part of it, on payment of such fee as may be prescribed.

(3)   A copy of any trust deed for securing an issue of debentures shall be forwarded to every holder of any such debentures at his request on payment of such fee as may be prescribed.

(4)   If inspection is refused, or a copy is refused or not forwarded, the company and every officer of it who is in default is liable to a fine and, for continued contravention, to a daily default fine.

(5)   Where a company is in default as above-mentioned, the court may by order compel an immediate inspection of the register or direct that the copies required be sent to the person requiring them.

(6)   For purposes of this section, a register is deemed to be duly closed if closed in accordance with provisions contained in the articles or in the debentures or, in the case of debenture stock, in the stock certificates, or in the trust deed or other document securing the debentures or debenture stock, during such period or periods, not exceeding in the whole 30 days in any year, as may be therein specified.

(7)   Liability incurred by a company from the making or deletion of an entry in its register of debenture holders, or from a failure to make or delete any such entry, is not enforceable more than 20 years after the date on which the entry was made or deleted or, in the case of any such failure, the failure first occurred.

This is without prejudice to any lesser period of limitation.

192.   Liability of trustees of debentures.

(1)   Subject to this section, any provision contained—
    (a)   in a trust deed for securing an issue of debentures, or
    (b)   in any contract with the holders of debentures secured by a trust deed,
is void in so far as it would have the effect of exempting a trustee of the deed from, or indemnifying him against, liability for breach of trust where he fails to show the degree of care and diligence required of him as trustee, having regard to the provisions of the trust deed conferring on him any powers, authorities or discretions.

(2)   Subsection (1) does not invalidate—
    (a)   a release otherwise validly given in respect of anything done or omitted to be done by a trustee before the giving of the release; or
    (b)   any provision enabling such a release to be given—
        (i)   on the agreement thereto of a majority of not less than three-fourths in value of the debenture holders present and voting in person or, where proxies are permitted, by proxy at a meeting summoned for the purpose, and
        (ii)   either with respect to specific acts or omissions or on the trustee dying or ceasing to act.

(3)   Subsection (1) does not operate—
    (a)   to invalidate any provision in force on 1 July 1948 so long as any person then entitled to the benefit of that provision or afterwards given the benefit of that provision under the following subsection remains a trustee of the deed in question; or
    (b)   to deprive any person of any exemption or right to be indemnified in respect of anything done or omitted to be done by him while any such provision was in force.

(4)   While any trustee of a trust deed remains entitled to the benefit of a provision saved by subsection (3), the benefit of that provision may be given either—
    (a)   to all trustees of the deed, present and future; or
    (b)   to any named trustees or proposed trustees of it,
by a resolution passed by a majority of not less than three-fourths in value of the debenture holders present in person or, where proxies are permitted, by proxy at a meeting summoned for the purpose in accordance with the provisions of the deed or, if the deed makes no provision for summoning meetings, a meeting summoned for the purpose in any manner approved by the court.

193.   Perpetual debentures.

A condition contained in debentures, or in a deed for securing debentures, is not invalid by reason only that the debentures are thereby made irredeemable or redeemable only on the happening of a contingency (however remote), or on the expiration of a period (however long), any rule of equity to the contrary notwithstanding.

This applies to debentures whenever issued, and to deeds whenever executed.

194. Power to reissue redeemed debentures.

(1)   Where (at any time) a company has redeemed debentures previously issued, then—

(a)   unless provision to the contrary, whether express or implied, is contained in the articles or in any contract entered into by the company; or

(b)   unless the company has, by passing a resolution to that effect or by some other act, manifested its intention that the debentures shall be cancelled,

the company has, and is deemed always to have had, power to reissue the debentures, either by reissuing the same debentures or by issuing other debentures in their place.

(2)   On a reissue of redeemed debentures, the person entitled to the debentures has, and is deemed always to have had, the same priorities as if the debentures had never been redeemed.

(3)   Where a company has (at any time) deposited any of its debentures to secure advances from time to time on current account or otherwise, the debentures are not deemed to have been redeemed by reason only of the company's account having ceased to be in debit while the debentures remained so deposited.

(4)   The reissue of a debenture or the issue of another debenture in its place under the power which by this section is given to or deemed to be possessed by a company is to be treated as the issue of a new debenture for purposes of stamp duty; but it is not to be so treated for the purposes of any provision limiting the amount or number of debentures to be issued.

This applies whenever the issue or reissue was made.

(5)   A person lending money on the security of a debenture reissued under this section which appears to be duly stamped may give the debenture in evidence in any proceedings for enforcing his security without payment of the stamp duty or any penalty in respect of it, unless he had notice (or, but for his negligence, might have discovered) that the debenture was not duly stamped; but in that case the company is liable to pay the proper stamp duty and penalty.

195. Contract to subscribe for debentures.

A contract with a company to take up and pay for debentures of the company may be enforced by an order for specific performance.

196.

(1)   The following applies in the case of a company registered in England and Wales, where debentures of the company are secured by a charge which, as created, was a floating charge.

(2)   If possession is taken, by or on behalf of the holders of any of the debentures, of any property comprised in or subject to the charge, and the company is not at that time in course of being wound up, the company's preferential debts shall be paid out of assets coming to the hands of the person taking possession in priority to any claims for principal or interest in respect of the debentures.

(3)   'Preferential debts' means the categories of debts listed in Schedule 6 to the Insolvency Act; and for the purposes of that Schedule 'the relevant date' is the date of possession being taken as above-mentioned.

(4)   Payments made under this section shall be recouped, as far as may be, out of the assets of the company available for payment of general creditors.

PART VI

DISCLOSURE OF INTERESTS IN SHARES

Individual and group acquisitions

198. Obligation of disclosure: the cases in which it may arise and 'the relevant time'.

(1)   Where a person either—

(a) to his knowledge acquires an interest in shares comprised in a public company's relevant share capital, or ceases to be interested in shares so comprised (whether or not retaining an interest in other shares so comprised), or

(b) becomes aware that he has acquired an interest in shares so comprised or that he has ceased to be interested in shares so comprised in which he was previously interested,

then in certain circumstances he comes under an obligation ('the obligation of disclosure') to make notification to the company with respect to his interests (if any) in its shares.

(2) In relation to a public company, 'relevant share capital' means the company's issued share capital of a class carrying rights to vote in all circumstances at general meetings of the company; and it is hereby declared for the avoidance of doubt that—

(a) where a company's share capital is divided into different classes of shares, references in this Part to a percentage of the nominal value of its relevant share capital are to a percentage of the nominal value of the issued shares comprised in each of the classes taken separately, and

(b) the temporary suspension of voting rights in respect of shares comprised in issued share capital of a company of any such class does not affect the application of this Part in relation to interests in those or any other shares comprised in that class.

(3) Where, otherwise than in circumstances within subsection (1), a person—

(a) is aware at the time when it occurs of any change of circumstances affecting facts relevant to the application of the next following section to an existing interest of his in shares comprised in a company's share capital of any description, or

(b) otherwise becomes aware of any such facts (whether or not arising from any such change of circumstances),

then in certain circumstances he comes under the obligation of disclosure.

(4) The existence of the obligation in a particular case depends (in part) on circumstances obtaining before and after whatever is in that case the relevant time; and that is—

(a) in a case within subsection (1)(a) or (3)(a), the time of the event or change of circumstances there mentioned, and

(b) in a case within subsection (1)(b) or (3)(b), the time at which the person became aware of the facts in question.

199. Interests to be disclosed.

(1) For purposes of the obligation of disclosure, the interests to be taken into account are those in relevant share capital of the company concerned.

(2) Where a person is interested in shares comprised in relevant share capital, then—

(a) if in some or all of those shares he has interests which are material interests, he has a notifiable interest at any time when the aggregate nominal value of the shares in which those material interests subsist is equal to or more than 3 per cent of the nominal value of that share capital; and

(b) he has a notifiable interest at any time when, not having such an interest by virtue of paragraph (a), the aggregate nominal value of the shares in which he has interests (whether or not including material interests) is equal to or more than 10 per cent of the nominal value of the relevant share capital.

(2A) For the purposes of this Part, a material interest is any interest other than—

(a) an interest which a person authorised to manage investments belonging to another has by virtue of having the management of such investments under an agreement in or evidenced in writing;

(b) an interest which a person has by virtue of being the operator of—

(i) an authorised unit trust scheme;

   (ii)   a recognised scheme; or

   (iii)   a UCITS (as defined in subsection (8));

(bb)   an interest belonging to an investment company with variable capital;

(c)   an interest in shares in a listed company which, if that company were not listed, would fall to be disregarded by virtue of section 209(10); or

(d)   an interest of another which a person is taken to have by virtue of the application of section 203 or 205, where the interest of that other person falls within paragraph (a), (b) or (c).

(3)   All facts relevant to determining whether a person has a notifiable interest at any time (or the percentage level of his interest) are taken to be what he knows the facts to be at that time.

(4)   The obligation of disclosure arises under section 198(1) or (3) where the person has a notifiable interest immediately after the relevant time, but did not have such an interest immediately before that time.

(5)   The obligation also arises under section 198(1) or (3) where—

(a)   the person had a notifiable interest immediately before the relevant time, but does not have such an interest immediately after it, or

(b)   he had a notifiable interest immediately before that time, and has such an interest immediately after it, but the percentage levels of his interest immediately before and immediately after that time are not the same.

(6)   For the purposes of subsection (2A), a person is authorised to manage investments belonging to another if—

(a)   he is an authorised person under Chapter III of Part I of the Financial Services Act 1986 and may manage that other's investments without contravening any prohibition mentioned in subsection (7); or

(b)   it is an authorised credit institution which may manage that other's investments without being in breach of its authorisation.

(7)   The prohibitions referred to in subsection (6)(a) are—

(a)   any prohibition contained in rules—

   (i)   which make provision of a description mentioned in section 48(2)(a) and (b) of the Financial Services Act 1986; and

   (ii)   which are made by the Secretary of State, the Treasury, a designated agency, a recognised professional body or a recognised self-regulating organisation; and

(b)   any prohibition imposed under section 65 of that Act.

(8)   In this Part 'UCITS' means a collective investment scheme which—

(a)   is constituted in a member State other than the United Kingdom, and

(b)   complies with the conditions necessary for it to enjoy the rights conferred by Council Directive 85/611/EEC coordinating the laws, regulations and administrative provisions relating to undertakings for collective investment in transferable securities;

and subsection (8) of section 86 of the Financial Services Act 1986 (meaning of 'constituted in a member State') applies for the purposes of paragraph (a) of this subsection as it applies for the purposes of that section.

200.   'Percentage level' in relation to notifiable interests.

(1)   Subject to the qualifications mentioned below, 'percentage level', in section 199(5)(b), means the percentage figure found by expressing the aggregate nominal value of all the shares comprised in the share capital concerned in which the person has material interests immediately before or (as the case may be) immediately after the relevant time as a percentage of the nominal value of that share capital and rounding that figure down, if it is not a whole number, to the next whole number.

(2)   In relation to a notifiable interest which a person has when the aggregate nominal value of the shares in which he is interested is equal to or more than 10 per cent

of the nominal value of that relevant share capital, subsection (1) shall have effect as if for the words 'has material interests' there were substituted 'is interested'.

(3) Where the nominal value of the share capital is greater immediately after the relevant time than it was immediately before, the percentage level of the person's interest immediately before (as well as immediately after) that time is determined by reference to the larger amount.

202. Particulars to be contained in notification.

(1) Where notification is required by section 198 with respect to a person's interest (if any) in shares comprised in relevant share capital of a public company, the obligation to make the notification must be performed within the period of 2 days next following the day on which that obligation arises; and the notification must be in writing to the company.

(2) The notification must specify the share capital to which it relates, and must also—

(a) subject to subsections (2A) and (2B), state the number of shares comprised in that share capital in which the person making the notification knows he had material interests immediately after the time when the obligation arose, or

(b) in a case where the person no longer has a notifiable interest in shares comprised in that share capital, state that he no longer has that interest.

(2A) Where, immediately after the relevant time, the aggregate nominal value of the shares in which the person making the notification is interested is equal to or more than 10 per cent of the nominal value of that relevant share capital, subsection (2)(a) shall have effect as if for the words 'had material interests' there were substituted 'was interested'.

(2B) Nothing in subsection (2) or (2A) requires a notification to state, in relation to any shares, whether the interest of the person making the notification is (or is not) a material interest.

(3) A notification (other than one stating that a person no longer has a notifiable interest) shall include the following particulars, so far as known to the person making the notification at the date when it is made—

(a) the identity of each registered holder of shares to which the notification relates and the number of such shares held by each of them, and

(b) the number of such shares in which the interest of the person giving the notification is such an interest as is mentioned in section 208(5).

(4) A person who has an interest in shares comprised in a company's relevant share capital, that interest being notifiable, is under obligation to notify the company in writing—

(a) of any particulars in relation to those shares which are specified in subsection (3), and

(b) of any change in those particulars,

of which in either case he becomes aware at any time after any interest notification date and before the first occasion following that date on which he comes under any further obligation of disclosure with respect to his interest in shares comprised in that share capital.

An obligation arising under this subsection must be performed within the period of 2 days next following the day on which it arises.

(5) The reference in subsection (4) to an interest notification date, in relation to a person's interest in shares comprised in a public company's relevant share capital, is to either of the following—

(a) the date of any notification made by him with respect to his interest under this Part, and

(b) where he has failed to make a notification, the date on which the period allowed for making it came to an end.

(6)   A person who at any time has an interest in shares which is notifiable is to be regarded under subsection (4) as continuing to have a notifiable interest in them unless and until he comes under obligation to make a notification stating that he no longer has such an interest in those shares.

203.   Notification of family and corporate interests.

(1)   For purposes of sections 198 to 202, a person is taken to be interested in any shares in which his spouse or any infant child or stepchild of his is interested; and 'infant' means, in relation to Scotland, pupil or minor.

(2)   For those purposes, a person is taken to be interested in shares if a body corporate is interested in them and—

(a)   that body or its directors are accustomed to act in accordance with his directions or instructions, or

(b)   he is entitled to exercise or control the exercise of one-third or more of the voting power at general meetings of that body corporate.

(3)   Where a person is entitled to exercise or control the exercise of one-third or more of the voting power at general meetings of a body corporate and that body corporate is entitled to exercise or control the exercise of any of the voting power at general meetings of another body corporate ('the effective voting power') then, for purposes of subsection (2)(b), the effective voting power is taken as exercisable by that person.

(4)   For purposes of subsections (2) and (3), a person is entitled to exercise or control the exercise of voting power if—

(a)   he has a right (whether subject to conditions or not) the exercise of which would make him so entitled, or

(b)   he is under an obligation (whether or not so subject) the fulfilment of which would make him so entitled.

204.   Agreement to acquire interests in a particular company.

(1)   In certain circumstances the obligation of disclosure may arise from an agreement between two or more persons which includes provision for the acquisition by any one or more of them of interests in shares of a particular public company ('the target company'), being shares comprised in the relevant share capital of that company.

(2)   This section applies to such an agreement if—

(a)   the agreement also includes provisions imposing obligations or restrictions on any one or more of the parties to it with respect to their use, retention or disposal of their interests in that company's shares acquired in pursuance of the agreement (whether or not together with any other interests of theirs in the company's shares to which the agreement relates), and

(b)   any interest in the company's shares is in fact acquired by any of the parties in pursuance of the agreement;

and in relation to such an agreement references below in this section, and in sections 205 and 206, to the target company are to the company which is the target company for that agreement in accordance with this and the previous subsection.

(3)   The reference in subsection (2)(a) to the use of interests in shares in the target company is to the exercise of any rights or of any control or influence arising from those interests (including the right to enter into any agreement for the exercise, or for control of the exercise, of any of those rights by another person).

(4)   Once any interest in shares in the target company has been acquired in pursuance of such an agreement as is mentioned above, this section continues to apply to that agreement irrespective of—

(a)   whether or not any further acquisitions of interests in the company's shares take place in pursuance of the agreement, and

(b)   any change in the persons who are for the time being parties to it, and

(c)   any variation of the agreement,

so long as the agreement continues to include provisions of any description mentioned in subsection (2)(a).

References in this subsection to the agreement include any agreement having effect (whether directly or indirectly) in substitution for the original agreement.

(5)   In this section, and also in references elsewhere in this Part to an agreement to which this section applies, 'agreement' includes any agreement or arrangement; and references in this section to provisions of an agreement—

(a)   accordingly include undertakings, expectations or understandings operative under any arrangement, and

(b)   (without prejudice to the above) also include any provisions, whether express or implied and whether absolute or not.

(6)   However, this section does not apply to an agreement which is not legally binding unless it involves mutuality in the undertakings, expectations or understandings of the parties to it; nor does the section apply to an agreement to underwrite or sub-underwrite any offer of shares in a company, provided the agreement is confined to that purpose and any matters incidental to it.

205.   Obligation of disclosure arising under s. 204.

(1)   In the case of an agreement to which section 204 applies, each party to the agreement is taken (for purposes of the obligation of disclosure) to be interested in all shares in the target company in which any other party to it is interested apart from the agreement (whether or not the interest of the other party in question was acquired, or includes any interest which was acquired, in pursuance of the agreement).

(2)   For those purposes, and also for those of the next section, an interest of a party to such an agreement in shares in the target company is an interest apart from the agreement if he is interested in those shares otherwise than by virtue of the application of section 204 and this section in relation to the agreement.

(3)   Accordingly, any such interest of the person (apart from the agreement) includes for those purposes any interest treated as his under section 203 or by the application of section 204 and this section in relation to any other agreement with respect to shares in the target company to which he is a party.

(4)   A notification with respect to his interest in shares in the target company made to that company under this Part by a person who is for the time being a party to an agreement to which section 204 applies shall—

(a)   state that the person making the notification is a party to such an agreement,

(b)   include the names and (so far as known to him) the addresses of the other parties to the agreement, identifying them as such, and

(c)   state whether or not any of the shares to which the notification relates are shares in which he is interested by virtue of section 204 and this section and, if so, the number of those shares.

(5)   Where a person makes a notification to a company under this part in consequence of ceasing to be interested in any shares of that company by virtue of the fact that he or any other person has ceased to be a party to an agreement to which section 204 applies, the notification shall include a statement that he or that other person has ceased to be a party to the agreement (as the case may require) and also (in the latter case) the name and (if known to him) the address of that other.

206.   Obligation of persons acting together to keep each other informed.

(1)   A person who is a party to an agreement to which section 204 applies is subject to the requirements of this section at any time when—

(a)   the target company is a public company, and he knows it to be so, and

(b)   the shares in that company to which the agreement relates consist of or include shares comprised in relevant share capital of the company, and he knows that to be the case; and

(c)   he knows the facts which make the agreement one to which section 204 applies.

(2)   Such a person is under obligation to notify every other party to the agreement, in writing, of the relevant particulars of his interest (if any) apart from the agreement in shares comprised in relevant share capital of the target company—

(a)   on his first becoming subject to the requirements of this section, and

(b)   on each occurrence after that time while he is still subject to those requirements of any event or circumstances within section 198(1) (as it applies to his case otherwise than by reference to interests treated as his under section 205 as applying to that agreement).

(3)   The relevant particulars to be notified under subsection (2) are—

(a)   the number of shares (if any) comprised in the target company's relevant share capital in which the person giving the notice would be required to state his interest if he were under the wide obligation of disclosure with respect to that interest (apart from the agreement) immediately after the time when the obligation to give notice under subsection (2) arose, and

(b)   the relevant particulars with respect to the registered ownership of those shares, so far as known to him at the date of the notice, and

(c)   except in the circumstance mentioned in subsection (3A), the number of shares (if any) out of the number given under paragraph (a) in which he knows that, immediately after the time when the obligation to give the notice arose, he had interests (apart from the agreement) which were not material interests.

(3A)   The circumstance referred to in subsection (3)(c) is that the aggregate nominal value of the shares comprised in relevant share capital in which the person is interested (apart from the agreement) is equal to or more than 10 per cent of the nominal value of the relevant share capital.

(3B)   For the purposes of subsection (3)(a) 'the wide obligation of disclosure' means the obligation to disclose the number of shares in which the person concerned has any interest (material or otherwise).

(4)   A person who is for the time being subject to the requirements of this section is also under obligation to notify every other party to the agreement, in writing—

(a)   of any relevant particulars with respect to the registered ownership of any shares comprised in relevant share capital of the target company in which he is interested apart from the agreement, and

(b)   of any change in those particulars,

of which in either case he becomes aware at any time after any interest notification date and before the first occasion following that date on which he becomes subject to any further obligation to give notice under subsection (2) with respect to his interest in shares comprised in that share capital.

(5)   The reference in subsection (4) to an interest notification date, in relation to a person's interest in shares comprised in the target company's relevant share capital, is to either of the following—

(a)   the date of any notice given by him with respect to his interest under subsection (2), and

(b)   where he has failed to give that notice, the date on which the period allowed by this section for giving the notice came to an end.

(6)   A person who is a party to an agreement to which section 204 applies is under an obligation to notify each other party to the agreement, in writing, of his current address—

(a)   on his first becoming subject to the requirements of this section, and

(b)   on any change in his address occurring after that time and while he is still subject to those requirements.

(7)   A reference to the relevant particulars with respect to the registered ownership of shares is to such particulars in relation to those shares as are mentioned in section 202(3)(a) or (b).

(8)   A person's obligation to give any notice required by this section to any other person must be performed within the period of 2 days next following the day on which that obligation arose.

207.   Interests in shares by attribution.

(1)   Where section 198 or 199 refers to a person acquiring an interest in shares or ceasing to be interested in shares, that reference in certain cases includes his becoming or ceasing to be interested in those shares by virtue of another person's interest.

(2)   Such is the case where he becomes or ceases to be interested by virtue of section 203 or (as the case may be) section 205 whether—

(a)   by virtue of the fact that the person who is interested in the shares becomes or ceases to be a person whose interests (if any) fall by virtue of either section to be treated as his, or

(b)   in consequence of the fact that such a person has become or ceased to be interested in the shares, or

(c)   in consequence of the fact that he himself becomes or ceases to be a party to an agreement to which section 204 applies to which the person interested in the shares is for the time being a party, or

(d)   in consequence of the fact that an agreement to which both he and that person are parties becomes or ceases to be one to which that section applies.

(3)   The person is then to be treated as knowing he has acquired an interest in the shares or (as the case may be) that he has ceased to be interested in them, if and when he knows both—

(a)   the relevant facts with respect to the other person's interest in the shares, and

(b)   the relevant facts by virtue of which he himself has become or ceased to be interested in them in accordance with section 203 or 205.

(4)   He has the knowledge referred to in subsection (3)(a) if he knows (whether contemporaneously or not) either of the subsistence of the other person's interest at any material time or of the fact that the other has become or ceased to be interested in the shares at any such time; and 'material time' is any time at which the other's interests (if any) fall or fell to be treated as his under section 203 or 205.

(5)   A person is to be regarded as knowing of the subsistence of another's interest in shares or (as the case may be) that another has become or ceased to be interested in shares if he has been notified under section 206 of facts with respect to the other's interest which indicate that he is or has become or ceased to be interested in the shares (whether on his own account or by virtue of a third party's interest in them).

208.   Interests in shares which are to be notified.

(1)   This section applies, subject to the section next following, in determining for purposes of sections 198 to 202 whether a person has a notifiable interest in shares.

(2)   A reference to an interest in shares is to be read as including an interest of any kind whatsoever in the shares; and accordingly there are to be disregarded any restraints or restrictions to which the exercise of any right attached to the interest is or may be subject.

(3)   Where property is held on trust and an interest in shares is comprised in the property, a beneficiary of the trust who apart from this subsection does not have an interest in the shares is to be taken as having such an interest.

(4)   A person is taken to have an interest in shares if—

(a)   he enters into a contract for their purchase by him (whether for cash or other consideration), or

(b)   not being the registered holder, he is entitled to exercise any right conferred by the holding of the shares or is entitled to control the exercise of any such right.

(5)   A person is taken to have an interest in shares if, otherwise than by virtue of having an interest under a trust—

(a)   he has a right to call for delivery of the shares to himself or to his order, or .

(b)   he has a right to acquire an interest in shares or is under an obligation to take an interest in shares,
whether in any case the right or obligation is conditional or absolute.

(6)   For purposes of subsection (4)(b), a person is entitled to exercise or control the exercise of any right conferred by the holding of shares if he—

(a)   has a right (whether subject to conditions or not) the exercise of which would make him so entitled, or

(b)   is under an obligation (whether so subject or not) the fulfilment of which would make him so entitled.

(7)   Persons having a joint interest are taken each of them to have that interest.

(8)   It is immaterial that shares in which a person has an interest are unidentifiable.

209.   Interests to be disregarded.

(1)   Subject to subsections (5) and (6), the following interests in shares are disregarded for the purposes of sections 198 to 202—

(a)   where property is held on trust and an interest in shares is comprised in that property, an interest of a person, being a discretionary interest or an interest in reversion or remainder or an interest of a bare trustee;

(b)   an interest which a person has by virtue of holding units in—

(i)   an authorised unit trust scheme;

(ii)   a recognised scheme; or

(iii)   a UCITS;

(c)   an interest of a person which is an exempt security interest within the meaning of subsection (2);

(d)   an interest which a person has by virtue of his being a beneficiary under a retirement benefits scheme as defined in section 611 of the Income and Corporation Taxes Act 1988;

(e)   an interest which a person has in shares as a result of the acceptance of a takeover offer made by him (either alone or jointly with one or more other persons) for shares where—

(i)   the offer is subject to a threshold acceptance condition; and

(ii)   the threshold acceptance condition is not fulfilled;

(f)   an interest of a person which is an exempt custodian interest within the meaning of subsection (4);

(g)   an interest which a person has by virtue of his being a personal representative of any estate;

(h)   an interest which a person has—

(i)   by virtue of his being a trustee of an authorised unit trust scheme,

(ii)   in relation to a recognised scheme or a UCITS, by virtue of his being entrusted with the custody of the property in question (whether or not under a trust), or

(iii)   by virtue of his being a depositary, within the meaning of the Open-Ended Investment Companies (Investment Companies with Variable Capital) Regulations 1996, of an investment company with variable capital.

(2)   An interest in shares is an exempt security interest for the purposes of subsection (1)(c)—

(a)   if it is held by a person who is—

(i)   a person authorised under Part I of the Banking Act 1987, an authorised credit institution, a person authorised under the law of a member State other than the United Kingdom to accept deposits who would, if he were to accept such deposits in the United Kingdom require authorisation under Part I of that Act, or an authorised insurance undertaking; or

(ii)   a person authorised under the law of a member State to deal in securities or derivatives, who deals in securities or derivatives on a relevant stock exchange or on a relevant investment exchange, whether as a member or otherwise; or

(iii)   a relevant stock exchange, a relevant investment exchange or a recognised clearing house; or

(b)   if it is held by the Bank of England or by the central bank of a member State other than the United Kingdom;

and it is held by way of security only for the purposes of a transaction entered into in the ordinary course of his or its business as such a person.

(3)   For the purposes of subsection (1)(e)—

(a)   'takeover offer' has the same meaning as in Part XIIIA; and

(b)   'a threshold acceptance condition' means a condition that acceptances are received in respect of such proportion of the shares for which the takeover offer is made as is specified in or determined in accordance with the terms of the takeover offer.

(4)   For the purposes of subsection (1)(f) an interest of a person is an exempt custodian interest if it is held by him—

(a)   as a custodian (whether under a trust or by a contract); or

(b)   under an arrangement pursuant to which he has issued, or is to issue, depositary receipts in respect of the shares concerned.

(5)   An interest referred to in any paragraph of subsection (1) (except for paragraph (c)) is disregarded only if the person referred to in the relevant paragraph or in subsection (4) is not entitled to exercise or control the exercise of voting rights in respect of the shares concerned; and for this purpose he is not so entitled if he is bound (whether by contract or otherwise) not to exercise the voting rights, or not to exercise them otherwise than in accordance with the instructions of another.

(6)   In the case of an interest referred to in paragraph (c) of subsection (1), an interest of a person referred to in subsection (2) is disregarded only if that person—

(a)   is not entitled (within the meaning of subsection (5)) to exercise or control the exercise of voting rights in respect of the shares concerned; or

(b)   is so entitled, but has not evidenced any intention to exercise them or control their exercise nor taken any step to do so.

(7)   For the purposes of subsection (5) and (6), voting rights which a person is entitled to exercise or of which he is entitled to control the exercise only in certain circumstances shall be taken into account only when the circumstances have arisen and for so long as they continue to obtain.

(8)   An interest in shares of a company is also disregarded for the purposes of sections 198 to 202—

(a)   if it is held by a market maker in securities or derivatives for the purposes of his business, but

(b)   only in so far as it is not used by him for the purpose of intervening in the management of the company.

(9)   For the purposes of subsection (8) a person is a market maker in securities or derivatives if—

(a)   he is authorised under the law of a member State to deal in securities or derivatives and so deals on a relevant stock exchange or on a relevant investment exchange (whether as a member or otherwise); and

(b)   he holds himself out at all normal times as willing to acquire and dispose of securities or derivatives at prices specified by him and in so doing is subject to the rules of that exchange;

and he holds an interest for the purposes of his business if he holds it for the purposes of a business carried on by him as a market maker in a member State.

(9A)   Where—

(a)   in pursuance of arrangements made with the operator of a relevant system—

(i)   securities of a particular aggregate value are on any day transferred by means of that system from a person ('A') to another person ('B');

(ii)   the securities are of kinds and amounts determined by the operator-system; and

(iii)   the securities, or securities of the same kinds and amounts, are on the following day transferred by means of the relevant system from B to A; and

(b)   the securities comprise any shares of a company,

any interest of B in those shares is also disregarded for the purposes of sections 198 to 202.

(9B)   For the purposes of subsection (9A)—

(a)   any day which, in England and Wales, is a non-business day for the purposes of the Bills of Exchange Act 1882 is disregarded; and

(b)   expressions which are used in the Uncertificated Securities Regulations 1995 have the same meanings as in those Regulations.

(10)   The following interests in shares in a public company which is not listed are also disregarded for the purposes of sections 198 to 202—

(a)   an interest which subsists by virtue of—

(i)   a scheme made under section 24 or 25 of the Charities Act 1993, section 25 of the Charities Act (Northern Ireland) 1964, section 11 of the Trustee Investments Act 1961 or section 42 of the Administration of Justice Act 1982, or

(ii)   the scheme set out in the Schedule to the Church Funds Investment Measure 1958;

(b)   an interest of the Church of Scotland General Trustees, the Church of Scotland Trust or the Church of Scotland Investors Trust in shares held by them or of any other person in shares held by those Trustees or Trusts otherwise than as simple trustees;

(c)   an interest for the life of himself or another of a person under a settlement in the case of which the property comprised in the settlement consists of or includes shares, and the conditions mentioned in subsection (11) are satisfied;

(e)   an interest of the Accountant General of the Supreme Court in shares held by him;

(f)   an interest of the Public Trustee;

(g)   an interest of the Probate Judge subsisting by virtue of section 3 of the Administration of Estates Act (Northern Ireland) 1955.

(11)   The conditions referred to in subsection (10)(c) are, in relation to a settlement—

(a)   that it is irrevocable, and

(b)   that the settlor (within the meaning of section 670 of the Income and Corporation Taxes Act 1988) has no interest in any income arising under, or property comprised in, the settlement.

(12)   A person is not by virtue of section 208(4)(b) taken to be interested in shares by reason only that he has been appointed a proxy to vote at a specified meeting of a company or of any class of its members and at any adjournment of that meeting, or has been appointed by a corporation to act as its representative at any meeting of a company or of any class of its members.

(13)   In the application of subsection (1)(a) to property held on trust according to the law of Scotland, for the words 'or remainder or an interest of a bare trustee' there shall be substituted 'or in fee or an interest of a simple trustee'.

210.   Other provisions about notification under this Part.

(1)   Where a person authorises another ('the agent') to acquire or dispose of, on his behalf, interests in shares comprised in relevant share capital of a public company, he

shall secure that the agent notifies him immediately of acquisitions or disposals effected by the agent which will or may give rise to any obligation of disclosure imposed on him by this Part with respect to his interest in that share capital.

(2) An obligation of disclosure imposed on a person by any provision of sections 198 to 202 is treated as not being fulfilled unless the notice by means of which it purports to be fulfilled identifies him and gives his address and, in a case where he is a director of the company, is expressed to be given in fulfilment of that obligation.

(3) A person who—

(a) fails to fulfil, within the proper period, an obligation of disclosure imposed on him by this Part, or

(b) in purported fulfilment of any such obligation makes to a company a statement which he knows to be false, or recklessly makes to a company a statement which is false, or

(c) fails to fulfil, within the proper period, an obligation to give another person a notice required by section 206, or

(d) fails without reasonable excuse to comply with subsection (1) of this section, is guilty of an offence and liable to imprisonment or a fine, or both.

(4) It is a defence for a person charged with an offence under subsection (3)(c) to prove that it was not possible for him to give the notice to the other person required by section 206 within the proper period, and either—

(a) that it has not since become possible for him to give the notice so required, or

(b) that he gave the notice as soon after the end of that period as it became possible for him to do so.

(5) Where a person is convicted of an offence under this section (other than an offence relating to his ceasing to be interested in a company's shares), the Secretary of State may by order direct that the shares in relation to which the offence was committed shall, until further order, be subject to the restrictions of Part XV of this Act; and such an order may be made notwithstanding any power in the company's memorandum or articles enabling the company to impose similar restrictions on those shares.

(5A) If the Secretary of State is satisfied that an order under subsection (5) may unfairly affect the rights of third parties in respect of shares then the Secretary of State, for the purpose of protecting such rights and subject to such terms as he thinks fit, may direct that such acts by such persons or descriptions of persons and for such purposes as may be set out in the order, shall not constitute a breach of the restrictions of Part XV of this Act.

(6) Sections 732 (restriction on prosecutions) and 733(2) and (3) (liability of directors, etc.) apply to offences under this section.

210A. Power to make further provision by regulations.

(1) The Secretary of State may by regulations amend—

(a) the definition of 'relevant share capital' (section 198(2)),

(b) the percentage giving rise to a 'notifiable interest' (section 199(2)),

(c) the periods within which an obligation of disclosure must be fulfilled or a notice must be given (sections 202(1) and (4) and 206(8)),

(d) the provisions as to what is taken to be an interest in shares (section 208) and what interests are to be disregarded (section 209), and

(e) the provisions as to company investigations (section 212); and the regulations may amend, replace or repeal the provisions referred to above and make such other consequential amendments or repeals of provisions of this part as appear to the Secretary of State to be appropriate.

(2) The regulations may in any case make different provision for different descriptions of company; and regulations under subsection (1)(b), (c) or (d) may make different provision for different descriptions of person, interest or share capital.

(3)   The regulations may contain such transitional and other supplementary and incidental provisions as appear to the Secretary of State to be appropriate, and may in particular make provision as to the obligations of a person whose interest in a company's shares becomes or ceases to be notifiable by virtue of the regulations.

(4)   Regulations under this section shall be made by statutory instrument.

(5)   No regulations shall be made under this section unless a draft of the regulations has been laid before and approved by a resolution of each House of Parliament.

Registration and investigation of share acquisitions and disposals

211.   Register of interests in shares.

(1)   Every public company shall keep a register for purposes of sections 198 to 202, and whenever the company receives information from a person in consequence of the fulfilment of an obligation imposed on him by any of those sections, it is under obligation to inscribe in the register, against that person's name, that information and the date of the inscription.

(2)   Without prejudice to subsection (1), where a company receives a notification under this Part which includes a statement that the person making the notification, or any other person, has ceased to be a party to an agreement to which section 204 applies, the company is under obligation to record that information against the name of that person in every place where his name appears in the register as a party to that agreement (including any entry relating to him made against another person's name).

(3)   An obligation imposed by subsection (1) or (2) must be fulfilled within the period of 3 days next following the day on which it arises.

(4)   The company is not, by virtue of anything done for the purposes of this section, affected with notice of, or put upon enquiry as to, the rights of any person in relation to any shares.

(5)   The register must be so made up that the entries against the several names entered in it appear in chronological order.

(6)   Unless the register is in such form as to constitute in itself an index, the company shall keep an index of the names entered in the register which shall in respect of each name contain a sufficient indication to enable the information entered against it to be readily found; and the company shall, within 10 days after the date on which a name is entered in the register, make any necessary alteration in the index.

(7)   If the company ceases to be a public company it shall continue to keep the register and any associated index until the end of the period of 6 years beginning with the day next following that on which it ceases to be such a company.

(8)   The register and any associated index—

(a)   shall be kept at the place at which the register required to be kept by the company by section 325 (register of directors' interests) is kept, and

(b)   subject to the next subsection, shall be available for inspection in accordance with section 219 below.

(9)   Neither the register nor any associated index shall be available for inspection in accordance with that section in so far as it contains information with respect to a company for the time being entitled to avail itself of the benefit conferred by section 231(3) (disclosure of shareholdings not required if it would be harmful to company's business).

(10)   If default is made in complying with subsection (1) or (2), or with any of subsections (5) to (7), the company and every officer of it who is in default is liable to a fine and, for continued contravention, to a daily default fine.

(11)   Any register kept by a company immediately before 15 June 1982 under section 34 of the Companies Act 1967 shall continue to be kept by the company under and for the purposes of this section.

212. Company investigations.

(1) A public company may by notice in writing require a person whom the company knows or has reasonable cause to believe to be or, at any time during the 3 years immediately preceding the date on which the notice is issued, to have been interested in shares comprised in the company's relevant share capital—

(a) to confirm that fact or (as the case may be) to indicate whether or not it is the case, and

(b) where he holds or has during that time held an interest in shares so comprised, to give such further information as may be required in accordance with the following subsection.

(2) A notice under this section may require the person to whom it is addressed—

(a) to give particulars of his own past or present interest in shares comprised in relevant share capital of the company (held by him at any time during the 3-year period mentioned in subsection (1)),

(b) where the interest is a present interest and any other interest in the shares subsists or, in any case, where another interest in the shares subsisted during that 3-year period at any time when his own interest subsisted, to give (so far as lies within his knowledge) such particulars with respect to that other interest as may be required by the notice,

(c) where his interest is a past interest, to give (so far as lies within his knowledge) particulars of the identity of the person who held that interest immediately upon his ceasing to hold it.

(3) The particulars referred to in subsection (2)(a) and (b) include particulars of the identity of persons interested in the shares in question and of whether persons interested in the same shares are or were parties to any agreement to which section 204 applies or to any agreement or arrangement relating to the exercise of any rights conferred by the holding of the shares.

(4) A notice under this section shall require any information given in response to the notice to be given in writing within such reasonable time as may be specified in the notice.

(5) Sections 203 to 205 and 208 apply for the purpose of construing references in this section to persons interested in shares and to interests in shares respectively, as they apply in relation to sections 198 to 201 (but with the omission of any reference to section 209).

(6) This section applies in relation to a person who has or previously had, or is or was entitled to acquire, a right to subscribe for shares in a public company which would on issue be comprised in relevant share capital of that company as it applies in relation to a person who is or was interested in shares so comprised; and references above in this section to an interest in shares so comprised and to shares so comprised are to be read accordingly in any such case as including respectively any such right and shares which would on issue be so comprised.

213. Registration of interests disclosed under s. 212.

(1) Whenever in pursuance of a requirement imposed on a person under section 212 a company receives information to which this section applies relating to shares comprised in its relevant share capital, it is under obligation to enter against the name of the registered holder of those shares, in a separate part of its register of interests in shares—

(a) the fact that the requirement was imposed and the date on which it was imposed, and

(b) any information to which this section applies received in pursuance of the requirement.

(2) This section applies to any information received in pursuance of a requirement imposed by section 212 which relates to the present interests held by any persons in shares comprised in relevant share capital of the company in question.

(3) Subsections (3) to (10) of section 211 apply in relation to any part of the register maintained in accordance with subsection (1) of this section as they apply in relation to the remainder of the register, reading references to subsection (1) of that section to include subsection (1) of this.

(4) In the case of a register kept by a company immediately before 15 June 1982 under section 34 of the Companies Act 1967, and part of the register so kept for the purposes of scetion 27 of the Companies Act 1976 shall continue to be kept by the company under and for the purposes of this section.

214. Company investigation on requisition by members.

(1) A company may be required to exercise its powers under section 212 on the requisition of members of the company holding at the date of the deposit of the requisition not less than one-tenth of such of the paid-up capital of the company as carries at that date the right of voting at general meetings of the company.

(2) The requisition must—

(a) state that the requisitions are requiring the company to exercise its powers under section 212,

(b) specify the manner in which they require those powers to be exercised, and

(c) give reasonable grounds for requiring the company to exercise those powers in the manner specified,

and must be signed by the requisitions and deposited at the company's registered office.

(3) The requisition may consist of several documents in like form each signed by one or more requisitionists.

(4) On the deposit of a requisition complying with this section it is the company's duty to exercise its powers under section 212 in the manner specified in the requisition.

(5) If default is made in complying with subsection (4), the company and every officer of it who is in default is liable to a fine.

215. Company report to members.

(1) On the conclusion of an investigation carried out by a company in pursuance of a requisition under section 214, it is the company's duty to cause a report of the information received in pursuance of that investigation to be prepared, and the report shall be made available at the company's registered office within a reasonable period after the conclusion of that investigation.

(2) Where—

(a) a company undertakes an investigation in pursuance of a requisition under section 214, and

(b) the investigation is not concluded before the end of 3 months beginning with the date immediately following the date of the deposit of the requisition,

it is the duty of the company to cause to be prepared, in respect of that period and each successive period of 3 months ending before the conclusion of the investigation, an interim report of the information received during that period in pursuance of the investigation. Each such report shall be made available at the company's registered office within a reasonable period after the end of the period to which it relates.

(3) The period for making any report prepared under this section available as required by subsection (1) or (2) shall not exceed 15 days.

(4) Such a report shall not include any information with respect to a company entitled to avail itself of the benefit conferred by section 231(3) (disclosure of shareholdings not required if it would be harmful to company's business); but where any such information is omitted, that fact shall be stated in the report.

(5) The company shall, within 3 days of making any report prepared under this section available at its registered office, notify the requisitionists that the report is so available.

(6) An investigation carried out by a company in pursuance of a requisition under section 214 is regarded for purposes of this section as concluded when the company has

made all such inquiries as are necessary or expedient for the purposes of the requisition and in the case of each such inquiry, either a response has been received by the company or the time allowed for a response has elapsed.

(7)   A report prepared under this section—

(a)   shall be kept at the company's registered office from the day on which it is first available there in accordance with subsection (1) or (2) until the expiration of 6 years beginning with the day next following that day, and

(b)   shall be available for inspection in accordance with section 219 below so long as it is so kept.

(8)   If default is made in complying with subsection (1), (2), (5) or (7)(a), the company and every officer of it who is in default is liable to a fine.

216.   Penalty for failure to provide information.

(1)   Where notice is served by a company under section 212 on a person who is or was interested in shares of the company and that person fails to give the company any information required by the notice within the time specified in it, the company may apply to the court for an order directing that the shares in question be subject to the restrictions of Part XV of this Act.

(1A)   On an application made under subsection (1) the court may make an interim order and any such order may be made unconditionally or on such terms as the court thinks fit.

(1B)   If the court is satisfied that an order under subsection (1) may unfairly affect the rights of third parties in respect of shares then the court, for the purpose of protecting such rights and subject to such terms as it thinks fit, may direct that such acts by such persons or descriptions of persons and for such purposes as may be set out in the order, shall not constitute a breach of the restrictions of Part XV of this Act.

(2)   An order under this section may be made by the court notwithstanding any power contained in the applicant company's memorandum or articles enabling the company itself to impose similar restrictions on the shares in question.

(3)   Subject to the following subsections, a person who fails to comply with a notice under section 212 or who, in purported compliance with such a notice, makes any statement which he knows to be false in a material particular or recklessly makes any statement which is false in a material particular is guilty of an offence and liable to imprisonment or a fine, or both.

Section 733(2) and (3) of this Act (liability of individuals for corporate default) apply to offences under this subsection.

(4)   A person is not guilty of an offence by virtue of failing to comply with a notice under section 212 if he proves that the requirement to give the information was frivolous or vexatious.

(5)   A person is not obliged to comply with a notice under section 212 if he is for the time being exempted by the Secretary of State from the operation of that section; but the Secretary of State shall not grant any such exemption unless—

(a)   he has consulted with the Governor of the Bank of England, and

(b)   he (the Secretary of State) is satisfied that, having regard to any undertaking given by the person in question with respect to any interest held or to be held by him in any shares, there are special reasons why that person should not be subject to the obligations imposed by that section.

217.   Removal of entries from register.

(1)   A company may remove an entry against a person's name from its register of interests in shares if more than 6 years have elapsed since the date of the entry being made, and either—

(a)   that entry recorded the fact that the person in question had ceased to have an interest notifiable under this Part in relevant share capital of the company, or

(b) it has been superseded by a later entry made under section 211 against the same person's name;
and in a case within paragraph (a) the company may also remove that person's name from the register.

(2) If a person in pursuance of an obligation imposed on him by any provision of this Part gives to a company the name and address of another person as being interested in shares in the company, the company shall, within 15 days of the date on which it was given that information, notify the other person that he has been so named and shall include in that notification—

(a) particulars of any entry relating to him made, in consequence of its being given that information, by the company in its register of interests in shares, and

(b) a statement informing him of his right to apply to have the entry removed in accordance with the following provisions of this section.

(3) A person who has been notified by a company in pursuance of subsection (2) that an entry relating to him has been made in the company's register of interests in shares may apply in writing to the company for the removal of that entry from the register; and the company shall remove the entry if satisfied that the information in pursuance of which the entry was made was incorrect.

(4) If a person who is identified in a company's register of interests in shares as being a party to an agreement to which section 204 applies (whether by an entry against his own name or by an entry relating to him made against another person's name as mentioned in subsection (2)(a)) ceases to be a party to that agreement, he may apply in writing to the company for the inclusion of that information in the register; and if the company is satisfied that he has ceased to be a party to the agreement, it shall record that information (if not already recorded) in every place where his name appears as a party to that agreement in the register.

(5) If an application under subsection (3) or (4) is refused (in a case within subsection (4), otherwise than on the ground that the information has already been recorded) the applicant may apply to the court for an order directing the company to remove the entry in question from the register or (as the case may be) to include the information in question in the register; and the court may, if it thinks fit, make such an order.

(6) Where a name is removed from a company's register of interests in shares in pursuance of subsection (1) or (3) or an order under subsection (5), the company shall within 14 days of the date of that removal make any necessary alteration in any associated index.

(7) If default is made in complying with subsection (2) or (6), the company and every officer of it who is in default is liable to a fine and, for continued contravention, to a daily default fine.

218. Otherwise, entries not to be removed.

(1) Entries in a company's register of interests in shares shall not be deleted except in accordance with section 217.

(2) If an entry is deleted from a company's register of interests in shares in contravention of subsection (1), the company shall restore that entry to the register as soon as is reasonably practicable.

(3) If default is made in complying with subsection (1) or (2), the company and every officer of it who is in default is liable to a fine and, for continued contravention of subsection (2), to a daily default fine.

219. Inspection of register and reports.

(1) Any register of interests in shares and any report which is required by section 215(7) to be available for inspection in accordance with this section shall be open to the inspection of any member of the company or of any other person without charge.

(2)   Any such member or other person may require a copy of any such register or report, or any part of it, on payment of such fee as may be prescribed; and the company shall cause any copy so required by a person to be sent to him before the expiration of the period of 10 days beginning with the day next following that on which the requirement is received by the company.

(3)   If an inspection required under this section is refused or a copy so required is not sent within the proper period, the company and every officer of it who is in default is liable to a fine and, for continued contravention, to a daily default fine.

(4)   In the case of a refusal of an inspection required under this section of any register or report, the court may by order compel an immediate inspection of it; and in the case of failure to send a copy required under this section, the court may by order direct that the copy required shall be sent to the person requiring it.

(5)   The Secretary of State may by regulations made by statutory instrument substitute a sum specified in the regulations for the sum for the time being mentioned in subsection (2).

[*No sum is now mentioned in s. 219(2), following amendment by the Companies Act 1989, s. 143(5)(b).*]

Supplementary

220.   Definitions for Part VI.

(1)   In this Part of this Act—

'associated index', in relation to a register, means the index kept in relation to that register in pursuance of section 211(6);

'authorised credit institution' means a credit institution as defined in Article 1 of Council Directive 77/780/EEC which is authorised to carry on the business of a credit institution by a competent authority of a member State other than the United Kingdom;

'authorised insurance undertaking' means an insurance undertaking which has been authorised in accordance with Article 6 or 23 of Council Directive 73/239/EEC or Article 6 or 27 of Council Directive 79/267/EEC, or is authorised under the law of a member State to carry on insurance business restricted to reinsurance;

'authorised unit trust scheme' has the same meaning as in Chapter VIII of Part I of the Financial Services Act 1986;

'depositary receipt' means a certificate or other record (whether or not in the form of a document)—

(a)   which is issued by or on behalf of a person who holds shares or who holds evidence of the right to receive shares, or has an interest in shares, in a particular company; and

(b)   which evidences or acknowledges that another person is entitled to rights in relation to those shares or shares of the same kind, which shall include the right to receive such shares (or evidence of the right to receive such shares) from the person mentioned in paragraph (a);

'derivatives' means—

(a)   options to acquire or dispose of shares; and

(b)   rights under a contract falling within paragraph 8 of Schedule 1 to the Financial Services Act 1986 (futures), where the property in question is shares;

'designated agency' has the same meaning as in the Financial Services Act 1986;

'investment company with variable capital' has the same meaning as in the Open-Ended Investment Companies (Investment Companies with Variable Capital) Regulations 1996;

'listed company' means a company any of the shares in which are officially listed on a relevant stock exchange and 'listed' shall be construed accordingly;

'material interest' shall be construed in accordance with section 199(2A);

'operator', in relation to a collective investment scheme, shall be construed in accordance with section 75(8) of the Financial Services Act 1986;

'recognised clearing house', 'recognised professional body', 'recognised scheme', and 'recognised self-regulating organisation' have the same meaning as in the Financial Services Act 1986;

'register of interest in shares' means the register kept in pursuance of section 211 including, except where the context otherwise requires, that part of the register kept in pursuance of section 213;

'relevant investment exchange' means an exchange situated or operating in a member State on which derivatives are traded;

'relevant share capital' has the meaning given by section 198(2);

'relevant stock exchange' means a stock exchange situated or operating in a member State;

'UCITS' has the meaning given by section 199(8);

'units' has the same meaning as in section 75 of the Financial Services Act 1986.

(2)   Where the period allowed by any provision of this Part for fulfilling an obligation is expressed as a number of days, any day that is a Saturday or Sunday or a bank holiday in any part of Great Britain is to be disregarded in reckoning that period.

PART VII
ACCOUNTS AND AUDIT

CHAPTER I
PROVISIONS APPLYING TO COMPANIES GENERALLY

Accounting records

221.   Duty to keep accounting records.

(1)   Every company shall keep accounting records which are sufficient to show and explain the company's transactions and are such as to—

(a)   disclose with reasonable accuracy, at any time, the financial position of the company at that time, and

(b)   enable the directors to ensure that any balance sheet and profit and loss account prepared under this Part complies with the requirements of this Act.

(2)   The accounting records shall in particular contain—

(a)   entries from day to day of all sums of money received and expended by the company, and the matters in respect of which the receipt and expenditure takes place, and

(b)   a record of the assets and liabilities of the company.

(3)   If the company's business involves dealing in goods, the accounting records shall contain—

(a)   statements of stock held by the company at the end of each financial year of the company,

(b)   all statements of stocktakings from which any such statement of stock as is mentioned in paragraph (a) has been or is to be prepared, and

(c)   except in the case of goods sold by way of ordinary retail trade, statements of all goods sold and purchased, showing the goods and the buyers and sellers in sufficient detail to enable all these to be identified.

(4)   A parent company which has a subsidiary undertaking in relation to which the above requirements do not apply shall take reasonable steps to secure that the undertaking keeps such accounting records as to enable the directors of the parent company to ensure that any balance sheet and profit and loss account prepared under this Part complies with the requirements of this Act.

(5)   If a company fails to comply with any provision of this section, every officer of the company who is in default is guilty of an offence unless he shows that he acted

honestly and that in the circumstances in which the company's business was carried on the default was excusable.

(6)   A person guilty of an offence under this section is liable to imprisonment or a fine, or both.

[*In s. 221(2)(a), it may be that 'the receipt and expenditure takes place' is a mistake for 'the receipt or expenditure takes place'.*]

222.   Where and for how long records to be kept.

(1)   A company's accounting records shall be kept at its registered office or such other place as the directors think fit, and shall at all times be open to inspection by the company's officers.

(2)   If accounting records are kept at a place outside Great Britain, accounts and returns with respect to the business dealt with in the accounting records so kept shall be sent to, and kept at, a place in Great Britain, and shall at all times be open to such inspection.

(3)   The accounts and returns to be sent to Great Britain shall be such as to—

(a)   disclose with reasonable accuracy the financial position of the business in question at intervals of not more than six months, and

(b)   enable the directors to ensure that the company's balance sheet and profit and loss account comply with the requirements of this Act.

(4)   If a company fails to comply with any provision of subsections (1) to (3), every officer of the company who is in default is guilty of an offence, and liable to imprisonment or a fine or both, unless he shows that he acted honestly and that in the circumstances in which the company's business was carried on the default was excusable.

(5)   Accounting records which a company is required by section 221 to keep shall be preserved by it—

(a)   in the case of a private company, for three years from the date on which they are made, and

(b)   in the case of a public company, for six years from the date on which they are made.

This is subject to any provision contained in rules made under section 411 of the Insolvency Act 1986 (company insolvency rules).

(6)   An officer of a company is guilty of an offence, and liable to imprisonment or a fine or both, if he fails to take all reasonable steps for securing compliance by the company with subsection (5) or intentionally causes any default by the company under that subsection.

A company's financial year and accounting reference periods

223.   A company's financial year.

(1)   A company's 'financial year' is determined as follows.

(2)   Its first financial year begins with the first day of its first accounting reference period and ends with the last day of that period or such other date, not more than seven days before or after the end of that period, as the directors may determine.

(3)   Subsequent financial years begin with the day immediately following the end of the company's previous financial year and end with the last day of its next accounting reference period or such other date, not more than seven days before or after the end of that period, as the directors may determine.

(4)   In relation to an undertaking which is not a company, references in this Act to its financial year are to any period in respect of which a profit and loss account of the undertaking is required to be made up (by its constitution or by the law under which it is established), whether that period is a year or not.

(5) The directors of a parent company shall secure that, except where in their opinion there are good reasons against it, the financial year of each of its subsidiary undertakings coincides with the company's own financial year.

224. Accounting reference periods and accounting reference date.

(1) A company's accounting reference periods are determined according to its accounting reference date.

(2) A company incorporated before 1 April 1996 may, at any time before the end of the period of nine months beginning with the date of its incorporation, by notice in the prescribed form given to the registrar specify its accounting reference date, that is, the date on which its accounting reference period ends in each calendar year.

(3) Failing such notice, the accounting reference date of such a company is—

    (a)   in the case of a company incorporated before 1 April 1990, 31 March;

    (b)   in the case of a company incorporated after 1 April 1990, the last day of the month in which the anniversary of its incorporation falls.

(3A) The accounting reference date of a company incorporated on or after 1 April 1996 is the last day of the month in which the anniversary of its incorporation falls.

(4) A company's first accounting reference period is the period of more than six months, but not more than 18 months, beginning with the date of its incorporation and ending with its accounting reference date.

(5) Its subsequent accounting reference periods are successive periods of twelve months beginning immediately after the end of the previous accounting reference period and ending with its accounting reference date.

(6) This section has effect subject to the provisions of section 225 relating to the alteration of accounting reference dates and the consequences of such alteration.

225. Alteration of accounting reference date.

(1) A company may by notice in the prescribed form given to the registrar specify a new accounting reference date having effect in relation to—

    (a)   the company's current accounting reference period and subsequent periods; or

    (b)   the company's previous accounting reference period and subsequent periods.

A company's 'previous accounting reference period' means that immediately preceding its current accounting reference period.

(3) The notice shall state whether the current or previous accounting reference period—

    (a)   is to be shortened, so as to come to an end on the first occasion on which the new accounting reference date falls or fell after the beginning of the period, or

    (b)   is to be extended, so as to come to an end on the second occasion on which that date falls or fell after the beginning of the period.

(4) A notice under subsection (1) stating that the current or previous accounting reference period is to be extended is ineffective, except as mentioned below, if given less than five years after the end of an earlier accounting reference period of the company which was extended by virtue of this section.

This subsection does not apply—

    (a)   to a notice given by a company which is a subsidiary undertaking or parent undertaking of another EEA undertaking if the new accounting reference date coincides with that of the other EEA undertaking or, where that undertaking is not a company, with the last day of its financial year, or

    (b)   where an administration order is in force under Part II of the Insolvency Act 1986,

or where the Secretary of State directs that it should not apply, which he may do with respect to a notice which has been given or which may be given.

(5)   A notice under subsection (1) may not be given in respect of a previous accounting reference period if the period allowed for laying and delivering accounts and reports in relation to that period has already expired.

(6)   An accounting reference period may not in any case, unless an administration order is in force under Part II of the Insolvency Act 1986, be extended so as to exceed 18 months and a notice under this section is ineffective if the current or previous accounting reference period as extended in accordance with the notice would exceed that limit.

(7)   In this section 'EEA undertaking' means an undertaking established under the law of any part of the United Kingdom or the law of any other EEA State.

Annual accounts

226.   Duty to prepare individual company accounts.

(1)   The directors of every company shall prepare for each financial year of the company—

    (a)   a balance sheet as at the last day of the year, and

    (b)   a profit and loss account.

Those accounts are referred to in this Part as the company's 'individual accounts'.

(2)   The balance sheet shall give a true and fair view of the state of affairs of the company as at the end of the financial year; and the profit and loss account shall give a true and fair view of the profit or loss of the company for the financial year.

(3)   A company's individual accounts shall comply with the provisions of Schedule 4 as to the form and content of the balance sheet and profit and loss account and additional information to be provided by way of notes to the accounts.

(4)   Where compliance with the provisions of that Schedule, and the other provisions of this Act as to the matters to be included in a company's individual accounts or in notes to those accounts, would not be sufficient to give a true and fair view, the necessary additional information shall be given in the accounts or in a note to them.

(5)   If in special circumstances compliance with any of those provisions is inconsistent with the requirement to give a true and fair view, the directors shall depart from that provision to the extent necessary to give a true and fair view.

Particulars of any such departure, the reasons for it and its effect shall be given in a note to the accounts.

227.   Duty to prepare group accounts.

(1)   If at the end of a financial year a company is a parent company the directors shall, as well as preparing individual accounts for the year, prepare group accounts.

(2)   Group accounts shall be consolidated accounts comprising—

    (a)   a consolidated balance sheet dealing with the state of affairs of the parent company and its subsidiary undertakings, and

    (b)   a consolidated profit and loss account dealing with the profit or loss of the parent company and its subsidiary undertakings.

(3)   The accounts shall give a true and fair view of the state of affairs as at the end of the financial year, and the profit or loss for the financial year, of the undertakings included in the consolidation as a whole, so far as concerns members of the company.

(4)   A company's group accounts shall comply with the provisions of Schedule 4A as to the form and content of the consolidated balance sheet and consolidated profit and loss account and additional information to be provided by way of notes to the accounts.

(5)   Where compliance with the provisions of that Schedule, and the other provisions of this Act, as to the matters to be included in a company's group accounts or in notes to those accounts, would not be sufficient to give a true and fair view, the necessary additional information shall be given in the accounts or in a note to them.

(6)   If in special circumstances compliance with any of those provisions is inconsistent with the requirement to give a true and fair view, the directors shall depart from that provision to the extent necessary to give a true and fair view.

Particulars of any such departure, the reasons for it and its effect shall be given in a note to the accounts.

228.   Exemption for parent companies included in accounts of larger group.

(1)   A company is exempt from the requirement to prepare group accounts if it is itself a subsidiary undertaking and its immediate parent undertaking is established under the law of a member State of the European Economic Community, in the following cases—

    (a)   where the company is a wholly-owned subsidiary of that parent undertaking;

    (b)   where that parent undertaking holds more than 50 per cent of the shares in the company and notice requesting the preparation of group accounts has not been served on the company by shareholders holding in aggregate—

        (i)   more than half of the remaining shares in the company, or

        (ii)   5 per cent of the total shares in the company.

Such notice must be served not later than six months after the end of the financial year before that to which it relates.

(2)   Exemption is conditional upon compliance with all of the following conditions—

    (a)   that the company is included in consolidated accounts for a larger group drawn up to the same date, or to an earlier date in the same financial year, by a parent undertaking established under the law of a member State of the European Economic Community;

    (b)   that those accounts are drawn up and audited, and that parent undertaking's annual report is drawn up, according to that law, in accordance with the provisions of the Seventh Directive (83/349/EEC) (where applicable as modified by the provisions of the Bank Accounts Directive (86/635/EEC) or the Insurance Accounts Directive (91/674/EEC));

    (c)   that the company discloses in its individual accounts that it is exempt from the obligation to prepare and deliver group accounts;

    (d)   that the company states in its individual accounts the name of the parent undertaking which draws up the group accounts referred to above and—

        (i)   if it is incorporated outside Great Britain, the country in which it is incorporated,

        (iii)   if it is unincorporated, the address of its principal place of business;

    (e)   that the company delivers to the registrar, within the period allowed for delivering its individual accounts, copies of those group accounts and of the parent undertaking's annual report, together with the auditors' report on them; and

    (f)   (subject to section 710B(6) (delivery of certain Welsh documents without a translation)) that if any document comprised in accounts and reports delivered in accordance with paragraph (e) is in a language other than English, there is annexed to the copy of that document delivered a translation of it into English, certified in the prescribed manner to be a correct translation.

(3)   The exemption does not apply to a company any of whose securities are listed on a stock exchange in any member State of the European Economic Community.

(4)   Shares held by directors of a company for the purpose of complying with any share qualification requirement shall be disregarded in determining for the purposes of subsection (1)(a) whether the company is a wholly-owned subsidiary.

(5)   For the purposes of subsection (1)(b) shares held by a wholly-owned subsidiary of the parent undertaking, or held on behalf of the parent undertaking or a wholly-owned subsidiary, shall be attributed to the parent undertaking.

(6) In subsection (3) 'securities' includes—

(a) shares and stock,

(b) debentures, including debenture stock, loan stock, bonds, certificates of deposit and other instruments creating or acknowledging indebtedness,

(c) warrants or other instruments entitling the holder to subscribe for securities falling within paragraph (a) or (b), and

(d) certificates or other instruments which confer—

(i) property rights in respect of a security falling within paragraph (a), (b) or (c),

(ii) any right to acquire, dispose of, underwrite or convert a security, being a right to which the holder would be entitled if he held any such security to which the certificate or other instrument relates, or

(iii) a contractual right (other than an option) to acquire any such security otherwise than by subscription.

229. Subsidiary undertakings included in the consolidation.

(1) Subject to the exceptions authorised or required by this section, all the subsidiary undertakings of the parent company shall be included in the consolidation.

(2) A subsidiary undertaking may be excluded from consolidation if its inclusion is not material for the purpose of giving a true and fair view; but two or more undertakings may be excluded only if they are not material taken together.

(3) In addition, a subsidiary undertaking may be excluded from consolidation where—

(a) severe long-term restrictions substantially hinder the exercise of the rights of the parent company over the assets or management of that undertaking, or

(b) the information necessary for the preparation of group accounts cannot be obtained without disproportionate expense or undue delay, or

(c) the interest of the parent company is held exclusively with a view to subsequent resale and the undertaking has not previously been included in consolidated group accounts prepared by the parent company.

The reference in paragraph (a) to the rights of the parent company and the reference in paragraph (c) to the interest of the parent company are, respectively, to rights and interests held by or attributed to the company for the purposes of section 258 (definition of 'parent undertaking') in the absence of which it would not be the parent company.

(4) Where the activities of one or more subsidiary undertakings are so different from those of other undertakings to be included in the consolidation that their inclusion would be incompatible with the obligation to give a true and fair view, those undertakings shall be excluded from consolidation.

This subsection does not apply merely because some of the undertakings are industrial, some commercial and some provide services, or because they carry on industrial or commercial activities involving different products or provide different services.

(5) Where all the subsidiary undertakings of a parent company fall within the above exclusions, no group accounts are required.

230. Treatment of individual profit and loss account where group accounts prepared.

(1) The following provisions apply with respect to the individual profit and loss account of a parent company where—

(a) the company is required to prepare and does prepare group accounts in accordance with this Act, and

(b) the notes to the company's individual balance sheet show the company's profit or loss for the financial year determined in accordance with this Act.

(2)   The profit and loss account need not contain the information specified in paragraphs 52 to 57 of Schedule 4 (information supplementing the profit and loss account).

(3)   The profit and loss account must be approved in accordance with section 233(1) (approval by board of directors) but may be omitted from the company's annual accounts for the purposes of the other provisions below in this Chapter.

(4)   The exemption conferred by this section is conditional upon its being disclosed in the company's annual accounts that the exemption applies.

231.   Disclosure required in notes to accounts: related undertakings.

(1)   The information specified in Schedule 5 shall be given in notes to a company's annual accounts.

(2)   Where the company is not required to prepare group accounts, the information specified in Part I of that Schedule shall be given; and where the company is required to prepare group accounts, the information specified in Part II of that Schedule shall be given.

(3)   The information required by Schedule 5 need not be disclosed with respect to an undertaking which—

(a)   is established under the law of a country outside the United Kingdom, or

(b)   carries on business outside the United Kingdom,

if in the opinion of the directors of the company the disclosure would be seriously prejudicial to the business of that undertaking, or to the business of the company or any of its subsidiary undertakings, and the Secretary of State agrees that the information need not be disclosed.

This subsection does not apply in relation to the information required under paragraph 6, 9A, 20 or 28A of that Schedule.

(4)   Where advantage is taken of subsection (3), that fact shall be stated in a note to the company's annual accounts.

(5)   If the directors of the company are of the opinion that the number of undertakings in respect of which the company is required to disclose information under any provision of Schedule 5 to this Act is such that compliance with that provision would result in information of excessive length being given, the information need only be given in respect of—

(a)   the undertakings whose results or financial position, in the opinion of the directors, principally affected the figures shown in the company's annual accounts, and

(b)   undertakings excluded from consolidation under section 229(3) or (4).

(6)   If advantage is taken of subsection (5)—

(a)   there shall be included in the notes to the company's annual accounts a statement that the information is given only with respect to such undertakings as are mentioned in that subsection, and

(b)   the full information (both that which is disclosed in the notes to the accounts and that which is not) shall be annexed to the company's next annual return.

For this purpose the 'next annual return' means that next delivered to the registrar after the accounts in question have been approved under section 233.

(7)   If a company fails to comply with subsection (6)(b), the company and every officer of it who is in default is liable to a fine and, for continued contravention, to a daily default fine.

232.   Disclosure required in notes to accounts: emoluments and other benefits of directors and others.

(1)   The information specified in Schedule 6 shall be given in notes to a company's annual accounts.

(2)   In that Schedule—

Part I   relates to the emoluments of directors (including emoluments waived), pensions of directors and past directors, compensation for loss of office to directors and past directors and sums paid to third parties in respect of directors' services,

Part II   relates to loans, quasi-loans and other dealings in favour of directors and connected persons, and

Part III   relates to transactions, arrangements and agreements made by the company or a subsidiary undertaking for officers of the company other than directors.

(3)   It is the duty of any director of a company, and any person who is or has at any time in the preceding five years been an officer of the company, to give notice to the company of such matters relating to himself as may be necessary for the purposes of Part I of Schedule 6.

(4)   A person who makes default in complying with subsection (3) commits an offence and is liable to a fine.

Approval and signing of accounts

233.   Approval and signing of accounts.

(1)   A company's annual accounts shall be approved by the board of directors and signed on behalf of the board by a director of the company.

(2)   The signature shall be on the company's balance sheet.

(3)   Every copy of the balance sheet which is laid before the company in general meeting, or which is otherwise circulated, published or issued, shall state the name of the person who signed the balance sheet on behalf of the board.

(4)   The copy of the company's balance sheet which is delivered to the registrar shall be signed on behalf of the board by a director of the company.

(5)   If annual accounts are approved which do not comply with the requirements of this Act, every director of the company who is party to their approval and who knows that they do not comply or is reckless as to whether they comply is guilty of an offence and liable to a fine.

For this purpose every director of the company at the time the accounts are approved shall be taken to be a party to their approval unless he shows that he took all reasonable steps to prevent their being approved.

(6)   If a copy of the balance sheet—

(a)   is laid before the company, or otherwise circulated, published or issued, without the balance sheet having been signed as required by this section or without the required statement of the signatory's name being included, or

(b)   is delivered to the registrar without being signed as required by this section,

the company and every officer of it who is in default is guilty of an offence and liable to a fine.

Directors' report

234.   Duty to prepare directors' report.

(1)   The directors of a company shall for each financial year prepare a report—

(a)   containing a fair review of the development of the business of the company and its subsidiary undertakings during the financial year and of their position at the end of it, and

(b)   stating the amount (if any) which they recommend should be paid as dividend.

(2)   The report shall state the names of the persons who, at any time during the financial year, were directors of the company, and the principal activities of the company and its subsidiary undertakings in the course of the year and any significant change in those activities in the year.

(3)   The report shall also comply with Schedule 7 as regards the disclosure of the matters mentioned there.

(4)   In Schedule 7—

Part I   relates to matters of a general nature, including changes in asset values, directors' shareholdings and other interests and contributions for political and charitable purposes,

Part II   relates to the acquisition by a company of its own shares or a charge on them,

Part III   relates to the employment, training and advancement of disabled persons,

Part V   relates to the involvement of employees in the affairs, policy and perform-ance of the company,

Part VI   relates to the company's policy and practice on the payment of creditors.

(5)   In the case of any failure to comply with the provisions of this Part as to the preparation of a directors' report and the contents of the report, every person who was a director of the company immediately before the end of the period of laying and delivering accounts and reports for the financial year in question is guilty of an offence and liable to a fine.

(6)   In proceedings against a person for an offence under this section it is a defence for him to prove that he took all reasonable steps for securing compliance with the requirements in question.

234A.   Approval and signing of directors' report.

(1)   The directors' report shall be approved by the board of directors and signed on behalf of the board by a director or the secretary of the company.

(2)   Every copy of the directors' report which is laid before the company in general meeting, or which is otherwise circulated, published or issued, shall state the name of the person who signed it on behalf of the board.

(3)   The copy of the directors' report which is delivered to the registrar shall be signed on behalf of the board by a director or the secretary of the company.

(4)   If a copy of the directors' report—

(a)   is laid before the company, or otherwise circulated, published or issued, without the report having been signed as required by this section or without the required statement of the signatory's name being included, or

(b)   is delivered to the registrar without being signed as required by this section, the company and every officer of it who is in default is guilty of an offence and liable to a fine.

Auditors' report

235.   Auditors' report.

(1)   A company's auditors shall make a report to the company's members on all annual accounts of the company of which copies are to be laid before the company in general meeting during their tenure of office.

(2)   The auditors' report shall state whether in the auditors' opinion the annual accounts have been properly prepared in accordance with this Act, and in particular whether a true and fair view is given—

(a)   in the case of an individual balance sheet, of the state of affairs of the company as at the end of the financial year,

(b)   in the case of an individual profit and loss account, of the profit or loss of the company for the financial year,

(c)   in the case of group accounts, of the state of affairs as at the end of the financial year, and the profit or loss for the financial year, of the undertakings included in the consolidation as a whole, so far as concerns members of the company.

(3)   The auditors shall consider whether the information given in the directors' report for the financial year for which the annual accounts are prepared is consistent with those accounts; and if they are of opinion that it is not they shall state that fact in their report.

236. Signature of auditors' report.

(1)   The auditors' report shall state the names of the auditors and be signed by them.

(2)   Every copy of the auditors' report which is laid before the company in general meeting, or which is otherwise circulated, published or issued, shall state the names of the auditors.

(3)   The copy of the auditors' report which is delivered to the registrar shall state the names of the auditors and be signed by them.

(4)   If a copy of the auditors' report—

(a)   is laid before the company, or otherwise circulated, published or issued, without the required statement of the auditors' names, or

(b)   is delivered to the registrar without the required statement of the auditors' names or without being signed as required by this section,

the company and every officer of it who is in default is guilty of an offence and liable to a fine.

(5)   References in this section to signature by the auditors are, where the office of auditor is held by a body corporate or partnership, to signature in the name of the body corporate or partnership by a person authorised to sign on its behalf.

237. Duties of auditors.

(1)   A company's auditors shall, in preparing their report, carry out such investigations as will enable them to form an opinion as to—

(a)   whether proper accounting records have been kept by the company and proper returns adequate for their audit have been received from branches not visited by them, and

(b)   whether the company's individual accounts are in agreement with the accounting records and returns.

(2)   If the auditors are of opinion that proper accounting records have not been kept, or that proper returns adequate for their audit have not been received from branches not visited by them, or if the company's individual accounts are not in agreement with the accounting records and returns, the auditors shall state the fact in their report.

(3)   If the auditors fail to obtain all the information and explanations which, to the best of their knowledge and belief, are necessary for the purposes of their audit, they shall state that fact in their report.

(4)   If the requirements of Schedule 6 (disclosure of information: emoluments and other benefits of directors and others) are not complied with in the annual accounts, the auditors shall include in their report, so far as they are reasonably able to do so, a statement giving the required particulars.

(4A)   If the directors of the company have taken advantage of the exemption conferred by section 248 (exemption for small and medium-sized groups from the need to prepare group accounts) and in the auditors' opinion they were not entitled so to do, the auditors shall state that fact in their report.

Publication of accounts and reports

238. Persons entitled to receive copies of accounts and reports.

(1)   A copy of the company's annual accounts, together with a copy of the directors' report for that financial year and of the auditors' report on those accounts, shall be sent to—

(a)   every member of the company,

(b)   every holder of the company's debentures, and

(c)   every person who is entitled to receive notice of general meetings,

not less than 21 days before the date of the meeting at which copies of those documents are to be laid in accordance with section 241.

(2)   Copies need not be sent—

(a)   to a person who is not entitled to receive notices of general meetings and of whose address the company is unaware, or

(b)   to more than one of the joint holders of shares or debentures none of whom is entitled to receive such notices, or

(c)   in the case of joint holders of shares or debentures some of whom are, and some not, entitled to receive such notices, to those who are not so entitled.

(3)   In the case of a company not having a share capital, copies need not be sent to anyone who is not entitled to receive notices of general meetings of the company.

(4)   If copies are sent less than 21 days before the date of the meeting, they shall, notwithstanding that fact, be deemed to have been duly sent if it is so agreed by all the members entitled to attend and vote at the meeting.

(5)   If default is made in complying with this section, the company and every officer of it who is in default is guilty of an offence and liable to a fine.

(6)   Where copies are sent out under this section over a period of days, references elsewhere in this Act to the day on which copies are sent out shall be construed as references to the last day of that period.

239.   Right to demand copies of accounts and reports.

(1)   Any member of a company and any holder of a company's debentures is entitled to be furnished, on demand and without charge, with a copy of the company's last annual accounts and directors' report and a copy of the auditors' report on those accounts.

(2)   The entitlement under this section is to a single copy of those documents, but that is in addition to any copy to which a person may be entitled under section 238.

(3)   If a demand under this section is not complied with within seven days, the company and every officer of it who is in default is guilty of an offence and liable to a fine and, for continued contravention, to a daily default fine.

(4)   If in proceedings for such an offence the issue arises whether a person had already been furnished with a copy of the relevant document under this section, it is for the defendant to prove that he had.

240.   Requirements in connection with publication of accounts.

(1)   If a company publishes any of its statutory accounts, they must be accompanied by the relevant auditors' report under section 235 or, as the case may be, the relevant report made for the purposes of section 249A(2).

(2)   A company which is required to prepare group accounts for a financial year shall not publish its statutory individual accounts for that year without also publishing with them its statutory group accounts.

(3)   If a company publishes non-statutory accounts, it shall publish with them a statement indicating—

(a)   that they are not the company's statutory accounts,

(b)   whether statutory accounts dealing with any financial year with which the non-statutory accounts purport to deal have been delivered to the registrar,

(c)   whether the company's auditors have made a report under section 235 on the statutory accounts for any such financial year and, if no such report has been made, whether the company's reporting accountant has made a report for the purposes of section 249A(2) on the statutory accounts for any such financial year, and

(d)   whether any auditors' report so made was qualified or contained a statement under section 237(2) or (3) (accounting records or returns inadequate, accounts not agreeing with records and returns or failure to obtain necessary information and explanations) or whether any report made for the purposes of section 249A(2) was qualified;

and it shall not publish with the non-statutory accounts any auditors' report under section 235 or any report made for the purposes of section 249A(2).

(4)   For the purposes of this section a company shall be regarded as publishing a document if it publishes, issues or circulates it or otherwise makes it available for public inspection in a manner calculated to invite members of the public generally, or any class of members of the public, to read it.

(5)   References in this section to a company's statutory accounts are to its individual or group accounts for a financial year as required to be delivered to the registrar under section 242; and references to the publication by a company of 'non-statutory accounts' are to the publication of—

(a)   any balance sheet or profit and loss account relating to, or purporting to deal with, a financial year of the company, or

(b)   an account in any form purporting to be a balance sheet or profit and loss account for the group consisting of the company and its subsidiary undertakings relating to, or purporting to deal with, a financial year of the company,

otherwise than as part of the company's statutory accounts.

(6)   A company which contravenes any provision of this section, and any officer of it who is in default, is guilty of an offence and liable to a fine.

Laying and delivering of accounts and reports

241.   Accounts and reports to be laid before company in general meeting.

(1)   The directors of a company shall in respect of each financial year lay before the company in general meeting copies of the company's annual accounts, the directors' report and the auditors' report on those accounts.

(2)   If the requirements of subsection (1) are not complied with before the end of the period allowed for laying and delivering accounts and reports, every person who immediately before the end of that period was a director of the company is guilty of an offence and liable to a fine and, for continued contravention, to a daily default fine.

(3)   It is a defence for a person charged with such an offence to prove that he took all reasonable steps for securing that those requirements would be complied with before the end of that period.

(4)   It is not a defence to prove that the documents in question were not in fact prepared as required by this Part.

242.   Accounts and reports to be delivered to the registrar.

(1)   The directors of a company shall in respect of each financial year deliver to the registrar a copy of the company's annual accounts together with a copy of the directors' report for that year and a copy of the auditors' report on those accounts.

If any document comprised in those accounts or reports is in a language other than English then, subject to section 710B(6) (delivery of certain Welsh documents without a translation), the directors shall annex to the copy of that document delivered a translation of it into English, certified in the prescribed manner to be a correct translation

(2)   If the requirements of subsection (1) are not complied with before the end of the period allowed for laying and delivering accounts and reports, every person who immediately before the end of that period was a director of the company is guilty of an offence and liable to a fine and, for continued contravention, to a daily default fine.

(3)   Further, if the directors of the company fail to make good the default within 14 days after the service of a notice on them requiring compliance, the court may on the application of any member or creditor of the company or of the registrar, make an order directing the directors (or any of them) to make good the default within such time as may be specified in the order.

The court's order may provide that all costs of and incidental to the application shall be borne by the directors.

(4)   It is a defence of a person charged with an offence under this section to prove that he took all reasonable steps for securing that the requirements of subsection (1)

would be complied with before the end of the period allowed for laying and delivering accounts and reports.

(5)   It is not a defence in any proceedings under this section to prove that the documents in question were not in fact prepared as required by this Part.

242A.   Civil penalty for failure to deliver accounts.

(1)   Where the requirements of section 242(1) are not complied with before the end of the period allowed for laying and delivering accounts and reports, the company is liable to a civil penalty.

This is in addition to any liability of the directors under section 242.

(2)   The amount of the penalty is determined by reference to the length of the period between the end of the period allowed for laying and delivering accounts and reports and the day on which the requirements are complied with, and whether the company is a public or private company, as follows:—

Length of period	Public company	Private company
Not more than 3 months.	£500	£100
More than 3 months but not more than 6 months.	£1,000	£250
More than 6 months but not more than 12 months.	£2,000	£500
More than 12 months.	£5,000	£1,000

(3)   The penalty may be recovered by the registrar and shall be paid by him into the Consolidated Fund.

(4)   It is not a defence in proceedings under this section to prove that the documents in question were not in fact prepared as required by this Part.

242B.   Delivery and publication of accounts in ECUs.

(1)   The amount set out in the annual accounts of a company may also be shown in the same accounts translated into ECUs.

(2)   When complying with section 242, the directors of a company may deliver to the registrar an additional copy of the company's annual accounts in which the amounts have been translated into ECUs.

(3)   In both cases—

(a)   the amounts must have been translated at the relevant exchange rate prevailing on the balance sheet date, and

(b)   that rate must be disclosed in the notes to the accounts.

(4)   For the purposes of section 240 any additional copy of the company's annual accounts delivered to the registrar under subsection (2) shall be treated as statutory accounts of the company and, in the case of such a copy, references in section 240 to the auditors' report under section 235 shall be read as references to the auditors' report on the annual accounts of which it is a copy.

(5)   In this section—

'ECU' means a unit with a value equal to the value of the unit of account known as the ecu used in the European Monetary System, and

'relevant exchange rate' means the rate of exchange used for translating the value of the ecu for the purposes of that System.

243.   Accounts of subsidiary undertakings to be appended in certain cases.

(1)   The following provisions apply where at the end of the financial year a parent company has as a subsidiary undertaking—

(a)   a body corporate incorporated outside Great Britain which does not have an established place of business in Great Britain, or

(b)   an unincorporated undertaking,

which is excluded from consolidation in accordance with section 229(4) (undertaking with activities different from the undertakings included in the consolidation).

(2)   There shall be appended to the copy of the company's annual accounts delivered to the registrar in accordance with section 242 a copy of the undertaking's latest individual accounts and, if it is a parent undertaking, its latest group accounts.

If the accounts appended are required by law to be audited, a copy of the auditors' report shall also be appended.

(3)   The accounts must be for a period ending not more than twelve months before the end of the financial year for which the parent company's accounts are made up.

(4)   If any document required to be appended is in a language other than English then, subject to section 710B(6) (delivery of certain Welsh documents without a translation), the directors shall annex to the copy of that document delivered a translation of it into English certified in the prescribed manner to be a correct translation.

(5)   The above requirements are subject to the following qualifications—

(a)   an undertaking is not required to prepare for the purposes of this section accounts which would not otherwise be prepared, and if no accounts satisfying the above requirements are prepared none need be appended;

(b)   a document need not be appended if it would not otherwise be required to be published, or made available for public inspection, anywhere in the world, but in that case the reason for not appending it shall be stated in a note to the company's accounts;

(c)   where an undertaking and all its subsidiary undertakings are excluded from consolidation in accordance with section 229(4), the accounts of such of the subsidiary undertakings of that undertaking as are included in its consolidated group accounts need not be appended.

(6)   Subsections (2) to (4) of section 242 (penalties, &c. in case of default) apply in relation to the requirements of this section as they apply in relation to the requirements of subsection (1) of that section.

244.   Period allowed for laying and delivering accounts and reports.

(1)   The period allowed for laying and delivering accounts and reports is—

(a)   for a private company, 10 months after the end of the relevant accounting reference period, and

(b)   for a public company, 7 months after the end of that period.

This is subject to the following provisions of this section.

(2)   If the relevant accounting reference period is the company's first and is a period of more than 12 months, the period allowed is—

(a)   10 months or 7 months, as the case may be, from the first anniversary of the incorporation of the company, or

(b)   3 months from the end of the accounting reference period,

whichever last expires.

(3)   Where a company carries on business, or has interests, outside the United Kingdom, the Channel Islands and the Isle of Man, the directors may, in respect of any financial year, give to the registrar before the end of the period allowed by subsection (1) or (2) a notice in the prescribed form—

(a)   stating that the company so carries on business or has such interests, and

(b)   claiming a 3 month extension of the period allowed for laying and delivering accounts and reports;

and upon such a notice being given the period is extended accordingly.

(4)   If the relevant accounting period is treated as shortened by virtue of a notice given by the company under section 225 (alteration of accounting reference date), the period allowed for laying and delivering accounts is that applicable in accordance with the above provisions or 3 months from the date of the notice under that section, whichever last expires.

(5)   If for any special reason the Secretary of State thinks fit he may, on an application made before the expiry of the period otherwise allowed, by notice in writing to a company extend that period by such further period as may be specified in the notice.

(6)   In this section 'the relevant accounting reference period' means the accounting reference period by reference to which the financial year for the accounts in question was determined.

Revision of defective accounts and reports

245.   Voluntary revision of annual accounts or directors' report.

(1)   If it appears to the directors of a company that any annual accounts of the company, or any directors' report, did not comply with the requirements of this Act, they may prepare revised accounts or a revised report.

(2)   Where copies of the previous accounts or report have been laid before the company in general meeting or delivered to the registrar, the revisions shall be confined to—

(a)   the correction of those respects in which the previous accounts or report did not comply with the requirements of this Act, and

(b)   the making of any necessary consequential alterations.

(3)   The Secretary of State may make provision by regulations as to the application of the provisions of this Act in relation to revised annual accounts or a revised directors' report.

(4)   The regulations may, in particular—

(a)   make different provision according to whether the previous accounts or report are replaced or are supplemented by a document indicating the corrections to be made;

(b)   make provision with respect to the functions of the company's auditors or reporting accountant in relation to the revised accounts or report;

(c)   require the directors to take such steps as may be specified in the regulations where the previous accounts or report have been—

(i)   sent out to members and others under section 238(1),

(ii)   laid before the company in general meeting, or

(iii)   delivered to the registrar,

or where a summary financial statement based on the previous accounts or report has been sent to members under section 251;

(d)   apply the provisions of this Act (including those creating criminal offences) subject to such additions, exceptions and modifications as are specified in the regulations.

(5)   Regulations under this section shall be made by statutory instrument which shall be subject to annulment in pursuance of a resolution of either House of Parliament.

245A.   Secretary of State's notice in respect of annual accounts.

(1)   Where copies of a company's annual accounts have been sent out under section 238, or a copy of a company's annual accounts has been laid before the company in general meeting or delivered to the registrar, and it appears to the Secretary of State that there is, or may be, a question whether the accounts comply with the requirements of this Act, he may give notice to the directors of the company indicating the respects in which it appears to him that such a question arises, or may arise.

(2)   The notice shall specify a period of not less than one month for the directors to give him an explanation of the accounts or prepare revised accounts.

(3)   If at the end of the specified period, or such longer period as he may allow, it appears to the Secretary of State that no satisfactory explanation of the accounts has been given and that the accounts have not been revised so as to comply with the requirements of this Act, he may if he thinks fit apply to the court.

(4)   The provisions of this section apply equally to revised annual accounts, in which case the references to revised accounts shall be read as references to further revised accounts.

245B. Application to court in respect of defective accounts.

(1) An application may be made to the court—

  (a) by the Secretary of State, after having complied with section 245A, or

  (b) by a person authorised by the Secretary of State for the purposes of this section,

for a declaration or declarator that the annual accounts of a company do not comply with the requirements of this Act and for an order requiring the directors of the company to prepare revised accounts.

(2) Notice of the application, together with a general statement of the matters at issue in the proceedings, shall be given by the applicant to the registrar for registration.

(3) If the court orders the preparation of revised accounts, it may give directions with respect to—

  (a) the auditing of the accounts,

  (b) the revision of any directors' report or summary financial statement, and

  (c) the taking of steps by the directors to bring the making of the order to the notice of persons likely to rely on the previous accounts,

and such other matters as the court thinks fit.

(4) If the court finds that the accounts did not comply with the requirements of this Act it may order that all or part of—

  (a) the costs (or in Scotland expenses) of and incidental to the application, and

  (b) any reasonable expenses incurred by the company in connection with or in consequence of the preparation of revised accounts,

shall be borne by such of the directors as were party to the approval of the defective accounts.

For this purpose every director of the company at the time the accounts were approved shall be taken to have been a party to their approval unless he shows that he took all reasonable steps to prevent their being approved.

(5) Where the court makes an order under subsection (4) it shall have regard to whether the directors party to the approval of the defective accounts knew or ought to have known that the accounts did not comply with the requirements of this Act, and it may exclude one or more directors from the order or order the payment of different amounts by different directors.

(6) On the conclusion of proceedings on an application under this section, the applicant shall give to the registrar for registration an office copy of the court order or, as the case may be, notice that the application has failed or been withdrawn.

(7) The provisions of this section apply equally to revised annual accounts, in which case the references to revised accounts shall be read as references to further revised accounts.

245C. Other persons authorised to apply to court.

(1) The Secretary of State may authorise for the purposes of section 245B any person appearing to him—

  (a) to have an interest in, and to have satisfactory procedures directed to securing, compliance by companies with the accounting requirements of this Act.

  (b) to have satisfactory procedures for receiving and investigating complaints about the annual accounts of companies, and

  (c) otherwise to be a fit and proper person to be authorised.

(2) A person may be authorised generally or in respect of particular classes of case, and different persons may be authorised in respect of different classes of case.

(3) The Secretary of State may refuse to authorise a person if he considers that his authorisation is unnecessary having regard to the fact that there are one or more other persons who have been or are likely to be authorised.

(4) Authorisation shall be by order made by statutory instrument which shall be subject to annulment in pursuance of a resolution of either House of Parliament.

(5)   Where authorisation is revoked, the revoking order may make such provision as the Secretary of State thinks fit with respect to pending proceedings.

(6)   Neither a person authorised under this section, nor any officer, servant or member of the governing body of such a person, shall be liable in damages for anything done or purporting to be done for the purposes of or in connection with—

(a)   the taking of steps to discover whether there are grounds for an application to the court,

(b)   the determination whether or not to make such an application, or

(c)   the publication of its reasons for any such decision,

unless the act or omission is shown to have been in bad faith.

CHAPTER II
EXEMPTIONS, EXCEPTIONS AND SPECIAL PROVISIONS

Small and medium-sized companies and groups

246.   Special provisions for small companies.

(1)   Subject to section 247A, this section applies where a company qualifies as a small company in relation to a financial year.

(2)   If the company's individual accounts for the year—

(a)   comply with the provisions of Schedule 8, or

(b)   fail to comply with those provisions only in so far as they comply instead with one more corresponding provisions of Schedule 4,

they need not comply with the provisions or, as the case may be, the remaining provisions of Schedule 4; and where advantage is taken of this subsection, references in section 226 to compliance with the provisions of Schedule 4 shall be construed accordingly.

(3)   The company's individual accounts for the year—

(a)   may give the total of the aggregates required by paragraphs (a), (c) and (d) of paragraph 1(1) of Schedule 6 (emoluments and other benefits etc. of directors) instead of giving those aggregates individually; and

(b)   need not give the information required by—

(i)   paragraph 4 of Schedule 5 (financial years of subsidiary undertakings);

(ii)   paragraph 1(2)(b) of Schedule 6 (numbers of directors exercising share options and receiving shares under long term incentive schemes);

(iii)   paragraph 2 of Schedule 6 (details of highest paid director's emoluments etc.); or

(iv)   paragraph 7 of Schedule 6 (excess retirement benefits of directors and past directors).

(4)   The directors' report for the year need not give the information required by—

(a)   section 234(1)(a) and (b) (fair review of business and amount to be paid as dividend);

(b)   paragraph 1(2) of Schedule 7 (statement of market value of fixed assets where substantially different from balance sheet amount);

(c)   paragraph 6 of Schedule 7 (miscellaneous disclosures); or

(d)   paragraph 11 of Schedule 7 (employee involvement).

(5)   Notwithstanding anything in section 242(1), the directors of the company need not deliver to the registrar any of the following, namely—

(a)   a copy of the company's profit and loss account for the year;

(b)   a copy of the directors' report for the year; and

(c)   if they deliver a copy of a balance sheet drawn up as at the last day of the year which complies with the requirements of Schedule 8A, a copy of the company's balance sheet drawn up as at that day.

(6)   Neither a copy of the company's accounts for the year delivered to the registrar under section 242(1), nor a copy of a balance sheet delivered to the registrar under subsection (5)(c), need give the information required by—

(a)   paragraph 4 of Schedule 5 (financial years of subsidiary undertakings);

(b)   paragraph 6 of Schedule 5 (shares of company held by subsidiary undertakings);

(c)   Part I of Schedule 6 (directors' and chairman's emoluments, pensions and compensation for loss of office); or

(d)   section 390A(3) (amount of auditors' remuneration).

(7)   The provisions of section 233 as to the signing of the copy of the balance sheet delivered to the registrar apply to a copy of a balance sheet delivered under subsection (5)(c).

(8)   Subject to subsection (9), each of the following, namely—

(a)   accounts prepared in accordance with subsection (2) or (3),

(b)   a report prepared in accordance with subsection (4), and

(c)   a copy of accounts delivered to the registrar in accordance with subsection (5) or (6),

shall contain a statement in a prominent position on the balance sheet, in the report or, as the case may be, on the copy of the balance sheet, above the signature required by section 233, 234A or subsection (7), that they are prepared in accordance with the special provisions of this Part relating to small companies.

(9)   Subsection (8) does not apply where the company is exempt by virtue of section 250 (dormant companies) from the obligation to appoint auditors.

246A.   Special provisions for medium-sized companies.

(1)   Subject to section 247A, this section applies where a company qualifies as a medium-sized company in relation to a financial year.

(2)   The company's individual accounts for the year need not comply with the requirements of paragraph 36A of Schedule 4 (disclosure with respect to compliance with accounting standards).

(3)   The company may deliver to the registrar a copy of the company's accounts for the year—

(a)   which includes a profit and loss account in which the following items listed in the profit and loss account formats set out in Part I of Schedule 4 are combined as one item under the heading 'gross profit or loss'—

Items 1, 2, 3 and 6 in Format 1;

Items 1 to 5 in Format 2;

Items A.1, B.1 and B.2 in Format 3;

Items A.1, A.2 and B.1 to B.4 in Format 4;

(b)   which does not contain the information required by paragraph 55 of Schedule 4 (particulars of turnover).

(4)   A copy of accounts delivered to the registrar in accordance with subsection (3) shall contain a statement in a prominent position on the copy of the balance sheet, above the signature required by section 233, that the accounts are prepared in accordance with the special provisions of this Part relating to medium-sized companies.

247.   Qualification of company as small or medium-sized.

(1)   A company qualifies as small or medium-sized in relation to a financial year if the qualifying conditions are met—

(a)   in the case of the company's first financial year, in that year, and

(b)   in the case of any subsequent financial year, in that year and the preceding year.

(2)   A company shall be treated as qualifying as small or medium-sized in relation to a financial year—

(a)   if it so qualified in relation to the previous financial year under subsection (1) above or was treated as so qualifying under paragraph (b) below; or

(b)   if it was treated as so qualifying in relation to the previous year by virtue of paragraph (a) and the qualifying conditions are met in the year in question.

(3)   The qualifying conditions are met by a company in a year in which it satisfies two or more of the following requirements—

Small company

1.	Turnover	Not more than £2.8 million
2.	Balance sheet total	Not more than £1.4 million
3.	Number of employees	Not more than 50

Medium-sized company

1.	Turnover	Not more than £11.2 million
2.	Balance sheet total	Not more than £5.6 million
3.	Number of employees	Not more than 250.

(4)   For a period which is a company's financial year but not in fact a year the maximum figures for turnover shall be proportionately adjusted.

(5)   The balance sheet total means—

(a)   where in the company's accounts Format 1 of the balance sheet formats set out in Part I of Schedule 4 or Part I of Schedule 8 is adopted, the aggregate of the amounts shown in the balance sheet under the headings corresponding to items A to D in that Format, and

(b)   where Format 2 is adopted, the aggregate of the amounts shown under the general heading 'Assets'.

(6)   The number of employees means the average number of persons employed by the company in the year (determined on a monthly basis).

That number shall be determined by applying the method of calculation prescribed by paragraph 56(2) and (3) of Schedule 4 for determining the corresponding number required to be stated in a note to the company's accounts.

247A.   Cases in which special provisions do not apply.

(1)   Nothing in section 246 or 246A shall apply where—

(a)   the company is, or was at any time within the financial year to which the accounts relate—

(i)   a public company,

(ii)   a banking or insurance company, or

(iii)   an authorised person under the Financial Services Act 1986; or

(b)   the company is, or was at any time during that year, a member of an ineligible group.

(2)   A group is ineligible if any of its members is—

(a)   a public company or a body corporate which (not being a company) has power under its constitution to offer its shares or debentures to the public and may lawfully exercise that power,

(b)   an authorised institution under the Banking Act 1987,

(c)   an insurance company to which Part II of the Insurance Companies Act 1982 applies, or

(d)   an authorised person under the Financial Services Act 1986.

(3)   A parent company shall not be treated as qualifying as a small company in relation to a financial year unless the group headed by it qualifies as a small group, and shall not be treated as qualifying as a medium-sized company in relation to a financial year unless that group qualifies as a medium-sized group (see section 249).

247B. Special auditors' report.

(1) This section applies where—

(a) the directors of a company propose to deliver to the registrar copies of accounts ('abbreviated accounts') prepared in accordance with section 246(5) or (6) or 246A(3) ('the relevant provision'),

(b) the directors have not taken advantage of the exemption from audit conferred by section 249A(1) or (2), and

(c) the company is not exempt by virtue of section 250 from the obligation to appoint auditors.

(2) If abbreviated accounts prepared in accordance with the relevant provision are delivered to the registrar, they shall be accompanied by a copy of a special report of the auditors stating that in their opinion—

(a) the company is entitled to deliver abbreviated accounts prepared in accordance with that provision, and

(b) the abbreviated accounts to be delivered are properly prepared in accordance with that provision.

(3) In such a case a copy of the auditors' report under section 235 need not be delivered, but—

(a) if that report was qualified, the special report shall set out that report in full together with any further material necessary to understand the qualification; and

(b) if that report contained a statement under—

(i) section 237(2) (accounts, records or returns inadequate or accounts not agreeing with records and returns), or

(ii) section 237(3) (failure to obtain necessary information and explanations), the special report shall set out that statement in full.

(4) Section 236 (signature of auditors' report) applies to a special report under this section as it applies to a report under section 235.

(5) If abbreviated accounts prepared in accordance with the relevant provision are delivered to the registrar, references in section 240 (requirements in connection with publication of accounts) to the auditors' report under section 235 shall be read as references to the special auditors' report under this section.

248. Exemption for small and medium-sized groups.

(1) A parent company need not prepare group accounts for a financial year in relation to which the group headed by that company qualifies as a small or medium-sized group and is not an ineligible group.

(2) A group is ineligible if any of its members is—

(a) a public company or a body corporate which (not being a company) has power under its constitution to offer its shares or debentures to the public and may lawfully exercise that power,

(b) an authorised institution under the Banking Act 1987,

(c) an insurance company to which Part II of the Insurance Companies Act 1982 applies, or

(d) an authorised person under the Financial Services Act 1986.

248A. Group accounts prepared by small company.

(1) This section applies where a small company—

(a) has prepared individual accounts for a financial year in accordance with section 246(2) or (3), and

(b) is preparing group accounts in respect of the same year.

(2) If the group accounts—

(a) comply with the provisions of Schedule 8, or

(b) fail to comply with those provisions only in so far as they comply instead with one or more corresponding provisions of Schedule 4, they need not comply with the provisions or, as the case may be, the remaining provisions of Schedule 4; and where advantage is taken of this subsection, references in Schedule 4A to compliance with the provisions of Schedule 4 shall be construed accordingly.

(3) For the purposes of this section, Schedule 8 shall have effect as if, in each balance sheet format set out in that Schedule, for item B.III there were substituted the following item—

'B.III   Investments
   1.   Shares in group undertakings
   2.   Interests in associated undertakings
   3.   Other participating interests
   4.   Loans to group undertakings and undertakings in which a participating interest is held
   5.   Other investments other than loans
   6.   Others.'

(4) The group accounts need not give the information required by the provisions specified in section 246(3).

(5) Group accounts prepared in accordance with this section shall contain a statement in a prominent position on the balance sheet, above the signature required by section 233, that they are prepared in accordance with the special provisions of this Part relating to small companies.

249.   Qualification of group as small or medium-sized.

(1) A group qualifies as small or medium-sized in relation to a financial year if the qualifying conditions are met—

   (a)   in the case of the parent company's first financial year, in that year, and

   (b)   in the case of any subsequent financial year, in that year and the preceding year.

(2) A group shall be treated as qualifying as small or medium-sized in relation to a financial year—

   (a)   if it so qualified in relation to the previous financial year under subsection (1) above or was treated as so qualifying under paragraph (b) below; or

   (b)   if it was treated as so qualifying in relation to the previous year by virtue of paragraph (a) and the qualifying conditions are met in the year in question.

(3) The qualifying conditions are met by a group in a year in which it satisfies two or more of the following requirements—

Small group

1.	Aggregate turnover	Not more than £2.8 million net (or £3.36 million gross)
2.	Aggregate balance sheet total	Not more than £1.4 million net (or £1.68 million gross)
3.	Aggregate number of employees	Not more than 50

Medium-sized group

1.	Aggregate turnover	Not more than £11.2 million net (or £13.44 million gross)
2.	Aggregate balance sheet total	Not more than £5.6 million net (or £6.72 million gross)
3.	Aggregate number of employees	Not more than 250.

(4) The aggregate figures shall be ascertained by aggregating the relevant figures determined in accordance with section 247 for each member of the group.

In relation to the aggregate figures for turnover and balance sheet total, 'net' means with the set-offs and other adjustments required by Schedule 4A in the case of group accounts and 'gross' means without those set-offs and other adjustments; and a company may satisfy the relevant requirement on the basis of either the net or the gross figure.

(5)   The figures for each subsidiary undertaking shall be those included in its accounts for the relevant financial year, that is—

(a)   if its financial year ends with that of the parent company, that financial year, and

(b)   if not, its financial year ending last before the end of the financial year of the parent company.

(6)   If those figures cannot be obtained without disproportionate expense or undue delay, the latest available figures shall be taken.

Exemptions from audit for certain categories of small company

249A.   Exemptions from audit.

(1)   Subject to section 249B, a company which meets the total exemption conditions set out below in respect of a financial year is exempt from the provisions of this Part relating to the audit of accounts in respect of that year.

(2)   Subject to section 249B, a company which is a charity and which meets the report conditions set out below in respect of a financial year is exempt from the provisions of this Part relating to the audit of accounts in respect of that year if the directors cause a report in respect of the company's individual accounts for that year to be prepared in accordance with section 249C and made to the company's members.

(3)   The total exemption conditions are met by a company in respect of a financial year if—

(a)   it qualifies as a small company in relation to that year for the purposes of section 246,

(b)   its turnover in that year is not more than £350,000, and

(c)   its balance sheet total for that year is not more than £1.4 million.

(3A)   In relation to any company which is a charity, subsection (3)(b) shall have effect with the substitution—

(a)   for the reference to turnover of a reference to gross income, and

(b)   for the reference to £350,000 of a reference to £90,000.

(4)   The report conditions are met by a company which is a charity in respect of a financial year if—

(a)   it qualifies as a small company in relation to that year for the purposes of section 246,

(b)   its gross income in that year is more than £90,000 but not more than £250,000, and

(c)   its balance sheet total for that year is not more than £1.4 million.

(6)   For a period which is a company's financial year but not in fact a year the maximum figures for turnover or gross income shall be proportionately adjusted.

(6A)   A company is entitled to the exemption conferred by subsection (1) or (2) notwithstanding that it falls within paragraph (a) or (b) of section 250(1).

(7)   In this section—

'balance sheet total' has the meaning given by section 247(5), and

'gross income' means the company's income from all sources, as shown in the company's income and expenditure account.

249B.   Cases where exemptions not available.

(1)   Subject to subsections (1A) to (1C), a company is not entitled to the exemption conferred by subsection (1) or (2) of section 249A in respect of a financial year if at any time within that year—

(a) it was a public company,

(b) it was a banking or insurance company,

(c) it was enrolled in the list maintained by the Insurance Brokers Registration Council under section 4 of the Insurance Brokers (Registration) Act 1977,

(d) it was an authorised person or an appointed representative under the Financial Services Act 1986,

(e) it was a special register body as defined in section 117(1) of the Trade Union and Labour Relations (Consolidation) Act 1992 or an employers' association as defined in section 122 of that Act, or

(f) it was a parent company or a subsidiary undertaking.

(1A) A company which, apart from this subsection, would fall within subsection (1)(f) by virtue of its being a subsidiary undertaking for any period within a financial year shall not be treated as so falling if it is dormant (within the meaning of section 250) throughout that period.

(1B) A company which, apart from this subsection, would fall within subsection (1)(f) by virtue of its being a parent company or a subsidiary undertaking for any period within a financial year, shall not be treated as so falling if throughout that period it was a member of a group meeting the conditions set out in subsection (1C).

(1C) The conditions referred to in subsection (1B) are—

(a) that the group qualifies as a small group, in relation to the financial year within which the period falls, for the purposes of section 249 and is not, and was not at any time within that year, an ineligible group within the meaning of section 248(2),

(b) that the group's aggregate turnover in that year (calculated in accordance with section 249) is not more than £350,000 net (or £420,000 gross), and

(c) that the group's aggregate balance sheet total for that year (calculated in accordance with section 249) is not more than £1.4 million net (or £1.68 million gross).

(2) Any member or members holding not less in the aggregate than 10 per cent in nominal value of the company's issued share capital or any class of it or, if the company does not have a share capital, not less than 10 per cent in number of the members of the company, may, by notice in writing deposited at the registered office of the company during a financial year but not later than one month before the end of that year, require the company to obtain an audit of its accounts for that year.

(3) Where a notice has been deposited under subsection (2), the company is not entitled to the exemption conferred by subsection (1) or (2) of section 249A in respect of the financial year to which the notice relates.

(4) A company is not entitled to the exemption conferred by subsection (1) or (2) of section 249A unless its balance sheet contains a statement by the directors—

(a) to the effect that for the year in question the company was entitled to exemption under subsection (1) or (2) (as the case may be) of section 249A,

(b) to the effect that no notice has been deposited under subsection (2) of this section in relation to its accounts for the financial year, and

(c) to the effect that the directors acknowledge their responsibilities for—

(i) ensuring that the company keeps accounting records which comply with section 221, and

(ii) preparing accounts which give a true and fair view of the state of affairs of the company as at the end of the financial year and of its profit or loss for the financial year in accordance with the requirements of section 226, and which otherwise comply with the requirements of this Act relating to accounts, so far as applicable to the company.

(5) The statement required by subsection (4) shall appear in the balance sheet above the signature required by section 233.

249E. Effect of exemptions.

(1) Where the directors of a company have taken advantage of the exemption conferred by section 249A(1)—

(a)   sections 238 and 239 (right to receive or demand copies of accounts and reports) shall have effect with the omission of references to the auditors' report;

(b)   no copy of an auditors' report need be delivered to the registrar or laid before the company in general meeting;

(c)   subsections (3) to (5) of section 271 (accounts by reference to which distribution to be justified) shall not apply.

. . .

Dormant companies

250. Resolution not to appoint auditors.

(1)   A company may by special resolution make itself exempt from the provisions of this Part relating to the audit of accounts in the following cases—

(a)   if the company has been dormant from the time of its formation;

(b)   if the company has been dormant since the end of the previous financial year and—

(i)   is entitled in respect of its individual accounts for that year to prepare accounts in accordance with section 246(2), or would be so entitled but for the application of subsection (1)(a)(i) or (b) of section 247A, and

(ii)   is not required to prepare group accounts for that year,

by a special resolution passed at a general meeting of the company at any time after copies of the annual accounts for that year have been sent out in accordance with section 238(1).

(2)   A company may not pass such a resolution if it is—

(b)   a banking or insurance company, or

(c)   an authorised person under the Financial Services Act 1986.

(3)   A company is 'dormant' during a period in which no significant accounting transaction occurs, that is, no transaction which is required by section 221 to be entered in the company's accounting records; and a company ceases to be dormant on the occurrence of such a transaction.

For this purpose there shall be disregarded any transaction arising from the taking of shares in the company by a subscriber to the memorandum in pursuance of an undertaking of his in the memorandum.

(4)   Where a company is, at the end of a financial year, exempt by virtue of this section from the provisions of this Part relating to the audit of accounts—

(a)   sections 238 and 239 (right to receive or demand copies of accounts and reports) have effect with the omission of references to the auditors' report;

(b)   no copies of an auditors' report need be laid before the company in general meeting;

(c)   no copy of an auditors' report need be delivered to the registrar, and if none is delivered, the copy of the balance sheet so delivered shall contain a statement by the directors, in a position above the signature required by section 233(4), to the effect that the company was dormant throughout the financial year; and

(d)   the company shall be treated as a company entitled to prepare accounts in accordance with section 246(2) notwithstanding that it is a member of an ineligible group.

(5)   Where a compay which is exempt by virtue of this section from the provisions of this Part relating to the audit of accounts—

(a)   ceases to be dormant, or

(b)   would no longer qualify (for any other reason) to make itself exempt by passing a resolution under this section,
it shall thereupon cease to be so exempt.

Listed public companies

251.   Provision of summary financial statement to shareholders.

(1)   A public company whose shares or debentures, or any class of whose shares or debentures, are listed need not, in such cases as may be specified by regulations made by the Secretary of State, and provided any conditions so specified are complied with, send copies of the documents referred to in section 238(1) to entitled persons, but may instead send them a summary financial statement.

In this section—

'entitled persons', in relation to a company, means such of the persons specified in paragraphs (a) to (c) of subsection (1) of section 238 as are or would apart from this section be entitled to be sent copies of those documents relating to the company which are referred to in that subsection; and

'listed' means admitted to the Official List of The International Stock Exchange of the United Kingdom and the Republic of Ireland Limited.

(2)   Copies of the documents referred to in section 238(1) shall, however, be sent to any entitled person who wishes to receive them; and the Secretary of State may by regulations make provision as to the manner in which it is to be ascertained (whether before or after he becomes an entitled person) whether an entitled person wishes to receive them.

(3)   The summary financial statement shall be derived from the company's annual accounts and the directors' report and shall be in such form and contain such information as may be specified by regulations made by the Secretary of State.

(4)   Every summary financial statement shall—

(a)   state that it is only a summary of information in the company's annual accounts and the directors' report;

(b)   contain a statement by the company's auditors of their opinion as to whether the summary financial statement is consistent with those accounts and that report and complies with the requirements of this section and regulations made under it;

(c)   state whether the auditors' report on the annual accounts was unqualified or qualified, and if it was qualified set out the report in full together with any further material needed to understand the qualification;

(d)   state whether the auditors' report on the annual accounts contained a statement under—

(i)   section 237(2) (accounting records or returns inadequate or accounts not agreeing with records and returns), or

(ii)   section 237(3) (failure to obtain necessary information and explanations), and if so, set out the statement in full.

(5)   Regulations under this section shall be made by statutory instrument which shall be subject to annulment in pursuance of a resolution of either House of Parliament.

(6)   If default is made in complying with this section or regulations made under it, the company and every officer of it who is in default is guilty of an offence and liable to a fine.

(7)   Section 240 (requirements in connection with publication of accounts) does not apply in relation to the provision to entitled persons of a summary financial statement in accordance with this section.

Private companies

252. Election to dispense with laying of accounts and reports before general meeting.

(1) A private company may elect (by elective resolution in accordance with section 379A) to dispense with the laying of accounts and reports before the company in general meeting.

(2) An election has effect in relation to the accounts and reports in respect of the financial year in which the election is made and subsequent financial years.

(3) Whilst an election is in force, the references in the following provisions of this Act to the laying of accounts before the company in general meeting shall be read as references to the sending of copies of the accounts to members and others under section 238(1)—

(a) section 235(1) (accounts on which auditors are to report),

(b) section 270(3) and (4) (accounts by reference to which distributions are justified), and

(c) section 320(2) (accounts relevant for determining company's net assets for purposes of ascertaining whether approval required for certain transactions);

and the requirement in section 271(4) that the auditors' statement under that provision be laid before the company in general meeting shall be read as a requirement that it be sent to members and others along with the copies of the accounts sent to them under section 238(1).

(4) If an election under this section ceases to have effect, section 241 applies in relation to the accounts and reports in respect of the financial year in which the election ceases to have effect and subsequent financial years.

253. Right of shareholder to require laying of accounts.

(1) Where an election under section 252 is in force, the copies of the accounts and reports sent out in accordance with section 238(1)—

(a) shall be sent not less than 28 days before the end of the period allowed for laying and delivering accounts and reports, and

(b) shall be accompanied, in the case of a member of the company, by a notice informing him of his right to require the laying of the accounts and reports before a general meeting;

and section 238(5) (penalty for default) applies in relation to the above requirements as to the requirements contained in that section.

(2) Before the end of the period of 28 days beginning with the day on which the accounts and reports are sent out in accordance with section 238(1), any member or auditor of the company may by notice in writing deposited at the registered office of the company require that a general meeting be held for the purpose of laying the accounts and reports before the company.

(3) If the directors do not within 21 days from the date of the deposit of such a notice proceed duly to convene a meeting, the person who deposited the notice may do so himself.

(4) A meeting so convened shall not be held more than three months from that date and shall be convened in the same manner, as nearly as possible, as that in which meetings are to be convened by directors.

(5) Where the directors do not duly convene a meeting, any reasonable expenses incurred by reason of that failure by the person who deposited the notice shall be made good to him by the company, and shall be recouped by the company out of any fees, or other remuneration in respect of their services, due or to become due to such of the directors as were in default.

(6) The directors shall be deemed not to have duly convened a meeting if they convene a meeting for a date more than 28 days after the date of the notice convening it.

Unlimited companies

254. Exemption from requirement to deliver accounts and reports.

(1)   The directors of an unlimited company are not required to deliver accounts and reports to the registrar in respect of a financial year if the following conditions are met.

(2)   The conditions are that at no time during the relevant accounting reference period—

(a)   has the company been, to its knowledge, a subsidiary undertaking of an undertaking which was then limited, or

(b)   have there been, to its knowledge, exercisable by or on behalf of two or more undertakings which were then limited, rights which if exercisable by one of them would have made the company a subsidiary undertaking of it, or

(c)   has the company been a parent company of an undertaking which was then limited.

The references above to an undertaking being limited at a particular time are to an undertaking (under whatever law established) the liability of whose members is at that time limited.

(3)   The exemption conferred by this section does not apply if—

(a)   the company is a banking or insurance company or the parent company of a banking or insurance group, or

(b)   the company is a qualifying company within the meaning of the Partnerships and Unlimited Companies (Accounts) Regulations 1993, or

(c)   at any time during the relevant accounting period the company carried on business as the promoter of a trading stamp scheme within the Trading Stamps Act 1964.

(4)   Where a company is exempt by virtue of this section from the obligation to deliver accounts, section 240 (requirements in connection with publication of accounts) has effect with the following modifications—

(a)   in subsection (3)(b) for the words from 'whether statutory accounts' to 'have been delivered to the registrar' substitute 'that the company is exempt from the requirement to deliver statutory accounts', and

(b)   in subsection (5) for 'as required to be delivered to the registrar under section 242' substitute 'as prepared in accordance with this Part and approved by the board of directors'.

CHAPTER III
SUPPLEMENTARY PROVISIONS

Accounting standards

256. Accounting standards.

(1)   In this Part 'accounting standards' means statements of standard accounting practice issued by such body or bodies as may be prescribed by regulations.

(2)   References in this Part to accounting standards applicable to a company's annual accounts are to such standards as are, in accordance with their terms, relevant to the company's circumstances and to the accounts.

(3)   The Secretary of State may make grants to or for the purposes of bodies concerned with—

(a)   issuing accounting standards,

(b)   overseeing and directing the issuing of such standards, or

(c)   investigating departures from such standards or from the accounting requirements of this Act and taking steps to secure compliance with them.

(4)   Regulations under this section may contain such transitional and other supplementary and incidental provisions as appear to the Secretary of State to be appropriate.

Power to alter accounting requirements

257. Power of Secretary of State to alter accounting requirements.

(1)   The Secretary of State may by regulations made by statutory instrument modify the provisions of this Part.

(2)   Regulations which—

(a)   add to the classes of documents required to be prepared, laid before the company in general meeting or delivered to the registrar,

(b)   restrict the classes of company which have the benefit of any exemption, exception or special provision,

(c)   require additional matter to be included in a document of any class, or

(d)   otherwise render the requirements of this Part more onerous,

shall not be made unless a draft of the instrument containing the regulations has been laid before Parliament and approved by a resolution of each House.

(3)   Otherwise, a statutory instrument containing regulations under this section shall be subject to annulment in pursuance of a resolution of either House of Parliament.

(4)   Regulations under this section may—

(a)   make different provision for different cases or classes of case,

(b)   repeal and re-enact provisions with modifications of form or arrangement, whether or not they are modified in substance,

(c)   make consequential amendments or repeals in other provisions of this Act, or in other enactments, and

(d)   contain such transitional and other incidental and supplementary provisions as the Secretary of State thinks fit.

(5)   Any modification by regulations under this section of section 258 or Schedule 10A (parent and subsidiary undertakings) does not apply for the purposes of enactments outside the Companies Acts unless the regulations so provide.

Parent and subsidiary undertakings

258. Parent and subsidiary undertakings.

(1)   The expressions 'parent undertaking' and 'subsidiary undertaking' in this Part shall be construed as follows; and a 'parent company' means a parent undertaking which is a company.

(2)   An undertaking is a parent undertaking in relation to another undertaking, a subsidiary undertaking, if—

(a)   it holds a majority of the voting rights in the undertaking, or

(b)   it is a member of the undertaking and has the right to appoint or remove a majority of its board of directors, or

(c)   it has the right to exercise a dominant influence over the undertaking—

(i)   by virtue of provisions contained in the undertaking's memorandum or articles, or

(ii)   by virtue of a control contract, or

(d)   it is a member of the undertaking and controls alone, pursuant to an agreement with other shareholders or members, a majority of the voting rights in the undertaking.

(3)   For the purposes of subsection (2) an undertaking shall be treated as a member of another undertaking—

(a)   if any of its subsidiary undertakings is a member of that undertaking, or

(b)   if any shares in that other undertaking are held by a person acting on behalf of the undertaking or any of its subsidiary undertakings.

(4)   An undertaking is also a parent undertaking in relation to another undertaking, a subsidiary undertaking, if it has a participating interest in the undertaking and—

(a)   it actually exercises a dominant influence over it, or

(b)   it and the subsidiary undertaking are managed on a unified basis.

(5)   A parent undertaking shall be treated as the parent undertaking of undertakings in relation to which any of its subsidiary undertakings are, or are to be treated as, parent undertakings; and references to its subsidiary undertakings shall be construed accordingly.

(6)   Schedule 10A contains provisions explaining expressions used in this section and otherwise supplementing this section.

Other interpretation provisions

259.   Meaning of 'undertaking' and related expressions.

(1)   In this Part 'undertaking' means—

(a)   a body corporate or partnership, or

(b)   an unincorporated association carrying on a trade or business, with or without a view to profit.

(2)   In this part references to shares—

(a)   in relation to an undertaking with a share capital, are to allotted shares;

(b)   in relation to an undertaking with capital but no share capital, are to rights to share in the capital of the undertaking; and

(c)   in relation to an undertaking without capital, are to interests—

(i)   conferring any right to share in the profits or liability or contribute to the losses of the undertaking, or

(ii)   giving rise to an obligation to contribute to the debts or expenses of the undertaking in the event of a winding up.

(3)   Other expressions appropriate to companies shall be construed, in relation to an undertaking which is not a company, as references to the corresponding persons, officers, documents or organs, as the case may be, appropriate to undertakings of that description.

This is subject to provision in any specific context providing for the translation of such expressions.

(4)   References in this part to 'fellow subsidiary undertakings' are to undertakings which are subsidiary undertakings of the same parent undertaking but are not parent undertakings or subsidiary undertakings of each other.

(5)   In this Part 'group undertaking', in relation to an undertaking, means an undertaking which is—

(a)   a parent undertaking or subsidiary undertaking of that undertaking, or

(b)   a subsidiary undertaking of any parent undertaking of that undertaking.

260.   Participating interests.

(1)   In this Part a 'participating interest' means an interest held by an undertaking in the shares of another undertaking which it holds on a long-term basis for the purpose of securing a contribution to its activities by the exercise of control or influence arising from or related to that interest.

(2)   A holding of 20 per cent or more of the shares of an undertaking shall be presumed to be a participating interest unless the contrary is shown.

(3)   The reference in subsection (1) to an interest in shares includes—

(a)   an interest which is convertible into an interest in shares, and

(b)   an option to acquire shares or any such interest;

and an interest or option falls within paragraph (a) or (b) notwithstanding that the shares to which it relates are, until the conversion or the exercise of the option, unissued.

(4)   For the purposes of this section an interest held on behalf of an undertaking shall be treated as held by it.

(5)   For the purposes of this section as it applies in relation to the expression 'participating interest' in section 258(4) (definition of 'subsidiary undertaking')—

(a)   there shall be attributed to an undertaking any interests held by any of its subsidiary undertakings, and

(b)   the references in subsection (1) to the purpose and activities of an undertaking include the purposes and activities of any of its subsidiary undertakings and of the group as a whole.

(6)   In the balance sheet and profit and loss formats set out in Part I of Schedule 4, Part I of Schedule 8, Schedule 8A, Chapter I of Part I of Schedule 9 and Chapter I of Part I of Schedule 9A, 'participating interest' does not include an interest in a group undertaking.

(7)   For the purposes of this section as it applies in relation to the expression 'participating interest'—

(a)   in those formats as they apply in relation to group accounts, and

(b)   in paragraph 20 of Schedule 4A (group accounts: undertakings to be accounted for as associated undertakings),

the references in subsections (1) to (4) to the interest held by, and the purposes and activities of, the undertaking concerned shall be construed as references to the interest held by, and the purposes and activities of, the group (within the meaning of paragraph 1 of that Schedule).

261.   Notes to the accounts.

(1)   Information required by this Part to be given in notes to a company's annual accounts may be contained in the accounts or in a separate document annexed to the accounts.

(2)   References in this Part to a company's annual accounts, or to a balance sheet or profit and loss account, include notes to the accounts giving information which is required by any provision of this Act, and required or allowed by any such provision to be given in a note to company accounts.

262.   Minor definitions.

(1)   In this Part—

'annual accounts' means—

(a)   the individual accounts required by section 226, and

(b)   any group accounts required by section 227,

(but see also section 230 (treatment of individual profit and loss account where group accounts prepared));

'annual report', in relation to a company, means the directors' report required by section 234;

'balance sheet date' means the date as at which the balance sheet was made up;

'capitalisation', in relation to work or costs, means treating that work or those costs as a fixed asset;

'credit institution' means a credit institution as defined in article 1 of the First Council Directive on the coordination of laws, regulations and administrative provisions relating to the taking up and pursuit of the business of credit institutions (77/780/EEC), that is to say an undertaking whose business is to receive deposits or other repayable funds from the public and to grant credits for its own account;

'fixed assets' means assets of a company which are intended for use on a continuing basis in the company's activities, and 'current assets' means assets not intended for such use;

'group' means a parent undertaking and its subsidiary undertakings;

'included in the consolidation', in relation to group accounts, or 'included in consolidated group accounts', means that the undertaking is included in the accounts by the method of full (and not proportional) consolidation, and references to an undertaking excluded from consolidation shall be construed accordingly;

'purchase price', in relation to an asset of a company or any raw materials or consumables used in the production of such an asset, includes any consideration (whether in cash or otherwise) given by the company in respect of that asset or those materials or consumables, as the case may be;

'qualified', in relation to an auditors' report, means that the report does not state the auditors' unqualified opinion that the accounts have been properly prepared in accordance with this Act or, in the case of an undertaking not required to prepare accounts in accordance with this Act, under any corresponding legislation under which it is required to prepare accounts;

'true and fair view' refers—

    (a)   in the case of individual accounts, to the requirement of section 226(2), and

    (b)   in the case of group accounts, to the requirement of section 227(3);

'turnover', in relation to a company, means the amounts derived from the provision of goods and services falling within the company's ordinary activities, after deduction of—

    (i)   trade discounts,

    (ii)   value added tax, and

    (iii)   any other taxes based on the amounts so derived.

(2)   In the case of an undertaking not trading for profit, any reference in this Part to a profit and loss account is to an income and expenditure account; and references to profit and loss and, in relation to group accounts, to a consolidated profit and loss account shall be construed accordingly.

(3)   References in this Part to 'realised profits' and 'realised losses', in relation to a company's accounts, are to such profits or losses of the company as fall to be treated as realised in accordance with principles generally accepted, at the time when the accounts are prepared, with respect to the determination for accounting purposes of realised profits or losses.

This is without prejudice to—

    (a)   the construction of any other expression (where appropriate) by reference to accepted accounting principles or practice, or

    (b)   any specific provision for the treatment of profits or losses of any description as realised.

262A. Index of defined expressions.

The following Table shows the provisions of this Part defining or otherwise explaining expressions used in this part (other than expressions used only in the same section or paragraph)—

the 1982 Act (in Schedule 9A)	paragraph 81 of Part I of that Schedule
accounting reference date and accounting reference period	section 224
accounting standards and applicable accounting standards	section 256
annual accounts	
(generally)	section 262(1)
(includes notes to the accounts)	section 261(2)
annual report	section 262(1)
associated undertaking (in Schedule 4A)	paragraph 20 of that Schedule
balance sheet (includes notes)	section 261(2)
balance sheet date	section 262(1)
banking group	section 255A(4)
capitalisation (in relation to work or costs)	section 262(1)
credit institution	section 262(1)

current assets	section 262(1)
fellow subsidiary undertaking	section 259(4)
financial fixed assets (in Schedule 9)	paragraph 82 of Part I of that Schedule
financial year	section 223
fixed assets	section 262(1)
general business (in Schedule 9A)	paragraph 81 of Part I of that Schedule
group	section 262(1)
group undertaking	section 259(5)
historical cost accounting rules	
— in Schedule 4	paragraph 29 of that Schedule
— in Schedule 8	paragraph 29 of that Schedule
— in Schedule 9	paragraph 39 of Part I of that Schedule
— in Schedule 9A	paragraph 20(1) of Part I of that Schedule
included in the consolidation and related expressions	section 262(1)
individual accounts	section 262(1)
insurance group	section 255A(5)
land of freehold tenure and land of leasehold tenure (in relation to Scotland)	
— in Schedule 4	paragraph 93 of that Schedule
— in Schedule 9	paragraph 86 of Part I of that Schedule
— in Schedule 9A	paragraph 85 of Part I of that Schedule
lease, long lease and short lease	
— in Schedule 4	paragraph 83 of that Schedule
— in Schedule 9	paragraph 82 of Part I of that Schedule
— in Schedule 9A	paragraph 81 of Part I of that Schedule
listed investment	
— in Schedule 4	paragraph 84 of that Schedule
— in Schedule 8	paragraph 54 of that Schedule
— in Schedule 9A	paragraph 81 of Part I of that Schedule
listed security (in Schedule 9)	paragraph 82 of Part I of that Schedule
long term business (in Schedule 9A)	paragraph 81 of Part I of that Schedule
long term fund (in Schedule 9A)	paragraph 81 of Part I of that Schedule
notes to the accounts	section 261(1)
parent undertaking (and parent company)	section 258 and Schedule 10A
participating interest	section 260
pension costs	
— in Schedule 4	paragraph 94(2) of that Schedule
— in Schedule 8	paragraph 59(2) of that Schedule

— in Schedule 9	paragraph 87(b) of Part I of that Schedule
— in Schedule 9A	paragraph 86(b) of Part I of that Schedule
period allowed for laying and delivering accounts and reports	section 244
policy holder (in Schedule 9A)	paragraph 81 of Part I of that Schedule
profit and loss account	
(includes notes)	section 261(2)
(in relation to a company not trading for profit)	section 262(2)
provision	
— in Schedule 4	paragraphs 88 and 89 of that Schedule
— in Schedule 8	paragraphs 57 and 58 of that Schedule
— in Schedule 9	paragraph 85 of Part I of that Schedule
— in Schedule 9A	paragraph 84 of Part I of that Schedule
provision for unexpired risks (in Schedule 9A)	paragraph 81 of Part I of that Schedule
purchase price	section 262(1)
qualified	section 262(1)
realised losses and realised profits	section 262(3)
repayable on demand (in Schedule 9)	paragraph 82 of Part I of that Schedule
reporting account	section 249C(1)
reserve (in Schedule 9A)	paragraph 32 of that Schedule *
sale and repurchase transaction (in Schedule 9)	paragraph 82 of Part I of that Schedule
sale and option to resell transaction (in Schedule 9)	paragraph 82 of Part I of that Schedule
shares	section 259(2)
social security costs	
— in Schedule 4	paragraph 94(1) and (3) of that Schedule
— in Schedule 8	paragraph 59(1) and (3) of that Schedule
— in Schedule 9	paragraph 87(a) and (c) of Part I of that Schedule
— in Schedule 9A	paragraph 86(a) and (c) of Part I of that Schedule
special provisions for banking and insurance companies and groups	sections 255 and 255A
subsidiary undertaking	section 258 and Schedule 10A
true and fair view	section 262(1)
turnover	section 262(1)
undertaking and related expressions	section 259(1) to (3)

[*This entry was not changed when a new sch. 9A was substituted by the Companies Act 1985 (Insurance Companies Accounts) Regulations 1993 (SI 1993/3246) and is no longer accurate.]

PART VIII
DISTRIBUTION OF PROFITS AND ASSETS

Limits of company's power of distribution

263. Certain distributions prohibited.

(1) A company shall not make a distribution except out of profits available for the purpose.

(2) In this Part, 'distribution' means every description of distribution of a company's assets to its members, whether in cash or otherwise, except distribution by way of—

(a) an issue of shares as fully or partly paid bonus shares,

(b) the redemption or purchase of any of the company's own shares out of capital (including the proceeds of any fresh issue of shares) or out of unrealised profits in accordance with Chapter VII of Part V,

(c) the reduction of share capital by extinguishing or reducing the liability of any of the members on any of the company's shares in respect of share capital not paid up, or by paying off paid-up share capital, and

(d) a distribution of assets to members of the company on its winding up.

(3) For purposes of this Part, a company's profits available for distribution are its accumulated, realised profits, so far as not previously utilised by distribution or capitalisation, less its accumulated, realised losses, so far as not previously written off in a reduction or reorganisation of capital duly made.

This is subject to the provision made by sections 265 and 266 for investment and other companies.

(4) A company shall not apply an unrealised profit in paying up debentures, or any amounts unpaid on its issued shares.

(5) Where the directors of a company are, after making all reasonable enquiries, unable to determine whether a particular profit made before 22 December 1980 is realised or unrealised, they may treat the profit as realised; and where after making such enquiries they are unable to determine whether a particular loss so made is realised or unrealised, they may treat the loss as unrealised.

264. Restriction on distribution of assets.

(1) A public company may only make a distribution at any time—

(a) if at that time the amount of its net assets is not less than the aggregate of its called-up share capital and undistributable reserves, and

(b) if, and to the extent that, the distribution does not reduce the amount of those assets to less than that aggregate.

This is subject to the provision made by sections 265 and 266 for investment and other companies.

(2) In subsection (1), 'net assets' means the aggregate of the company's assets less the aggregate of its liabilities ('liabilities' to include any provision for liabilities or charges within paragraph 89 of Schedule 4).

(3) A company's undistributable reserves are—

(a) the share premium account,

(b) the capital redemption reserve,

(c) the amount by which the company's accumulated, unrealised profits, so far as not previously utilised by capitalisation of a description to which this paragraph applies, exceed its accumulated, unrealised losses (so far as not previously written off in a reduction or reorganisation of capital duly made), and

(d) any other reserve which the company is prohibited from distributing by any enactment (other than one contained in this Part) or by its memorandum or articles; and paragraph (c) applies to every description of capitalisation except a transfer of profits of the company to its capital redemption reserve on or after 22 December 1980.

(4)   A public company shall not include any uncalled share capital as an asset in any accounts relevant for purposes of this section.

265.   Other distributions by investment companies.

(1)   Subject to the following provisions of this section, an investment company (defined in section 266) may also make a distribution at any time out of its accumulated, realised revenue profits, so far as not previously utilised by distribution or capitalisation, less its accumulated revenue losses (whether realised or unrealised), so far as not previously written off in a reduction or reorganisation of capital duly made—

(a)   if at that time the amount of its assets is at least equal to one and a half times the aggregate of its liabilities, and

(b)   if, and to the extent that, the distribution does not reduce that amount to less than one and a half times that aggregate.

(2)   In subsection (1)(a), 'liabilities' includes any provision for liabilities or charges (within the meaning of paragraph 89 of Schedule 4).

(3)   The company shall not include any uncalled share capital as an asset in any accounts relevant for purposes of this section.

(4)   An investment company may not make a distribution by virtue of subsection (1) unless—

(a)   its shares are listed on a recognised investment exchange other than an overseas investment exchange within the meaning of the Financial Services Act 1986, and

(b)   during the relevant period it has not—
  (i)   distributed any of its capital profits, or
  (ii)   applied any unrealised profits or any capital profits (realised or unrealised) in paying up debentures or amounts unpaid on its issued shares.

(5)   The 'relevant period' under subsection (4) is the period beginning with—

(a)   the first day of the accounting reference period immediately preceding that in which the proposed distribution is to be made, or

(b)   where the distribution is to be made in the company's first accounting reference period, the first day of that period,
and ending with the date of the distribution.

(6)   An investment company may not make a distribution by virtue of subsection (1) unless the company gave to the registrar of companies the requisite notice (that is, notice under section 266(1)) of the company's intention to carry on business as an investment company—

(a)   before the beginning of the relevant period under subsection (4), or

(b)   in the case of a company incorporated on or after 22 December 1980, as soon as may have been reasonably practicable after the date of its incorporation.

266.   Meaning of 'investment company'.

(1)   In section 265 'investment company' means a public company which has given notice in the prescribed form (which has not been revoked) to the registrar of companies of its intention to carry on business as an investment company, and has since the date of that notice complied with the requirements specified below.

(2)   Those requirements are—

(a)   that the business of the company consists of investing its funds mainly in securities, with the aim of spreading investment risk and giving members of the company the benefit of the results of the management of its funds,

(b)   that none of the company's holdings in companies (other than those which are for the time being in investment companies) represents more than 15 per cent by value of the investing company's investments,

(c)   that distribution of the company's capital profits is prohibited by its memorandum or articles of association,

(d) that the company has not retained, otherwise than in compliance with this Part, in respect of any accounting reference period more than 15 per cent of the income it derives from securities.

(3) Notice to the registrar of companies under subsection (1) may be revoked at any time by the company on giving notice in the prescribed form to the registrar that it no longer wishes to be an investment company within the meaning of this section; and, on giving such notice, the company ceases to be such a company.

(4) Subsections (1A) to (3) of section 842 of the Income and Corporation Taxes Act 1988 apply for the purposes of subsection (2)(b) above as for those of subsection (1)(b) of that section.

267. Extension of ss. 265, 266 to other companies.

(1) The Secretary of State may by regulations in a statutory instrument extend the provisions of sections 265 and 266 (with or without modifications) to companies whose principal business consists of investing their funds in securities, land or other assets with the aim of spreading investment risk and giving their members the benefit of the results of the management of the assets.

(2) Regulations under this section—

(a) may make different provision for different classes of companies and may contain such transitional and supplemental provisions as the Secretary of State considers necessary, and

(b) shall not be made unless a draft of the statutory instrument containing them has been laid before Parliament and approved by a resolution of each House.

269. Treatment of development costs.

(1) Subject as follows, where development costs are shown as an asset in a company's accounts, any amount shown in respect of those costs is to be treated—

(a) under section 263, as a realised loss, and

(b) under section 265, as a realised revenue loss.

(2) This does not apply to any part of that amount representing an unrealised profit made on revaluation of those costs; nor does it apply if—

(a) there are special circumstances in the company's case justifying the directors in deciding that the amount there mentioned is not to be treated as required by subsection (1), and

(b) the note to the accounts required by paragraph 20 of Schedule 4 [or] paragraph 20 of Schedule 8 (reasons for showing development costs as an asset) states that the amount is not to be so treated and explains the circumstances relied upon to justify the decision of the directors to that effect.

[*It is clear that the word 'or' has been accidentally omitted from s. 269(2)(b).*]

Relevant accounts

270. Distribution to be justified by reference to company's accounts.

(1) This section and sections 271 to 276 below are for determining the question whether a distribution may be made by a company without contravening sections 263, 264 or 265.

(2) The amount of a distribution which may be made is determined by reference to the following items as stated in the company's accounts—

(a) profits, losses, assets and liabilities,

(b) provisions of any of the kinds mentioned in paragraphs 88 and 89 of Schedule 4 (depreciation, diminution in value of assets, retentions to meet liabilities, etc.), and

(c) share capital and reserves (including undistributable reserves).

(3) Except in a case falling within the next subsection, the company's accounts which are relevant for this purpose are its last annual accounts, that is to say those prepared under Part VII which were laid in respect of the last preceding accounting

reference period in respect of which accounts so prepared were laid; and for this purpose accounts are laid if section 241(1) has been complied with in relation to them.

(4)   In the following two cases—

(a)   where the distribution would be found to contravene the relevant section if reference were made only to the company's last annual accounts, or

(b)   where the distribution is proposed to be declared during the company's first accounting reference period, or before any accounts are laid in respect of that period, the accounts relevant under this section (called 'interim accounts' in the first case, and 'initial accounts' in the second) are those necessary to enable a reasonable judgment to be made as to the amounts of the items mentioned in subsection (2) above.

(5)   The relevant section is treated as contravened in the case of a distribution unless the statutory requirements about the relevant accounts (that is, the requirements of this and the following three sections, as and where applicable) are complied with in relation to that distribution.

271.   Requirements for last annual accounts.

(1)   If the company's last annual accounts constitute the only accounts relevant under section 270, the statutory requirements in respect of them are as follows.

(2)   The accounts must have been properly prepared in accordance with this Act, or have been so prepared subject only to matters which are not material for determining, by reference to items mentioned in section 270(2), whether the distribution would contravene the relevant section; and, without prejudice to the foregoing—

(a)   so much of the accounts as consists of a balance sheet must give a true and fair view of the state of the company's affairs as at the balance sheet date, and

(b)   so much of the accounts as consists of a profit and loss account must give a true and fair view of the company's profit or loss for the period in respect of which the accounts were prepared.

(3)   The auditors must have made their report on the accounts under section 235; and the following subsection applies if the report is a qualified report, that is to say, it is not a report without qualification to the effect that in the auditors' opinion the accounts have been properly prepared in accordance with this Act.

(4)   The auditors must in that case also have stated in writing (either at the time of their report or subsequently) whether, in their opinion, the matter in respect of which their report is qualified is material for determining, by reference to items mentioned in section 270(2), whether the distribution would contravene the relevant section; and a copy of the statement must have been laid before the company in general meeting.

(5)   A statement under subsection (4) suffices for purposes of a particular distribution not only if it relates to a distribution which has been proposed but also if it relates to distributions of any description which includes that particular distribution, notwithstanding that at the time of the statement it has not been proposed.

272.   Requirements for interim accounts.

(1)   The following are the statutory requirements in respect of interim accounts prepared for a proposed distribution by a public company.

(2)   The accounts must have been properly prepared, or have been so prepared subject only to matters which are not material for determining, by reference to items mentioned in section 270(2), whether the proposed distribution would contravene the relevant section.

(3)   'Properly prepared' means that the accounts must comply with section 226 (applying that section and Schedule 4 with such modifications as are necessary because the accounts are prepared otherwise than in respect of an accounting reference period) and any balance sheet comprised in the accounts must have been signed in accordance with section 233; and, without prejudice to the foregoing—

(a)   so much of the accounts as consists of a balance sheet must give a true and fair view of the state of the company's affairs as at the balance sheet date, and

(b)   so much of the accounts as consists of a profit and loss account must give a true and fair view of the company's profit or loss for the period in respect of which the accounts were prepared.

(4)   A copy of the accounts must have been delivered to the registrar of companies.

(5)   If the accounts are in a language other than English and the second sentence of section 242(1) (translation) does not apply then, subject to section 710B(6) (delivery of certain Welsh documents without a translation), a translation into English of the accounts, certified in the prescribed manner to be a correct translation, must also have been delivered to the registrar.

273.   Requirements for initial accounts.

(1)   The following are the statutory requirements in respect of initial accounts prepared for a proposed distribution by a public company.

(2)   The accounts must have been properly prepared, or they must have been so prepared subject only to matters which are not material for determining, by reference to items mentioned in section 270(2), whether the proposed distribution would contravene the relevant section.

(3)   Section 272(3) applies as respects the meaning of 'properly prepared'.

(4)   The company's auditors must have made a report stating whether, in their opinion, the accounts have been properly prepared; and the following subsection applies if their report is a qualified report, that is to say it is not a report without qualification to the effect that in the auditors' opinion the accounts have been so prepared.

(5)   The auditors must in that case also have stated in writing whether, in their opinion, the matter in respect of which their report is qualified is material for determining, by reference to items mentioned in section 270(2), whether the distribution would contravene the relevant section.

(6)   A copy of the accounts, of the auditors' report under subsection (4) and of the auditors' statement (if any) under subsection (5) must have been delivered to the registrar of companies.

(7)   If the accounts are, or the auditors' report under subsection (4) or their statement (if any) under subsection (5) is, in a language other than English and the second sentence of section 242(1) (translation) does not apply then, subject to section 710B(6) (delivery of certain Welsh documents without a translation), a translation into English of the accounts, the report or the statement (as the case may be), certified in the prescribed manner to be a correct translation, must also have been delivered to the registrar

274.   Method of applying s. 270 to successive distributions.

(1)   For the purpose of determining by reference to particular accounts whether a proposed distribution may be made by a company, section 270 has effect, in a case where one or more distributions have already been made in pursuance of determinations made by reference to those same accounts, as if the amount of the proposed distribution was increased by the amount of the distributions so made.

(2)   Subsection (1) of this section applies (if it would not otherwise do so) to—

(a)   financial assistance lawfully given by a public company out of its distributable profits in a case where the assistance is required to be so given by section 154,

(b)   financial assistance lawfully given by a private company out of its distributable profits in a case where the assistance is required to be so given by section 155(2),

(c)   financial assistance given by a company in contravention of section 151, in a case where the giving of that assistance reduces the company's net assets or increases its net liabilities,

(d)   a payment made by a company in respect of the purchase by it of shares in the company (except a payment lawfully made otherwise than out of distributable profits), and

(e)   a payment of any description specified in section 168 (company's purchase of right to acquire its own shares, etc.),

being financial assistance given or payment made since the relevant accounts were prepared, as if any such financial assistance or payment were a distribution already made in pursuance of a determination made by reference to those accounts.

(3)   In this section the following definitions apply—

'financial assistance' means the same as in Chapter VI of Part V;

'net assets' has the meaning given by section 154(2)(a); and

'net liabilities', in relation to the giving of financial assistance by a company, means the amount by which the aggregate amount of the company's liabilities (within the meaning of section 154(2)(b)) exceeds the aggregate amount of its assets, taking the amount of the assets and liabilities to be as stated in the company's accounting records immediately before the financial assistance is given.

(4)   Subsections (2) and (3) of this section are deemed to be included in Chapter VII of Part V for purposes of the Secretary of State's power to make regulations under section 179.

275.   Treatment of assets in the relevant accounts.

(1)   For purposes of sections 263 and 264, a provision of any kind mentioned in paragraphs 88 and 89 of Schedule 4, other than one in respect of a diminution in value of a fixed asset appearing on a revaluation of all the fixed assets of the company, or of all of its fixed assets other than goodwill, is treated as a realised loss.

(2)   If, on the revaluation of a fixed asset, an unrealised profit is shown to have been made and, on or after the revaluation, a sum is written off or retained for depreciation of that asset over a period, then an amount equal to the amount by which that sum exceeds the sum which would have been so written off or retained for the depreciation of that asset over that period, if that profit had not been made, is treated for purposes of sections 263 and 264 as a realised profit made over that period.

(3)   Where there is no record of the original cost of an asset, or a record cannot be obtained without unreasonable expense or delay, then for the purpose of determining whether the company has made a profit or loss in respect of that asset, its cost is taken to be the value ascribed to it in the earliest available record of its value made on or after its acquisition by the company.

(4)   Subject to subsection (6), any consideration by the directors of the value at a particular time of a fixed asset is treated as a revaluation of the asset for the purposes of determining whether any such revaluation of the company's fixed assets as is required for purposes of the exception from subsection (1) has taken place at that time.

(5)   But where any such assets which have not actually been revalued are treated as revalued for those purposes under subsection (4), that exception applies only if the directors are satisfied that their aggregate value at the time in question is not less than the aggregate amount at which they are for the time being stated in the company's accounts.

(6)   Where section 271(2), 272(2) or 273(2) applies to the relevant accounts, subsections (4) and (5) above do not apply for the purpose of determining whether a revaluation of the company's fixed assets affecting the amount of the relevant items (that is, the items mentioned in section 270(2)) as stated in those accounts has taken place, unless it is stated in a note to the accounts—

(a)   that the directors have considered the value at any time of any fixed assets of the company, without actually revaluing those assets,

(b)   that they are satisfied that the aggregate value of those assets at the time in question is or was not less than the aggregate amount at which they are or were for the time being stated in the company's accounts, and

(c)   that the relevant items in question are accordingly stated in the relevant accounts on the basis that a revaluation of the company's fixed assets which by virtue of subsections (4) and (5) included the assets in question took place at that time.

276.   Distributions in kind.

Where a company makes a distribution of or including a non-cash asset, and any part of the amount at which that asset is stated in the accounts relevant for the purposes of the distribution in accordance with sections 270 to 275 represents an unrealised profit, that profit is to be treated as a realised profit—

(a)   for the purpose of determining the lawfulness of the distribution in accordance with this Part (whether before or after the distribution takes place), and

(b)   for the purpose of the application of paragraphs 12(a) and 34(3)(a) of Schedule 4 or paragraphs 12(a) and 34(3)(a) of Schedule 8 (only realised profits to be included in or transferred to the profit and loss account) in relation to anything done with a view to or in connection with the making of that distribution.

Supplementary

277.   Consequences of unlawful distribution.

(1)   Where a distribution, or part of one, made by a company to one of its members is made in contravention of this Part and, at the time of the distribution, he knows or has reasonable grounds for believing that it is so made, he is liable to repay it (or that part of it, as the case may be) to the company or (in the case of a distribution made otherwise than in cash) to pay the company a sum equal to the value of the distribution (or part) at that time.

(2)   The above is without prejudice to any obligation imposed apart from this section on a member of a company to repay a distribution unlawfully made to him; but this section does not apply in relation to—

(a)   financial assistance given by a company in contravention of section 151, or

(b)   any payment made by a company in respect of the redemption or purchase by the company of shares in itself.

(3)   Subsection (2) of this section is deemed included in Chapter VII of Part V for purposes of the Secretary of State's power to make regulations under section 179.

278.   Saving for provision in articles operative before Act of 1980.

Where immediately before 22 December 1980 a company was authorised by a provision of its articles to apply its unrealised profits in paying up in full or in part unissued shares to be allotted to members of the company as fully or partly paid bonus shares, that provision continues (subject to any alteration of the articles) as authority for those profits to be so applied after that date.

280.   Definitions for Part VIII.

(1)   The following has effect for the interpretation of this Part.

(2)   'Capitalisation', in relation to a company's profits, means any of the following operations (whenever carried out)—

(a)   applying the profits in wholly or partly paying up unissued shares in the company to be allotted to members of the company as fully or partly paid bonus shares, or

(b)   transferring the profits to capital redemption reserve.

(3)   References to profits and losses of any description are (respectively) to profits and losses of that description made at any time and, except where the context otherwise requires, are (respectively) to revenue and capital profits and revenue and capital losses.

281. Saving for other restraints on distribution.

The provisions of this Part are without prejudice to any enactment or rule of law, or any provision of a company's memorandum or articles, restricting the sums out of which, or the cases in which, a distribution may be made.

PART IX
A COMPANY'S MANAGEMENT; DIRECTORS AND SECRETARIES; THEIR QUALIFICATIONS, DUTIES AND RESPONSIBILITIES

Officers and registered office

282. Directors.

(1)   Every company registered on or after 1 November 1929 (other than a private company) shall have at least two directors.

(2)   Every company registered before that date (other than a private company) shall have at least one director.

(3)   Every private company shall have at least one director.

283. Secretary.

(1)   Every company shall have a secretary.

(2)   A sole director shall not also be secretary.

(3)   Anything required or authorised to be done by or to the secretary may, if the office is vacant or there is for any other reason no secretary capable of acting, be done by or to any assistant or deputy secretary or, if there is no assistant or deputy secretary capable of acting, by or to any officer of the company authorised generally or specially in that behalf by the directors.

(4)   No company shall—

(a)   have as secretary to the company a corporation the sole director of which is a sole director of the company;

(b)   have as sole director of the company a corporation the sole director of which is secretary to the company.

284. Acts done by person in dual capacity.

A provision requiring or authorising a thing to be done by or to a director and the secretary is not satisfied by its being done by or to the same person acting both as director and as, or in place of, the secretary.

285. Validity of acts of directors.

The acts of a director or manager are valid notwithstanding any defect that may afterwards be discovered in his appointment or qualification; and this provision is not excluded by section 292(2) (void resolution to appoint).

286. Qualifications of company secretaries.

(1)   It is the duty of the directors of a public company to take all reasonable steps to secure that the secretary (or each joint secretary) of the company is a person who appears to them to have the requisite knowledge and experience to discharge the functions of secretary of the company and who—

(a)   on 22 December 1980 held the office of secretary or assistant or deputy secretary of the company; or

(b)   for at least 3 of the 5 years immediately preceding his appointment as secretary held the office of secretary of a company other than a private company; or

(c)   is a member of any of the bodies specified in the following subsection; or

(d)   is a barrister, advocate or solicitor called or admitted in any part of the United Kingdom; or

(e)   is a person who, by virtue of his holding or having held any other position or his being a member of any other body, appears to the directors to be capable of discharging those functions.

(2)   The bodies referred to in subsection (1)(c) are—

    (a)   the Institute of Chartered Accountants in England and Wales;

    (b)   the Institute of Chartered Accountants of Scotland;

    (c)   the Chartered Association of Certified Accountants;

    (d)   the Institute of Chartered Accountants in Ireland;

    (e)   the Institute of Chartered Secretaries and Administrators;

    (f)   the Institute of Cost and Management Accountants;

    (g)   the Chartered Institute of Public Finance and Accountancy.

287.   Registered office.

(1)   A company shall at all times have a registered office to which all communications and notices may be addressed.

(2)   On incorporation the situation of the company's registered office is that specified in the statement sent to the registrar under section 10.

(3)   The company may change the situation of its registered office from time to time by giving notice in the prescribed form to the registrar.

(4)   The change takes effect upon the notice being registered by the registrar, but until the end of the period of 14 days beginning with the date on which it is registered a person may validly serve any document on the company at its previous registered office.

(5)   For the purposes of any duty of a company—

    (a)   to keep at its registered office, or make available for public inspection there, any register, index or other document, or

    (b)   to mention the address of its registered office in any document,

a company which has given notice to the registrar of a change in the situation of its registered office may act on the change as from such date, not more than 14 days after the notice is given, as it may determine.

(6)   Where a company unavoidably ceases to perform at its registered office any such duty as is mentioned in subsection (5)(a) in circumstances in which it was not practicable to give prior notice to the registrar of a change in the situation of its registered office, but—

    (a)   resumes performance of that duty at other premises as soon as practicable, and

    (b)   gives notice accordingly to the registrar of a change in the situation of its registered office within 14 days of doing so,

it shall not be treated as having failed to comply with that duty.

(7)   In proceedings for an offence of failing to comply with any such duty as is mentioned in subsection (5), it is for the person charged to show that by reason of the matters referred to in that subsection or subsection (6) no offence was committed.

288.   Register of directors and secretaries.

(1)   Every company shall keep at its registered office a register of its directors and secretaries; and the register shall, with respect to the particulars to be contained in it of those persons, comply with sections 289 and 290 below.

(2)   The company shall, within the period of 14 days from the occurrence of—

    (a)   any change among its directors or in its secretary, or

    (b)   any change in the particulars contained in the register,

send to the registrar of companies a notification in the prescribed form of the change and of the date on which it occurred; and a notification of a person having become a director or secretary, or one of joint secretaries, of the company shall contain a consent, signed by that person, to act in the relevant capacity.

(3) The register shall be open to the inspection of any member of the company without charge and of any other person on payment of such fee as may be prescribed.

(4) If an inspection required under this section is refused, or if default is made in complying with subsection (1) or (2), the company and every officer of it who is in default is liable to a fine and, for continued contravention, to a daily default fine.

(5) In the case of a refusal of inspection of the register, the court may by order compel an immediate inspection of it.

(6) For purposes of this and the next section, a shadow director of a company is deemed a director and officer of it.

289. Particulars of directors to be registered under s. 288.

(1) Subject to the provisions of this section, the register kept by a company under section 288 shall contain the following particulars with respect to each director—

    (a)   in the case of an individual—
        (i)   his present name,
        (ii)   any former name,
        (iii) his usual residential address,
        (iv) his nationality,
        (v)   his business occupation (if any),
        (vi) particulars of any other directorships held by him or which have been held by him, and
        (vii) the date of his birth;
    (b)   in the case of a corporation or Scottish firm, its corporate or firm name and registered or principal office.

(2) In subsection (1)(a)—

    (a)   'name' means a person's Christian name (or other forename) and surname, except that in the case of a peer, or an individual usually known by a title, the title may be stated instead of his Christian name (or other forename) and surname, or in addition to either or both of them; and

    (b)   the reference to a former name does not include—
        (i)   in the case of a peer, or an individual normally known by a British title, the name by which he was known previous to the adoption of or succession to the title, or
        (ii)   in the case of any person, a former name which was changed or disused before he attained the age of 18 years or which has been changed or disused for 20 years or more, or
        (iii) in the case of a married woman, the name by which she was known previous to the marriage.

(3) It is not necessary for the register to contain on any day particulars of a directorship—

    (a)   which has not been held by a director at any time during the 5 years preceding that day,

    (b)   which is held by a director in a company which—
        (i)   is dormant or grouped with the company keeping the register, and
        (ii)   if he also held that directorship for any period during those 5 years, was for the whole of that period either dormant or so grouped,

    (c)   which was held by a director for any period during those 5 years in a company which for the whole of that period was either dormant or grouped with the company keeping the register.

(4) For purposes of subsection (3), 'company' includes any body corporate incorporated in Great Britain; and—

    (a)   section 250(3) applies as regards whether and when a company is or has been dormant, and

    (b)   a company is to be regarded as being, or having been, grouped with another at any time if at that time it is or was a company of which the other is or was a wholly-owned subsidiary, or if it is or was a wholly-owned subsidiary of the other or of another company of which that other is or was a wholly-owned subsidiary.

290. Particulars of secretaries to be registered under s. 288.

(1)   The register to be kept by a company under section 288 shall contain the following particulars with respect to the secretary or, where there are joint secretaries, with respect to each of them—

(a)   in the case of an individual, his present name, any former name and his usual residential address, and

(b)   in the case of a corporation or a Scottish firm, its corporate or firm name and registered or principal office.

(2)   Where all the partners in a firm are joint secretaries, the name and principal office of the firm may be stated instead of the particulars specified above.

(3)   Section 289(2)(a) and (b) apply for the purposes of the obligation under subsection (1)(a) of this section to state the name or former name of an individual.

Provisions governing appointment of directors

291.   Share qualification of directors.

(1)   It is the duty of every director who is by the company's articles required to hold a specified share qualification, and who is not already qualified, to obtain his qualification within 2 months after his appointment, or such shorter time as may be fixed by the articles.

(2)   For the purpose of any provision of the articles requiring a director or manager to hold any specified share qualification, the bearer of a share warrant is not deemed the holder of the shares specified in the warrant.

(3)   The office of director of a company is vacated if the director does not within 2 months from the date of his appointment (or within such shorter time as may be fixed by the articles) obtain his qualification, or if after the expiration of that period or shorter time he ceases at any time to hold his qualification.

(4)   A person vacating office under this section is incapable of being reappointed to be a director of the company until he has obtained his qualification.

(5)   If after the expiration of that period or shorter time any unqualified person acts as a director of the company, he is liable to a fine and, for continued contravention, to a daily default fine.

292.   Appointment of directors to be voted on individually.

(1)   At a general meeting of a public company, a motion for the appointment of two or more persons as directors of the company by a single resolution shall not be made, unless a resolution that it shall be so made has first been agreed to by the meeting without any vote being given against it.

(2)   A resolution moved in contravention of this section is void, whether or not its being so moved was objected to at the time; but where a resolution so moved is passed, no provision for the automatic reappointment of retiring directors in default of another appointment applies.

(3)   For purposes of this section, a motion for approving a person's appointment, or for nominating a person for appointment, is to be treated as a motion for his appointment.

(4)   Nothing in this section applies to a resolution altering the company's articles.

293.   Age limit for directors.

(1)   A company is subject to this section if—

(a)   it is a public company, or

(b)   being a private company, it is a subsidiary of a public company or of a body corporate registered under the law relating to companies for the time being in force in Northern Ireland as a public company.

(2)   No person is capable of being appointed a director of a company which is subject to this section if at the time of his appointment he has attained the age of 70.

(3)   A director of such a company shall vacate his office at the conclusion of the annual general meeting commencing next after he attains the age of 70; but acts done by a person as director are valid notwithstanding that it is afterwards discovered that his appointment had terminated under this subsection.

(4)   Where a person retires under subsection (3), no provision for the automatic reappointment of retiring directors in default of another appointment applies; and if at the meeting at which he retires the vacancy is not filled, it may be filled as a casual vacancy.

(5)   Nothing in subsections (2) to (4) prevents the appointment of a director at any age, or requires a director to retire at any time, if his apointment is or was made or approved by the company in general meeting; but special notice is required of a resolution appointing or approving the appointment of a director for it to have effect under this subsection, and the notice of the resolution given to the company, and by the company to its members, must state, or have stated, the age of the person to whom it relates.

(6)   A person reappointed director on retiring under subsection (3), or appointed in place of a director so retiring, is to be treated, for the purpose of determining the time at which he or any other director is to retire, as if he had become director on the day on which the retiring director was last appointed before his retirement.

Subject to this, the retirement of a director out of turn under subsection (3) is to be disregarded in determining when any other directors are to retire.

(7)   In the case of a company first registered after the beginning of 1947, this section has effect subject to the provisions of the company's articles; and in the case of a company first registered before the beginning of that year—

(a)   this section has effect subject to any alterations of the company's articles made after the beginning of that year; and

(b)   if at the beginning of that year the company's articles contained provision for retirement of directors under an age limit, or for preventing or restricting appointments of directors over a given age, this section does not apply to directors to whom that provision applies.

294.   Duty of director to disclose his age.

(1)   A person who is appointed or to his knowledge proposed to be appointed director of a company subject to section 293 at a time when he has attained any retiring age applicable to him under that section or under the company's articles shall give notice of his age to the company.

(2)   For purposes of this section, a company is deemed subject to section 293 notwithstanding that all or any of the section's provisions are excluded or modified by the company's articles.

(3)   Subsection (1) does not apply in relation to a person's reappointment on the termination of a previous appointment as director of the company.

(4)   A person who—

(a)   fails to give notice of his age as required by this section; or

(b)   acts as director under any appointment which is invalid or has terminated by reason of his age,

is liable to a fine and, for continued contravention, to a daily default fine.

(5)   For purposes of subsection (4), a person who has acted as director under an appointment which is invalid or has terminated is deemed to have continued so to act throughout the period from the invalid appointment or the date on which the appointment terminated (as the case may be), until the last day on which he is shown to have acted thereunder.

Removal of directors

303. Resolution to remove director.

(1)   A company may by ordinary resolution remove a director before the expiration of his period of office, notwithstanding anything in its articles or in any agreement between it and him.

(2)   Special notice is required of a resolution to remove a director under this section or to appoint somebody instead of a director so removed at the meeting at which he is removed.

(3)   A vacancy created by the removal of a director under this section, if not filled at the meeting at which he is removed, may be filled as a casual vacancy.

(4)   A person appointed director in place of a person removed under this section is treated, for the purpose of determining the time at which he or any other director is to retire, as if he had become director on the day on which the person in whose place he is appointed was last appointed a director.

(5)   This section is not to be taken as depriving a person removed under it of compensation or damages payable to him in respect of the termination of his appointment as director or of any appointment terminating with that as director, or as derogating from any power to remove a director which may exist apart from this section.

304. Director's right to protest removal.

(1)   On receipt of notice of an intended resolution to remove a director under section 303, the company shall forthwith send a copy of the notice to the director concerned; and he (whether or not a member of the company) is entitled to be heard on the resolution at the meeting.

(2)   Where notice is given of an intended resolution to remove a director under that section, and the director concerned makes with respect to it representations in writing to the company (not exceeding a reasonable length) and requests their notification to members of the company, the company shall, unless the representations are received by it too late for it to do so—

(a)   in any notice of the resolution given to members of the company state the fact of the representations having been made; and

(b)   send a copy of the representations to every member of the company to whom notice of the meeting is sent (whether before or after receipt of the representations by the company).

(3)   If a copy of the representations is not sent as required by subsection (2) because received too late or because of the company's default, the director may (without prejudice to his right to be heard orally) require that the representations shall be read out at the meeting.

(4)   But copies of the representations need not be sent out and the representations need not be read out at the meeting if, on the application either of the company or of any other person who claims to be aggrieved, the court is satisfied that the rights conferred by this section are being abused to secure needless publicity for defamatory matter.

(5)   The court may order the company's costs on an application under this section to be paid in whole or in part by the director, notwithstanding that he is not a party to the application.

Other provisions about directors and officers

305. Directors' names on company correspondence, etc.

(1)   A company to which this section applies shall not state, in any form, the name of any of its directors (otherwise than in the text or as a signatory) on any business letter on which the company's name appears unless it states on the letter in legible characters the name of every director of the company.

(2)   This section applies to—

(a)   every company registered under this Act or under the former Companies Acts (except a company registered before 23 November 1916); and

(b)   every company incorporated outside Great Britain which has an established place of business within Great Britain, unless it had established such a place of business before that date.

(3)   If a company makes default in complying with this section, every officer of the company who is in default is liable for each offence to a fine; and for this purpose, where a corporation is an officer of the company, any officer of the corporation is deemed an officer of the company.

(4)   For the purposes of the obligation under subsection (1) to state the name of every director of the company, a person's 'name' means—

(a)   in the case of an individual, his Christian name (or other forename) and surname; and

(b)   in the case of a corporation or Scottish firm, its corporate or firm name.

(5)   The initial or a recognised abbreviation of a person's Christian name or other forename may be stated instead of the full Christian name or other forename.

(6)   In the case of a peer, or an individual usually known by a title, the title may be stated instead of his Christian name (or other forename) and surname or in addition to either or both of them.

(7)   In this section 'director' includes a shadow director and the reference in subsection (3) to an 'officer' shall be construed accordingly.

306.   Limited company may have directors with unlimited liability.

(1)   In the case of a limited company the liability of the directors or managers, or of the managing director, may, if so provided by the memorandum, be unlimited.

(2)   In the case of a limited company in which the liability of a director or manager is unlimited, the directors and any managers of the company and the member who proposes any person for election or appointment to the office of director or manager, shall add to that proposal a statement that the liability of the person holding that office will be unlimited.

(3)   Before the person accepts the office or acts in it, notice in writing that his liability will be unlimited shall be given to him by the following or one of the following persons, namely—

(a)   the promoters of the company,

(b)   the directors of the company,

(c)   any managers of the company,

(d)   the company secretary.

(4)   If a director, manager or proposer makes default in adding such a statement, or if a promoter, director, manager or secretary makes default in giving the notice required by subsection (3), then—

(a)   he is liable to a fine, and

(b)   he is also liable for any damage which the person so elected or appointed may sustain from the default;

but the liability of the person elected or appointed is not affected by the default.

307.   Special resolution making liability of directors unlimited.

(1)   A limited company, if so authorised by its articles, may by special resolution after its memorandum so as to render unlimited the liability of its directors or managers, or of any managing director.

(2)   When such a special resolution is passed, its provisions are as valid as if they had been originally contained in the memorandum.

308.   Assignment of office by directors.

If provision is made by a company's articles, or by any agreement entered into between any person and the company, for empowering a director or manager of the company to assign his office as such to another person, any assignment of office made in pursuance of that provision is (notwithstanding anything to the contrary contained in the provision) of no effect unless and until it is approved by a special resolution of the company.

309. Directors to have regard to interests of employees.

(1)   The matters to which the directors of a company are to have regard in the performance of their functions include the interests of the company's employees in general, as well as the interests of its members.

(2)   Accordingly, the duty imposed by this section on the directors is owed by them to the company (and the company alone) and is enforceable in the same way as any other fiduciary duty owed to a company by its directors.

(3)   This section applies to shadow directors as it does to directors.

310. Provisions exempting officers and auditors from liability.

(1)   This section applies to any provision, whether contained in a company's articles or in any contract with the company or otherwise, for exempting any officer of the company or any person (whether an officer or not) employed by the company as auditor from, or indemnifying him against, any liability which by virtue of any rule of law would otherwise attach to him in respect of any negligence, default, breach of duty or breach of trust of which he may be guilty in relation to the company.

(2)   Except as provided by the following subsection, any such provision is void.

(3)   This section does not prevent a company—

(a)   from purchasing and maintaining for any such officer or auditor insurance against any such liability, or

(b)   from indemnifying any such officer or auditor against any liability incurred by him—

(i)   in defending any proceedings (whether civil or criminal) in which judgment is given in his favour or he is acquitted, or

(ii)   in connection with any application under section 144(3) or (4) (acquisition of shares by innocent nominee) or section 727 (general power to grant relief in case of honest and reasonable conduct) in which relief is granted to him by the court.

PART X
ENFORCEMENT OF FAIR DEALING BY DIRECTORS

Restrictions on directors taking financial advantage

311. Prohibition on tax-free payments to directors.

(1)   It is not lawful for a company to pay a director remuneration (whether as director or otherwise) free of income tax, or otherwise calculated by reference to or varying with the amount of his income tax, or to or with any rate of income tax.

(2)   Any provision contained in a company's articles, or in any contract, or in any resolution of a company or a company's directors, for payment to a director of remuneration as above-mentioned has effect as if it provided for payment, as a gross sum subject to income tax, of the net sum for which it actually provides.

312. Payment to director for loss of office etc.

It is not lawful for a company to make to a director of the company any payment by way of compensation for loss of office, or as consideration for or in connection with his retirement from office, without particulars of the proposed payment (including its amount) being disclosed to members of the company and the proposal being approved by the company.

313. Company approval for property transfer.

(1)   It is not lawful, in connection with the transfer of the whole or any part of the undertaking or property of a company, for any payment to be made to a director of the

company by way of compensation for loss of office, or as consideration for or in connection with his retirement from office, unless particulars of the proposed payment (including its amount) have been disclosed to members of the company and the proposal approved by the company.

(2)   Where a payment unlawful under this section is made to a director, the amount received is deemed to be received by him in trust for the company.

314.   Director's duty of disclosure on takeover, etc.

(1)   This section applies where, in connection with the transfer to any persons of all or any of the shares in a company, being a transfer resulting from—

(a)   an offer made to the general body of shareholders; or

(b)   an offer made by or on behalf of some other body corporate with a view to the company becoming its subsidiary or a subsidiary of its holding company; or

(c)   an offer made by or on behalf of an individual with a view to his obtaining the right to exercise or control the exercise of not less than one-third of the voting power at any general meeting of the company; or

(d)   any other offer which is conditional on acceptance to a given extent,

a payment is to be made to a director of the company by way of compensation for loss of office, or as consideration for or in connection with his retirement from office.

(2)   It is in those circumstances the director's duty to take all reasonable steps to secure that particulars of the proposed payment (including its amount) are included in or sent with any notice of the offer made for their shares which is given to any shareholders.

(3)   If—

(a)   the director fails to take those steps, or

(b)   any person who has been properly required by the director to include those particulars in or send them with the notice required by subsection (2) fails to do so, he is liable to a fine.

315.   Consequences of non-compliance with s. 314.

(1)   If in the case of any such payment to a director as is mentioned in section 314(1)—

(a)   his duty under that section is not complied with, or

(b)   the making of the proposed payment is not, before the transfer of any shares in pursuance of the offer, approved by a meeting (summoned for the purpose) of the holders of the shares to which the offer relates and of other holders of shares of the same class as any of those shares,

any sum received by the director on account of the payment is deemed to have been received by him in trust for persons who have sold their shares as a result of the offer made; and the expenses incurred by him in distributing that sum amongst those persons shall be borne by him and not retained out of that sum.

(2)   Where—

(a)   the shareholders referred to in subsection (1)(b) are not all the members of the company, and

(b)   no provision is made by the articles for summoning or regulating the meeting referred to in that paragraph,

the provisions of this Act and of the company's articles relating to general meetings of the company apply (for that purpose) to the meeting either without modification or with such modifications as the Secretary of State on the application of any person concerned may direct for the purpose of adapting them to the circumstances of the meeting.

(3)   If at a meeting summoned for the purpose of approving any payment as required by subsection (1)(b) a quorum is not present and, after the meeting has been adjourned to a later date, a quorum is again not present, the payment is deemed for the purposes of that subsection to have been approved.

316.   Provisions supplementing ss. 312 to 315.

(1)   Where in proceedings for the recovery of any payment as having, by virtue of section 313(2) or 315(1), been received by any person in trust, it is shown that—

(a)   the payment was made in pursuance of any arrangement entered into as part of the agreement for the transfer in question, or within one year before or two years after that agreement or the offer leading to it; and

(b)   the company or any person to whom the transfer was made was privy to that arrangement,

the payment is deemed, except in so far as the contrary is shown, to be one to which the provisions mentioned above in this subsection apply.

(2)   If in connection with any such transfer as is mentioned in any of sections 313 to 315—

(a)   the price to be paid to a director of the company whose office is to be abolished or who is to retire from office for any shares in the company held by him is in excess of the price which could at the time have been obtained by other holders of the like shares; or

(b)   any valuable consideration is given to any such director,

the excess or the money value of the consideration (as the case may be) is deemed for the purposes of that section to have been a payment made to him by way of compensation for loss of office or as consideration for or in conection with his retirement from office.

(3)   References in sections 312 to 315 to payments made to a director by way of compensation for loss of office or as consideration for or in connection with his retirement from office, do not include any bona fide payment by way of damages for breach of contract or by way of pension in respect of past services.

'Pension' here includes any superannuation allowance, superannuation gratuity or similar payment.

(4)   Nothing in sections 313 to 315 prejudices the operation of any rule of law requiring disclosure to be made with respect to such payments as are there mentioned, or with respect to any other like payments made or to be made to a company's directors.

317.   Directors to disclose interest in contracts.

(1)   It is the duty of a director of a company who is in any way, whether directly or indirectly, interested in a contract or proposed contract with the company to declare the nature of his interest at a meeting of the directors of the company.

(2)   In the case of a proposed contract, the declaration shall be made—

(a)   at the meeting of the directors at which the question of entering into the contract is first taken into consideration; or

(b)   if the director was not at the date of that meeting interested in the proposed contract, at the next meeting of the directors held after he became so interested;

and, in a case where the director becomes interested in a contract after it is made, the declaration shall be made at the first meeting of the directors held after he becomes so interested.

(3)   For purposes of this section, a general notice given to the directors of a company by a director to the effect that—

(a)   he is a member of a specified company or firm and is to be regarded as interested in any contract which may, after the date of the notice, be made with that company or firm; or

(b)   he is to be regarded as interested in any contract which may after the date of the notice be made with a specified person who is connected with him (within the meaning of section 346 below),

is deemed a sufficient declaration of interest in relation to any such contract.

(4)   However, no such notice is of effect unless either it is given at a meeting of the directors or the director takes reasonable steps to secure that it is brought up and read at the next meeting of the directors after it is given.

(5)   A reference in this section to a contract includes any transaction or arrangement (whether or not constituting a contract) made or entered into on or after 22 December 1980.

(6)   For purposes of this section, a transaction or arrangement of a kind described in section 330 (prohibition of loans, quasi-loans etc. to directors) made by a company for a director of the company or a person connected with such a director is treated (if it would not otherwise be so treated, and whether or not it is prohibited by that section) as a transaction or arrangement in which that director is interested.

(7)   A director who fails to comply with this section is liable to a fine.

(8)   This section applies to a shadow director as it applies to a director, except that a shadow director shall declare his interest, not at a meeting of the directors, but by a notice in writing to the directors which is either—

(a)   a specific notice given before the date of the meeting at which, if he had been a director, the declaration would be required by subsection (2) to be made; or

(b)   a notice which under subsection (3) falls to be treated as a sufficient declaration of that interest (or would fall to be so treated apart from subsection (4)).

(9)   Nothing in this section prejudices the operation of any rule of law restricting directors of a company from having an interest in contracts with the company.

318.   Directors' service contracts to be open to inspection.

(1)   Subject to the following provisions, every company shall keep at an appropriate place—

(a)   in the case of each director whose contract of service with the company is in writing, a copy of that contract;

(b)   in the case of each director whose contract of service with the company is not in writing, a written memorandum setting out its terms; and

(c)   in the case of each director who is employed under a contract of service with a subsidiary of the company, a copy of that contract or, if it is not in writing, a written memorandum setting out its terms.

(2)   All copies and memoranda kept by a company in pursuance of subsection (1) shall be kept at the same place.

(3)   The following are appropriate places for the purposes of subsection (1)—

(a)   the company's registered office;

(b)   the place where its register of members is kept (if other than its registered office);

(c)   its principal place of business, provided that is situated in that part of Great Britain in which the company is registered.

(4)   Every company shall send notice in the prescribed form to the registrar of companies of the place where copies and memoranda are kept in compliance with subsection (1), and of any change in that place, save in a case in which they have at all times been kept at the company's registered office.

(5)   Subsection (1) does not apply to a director's contract of service with the company or with a subsidiary of it if that contract required him to work wholly or mainly outside the United Kingdom; but the company shall keep a memorandum—

(a)   in the case of a contract of service with the company, giving the director's name and setting out the provisions of the contract relating to its duration;

(b)   in the case of a contract of service with a subsidiary, giving the director's name and the name and place of incorporation of the subsidiary, and setting out the provisions of the contract relating to its duration,

at the same place as copies and memoranda are kept by the company in pursuance of subsection (1).

(6)   A shadow director is treated for purposes of this section as a director.

(7)   Every copy and memorandum required by subsection (1) or (5) to be kept shall be open to inspection of any member of the company without charge.

(8)   If—

(a)   default is made in complying with subsection (1) or (5), or

(b)   an inspection required under subsection (7) is refused, or

(c)   default is made for 14 days in complying with subsection (4),

the company and every officer of it who is in default is liable to a fine and, for continued contravention, to a daily default fine.

(9)   In the case of a refusal of an inspection required under subsection (7) of a copy or memorandum, the court may by order compel an immediate inspection of it.

(10)   Subsections (1) and (5) apply to a variation of a director's contract of service as they apply to the contract.

(11)   This section does not require that there be kept a copy of, or memorandum setting out the terms of, a contract (or its variation) at a time when the unexpired portion of the term for which the contract is to be in force is less than 12 months, or at a time at which the contract can, within the next ensuing 12 months, be terminated by the company without payment of compensation.

319.   Director's contract of employment for more than 5 years.

(1)   This section applies in respect of any term of an agreement whereby a director's employment with the company of which he is a director or, where he is the director of a holding company, his employment within the group is to continue, or may be continued, otherwise than at the instance of the company (whether under the original agreement or under a new agreement entered into in pursuance of it), for a period of more than 5 years during which the employment—

(a)   cannot be terminated by the company by notice; or

(b)   can be so terminated only in specified circumstances.

(2)   In any case where—

(a)   a person is or is to be employed with a company under an agreement which cannot be terminated by the company by notice or can be so terminated only in specified circumstances; and

(b)   more than 6 months before the expiration of the period for which he is or is to be so employed, the company enters into a further agreement (otherwise than in pursuance of a right conferred by or under the original agreement on the other party to it) under which he is to be employed with the company or, where he is a director of a holding company, within the group,

this section applies as if to the period for which he is to be employed under that further agreement there were added a further period equal to the unexpired period of the original agreement.

(3)   A company shall not incorporate in an agreement such a term as is mentioned in subsection (1), unless the term is first approved by a resolution of the company in general meeting and, in the case of a director of a holding company, by a resolution of that company in general meeting.

(4)   No approval is required to be given under this section by any body corporate unless it is a company within the meaning of this Act, or is registered under section 680, or if it is a wholly-owned subsidiary of any body corporate, wherever incorporated.

(5)   A resolution of a company approving such a term as is mentioned in subsection (1) shall not be passed at a general meeting of the company unless a written memorandum setting out the proposed agreement incorporating the term is available for inspection by members of the company both—

(a)   at the company's registered office for not less than 15 days ending with the date of the meeting; and

(b)   at the meeting itself.

(6)   A term incorporated in an agreement in contravention of this section is, to the extent that it contravenes the section, void; and that agreement and, in a case where subsection (2) applies, the original agreement are deemed to contain a term entitling the company to terminate it at any time by the giving of reasonable notice.

(7)   In this section—

(a)   'employment' includes employment under a contract for services; and

(b)   'group', in relation to a director of a holding company, means the group which consists of that company and its subsidiaries;

and for purposes of this section a shadow director is treated as a director.

320.   Substantial property transactions involving directors, etc.

(1)   With the exceptions provided by the section next following, a company shall not enter into an arrangement—

(a)   whereby a director of the company or its holding company, or a person connected with such a director, acquires or is to acquire one or more non-cash assets of the requisite value from the company; or

(b)   whereby the company acquires or is to acquire one or more non-cash assets of the requisite value from such a director or a person so connected,

unless the arrangement is first approved by a resolution of the company in general meeting and, if the director or connected person is a director of its holding company or a person connected with such a director, by a resolution in general meeting of the holding company.

(2)   For this purpose a non-cash asset is of the requisite value if at the time the arrangement in question is entered into its value is not less than £2,000 but (subject to that) exceeds £100,000 or 10 per cent of the company's asset value, that is—

(a)   except in a case falling within paragraph (b) below, the value of the company's net assets determined by reference to the accounts prepared and laid under Part VII in respect of the last preceding financial year in respect of which such accounts were so laid; and

(b)   where no accounts have been so prepared and laid before that time, the amount of the company's called-up share capital.

(3)   For purposes of this section and sections 321 and 322, a shadow director is treated as a director.

321.   Exceptions from s. 320.

(1)   No approval is required to be given under section 320 by any body corporate unless it is a company within the meaning of this Act or registered under section 680 or, if it is a wholly-owned subsidiary of any body corporate, wherever incorporated.

(2)   Section 320(1) does not apply to an arrangement for the acquisition of a non-cash asset—

(a)   if the asset is to be acquired by a holding company from any of its wholly-owned subsidiaries or from a holding company by any of its wholly-owned subsidiaries, or by one wholly-owned subsidiary of a holding company from another wholly-owned subsidiary of that same holding company, or

(b)   if the arrangement is entered into by a company which is being wound up, unless the winding up is a member's voluntary winding up.

(3)   Section 320(1)(a) does not apply to an arrangement whereby a person is to acquire an asset from a company of which he is a member, if the arrangement is made with that person in his character as a member.

(4)   Section 320(1) does not apply to a transaction on a recognised investment exchange which is effected by a director, or a person connected with him, through the agency of a person who in relation to the transaction acts as an independent broker.

For this purpose an 'independent broker' means—

(a)   in relation to a transaction on behalf of a director, a person who independently of the director selects the person with whom the transaction is to be effected, and

(b)   in relation to a transaction on behalf of a person connected with a director, a person who independently of that person or the director selects the person with whom the transaction is to be effected;

and 'recognised', in relation to an investment exchange, means recognised under the Financial Services Act 1986.

322.   Liabilities arising from contravention of s. 320.

(1)   An arrangement entered into by a company in contravention of section 320, and any transaction entered into in pursuance of the arrangement (whether by the company or any other person) is voidable at the instance of the company unless one or more of the conditions specified in the next subsection is satisfied.

(2)   Those conditions are that—

(a)   restitution of any money or other asset which is the subject matter of the arrangement or transaction is no longer possible or the company has been indemnified in pursuance of this section by any other person for the loss or damage suffered by it; or

(b)   any rights acquired bona fide for value and without actual notice of the contravention by any person who is not a party to the arrangement or transaction would be affected by its avoidance; or

(c)   the arrangement is, within a reasonable period, affirmed by the company in general meeting and, if it is an arrangement for the transfer of an asset to or by a director of its holding company or a person who is connected with such a director, is so affirmed with the approval of the holding company given by a resolution in general meeting.

(3)   If an arrangement is entered into with a company by a director of the company or its holding company or a person connected with him in contravention of section 320, that director and the person so connected, and any other director of the company who authorised the arrangement or any transaction entered into in pursuance of such an arrangement, is liable—

(a)   to account to the company for any gain which he has made directly or indirectly by the arrangement or transaction, and

(b)   (jointly and severally with any other person liable under this subsection) to indemnify the company for any loss or damage resulting from the arrangement or transaction.

(4)   Subsection (3) is without prejudice to any liability imposed otherwise than by that subsection, and is subject to the following two subsections; and the liability under subsection (3) arises whether or not the arrangement or transaction entered into has been avoided in pursuance of subsection (1).

(5)   If an arrangement is entered into by a company and a person connected with a director of the company or its holding company in contravention of section 320, that director is not liable under subsection (3) if he shows that he took all reasonable steps to secure the company's compliance with that section.

(6)   In any case, a person so connected and any such other director as is mentioned in subsection (3) is not so liable if he shows that, at the time the arrangement was entered into, he did not know the relevant circumstances constituting the contravention.

322A.   Invalidity of certain transactions involving directors, etc.

(1)   This section applies where a company enters into a transaction to which the parties include—

(a)   a director of the company or of its holding company, or

(b)   a person connected with such a director or a company with whom such a director is associated,

and the board of directors, in connection with the transaction, exceed any limitation on their powers under the company's constitution.

(2)   The transaction is voidable at the instance of the company.

(3)   Whether or not it is avoided, any such party to the transaction as is mentioned in subsection (1)(a) or (b), and any director of the company who authorised the transaction, is liable—

(a)   to account to the company for any gain which he has made directly or indirectly by the transaction, and

(b)   to indemnify the company for any loss or damage resulting from the transaction.

(4)   Nothing in the above provisions shall be construed as excluding the operation of any other enactment or rule of law by virtue of which the transaction may be called in question or any liability to the company may arise.

(5)   The transaction ceases to be voidable if—

(a)   restitution of any money or other asset which was the subject matter of the transaction is no longer possible, or

(b)   the company is indemnified for any loss or damage resulting from the transaction, or

(c)   rights acquired bona fide for value and without actual notice of the directors' exceeding their powers by a person who is not party to the transaction would be affected by the avoidance, or

(d)   the transaction is ratified by the company in general meeting, by ordinary or special resolution or otherwise as the case may require.

(6)   A person other than a director of the company is not liable under subsection (3) if he shows that at the time the transaction was entered into he did not know that the directors were exceeding their powers.

(7)   This section does not affect the operation of section 35A in relation to any party to the transaction not within subsection (1)(a) or (b).

But where a transaction is voidable by virtue of this section and valid by virtue of that section in favour of such a person, the court may, on the application of that person or of the company, make such order affirming, severing or setting aside the transaction, on such terms, as appear to the court to be just.

(8)   In this section 'transaction' includes any act; and the reference in subsection (1) to limitations under the company's constitution includes limitations deriving—

(a)   from a resolution of the company in general meeting or a meeting of any class of shareholders, or

(b)   from any agreement between the members of the company or of any class of shareholders.

322B.   Contracts with sole members who are directors.

(1)   Subject to subsection (2), where a private company limited by shares or by guarantee having only one member enters into a contract with the sole member of the company and the sole member is also a director of the company, the company shall, unless the contract is in writing, ensure that the terms of the contract are either set out in a written memorandum or are recorded in the minutes of the first meeting of the directors of the company following the making of the contract.

(2)   Subsection (1) shall not apply to contracts entered into in the ordinary course of the company's business.

(3)   For the purposes of this section a sole member who is a shadow director is treated as a director.

(4)   If a company fails to comply with subsection (1), the company and every officer of it who is in default is liable to a fine.

(5)   Subject to subsection (6), nothing in this section shall be construed as excluding the operation of any other enactment or rule of law applying to contracts between a company and a director of that company.

(6)   Failure to comply with subsection (1) with respect to a contract shall not affect the validity of that contract.

Share dealings by directors and their families

323.   Prohibition on directors dealing in share options.

(1)   It is an offence for a director of a company to buy—

(a)   a right to call for delivery at a specified price and within a specified time of a specified number of relevant shares or a specified amount of relevant debentures; or

(b)   a right to make delivery at a specified price and within a specified time of a specified number of relevant shares or a specified amount of relevant debentures; or

(c)   a right (as he may elect) to call for delivery at a specified price and within a specified time or to make delivery at a specified price and within a specified time of a specified number of relevant shares or a specified amount of relevant debentures.

(2)   A person guilty of an offence under subsection (1) is liable to imprisonment or a fine, or both.

(3)   In subsection (1)—

(a)   'relevant shares', in relation to a director of a company, means shares in the company or in any other body corporate, being the company's subsidiary or holding company, or a subsidiary of the company's holding company, being shares as respects which there has been granted a listing on a stock exchange (whether in Great Britain or elsewhere);

(b)   'relevant debentures', in relation to a director of a company, means debentures of the company or of any other body corporate, being the company's subsidiary or holding company or a subsidiary of the company's holding company, being debentures as respects which there has been granted such a listing; and

(c)   'price' includes any consideration other than money.

(4)   This section applies to a shadow director as to a director.

(5)   This section is not to be taken as penalising a person who buys a right to subscribe for shares in, or debentures of, a body corporate or buys debentures of a body corporate that confer upon the holder of them a right to subscribe for, or to convert the debentures (in whole or in part) into, shares of that body.

324.   Duty of director to disclose shareholdings in own company.

(1)   A person who becomes a director of a company and at the time when he does so is interested in shares in, or debentures of, the company or any other body corporate, being the company's subsidiary or holding company or a subsidiary of the company's holding company, is under obligation to notify the company in writing—

(a)   of the subsistence of his interests at that time; and

(b)   of the number of shares of each class in, and the amount of debentures of each class of, the company or other such body corporate in which each interest of his subsists at that time.

(2)   A director of a company is under obligation to notify the company in writing of the occurrence, while he is a director, of any of the following events—

(a)   any event in consequence of whose occurrence he becomes, or ceases to be, interested in shares in, or debentures of, the company or any other body corporate, being the company's subsidiary or holding company or a subsidiary of the company's holding company;

(b)   the entering into by him of a contract to sell any such shares or debentures;

(c)   the assignment by him of a right granted to him by the company to subscribe for shares in, or debentures of, the company; and

(d)   the grant to him by another body corporate, being the company's subsidiary or holding company or a subsidiary of the company's holding company, of a right to subscribe for shares in, or debentures of, that other body corporate, the exercise of such a right granted to him and the assignment by him of such a right so granted;

and notification to the company must state the number or amount, and class, of shares or debentures involved.

(3)   Schedule 13 has effect in connection with subsections (1) and (2) above; and of that Schedule—

(a)   Part I contains rules for the interpretation of, and otherwise in relation to, those subsections and applies in determining, for purposes of those subsections, whether a person has an interest in shares or debentures;

(b)   Part II applies with respect to the periods within which obligations imposed by the subsections must be fulfilled; and

(c)   Part III specifies certain circumstances in which obligations arising from subsection (2) are to be treated as not discharged;

and subsections (1) and (2) are subject to any exceptions for which provision may be made by regulations made by the Secretary of State by statutory instrument.

(4)   Subsection (2) does not require the notification by a person of the occurrence of an event whose occurrence comes to his knowledge after he has ceased to be a director.

(5)   An obligation imposed by this section is treated as not discharged unless the notice by means of which it purports to be discharged is expressed to be given in fulfilment of that obligation.

(6)   This section applies to shadow directors as to directors; but nothing in it operates so as to impose an obligation with respect to shares in a body corporate which is the wholly-owned subsidiary of another body corporate.

(7)   A person who—

(a)   fails to discharge, within the proper period, an obligation to which he is subject under subsection (1) or (2), or

(b)   in purported discharge of an obligation to which he is so subject, makes to the company a statement which he knows to be false, or recklessly makes to it a statement which is false,

is guilty of an offence and liable to imprisonment or a fine, or both.

(8)   Section 732 (restriction on prosecutions) applies to an offence under this section.

325.   Register of directors' interests notified under s. 324.

(1)   Every company shall keep a register for the purposes of section 324.

(2)   Whenever a company receives information from a director given in fulfilment of an obligation imposed on him by that section, it is under obligation to enter in the register, against the director's name, the information received and the date of the entry.

(3)   The company is also under obligation, whenever it grants to a director a right to subscribe for shares in, or debentures of, the company to enter in the register against his name—

(a)   the date on which the right is granted,

(b)   the period during which, or time at which, it is exercisable,

(c)   the consideration for the grant (or, if there is no consideration, that fact), and

(d)   the description of shares or debentures involved and the number or amount of them, and the price to be paid for them (or the consideration, if otherwise than in money).

(4)   Whenever such a right as is mentioned above is exercised by a director, the company is under obligation to enter in the register against his name that fact

(identifying the right), the number or amount of shares or debentures in respect of which it is exercised and, if they were registered in his name, that fact and, if not, the name or names of the person or persons in whose name or names they were registered, together (if they were registered in the names of two persons or more) with the number or amount of the shares or debentures registered in the name of each of them.

(5)   Part IV of Schedule 13 has effect with respect to the register to be kept under this section, to the way in which entries in it are to be made, to the right of inspection, and generally.

(6)   For purposes of this section, a shadow director is deemed a director.

326.   Sanctions for non-compliance.

(1)   The following applies with respect to defaults in complying with, and to contraventions of, section 325 and Part IV of Schedule 13.

(2)   If default is made in complying with any of the following provisions—
    (a)   section 325(1), (2), (3) or (4), or
    (b)   Schedule 13, paragraph 21, 22 or 28,
the company and every officer of it who is in default is liable to a fine and, for continued contravention, to a daily default fine.

(3)   If an inspection of the register required under paragraph 25 of the Schedule is refused, or a copy required under paragraph 26 is not sent within the proper period, the company and every officer of it who is in default is liable to a fine and, for continued contravention, to a daily default fine.

(4)   If default is made for 14 days in complying with paragraph 27 of the Schedule (notice to registrar of where register is kept), the company and every officer of it who is in default is liable to a fine and, for continued contravention, to a daily default fine.

(5)   If default is made in complying with paragraph 29 of the Schedule (register to be produced at annual general meeting), the company and every officer of it who is in default is liable to a fine.

(6)   In the case of a refusal of an inspection of the register required under paragraph 25 of the Schedule, the court may by order compel an immediate inspection of it; and in the case of failure to send within the proper period a copy required under paragraph 26, the court may by order direct that the copy be sent to the person requiring it.

327.   Extension of s. 323 to spouses and children.

(1)   Section 323 applies to—
    (a)   the wife or husband of a director of a company (not being herself or himself a director of it), and
    (b)   an infant son or infant daughter of a director (not being himself or herself a director of the company),
as it applies to the director; but it is a defence for a person charged by virtue of this section with an offence under section 323 to prove that he (she) had no reason to believe that his (her) spouse or, as the case may be, parent was a director of the company in question.

(2)   For purposes of this section—
    (a)   'son' includes stepson and 'daughter' includes stepdaughter ('parent' being construed accordingly),
    (b)   'infant' means, in relation to Scotland, pupil or minor, and
    (c)   a shadow director of a company is deemed a director of it.

328.   Extension of s. 324 to spouses and children.

(1)   For the purposes of section 324—
    (a)   an interest of the wife or husband of a director of a company (not being herself or himself a director of it) in shares or debentures is to be treated as the director's interest; and

(b)   the same applies to an interest of an infant son or infant daughter of a director of a company (not being himself or herself a director of it) in shares or debentures.

(2)   For those purposes—

(a)   a contract, assignment or right of subscription entered into, exercised or made by, or a grant made to, the wife or husband of a director of a company (not being herself or himself a director of it) is to be treated as having been entered into, exercised or made by, or (as the case may be) as having been made to, the director; and

(b)   the same applies to a contract, assignment or right of subscription entered into, exercised or made by, or grant made to, an infant son or infant daughter of a director of a company (not being himself or herself a director of it).

(3)   A director of a company is under obligation to notify the company in writing of the occurrence while he or she is a director, of either of the following events, namely—

(a)   the grant by the company to his (her) spouse, or to his or her infant son or infant daughter, of a right to subscribe for shares in, or debentures of, the company; and

(b)   the exercise by his (her) spouse or by his or her infant son or infant daughter of such a right granted by the company to the wife, husband, son or daughter.

(4)   In a notice given to the company under subsection (3) there shall be stated—

(a)   in the case of the grant of a right, the like information as is required by section 324 to be stated by the director on the grant to him by another body corporate of a right to subscribe for shares in, or debentures of, that other body corporate; and

(b)   in the case of the exercise of a right, the like information as is required by that section to be stated by the director on the exercise of a right granted to him by another body corporate to subscribe for shares in, or debentures of, that other body corporate.

(5)   An obligation imposed by subsection (3) on a director must be fulfilled by him before the end of 5 days beginning with the day following that on which the occurrence of the event giving rise to it comes to his knowledge; but in reckoning that period of days there is disregarded any Saturday or Sunday, and any day which is a bank holiday in any part of Great Britain.

(6)   A person who—

(a)   fails to fulfil, within the proper period, an obligation to which he is subject under subsection (3), or

(b)   in purported fulfiment of such an obligation, makes to a company a statement which he knows to be false, or recklessly makes to a company a statement which is false, is guilty of an offence and liable to imprisonment or a fine, or both.

(7)   The rules set out in Part I of Schedule 13 have effect for the interpretation of, and otherwise in relation to, subsections (1) and (2); and subsections (5), (6) and (8) of section 324 apply with any requisite modification.

(8)   In this section, 'son' includes stepson 'daughter' includes stepdaughter, and 'infant' means, in relation to Scotland, pupil or minor.

(9)   For purposes of section 325, an obligation imposed on a director by this section is to be treated as if imposed by section 324.

329.   Duty to notify stock exchange of matters notified under preceding sections.

(1)   Whenever a company whose shares or debentures are listed on a recognised investment exchange other than an overseas investment exchange within the meaning of the Financial Services Act 1986 is notified of any matter by a director in consequence of the fulfilment of an obligation imposed by section 324 or 328, and that matter relates to shares or debentures so listed, the company is under obligation to notify that investment exchange of that matter; and the investment exchange may publish, in such manner as it may determine, any information received by it under this subsection.

(2)   An obligation imposed by subsection (1) must be fulfilled before the end of the day next following that on which it arises; but there is disregarded for this purpose a day which is a Saturday or a Sunday or a bank holiday in any part of Great Britain.

(3)   If default is made in complying with this section, the company and every officer of it who is in default is guilty of an offence and liable to a fine and, for continued contravention, to a daily default fine.

Section 732 (restriction on prosecutions) applies to an offence under this section.

Restrictions on a company's power to make loans, etc., to directors and persons connected with them

330.   General restriction on loans etc. to directors and persons connected with them.

(1)   The prohibitions listed below in this section are subject to the exceptions in sections 332 to 338.

(2)   A company shall not—

(a)   make a loan to a director of the company or of its holding company;

(b)   enter into any guarantee or provide any security in connection with a loan made by any person to such a director.

(3)   A relevant company shall not—

(a)   make a quasi-loan to a director of the company or of its holding company;

(b)   make a loan or a quasi-loan to a person connected with such a director;

(c)   enter into a guarantee or provide any security in connection with a loan or quasi-loan made by any other person for such a director or a person so connected.

(4)   A relevant company shall not—

(a)   enter into a credit transaction as creditor for such a director or a person so connected;

(b)   enter into any guarantee or provide any security in connection with a credit transaction made by any other person for such a director or a person so connected.

(5)   For purposes of sections 330 to 346, a shadow director is treated as a director.

(6)   A company shall not arrange for the assignment to it, or the assumption by it, of any rights, obligations or liabilities under a transaction which, if it had been entered into by the company, would have contravened subsection (2), (3) or (4); but for the purposes of sections 330 to 347 the transaction is to be treated as having been entered into on the date of the arrangement.

(7)   A company shall not take part in any arrangement whereby—

(a)   another person enters into a transaction which, if it had been entered into by the company, would have contravened any of subsections (2), (3), (4) or (6); and

(b)   that other person, in pursuance of the arrangement, has obtained or is to obtain any benefit from the company or its holding company or a subsidiary of the company or its holding company.

331.   Definitions for ss. 330 ff.

(1)   The following subsections apply for the interpretation of sections 330 to 346.

(2)   'Guarantee' includes indemnity, and cognate expressions are to be construed accordingly.

(3)   A quasi-loan is a transaction under which one party ('the creditor') agrees to pay, or pays otherwise than in pursuance of an agreement, a sum for another ('the borrower') or agrees to reimburse, or reimburses otherwise than in pursuance of an agreement, expenditure incurred by another party for another ('the borrower')—

(a)   on terms that the borrower (or a person on his behalf) will reimburse the creditor; or

(b)   in circumstances giving rise to a liability on the borrower to reimburse the creditor.

(4)   Any reference to the person to whom a quasi-loan is made is a reference to the borrower; and the liabilities of a borrower under a quasi-loan include the liabilities of any person who has agreed to reimburse the creditor on behalf of the borrower.

(6)   'Relevant company' means a company which—

    (a)   is a public company, or

    (b)   is a subsidiary of a public company, or

    (c)   is a subsidiary of a company which has as another subsidiary a public company, or

    (d)   has a subsidiary which is a public company.

(7)   A credit transaction is a transaction under which one party ('the creditor')—

    (a)   supplies any goods or sells any land under a hire-purchase agreement or a conditional sale agreement;

    (b)   leases or hires any land or goods in return for periodical payments;

    (c)   otherwise disposes of land or supplies goods or services on the understanding that payment (whether in a lump sum or instalments or by way of periodical payments or otherwise) is to be deferred.

(8)   'Services' means anything other than goods or land.

(9)   A transaction or arrangement is made 'for' a person if—

    (a)   in the case of a loan or quasi-loan, it is made to him;

    (b)   in the case of a credit transaction, he is the person to whom goods or services are supplied, or land is sold or otherwise disposed of, under the transaction;

    (c)   in the case of a guarantee or security, it is entered into or provided in connection with a loan or quasi-loan made to him or a credit transaction made for him;

    (d)   in the case of an arrangement within subsection (6) or (7) of section 330, the transaction to which the arrangement relates was made for him; and

    (e)   in the case of any other transaction or arrangement for the supply or transfer of, or of any interest in, goods, land or services, he is the person to whom the goods, land or services (or the interest) are supplied or transferred.

(10)   'Conditional sale agreement' means the same as in the Consumer Credit Act 1974.

332.   Short-term quasi-loans.

(1)   Subsection (3) of section 330 does not prohibit a company ('the creditor') from making a quasi-loan to one of its directors or to a director of its holding company if—

    (a)   the quasi-loan contains a term requiring the director or a person on his behalf to reimburse the creditor his expenditure within 2 months of its being incurred; and

    (b)   the aggregate of the amount of that quasi-loan and of the amount outstanding under each relevant quasi-loan does not exceed £5,000.

(2)   A quasi-loan is relevant for this purpose if it was made to the director by virtue of this section by the creditor or its subsidiary or, where the director is a director of the creditor's holding company, any other subsidiary of that company; and 'the amount outstanding' is the amount of the outstanding liabilities of the person to whom the quasi-loan was made.

333.   Inter-company loans in same group.

In the case of a relevant company which is a member of a group of companies (meaning a holding company and its subsidiaries), paragraphs (b) and (c) of section 330(3) do not prohibit the company from—

    (a)   making a loan or quasi-loan to another member of that group; or

    (b)   entering into a guarantee or providing any security in connection with a loan or quasi-loan made by any person to another member of the group,

by reason only that a director of one member of the group is associated with another.

334. Loans of small amounts.

Without prejudice to any other provision of sections 332 to 338, paragraph (a) of section 330(2) does not prohibit a company from making a loan to a director of the company or of its holding company if the aggregate of the relevant amounts does not exceed £5,000.

335. Minor and business transactions.

(1) Section 330(4) does not prohibit a company from entering into a transaction for a person if the aggregate of the relevant amounts does not exceed £10,000.

(2) Section 330(4) does not prohibit a company from entering into a transaction for a person if—

(a) the transaction is entered into by the company in the ordinary course of its business; and

(b) the value of the transaction is not greater, and the terms on which it is entered into are no more favourable, in respect of the person for whom the transaction is made, than that or those which it is reasonable to expect the company to have offered to or in respect of a person of the same financial standing but unconnected with the company.

336. Transactions at behest of holding company.

The following transactions are excepted from the prohibitions of section 330—

(a) a loan or quasi-loan by a company to its holding company, or a company entering into a guarantee or providing any security in connection with a loan or quasi-loan made by any person to its holding company;

(b) a company entering into a credit transaction as creditor for its holding company, or entering into a guarantee or providing any security in connection with a credit transaction made by any other person for its holding company.

337. Funding of director's expenditure on duty to company.

(1) A company is not prohibited by section 330 from doing anything to provide a director with funds to meet expenditure incurred or to be incurred by him for the purposes of the company or for the purpose of enabling him properly to perform his duties as an officer of the company.

(2) Nor does the section prohibit a company from doing anything to enable a director to avoid incurring such expenditure.

(3) Subsections (1) and (2) apply only if one of the following conditions is satisfied—

(a) the thing in question is done with prior approval of the company given at a general meeting at which there are disclosed all the matters mentioned in the next subsection;

(b) that thing is done on condition that, if the approval of the company is not so given at or before the next annual general meeting, the loan is to be repaid, or any other liability arising under any such transaction discharged, within 6 months from the conclusion of that meeting;

but those subsections do not authorise a relevant company to enter into any transaction if the aggregate of the relevant amounts exceeds £20,000.

(4) The matters to be disclosed under subsection (3)(a) are—

(a) the purpose of the expenditure incurred or to be incurred, or which would otherwise be incurred, by the director,

(b) the amount of the funds to be provided by the company, and

(c) the extent of the company's liability under any transaction which is or is connected with the thing in question.

338. Loan or quasi-loan by money-lending company.

(1) There is excepted from the prohibitions in section 330—

(a) a loan or quasi-loan made by a money-lending company to any person; or

(b) a money-lending company entering into a guarantee in connection with any other loan or quasi-loan.

(2) 'Money-lending company' means a company whose ordinary business includes the making of loans or quasi-loans, or the giving of guarantees in connection with loans or quasi-loans.

(3) Subsection (1) applies only if both the following conditions are satisfied—

(a) the loan or quasi-loan in question is made by the company, or it enters into the guarantee, in the ordinary course of the company's business; and

(b) the amount of the loan or quasi-loan, or the amount guaranteed, is not greater, and the terms of the loan, quasi-loan or guarantee are not more favourable, in the case of the person to whom the loan or quasi-loan is made or in respect of whom the guarantee is entered into, than that or those which it is reasonable to expect that company to have offered to or in respect of a person of the same financial standing but unconnected with the company.

(4) But subsection (1) does not authorise a relevant company (unless it is a banking company) to enter into any transaction if the aggregate of the relevant amounts exceeds £100,000.

(5) In determining that aggregate, a company which a director does not control is deemed not to be connected with him.

(6) The condition specified in subsection (3)(b) does not of itself prevent a company from making a loan to one of its directors or a director of its holding company—

(a) for the purpose of facilitating the purchase, for use as that director's only or main residence, of the whole or part of any dwelling house together with any land to be occupied and enjoyed with it;

(b) for the purpose of improving a dwelling house or part of a dwelling house so used or any land occupied and enjoyed with it;

(c) in substitution for any loan made by any person and falling within paragraph (a) or (b) of this subsection,

if loans of that description are ordinarily made by the company to its employees and on terms no less favourable than those on which the transaction in question is made, and the aggregate of the relevant amounts does not exceed £100,000.

339. 'Relevant amounts' for purposes of ss. 334 ff.

(1) This section has effect for defining the 'relevant amounts' to be aggregated under sections 334, 335(1), 337(3) and 338(4); and in relation to any proposed transaction or arrangement and the question whether it falls within one or other of the exceptions provided by those sections, 'the relevant exception' is that exception; but where the relevant exception is the one provided by section 334 (loan of small amount), references in this section to a person connected with a director are to be disregarded.

(2) Subject as follows, the relevant amounts in relation to a proposed transaction or arrangement are—

(a) the value of the proposed transaction or arrangement,

(b) the value of any existing arrangement which—

(i) falls within subsection (6) or (7) of section 330, and

(ii) also falls within subsection (3) of this section, and

(iii) was entered into by virtue of the relevant exception by the company or by a subsidiary of the company or, where the proposed transaction or arrangement is to be made for a director of its holding company or a person connected with such a director, by that holding company or any of its subsidiaries;

(c) the amount outstanding under any other transaction—

(i) falling within subsection (3) below, and

(ii) made by virtue of the relevant exception, and

(iii)   made by the company or by a subsidiary of the company or, where the proposed transaction or arrangement is to be made for a director of its holding company or a person connected with such a director, by that holding company or any of its subsidiaries.

(3)   A transaction falls within this subsection if it was made—

(a)   for the director for whom the proposed transaction or arrangement is to be made, or for any person connected with that director; or

(b)   where the proposed transaction or arrangement is to be made for a person connected with a director of a company, for that director or any person connected with him;

and an arrangement also falls within this subsection if it relates to a transaction which does so.

(4)   But where the proposed transaction falls within section 338 and is one which a banking company proposes to enter into under subsection (6) of that section (housing loans, etc.), any other transaction or arrangement which apart from this subsection would fall within subsection (3) of this section does not do so unless it was entered into in pursuance of section 338(6).

(5)   A transaction entered into by a company which is (at the time of that transaction being entered into) a subsidiary of the company which is to make the proposed transaction, or is a subsidiary of that company's holding company, does not fall within subsection (3) if at the time when the question arises (that is to say, the question whether the proposed transaction or arrangement falls within any relevant exception), it no longer is such a subsidiary.

(6)   Values for purposes of subsection (2) of this section are to be determined in accordance with the section next following; and 'the amount outstanding' for purposes of subsection (2)(c) above is the value of the transaction less any amount by which that value has been reduced.

340.   'Value' of transactions and arrangements.

(1)   This section has effect for determining the value of a transaction or arrangement for purposes of sections 330 to 339.

(2)   The value of a loan is the amount of its principal.

(3)   The value of a quasi-loan is the amount, or maximum amount, which the person to whom the quasi-loan is made is liable to reimburse the creditor.

(4)   The value of a guarantee or security is the amount guaranteed or secured.

(5)   The value of an arrangement to which section 330(6) or (7) applies is the value of the transaction to which the arrangement relates less any amount by which the liabilities under the arrangement or transaction of the person for whom the transaction was made have been reduced.

(6)   The value of a transaction or arrangement not falling within subsections (2) to (5) above is the price which it is reasonable to expect could be obtained for the goods, land or services to which the transaction or arrangement relates if they had been supplied (at the time the transaction or arrangement is entered into) in the ordinary course of business and on the same terms (apart from price) as they have been supplied, or are to be supplied, under the transaction or arrangement in question.

(7)   For purposes of this section, the value of a transaction or arrangement which is not capable of being expressed as a specific sum of money (because the amount of any liability arising under the transaction or arrangement is unascertainable, or for any other reason), whether or not any liability under the transaction or arrangement has been reduced, is deemed to exceed £100,000.

341.   Civil remedies for breach of s. 330.

(1)   If a company enters into a transaction or arrangement in contravention of section 330, the transaction or arrangement is voidable at the instance of the company unless—

(a) restitution of any money or any other asset which is the subject matter of the arrangement or transaction is no longer possible, or the company has been indemnified in pursuance of subsection (2)(b) below for the loss or damage suffered by it, or

(b) any rights acquired bona fide for value and without actual notice of the contravention by a person other than the person for whom the transaction or arrangement was made would be affected by its avoidance.

(2) Where an arrangement or transaction is made by a company for a director of the company or its holding company or a person connected with such a director in contravention of section 330, that director and the person so connected and any other director of the company who authorised the transaction or arrangement (whether or not it has been avoided in pursuance of subsection (1)) is liable—

(a) to account to the company for any gain which he has made directly or indirectly by the arrangement or transaction; and

(b) (jointly and severally with any other person liable under this subsection) to indemnify the company for any loss or damage resulting from the arrangement or transaction.

(3) Subsection (2) is without prejudice to any liability imposed otherwise than by that subsection, but is subject to the next two subsections.

(4) Where an arrangement or transaction is entered into by a company and a person connected with a director of the company or its holding company in contravention of section 330, that director is not liable under subsection (2) of this section if he shows that he took all reasonable steps to secure the company's compliance with that section.

(5) In any case, a person so connected and any such other director as is mentioned in subsection (2) is not so liable if he shows that, at the time the arrangement or transaction was entered into, he did not know the relevant circumstances constituting the contravention.

342. Criminal penalties for breach of s. 330.

(1) A director of a relevant company who authorises or permits the company to enter into a transaction or arrangement knowing or having reasonable cause to believe that the company was thereby contravening section 330 is guilty of an offence.

(2) A relevant company which enters into a transaction or arrangement for one of its directors or for a director of its holding company in contravention of section 330 is guilty of an offence.

(3) A person who procures a relevant company to enter into a transaction or arrangement knowing or having reasonable cause to believe that the company was thereby contravening section 330 is guilty of an offence.

(4) A person guilty of an offence under this section is liable to imprisonment or a fine, or both.

(5) A relevant company is not guilty of an offence under subsection (2) if it shows that, at the time the transaction or arrangement was entered into, it did not know the relevant circumstances.

Supplementary

345. Power to increase financial limits.

(1) The Secretary of State may by order in a statutory instrument substitute for any sum of money specified in this Part a larger sum specified in the order.

(2) An order under this section is subject to annulment in pursuance of a resolution of either House of Parliament.

(3) Such an order does not have effect in relation to anything done or not done before its coming into force; and accordingly, proceedings in respect of any liability (whether civil or criminal) incurred before that time may be continued or instituted as if the order had not been made.

346. 'Connected persons', etc.

(1)   This section has effect with respect to references in this Part to a person being 'connected' with a director of a company, and to a director being 'associated with' or 'controlling' a body corporate.

(2)   A person is connected with a director of a company if, but only if, he (not being himself a director of it) is—

(a)   that director's spouse, child or stepchild; or

(b)   except where the context otherwise requires, a body corporate with which the director is associated; or

(c)   a person acting in his capacity as trustee of any trust the beneficiaries of which include—

(i)   the director, his spouse or any children or stepchildren of his, or

(ii)   a body corporate with which he is associated,

or of a trust whose terms confer a power on the trustees that may be exercised for the benefit of the director, his spouse, or any children or stepchildren of his, or any such body corporate; or

(d)   a person acting in his capacity as partner of that director or of any person who, by virtue of paragraph (a), (b) or (c) of this subsection, is connected with that director; or

(e)   a Scottish firm in which—

(i)   that director is a partner,

(ii)   a partner is a person who, by virtue of paragraph (a), (b) or (c) above, is connected with that director, or

(iii)   a partner is a Scottish firm in which that director is a partner or in which there is a partner who, by virtue of paragraph (a), (b) or (c) above, is connected with that director.

(3)   In subsection (2)—

(a)   a reference to the child or stepchild of any person includes an illegitimate child of his, but does not include any person who has attained the age of 18; and

(b)   paragraph (c) does not apply to a person acting in his capacity as trustee under an employees' share scheme or a pension scheme.

(4)   A director of a company is associated with a body corporate if, but only if, he and the persons connected with him, together—

(a)   are interested in shares comprised in the equity share capital of that body corporate of a nominal value equal to at least one-fifth of that share capital; or

(b)   are entitled to exercise or control the exercise of more than one-fifth of the voting power at any general meeting of that body.

(5)   A director of a company is deemed to control a body corporate if, but only if—

(a)   he or any person connected with him is interested in any part of the equity share capital of that body or is entitled to exercise or control the exercise of any part of the voting power at any general meeting of that body; and

(b)   that director, the persons connected with him and the other directors of that company, together, are interested in more than one-half of that share capital or are entitled to exercise or control the exercise of more than one-half of that voting power.

(6)   For purposes of subsections (4) and (5)—

(a)   a body corporate with which a director is associated is not to be treated as connected with that director unless it is also connected with him by virtue of subsection (2)(c) or (d); and

(b)   a trustee of a trust the beneficiaries of which include (or may include) a body corporate with which a director is associated is not to be treated as connected with a director by reason only of that fact.

(7)   The rules set out in Part I of Schedule 13 apply for the purposes of subsections (4) and (5).

(8)   References in those subsections to voting power the exercise of which is controlled by a director include voting power whose exercise is controlled by a body corporate controlled by him; but this is without prejudice to other provisions of subsections (4) and (5).

347.   Transactions under foreign law.

For purposes of sections 319 to 322 and 330 to 343, it is immaterial whether the law which (apart from this Act) governs any arrangement or transaction is the law of the United Kingdom, or of a part of it, or not.

PART XI
COMPANY ADMINISTRATION AND PROCEDURE

CHAPTER I
COMPANY IDENTIFICATION

348.   Company name to appear outside place of business.

(1)   Every company shall paint or affix, and keep painted or affixed, its name on the outside of every office or place in which its business is carried on, in a conspicuous position and in letters easily legible.

(2)   If a company does not paint or affix its name as required above, the company and every officer of it who is in default is liable to a fine; and if a company does not keep its name painted or affixed as so required, the company and every officer of it who is in default is liable to a fine and, for continued contravention, to a daily default fine.

349.   Company's name to appear in its correspondence, etc.

(1)   Every company shall have its name mentioned in legible characters—
    (a)   in all business letters of the company,
    (b)   in all its notices and other official publications,
    (c)   in all bills of exchange, promissory notes, endorsements, cheques and orders for money or goods purporting to be signed by or on behalf of the company, and
    (d)   in all its bills of parcels, invoices, receipts and letters of credit.

(2)   If a company fails to comply with subsection (1) it is liable to a fine.

(3)   If an officer of a company or a person on its behalf—
    (a)   issues or authorises the issue of any business letter of the company, or any notice or other official publication of the company, in which the company's name is not mentioned as required by subsection (1), or
    (b)   issues or authorises the issue of any bill of parcels, invoice, receipt or letter of credit of the company in which its name is not so mentioned,
he is liable to a fine.

(4)   If an officer of a company or a person on its behalf signs or authorises to be signed on behalf of the company any bill of exchange, promissory note, endorsement, cheque or order for money or goods in which the company's name is not mentioned as required by subsection (1), he is liable to a fine; and he is further personally liable to the holder of the bill of exchange, promissory note, cheque or order for money or goods for the amount of it (unless it is duly paid by the company).

350.   Company seal.

(1)   A company which has a common seal shall have its name engraved in legible characters on the seal; and if it fails to comply with this subsection it is liable to a fine.

(2)   If an officer of a company or a person on its behalf uses or authorises the use of any seal purporting to be a seal of the company on which its name is not engraved as required by subsection (1), he is liable to a fine.

351. Particulars in correspondence, etc.

(1) Every company shall have the following particulars mentioned in legible characters in all business letters and order forms of the company, that is to say—

  (a)   the company's place of registration and the number with which it is registered,

  (b)   the address of its registered office,

  (c)   in the case of an investment company (as defined in section 266), the fact that it is such a company, and

  (d)   in the case of a limited company exempt from the obligation to use the word 'limited' as part of its name, the fact that it is a limited company.

(2) If in the case of a company having a share capital there is on the stationery used for any such letters, or on the company's order forms, a reference to the amount of share capital, the reference must be to paid-up share capital.

(5) As to contraventions of this section, the following applies—

  (a)   if a company fails to comply with subsection (1) or (2), it is liable to a fine,

  (b)   if an officer of a company or a person on its behalf issues or authorises the issue of any business letter or order form not complying with those subsections, he is liable to a fine.

CHAPTER II
REGISTER OF MEMBERS

352. Obligation to keep and enter up register.

(1) Every company shall keep a register of its members and enter in it the particulars required by this section.

(2) There shall be entered in the register—

  (a)   the names and addresses of the members;

  (b)   the date on which each person was registered as a member; and

  (c)   the date at which any person ceased to be a member.

(3) The following applies in the case of a company having a share capital—

  (a)   with the names and addresses of the members there shall be entered a statement—

       (i)   of the shares held by each member, distinguishing each share by its number (so long as the share has a number) and, where the company has more than one class of issued shares, by its class, and

       (ii)   of the amount paid or agreed to be considered as paid on the shares of each member;

  (b)   where the company has converted any of its shares into stock and given notice of the conversion to the registrar of companies, the register shall show the amount and class of stock held by each member, instead of the amount of shares and the particulars relating to shares specified in paragraph (a).

(4) In the case of a company which does not have a share capital but has more than one class of members, there shall be entered in the register, with the names and addresses of the members, the class to which each member belongs.

(5) If a company makes default in complying with this section, the company and every officer of it who is in default is liable to a fine and, for continued contravention, to a daily default fine.

(6) An entry relating to a former member of the company may be removed from the register after the expiration of 20 years from the date on which he ceased to be a member.

(7) Liability incurred by a company from the making or deletion of an entry in its register of members, or from a failure to make or delete any such entry, is not enforceable more than 20 years after the date on which the entry was made or deleted or, in the case of any such failure, the failure first occurred.

This is without prejudice to any lesser period of limitation.

352A. Statement that company has only one member.

(1) If the number of members of a private company limited by shares or by guarantee falls to one there shall upon the occurrence of that event be entered in the company's register of members with the name and address of the sole member—

(i)   a statement that the company has only one member, and

(ii)   the date on which the company became a company having only one member.

(2) If the membership of a private company limited by shares or by guarantee increases from one to two or more members there shall upon the occurrence of that event be entered in the company's register of members, with the name and address of the person who was formerly the sole member, a statement that the company has ceased to have only one member together with the date on which that event occurred.

(3) If a company makes default in complying with this section, the company and every officer of it who is in default is liable to a fine and, for continued contravention, to a daily default fine.

353. Location of register.

(1) A company's register of members shall be kept at its registered office, except that—

(a)   if the work of making it up is done at another office of the company, it may be kept there; and

(b)   if the company arranges with some other person for the making up of the register to be undertaken on its behalf by that other, it may be kept at the office of the other at which the work is done;

but it must not be kept, in the case of a company registered in England and Wales, at any place elsewhere than in England and Wales or, in the case of a company registered in Scotland, at any place elsewhere than in Scotland.

(2) Subject as follows, every company shall send notice in the prescribed form to the registrar of companies of the place where its register of members is kept, and of any change in that place.

(3) The notice need not be sent if the register has, at all times since it came into existence (or, in the case of a register in existence on 1 July 1948, at all times since then) been kept at the company's registered office.

(4) If a company makes default for 14 days in complying with subsection (2), the company and every officer of it who is in default is liable to a fine and, for continued contravention, to a daily default fine.

354. Index of members.

(1) Every company having more than 50 members shall, unless the register of members is in such a form as to constitute in itself an index, keep an index of the names of the members of the company and shall, within 14 days after the date on which any alteration is made in the register of members, make any necessary alteration in the index.

(2) The index shall in respect of each member contain a sufficient indication to enable the account of that member in the register to be readily found.

(3) The index shall be at all times kept at the same place as the register of members.

(4) If default is made in complying with this section, the company and every officer of it who is in default is liable to a fine and, for continued contravention, to a daily default fine.

355. Entries in register in relation to share warrants.

(1) On the issue of a share warrant the company shall strike out of its register of members the name of the member then entered in it as holding the shares specified in the warrant as if he had ceased to be a member, and shall enter in the register the following particulars, namely—

(a) the fact of the issue of the warrant;

(b) a statement of the shares included in the warrant, distinguishing each share by its number so long as the share has a number; and

(c) the date of the issue of the warrant.

(2) Subject to the company's articles, the bearer of a share warrant is entitled, on surrendering it for cancellation, to have his name entered as a member in the register of members.

(3) The company is responsible for any loss incurred by any person by reason of the company entering in the register the name of a bearer of a share warrant in respect of the shares specified in it without the warrant being surrendered and cancelled.

(4) Until the warrant is surrendered, the particulars specified in subsection (1) are deemed to be those required by this Act to be entered in the register of members; and, on the surrender, the date of the surrender must be entered.

(5) Except as provided by section 291(2) (director's share qualification), the bearer of a share warrant may, if the articles of the company so provide, be deemed a member of the company within the meaning of this Act, either to the full extent or for any purposes defined in the articles.

356. Inspection of register and index.

(1) Except when the register of members is closed under the provisions of this Act, the register and the index of members' names shall be open to the inspection of any member of the company without charge, and of any other person on payment of such fee as may be prescribed.

(3) Any member of the company or other person may require a copy of the register, or of any part of it, on payment of such fee as may be prescribed; and the company shall cause any copy so required by a person to be sent to him within 10 days beginning with the day next following that on which the requirement is received by the company.

(5) If an inspection required under this section is refused, or if a copy so required is not sent within the proper period, the company and every officer of it who is in default is liable in respect of each offence to a fine.

(6) In the case of such refusal or default, the court may by order compel an immediate inspection of the register and index, or direct that the copies required be sent to the persons requiring them.

357. Non-compliance with ss. 353, 354, 356; agent's default.

Where under section 353(1)(b), the register of members is kept at the office of some person other than the company, and by reason of any default of his the company fails to comply with—

section 353(2) (notice to registrar),

section 354(3) (index to be kept with register), or

section 356 (inspection),

or with any requirement of this Act as to the production of the register, that other person is liable to the same penalties as if he were an officer of the company who was in default, and the power of the court under section 356(6) extends to the making of orders against that other and his officers and servants.

358. Power to close register.

A company may, on giving notice by advertisement in a newspaper circulating in the district in which the company's registered office is situated, close the register of members for any time or times not exceeding in the whole 30 days in each year.

359. Power of court to rectify register.

(1) If—

(a) the name of any person is, without sufficient cause, entered in or omitted from a company's register of members, or

(b)   default is made or unnecessary delay takes place in entering on the register the fact of any person having ceased to be a member,

the person aggrieved, or any member of the company, or the company, may apply to the court for rectification of the register.

(2)   The court may either refuse the application or may order rectification of the register and payment by the company of any damages sustained by any party aggrieved.

(3)   On such an application the court may decide any question relating to the title of a person who is a party to the application to have his name entered in or omitted from the register, whether the question arises between members or alleged members, or between members or alleged members on the one hand and the company on the other hand, and generally may decide any question necessary or expedient to be decided for rectification of the register.

(4)   In the case of a company required by this Act to send a list of its members to the registrar of companies, the court, when making an order for rectification of the register, shall by its order direct notice of the rectification to be given to the registrar.

360.   Trusts not to be entered on register in England and Wales.

No notice of any trust, expressed, implied or constructive, shall be entered on the register, or be receivable by the registrar, in the case of companies registered in England and Wales.

361.   Register to be evidence.

The register of members is prima facie evidence of any matters which are by this Act directed or authorised to be inserted in it.

CHAPTER III
ANNUAL RETURN

363.   Duty to deliver annual returns.

(1)   Every company shall deliver to the registrar successive annual returns each of which is made up to a date not later than the date which is from time to time the company's 'return date', that is—

(a)   the anniversary of the company's incorporation, or

(b)   if the company's last return delivered in accordance with this Chapter was made up to a different date, the anniversary of that date.

(2)   Each return shall—

(a)   be in the prescribed form,

(b)   contain the information required by or under the following provisions of this Chapter, and

(c)   be signed by a director or the secretary of the company;

and it shall be delivered to the registrar within 28 days after the date to which it is made up.

(3)   If a company fails to deliver an annual return in accordance with this Chapter before the end of the period of 28 days after a return date, the company is guilty of an offence and liable to a fine and, in the case of continued contravention, to a daily default fine.

The contravention continues until such time as an annual return made up to that return date and complying with the requirements of subsection (2) (except as to date of delivery) is delivered by the company to the registrar.

(4)   Where a company is guilty of an offence under subsection (3), every director or secretary of the company is similarly liable unless he shows that he took all reasonable steps to avoid the commission or continuation of the offence.

(5)   The references in this section to a return being delivered 'in accordance with this Chapter' are—

(a)   in relation to a return made on or after 1 October 1990, to a return with respect to which all the requirements of subsection (2) are complied with;

(b)   in relation to a return made before 1 October 1990, to a return with respect to which the formal and substantive requirements of this Chapter as it then had effect were complied with, whether or not the return was delivered in time.

364.   Contents of annual return: general.

(1)   Every annual return shall state the date to which it is made up and shall contain the following information—

(a)   the address of the company's registered office;

(b)   the type of company it is and its principal business activities;

(c)   the name and address of the company secretary;

(d)   the name and address of every director of the company;

(e)   in the case of each individual director—

(i)   his nationality, date of birth and business occupation, and

(ii)   such particulars of other directorships and former names as are required to be contained in the company's register of directors;

(f)   in the case of any corporate director, such particulars of other directorships as would be required to be contained in that register in the case of an individual;

(g)   if the register of members is not kept at the company's registered office, the address of the place where it is kept;

(h)   if any register of debenture holders (or a duplicate of any such register or a part of it) is not kept at the company's registered office, the address of the place where it is kept;

(i)   if the company has elected—

(i)   to dispense under section 252 with the laying of accounts and reports before the company in general meeting, or

(ii)   to dispense under section 366A with the holding of annual general meetings,

a statement to that effect.

(2)   The information as to the company's type shall be given by reference to the classification scheme prescribed for the purposes of this section.

(3)   The information as to the company's principal business activities may be given by reference to one or more categories of any prescribed system of classifying business activities.

(4)   A person's 'name' and 'address' mean, respectively—

(a)   in the case of an individual, his Christian name (or other forename) and surname and his usual residential address;

(b)   in the case of a corporation or Scottish firm, its corporate or firm name and its registered or principal office.

(5)   In the case of a peer, or an individual usually known by a title, the title may be stated instead of his Christian name (or other forename) and surname or in addition to either or both of them.

(6)   Where all the partners in a firm are joint secretaries, the name and principal office of the firm may be stated instead of the names and addresses of the partners.

364A   Contents of annual return: particulars of share capital and shareholders.

(1)   The annual return of a company having a share capital shall contain the following information with respect to its share capital and members.

(2)   The return shall state the total number of issued shares of the company at the date to which the return is made up and the aggregate nominal value of those shares.

(3)   The return shall state with respect to each class of shares in the company—

(a)   the nature of the class, and

(b)   the total number and aggregate nominal value of issued shares of that class at the date to which the return is made up.

(4)   The return shall contain a list of the names and addresses of every person who—

(a)   is a member of the company on the date to which the return is made up, or

(b)   has ceased to be a member of the company since the date to which the last return was made up (or, in the case of the first return, since the incorporation of the company);

and if the names are not arranged in alphabetical order the return shall have annexed to it an index sufficient to enable the name of any person in the list to be easily found.

(5)   The return shall also state—

(a)   the number of shares of each class held by each member of the company at the date to which the return is made up, and

(b)   the number of shares of each class transferred since the date to which the last return was made up (or, in the case of the first return, since the incorporation of the company) by each member or person who has ceased to be a member, and the dates of registration of the transfers.

(6)   The return may, if either of the two immediately preceding returns has given the full particulars required by subsection (4) and (5), give only such particulars as relate to persons ceasing to be or becoming members since the date of the last return and to shares transferred since that date.

(7)   Subsections (4) and (5) do not require the inclusion of particulars entered in an overseas branch register if copies of those entries have not been received at the company's registered office by the date to which the return is made up.

Those particulars shall be included in the company's next annual return after they are received.

(8)   Where the company has converted any of its shares into stock, the return shall give the corresponding information in relation to that stock, stating the amount of stock instead of the number or nominal value of shares.

365.   Supplementary provisions: regulations and interpretation.

(1)   The Secretary of State may by regulations make further provision as to the information to be given in a company's annual return, which may amend or repeal the provisions of sections 364 and 364A.

(2)   Regulations under this section shall be made by statutory instrument which shall be subject to annulment in pursuance of a resolution of either House of Parliament.

(3)   For the purposes of this Chapter, except section 363(2)(c) (signature of annual return), a shadow director shall be deemed to be a director.

CHAPTER IV
MEETINGS AND RESOLUTIONS

Meetings

366.   Annual general meeting.

(1)   Every company shall in each year hold a general meeting as its annual general meeting in addition to any other meetings in that year, and shall specify the meeting as such in the notices calling it.

(2)   However, so long as a company holds its first annual general meeting within 18 months of its incorporation, it need not hold it in the year of its incorporation or in the following year.

(3)   Not more than 15 months shall elapse between the date of one annual general meeting of a company and that of the next.

(4)   If default is made in holding a meeting in accordance with this section, the company and every officer of it who is in default is liable to a fine.

366A.   Election by private company to dispense with annual general meetings.

(1)   A private company may elect (by elective resolution in accordance with section 379A) to dispense with the holding of annual general meetings.

(2)   An election has effect for the year in which it is made and subsequent years, but does not affect any liability already incurred by reason of default in holding an annual general meeting.

(3)   In any year in which an annual general meeting would be required to be held but for the election, and in which no such meeting has been held, any member of the company may, by notice to the company not later than three months before the end of the year, require the holding of an annual general meeting in that year.

(4)   If such a notice is given, the provisions of section 366(1) and (4) apply with respect to the calling of the meeting and the consequences of default.

(5)   If the election ceases to have effect, the company is not obliged under section 366 to hold an annual general meeting in that year if, when the election ceases to have effect, less than three months of the year remains.

This does not affect any obligation of the company to hold an annual general meeting in that year in pursuance of a notice given under subsection (3).

367.   Secretary of State's power to call meeting in default.

(1)   If default is made in holding a meeting in accordance with section 366, the Secretary of State may, on the application of any member of the company, call, or direct the calling of, a general meeting of the company and give such ancillary or consequential directions as he thinks expedient, including directions modifying or supplementing, in relation to the calling, holding and conduct of the meeting, the operation of the company's articles.

(2)   The directions that may be given under subsection (1) include a direction that one member of the company present in person or by proxy shall be deemed to constitute a meeting.

(3)   If default is made in complying with directions of the Secretary of State under subsection (1), the company and every officer of it who is in default is liable to a fine.

(4)   A general meeting held under this section shall, subject to any directions of the Secretary of State, be deemed to be an annual general meeting of the company; but, where a meeting so held is not held in the year in which the default in holding the company's annual general meeting occurred, the meeting so held shall not be treated as the annual general meeting for the year in which it is held unless at that meeting the company resolves that it be so treated.

(5)   Where a company so resolves, a copy of the resolution shall, within 15 days after its passing, be forwarded to the registrar of companies and recorded by him; and if default is made in complying with this subsection, the company and every officer of it who is in default is liable to a fine and, for continued contravention, to a daily default fine.

368.   Extraordinary general meeting on members' requisition.

(1)   The directors of a company shall, on a members' requisition, forthwith proceed duly to convene an extraordinary general meeting of the company.

This applies notwithstanding anything in the company's articles.

(2)   A members' requisition is a requisition of—

(a)   members of the company holding at the date of the deposit of the requisition not less than one-tenth of such of the paid-up capital of the company as at that date carries the right of voting at general meetings of the company; or

(b)   in the case of a company not having a share capital, members of it representing not less than one-tenth of the total voting rights of all the members having at the date of deposit of the requisition a right to vote at general meetings.

(3)   The requisition must state the objects of the meeting, and must be signed by the requisitionists and deposited at the registered office of the company, and may consist of several documents in like form each signed by one or more requisitionists.

(4)   If the directors do not within 21 days from the date of the deposit of the requisition proceed duly to convene a meeting, the requisitionists, or any of them representing more than one-half of the total voting rights of all of them, may themselves convene a meeting, but any meeting so convened shall not be held after the expiration of 3 months from that date.

(5)   A meeting convened under this section by requisitionists shall be convened in the same manner, as nearly as possible, as that in which meetings are to be convened by directors.

(6)   Any reasonable expenses incurred by the requisitionists by reason of the failure of the directors duly to convene a meeting shall be repaid to the requisitionists by the company, and any sum so repaid shall be retained by the company out of any sums due or to become due from the company by way of fees or other remuneration in respect of their services to such of the directors as were in default.

(7)   In the case of a meeting at which a resolution is to be proposed as a special resolution, the directors are deemed not to have duly convened the meeting if they do not give the notice required for special resolutions by section 378(2).

(8)   The directors are deemed not to have duly convened a meeting if they convene a meeting for a date more than 28 days after the date of the notice convening the meeting.

369.   Length of notice for calling meetings.

(1)   A provision of a company's articles is void in so far as it provides for the calling of a meeting of the company (other than an adjourned meeting) by a shorter notice than—

    (a)   in the case of the annual general meeting, 21 days' notice in writing; and

    (b)   in the case of a meeting other than an annual general meeting or a meeting for the passing of a special resolution—

        (i)   7 days' notice in writing in the case of an unlimited company, and

        (ii)   otherwise, 14 days' notice in writing.

(2)   Save in so far as the articles of a company make other provision in that behalf (not being a provision avoided by subsection (1)), a meeting of the company (other than an adjourned meeting) may be called—

    (a)   in the case of the annual general meeting, by 21 days' notice in writing; and

    (b)   in the case of a meeting other than an annual general meeting or a meeting for the passing of a special resolution—

        (i)   by 7 days' notice in writing in the case of an unlimited company, and

        (ii)   otherwise, 14 days' notice in writing.

(3)   Notwithstanding that a meeting is called by shorter notice than that specified in subsection (2) or in the company's articles (as the case may be), it is deemed to have been duly called if it is so agreed—

    (a)   in the case of a meeting called as the annual general meeting, by all the members entitled to attend and vote at it; and

    (b)   otherwise by the requisite majority.

(4)   The requisite majority for this purpose is a majority in number of the members having a right to attend and vote at the meeting, being a majority—

    (a)   together holding not less than 95 per cent in nominal value of the shares giving a right to attend and vote at the meeting; or

    (b)   in the case of a company not having a share capital, together representing not less than 95 per cent of the total voting rights at that meeting of all the members.

A private company may elect (by elective resolution in accordance with section 379A) that the above provisions shall have effect in relation to the company as if for the references to 95 per cent there were substituted references to such lesser percentage, but not less than 90 per cent, as may be specified in the resolution or subsequently determined by the company in general meeting.

370.   General provisions as to meetings and votes.

(1)   The following provisions have effect in so far as the articles of the company do not make other provision in that behalf.

(2)   Notice of the meeting of a company shall be served on every member of it in the manner in which notices are required to be served by Table A (as for the time being in force).

(3)   Two or more members holding not less than one-tenth of the issued share capital or, if the company does not have a share capital, not less than 5 per cent in number of the members of the company may call a meeting.

(4)   Two members personally present are a quorum.

(5)   Any member elected by the members present at a meeting may be chairman of it.

(6)   In the case of a company originally having a share capital, every member has one vote in respect of each share or each £10 of stock held by him; and in any other case every member has one vote.

370A.   Quorum at meetings of the sole member.

Notwithstanding any provision to the contrary in the articles of a private company limited by shares or by guarantee having only one member, one member present in person or by proxy shall be a quorum.

371.   Power of court to order meeting.

(1)   If for any reason it is impracticable to call a meeting of a company in any manner in which meetings of that company may be called, or to conduct the meeting in manner prescribed by the articles or this Act, the court may, either of its own motion or on the application—

(a)   of any director of the company, or

(b)   of any member of the company who would be entitled to vote at the meeting,

order a meeting to be called, held and conducted in any manner the court thinks fit.

(2)   Where such an order is made, the court may give such ancillary or consequential directions as it thinks expedient; and these may include a direction that one member of the company present in person or by proxy be deemed to constitute a meeting.

(3)   A meeting called, held and conducted in accordance with an order under subsection (1) is deemed for all purposes a meeting of the company duly called, held and conducted.

372.   Proxies.

(1)   Any member of a company entitled to attend and vote at a meeting of it is entitled to appoint another person (whether a member or not) as his proxy to attend and vote instead of him; and in the case of a private company a proxy appointed to attend and vote instead of a member has also the same right as the member to speak at the meeting.

(2)   But, unless the articles otherwise provide—

(a)   subsection (1) does not apply in the case of a company not having a share capital; and

(b)   a member of a private company is not entitled to appoint more than one proxy to attend on the same occasion; and

(c)   a proxy is not entitled to vote except on a poll.

(3)   In the case of a company having a share capital, in every notice calling a meeting of the company there shall appear with reasonable prominence a statement that a member entitled to attend and vote is entitled to appoint a proxy or, where that is

allowed, one or more proxies to attend and vote instead of him, and that a proxy need not also be a member.

(4) If default is made in complying with subsection (3) as respects any meeting, every officer of the company who is in default is liable to a fine.

(5) A provision contained in a company's articles is void in so far as it would have the effect of requiring the instrument appointing a proxy, or any other document necessary to show the validity of, or otherwise relating to, the appointment of a proxy, to be received by the company or any other person more than 48 hours before a meeting or adjourned meeting in order that the appointment may be effective.

(6) If for the purpose of any meeting of a company invitations to appoint as proxy a person or one of a number of persons specified in the invitations are issued at the company's expense to some only of the members entitled to be sent a notice of the meeting and to vote at it by proxy, then every officer of the company who knowingly and wilfully authorises or permits their issue in that manner is liable to a fine.

However, an officer is not so liable by reason only of the issue to a member at his request in writing of a form of appointment naming the proxy, or of a list of persons willing to act as proxy, if the form or list is available on request in writing to every member entitled to vote at the meeting by proxy.

(7) This section applies to meetings of any class of members of a company as it applies to general meetings of the company.

373. Right to demand a poll.

(1) A provision contained in a company's articles is void in so far as it would have the effect either—

(a) of excluding the right to demand a poll at a general meeting on any question other than the election of the chairman of the meeting or the adjournment of the meeting; or

(b) of making ineffective a demand for a poll on any such question which is made either—

(i) by not less than 5 members having the right to vote at the meeting; or

(ii) by a member or members representing not less than one-tenth of the total voting rights of all the members having the right to vote at the meeting; or

(iii) by a member or members holding shares in the company conferring a right to vote at the meeting, being shares on which an aggregate sum has been paid up equal to not less than one-tenth of the total sum paid up on all the shares conferring that right.

(2) The instrument appointing a proxy to vote at a meeting of a company is deemed also to confer authority to demand or join in demanding a poll; and for the purposes of subsection (1) a demand by a person as proxy for a member is the same as a demand by the member.

374. Voting on a poll.

On a poll taken at a meeting of a company or a meeting of any class of members of a company, a member entitled to more than one vote need not, if he votes, use all his votes or cast all the votes he uses in the same way.

375. Representation of corporations at meetings.

(1) A corporation, whether or not a company within the meaning of this Act, may—

(a) if it is a member of another corporation, being such a company, by resolution of its directors or other governing body authorise such person as it thinks fit to act as its representative at any meeting of the company or at any meeting of any class of members of the company;

(b) if it is a creditor (including a holder of debentures) of another corporation, being such a company, by resolution of its directors or other governing body authorise such person as it thinks fit to act as its representative at any meeting of creditors of the company held in pursuance of this Act or of rules made under it, or in pursuance of the provisions contained in any debenture or trust deed, as the case may be.

(2)   A person so authorised is entitled to exercise the same powers on behalf of the corporation which he represents as that corporation could exercise if it were an individual shareholder, creditor or debenture-holder of the other company.

Resolutions

376.   Circulation of members' resolutions.

(1)   Subject to the section next following, it is the duty of a company, on the requisition in writing of such number of members as is specified below and (unless the company otherwise resolves) at the expense of the requisitionists—

(a)   to give to members of the company entitled to receive notice of the next annual general meeting notice of any resolution which may properly be moved and is intended to be moved at that meeting;

(b)   to circulate to members entitled to have notice of any general meeting sent to them any statement of not more than 1,000 words with respect to the matter referred to in any proposed resolution or the business to be dealt with at that meeting.

(2)   The number of members necessary for a requisition under subsection (1) is—

(a)   any number representing not less than one-twentieth of the total voting rights of all the members having at the date of the requisition a right to vote at the meeting to which the requisition relates; or

(b)   not less than 100 members holding shares in the company on which there has been paid up an average sum, per member, of not less than £100.

(3)   Notice of any such resolution shall be given, and any such statement shall be circulated, to members of the company entitled to have notice of the meeting sent to them, by serving a copy of the resolution or statement on each such member in any manner permitted for service of notice of the meeting.

(4)   Notice of any such resolution shall be given to any other member of the company by giving notice of the general effect of the resolution in any manner permitted for giving him notice of meetings of the company.

(5)   For compliance with subsections (3) and (4), the copy must be served, or notice of the effect of the resolution be given (as the case may be), in the same manner and (so far as practicable) at the same time as notice of the meeting; and, where it is not practicable for it to be served or given at the same time, it must be served or given as soon as practicable thereafter.

(6)   The business which may be dealt with at an annual general meeting includes any resolution of which notice is given in accordance with this section; and for purposes of this subsection notice is deemed to have been so given notwithstanding the accidental omission, in giving it, of one or more members. This has effect notwithstanding anything in the company's articles.

(7)   In the event of default in complying with this section, every officer of the company who is in default is liable to a fine.

377.   In certain cases, compliance with s. 376 not required.

(1)   A company is not bound under section 376 to give notice of a resolution or to circulate a statement unless—

(a)   a copy of the requisition signed by the requisitionists (or two or more copies which between them contain the signatures of all the requisitionists) is deposited at the registered office of the company—

(i)   in the case of a requisition requiring notice of a resolution, not less than 6 weeks before the meeting, and

(ii)   otherwise, not less than one week before the meeting; and

(b)   there is deposited or tendered with the requisition a sum reasonably sufficient to meet the company's expenses in giving effect to it.

(2)   But if, after a copy of a requisition requiring notice of a resolution has been deposited at the company's registered office, an annual general meeting is called for a date 6 weeks or less after the copy has been deposited, the copy (though not deposited within the time required by subsection (1)) is deemed properly deposited for the purposes of that subsection.

(3)   The company is also not bound under section 376 to circulate a statement if, on the application either of the company or of any other person who claims to be aggrieved, the court is satisfied that the rights conferred by that section are being abused to secure needless publicity for defamatory matter; and the court may order the company's costs on such an application to be paid in whole or in part by the requisitionists, notwithstanding that they are not parties to the application.

378.   Extraordinary and special resolutions.

(1)   A resolution is an extraordinary resolution when it has been passed by a majority of not less than three-fourths of such members as (being entitled to do so) vote in person or, where proxies are allowed, by proxy, at a general meeting of which notice specifying the intention to propose the resolution as an extraordinary resolution has been duly given.

(2)   A resolution is a special resolution when it has been passed by such a majority as is required for the passing of an extraordinary resolution and at a general meeting of which not less than 21 days' notice, specifying the intention to propose the resolution as a special resolution, has been duly given.

(3)   If it is so agreed by a majority in number of the members having the right to attend and vote at such a meeting, being a majority—

(a)   together holding not less than 95 per cent in nominal value of the shares giving that right; or

(b)   in the case of a company not having a share capital, together representing not less than 95 per cent of the total voting rights at that meeting of all the members,

a resolution may be proposed and passed as a special resolution at a meeting of which less than 21 days' notice has been given.

A private company may elect (by elective resolution in accordance with section 379A) that the above provisions shall have effect in relation to the company as if for the references to 95 per cent there were substituted references to such lesser percentage, but not less than 90 per cent, as may be specified in the resolution or subsequently determined by the company in general meeting.

(4)   At any meeting at which an extraordinary resolution or a special resolution is submitted to be passed, a declaration by the chairman that the resolution is carried is, unless a poll is demanded, conclusive evidence of the fact without proof of the number or proportion of the votes recorded in favour of or against the resolution.

(5)   In computing the majority on a poll demanded on the question that an extraordinary resolution or a special resolution be passed, reference is to be had to the number of votes cast for and against the resolution.

(6)   For purposes of this section, notice of a meeting is deemed duly given, and the meeting duly held, when the notice is given and the meeting held in the manner provided by this Act or the company's articles.

379.   Resolution requiring special notice.

(1)   Where by any provision of this Act special notice is required of a resolution, the resolution is not effective unless notice of the intention to move it has been given to the company at least 28 days before the meeting at which it is moved.

(2)   The company shall give its members notice of any such resolution at the same time and in the same manner as it gives notice of the meeting or, if that is not practicable,

shall give them notice either by advertisement in a newspaper having an appropriate circulation or in any other mode allowed by the company's articles, at least 21 days before the meeting.

(3)   If, after notice of the intention to move such a resolution has been given to the company, a meeting is called for a date 28 days or less after the notice has been given, the notice is deemed properly given, though not given within the time required.

379A.   Elective resolution of private company.

(1)   An election by a private company for the purposes of—

    (a)   section 80A (election as to duration of authority to allot shares),

    (b)   section 252 (election to dispense with laying of accounts and reports before general meeting),

    (c)   section 366A (election to dispense with holding of annual general meeting),

    (d)   section 369(4) or 378(3) (election as to majority required to authorise short notice of meeting), or

    (e)   section 386 (election to dispense with appointment of auditors annually), shall be made by resolution of the company in general meeting in accordance with this section.

Such a resolution is referred to in this Act as an 'elective resolution'.

(2)   An elective resolution is not effective unless—

    (a)   at least 21 days' notice in writing is given of the meeting, stating that an elective resolution is to be proposed and stating the terms of the resolution, and

    (b)   the resolution is agreed to at the meeting, in person or by proxy, by all the members entitled to attend and vote at the meeting.

(2A)   An elective resolution is effective notwithstanding the fact that less than 21 days' notice in writing of the meeting is given if all the members entitled to attend and vote at the meeting so agree.

(3)   The company may revoke an elective resolution by passing an ordinary resolution to that effect.

(4)   An elective resolution shall cease to have effect if the company is re-registered as a public company.

(5)   An elective resolution may be passed or revoked in accordance with this section, and the provisions referred to in subsection (1) have effect, notwithstanding any contrary provision in the company's articles of association.

380.   Registration, etc. of resolutions and agreements.

(1)   A copy of every resolution or agreement to which this section applies shall, within 15 days after it is passed or made, be forwarded to the registrar of companies and recorded by him; and it must be either a printed copy or else a copy in some other form approved by the registrar.

(2)   Where articles have been registered, a copy of every such resolution or agreement for the time being in force shall be embodied in or annexed to every copy of the articles issued after the passing of the resolution or the making of the agreement.

(3)   Where articles have not been registered, a printed copy of every such resolution or agreement shall be forwarded to any member at his request on payment of 5 pence or such less sum as the company may direct.

(4)   This section applies to—

    (a)   special resolutions;

    (b)   extraordinary resolutions;

    (bb)   an elective resolution or a resolution revoking such a resolution;

    (c)   resolutions or agreements which have been agreed to by all the members of a company but which, if not so agreed to, would not have been effective for their purpose unless (as the case may be) they had been passed as special resolutions or as extraordinary resolutions;

(d)   resolutions or agreements which have been agreed to by all the members of some class of shareholders but which, if not so agreed to, would not have been effective for their purpose unless they had been passed by some particular majority or otherwise in some particular manner, and all resolutions or agreements which effectively bind all the members of any class of shareholders though not agreed to by all those members;

(e)   a resolution passed by the directors of a company in compliance with a direction under section 31(2) (change of name on Secretary of State's direction);

(f)   a resolution of a company to give, vary, revoke or renew an authority to the directors for the purposes of section 80 (allotment of relevant securities);

(g)   a resolution of the directors passed under section 147(2) (alteration of memorandum on company ceasing to be a public company, following acquisition of its own shares);

(h)   a resolution conferring, varying, revoking or renewing authority under section 166 (market purchase of company's own shares);

(j)   a resolution for voluntary winding up, passed under section 84(1)(a) of the Insolvency Act;

(k)   a resolution passed by the directors of an old public company, under section 2(1) of the Consequential Provisions Act, that the company should be re-registered as a public company;

(l)   a resolution of the directors passed by virtue of regulation 16(2) of the Uncertificated Securities Regulations 1995 (which allow title to a company's shares to be evidenced and transferred without written instrument); and

(m)   a resolution of a company passed by virtue of regulation 16(6) of the Uncertificated Securities Regulations 1995 (which prevents or reverses a resolution of the directors under regulation 16(2) of those Regulations).

(5)   If a company fails to comply with subsection (1), the company and every officer of it who is in default is liable to a fine and, for continued contravention, to a daily default fine.

(6)   If a company fails to comply with subsection (2) or (3), the company and every officer of it who is in default is liable to a fine.

(7)   For purposes of subsections (5) and (6), a liquidator of a company is deemed an officer of it.

381.   Resolution passed at adjourned meeting.
Where a resolution is passed at an adjourned meeting of—
(a)   a company;
(b)   the holders of any class of shares in a company;
(c)   the directors of a company;
the resolution is for all purposes to be treated as having been passed on the date on which it was in fact passed, and is not to be deemed passed on any earlier date.

Written resolutions of private companies

381A.   Written resolutions of private companies.
(1)   Anything which in the case of a private company may be done—
(a)   by resolution of the company in general meeting, or
(b)   by resolution of a meeting of any class of members of the company,
may be done, without a meeting and without any previous notice being required, by resolution in writing signed by or on behalf of all the members of the company who at the date of the resolution would be entitled to attend and vote at such meeting.

(2)   The signatures need not be on a single document provided each is on a document which accurately states the terms of the resolution.

(3) The date of the resolution means when the resolution is signed by or on behalf of the last member to sign.

(4) A resolution agreed to in accordance with this section has effect as if passed—

    (a) by the company in general meeting, or

    (b) by a meeting of the relevant class of members of the company,

as the case may be; and any reference in any enactment to a meeting at which a resolution is passed or to members voting in favour of a resolution shall be construed accordingly.

(5) Any reference in any enactment to the date of passing of a resolution is, in relation to a resolution agreed to in accordance with this section, a reference to the date of the resolution.

(6) A resolution may be agreed to in accordance with this section which would otherwise be required to be passed as a special, extraordinary or elective resolution; and any reference in any enactment to a special, extraordinary or elective resolution includes such a resolution.

(7) This section has effect subject to the exceptions specified in Part I of Schedule 15A; and in relation to certain descriptions of resolution under this section the procedural requirements of this Act have effect with the adaptations specified in Part II of that Schedule.

381B. Duty to notify auditors of proposed written resolution.

(1) If a director or secretary of a company—

    (a) knows that it is proposed to seek agreement to a resolution in accordance with section 381A, and

    (b) knows the terms of the resolution,

he shall, if the company has auditors, secure that a copy of the resolution is sent to them, or that they are otherwise notified of its contents, at or before the time the resolution is supplied to a member for signature.

(2) A person who fails to comply with subsection (1) is liable to a fine.

(3) In any proceedings for an offence under this section it is a defence for the accused to prove—

    (a) that the circumstances were such that it was not practicable for him to comply with subsection (1), or

    (b) that he believed on reasonable grounds that a copy of the resolution had been sent to the company's auditors or that they had otherwise been informed of its contents.

(4) Nothing in this section affects the validity of any resolution.

381C. Written resolutions: supplementary provisions.

(1) Sections 381A and 381B have effect notwithstanding any provision of the company's memorandum or articles, but do not prejudice any power conferred by any such provision.

(2) Nothing in those sections affects any enactment or rule of law as to—

    (a) things done otherwise than by passing a resolution, or

    (b) cases in which a resolution is treated as having been passed, or a person is precluded from alleging that a resolution has not been duly passed.

Records of proceedings

382. Minutes of meetings.

(1) Every company shall cause minutes of all proceedings of general meetings, all proceedings at meetings of its directors and, where there are managers, all proceedings at meetings of its managers to be entered in books kept for that purpose.

(2) Any such minute, if purporting to be signed by the chairman of the meeting at which the proceedings were had, or by the chairman of the next succeeding meeting, is evidence of the proceedings.

(3)   Where a shadow director by means of a notice required by section 317(8) declares an interest in a contract or proposed contract, this section applies—

(a)   if it is a specific notice under paragraph (a) of that subsection, as if the declaration had been made at the meeting there referred to, and

(b)   otherwise, as if it had been made at the meeting of the directors next following the giving of the notice;

and the making of the declaration is in either case deemed to form part of the proceedings at the meeting.

(4)   Where minutes have been made in accordance with this section of the proceedings at any general meeting of the company or meeting of directors or managers, then, until the contrary is proved, the meeting is deemed duly held and convened, and all proceedings had at the meeting to have been duly had; and all appointments of directors, managers or liquidators are deemed valid.

(5)   If a company fails to comply with subsection (1), the company and every officer of it who is in default is liable to a fine and, for continued contravention, to a daily default fine.

382A.   Recording of written resolutions.

(1)   Where a written resolution is agreed to in accordance with section 381A which has effect as if agreed by the company in general meeting, the company shall cause a record of the resolution (and of the signatures) to be entered in a book in the same way as minutes of proceedings of a general meeting of the company.

(2)   Any such record, if purporting to be signed by a director of the company or by the company secretary, is evidence of the proceedings in agreeing to the resolution; and where a record is made in accordance with this section, then, until the contrary is proved, the requirements of this Act with respect to those proceedings shall be deemed to be complied with.

(3)   Section 382(5) (penalties) applies in relation to a failure to comply with subsection (1) above as it applies in relation to a failure to comply with subsection (1) of that section; and section 383 (inspection of minute books) applies in relation to a record made in accordance with this section as it applies in relation to the minutes of a general meeting.

382B.   Recording of decisions by the sole member.

(1)   Where a private company limited by shares or by guarantee has only one member and he takes any decision which may be taken by the company in general meeting and which has effect as if agreed by the company in general meeting, he shall (unless that decision is taken by way of a written resolution) provide the company with a written record of that decision.

(2)   If the sole member fails to comply with subsection (1) he shall be liable to a fine.

(3)   Failure by the sole member to comply with subsection (1) shall not affect the validity of any decision referred to in that subsection.

383.   Inspection of minute books.

(1)   The books containing the minutes of proceedings of any general meeting of a company held on or after 1 November 1929 shall be kept at the company's registered office, and shall be open to the inspection of any member without charge.

(3)   Any member shall be entitled on payment of such fee as may be prescribed to be furnished, within 7 days after he has made a request in that behalf to the company, with a copy of any such minutes as are referred to above.

(4)   If an inspection required under this section is refused or if a copy required under this section is not sent within the proper time, the company and every officer of it who is in default is liable in respect of each offence to a fine.

(5) In the case of any such refusal or default, the court may by order compel an immediate inspection of the books in respect of all proceedings of general meetings, or direct that the copies required be sent to the persons requiring them.

CHAPTER V
AUDITORS

Appointment of auditors

384. Duty to appoint auditors.

(1) Every company shall appoint an auditor or auditors in accordance with this Chapter.

This is subject to section 388A (certain companies exempt from obligation to appoint auditors).

(2) Auditors shall be appointed in accordance with section 385 (appointment at general meeting at which accounts are laid), except in the case of a private company which has elected to dispense with the laying of accounts in which case the appointment shall be made in accordance with section 385A.

(3) References in this Chapter to the end of the time for appointing auditors are to the end of the time within which an appointment must be made under section 385(2) or 385A(2), according to whichever of those sections applies.

(4) Sections 385 and 385A have effect subject to section 386 under which a private company may elect to dispense with the obligation to appoint auditors annually.

385. Appointment at general meeting at which accounts laid.

(1) This section applies to every public company and to a private company which has not elected to dispense with the laying of accounts.

(2) The company shall, at each general meeting at which accounts are laid, appoint an auditor or auditors to hold office from the conclusion of that meeting until the conclusion of the next general meeting at which accounts are laid.

(3) The first auditors of the company may be appointed by the directors at any time before the first general meeting of the company at which accounts are laid; and auditors so appointed shall hold office until the conclusion of that meeting.

(4) If the directors fail to exercise their powers under subsection (3), the powers may be exercised by the company in general meeting.

385A. Appointment by private company which is not obliged to lay accounts.

(1) This section applies to a private company which has elected in accordance with section 252 to dispense with the laying of accounts before the company in general meeting.

(2) Auditors shall be appointed by the company in general meeting before the end of the period of 28 days beginning with the day on which copies of the company's annual accounts for the previous financial year are sent to members under section 238 or, if notice is given under section 253(2) requiring the laying of the accounts before the company in general meeting, the conclusion of that meeting.

Auditors so appointed shall hold office from the end of that period or, as the case may be, the conclusion of that meeting until the end of the time for appointing auditors for the next financial year.

(3) The first auditors of the company may be appointed by the directors at any time before—

(a) the end of the period of 28 days beginning with the day on which copies of the company's first annual accounts are sent to members under section 238, or

(b) if notice is given under section 253(2) requiring the laying of the accounts before the company in general meeting, the beginning of that meeting;

and auditors so appointed shall hold office until the end of that period or, as the case may be, the conclusion of that meeting.

(4)   If the directors fail to exercise their powers under subsection (3), the powers may be exercised by the company in general meeting.

(5)   Auditors holding office when the election is made shall, unless the company in general meeting determines otherwise, continue to hold office until the end of the time for appointing auditors for the next financial year; and auditors holding office when an election ceases to have effect shall continue to hold office until the conclusion of the next general meeting of the company at which accounts are laid.

386.   Election by private company to dispense with annual appointment.

(1)   A private company may elect (by elective resolution in accordance with section 379A) to dispense with the obligation to appoint auditors annually.

(2)   When such an election is in force the company's auditors shall be deemed to be reappointed for each succeeding financial year on the expiry of the time for appointing auditors for that year, unless—

(a)   a resolution has been passed under section 250 by virtue of which the company is exempt from the obligation to appoint auditors, or

(b)   a resolution has been passed under section 393 to the effect that their appointment should be brought to an end.

(3)   If the election ceases to be in force, the auditors then holding office shall continue to hold office—

(a)   where section 385 then applies, until the conclusion of the next general meeting of the company at which accounts are laid;

(b)   where section 385A then applies, until the end of the time for appointing auditors for the next financial year under that section.

(4)   No account shall be taken of any loss of the opportunity of further deemed reappointment under this section in ascertaining the amount of any compensation or damages payable to an auditor on his ceasing to hold office for any reason.

387.   Appointment by Secretary of State in default of appointment by company.

(1)   If in any case no auditors are appointed, reappointed or deemed to be reappointed before the end of the time for appointing auditors, the Secretary of State may appoint a person to fill the vacancy.

(2)   In such a case the company shall within one week of the end of the time for appointing auditors give notice to the Secretary of State of his power having become exercisable.

If a company fails to give the notice required by this subsection, the company and every officer of it who is in default is guilty of an offence and liable to a fine and, for continued contravention, to a daily default fine.

388.   Filling of casual vacancies.

(1)   The directors, or the company in general meeting, may fill a casual vacancy in the office of auditor.

(2)   While such a vacancy continues, any surviving or continuing auditor or auditors may continue to act.

(3)   Special notice is required for a resolution at a general meeting of a company—

(a)   filling a casual vacancy in the office of auditor, or

(b)   reappointing as auditor a retiring auditor who was appointed by the directors to fill a casual vacancy.

(4)   On receipt of notice of such an intended resolution the company shall forthwith send a copy of it—

(a)   to the person proposed to be appointed, and

(b)   if the casual vacancy was caused by the resignation of an auditor, to the auditor who resigned.

388A. Certain companies exempt from obligation to appoint auditors.

(1) A company which by virtue of section 249A (certain categories of small company) or section 250 (dormant companies) is exempt from the provisions of Part VII relating to the audit of accounts is also exempt from the obligation to appoint auditors.

(2) The following provisions apply if a company which has been exempt from those provisions ceases to be so exempt.

(3) Where section 385 applies (appointment at general meeting at which accounts are laid), the directors may appoint auditors at any time before the next meeting of the company at which accounts are to be laid; and auditors so appointed shall hold office until the conclusion of that meeting.

(4) Where section 385A applies (appointment by private company not obliged to lay accounts), the directors may appoint auditors at any time before—

(a) the end of the period of 28 days beginning with the day on which copies of the company's annual accounts are next sent to members under section 238, or

(b) if notice is given under section 253(2) requiring the laying of the accounts before the company in general meeting, the beginning of that meeting;

and auditors so appointed shall hold office until the end of that period or, as the case may be, the conclusion of that meeting.

(5) If the directors fail to exercise their powers under subsection (3) or (4), the powers may be exercised by the company in general meeting.

Rights of auditors

389A. Rights to information.

(1) The auditors of a company have a right of access at all times to the company's books, accounts and vouchers, and are entitled to require from the company's officers such information and explanations as they think necessary for the performance of their duties as auditors.

(2) An officer of a company commits an offence if he knowingly or recklessly makes to the company's auditors a statement (whether written or oral) which—

(a) conveys or purports to convey any information or explanations which the auditors require, or are entitled to require, as auditors of the company, and

(b) is misleading, false or deceptive in a material particular.

A person guilty of an offence under this subsection is liable to imprisonment or a fine, or both.

(3) A subsidiary undertaking which is a body corporate incorporated in Great Britain, and the auditors of such an undertaking, shall give to the auditors of any parent company of the undertaking such information and explanations as they may reasonably require for the purposes of their duties as auditors of that company.

If a subsidiary undertaking fails to comply with this subsection, the undertaking and every officer of it who is in default is guilty of an offence and liable to a fine; and if an auditor fails without reasonable excuse to comply with this subsection he is guilty of an offence and liable to a fine.

(4) A parent company having a subsidiary undertaking which is not a body corporate incorporated in Great Britain shall, if required by its auditors to do so, take all such steps as are reasonably open to it to obtain from the subsidiary undertaking such information and explanations as they may reasonably require for the purposes of their duties as auditors of that company.

If a parent company fails to comply with this subsection, the company and every officer of it who is in default is guilty of an offence and liable to a fine.

(5) Section 734 (criminal proceedings against unincorporated bodies) applies to an offence under subsection (3).

390. Right to attend company meetings, &c.

(1)   A company's auditors are entitled—

(a)   to receive all notices of, and other communications relating to, any general meeting which a member of the company is entitled to receive;

(b)   to attend any general meeting of the company; and

(c)   to be heard at any general meeting which they attend on any part of the business of the meeting which concerns them as auditors.

(2)   In relation to a written resolution proposed to be agreed to by a private company in accordance with section 381A, the company's auditors are entitled—

(a)   to receive all such communications relating to the resolution as, by virtue of any provision of Schedule 15A, are required to be supplied to a member of the company.

(3)   The right to attend or be heard at a meeting is exercisable in the case of a body corporate or partnership by an individual authorised by it in writing to act as its representative at the meeting.

Remuneration of auditors

390A. Remuneration of auditors.

(1)   The remuneration of auditors appointed by the company in general meeting shall be fixed by the company in general meeting or in such manner as the company in general meeting may determine.

(2)   The remuneration of auditors appointed by the directors or the Secretary of State shall be fixed by the directors or the Secretary of State, as the case may be.

(3)   There shall be stated in a note to the company's annual accounts the amount of the remuneration of the company's auditors in their capacity as such.

(4)   For the purposes of this section 'remuneration' includes sums paid in respect of expenses.

(5)   This section applies in relation to benefits in kind as to payments in cash, and in relation to any such benefit references to its amount are to its estimated money value.

The nature of any such benefit shall also be disclosed.

390B. Remuneration of auditors or their associates for non-audit work.

(1)   The Secretary of State may make provision by regulations for securing the disclosure of the amount of any remuneration received or receivable by a company's auditors or their associates in respect of services other than those of auditors in their capacity as such.

(2)   The regulations may—

(a)   provide that 'remuneration' includes sums paid in respect of expenses,

(b)   apply in relation to benefits in kind as to payments in cash, and in relation to any such benefit require disclosure of its nature and its estimated money value,

(c)   define 'associate' in relation to an auditor,

(d)   require the disclosure of remuneration in respect of services rendered to associated undertakings of the company, and

(e)   define 'associated undertaking' for that purpose.

(3)   The regulations may require the auditors to disclose the relevant information in their report or require the relevant information to be disclosed in a note to the company's accounts and require the auditors to supply the directors of the company with such information as is necessary to enable that disclosure to be made.

(4)   The regulations may make different provision for different cases.

(5)   Regulations under this section shall be made by statutory instrument which shall be subject to annulment in pursuance of a resolution of either House of parliament.

Removal, resignation, &c. of auditors

391.   Removal of auditors.

(1)   A company may by ordinary resolution at any time remove an auditor from office, notwithstanding anything in any agreement between it and him.

(2)   Where a resolution removing an auditor is passed at a general meeting of a company, the company shall within 14 days give notice of that fact in the prescribed form to the registrar.

If a company fails to give the notice required by this subsection, the company and every officer of it who is in default is guilty of an offence and liable to a fine and, for continued contravention, to a daily default fine.

(3)   Nothing in this section shall be taken as depriving a person removed under it of compensation or damages payable to him in respect of the termination of his appointment as auditor or of any appointment terminating with that as auditor.

(4)   An auditor of a company who has been removed has, notwithstanding his removal, the rights conferred by section 390 in relation to any general meeting of the company—

   (a)   at which his term of office would otherwise have expired, or

   (b)   at which it is proposed to fill the vacancy caused by his removal.

In such a case the references in that section to matters concerning the auditors as auditors shall be construed as references to matters concerning him as a former auditor.

391A.   Rights of auditors who are removed or not reappointed.

(1)   Special notice is required for a resolution at a general meeting of a company—

   (a)   removing an auditor before the expiration of his term of office, or

   (b)   appointing as auditor a person other than a retiring auditor.

(2)   On receipt of notice of such an intended resolution the company shall forthwith send a copy of it to the person proposed to be removed or, as the case may be, to the person proposed to be appointed and to the retiring auditor.

(3)   The auditor proposed to be removed or (as the case may be) the retiring auditor may make with respect to the intended resolution representations in writing to the company (not exceeding a reasonable length) and request their notification to members of the company.

(4)   The company shall (unless the representations are received by it too late for it to do so)—

   (a)   in any notice of the resolution given to members of the company, state the fact of the representations having been made, and

   (b)   send a copy of the representations to every member of the company to whom notice of the meeting is or has been sent.

(5)   If a copy of any such representations is not sent out as required because received too late or because of the company's default, the auditor may (without prejudice to his right to be heard orally) require that the representations be read out at the meeting.

(6)   Copies of the representtions need not be sent out and the representations need not be read at the meeting if, on the application either of the company or of any other person claiming to be aggrieved, the court is satisfied that the rights conferred by this section are being abused to secure needless publicity for defamatory matter; and the court may order the company's costs on the application to be paid in whole or in part by the auditor, notwithstanding that he is not a party to the application.

392.   Resignation of auditors.

(1)   An auditor of a company may resign his office by depositing a notice in writing to that effect at the company's registered office.

The notice is not effective unless it is accompanied by the statement required by section 394.

(2)   An effective notice of resignation operates to bring the auditor's term of office to an end as of the date on which the notice is deposited or on such later date as may be specified in it.

(3)   The company shall within 14 days of the deposit of a notice of resignation send a copy of the notice to the registrar of companies.

If default is made in complying with this subsection, the company and every officer of it who is in default is guilty of an offence and liable to a fine and, for continued contravention, a daily default fine.

392A   Rights of resigning auditors.

(1)   This section applies where an auditor's notice of resignation is accompanied by a statement of circumstances which he considers should be brought to the attention of members or creditors of the company.

(2)   He may deposit with the notice a signed requisition calling on the directors of the company forthwith duly to convene an extraordinary general meeting of the company for the purpose of receiving and considering such explanation of the circumstances connected with his resignation as he may wish to place before the meeting.

(3)   He may request the company to circulate to its members—
(a)   before the meeting convened on his requisition, or
(b)   before any general meeting at which his term of office would otherwise have expired or at which it is proposed to fill the vacancy caused by his resignation,
a statement in writing (not exceeding a reasonable length) of the circumstances connected with his resignation.

(4)   The company shall (unless the statement is received too late for it to comply)—
(a)   in any notice of the meeting given to members of the company, state the fact of the statement having been made, and
(b)   send a copy of the statement to every member of the company to whom notice of the meeting is or has been sent.

(5)   If the directors do not within 21 days from the date of the deposit of a requisition under this section proceed duly to convene a meeting for a day not more than 28 days after the date on which the notice convening the meeting is given, every director who failed to take all reasonable steps to secure that a meeting was convened as mentioned above is guilty of an offence and liable to a fine.

(6)   If a copy of the statement mentioned above is not sent out as required because received too late or because of the company's default, the auditor may (without prejudice to his right to be heard orally) require that the statement be read out at the meeting.

(7)   Copies of a statement need not be sent out and the statement need not be read out at the meeting if, on the application either of the company or of any other person who claims to be aggrieved, the court is satisfied that the rights conferred by this section are being abused to secure needless publicity for defamatory matters; and the court may order the company's costs on such an application to be paid in whole or in part by the auditor, notwithstanding that he is not a party to the application.

(8)   An auditor who has resigned has, notwithstanding his resignation, the rights conferred by section 390 in relation to any such general meeting of the company as is mentioned in subsection (3)(a) or (b).

In such a case the references in that section to matters concerning the auditors as auditors shall be construed as references to matters concerning him as a former auditor.

393.   Termination of appointment of auditors not appointed annually.

(1)   When an election is in force under section 386 (election by private company to dispense with annual appointment), any member of the company may deposit notice in

writing at the company's registered office proposing that the appointment of the company's auditors be brought to an end.

No member may deposit more than one such notice in any financial year of the company.

(2)   If such a notice is deposited it is the duty of the directors—

(a)   to convene a general meeting of the company for a date not more than 28 days after the date on which the notice was given, and

(b)   to propose at the meeting a resolution in a form enabling the company to decide whether the appointment of the company's auditors should be brought to an end.

(3)   If the decision of the company at the meeting is that the appointment of the auditors should be brought to an end, the auditors shall not be deemed to be reappointed when next they would be and, if the notice was deposited within the period immediately following the distribution of accounts, any deemed reappointment for the financial year following that to which those accounts relate which has already occurred shall cease to have effect.

The period immediately following the distribution of accounts means the period beginning with the day on which copies of the company's annual accounts are sent to members of the company under section 238 and ending 14 days after that day.

(4)   If the directors do not within 14 days from the date of the deposit of the notice proceed duly to convene a meeting, the member who deposited the notice (or, if there was more than one, any of them) may himself convene the meeting; but any meeting so convened shall not be held after the expiration of three months from that date.

(5)   A meeting convened under this section by member shall be convened in the same manner, as nearly as possible, as that in which meetings are to be convened by directors.

(6)   Any reasonable expenses incurred by a member by reason of the failure of the directors duly to convene a meeting shall be made good to him by the company; and any such sums shall be recouped by the company from such of the directors as were in default out of any sums payable, or to become payable, by the company by way of fees or other remuneration in respect of their services.

(7)   This section has effect notwithstanding anything in any agreement between the company and its auditors; and no compensation or damages shall be payable by reason of the auditors' appointment being terminated under this section.

394.   Statement by person ceasing to hold office as auditor.

(1)   Where an auditor ceases for any reason to hold office, he shall deposit at the company's registered office a statement of any circumstances connected with his ceasing to hold office which he considers should be brought to the attention of the members or creditors of the company or, if he considers that there are no such circumstances, a statement that there are none.

 · (2)   In the case of resignation, the statement shall be deposited along with the notice of resignation; in the case of failure to seek reappointment, the statement shall be deposited not less than 14 days before the end of the time allowed for next appointing auditors; in any other case, the statement shall be deposited not later than the end of the period of 14 days beginning with the date on which he ceases to hold office.

(3)   If the statement is of circumstances which the auditor considers should be brought to the attention of the members or creditors of the company, the company shall within 14 days of the deposit of the statement either—

(a)   send a copy of it to every person who under section 238 is entitled to be sent copies of the accounts, or

(b)   apply to the court.

(4)   The company shall if it applies to the court notify the auditor of the application.

(5) Unless the auditor receives notice of such an application before the end of the period of 21 days beginning with the day on which he deposited the statement, he shall within a further seven days send a copy of the statement to the registrar.

(6) If the court is satisfied that the auditor is using the statement to secure needless publicity for defamatory matter—

  (a) it shall direct that copies of the statement need not be sent out, and

  (b) it may further order the company's costs on the application to be paid in whole or in part by the auditor, notwithstanding that he is not a party to the application;

and the company shall within 14 days of the court's decision send to the persons mentioned in subsection (3)(a) a statement setting out the effect of the order.

(7) If the court is not so satisfied, the company shall within 14 days of the court's decision—

  (a) send copies of the statement to the persons mentioned in subsection (3)(a), and

  (b) notify the auditor of the court's decision;

and the auditor shall within seven days of receiving such notice send a copy of the statement to the registrar.

394A.   Offences of failing to comply with s. 394.

(1) If a person ceasing to hold office as auditor fails to comply with section 394 he is guilty of an offence and liable to a fine.

(2) In proceedings for an offence under subsection (1) it is a defence for the person charged to show that he took all reasonable steps and exercised all due diligence to avoid the commission of the offence.

(3) Sections 733 (liability of individuals for corporate default) and 734 (criminal proceedings against unincorporated bodies) apply to an offence under subsection (1).

(4) If a company makes default in complying with section 394, the company and every officer of it who is in default is guilty of an offence and liable to a fine and, for continued contravention, to a daily default fine.

PART XII
REGISTRATION OF CHARGES

[Part XII would be replaced by new provisions if Part IV of the Companies Act 1989 were brought into force. The Department of Trade and Industry has indicated that Part IV of the 1989 Act will not be brought into force.]

CHAPTER I
REGISTRATION OF CHARGES (ENGLAND AND WALES)

395.   Certain charges void if not registered.

(1) Subject to the provisions of this Chapter, a charge created by a company registered in England and Wales and being a charge to which this section applies is, so far as any security on the company's property or undertaking is conferred by the charge, void against the liquidator or administrator and any creditor of the company, unless the prescribed particulars of the charge together with the instrument (if any) by which the charge is created or evidenced, are delivered to or received by the registrar of companies for registration in the manner required by this Chapter within 21 days after the date of the charge's creation.

(2) Subsection (1) is without prejudice to any contract or obligation for repayment of the money secured by the charge; and when a charge becomes void under this section, the money secured by it immediately becomes payable.

396.   Charges which have to be registered.

(1) Section 395 applies to the following charges—

  (a) a charge for the purpose of securing any issue of debentures,

    (b)   a charge on uncalled share capital of the company,

    (c)   a charge created or evidenced by an instrument which, if executed by an individual, would require registration as a bill of sale,

    (d)   a charge on land (wherever situated) or any interest in it, but not including a charge for any rent or other periodical sum issuing out of the land,

    (e)   a charge on book debts of the company,

    (f)   a floating charge on the company's undertaking or property,

    (g)   a charge on calls made but not paid,

    (h)   a charge on a ship or aircraft, or any share in a ship,

    (j)   a charge on goodwill, or on any intellectual property.

(2)   Where a negotiable instrument has been given to secure the payment of any book debts of a company, the deposit of the instrument for the purpose of securing an advance to the company is not, for purposes of section 395, to be treated as a charge on those book debts.

(3)   The holding of debentures entitling the holder to a charge on land is not for purposes of this section deemed to be an interest in land.

(3A)   The following are 'intellectual property' for the purposes of this section—

    (a)   any patent, trade mark, registered design, copyright or design right;

    (b)   any licence under or in respect of any such right.

(4)   In this Chapter, 'charge' includes mortgage.

397.   Formalities of registration (debentures).

(1)   Where a series of debentures containing, or giving by reference to another instrument, any charge to the benefit of which the debenture holders of that series are entitled *pari passu* is created by a company, it is for purposes of section 395 sufficient if there are delivered to or received by the registrar, within 21 days after the execution of the deed containing the charge (or, if there is no such deed, after the execution of any debentures of the series), the following particulars in the prescribed form—

    (a)   the total amount secured by the whole series, and

    (b)   the dates of the resolutions authorising the issue of the series and the date of the covering deed (if any) by which the security is created or defined, and

    (c)   a general description of the property charged, and

    (d)   the names of the trustees (if any) for the debenture holders,

together with the deed containing the charge or, if there is no such deed, one of the debentures of the series:

Provided that there shall be sent to the registrar of companies, for entry in the register, particulars in the prescribed form of the date and amount of each issue of debentures of the series, but any omission to do this does not affect the validity of any of those debentures.

(2)   Where any commission, allowance or discount has been paid or made either directly or indirectly by a company to a person in consideration of his—

    (a)   subscribing or agreeing to subscribe, whether absolutely or conditionally, for debentures of the company, or

    (b)   procuring or agreeing to procure subscriptions, whether absolute or conditional, for such debentures,

the particulars required to be sent for registration under section 395 shall include particulars as to the amount or rate per cent of the commission, discount or allowance so paid or made, but omission to do this does not affect the validity of the debentures issued.

(3)   The deposit of debentures as security for a debt of the company is not, for the purposes of subsection (2), treated as the issue of the debentures at a discount.

398.   Verification of charge on property outside United Kingdom.

(1)   In the case of a charge created out of the United Kingdom comprising property situated outside the United Kingdom, the delivery to and the receipt by the registrar of

companies of the copy (verified in the prescribed manner) of the instrument by which the charge is created or evidenced has the same effect for purposes of sections 395 to 398 as the delivery and receipt of the instrument itself.

(2)   In that case, 21 days after the date on which the instrument or copy could, in due course of post (and if dispatched with due diligence), have been received in the United Kingdom are substituted for the 21 days mentioned in section 395(1) (or as the case may be, section 397(1)) as the time within which the particulars and instrument or copy are to be delivered to the registrar.

(3)   Where a charge is created in the United Kingdom but comprises property outside the United Kingdom, the instrument creating or purporting to create the charge may be sent for registration under section 395 notwithstanding that further proceedings may be necessary to make the charge valid or effectual according to the law of the country in which the property is situated.

(4)   Where a charge comprises property situated in Scotland or Northern Ireland and registration in the country where the property is situated is necessary to make the charge valid or effectual according to the law of that country, the delivery to and the receipt by the registrar of a copy (verified in the prescribed manner) of the instrument by which the charge is created or evidenced, together with a certificate in the prescribed form stating that the charge was presented for registration in Scotland or Northern Ireland (as the case may be) on the date on which it was so presented has, for purposes of sections 395 to 398, the same effect as the delivery and receipt of the instrument itself.

399.   Company's duty to register charges it creates.

(1)   It is a company's duty to send to the registrar of companies for registration the particulars of every charge created by the company and of the issues of debentures of a series requiring registration under sections 395 to 398; but registration of any such charge may be effected on the application of any person interested in it.

(2)   Where registration is effected on the application of some person other than the company, that person is entitled to recover from the company the amount of any fees properly paid by him to the registrar on the registration.

(3)   If a company fails to comply with subsection (1), then, unless the registration has been effected on the application of some other person, the company and every officer of it who is in default is liable to a fine and, for continued contravention, to a daily default fine.

400.   Charges existing on property acquired.

(1)   This section applies where a company registered in England and Wales acquires property which is subject to a charge of any such kind as would, if it had been created by the company after the acquisition of the property, have been required to be registered under this Chapter.

(2)   The company shall cause the prescribed particulars of the charge, together with a copy (certified in the prescribed manner to be a correct copy) of the instrument (if any) by which the charge was created or is evidenced, to be delivered to the registrar of companies for registration in manner required by this Chapter within 21 days after the date on which the acquisition is completed.

(3)   However, if the property is situated and the charge was created outside Great Britain, 21 days after the date on which the copy of the instrument could in due course of post, and if dispatched with due diligence, have been received in the United Kingdom is substituted for the 21 days above-mentioned as the time within which the particulars and copy of the instrument are to be delivered to the registrar.

(4)   If default is made in complying with this section, the company and every officer of it who is in default is liable to a fine and, for continued contravention, to a daily default fine.

401. Register of charges to be kept by registrar of companies.

(1)   The registrar of companies shall keep, with respect to each company, a register in the prescribed form of all the charges requiring registration under this Chapter; and he shall enter in the register with respect to such charges the following particulars—

(a)   in the case of a charge to the benefit of which the holders of a series of debentures are entitled, the particulars specified in section 397(1),

(b)   in the case of any other charge—

(i)   if it is a charge created by the company, the date of its creation, and if it is a charge which was existing on property acquired by the company, the date of the acquisition of the property, and

(ii)   the amount secured by the charge, and

(iii)   short particulars of the property charged, and

(iv)   the persons entitled to the charge.

(2)   The registrar shall give a certificate of the registration of any charge registered in pursuance of this Chapter, stating the amount secured by the charge.

The certificate—

(a)   shall be either signed by the registrar, or authenticated by his official seal, and

(b)   is conclusive evidence that the requirements of this Chapter as to registration have been satisfied.

(3)   The register kept in pursuance of this section shall be open to inspection by any person.

402. Endorsement of certificate on debentures.

(1)   The company shall cause a copy of every certificate of registration given under section 401 to be endorsed on every debenture or certificate of debenture stock which is issued by the company, and the payment of which is secured by the charge so registered.

(2)   But this does not require a company to cause a certificate of registration of any charge so given to be endorsed on any debenture or certificate of debenture stock issued by the company before the charge was created.

(3)   If a person knowingly and wilfully authorises or permits the delivery of a debenture or certificate of debenture stock which under this section is required to have endorsed on it a copy of a certificate of registration, without the copy being so endorsed upon it, he is liable (without prejudice to any other liability) to a fine.

403. Entries of satisfaction and release.

(1)   The registrar of companies, on receipt of a statutory declaration in the prescribed form verifying, with respect to a registered charge,—

(a)   that the debt for which the charge was given has been paid or satisfied in whole or in part, or

(b)   that part of the property or undertaking charged has been released from the charge or has ceased to form part of the company's property or undertaking,

may enter on the register a memorandum of satisfaction in whole or in part, or of the fact that part of the property or undertaking has been released from the charge or has ceased to form part of the company's property or undertaking (as the case may be).

(2)   Where the registrar enters a memorandum of satisfaction in whole, he shall if required furnish the company with a copy of it.

404. Rectification of register of charges.

(1)   The following applies if the court is satisfied that the omission to register a charge within the time required by this Chapter or that the omission or misstatement of any particular with respect to any such charge or in a memorandum of satisfaction was accidental, or due to inadvertence or to some other sufficient cause, or is not of a nature

to prejudice the position of creditors or shareholders of the company, or that on other grounds it is just and equitable to grant relief.

(2)   The court may, on the application of the company or a person interested, and on such terms and conditions as seem to the court just and expedient, order that the time for registration shall be extended or, as the case may be, that the omission or misstatement shall be rectified.

405.   Registration of enforcement of security.

(1)   If a person obtains an order for the appointment of a receiver or manager of a company's property, or appoints such a receiver or manager under powers contained in an instrument, he shall within 7 days of the order or of the appointment under those powers, give notice of the fact to the registrar of companies; and the registrar shall enter the fact in the register of charges.

(2)   Where a person appointed receiver or manager of a company's property under powers contained in an instrument ceases to act as such receiver or manager, he shall, on so ceasing, give the registrar notice to that effect, and the registrar shall enter the fact in the register of charges.

(3)   A notice under this section shall be in the prescribed form.

(4)   If a person makes default in complying with the requirements of this section, he is liable to a fine and, for continued contravention, to a daily default fine.

406.   Companies to keep copies of instruments creating charges.

(1)   Every company shall cause a copy of every instrument creating a charge requiring registration under this Chapter to be kept at its registered office.

(2)   In the case of a series of uniform debentures, a copy of one debenture of the series is sufficient.

407.   Company's register of charges.

(1)   Every limited company shall keep at its registered office a register of charges and enter in it all charges specifically affecting property of the company and all floating charges on the company's undertaking or any of its property.

(2)   The entry shall in each case give a short description of the property charged, the amount of the charge and, except in the case of securities to bearer, the names of the persons entitled to it.

(3)   If an officer of the company knowingly and wilfully authorises or permits the omission of an entry required to be made in pursuance of this section, he is liable to a fine.

408.   Right to inspect instruments which create charges, etc.

(1)   The copies of instruments creating any charge requiring registration under this Chapter with the registrar of companies, and the register of charges kept in pursuance of section 407, shall be open during business hours (but subject to such reasonable restrictions as the company in general meeting may impose, so that not less than 2 hours in each day be allowed for inspection) to the inspection of any creditor or member of the company without fee.

(2)   The register of charges shall also be open to the inspection of any other person on payment of such fee, not exceeding 5 pence, for each inspection, as the company may prescribe.

(3)   If inspection of the copies referred to, or of the register, is refused, every officer of the company who is in default is liable to a fine and, for continued contravention, to a daily default fine.

(4)   If such a refusal occurs in relation to a company registered in England and Wales, the court may by order compel an immediate inspection of the copies or register.

PART XIII
ARRANGEMENTS AND RECONSTRUCTIONS

425. Power of company to compromise with creditors and members.

(1)   Where a compromise or arrangement is proposed between a company and its creditors, or any class of them, or between the company and its members, or any class of them, the court may on the application of the company or any creditor or member of it or, in the case of a company being wound up or an administration order being in force in relation to a company, of the liquidator or administrator, order a meeting of the creditors or class of creditors, or of the members of the company or class of members (as the case may be), to be summoned in such manner as the court directs.

(2)   If a majority in number representing three-fourths in value of the creditors or class of creditors or members or class of members (as the case may be), present and voting either in person or by proxy at the meeting, agree to any compromise or arrangement, the compromise or arrangement, if sanctioned by the court, is binding on all creditors or the class of creditors or on the members or class of members (as the case may be), and also on the company or, in the case of a company in the course of being wound up, on the liquidator and contributories of the company.

(3)   The court's order under subsection (2) has no effect until an office copy of it has been delivered to the registrar of companies for registration; and a copy of every such order shall be annexed to every copy of the company's memorandum issued after the order has been made or, in the case of a company not having a memorandum, of every copy so issued of the instrument constituting the company or defining its constitution.

(4)   If a company makes default in complying with subsection (3), the company and every officer of it who is in default is liable to a fine.

. . .

(6)   In this section and the next—

(a)   'company' means any company liable to be wound up under this Act, and

(b)   'arrangement' includes a reorganisation of the company's share capital by the consolidation of shares of different classes or by the division of shares into shares of different classes, or by both of those methods.

426. Information as to compromise to be circulated.

(1)   The following applies where a meeting of creditors or any class of creditors, or of members or any class of members, is summoned under section 425.

(2)   With every notice summoning the meeting which is sent to a creditor or member there shall be sent also a statement explaining the effect of the compromise or arrangement and in particular stating any material interests of the directors of the company (whether as directors or as members or as creditors of the company or otherwise) and the effect on those interests of the compromise or arrangement, in so far as it is different from the effect on the like interests of other persons.

(3)   In every notice summoning the meeting which is given by advertisement there shall be included either such a statement as above-mentioned or a notification of the place at which, and the manner in which, creditors or members entitled to attend the meeting may obtain copies of the statement.

(4)   Where the compromise or arrangement affects the rights of debenture holders of the company, the statement shall give the like explanation as respects the trustees of any deed for securing the issue of the debentures as it is required to give as respects the company's directors.

(5)   Where a notice given by advertisement includes a notification that copies of a statement explaining the effect of the compromise or arrangement proposed can be obtained by creditors or members entitled to attend the meeting, every such creditor or member shall, on making application in the manner indicated by the notice, be furnished by the company free of charge with a copy of the statement.

(6)   If a company makes default in complying with any requirement of this section, the company and every officer of it who is in default is liable to a fine; and for this purpose a liquidator or administrator of the company and a trustee of a deed for securing the issue of debentures of the company is deemed an officer of it.

However, a person is not liable under this subsection if he shows that the default was due to the refusal of another person, being a director or trustee for debenture holders, to supply the necessary particulars of his interests.

(7)   It is the duty of any director of the company, and of any trustee for its debenture holders, to give notice to the company of such matters relating to himself as may be necessary for purposes of this section; and any person who makes default in complying with this subsection is liable to a fine.

427.   Provisions for facilitating company reconstruction or amalgamation.

(1)   The following applies where application is made to the court under section 425 for the sanctioning of a compromise or arrangement proposed between a company and any such persons as are mentioned in that section.

(2)   If it is shown—

(a)   that the compromise or arrangement has been proposed for the purposes of, or in connection with, a scheme for the reconstruction of any company or companies, or the amalgamation of any two or more companies, and

(b)   that under the scheme the whole or any part of the undertaking or the property of any company concerned in the scheme ('a transferor company') is to be transferred to another company ('the transferee company'),

the court may, either by the order sanctioning the compromise or arrangement or by any subsequent order, make provision for all or any of the following matters.

(3)   The matters for which the court's order may make provision are—

(a)   the transfer to the transferee company of the whole or any part of the undertaking and of the property or liabilities of any transferor company,

(b)   the allotting or appropriation by the transferee company of any shares, debentures, policies or other like interests in that company which under the compromise or arrangement are to be allotted or appropriated by that company to or for any person,

(c)   the continuation by or against the transferee company of any legal proceedings pending by or against any transferor company,

(d)   the dissolution, without winding up, of any transferor company,

(e)   the provision to be made for any persons who, within such time and in such manner as the court directs, dissent from the compromise or arrangement,

(f)   such incidental, consequential and supplemental matters as are necessary to secure that the reconstruction or amalgamation is fully and effectively carried out.

(4)   If an order under this section provides for the transfer of property or liabilities, then—

(a)   that property is by virtue of the order transferred to, and vests in, the transferee company, and

(b)   those liabilities are, by virtue of the order, transferred to and become liabilities of that company;

and property (if the order so directs) vests freed from any charge which is by virtue of the compromise or arrangement to cease to have effect.

(5)   Where an order is made under this section, every company in relation to which the order is made shall cause an office copy of the order to be delivered to the registrar of companies for registration within 7 days after its making; and if default is made in complying with this subsection, the company and every officer of it who is in default is liable to a fine and, for continued contravention, to a daily default fine.

(6) In this section the expression 'property' includes property, rights and powers of every description; the expression 'liabilities' includes duties and 'company' includes only a company as defined in section 735(1).

PART XIIIA
TAKEOVER OFFERS

428. 'Takeover offers'.

(1) In this Part of this Act 'a takeover offer' means an offer to acquire all the shares, or all the shares of any class or classes, in a company (other than shares which at the date of the offer are already held by the offeror), being an offer on terms which are the same in relation to all the shares to which the offer relates or, where those shares include shares of different classes, in relation to all the shares of each class.

(2) In subsection (1) 'shares' means shares which have been allotted on the date of the offer but a takeover offer may include among the shares to which it relates all or any shares that are subsequently allotted before a date specified in or determined in accordance with the terms of the offer.

(3) The terms offered in relation to any shares shall for the purposes of this section be treated as being the same in relation to all the shares or, as the case may be, all the shares of a class to which the offer relates notwithstanding any variation permitted by subsection (4).

(4) A variation is permitted by this subsection where—

(a) the law of a country or territory outside the United Kingdom precludes an offer of consideration in the form or any of the forms specified in the terms in question or precludes it except after compliance by the offeror with conditions with which he is unable to comply or which he regards as unduly onerous; and

(b) the variation is such that the persons to whom an offer of consideration in that form is precluded are able to receive consideration otherwise than in that form but of substantially equivalent value.

(5) The reference in subsection (1) to shares already held by the offeror includes a reference to shares which he has contracted to acquire but that shall not be construed as including shares which are the subject of a contract binding the holder to accept the offer when it is made, being a contract entered into by the holder either for no consideration and under seal or for no consideration other than a promise by the offeror to make the offer.

(6) In the application of subsection (5) to Scotland, the words 'and under seal' shall be omitted.

(7) Where the terms of an offer make provision for their revision and for acceptances on the previous terms to be treated as acceptances on the revised terms, the revision shall not be regarded for the purposes of this Part of this Act as the making of a fresh offer and references in this part of this Act to the date of the offer shall accordingly be construed as references to the date on which the original offer was made.

(8) In this Part of this Act 'the offeror' means, subject to section 430D, the person making a takeover offer and 'the company' means the company whose shares are the subject of the offer.

429. Right of offeror to buy out minority shareholders.

(1) If, in a case in which a takeover offer does not relate to shares of different classes, the offeror has by virtue of acceptances of the offer acquired or contracted to acquire not less than nine-tenths in value of the shares to which the offer relates he may give notice to the holder of any shares to which the offer relates which the offeror has not acquired or contracted to acquire that he desires to acquire those shares.

(2) If, in a case in which a takeover offer relates to shares of different classes, the offeror has by virtue of acceptances of the offer acquired or contracted to acquire not less

than nine-tenths in value of the shares of any class to which the offer relates, he may give notice to the holder of any shares of that class which the offeror has not acquired or contracted to acquire that he desires to acquire those shares.

(3)   No notice shall be given under subsection (1) or (2) unless the offeror has acquired or contracted to acquire the shares necessary to satisfy the minimum specified in that subsection before the end of the period of four months beginning with the date of the offer; and no such notice shall be given after the end of the period of two months beginning with the date on which he has acquired or contracted to acquire shares which satisfy that minimum.

(4)   Any notice under this section shall be given in the prescribed manner; and when the offeror gives the first notice in relation to an offer he shall send a copy of it to the company together with a statutory declaration by him in the prescribed form stating that the conditions for the giving of the notice are satisfied.

(5)   Where the offeror is a company (whether or not a company within the meaning of this Act) the statutory declaration shall be signed by a director.

(6)   Any person who fails to send a copy of a notice or a statutory declaration as required by subsection (4) or makes such a declaration for the purposes of that subsection knowing it to be false or without having reasonable grounds for believing it to be true shall be liable to imprisonment or a fine, or both, and for continued failure to send the copy or declaration, to a daily default fine.

(7)   If any person is charged with an offence for failing to send a copy of a notice as required by subsection (4) it is a defence for him to prove that he took reasonable steps for securing compliance with that subsection.

(8)   Where during the period within which a takeover offer can be accepted the offeror acquires or contracts to acquire any of the shares to which the offer relates but otherwise than by virtue of acceptances of the offer, then, if—

(a)   the value of the consideration for which they are acquired or contracted to be acquired ('the acquisition consideration') does not at that time exceed the value of the consideration specified in the terms of the offer; or

(b)   those terms are subsequently revised so that when the revision is announced the value of the acquisition consideration, at the time mentioned in paragraph (a) above, no longer exceeds the value of the consideration specified in those terms,

the offeror shall be treated for the purposes of this section as having acquired or contracted to acquire those shares by virtue of acceptances of the offer; but in any other case those shares shall be treated as excluded from those to which the offer relates.

430.   Effect of notice under s. 429.

(1)   The following provisions shall, subject to section 430C, have effect where a notice is given in respect of any shares under section 429.

(2)   The offeror shall be entitled and bound to acquire those shares on the terms of the offer.

(3)   Where the terms of an offer are such as to give the holder of any shares a choice of consideration the notice shall give particulars of the choice and state—

(a)   that the holder of the shares may within six weeks from the date of the notice indicate his choice by a written communication sent to the offeror at an address specified in the notice; and

(b)   which consideration specified in the offer is to be taken as applying in default of his indicating a choice as aforesaid;

and the terms of the offer mentioned in subsection (2) shall be determined accordingly.

(4)   Subsection (3) applies whether or not any time limit or other conditions applicable to the choice under the terms of the offer can still be complied with; and if the consideration chosen by the holder of the shares—

    (a)   is not cash and the offeror is no longer able to provide it; or

    (b)   was to have been provided by a third party who is no longer bound or able to provide it,

the consideration shall be taken to consist of an amount of cash payable by the offeror which at the date of the notice is equivalent to the chosen consideration.

    (5)   At the end of six weeks from the date of the notice the offeror shall forthwith—

    (a)   send a copy of the notice to the company; and

    (b)   pay or transfer to the company the consideration for the shares to which the notice relates.

    (6)   If the shares to which the notice relates are registered the copy of the notice sent to the company under subsection (5)(a) shall be accompanied by an instrument of transfer executed on behalf of the shareholder by a person appointed by the offeror; and on receipt of that instrument the company shall register the offeror as the holder of those shares.

    (7)   If the shares to which the notice relates are transferable by the delivery of warrants or other instruments the copy of the notice sent to the company under subsection (5)(a) shall be accompanied by a statement to that effect; and the company shall on receipt of the statement issue the offeror with warrants or other instruments in respect of the shares and those already in issue in respect of the shares shall become void.

    (8)   Where the consideration referred to in paragraph (b) of subsection (5) consists of shares or securities to be allotted by the offeror the reference in that paragraph to the transfer of the consideration shall be construed as a reference to the allotment of the shares or securities to the company.

    (9)   Any sum received by a company under paragraph (b) of subsection (5) and any other consideration received under that paragraph shall be held by the company on trust for the person entitled to the shares in respect of which the sum or other consideration was received.

    (10)   Any sum received by a company under paragraph (b) of subsection (5), and any dividend or other sum accruing from any other consideration received by a company under that paragraph, shall be paid into a separate bank account, being an account the balance on which bears interest at an appropriate rate and can be withdrawn by such notice (if any) as is appropriate.

    (11)   Where after reasonable enquiry made at such intervals as are reasonable the person entitled to any consideration held on trust by virtue of subsection (9) cannot be found and twelve years have elapsed since the consideration was received or the company is wound up the consideration (together with any interest, dividend or other benefit that has accrued from it) shall be paid into court.

    (12)   In relation to a company registered in Scotland, subsections (13) and (14) shall apply in place of subsection (11).

    (13)   Where after reasonable enquiry made at such intervals as are reasonable the person entitled to any consideration held on trust by virtue of subsection (9) cannot be found and twelve years have elapsed since the consideration was received or the company is wound up—

    (a)   the trust shall terminate;

    (b)   the company or, as the case may be, the liquidator shall sell any consideration other than cash and any benefit other than cash that has accrued from the consideration; and

    (c)   a sum representing—

       (i)   the consideration so far as it is cash;

       (ii)   the proceeds of any sale under paragraph (b) above; and

       (iii)   any interest, dividend or other benefit that has accrued from the consideration,

shall be deposited in the name of the Accountant of Court in a bank account such as is referred to in subsection (10) and the receipt for the deposit shall be transmitted to the Accountant of Court.

(14)   Section 58 of the Bankruptcy (Scotland) Act 1985 (so far as consistent with this Act) shall apply with any necessary modifications to sums deposited under subsection (13) as that section applies to sums deposited under section 57(1)(a) of that Act.

(15)   The expenses of any such enquiry as is mentioned in subsection (11) or (13) may be defrayed out of the money or other property held on trust for the person or persons to whom the enquiry relates.

430A.   Right of minority shareholder to be bought out by offeror.

(1)   If a takeover offer relates to all the shares in a company and at any time before the end of the period within which the offer can be accepted—

(a)   the offeror has by virtue of acceptances of the offer acquired or contracted to acquire some (but not all) of the shares to which the offer relates; and

(b)   those shares, with or without any other shares in the company which he has acquired or contracted to acquire, amount to not less than nine-tenths in value of all the shares in the company,

the holder of any shares to which the offer relates who has not accepted the offer may by a written communication addressed to the offeror require him to acquire those shares.

(2)   If a takeover offer relates to shares of any class or classes and at any time before the end of the period within which the offer can be accepted—

(a)   the offeror has by virtue of acceptances of the offer acquired or contracted to acquire some (but not all) of the shares of any class to which the offer relates; and

(b)   those shares, with or without any other shares of that class which he has acquired or contracted to acquire, amount to not less than nine-tenths in value of all the shares of that class,

the holder of any shares of that class who has not accepted the offer may by a written communication addressed to the offeror require him to acquire those shares.

(3)   Within one month of the time specified in subsection (1) or, as the case may be, subsection (2) the offeror shall give any shareholder who has not accepted the offer notice in the prescribed manner of the rights that are exercisable by him under that subsection; and if the notice is given before the end of the period mentioned in that subsection it shall state that the offer is still open for acceptance.

(4)   A notice under subsection (3) may specify a period for the exercise of the rights conferred by this section and in that event the rights shall not be exercisable after the end of that period; but no such period shall end less than three months after the end of the period within which the offer can be accepted.

(5)   Subsection (3) does not apply if the offeror has given the shareholder a notice in respect of the shares in question under section 429.

(6)   If the offeror fails to comply with subsection (3) he and, if the offeror is a company, every officer of the company who is in default or to whose neglect the failure is attributable, shall be liable to a fine and, for continued contravention, to a daily default fine.

(7)   If an offeror other than a company is charged with an offence for failing to comply with subsection (3) it is a defence for him to prove that he took all reasonable steps for securing compliance with that subsection.

430B.   Effect of requirement under s. 430A.

(1)   The following provisions shall, subject to section 430C, have effect where a shareholder exercises his rights in respect of any shares under section 430A.

(2)   The offeror shall be entitled and bound to acquire those shares on the terms of the offer or on such other terms as may be agreed.

(3)   Where the terms of an offer are such as to give the holder of shares a choice of consideration the holder of the shares may indicate his choice when requiring the offeror to acquire them and the notice given to the holder under section 430A(3)—

(a) shall give particulars of the choice and of the rights conferred by this subsection; and

(b) may state which consideration specified in the offer is to be taken as applying in default of his indicating a choice;

and the terms of the offer mentioned in subsection (2) shall be determined accordingly.

(4) Subsection (3) applies whether or not any time limit or other conditions applicable to the choice under the terms of the offer can still be complied with; and if the consideration chosen by the holder of the shares—

(a) is not cash and the offeror is no longer able to provide it; or

(b) was to have been provided by a third party who is no longer bound or able to provide it,

the consideration shall be taken to consist of an amount of cash payable by the offeror which at the date when the holder of the shares requires the offeror to acquire them is equivalent to the chosen consideration.

430C. Applications to the court.

(1) Where a notice is given under section 429 to the holder of any shares the court may, on an application made by him within six weeks from the date on which the notice was given—

(a) order that the offeror shall not be entitled and bound to acquire the shares; or

(b) specify terms of acquisition different from those of the offer.

(2) If an application to the court under subsection (1) is pending at the end of the period mentioned in subsection (5) of section 430 that subsection shall not have effect until the application has been disposed of.

(3) Where the holder of any shares exercises his rights under section 430A the court may, on an application made by him or the offeror, order that the terms on which the offeror is entitled and bound to acquire the shares shall be such as the court thinks fit.

(4) No order for costs or expenses shall be made against a shareholder making an application under subsection (1) or (3) unless the court considers—

(a) that the application was unnecessary, improper or vexatious; or

(b) that there has been unreasonable delay in making the application or unreasonable conduct on his part in conducting the proceedings on the application.

(5) Where a takeover offer has not been accepted to the extent necessary for entitling the offeror to give notices under subsection (1) or (2) of section 429 the court may, on the application of the offeror, make an order authorising him to give notices under that subsection if satisfied—

(a) that the offeror has after reasonable enquiry been unable to trace one or more of the persons holding shares to which the offer relates;

(b) that the shares which the offeror has acquired or contracted to acquire by virtue of acceptances of the offer, together with the shares held by the person or persons mentioned in paragraph (a), amount to not less than the minimum specified in that subsection; and

(c) that the consideration offered is fair and reasonable;

but the court shall not make an order under this subsection unless it considers that it is just and equitable to do so having regard, in particular, to the number of shareholders who have been traced but who have not accepted the offer.

430D. Joint offers.

(1) A takeover offer may be made by two or more persons jointly and in that event this Part of this Act has effect with the following modifications.

(2) The conditions for the exercise of the rights conferred by sections 429 and 430A shall be satisfied by the joint offerors acquiring or contracting to acquire the necessary shares jointly (as respects acquisitions by virtue of acceptances of the offer) and either

jointly or separately (in other cases); and, subject to the following provisions, the rights and obligations of the offeror under those sections and sections 430 and 430B shall be respectively joint rights and joint and several obligations of the joint offerors.

(3)   It shall be a sufficient compliance with any provision of those sections requiring or authorising a notice or other document to be given or sent by or to the joint offerors that it is given or sent by or to any of them; but the statutory declaration required by section 429(4) shall be made by all of them and, in the case of a joint offeror being a company, signed by a director of that company.

(4)   In sections 428, 430(8) and 430E references to the offeror shall be construed as references to the joint offerors or any of them.

(5)   In section 430(6) and (7) references to the offeror shall be construed as references to the joint offerors or such of them as they may determine.

(6)   In sections 430(4)(a) and 430B(4)(a) references to the offeror being no longer able to provide the relevant consideration shall be construed as references to none of the joint offerors being able to do so.

(7)   In section 430C references to the offeror shall be construed as references to the joint offerors except that any application under subsection (3) or (5) may be made by any of them and the reference in subsection (5)(a) to the offeror having been unable to trace one or more of the persons holding shares shall be construed as a reference to none of the offerors having been able to do so.

430E.   Associates.

(1)   The requirement in section 428(1) that a takeover offer must extend to all the shares, or all the shares of any class or classes, in a company shall be regarded as satisfied notwithstanding that the offer does not extend to shares which associates of the offeror hold or have contracted to acquire; but, subject to subsection (2), shares which any such associate holds or has contracted to acquire, whether at the time when the offer is made or subsequently, shall be disregarded for the purposes of any reference in this Part of this Act to the shares to which a takeover offer relates.

(2)   Where during the period within which a takeover offer can be accepted any associate of the offeror acquires or contracts to acquire any of the shares to which the offer relates, then, if the condition specified in subsection (8)(a) or (b) of section 429 is satisfied as respects those shares they shall be treated for the purposes of that section as shares to which the offer relates.

(3)   In section 430A(1)(b) and (2)(b) the reference to shares which the offeror has acquired or contracted to acquire shall include a reference to shares which any associate of his has acquired or contracted to acquire.

(4)   In this section 'associate', in relation to an offeror means—

(a)   a nominee of the offeror;

(b)   a holding company, subsidiary or fellow subsidiary of the offeror or a nominee of such a holding company, subsidiary or fellow subsidiary;

(c)   a body corporate in which the offeror is substantially interested; or

(d)   any person who is, or is a nominee of, a party to an agreement with the offeror for the acquisition of, or of an interest in, the shares which are the subject of the takeover offer, being an agreement which includes provisions imposing obligations or restrictions such as are mentioned in section 204(2)(a).

(5)   For the purposes of subsection (4)(b) a company is a fellow subsidiary of another body corporate if both are subsidiaries of the same body corporate but neither is a subsidiary of the other.

(6)   For the purposes of subsection (4)(c) an offeror has a substantial interest in a body corporate if—

(a)   that body or its directors are accustomed to act in accordance with his directions or instructions; or

(b)   he is entitled to exercise or control the exercise of one-third or more of the voting power at general meetings of that body.

(7)   Subsections (5) and (6) of section 204 shall apply to subsection (4)(d) above as they apply to that section and subsections (3) and (4) of section 203 shall apply for the purposes of subsection (6) above as they apply for the purposes of subsection (2)(b) of that section.

(8)   Where the offeror is an individual his associates shall also include his spouse and any minor child or stepchild of his.

430F.   Convertible securities.

(1)   For the purposes of this Part of this Act securities of a company shall be treated as shares in the company if they are convertible into or entitle the holder to subscribe for such shares; and references to the holder of shares or a shareholder shall be construed accordingly.

(2)   Subsection (1) shall not be construed as requiring any securities to be treated—

(a)   as shares of the same class as those into which they are convertible or for which the holder is entitled to subscribe; or

(b)   as shares of the same class as other securities by reason only that the shares into which they are convertible or for which the holder is entitled to subscribe are of the same class.

PART XIV

INVESTIGATION OF COMPANIES AND THEIR AFFAIRS; REQUISITION OF DOCUMENTS

Appointment and functions of inspectors

431.   Investigation of a company on its own application or that of its members.

(1)   The Secretary of State may appoint one or more competent inspectors to investigate the affairs of a company and to report on them in such manner as he may direct.

(2)   The appointment may be made—

(a)   in the case of a company having a share capital, on the application either of not less than 200 members or of members holding not less than one-tenth of the shares issued,

(b)   in the case of a company not having a share capital, on the application of not less than one-fifth in number of the persons on the company's register of members, and

(c)   in any case, on application of the company.

(3)   The application shall be supported by such evidence as the Secretary of State may require for the purpose of showing that the applicant or applicants have good reason for requiring the investigation.

(4)   The Secretary of State may, before appointing inspectors, require the applicant or applicants to give security, to an amount not exceeding £5,000, or such other sum as he may by order specify, for payment of the costs of the investigation.

An order under this subsection shall be made by statutory instrument subject to annulment in pursuance of a resolution of either House of Parliament.

432.   Other company investigations.

(1)   The Secretary of State shall appoint one or more competent inspectors to investigate the affairs of a company and report on them in such manner as he directs, if the court by order declares that its affairs ought to be so investigated.

(2)   The Secretary of State may make such an appointment if it appears to him that there are circumstances suggesting—

(a)   that the company's affairs are being or have been conducted with intent to defraud its creditors or the creditors of any other person, or otherwise for a fraudulent or unlawful purpose, or in a manner which is unfairly prejudicial to some part of its members, or

(b)   that any actual or proposed act or omission of the company (including an act or omission on its behalf) is or would be so prejudicial, or that the company was formed for any fraudulent or unlawful purpose, or

(c)   that persons concerned with the company's formation or the management of its affairs have in connection therewith been guilty of fraud, misfeasance or other misconduct towards it or towards its members, or

(d)   that the company's members have not been given all the information with respect to its affairs which they might reasonably expect.

(2A)   Inspectors may be appointed under subsection (2) on terms that any report they may make is not for publication; and in such a case, the provisions of section 437(3) (availability and publication of inspectors' reports) do not apply.

(3)   Subsections (1) and (2) are without prejudice to the powers of the Secretary of State under section 431; and the power conferred by subsection (2) is exercisable with respect to a body corporate notwithstanding that it is in course of being voluntarily wound up.

(4)   The reference in subsection (2)(a) to a company's members includes any person who is not a member but to whom shares in the company have been transferred or transmitted by operation of law.

433.   Inspectors' powers during investigation.

(1)   If inspectors appointed under section 431 or 432 to investigate the affairs of a company think it necessary for the purposes of their investigation to investigate also the affairs of another body corporate which is or at any relevant time has been the company's subsidiary or holding company, or a subsidiary of its holding company or a holding company of its subsidiary, they have power to do so; and they shall report on the affairs of the other body corporate so far as they think that the results of their investigation of its affairs are relevant to the investigation of the affairs of the company first mentioned above.

434.   Production of documents and evidence to inspectors.

(1)   When inspectors are appointed under section 431 or 432, it is the duty of all officers and agents of the company, and of all officers and agents of any other body corporate whose affairs are investigated under section 433(1)—

(a)   to produce to the inspectors all documents of or relating to the company or, as the case may be, the other body corporate which are in their custody or power,

(b)   to attend before the inspectors when required to do so, and

(c)   otherwise to give the inspectors all assistance in connection with the investigation which they are reasonably able to give.

(2)   If the inspectors consider that an officer or agent of the company or other body corporate, or any other person, is or may be in possession of information relating to a matter which they believe to be relevant to the investigation, they may require him—

(a)   to produce to them any documents in his custody or power relating to that matter,

(b)   to attend before them, and

(c)   otherwise to give them all assistance in connection with the investigation which he is reasonably able to give;
and it is that person's duty to comply with the requirement.

(3)   An insepctor may for the purposes of the investigation examine any person on oath, and may administer an oath accordingly.

(4)   In this section a reference to officers or to agents includes past, as well as present, officers or agents (as the case may be); and 'agents', in relation to a company or other body corporate, includes its bankers and solicitors and persons employed by it as

auditors, whether these persons are or are not officers of the company or other body corporate.

(5)   An answer given by a person to a question put to him in exercise of powers conferred by this section (whether as it has effect in relation to an investigation under any of sections 431 to 433, or as applied by any other section in this Part) may be used in evidence against him.

(6)   In this section 'documents' includes information recorded in any form; and, in relation to information recorded otherwise than in legible form, the power to require its production includes power to require the production of a copy of the information in legible form.

436.   Obstruction of inspectors treated as contempt of court.

(1)   If any person—

    (a)   fails to comply with section 434(1)(a) or (c),

    (b)   refuses to compy with a requirement under section 434(1)(b) or (2), or

    (c)   refuses to answer any question put to him by the inspectors for the purposes of the investigation,

the inspectors may certify that fact in writing to the court.

(2)   If that person—

    (a)   refuses to produce any book or document which it is his duty under section 434 or 435 to produce, or

    (b)   refuses to attend before the inspectors when required to do so, or

    (c)   refuses to answer any question put to him by the inspectors with respect to the affairs of the company or other body corporate (as the case may be),

the inspectors may certify the refusal in writing to the court.

(3)   The court may thereupon enquire into the case; and, after hearing any witnesses who may be produced against or on behalf of the alleged offender and after hearing any statement which may be offered in defence, the court may punish the offender in like manner as if he had been guilty of contempt of the court.

437.   Inspectors' reports.

(1)   The inspectors may, and if so directed by the Secretary of State shall, make interim reports to the Secretary of State, and on the conclusion of their investigation shall make a final report to him.

Any such report shall be written or printed, as the Secretary of State directs.

(1A)   Any persons who have been appointed under section 431 or 432 may at any time and, if the Secretary of State directs them to do so, shall inform him of any matters coming to their knowledge as a result of their investigations.

(1B)   If it appears to the Secretary of State that matters have come to light in the course of the inspectors' investigation which suggest that a criminal offence has been committed, and those matters have been referred to the appropriate prosecuting authority, he may direct the inspectors to take no further steps in the investigation or to take only such further steps as are specified in the direction.

(1C)   Where an investigation is the subject of a direction under subsection (1B), the inspectors shall make a final report to the Secretary of State only where—

    (a)   they were appointed under section 432(1) (appointment in pursuance of an order of the court), or

    (b)   the Secretary of State directs them to do so.

(2)   If the inspectors were appointed under section 432 in pursuance of an order of the court, the Secretary of State shall furnish a copy of any report of theirs to the court.

(3)   In any case the Secretary of State may, if he thinks fit—

    (a)   forward a copy of any report made by the inspectors to the company's registered office,

    (b)   furnish a copy on request and on payment of the prescribed fee to—

(i)   any member of the company or other body corporate which is the subject of the report,

(ii)   any person whose conduct is referred to in the report,

(iii)   the auditors of that company or body corporate,

(iv)   the applicants for the investigation,

(v)   any other person whose financial interests appear to the Secretary of State to be affected by the matters dealt with in the report, whether as a creditor of the company or body corporate, or otherwise, and

(c)   cause any such report to be printed and published.

438.   Power to bring civil proceedings on company's behalf.

(1)   If from any report made or information obtained under this Part it appears to the Secretary of State that any civil proceedings ought in the public interest to be brought by any body corporate, he may himself bring such proceedings in the name and on behalf of the body corporate.

(2)   The Secretary of State shall indemnify the body corporate against any costs or expenses incurred by it in or in connection with proceedings brought under this section.

439.   Expenses of investigating a company's affairs.

(1)   The expenses of an investigation under any of the powers conferred by this Part shall be defrayed in the first instance by the Secretary of State, but he may recover those expenses from the persons liable in accordance with this section.

There shall be treated as expenses of the investigation, in particular, such reasonable sums as the Secretary of State may determine in respect of general staff costs and overheads.

(2)   A person who is convicted on a prosecution instituted as a result of the investigation, or is ordered to pay the whole or any part of the costs of proceedings brought under section 438, may in the same proceedings be ordered to pay those expenses to such extent as may be specified in the order.

(3)   A body corporate in whose name proceedings are brought under that section is liable to the amount or value of any sums or property recovered by it as a result of those proceedings; and any amount for which a body corporate is liable under this subsection is a first charge on the sums or property recovered.

(4)   A body corporate dealt with by an inspectors' report, where the inspectors were appointed otherwise than of the Secretary of State's own motion, is liable except where it was the applicant for the investigation, and except so far as the Secretary of State otherwise directs.

(5)   Where inspectors were appointed—

(a)   under section 431, or

(b)   on an application under section 442(3),

the applicant or applicants for the investigation is or are liable to such extent (if any) as the Secretary of State may direct.

(6)   The report of inspectors appointed otherwise than of the Secretary of State's own motion may, if they think fit, and shall if the Secretary of State so directs, include a recommendation as to the directions (if any) which they think appropriate, in the light of their investigation, to be given under subsection (4) or (5) of this section.

(7)   For purposes of this section, any costs or expenses incurred by the Secretary of State in or in connection with proceedings brought under section 438 (including expenses incurred under subsection (2) of it) are to be treated as expenses of the investigation giving rise to the proceedings.

(8)   Any liability to repay the Secretary of State imposed by subsection (2) and (3) above is (subject to satisfaction of his right to repayment) a liability also to indemnify all persons against liability under subsections (4) and (5); and any such liability imposed by

subsection (2) is (subject as mentioned above) a liability also to indemnify all persons against liability under subsection (3).

(9)   A person liable under any one of those subsections is entitled to contribution from any other person liable under the same subsection, according to the amount of their respective liabilities under it.

(10)   Expenses to be defrayed by the Secretary of State under this section shall, so far as not recovered under it, be paid out of money provided by Parliament.

441.   Inspectors' report to be evidence.

(1)   A copy of any report of inspectors appointed under this Part, certified by the Secretary of State to be a true copy, is admissible in any legal proceedings as evidence of the opinion of the inspectors in relation to any matter contained in the report and, in proceedings on an application under section 8 of the Company Directors Disqualification Act 1986, as evidence of any fact stated therein.

(2)   A document purporting to be such a certificate as is mentioned above shall be received in evidence and be deemed to be such a certificate, unless the contrary is proved.

Other powers of investigation available to the Secretary of State

442.   Power to investigate company ownership.

(1)   Where it appears to the Secretary of State that there is good reason to do so, he may appoint one or more competent inspectors to investigate and report on the membership of any company, and otherwise with respect to the company, for the purpose of determining the true persons who are or have been financially interested in the success or failure (real or apparent) of the company or able to control or materially to influence its policy.

(2)   The appointment of inspectors under this section may define the scope of their investigation (whether as respects the matter or the period to which it is to extend or otherwise) and in particular may limit the investigation to matters connected with particular shares or debentures.

(3)   If an application for investigation under this section with respect to particular shares or debentures of a company is made to the Secretary of State by members of the company, and the number of applicants or the amount of shares held by them is not less than that required for an application for the appointment of inspectors under section 431(2)(a) or (b), then, subject to the following provisions, the Secretary of State shall appoint inspectors to conduct the investigation applied for.

(3A)   The Secretary of State shall not appoint inspectors if he is satisfied that the application is vexatious; and where inspectors are appointed their terms of appointment shall exclude any matter in so far as the Secretary of State is satisfied that it is unreasonable for it to be investigated.

(3B)   The Secretary of State may, before appointing inspectors, require the applicant or applicants to give security, to an amount not exceeding £5,000, or such other sum as he may by order specify, for payment of the costs of the investigation.

An order under this subsection shall be made by statutory instrument which shall be subject to annulment in pursuance of a resolution of either House of Parliament.

(3C)   If on an application under subsection (3) it appears to the Secretary of State that the powers conferred by section 444 are sufficient for the purposes of investigating the matters which inspectors would be appointed to investigate, he may instead conduct the investigation under that section.

(4)   Subject to the terms of their appointment, the inspectors' powers extend to the investigation of any circumstances suggesting the existence of an arrangement or understanding which, though not legally binding, is or was observed or likely to be observed in practice and which is relevant to the purposes of the investigation.

443. Provisions applicable on investigation under s. 442.

(1) For purposes of an investigation under section 442, sections 433(1), 434, 436 and 437 apply with the necessary modifications of references to the affairs of the company or to those of any other body corporate, subject however to the following subsections.

(2) Those sections apply to—

(a) all persons who are or have been, or whom the inspector has reasonable cause to believe to be or have been, financially interested in the success or failure or the apparent success or failure of the company or any other body corporate whose membership is investigated with that of the company, or able to control or materially influence its policy (including persons concerned only on behalf of others), and

(b) any other person whom the inspector has reasonable cause to believe possesses information relevant to the investigation,

as they apply in relation to officers and agents of the company or the other body corporate (as the case may be).

(3) If the Secretary of State is of opinion that there is good reason for not divulging any part of a report made by virtue of section 442 and this section, he may under section 437 disclose the report with the omission of that part; and he may cause to be kept by the registrar of companies a copy of the report with that part omitted or, in the case of any other such report, a copy of the whole report.

444. Power to obtain information as to those interested in shares, etc.

(1) If it appears to the Secretary of State that there is good reason to investigate the ownership of any shares in or debentures of a company and that it is unnecessary to appoint inspectors for the purpose, he may require any person whom he has reasonable cause to believe to have or to be able to obtain any information as to the present and past interests in those shares or debentures and the names and addresses of the persons interested and of any persons who act or have acted on their behalf in relation to the shares or debentures to give any such information to the Secretary of State.

(2) For this purpose a person is deemed to have an interest in shares or debentures if he has any right to acquire or dispose of them or of any interest in them, or to vote in respect of them, or if his consent is necessary for the exercise of any of the rights of other persons interested in them, or if other persons interested in them can be required, or are accustomed, to exercise their rights in accordance with his instructions.

(3) A person who fails to give information required of him under this section, or who in giving such information makes any statement which he knows to be false in a material particular, or recklessly makes any statement which is false in a material particular, is liable to imprisonment or a fine, or both.

445. Power to impose restrictions on shares and debentures.

(1) If in connection with an investigation under either section 442 or 444 it appears to the Secretary of State that there is difficulty in finding out the relevant facts about any shares (whether issued or to be issued), he may by order direct that the shares shall until further order be subject to the restrictions of Part XV of this Act.

(1A) If the Secretary of State is satisfied that an order under subsection (1) may unfairly affect the rights of third parties in respect of shares then the Secretary of State, for the purpose of protecting such rights and subject to such terms as he thinks fit, may direct that such acts by such persons or descriptions of persons and for such purposes as may be set out in the order, shall not constitute a breach of the restrictions of Part XV of this Act.

(2) This section, and Part XV in its application to orders under it, apply in relation to debentures as in relation to shares save that subsection (1A) shall not so apply.

446.　Investigation of share dealings.

(1)　If it appears to the Secretary of State that there are circumstances suggesting that contraventions may have occurred, in relation to a company's shares or debentures, of section 323 or 324 (taken with Schedule 13), or of subsections (3) to (5) of section 328 (restrictions on share dealings by directors and their families; obligation of director to disclose shareholding in his own company), he may appoint one or more competent inspectors to carry out such investigations as are requisite to establish whether or not such contraventions have occurred and to report the result of their investigations to him.

(2)　The appointment of inspectors under this section may limit the period to which their investigation is to extend or confine it to shares or debentures of a particular class, or both.

(3)　For purposes of an investigation under this section, sections 434 to 437 apply—

(a)　with the substitution, for references to any other body corporate whose affairs are investigated under section 433(1), of a reference to any other body corporate which is, or has at any relevant time been, the company's subsidiary or holding company, or a subsidiary of its holding company.

(4)　Sections 434 to 436 apply under the preceding subsection—

(a)　to any individual who is an authorised person within the meaning of the Financial Services Act 1986;

(b)　to any individual who holds a permission granted under paragraph 23 of Schedule 1 to that Act;

(c)　to any officer (whether past or present) of a body corporate which is such an authorised person or holds such a permission;

(d)　to any partner (whether past or present) in a partnership which is such an authorised person or holds such a permission;

(e)　to any member of the governing body or officer (in either case whether past or present) of an unincorporated association which is such an authorised person or holds such a permission,

as they apply to officers of the company or of the other body corporate.

Requisition and seizure of books and papers

447.　Secretary of State's power to require production of documents.

(2)　The Secretary of State may at any time, if he thinks there is good reason to do so, give directions to a company requiring it, at such time and place as may be specified in the directions, to produce such documents as may be so specified.

(3)　The Secretary of State may at any time, if he thinks there is good reason to do so, authorise an officer of his or any other competent person, on producing (if so required) evidence of his authority, to require a company to produce to him (the officer or other person) forthwith any documents which he (the officer or other person) may specify.

(4)　Where by virtue of subsection (2) or (3) the Secretary of State or an officer of his or other person has power to require the production of documents from a company, he or the officer or other person has the like power to require production of those documents from any person who appears to him or the officer or other person to be in possession of them; but where any such person claims a lien on books or papers produced by him, the production is without prejudice to the lien.

(5)　The power under this section to require a company or other person to produce documents includes power—

(a)　if the documents are produced—

(i)　to take copies of them or extracts from them, and

(ii)　to require that person, or any other person who is a present or past officer of, or is or was at any time employed by, the company in question, to provide an explanation of any of them;

(b)   if the documents are not produced, to require the person who was required to produce them to state, to the best of his knowledge and belief, where they are.

(6)   If the requirement to produce documents or provide an explanation or make a statement is not complied with, the company or other person on whom the requirement was so imposed is guilty of an offence and liable to a fine.

Sections 732 (restriction on prosecutions), 733 (liability of individuals for corporate default) and 734 (criminal proceedings against unincorporated bodies) apply to this offence.

(7)   However, where a person is charged with an offence under subsection (6) in respect of a requirement to produce any documents, it is a defence to prove that they were not in his possession or under his control and that it was not reasonably practicable for him to comply with the requirement.

(8)   A statement made by a person in compliance with such a requirement may be used in evidence against him.

(9)   In this section 'documents' includes information recorded in any form; and, in relation to information recorded otherwise than in legible form, the power to require its production includes power to require the production of a copy of it in legible form.

448.   Entry and search of premises.

(1)   A justice of the peace may issue a warrant under this section if satisfied on information on oath given by or on behalf of the Secretary of State, or by a person appointed or authorised to exercise powers under this Part, that there are reasonable grounds for believing that there are on any premises documents whose production has been required under this Part and which have not been produced in compliance with the requirement.

(2)   A justice of the peace may also issue a warrant under this section if satisfied on information on oath given by or on behalf of the Secretary of State, or by a person appointed or authorised to exercise powers under this Part—

(a)   that there are reasonable grounds for believing that an offence has been committed for which the penalty on conviction on indictment is imprisonment for a term of not less than two years and that there are on any premises documents relating to whether the offence has been committed,

(b)   that the Secretary of State, or the person so appointed or authorised, has power to require the production of the documents under this Part, and

(c)   that there are reasonable grounds for believing that if production was so required the documents would not be produced but would be removed from the premises, hidden, tampered with or destroyed.

(3)   A warrant under this section shall authorise a constable, together with any other person named in it and any other constables—

(a)   to enter the premises specified in the information, using such force as is reasonably necessary for the purpose;

(b)   to search the premises and take possession of any documents appearing to be such documents as are mentioned in subsection (1) or (2), as the case may be, or to take, in relation to any such documents, any other steps which may appear to be necessary for preserving them or preventing interference with them;

(c)   to take copies of any such documents; and

(d)   to require any person named in the warrant to provide an explanation of them or to state where they may be found.

(4)   If in the case of a warrant under subsection (2) the justice of the peace is satisfied on information on oath that there are reasonable grounds for believing that there are also on the premises other documents relevant to the investigation, the warrant shall also authorise the actions mentioned in subsection (3) to be taken in relation to such documents.

(5)   A warrant under this section shall continue in force until the end of the period of one month beginning with the day on which it is issued.

(6)   Any documents of which possession is taken under this section may be retained—

(a)   for a period of three months; or

(b)   if within that period proceedings to which the documents are relevant are commenced against any person for any criminal offence, until the conclusion of those proceedings.

(7)   Any person who intentionally obstructs the exercise of any rights conferred by a warrant issued under this section or fails without reasonable excuse to comply with any requirement imposed in accordance with subsection (3)(d) is guilty of an offence and liable to a fine.

Sections 732 (restriction on prosecutions), 733 (liability of individuals for corporate default) and 734 (criminal proceedings against unincorporated bodies) apply to this offence.

(8)   For the purposes of sections 449 and 451A (provision for security of information) documents obtained under this section shall be treated as if they had been obtained under the provision of this Part under which their production was or, as the case may be, could have been required.

(9)   In the application of this section to Scotland for the references to a justice of the peace substitute references to a justice of the peace or a sheriff, and for the references to information on oath substitute references to evidence on oath.

(10)   In this section 'document' includes information recorded in any form.

449.   Provision for security of information obtained.

(1)   No information or document relating to a company which has been obtained under section 447 shall, without the previous consent in writing of that company, be published or disclosed, except to a competent authority, unless the publication or disclosure is required—

(a)   with a view to the institution of or otherwise for the purposes of criminal proceedings;

(ba)   with a view to the institution of, or otherwise for the purposes of, any proceedings on an application under section 6, 7 or 8 of the Company Directors Disqualification Act 1986;

(c)   for the purposes of enabling or assisting any inspector appointed under this Part, or under section 94 or 177 of the Financial Services Act 1986, to discharge his functions;

(cc)   for the purpose of enabling or assisting any person authorised to exercise powers or appointed under section 43A or 44 of the Insurance Companies Act 1982, section 447 of this Act, section 106 of the Financial Services Act 1986 or section 84 of the Companies Act 1989 to discharge his functions;

(d)   for the purpose of enabling or assisting the Secretary of State or the Treasury to exercise any of their functions under this Act, the insider dealing legislation, *the Prevention of Fraud (Investments) Act 1958*, the Insurance Companies Act 1982, the Insolvency Act 1986, the Company Directors Disqualification Act 1986, the Financial Services Act 1986 or Part II, III or VII of the Companies Act 1989;

(dd)   for the purpose of enabling or assisting the Department of Economic Development for Northern Ireland to exercise any powers conferred on it by the enactments relating to companies or insolvency or for the purpose of enabling or assisting any inspector appointed by it under the enactments relating to companies to discharge his functions;

(de)   for the purpose of enabling or assisting the Chief Registrar of friendly societies or the Assistant Registrar of friendly societies for Scotland to discharge his functions under the enactments relating to friendly societies;

(df)   for the purpose of enabling or assisting the Friendly Societies Commission to discharge its functions under the Financial Services Act 1986;

(dg)   for the purpose of enabling or assisting the Occupational Pensions Regulatory Authority to discharge their functions under the Pension Schemes Act 1993 or the Pensions Act 1995 or any enactment in force in Northern Ireland corresponding to either of them;

(f)   for the purpose of enabling or assisting the Bank of England to discharge its functions;

(fa)   for the purpose of enabling or assisting the Financial Services Authority to discharge—

(i)   any functions under the Financial Services Act 1986, other than as a designated agency within the meaning of that Act,

(ii)   its functions under the Banking Act 1987, or

(iii)   its functions under section 171 of the Companies Act 1989;

(g)   for the purpose of enabling or assisting the Deposit Protection Board to discharge its functions under that Act;

(h)   for any purpose mentioned in section 180(1)(b), (e), (h) or (n) of the Financial Services Act 1986;

(hh)   for the purpose of enabling or assisting a body established by order under section 46 of the Companies Act 1989 to discharge its functions under Part II of that Act, or of enabling or assisting a recognised supervisory or qualifying body within the meaning of that Part to discharge its functions as such;

(i)   for the purpose of enabling or assisting the Industrial Assurance Commissioner or the Industrial Assurance Commissioner for Northern Ireland to discharge his functions under the enactments relating to industrial assurance;

(j)   for the purpose of enabling or assisting the Insurance Brokers Registration Council to discharge its functions under the Insurance Brokers (Registration) Act 1977;

(k)   for the purpose of enabling or assisting an official receiver to discharge his functions under the enactments relating to insolvency or for the purpose of enabling or assisting a body which is for the time being a recognised professional body for the purposes of section 391 of the Insolvency Act 1986 to discharge its functions as such;

(l)   with a view to the institution of, or otherwise for the purposes of, any disciplinary proceedings relating to the exercise by a solicitor, auditor, accountant, valuer or actuary of his professional duties;

(ll)   with a view to the institution of, or otherwise for the purposes of, any disciplinary proceedings relating to the discharge by a public servant of his duties;

(m)   for the purpose of enabling or assisting an overseas regulatory authority to exercise its regulatory functions.

(1A)   In subsection (1)—

(a)   in paragraph (ll) 'public servant' means an officer or servant of the Crown or of any public or other authority for the time being designated for the purposes of that paragraph by the Secretary of State by order made by statutory instrument; and

(b)   in paragraph (m) 'overseas regulatory authority' and 'regulatory functions' have the same meaning as in section 82 of the Companies Act 1989.

(1B)   Subject to subsection (1C), subsection (1) shall not preclude publication or disclosure for the purpose of enabling or assisting any public or other authority for the time being designated for the purposes of this subsection by the Secretary of State by an order in a statutory instrument to discharge any functions which are specified in the order.

(1C)   An order under subsection (1B) designating an authority for the purpose of that subsection may—

(a)   impose conditions subject to which the publication or disclosure of any information or document is permitted by that subsection; and

(b) otherwise restrict the circumstances in which that subsection permits publication or disclosure.

(1D) Subsection (1) shall not preclude the publication or disclosure of any such information as is mentioned in section 180(5) of the Financial Services Act 1986 by any person who by virtue of that section is not precluded by section 179 of that Act from disclosing it.

(2) A person who publishes or discloses any information or document in contravention of this section is guilty of an offence and liable to imprisonment or a fine, or both.

Sections 732 (restriction on prosecutions), 733 (liability of individuals for corporate default) and 734 (criminal proceedings against unincorporated bodies) apply to this offence.

(3) For the purposes of this section each of the following is a competent authority—

    (a) the Secretary of State,

    (b) an inspector appointed under this Part or under section 94 or 177 of the Financial Services Act 1986,

    (c) any person authorised to exercise powers under section 44 of the Insurance Companies Act 1982, section 447 of this Act, section 106 of the Financial Services Act 1986 or section 84 of the Companies Act 1989,

    (d) the Department of Economic Development in Northern Ireland,

    (e) the Treasury,

    (f) the Bank of England,

    (g) the Lord Advocate,

    (h) the Director of Public Prosecutions and the Director of Public Prosecutions for Northern Ireland,

    (ha) the Financial Services Authority, other than in its capacity as a designated agency within the meaning of the Financial Services Act 1986,

    (i) any designated agency or transferee body within the meaning of the Financial Services Act 1986, and any body administering a scheme under section 54 of or paragraph 18 of Schedule 11 to that Act (schemes for compensation of investors),

    (j) the Chief Registrar of Friendly Societies,

    (jj) the Friendly Societies Commission,

    (k) the Industrial Assurance Commissioner,

    (l) any constable,

    (m) any procurator fiscal.

(3A) Any information which may by virtue of this section be disclosed to a competent authority may be disclosed to any officer or servant of the authority.

(4) A statutory instrument containing an order under subsection (1A)(a) or (1B) is subject to annulment in pursuance of a resolution of either House of Parliament.

[*The words in italics in s. 449(1)(d) ('the Prevention of Fraud (Investments) Act 1958,') were repealed by the Financial Services Act 1986, sch. 17, part I, but this repeal has been brought into force only in so far as the words apply to a prospectus offering for subscription, or to any form of application for, units in a body corporate which is a recognised scheme (Financial Services Act 1986 (Commencement) (No. 8) Order 1988 (SI 1988/740), art. 2 and sch.). Section 449(1)(hh) has not been brought into force to the extent that it refers to a body established by order under the Companies Act 1989, s. 46.*]

450. Punishment for destroying, mutilating etc. company documents.

(1) An officer of a company or of an insurance company to which Part II of the Insurance Companies Act 1982 applies, who—

(a)   destroys, mutilates or falsifies, or is privy to the destruction, mutilation or falsification of a document affecting or relating to the company's property or affairs, or

(b)   makes, or is privy to the making of, a false entry in such a document,
is guilty of an offence, unless he proves that he had no intention to conceal the state of affairs of the company or to defeat the law.

(2)   Such a person as above mentioned who fraudulently either parts with, alters or makes an omission in any such document or is privy to fraudulent parting with, fraudulent altering or fraudulent making of an omission in, any such document, is guilty of an offence.

(3)   A person guilty of an offence under this section is liable to imprisonment or a fine, or both.

(4)   Sections 732 (restriction on prosecutions), 733 (liability of individuals for corporate default) and 734 (criminal proceedings against unincorporated bodies) apply to an offence under this section.

(5)   In this section 'document' includes information recorded in any form.

451.   Punishment for furnishing false information.
A person who, in purported compliance with a requirement imposed under section 447 to provide an explanation or make a statement, provides or makes an explanation or statement which he knows to be false in a material particular or recklessly provides or makes an explanation or statement which is so false, is guilty of an offence and liable to imprisonment or a fine, or both.

Sections 732 (restriction on prosecutions), 733 (liability of individuals for corporate default) and 734 (criminal proceedings against unincorporated bodies) apply to this offence.

451A.   Disclosure of information by Secretary of State or inspector.
(1)   This section applies to information obtained under sections 434 to 446.

(2)   The Secretary of State may, if he thinks fit—

(a)   disclose any information to which this section applies to any person to whom, or for any purpose for which, disclosure is permitted under section 449, or

(b)   authorise or require an inspector appointed under this Part to disclose such information to any such person or for any such purpose.

(3)   Information to which this section applies may also be disclosed by an inspector appointed under this Part to—

(a)   another inspector appointed under this Part or an inspector appointed under section 94 or 177 of the Financial Services Act 1986, or

(b)   a person authorised to exercise powers or appointed under section 43A or 44 of the Insurance Companies Act 1982, section 447 of this Act, section 106 of the Financial Services Act 1986 or section 84 of the Companies Act 1989.

(4)   Any information which may by virtue of subsection (3) be disclosed to any person may be disclosed to any officer or servant of that person.

(5)   The Secretary of State may, if he thinks fit, disclose any information obtained under section 444 to—

(a)   the company whose ownership was the subject of the investigation,

(b)   any member of the company,

(c)   any person whose conduct was investigated in the course of the investigation,

(d)   the auditors of the company, or

(e)   any person whose financial interests appear to the Secretary of State to be affected by matters covered by the investigation.

Supplementary

452.   Privileged information.
(1)   Nothing in sections 431 to 446 requires the disclosure to the Secretary of State or to an inspector appointed by him—

(a) by any person of information which he would in an action in the High Court or the Court of Session be entitled to refuse to disclose on grounds of legal professional privilege except, if he is a lawyer, the name and address of his client.

(1A) Nothing in section 434, 443 or 446 requires a person (except as mentioned in subsection (1B) below) to disclose information or produce documents in respect of which he owes an obligation of confidence by virtue of carrying on the business of banking unless—

(a) the person to whom the obligation of confidence is owed is the company or other body corporate under investigation,

(b) the person to whom the obligation of confidence is owed consents to the disclosure or production, or

(c) the making of the requirement is authorised by the Secretary of State.

(1B) Subsection (1A) does not apply where the person owing the obligation of confidence is the company or other body corporate under investigation under section 431, 432 or 433.

(2) Nothing in section 447 to 451 compels the production by any person of a document which he would in an action in the High Court or the Court of Session be entitled to refuse to produce on grounds of legal professional privilege, or authorises the taking of possession of any such document which is in the person's possession.

(3) The Secretary of State shall not under section 447 require, or authorise an officer of his or other person to require, the production by a person carrying on the business of banking of a document relating to the affairs of a customer of his unless either it appears to the Secretary of State that it is necessary to do so for the purpose of investigating the affairs of the first-mentioned person, or the customer is a person on whom a requirement has been imposed under that section, or under section 43A or 44(2) to (4) of the Insurance Companies Act 1982 (provision corresponding to section 447).

453. Investigation of oversea companies.

(1) The provisions of this Part apply to bodies corporate incorporated outside Great Britain which are carrying on business in Great Britain, or have at any time carried on business there, as they apply to companies under this Act; but subject to the following exceptions, adaptations and modifications.

(1A) The following provisions do not apply to such bodies—

(a) section 431 (investigation on application of company or its members),

(b) section 438 (power to bring civil proceedings on the company's behalf),

(c) sections 442 to 445 (investigation of company ownership and power to obtain information as to those interested in shares, &c.), and

(d) section 446 (investigation of share dealings).

(1B) The other provisions of this Part apply to such bodies subject to such adaptations and modifications as may be specified by regulations made by the Secretary of State.

(2) Regulations under this section shall be made by statutory instrument subject to annulment in pursuance of a resolution of either House of Parliament.

PART XV
ORDERS IMPOSING RESTRICTIONS ON SHARES (SECTIONS 210, 216, 445)

454. Consequence of order imposing restrictions.

(1) So long as any shares are directed to be subject to the restrictions of this Part then, subject to any directions made in relation to an order pursuant to sections 210(5A), 216(1B), 445(1A) or 456(1A) or subject in the case of an interim order pursuant to section 216(1A) to the terms of that order—

(a)   any transfer of those shares or, in the case of unissued shares, any transfer of the right to be issued with them, and any issue of them, is void;

(b)   no voting rights are exercisable in respect of the shares;

(c)   no further shares shall be issued in right of them or in pursuance of any offer made to their holder; and

(d)   except in a liquidation, no payment shall be made of any sums due from the company on the shares, whether in respect of capital or otherwise.

(2)   Where shares are subject to the restrictions of subsection (1)(a), any agreement to transfer the shares or, in the case of unissued shares, the right to be issued with them is void (except such agreement or right as may be made or exercised under the terms of directions made by the Secretary of State or the court under sections 210(5A), 216(1B), 445(1A), 456(1A) or of an interim order made under section 216(1A) or an agreement to transfer the shares on the making of an order under section 456(3)(b) below).

(3)   Where shares are subject to the restrictions of subsection (1)(c) or (d), an agreement to transfer any right to be issued with other shares in right of those shares, or to receive any payment on them (otherwise than in a liquidation) is void (except such agreement or right as may be made or exercised under the terms of directions made by the Secretary of State or the court under sections 210(5A), 216(1B), 445(1A), 456(1A) or of an interim order made under section 216(1A) or an agreement to transfer any such right on the transfer of the shares on the making of an order under section 456(3)(b) below).

455. Punishment for attempted evasion of restrictions.

(1)   Subject to the terms of any directions made under sections 210(5A), 216(1B) or 445(1A) or 456 or of an interim order made under section 216(1A) a person is liable to a fine if he—

(a)   exercises or purports to exercise any right to dispose of any shares which, to his knowledge, are for the time being subject to the restrictions of this Part or of any right to be issued with any such shares, or

(b)   votes in respect of any such shares (whether as holder or proxy), or appoints a proxy to vote in respect of them, or

(c)   being the holder of any such shares, fails to notify of their being subject to those restrictions any person whom he does not know to be aware of that fact but does know to be entitled (apart from the restrictions) to vote in respect of those shares whether as holder or as proxy, or

(d)   being the holder of any such shares, or being entitled to any right to be issued with other shares in right of them, or to receive any payment on them (otherwise than in a liquidation), enters into any agreement which is void under section 454(2) or (3).

(2)   Subject to the terms of any directions made under sections 210(5A), 216(1B), 445(1A) or 456 or of an interim order made under section 216(1A) if shares in a company are issued in contravention of the restrictions, the company and every officer of it who is in default is liable to a fine.

(3)   Section 732 (restriction on prosecutions) applies to an offence under this section.

456. Relaxation and removal of restrictions.

(1)   Where shares in a company are by order made subject to the restrictions of this Part, application may be made to the court for an order directing that the shares be no longer so subject.

(1A)   Where the court is satisfied that an order subjecting the shares to the restrictions of this Part unfairly affects the rights of third parties in respect of shares then the court, for the purpose of protecting such rights and subject to such terms as it thinks fit and in addition to any order it may make under subsection (1), may direct on an application made under that subsection that such acts by such persons or descriptions of persons and for such purposes, as may be set out in the order, shall not constitute a breach of the restrictions of Part XV of this Act.

Subsection (3) does not apply to an order made under this subsection.

(2) If the order applying the restrictions was made by the Secretary of State, or he has refused to make an order disapplying them, the application may be made by any person aggrieved; and if the order was made by the court under section 216 (non-disclosure of share holding), it may be made by any such person or by the company.

(3) Subject as follows, an order of the court or the Secretary of State directing that shares shall cease to be subject to the restrictions may be made only if—

(a) the court or (as the case may be) the Secretary of State is satisfied that the relevant facts about the shares have been disclosed to the company and no unfair advantage has accrued to any person as a result of the earlier failure to make that disclosure, or

(b) the shares are to be transferred for valuable consideration and the court (in any case) or the Secretary of State (if the order was made under section 210 or 445) approves the transfer.

(4) Without prejudice to the power of the court to give directions under subsection (1A), where shares in a company are subject to the restrictions, the court may on application order the shares to be sold, subject to the court's approval as to the sale, and may also direct that the shares shall cease to be subject to the restrictions.

An application to the court under this subsection may be made by the Secretary of State (unless the restrictions were imposed by court order under section 216), or by the company.

(5) Where an order has been made under subsection (4), the court may on application make such further order relating to the sale or transfer of the shares as it thinks fit.

An application to the court under this subsection may be made—

(a) by the Secretary of State (unless the restrictions on the shares were imposed by court order under section 216), or

(b) by the company, or

(c) by the person appointed by or in pursuance of the order to effect the sale, or

(d) by any person interested in the shares.

(6) An order (whether of the Secretary of State or the court) directing that shares shall cease to be subject to the restrictions of this Part, if it is—

(a) expressed to be made with a view to permitting a transfer of the shares, or

(b) made under subsection (4) of this section,

may continue the restrictions mentioned in paragraphs (c) and (d) or section 454(1), either in whole or in part, so far as they relate to any right acquired or offer made before the transfer.

(7) Subsection (3) does not apply to an order directing that shares shall cease to be subject to any restrictions which have been continued in force in relation to those shares under subsection (6).

457. Further provisions on sale by court order of restricted shares.

(1) Where shares are sold in pursuance of an order of the court under section 456(4) the proceeds of sale, less the costs of the sale, shall be paid into court for the benefit of the persons who are beneficially interested in the shares; and any such person may apply to the court for the whole or part of those proceeds to be paid to him.

(2) On application under subsection (1) the court shall (subject as provided below) order the payment to the applicant of the whole of the proceeds of sale together with any interest thereon or, if any other person had a beneficial interest in the shares at the time

of their sale, such proportion of those proceeds and interest as is equal to the proportion which the value of the applicant's interest in the shares bears to the total value of the shares.

(3)   On granting an application for an order under section 456(4) or (5) the court may order that the applicant's costs be paid out of the proceeds of sale; and if that order is made, the applicant is entitled to payment of his costs out of those proceeds before any person interested in the shares in question receives any part of those proceeds.

PART XVI
FRAUDULENT TRADING BY A COMPANY

458.   Punishment for fraudulent trading.

If any business of a company is carried on with intent to defraud creditors of the company or creditors of any other person, or for any fraudulent purpose, every person who was knowingly a party to the carrying on of the business in that manner is liable to imprisonment or a fine, or both.

This applies whether or not the company has been, or is in the course of being, wound up.

PART XVII
PROTECTION OF COMPANY'S MEMBERS AGAINST UNFAIR PREJUDICE

459.   Order on application of company member.

(1)   A member of a company may apply to the court by petition for an order under this Part on the ground that the company's affairs are being or have been conducted in a manner which is unfairly prejudicial to the interests of its members generally or of some part of its members (including at least himself) or that any actual or proposed act or omission of the company (including an act or omission on its behalf) is or would be so prejudicial.

(2)   The provisions of this Part apply to a person who is not a member of a company but to whom shares in the company have been transferred or transmitted by operation of law, as those provisions apply to a member of the company; and references to a member or members are to be construed accordingly.

(3)   In this section (and so far as applicable for the purposes of this section, in section 461(2)) 'company' means any company within the meaning of this Act or any company which is not such a company but is a statutory water company within the meaning of the Statutory Water Companies Act 1991.

460.   Order on application of Secretary of State.

(1)   If in the case of any company—

(a)   the Secretary of State has received a report under section 437, or exercised his powers under section 447 or 448 of this Act or section 43A or 44(2) to (6) of the Insurance Companies Act 1982, and

(b)   it appears to him that the company's affairs are being or have been conducted in a manner which is unfairly prejudicial to the interests of its members generally or of some part of its members, or that any actual or proposed act or omission of the company (including an act or omission on its behalf) is or would be so prejudicial,

he may himself (in addition to or instead of presenting a petition for the winding up of the company) apply to the court by petition for an order under this Part.

(2)   In this section (and, so far as applicable for its purposes, in the section next following) 'company' means any body corporate which is liable to be wound up under this Act.

461.   Provisions as to petitions and orders under this Part.

(1)   If the court is satisfied that a petition under this Part is well founded, it may make such order as it thinks fit for giving relief in respect of the matters complained of.

(2)   Without prejudice to the generality of subsection (1), the court's order may—

    (a)   regulate the conduct of the company's affairs in the future,

    (b)   require the company to refrain from doing or continuing an act complained of by the petitioner or to do an act which the petitioner has complained it has omitted to do,

    (c)   authorise civil proceedings to be brought in the name and on behalf of the company by such person or persons and on such terms as the court may direct,

    (d)   provide for the purchase of the shares of any members of the company by other members or by the company itself and, in the case of a purchase by the company itself, the reduction of the company's capital accordingly.

(3)   If an order under this Part requires the company not to make any, or any specified, alteration in the memorandum or articles, the company does not then have power without leave of the court to make any such alteration in breach of that requirement.

(4)   Any alteration in the company's memorandum or articles made by virtue of an order under this Part is of the same effect as if duly made by resolution of the company, and the provisions of this Act apply to the memorandum or articles as so altered accordingly.

(5)   An office copy of an order under this part altering, or giving leave to alter, a company's memorandum or articles shall, within 14 days from the making of the order or such longer period as the court may allow, be delivered by the company to the registrar of companies for registration; and if a company makes default in complying with this subsection, the company and every officer of it who is in default is liable to a fine and, for continued contravention, to a daily default fine.

(6)   The power under section 411 of the Insolvency Act to make rules shall, so far as it relates to a winding-up petition, apply for the purposes of a petition under this Part.

PART XX
WINDING UP OF COMPANIES REGISTERED UNDER THIS ACT OR THE FORMER COMPANIES ACTS

CHAPTER VI
MATTERS ARISING SUBSEQUENT TO WINDING UP

651.   Power of court to declare dissolution of company void.

(1)   Where a company has been dissolved, the court may, on an application made for the purpose by the liquidator of the company or by any other person appearing to the court to be interested, make an order, on such terms as the court thinks fit, declaring the dissolution to have been void.

(2)   Thereupon such proceedings may be taken as might have been taken if the company had not been dissolved.

(3)   It is the duty of the person on whose application the order was made, within 7 days after its making (or such further time as the court may allow), to deliver to the registrar of companies for registration an office copy of the order.

If the person fails to do so, he is liable to a fine and, for continued contravention, to a daily default fine.

(4)   Subject to the following provisions, an application under this section may not be made after the end of the period of two years from the date of the dissolution of the company.

(5)   An application for the purpose of bringing proceedings against the company—

    (a)   for damages in respect of personal injuries (including any sum claimed by virtue of section 1(2)(c) of the Law Reform (Miscellaneous Provisions) Act 1934 (funeral expenses)), or

(b)   for damages under the Fatal Accidents Act 1976 or the Damages (Scotland) Act 1976,

may be made at any time; but no order shall be made on such an application if it appears to the court that the proceedings would fail by virtue of any enactment as to the time within which proceedings must be brought.

(6)   Nothing in subsection (5) affects the power of the court on making an order under this section to direct that the period between the dissolution of the company and the making of the order shall not count for the purposes of any such enactment.

(7)   In subsection (5)(a) 'personal injuries' includes any disease and any impairment of a person's physical or mental condition.

652.   Registrar may strike defunct company off register.

(1)   If the registrar of companies has reasonable cause to believe that a company is not carrying on business or in operation, he may send to the company by post a letter inquiring whether the company is carrying on business or in operation.

(2)   If the registrar does not within one month of sending the letter receive any answer to it, he shall within 14 days after the expiration of that month send to the company by post a registered letter referring to the first letter, and stating that no answer to it has been received, and that if an answer is not received to the second letter within one month from its date, a notice will be published in the Gazette with a view to striking the company's name off the register.

(3)   If the registrar either receives an answer to the effect that the company is not carrying on business or in operation, or does not within one month after sending the second letter receive any answer, he may publish in the Gazette, and send to the company by post, a notice that at the expiration of 3 months from the date of that notice the name of the company mentioned in it will, unless cause is shown to the contrary, be struck off the register and the company will be dissolved.

(4)   If, in a case where a company is being wound up, the registrar has reasonable cause to believe either that no liquidator is acting, or that the affairs of the company are fully wound up, and the returns required to be made by the liquidator have not been made for a period of 6 consecutive months, the registrar shall publish in the Gazette and send to the company or the liquidator (if any) a like notice as is provided in subsection (3).

(5)   At the expiration of the time mentioned in the notice the registrar may, unless cause to the contrary is previously shown by the company, strike its name off the register, and shall publish notice of this in the Gazette; and on the publication of that notice in the Gazette the company is dissolved.

(6)   However—

(a)   the liability (if any) of every director, managing officer and member of the company continues and may be enforced as if the company had not been dissolved, and

(b)   nothing in subsection (5) affects the power of the court to wind up a company the name of which has been struck off the register.

(7)   A notice to be sent to a liquidator under this section may be addressed to him at his last known place of business; and a letter or notice to be sent under this section to a company may be addressed to the company at its registered office or, if no office has been registered, to the care of some officer of the company.

If there is no officer of the company whose name and address are known to the registrar of companies, the letter or notice may be sent to each of the persons who subscribed the memorandum, addressed to him at the address mentioned in the memorandum.

652A.   Registrar may strike private company off register on application.

(1)   On application by a private company, the registrar of companies may strike the company's name off the register.

(2)   An application by a company under this section shall—
  (a)   be made on its behalf by its directors or by a majority of them,
  (b)   be in the prescribed form, and
  (c)   contain the prescribed information.

(3)   The registrar shall not strike a company off under this section until after the expiration of 3 months from the publication by him in the Gazette of a notice—
  (a)   stating that he may exercise his power under this section in relation to the company, and
  (b)   inviting any person to show cause why he should not do so.

(4)   Where the registrar strikes a company off under this section, he shall publish notice of that fact in the Gazette.

(5)   On the publication in the Gazette of a notice under subsection (4), the company to which the notice relates is dissolved.

(6)   However, the liability (if any) of every director, managing officer and member of the company continues and may be enforced as if the company had not been dissolved.

(7)   Nothing in this section affects the power of the court to wind up a company the name of which has been struck off the register.

652B.   Duties in connection with making application under section 652A.

(1)   A person shall not make an application under section 652A on behalf of a company if, at any time in the previous 3 months, the company has—
  (a)   changed its name,
  (b)   traded or otherwise carried on business,
  (c)   made a disposal for value of property or rights which, immediately before ceasing to trade or otherwise carry on business, it held for the purpose of disposal for gain in the normal course of trading or otherwise carrying on business, or
  (d)   engaged in any other activity, except one which is—
    (i)   necessary or expedient for the purpose of making an application under section 652A, or deciding whether to do so,
    (ii)   necessary or expedient for the purpose of concluding the affairs of the company,
    (iii)   necessary or expedient for the purpose of complying with any statutory requirement, or
    (iv)   specified by the Secretary of State by order for the purposes of this sub-paragraph.

(2)   For the purposes of subsection (1), a company shall not be treated as trading or otherwise carrying on business by virtue only of the fact that it makes a payment in respect of a liability incurred in the course of trading or otherwise carrying on business.

(3)   A person shall not make an application under section 652A on behalf of a company at a time when any of the following is the case—
  (a)   an application has been made to the court under section 425 on behalf of the company for the sanctioning of a compromise or arrangement and the matter has not been finally concluded;
  (b)   a voluntary arrangement in relation to the company has been proposed under Part I of the Insolvency Act 1986 and the matter has not been finally concluded;
  (c)   an administration order in relation to the company is in force under Part II of that Act or a petition for such an order has been presented and not finally dealt with or withdrawn;
  (d)   the company is being wound up under Part IV of that Act, whether voluntarily or by the court, or a petition under that Part for the winding up of the company by the court has been presented and not finally dealt with or withdrawn;
  (e)   there is a receiver or manager of the company's property;
  (f)   the company's estate is being administered by a judicial factor.

(4)   For the purposes of subsection (3)(a), the matter is finally concluded if—

(a)   the application has been withdrawn,

(b)   the application has been finally dealt with without a compromise or arrangement being sanctioned by the court, or

(c)   a compromise or arrangement has been sanctioned by the court and has, together with anything required to be done under any provision made in relation to the matter by order of the court, been fully carried out.

(5)   For the purposes of subsection (3)(b), the matter is finally concluded if—

(a)   no meetings are to be summoned under section 3 of the Insolvency Act 1986,

(b)   meetings summoned under that section fail to approve the arrangement with no, or the same modifications,

(c)   an arrangement approved by meetings summoned under that section, or in consequence of a direction under section 6(4)(b) of that Act, has been fully implemented, or

(d)   the court makes an order under subsection (5) of section 6 of that Act revoking approval given at previous meetings and, if the court gives any directions under subsection (6) of that section, the company has done whatever it is required to do under those directions.

(6)   A person who makes an application under section 652A on behalf of a company shall secure that a copy of the application is given, within 7 days from the day on which the application is made, to every person who, at any time on that day, is—

(a)   a member of the company,

(b)   an employee of the company,

(c)   a creditor of the company,

(d)   a director of the company,

(e)   a manager or trustee of any pension fund established for the benefit of employees of the company, or

(f)   a person of a description specified for the purposes of this paragraph by regulations made by the Secretary of State.

(7)   Subsection (6) shall not require a copy of the application to be given to a director who is a party to the application.

(8)   The duty imposed by subection (6) shall cease to apply if the application is withdrawn before the end of the period for giving the copy application.

(9)   The Secretary of State may by order amend subsection (1) for the purpose of altering the period in relation to which the doing of the things mentioned in paragraphs (a) to (d) of that subsection is relevant.

652C.   Directors' duties following application under section 652A.

(1)   Subsection (2) applies in relation to any time after the day on which a company makes an application under section 652A and before the day on which the application is finally dealt with or withdrawn.

(2)   A person who is a director of the company at the end of a day on which a person other than himself becomes—

(a)   a member of the company,

(b)   an employee of the company,

(c)   a creditor of the company,

(d)   a director of the company,

(e)   a manager or trustee of any pension fund established for the benefit of employees of the company, or

(f)   a person of a description specified for the purposes of this paragraph by regulations made by the Secretary of State,

shall secure that a copy of the application is given to that person within 7 days from that day.

(3)   The duty imposed by subsection (2) shall cease to apply if the application is finally dealt with or withdrawn before the end of the period for giving the copy application.

(4)   Subsection (5) applies where, at any time on or after the day on which a company makes an application under section 652A and before the day on which the application is finally dealt with or withdrawn—

(a)   the company—

    (i)   changes its name,

    (ii)   trades or otherwise carries on business,

    (iii)   makes a disposal for value of any property or rights other than those which it was necessary or expedient for it to hold for the purpose of making, or proceeding with, an application under section 652A, or

    (iv)   engages in any other activity, except one to which subsection (6) applies;

(b)   an application is made to the court under section 425 on behalf of the company for the sanctioning of a compromise or arrangement;

(c)   a voluntary arrangement in relation to the company is proposed under Part I of the Insolvency Act 1986;

(d)   a petition is presented for the making of an administration order under Part II of that Act in relation to the company;

(e)   there arise any of the circumstances in which, under section 84(1) of that Act, the company may be voluntarily wound up;

(f)   a petition is presented for the winding up of the company by the court under Part IV of that Act;

(g)   a receiver or manager of the company's property is appointed; or

(h)   a judicial factor is appointed to administer the company's estate.

(5)   A person who, at the end of a day on which an event mentioned in any of paragraphs (a) to (h) of subsection (4) occurs, is a director of the company shall secure that the company's application is withdrawn forthwith.

(6)   This subsection applies to any activity which is—

(a)   necessary or expedient for the purpose of making, or proceeding with, an application under section 652A.

(b)   necessary or expedient for the purpose of concluding affairs of the company which are outstanding because of what has been necessary or expedient for the purpose of making, or proceeding with, such an application,

(c)   necessary or expedient for the purpose of complying with any statutory requirement, or

(d)   specified by the Secretary of State by order for the purposes of this subsection.

(7)   For the purposes of subsection (4)(a), a company shall not be treated as trading or otherwise carrying on business by virtue only of the fact that it makes a payment in respect of a liability incurred in the course of trading or otherwise carrying on business.

652D.   Sections 652B and 652C: supplementary provisions.

(1)   For the purposes of sections 652B(6) and 652C(2), a document shall be treated as given to a person if it is delivered to him or left at his proper address or sent by post to him at that address.

(2)   For the purposes of subsection (1) and section 7 of the Interpretation Act 1978 (which relates to the service of documents by post) in its application to that subsection, the proper address of any person shall be his last known address, except that—

(a)   in the case of a body corporate, other than one to which subsection (3) applies, it shall be the address of its registered or principal office,

(b)   in the case of a partnership, other than one to which subsection (3) applies, it shall be the address of its principal office, and

(c)   in the case of a body corporate or partnership to which subsection (3) applies, it shall be the address of its principal office in the United Kingdom.

(3)   This subsection applies to a body corporate or partnership which—
    (a)   is incorporated or formed under the law of a country or territory outside the United Kingdom, and
    (b)   has a place of business in the United Kingdom.

(4)   Where a creditor of the company has more than one place of business, subsection (1) shall have effect, so far as concerns the giving of a document to him, as if for the words from 'delivered' to the end there were substituted 'left, or sent by post to him, at each place of business of his with which the company has had dealings in relation to a matter by virtue of which he is a creditor of the company'.

(5)   Any power to make an order or regulations under section 652B or 652C shall—
    (a)   include power to make different provision for different cases or classes of case,
    (b)   include power to make such transitional provisions as the Secretary of State considers appropriate, and
    (c)   be exercisable by statutory instrument subject to annulment in pursuance of a resolution of either House of Parliament.

(6)   For the purposes of sections 652B and 652C, an application under section 652A is withdrawn if notice of withdrawal in the prescribed form is given to the registrar of companies.

(7)   In sections 652B and 652C, 'disposal' includes part disposal.

(8)   In sections 652B and 652C and this section, 'creditor' includes a contingent or prospective creditor.

652E.   Sections 652B and 652C: enforcement.

(1)   A person who breaches or fails to perform a duty imposed on him by section 652B or 652C is guilty of an offence and liable to a fine.

(2)   A person who fails to perform a duty imposed on him by section 652B(6) or 652C(2) with the intention of concealing the making of the application in question from the person concerned is guilty of an offence and liable to imprisonment or a fine, or both.

(3)   In any proceedings for an offence under subsection (1) consisting of breach of a duty imposed by section 652B(1) or (3), it shall be a defence for the accused to prove that he did not know, and could not reasonably have known, of the existence of the facts which led to the breach.

(4)   In any proceedings for an offence under subsection (1) consisting of failure to perform the duty imposed by section 652B(6), it shall be a defence for the accused to prove that he took all reasonable steps to perform the duty.

(5)   In any proceedings for an offence under subsection (1) consisting of failure to perform a duty imposed by section 652C(2) or (5), it shall be a defence for the accused to prove—
    (a)   that at the time of the failure he was not aware of the fact that the company had made an application under section 652A, or
    (b)   that he took all reasonable steps to perform the duty.

652F.   Other offences connected with section 652A.

(1)   Where a company makes an application under section 652A, any person who, in connection with the application, knowingly or recklessly furnishes any information to the registrar of companies which is false or misleading in a material particular is guilty of an offence and liable to a fine.

(2)   Any person who knowingly or recklessly makes an application to the registrar of companies which purports to be an application under section 652A, but which is not, is guilty of an offence and liable to a fine.

653.   Objection to striking off by person aggrieved.

(1)   Subsection (2) applies if a company or any member or creditor of it feels aggrieved by the company having been struck off the register under section 652.

(2)   The court, on an application by the company or the member or creditor made before the expiration of 20 years from publication in the Gazette of notice under section 652, may, if satisfied that the company was at the time of the striking off carrying on business or in operation, or otherwise that it is just that the company be restored to the register, order the company's name to be restored.

(2A)   Subsections (2B) and (2D) apply if a company has been struck off the register under section 652A.

(2B)   The court, on an application by a notifiable person made before the expiration of 20 years from publication in the Gazette of notice under section 652A(4), may, if satisfied—

(a)   that any duty under section 652B or 652C with respect to the giving to that person of a copy of the company's application under section 652A was not performed,

(b)   that the making of the company's application under section 652A involved a breach of duty under section 652B(1) or (3), or

(c)   that it is for some other reason just to do so,

order the company's name to be restored to the register.

(2C)   In subsection (2B), 'notifiable person' means a person to whom a copy of the company's application under section 652A was required to be given under section 652B or 652C.

(2D)   The court, on an application by the Secretary of State made before the expiration of 20 years from publication in the Gazette of notice under section 652A(4), may, if satisfied that it is in the public interest to do so, order the company's name to be restored.

(3)   On an office copy of an order under subsection (2), (2B) or (2D) being delivered to the registrar of companies for registration the company to which the order relates is deemed to have continued in existence as if its name had not been struck off; and the court may by the order give such directions and make such provisions as seem just for placing the company and all other persons in the same position (as nearly as may be) as if the company's name had not been struck off.

654.   Property of dissolved company to be bona vacantia.

(1)   When a company is dissolved, all property and rights whatsoever vested in or held on trust for the company immediately before its dissolution (including leasehold property, but not including property held by the company on trust for any other person) are deemed to be bona vacantia and—

(a)   accordingly belong to the Crown, or to the Duchy of Lancaster or to the Duke of Cornwall for the time being (as the case may be), and

(b)   vest and may be dealt with in the same manner as other bona vacantia accruing to the Crown, to the Duchy of Lancaster or to the Duke of Cornwall.

(2)   Except as provided by the section next following, the above has effect subject and without prejudice to any order made by the court under section 651 or 653.

655.   Effect on s. 654 of company's revival after dissolution.

(1)   The person in whom any property or right is vested by section 654 may dispose of, or of an interest in, that property or right notwithstanding that an order may be made under section 651 or 653.

(2)   Where such an order is made—

(a)   it does not affect the disposition (but without prejudice to the order so far as it relates to any other property or right previously vested in or held on trust for the company), and

(b)   the Crown or, as the case may be, the Duke of Cornwall shall pay to the company an amount equal to—

(i)   the amount of any consideration received for the property or right, or interest therein, or

(ii)   the value of any such consideration at the time of the disposition,
or, if no consideration was received, an amount equal to the value of the property, right
or interest disposed of, as at the date of the disposition.

(3)   Where a liability accrues under subsection (2) in respect of any property or right
which, before the order under section 651 or 653 was made, had accrued as bona
vacantia to the Duchy of Lancaster, the Attorney General of the Duchy shall represent
Her Majesty in any proceedings arising in connection with that liability.

(4)   Where a liability accrues under subsection (2) in respect of any property or right
which, before the order under section 651 or 653 was made, had accrued as bona
vacantia to the Duchy of Cornwall, such persons as the Duke of Cornwall (or other
possessor for the time being of the Duchy) may appoint shall represent the Duke (or
other possessor) in any proceedings arising out of that liability.

(5)   This section applies in relation to the disposition of any property, right or
interest on or after 22 December 1981, whether the company concerned was dissolved
before, on or after that day.

656.   Crown disclaimer of property vesting as bona vacantia.

(1)   Where property vests in the Crown under section 654, the Crown's title to it
under that section may be disclaimed by a notice signed by the Crown representative,
that is to say the Treasury Solicitor, or, in relation to property in Scotland, the Queen's
and Lord Treasurer's Remembrancer.

(2)   The right to execute a notice of disclaimer under this section may be waived by
or on behalf of the Crown either expressly or by taking possession or other act evincing
that intention.

(3)   A notice of disclaimer under this section is of no effect unless it is executed—

(a)   within 12 months of the date on which the vesting of the property under
section 654 came to the notice of the Crown representative, or

(b)   if an application in writing is made to the Crown representative by any person
interested in the property requiring him to decide whether he will or will not disclaim,
within a period of 3 months after the receipt of the application or such further period as
may be allowed by the court which would have had jurisdiction to wind up the company
if it had not been dissolved.

(4)   A statement in a notice of disclaimer of any property under this section that the
vesting of it came to the notice of the Crown representative on a specified date, or that
no such application as above mentioned was received by him with respect to the
property before a specified date, is sufficient evidence of the fact stated, until the
contrary is proved.

(5)   A notice of disclaimer under this section shall be delivered to the registrar of
companies and retained and registered by him; and copies of it shall be published in the
Gazette and sent to any persons who have given the Crown representative notice that
they claim to be interested in the property.

(6)   This section applies to property vested in the Duchy of Lancaster or the Duke
of Cornwall under section 654 as if for references to the Crown and the Crown
representative there were respectively substituted references to the Duchy of Lancaster
and to the Solicitor to that Duchy, or to the Duke of Cornwall and to the Solicitor to the
Duchy of Cornwall, as the case may be.

657.   Effect of Crown disclaimer under s. 656.

(1)   Where notice of disclaimer is executed under section 656 as respects any
property, that property is deemed not to have vested in the Crown under section 654.

(2)   As regards property in England and Wales, section 178(4) and sections 179 to
182 of the Insolvency Act shall apply as if the property had been disclaimed by the
liquidator under the said section 91 immediately before the dissolution of the company.
[*Before an amendment was made by the Insolvency Act 1986, sch. 13, this subsection read:*

As regards property in England and Wales, subsections (3) and (5) to (7) of section 91 of the Insolvency Act 1985 and section 92 of that Act shall apply as if the property had been disclaimed by the liquidator under the said section 91 immediately before the dissolution of the company.]

(3)   As regards property in Scotland, the following 4 subsections apply.

(4)   The Crown's disclaimer operates to determine, as from the date of the disclaimer, the rights, interests and liabilities of the company, and the property of the company, in or in respect of the property disclaimed; but it does not (except so far as is necessary for the purpose of releasing the company and its property from liability) affect the rights or liabilities of any other person.

(5)   The court may, on application by a person who either claims an interest in disclaimed property or is under a liability not discharged by this Act in respect of disclaimed property, and on hearing such persons as it thinks fit, make an order for the vesting of the property in or its delivery to any persons entitled to it, or to whom it may seem just that the property should be delivered by way of compensation for such liability, or a trustee for him, and on such terms as the court thinks just.

(6)   On such a vesting order being made, the property comprised in it vests accordingly in the person named in that behalf in the order, without conveyance or assignation for that purpose.

(7)   Part II of Schedule 20 has effect for the protection of third parties where the property disclaimed is held under a lease.

658.   Liability for rentcharge on company's land after dissolution.

(1)   Section 180 of the Insolvency Act shall apply to land in England and Wales which by operation of law vests subject to a rentcharge in the Crown or any other person on the dissolution of a company as it applies to land so vesting on a disclaimer under that section.

(2)   In this section 'company' includes any body corporate.

PART XXII
BODIES CORPORATE SUBJECT, OR BECOMING SUBJECT, TO THIS ACT
(OTHERWISE THAN BY ORIGINAL FORMATION UNDER PART I)

CHAPTER I
COMPANIES FORMED OR REGISTERED UNDER FORMER
COMPANIES ACTS

675.   Companies formed and registered under former Companies Acts.

(1)   In its application to existing companies, this Act applies in the same manner—

(a)   in the case of a limited company (other than a company limited by guarantee), as if the company had been formed and registered under Part I of this Act as a company limited by shares,

(b)   in the case of a company limited by guarantee, as if the company had been formed and registered under that Part as a company limited by guarantee, and

(c)   in the case of a company other than a limited company, as if the company had been formed and registered under that Part as an unlimited company.

(2)   But reference, express or implied, to the date of registration is to be read as the date at which the company was registered under the Joint Stock Companies Acts, the Companies Act 1862, the Companies (Consolidation) Act 1908, the Companies Act 1929, or the Companies Act 1948.

679.   Northern Ireland and Irish companies.

Nothing in sections 675 to 678 applies to companies registered in Northern Ireland or the Republic of Ireland.

PART XXIII
OVERSEA COMPANIES

CHAPTER I
REGISTRATION, ETC.

698. Definitions.

. . .

(2) For the purposes of this Part (except section 699A and Schedule 21C):

. . .

(b) 'branch' means a branch within the meaning of the Council Directive concerning disclosure requirements in respect of branches opened in a Member State by certain types of company governed by the law of another State (the Eleventh Company Law Directive, 89/666/EEC).

PART XXIV
THE REGISTRAR OF COMPANIES, HIS FUNCTIONS AND OFFICES

704. Registration offices.

(1) For the purposes of the registration of companies under the Companies Acts, there shall continue to be offices in England and Wales and in Scotland, at such places as the Secretary of State thinks fit.

(2) The Secretary of State may appoint such registrars, assistant registrars, clerks and servants as he thinks necessary for that purpose, and may make regulations with respect to their duties, and may remove any persons so appointed.

(3) The salaries of the persons so appointed continue to be fixed by the Secretary of State, with the concurrence of the Treasury, and shall be paid out of money provided by Parliament.

(4) The Secretary of State may direct a seal or seals to be prepared for the authentication of documents required for or in connection with the registration of companies; and any seal so prepared is referred to in this Act as the Registrar's official seal.

(5) Wherever any act is by the Companies Acts directed to be done to or by the registrar of companies, it shall (until the Secretary of State otherwise directs) be done to or by the existing registrar of companies in England and Wales or in Scotland (as the case may be), or to or by such person as the Secretary of State may for the time being authorise.

(6) In the event of the Secretary of State altering the constitution of the existing registration offices or any of them, any such act shall be done to or by such officer and at such place with reference to the local situation of the registered offices of the companies to be registered as the Secretary of State may appoint.

(7) Subsection (8) below applies where by virtue of an order made under section 69 of the Deregulation and Contracting Out Act 1994 a person is authorised by the registrar of companies to accept delivery of any class of documents which are under any provision of the Companies Acts to be delivered to the registrar.

(8) If—

(a) the registrar directs that documents of that class shall be delivered to a specified address of the authorised person; and

(b) the direction is printed and made available to the public (with or without payment),

any document of that class which is delivered to an address other than the specified address shall be treated for the purposes of those Acts as not having been delivered.

705. Companies' registered numbers.

(1) The registrar shall allocate to every company a number, which shall be known as the company's registered number.

(2)   Companies' registered numbers shall be in such form, consisting of one or more sequences of figures or letters, as the registrar may from time to time determine.

(3)   The registrar may upon adopting a new form of registered number make such changes of existing registered numbers as appear to him necessary.

(4)   A change of a company's registered number has effect from the date on which the company is notified by the registrar of the change; but for a period of three years beginning with the date on which that notification is sent by the registrar the requirement of section 351(1)(a) as to the use of the company's registered number on business letters and order forms is satisfied by the use of either the old number or the new.

(5)   In this section 'company' includes—

(za)   any oversea company which has complied with paragraph 1 of Schedule 21A other than a company which appears to the registrar not to have a branch in Great Britain;

(a)   any oversea company which has complied with section 691 (delivery of statutes to registrar, &c.), other than a company which appears to the registrar not to have a place of business in Great Britain; and

(b)   any body to which any provision of this Act applies by virtue of section 718 (unregistered companies).

706.   Delivery to the registrar of documents in legible form.

(1)   This section applies to the delivery to the registrar under any provision of the Companies Acts of documents in legible form.

(2)   The document must—

(a)   state in a prominent position the registered number of the company to which it relates, and, if the document is delivered under sections 659A(3), 703P or 703Q or Schedules 21A or 21D the registered number of the branch to which it relates,

(b)   satisfy any requirements prescribed by regulations for the purposes of this section, and

(c)   conform to such requirements as the registrar may specify for the purpose of enabling him to copy the document.

(3)   If a document is delivered to the registrar which does not comply with the requirements of this section, he may serve on the person by whom the document was delivered (or, if there are two or more such persons, on any of them) a notice indicating the respect in which the document does not comply.

(4)   Where the registrar serves such a notice, then, unless a replacement document—

(a)   is delivered to him within 14 days after the service of the notice, and

(b)   complies with the requirements of this section (or section 707) or is not rejected by him for failure to comply with those requirements,
the original document shall be deemed not to have been delivered to him.

But for the purposes of any enactment imposing a penalty for failure to deliver, so far as it imposes a penalty for continued contravention, no account shall be taken of the period between the delivery of the original document and the end of the period of 14 days after service of the registrar's notice.

(5)   Regulations made for the purposes of this section may make different provision with respect to different descriptions of document.

707.   Delivery to the registrar of documents otherwise than in legible form.

(1)   This section applies to the delivery to the registrar under any provision of the Companies Acts of documents otherwise than in legible form.

(2)   Any requirement to deliver a document to the registrar, or to deliver a document in the prescribed form, is satisfied by the communication to the registrar of the requisite information in any non-legible form prescribed for the purposes of this section by regulations or approved by the registrar.

(3)   Where the document is required to be signed or sealed, it shall instead be authenticated in such manner as may be prescribed by regulations or approved by the registrar.

(4)   The document must—

(a)   contain in a prominent position the registered number of the company to which it relates, and, if the document is delivered under sections 695A(3), 703P or 703Q or Schedules 21A or 21D the registered number of the branch to which it relates,

(b)   satisfy any requirements prescribed by regulations for the purposes of this section, and

(c)   be furnished in such manner, and conform to such requirements, as the registrar may specify for the purpose of enabling him to read and copy the document.

(5)   If a document is delivered to the registrar which does not comply with the requirements of this section, he may serve on the person by whom the document was delivered (or, if there are two or more such persons, on any of them) a notice indicating the respect in which the document does not comply.

(6)   Where the registrar serves such a notice, then, unless a replacement document—

(a)   is delivered to him within 14 days after the service of the notice, and

(b)   complies with the requirements of this section (or section 706) or is not rejected by him for failure to comply with those requirements,

the original document shall be deemed not to have been delivered to him.

But for the purposes of any enactment imposing a penalty for failure to deliver, so far as it imposes a penalty for continued contravention, no account shall be taken of the period between the delivery of the original document and the end of the period of 14 days after service of the registrar's notice.

(7)   The Secretary of State may by regulations make further provision with respect to the application of this section in relation to instantaneous forms of communication.

(8)   Regulations made for the purposes of this section may make different provision with respect to different descriptions of document and different forms of communication, and as respects delivery to the registrar for England and Wales and delivery to the registrar for Scotland.

707A.   The keeping of company records by the registrar.

(1)   The information contained in a document delivered to the registrar under the Companies Acts may be recorded and kept by him in any form he thinks fit, provided it is possible to inspect the information and to produce a copy of it in legible form.

This is sufficient compliance with any duty of his to keep, file or register the document.

(2)   The originals of documents delivered to the registrar in legible form shall be kept by him for ten years, after which they may be destroyed.

(3)   Where a company has been dissolved, the registrar may, at any time after the expiration of two years from the date of the dissolution, direct that any records in his custody relating to the company may be removed to the Public Record Office; and records in respect of which such a direction is given shall be disposed of in accordance with the enactments relating to that Office and the rules made under them.

This subsection does not extend to Scotland.

(4)   In subsection (3) 'company' includes a company provisionally or completely registered under the Joint Stock Companies Act 1844.

708.   Fees payable to registrar.

(1)   The Secretary of State may by regulations made by statutory instrument require the payment to the registrar of companies of such fees as may be specified in the regulations in respect of—

(a)   the performance by the registrar of such functions under the Companies Acts as may be so specified, including the receipt by him of any document which under those Acts is required to be delivered to him,

(b)   the inspection of documents kept by him under those Acts.

(2)   A statutory instrument containing regulations under this section requiring the payment of a fee in respect of a matter for which no fee was previously payable, or increasing a fee, shall be laid before Parliament after being made and shall cease to have effect at the end of the period of 28 days beginning with the day on which the regulations were made (but without prejudice to anything previously done under the regulations or to the making of further regulations) unless in that period the regulations are approved by resolution of each House of Parliament.

In reckoning that period of 28 days no account is to be taken of any time during which Parliament is dissolved or prorogued or during which both Houses are adjourned for more than 4 days.

(3)   A statutory instrument containing regulations under this section, where subsection (2) does not apply, is subject to annulment in pursuance of a resolution of either House of Parliament.

(4)   Fees paid to the registrar under the Companies Acts shall be paid into the Consolidated Fund.

(5)   It is hereby declared that the registrar may charge a fee for any services provided by him otherwise than in pursuance of an obligation on him by law.

709.   Inspection, &c. of records kept by the registrar.

(1)   Any person may inspect any records kept by the registrar for the purposes of the Companies Acts and may require—
    (a)   a copy, in such form as the registrar considers appropriate, of any information contained in those records, or
    (b)   a certified copy of, or extract from, any such record.

(2)   The right of inspection extends to the originals of documents delivered to the registrar in legible form only where the record kept by the registrar of the contents of the documents is illegible or unavailable.

(3)   A copy of or extract from a record kept at any of the offices for the registration of companies in England and Wales or Scotland, certified in writing by the registrar (whose official position it is unnecessary to prove) to be an accurate record of the contents of any document delivered to him under the Companies Acts, is in all legal proceedings admissible in evidence as of equal validity with the original document and as evidence of any fact stated therein of which direct oral evidence would be admissible.

In England and Wales this is subject, in the case of proceedings to which section 69 of the Police and Criminal Evidence Act 1984 applies, to compliance with any applicable rules of court under subsection (2) of that section (which relates to evidence from computer records).

(4)   Copies of or extracts from records furnished by the registrar may, instead of being certified by him in writing to be an accurate record, be sealed with his official seal.

(5)   No process for compelling the production of a record kept by the registrar shall issue from any court except with the leave of the court; and any such process shall bear on it a statement that it is issued with the leave of the court.

710.   Certificate of incorporation.

Any person may require a certificate of the incorporation of a company, signed by the registrar or authenticated by his official seal.

710A.   Provision and authentication by registrar of documents in non-legible form.

(1)   Any requirement of the Companies Acts as to the supply by the registrar of a document may, if the registrar thinks fit, be satisfied by the communication by the registrar of the requisite information in any non-legible form prescribed for the purposes of this section by regulations or approved by him.

(2)   Where the document is required to be signed by him or sealed with his official seal, it shall instead be authenticated in such manner as may be prescribed by regulations or approved by the registrar.

710B.   Documents relating to Welsh companies.

(1)   This section applies to any document which—

(a)   is delivered to the registrar under this Act or the Insolvency Act 1986, and

(b)   relates to a company (whether already registered or to be registered) whose memorandum states that its registered office is to be situated in Wales.

(2)   A document to which this section applies may be in Welsh but, subject to subsection (3), shall on delivery to the registrar be accompanied by a certified translation into English.

(3)   The requirement for a translation imposed by subsection (2) shall not apply—

(a)   to documents of such descriptions as may be prescribed for the purposes of this paragraph, or

(b)   to documents in a form prescribed in Welsh (or partly in Welsh and partly in English) by virtue of section 26 of the Welsh Language Act 1993.

(4)   Where by virtue of subsection (3) the registrar receives a document in Welsh without a certified translation into English, he shall, if that document is to be available for inspection, himself obtain such a translation; and that translation shall be treated as delivered to him in accordance with the same provision as the original.

(5)   A company whose memorandum states that its registered office is to be situated in Wales may deliver to the registrar a certified translation into Welsh of any document in English which relates to the company and which is or has been delivered to the registrar.

(6)   The provisions within subsection (7) (which require certified translations into English of certain documents delivered to the registrar) shall not apply where a translation is required by subsection (2) or would be required but for subsection (3).

(7)   The provisions within this subsection are section 228(2)(f), the second sentence of section 242(1), sections 243(4), 272(5) and 273(7) and paragraph 7(3) of Part II of Schedule 9.

(8)   In this section 'certified translation' means a translation certified in the prescribed manner to be a correct translation.

711.   Public notice by registrar of receipt and issue of certain documents.

(1)   The registrar of companies shall cause to be published in the Gazette notice of the issue or receipt by him of documents of any of the following descriptions (stating in the notice the name of the company, the description of document and the date of issue or receipt)—

(a)   any certificate of incorporation of a company,

(b)   any document making or evidencing an alteration in a company's memorandum or articles,

(c)   any notification of a change among the directors of a company,

(d)   any copy of a resolution of a public company which gives, varies, revokes or renews an authority for the purposes of section 80 (allotment of relevant securities),

(e)   any copy of a special resolution of a public company passed under section 95(1), (2) or (3) (disapplication of pre-emption rights),

(f)   any report under section 103 or 104 as to the value of a non-cash asset,

(g)   any statutory declaration delivered under section 117 (public company share capital requirements),

(h)   any notification (given under section 122) of the redemption of shares,

(j)   any statement or notice delivered by a public company under section 128 (registration of particulars of special rights),

(k)   any documents delivered by a company under section 242(1) (accounts and reports),

(l)   a copy of any resolution or agreement to which section 380 applies and which—

(i)   states the rights attached to any shares in a public company, other than shares which are in all respects uniform (for purposes of section 128) with shares previously allotted, or

(ii)   varies rights attached to any shares in a public company, or

(iii)   assigns a name or other designation, or a new name or designation, to any class of shares in a public company,

(m)   any return of allotments of a public company,

(n)   any notice of a change in the situation of a company's registered office,

(p)   any copy of a winding-up order in respect of a company,

(q)   any order for the dissolution of a company on a winding up,

(r)   any return by a liquidator of the final meeting of a company on a winding up,

(s)   any copy of a draft of the terms of a scheme delivered to the registrar of companies under paragraph 2(1) of Schedule 15A,

(t)   any copy of an order under section 425(2) or section 427 in respect of a compromise or arrangement to which section 427A(1) applies,

(u)   any return delivered under paragraph 1, 7 or 8 of Schedule 21A (branch registration),

(v)   any document delivered under paragraph 1 or 8 of that Schedule,

(w)   any notice under section 695A(3) of the closure of a branch,

(x)   any document delivered under Schedule 21C (accounts and reports of foreign credit and financial institutions),

(y)   any document delivered under Schedule 21D (accounts and reports of oversea companies subject to branch registration, other than credit and financial institutions),

(z)   any return delivered under section 703P (particulars of winding up of oversea companies subject to branch registration).

(2)   In section 42 'official notification' means—

(a)   in relation to anything stated in a document of any of the above descriptions, the notification of that document in the Gazette under this section, and

(b)   in relation to the appointment of a liquidator in a voluntary winding up, the notification of it in the Gazette under section 109 of the Insolvency Act;

and 'officially notified' is to be construed accordingly.

[*A new s. 711A would be inserted if s. 142(1) of the Companies Act 1989 were brought into force.*]

713.   Enforcement of company's duty to make returns.

(1)   If a company, having made default in complying with any provision of the Companies Acts which requires it to deliver a document to the registrar of companies, or to give notice to him of any matter, fails to make good the default within 14 days after the service of a notice on the company requiring it to do so, the court may, on an application made to it by any member or creditor of the company or by the registrar of companies, make an order directing the company and any officer of it to make good the default within such time as may be specified in the order.

(2)   The court's order may provide that all costs of and incidental to the application shall be borne by the company or by any officers of it responsible for the default.

(3)   Nothing in this section prejudices the operation of any enactment imposing penalties on a company or its officers in respect of any such default as is mentioned above.

714.   Registrar's index of company and corporate names.

(1)   The registrar of companies shall keep an index of the names of the following bodies—

(a)   companies as defined by this Act,

(aa)   companies incorporated outside the United Kingdom and Gibraltar which have complied with paragraph 1 of Schedule 21A and which do not appear to the registrar of companies not to have a branch in Great Britain,

(b)   companies incorporated outside Great Britain which have complied with section 691 and which do not appear to the registrar of companies not to have a place of business in Great Britain,

(c)   incorporated and unincorporated bodies to which any provision of this Act applies by virtue of section 718 (unregistered companies),

(d)   limited partnerships registered under the Limited Partnerships Act 1907,

(e)   companies within the meaning of the Companies Act (Northern Ireland) 1960,

(f)   companies incorporated outside Northern Ireland which have complied with section 356 of that Act (which corresponds with section 691 of this Act), and which do not appear to the registrar not to have a place of business in Northern Ireland, and

(g)   societies registered under the Industrial and Provident Societies Act 1965 or the Industrial and Provident Societies Act (Northern Ireland) 1969.

(2)   The Secretary of State may by order in a statutory instrument vary subsection (1) by the addition or deletion of any class of body, except any within paragraph (a) or (b) of the subsection, whether incorporated or unincorporated; and any such statutory instrument is subject to annulment in pursuance of a resolution of either House of Parliament.

715A.   Interpretation.

(1)   In this Part—

'document' includes information recorded in any form; and

'legible', in the context of documents in legible or non-legible form, means capable of being read with the naked eye.

(2)   References in this Part to delivering a document include sending, forwarding, producing or (in the case of a notice) giving it.

PART XXV
MISCELLANEOUS AND SUPPLEMENTARY PROVISIONS

716.   Prohibition of partnerships with more than 20 members.

(1)   No company, association or partnership consisting of more than 20 persons shall be formed for the purpose of carrying on any business that has for its object the acquisition of gain by the company, association or partnership, or by its individual members, unless it is registered as a company under this Act, or is formed in pursuance of some other Act of Parliament, or of letters patent.

(2)   However, this does not prohibit the formation—

(a)   for the purpose of carrying on practice as solicitors, of a partnership consisting of persons each of whom is a solicitor;

(b)   for the purpose of carrying on practice as accountants, of a partnership which is eligible for appointment as a company auditor under section 25 of the Companies Act 1989;

(c)   for the purpose of carrying on business as members of a recognised stock exchange, of a partnership consisting of persons each of whom is a member of that stock exchange;

(d)   for any purpose prescribed by regulations (which may include a purpose mentioned above), of a partnership of a description so prescribed;

(e)   of an investment company with variable capital within the meaning of the Open-Ended Investment Companies (Investment Companies with Variable Capital) Regulations 1996.

(3)   In subsection (2)(a) 'solicitor'—

(a)   in relation to England and Wales, means solicitor of the Supreme Court, and

(b)   in relation to Scotland, means a person enrolled or deemed enrolled as a solicitor in pursuance of the Solicitors (Scotland) Act 1980.

(4)   In subsection (2)(c) 'recognised stock exchange' means—

(a)   The International Stock Exchange of the United Kingdom and the Republic of Ireland Limited, and

(b)   any other stock exchange for the time being recognised for the purposes of this section by the Secretary of State by order made by statutory instrument.

719.   Power of company to provide for employees on cessation or transfer of business.

(1)   The powers of a company include (if they would not otherwise do so apart from this section) power to make the following provision for the benefit of persons employed or formerly employed by the company or any of its subsidiaries, that is to say, provision in connection with the cessation or the transfer to any person of the whole or part of the undertaking of the company or that subsidiary.

(2)   The power conferred by subsection (1) is exercisable notwithstanding that its exercise is not in the best interests of the company.

(3)   The power which a company may exercise by virtue only of subsection (1) shall only be exercised by the company if sanctioned—

(a)   in a case not falling within paragraph (b) or (c) below, by an ordinary resolution of the company, or

(b)   if so authorised by the memorandum or articles, a resolution of the directors, or

(c)   if the memorandum or articles require the exercise of the power to be sanctioned by a resolution of the company of some other description for which more than a simple majority of the members voting is necessary, with the sanction of a resolution of that description;

and in any case after compliance with any other requirements of the memorandum or articles applicable to its exercise.

(4)   Any payment which may be made by a company under this section may, if made before the commencement of any winding up of the company, be made out of profits of the company which are available for dividend.

722.   Form of company registers, etc.

(1)   Any register, index, minute book or accounting records required by the Companies Acts to be kept by a company may be kept either by making entries in bound books or by recording the matters in question in any other manner.

(2)   Where any such register, index, minute book or accounting record is not kept by making entries in a bound book, but by some other means, adequate precautions shall be taken for guarding against falsification and facilitating its discovery.

(3)   If default is made in complying with subsection (2), the company and every officer of it who is in default is liable to a fine and, for continued contravention, to a daily default fine.

723.   Use of computers for company records.

(1)   The power conferred on a company by section 722(1) to keep a register or other record by recording the matters in question otherwise than by making entries in bound books includes power to keep the register or other record by recording those matters otherwise than in a legible form, so long as the recording is capable of being reproduced in a legible form.

(2)   Any provision of an instrument made by a company before 12 February 1979 which requires a register of holders of the company's debentures to be kept in a legible form is to be read as requiring the register to be kept in a legible or non-legible form.

(3)   If any such register or other record of a company as is mentioned in section 722(1), or a register of holders of a company's debentures, is kept by the company by recording the matters in question otherwise than in a legible form, any duty imposed on the company by this Act to allow inspection of, or to furnish a copy of, the register or other record or any part of it is to be treated as a duty to allow inspection of, or to furnish, a reproduction of the recording or of the relevant part of it in a legible form.

(4)   The Secretary of State may by regulations in a statutory instrument make such provision in addition to subsection (3) as he considers appropriate in connection with such registers or other records as are mentioned in that subsection, and are kept as so mentioned; and the regulations may make modifications of provisions of this Act relating to such registers or other records.

(5)   A statutory instrument under subsection (4) is subject to annulment in pursuance of a resolution of either House of Parliament.

723A.   Obligations of company as to inspection of registers, &c.

(1)   The Secretary of State may make provision by regulations as to the obligations of a company which is required by any provision of this Act—
    (a)   to make available for inspection any register, index or document, or
    (b)   to provide copies of any such register, index or document, or part of it;
and a company which fails to comply with the regulations shall be deemed to have refused inspection or, as the case may be, to have failed to provide a copy.

(2)   The regulations may make provision as to the time, duration and manner of inspection, including the circumstances in which and extent to which the copying of information is permitted in the course of inspection.

(3)   The regulations may define what may be required of the company as regards the nature, extent and manner of extracting or presenting any information for the purposes of inspection or the provision of copies.

(4)   Where there is power to charge a fee, the regulations may make provision as to the amount of the fee and the basis of its calculation.

(5)   Regulations under this section may make different provision for different classes of case.

(6)   Nothing in any provision of this Act or in the regulations shall be construed as preventing a company from affording more extensive facilities than are required by the regulations or, where a fee may be charged, from charging a lesser fee than that prescribed or no fee at all.

(7)   Regulations under this section shall be made by statutory instrument which shall be subject to annulment in pursuance of a resolution of either House of Parliament.

725.   Service of documents.

(1)   A document may be served on a company by leaving it at, or sending it by post to, the company's registered office.

(2)   Where a company registered in Scotland carries on business in England and Wales, the process of any court in England and Wales may be served on the company by leaving it at, or sending it by post to, the company's principal place of business in England and Wales, addressed to the manager or other head officer in England and Wales of the company.

(3)   Where process is served on a company under subsection (2), the person issuing out the process shall send a copy of it by post to the company's registered office.

726.   Costs and expenses in actions by certain limited companies.

(1)   Where in England and Wales a limited company is plaintiff in an action or other legal proceeding, the court having jurisdiction in the matter may, if it appears by credible testimony that there is reason to believe that the company will be unable to pay the defendant's costs if successful in his defence, require sufficient security to be given for those costs, and may stay all proceedings until the security is given.

(2)   Where in Scotland a limited company is pursuer in an action or other legal proceeding, the court having jurisdiction in the matter may, if it appears by credible testimony that there is reason to believe that the company will be unable to pay the defender's expenses if successful in his defence, order the company to find caution and sist the proceedings until caution is found.

727.   Power of court to grant relief in certain cases.

(1)   If in any proceedings for negligence, default, breach of duty or breach of trust against an officer of a company or a person employed by a company as auditor (whether he is or is not an officer of the company) it appears to the court hearing the case that that officer or person is or may be liable in respect of the negligence, default, breach of duty or breach of trust, but that he has acted honestly and reasonably, and that having regard to all the circumstances of the case (including those connected with his appointment) he ought fairly to be excused for the negligence, default, breach of duty or breach of trust, that court may relieve him, either wholly or partly, from his liability on such terms as it thinks fit.

(2)   If any such officer or person as above-mentioned has reason to apprehend that any claim will or might be made against him in respect of any negligence, default, breach of duty or breach of trust, he may apply to the court for relief; and the court on the application has the same power to relieve him as under this section it would have had if it had been a court before which proceedings against that person for negligence, default, breach of duty or breach of trust had been brought.

(3)   Where a case to which subsection (1) applies is being tried by a judge with a jury, the judge, after hearing the evidence, may, if he is satisfied that the defendant or defender ought in pursuance of that subsection to be relieved either in whole or in part from the liability sought to be enforced against him, withdraw the case in whole or in part from the jury and forthwith direct judgment to be entered for the defendant or defender on such terms as to costs or otherwise as the judge may think proper.

728.   Enforcement of High Court orders.

Orders made by the High Court under this Act may be enforced in the same manner as orders made in an action pending in that court.

729.   Annual report by Secretary of State.

The Secretary of State shall cause a general annual report of matters within the Companies Acts to be prepared and laid before both Houses of Parliament.

730.   Punishment of offences.

(1)   Schedule 24 to this Act has effect with respect to the way in which offences under this Act are punishable on conviction.

(2)   In relation to an offence under a provision of this Act specified in the first column of the Schedule (the general nature of the offence being described in the second column), the third column shows whether the offence is punishable on conviction on indictment, or on summary conviction, or either in the one way or the other.

(3)   The fourth column of the Schedule shows, in relation to an offence, the maximum punishment by way of fine or imprisonment under this Act which may be imposed on a person convicted of the offence in the way specified in relation to it in the third column (that is to say, on indictment or summarily), a reference to a period of years or months being to a term of imprisonment of that duration.

(4)   The fifth column shows (in relation to an offence for which there is an entry in that column) that a person convicted of the offence after continued contravention is liable to a daily default fine; that is to say, he is liable on a second or subsequent summary conviction of the offence to the fine specified in that column for each day on which the contravention is continued (instead of the penalty specified for the offence in the fourth column·of the Schedule).

(5)   For the purpose of any enactment in the Companies Acts which provides that an officer of a company or other body who is in default is liable to a fine or penalty, the expression 'officer who is in default' means any officer of the company or other body who knowingly and wilfully authorises or permits the default, refusal or contravention mentioned in the enactment.

731.   Summary proceedings.

(1)   Summary proceedings for any offence under the Companies Acts may (without prejudice to any jurisdiction exercisable apart from this subsection) be taken against a body corporate at any place at which the body has a place of business, and against any other person at any place at which he is for the time being.

(2)   Notwithstanding anything in section 127(1) of the Magistrates' Courts Act 1980, an information relating to an offence under the Companies Acts which is triable by a magistrates' court in England and Wales may be so tried if it is laid at any time within 3 years after the commission of the offence and within 12 months after the date on which evidence sufficient in the opinion of the Director of Public Prosecutions or the Secretary of State (as the case may be) to justify the proceedings comes to his knowledge.

(3)   Summary proceedings in Scotland for an offence under the Companies Acts shall not be commenced after the expiration of 3 years from the commission of the offence.

Subject to this (and notwithstanding anything in section 136 of the Criminal Procedure (Scotland) Act 1995), such proceedings may (in Scotland) be commenced at any time within 12 months after the date on which evidence sufficient in the Lord Advocate's opinion to justify the proceedings came to his knowledge or, where such evidence was reported to him by the Secretary of State, within 12 months after the date on which it came to the knowledge of the latter; and subsection (3) of that section applies for the purpose of this subsection as it applies for the purpose of that section.

(4)   For purposes of this section, a certificate of the Director of Public Prosecutions, the Lord Advocate or the Secretary of State (as the case may be) as to the date on which such evidence as is referred to above came to his knowledge is conclusive evidence.

732.   Prosecution by public authorities.

(1)   In respect of an offence under any of sections 210, 324, 329, 447 to 451 and 455, proceedings shall not, in England and Wales, be instituted except by or with the consent of the appropriate authority.

(2)   That authority is—

(a)   for an offence under any of sections 210, 324 and 329, the Secretary of State or the Director of Public Prosecutions,

(b)   for an offence under any of sections 447 to 451, either one of those two persons or the Industrial Assurance Commissioner, and

(c)   for an offence under section 455, the Secretary of State.

(3)   Where proceedings are instituted under the Companies Acts against any person by the Director of Public Prosecutions or by or on behalf of the Secretary of State or the Lord Advocate, nothing in those acts is to be taken to require any person to disclose any information which he is entitled to refuse to disclose on grounds of legal professional privilege.

733.   Offences by bodies corporate.

(1)   The following applies to offences under any of sections 210, 216(3), 394A(1) and 447 to 451.

(2)   Where a body corporate is guilty of such an offence and it is proved that the offence occurred with the consent or connivance of, or was attributable to any neglect on the part of any director, manager, secretary or other similar officer of the body, or any person who was purporting to act in any such capacity, he as well as the body corporate is guilty of that offence and is liable to be proceeded against and punished accordingly.

(3)   Where the affairs of a body corporate are managed by its members, subsection (2) above applies in relation to the acts and defaults of a member in connection with his functions of management as if he were a director of the body corporate.

(4)   In this section 'director', in relation to an offence under any of sections 447 to 451, includes a shadow director.

734.   Criminal proceedings against unincorporated bodies.

(1)   Proceedings for an offence alleged to have been committed under section 389A(3) or section 394A(1) or any of sections 447 to 451 by an unincorporated body shall be brought in the name of that body (and not in that of any of its members), and for the purposes of any such proceedings, any rules of court relating to the service of documents apply as if that body were a corporation.

(2)   A fine imposed on an unincorporated body on its conviction of such an offence shall be paid out of the funds of that body.

(3)   In a case in which an unincorporated body is charged in England and Wales with such an offence, section 33 of the Criminal Justice Act 1925 and Schedule 3 to the Magistrates' Courts Act 1980 (procedure on charge of an offence against a corporation) have effect in like manner as in the case of a corporation so charged.

(4)   In relation to proceedings on indictment in Scotland for such an offence alleged to have been committed by an unincorporated body, section 70 of the Criminal Procedure (Scotland) Act 1995 (proceedings on indictment against bodies corporate) has effect as if that body were a body corporate.

(5)   Where such an offence committed by a partnership is proved to have been committed with the consent or connivance of, or to be attributable to any neglect on the part of, a partner, he as well as the partnership is guilty of the offence and liable to be proceeded against and punished accordingly.

(6)   Where such an offence committed by an unincorporated body (other than a partnership) is proved to have been committed with the consent or connivance of, or to be attributable to any neglect on the part of, any officer of the body or any member of its governing body, he as well as the body is guilty of the offence and liable to be proceeded against and punished accordingly.

PART XXVI
INTERPRETATION

735.   'Company'.

(1)   In this Act—
   (a)   'company' means a company formed and registered under this Act, or an existing company;
   (b)   'existing company' means a company formed and registered under the former Companies Acts, but does not include a company registered under the Joint Stock Companies Acts, the Companies Act 1862 or the Companies (Consolidation) Act 1908 in what was then Ireland;
   (c)   'the former Companies Acts' means the Joint Stock Companies Acts, the Companies Act 1862, the Companies (Consolidation) Act 1908, the Companies Act 1929 and the Companies Acts 1948 to 1983.

(2)   'Public company' and 'private company' have the meanings given by section 1(3).

(3)   'The Joint Stock Companies Acts' means the Joint Stock Companies Act 1856, the Joint Stock Companies Acts 1856, 1857, the Joint Stock Banking Companies Act 1857 and the Act to enable Joint Stock Banking Companies to be formed on the principle of limited liability, or any one or more of those Acts (as the case may require), but does not include the Joint Stock Companies Act 1844.

(4)   The definitions in this section apply unless the contrary intention appears.

735A.   Relationship of this Act to Insolvency Act.

(1)   In this Act 'the Insolvency Act' means the Insolvency Act 1986; and in the following provisions of this Act, namely, sections 375(1)(b), 425(6)(a), 460(2), 675, 676, 677, 699(1), 728 and Schedule 21, paragraph 6(1), the words 'this Act' are to be read as including Parts I to VII of that Act, sections 411, 413, 414, 416 and 417 in Part XV of that Act, and also the Company Directors Disqualification Act 1986.

(2)   In sections 704(5), (7) and (8), 706(1), 707(1), 707A(1), 708(1)(a) and (4), 709(1) and (3), 710A, 713(1), 729 and 732(3) references to the Companies Acts include Parts I to VII of the Insolvency Act, sections 411, 413, 414, 416 and 417 in Part XV of that Act, and also the Company Directors Disqualification Act 1986.

(3)   Subsections (1) and (2) apply unless the contrary intention appears.

735B.   Relationship of this Act to Parts IV and V of the Financial Services Act 1986.

In sections 704(5), (7) and (8), 706(1), 707(1), 707A(1), 708(1)(a) and (4), 709(1) and (3), 710A and 713(1) references to the Companies Acts include Parts IV and V of the Financial Services Act 1986.

736.   'Subsidiary', 'holding company' and 'wholly-owned subsidiary'.

(1)   A company is a 'subsidiary' of another company, its 'holding company', if that other company—

(a)   holds a majority of the voting rights in it, or

(b)   is a member of it and has the right to appoint or remove a majority of its board of directors, or

(c)   is a member of it and controls alone, pursuant to an agreement with other shareholders or members, a majority of the voting rights in it,

or if it is a subsidiary of a company which is itself a subsidiary of that other company.

(2)   A company is a 'wholly-owned subsidiary' of another company if it has no members except that other and that other's wholly-owned subsidiaries or persons acting on behalf of that other or its wholly-owned subsidiaries.

(3)   In this section 'company' includes any body corporate.

736A.   Provisions supplementing s. 736.

(1)   The provisions of this section explain expressions used in section 736 and otherwise supplement that section.

(2)   In section 736(1)(a) and (c) the references to the voting rights in a company are to the rights conferred on shareholders in respect of their shares or, in the case of a company not having a share capital, on members, to vote at general meetings of the company on all, or substantially all, matters.

(3)   In section 736(1)(b) the reference to the right to appoint or remove a majority of the board of directors is to the right to appoint or remove directors holding a majority of the voting rights at meetings of the board on all, or substantially all, matters; and for the purposes of that provision—

(a)   a company shall be treated as having the right to appoint to a directorship if—

(i)   a person's appointment to it follows necessarily from his appointment as director of the company, or

(ii)   the directorship is held by the company itself; and

(b)   a right to appoint or remove which is exercisable only with the consent or concurrence of another person shall be left out of account unless no other person has a right to appoint or, as the case may be, remove in relation to that directorship.

(4)   Rights which are exercisable only in certain circumstances shall be taken into account only—

(a)   when the circumstances have arisen, and for so long as they continue to obtain, or

(b)   when the circumstances are within the control of the person having the rights; and rights which are normally exercisable but are temporarily incapable of exercise shall continue to be taken into account.

(5)   Rights held by a person in a fiduciary capacity shall be treated as not held by him.

(6)   Rights held by a person as nominee for another shall be treated as held by the other; and rights shall be regarded as held as nominee for another if they are exercisable only on his instructions or with his consent or concurrence.

(7)   Rights attached to shares held by way of security shall be treated as held by the person providing the security—

(a)   where apart from the right to exercise them for the purpose of preserving the value of the security, or of realising it, the rights are exercisable only in accordance with his instructions;

(b)   where the shares are held in connection with the granting of loans as part of normal business activities and apart from the right to exercise them for the purpose of preserving the value of the security, or of realising it, the rights are exercisable only in his interests.

(8)   Rights shall be treated as held by a company if they are held by any of its subsidiaries; and nothing in subsection (6) or (7) shall be construed as requiring rights held by a company to be treated as held by any of its subsidiaries.

(9)   For the purposes of subsection (7) rights shall be treated as being exercisable in accordance with the instructions or in the interests of a company if they are exercisable in accordance with the instructions of or, as the case may be, in the interests of—

(a)   any subsidiary or holding company of that company, or

(b)   any subsidiary of a holding company of that company.

(10)   The voting rights in a company shall be reduced by any rights held by the company itself.

(11)   References in any provision of subsections (5) to (10) to rights held by a person include rights falling to be treated as held by him by virtue of any other provision of those subsections but not rights which by virtue of any such provision are to be treated as not held by him.

(12)   In this section 'company' includes any body corporate.

736B.   Power to amend ss. 736 and 736A.

(1)   The Secretary of State may by regulations amend sections 736 and 736A so as to alter the meaning of the expressions 'holding company', 'subsidiary' or 'wholly-owned subsidiary'.

(2)   The regulations may make different provision for different cases or classes of case and may contain such incidental and supplementary provisions as the Secretary of State thinks fit.

(3)   Regulations under this section shall be made by statutory instrument which shall be subject to annulment in pursuance of a resolution of either House of Parliament.

(4)   Any amendment made by regulations under this section does not apply for the purposes of enactments outside the Companies Acts unless the regulations so provide.

(5)   So much of section 23(3) of the Interpretation Act 1978 as applies section 17(2)(a) of that Act (effect of repeal and re-enactment) to deeds, instruments and

documents other than enactments shall not apply in relation to any repeal and re-enactment effected by regulations made under this section.

737. 'Called-up share capital'.

(1)   In this Act, 'called-up share capital', in relation to a company, means so much of its share capital as equals the aggregate amount of the calls made on its shares (whether or not those calls have been paid), together with any share capital paid up without being called and any share capital to be paid on a specified future date under the articles, the terms of allotment of the relevant shares or any other arrangements for payment of those shares.

(2)   'Uncalled share capital' is to be construed accordingly.

(3)   The definitions in this section apply unless the contrary intention appears.

738. 'Allotment' and 'paid up'.

(1)   In relation to an allotment of shares in a company, the shares are to be taken for the purposes of this Act to be allotted when a person acquires the unconditional right to be included in the company's register of members in respect of those shares.

(2)   For purposes of this Act, a share in a company is deemed paid up (as to its nominal value or any premium on it) in cash, or allotted for cash, if the consideration for the allotment or payment up is cash received by the company, or is a cheque received by it in good faith which the directors have no reason for suspecting will not be paid, or is a release of a liability of the company for a liquidated sum, or is an undertaking to pay cash to the company at a future date.

(3)   In relation to the allotment or payment up of any shares in a company, references in this Act (except sections 89 to 94) to consideration other than cash and to the payment up of shares and premiums on shares otherwise than in cash include the payment of, or any undertaking to pay, cash to any person other than the company.

(4)   For the purpose of determining whether a share is or is to be allotted for cash, or paid up in cash, 'cash' includes foreign currency.

739. 'Non-cash asset'.

(1)   In this Act 'non-cash asset' means any property or interest in property other than cash; and for this purpose 'cash' includes foreign currency.

(2)   A reference to the transfer or acquisition of a non-cash asset includes the creation or extinction of an estate or interest in, or a right over, any property and also the discharge of any person's liability, other than a liability for a liquidated sum.

740. 'Body corporate' and 'corporation'.

References in this Act to a body corporate or to a corporation do not include a corporation sole, but include a company incorporated elsewhere than in Great Britain.

Such references to a body corporate do not include a Scottish firm.

741. 'Director' and 'shadow director'.

(1)   In this Act, 'director' includes any person occupying the position of director, by whatever name called.

(2)   In relation to a company, 'shadow director' means a person in accordance with whose directions or instructions the directors of the company are accustomed to act.

However, a person is not deemed a shadow director by reason only that the directors act on advice given by him in a professional capacity.

(3)   For the purposes of the following provisions of this Act, namely—
section 309 (directors' duty to have regard to interests of employees),
section 319 (directors' long-term contracts of employment),
sections 320 to 322 (substantial property transactions involving directors),
section 322B (contracts with sole members who are directors), and
sections 330 to 346 (general restrictions on power of companies to make loans, etc., to directors and others connected with them),

(being provisions under which shadow directors are treated as directors), a body corporate is not to be treated as a shadow director of any of its subsidiary companies by reason only that the directors of the subsidiary are accustomed to act in accordance with its directions or instructions.

742. Expressions used in connection with accounts.
(1) In this Act, unless a contrary intention appears, the following expressions have the same meaning as in Part VII (accounts)—
'annual accounts',
'accounting reference date' and 'accounting reference period',
'balance sheet' and 'balance sheet date',
'current assets',
'financial year', in relation to a company,
'fixed assets',
'parent company' and 'parent undertaking',
'profit and loss account', and
'subsidiary undertaking'.
(2) References in this Act to 'realised profits' and 'realised losses', in relation to a company's accounts, shall be construed in accordance with section 262(3).

743. 'Employees' share scheme'.
For purposes of this Act, an employees' share scheme is a scheme for encouraging or facilitating the holding of shares or debentures in a company by or for the benefit of—
(a) the bona fide employees or former employees of the company, the company's subsidiary or holding company or a subsidiary of the company's holding company, or
(b) the wives, husbands, widows, widowers or children or stepchildren under the age of 18 of such employees or former employees.

744. Expressions used generally in this Act.
In this Act, unless the contrary intention appears, the following definitions apply—
'agent' does not include a person's counsel acting as such;
'articles' means, in relation to a company, its articles of association, as originally framed or as altered by resolution, including (so far as applicable to the company) regulations contained in or annexed to any enactment relating to companies passed before this Act, as altered by or under any such enactment;
'authorised minimum' has the meaning given by section 118;
'bank holiday' means a holiday under the Banking and Financial Dealings Act 1971;
'banking company' means a company which is authorised under the Banking Act 1987;
'books and papers' and 'books or papers' include accounts, deeds, writings and documents;
'the Companies Acts' means this Act, the insider dealing legislation and the Consequential Provisions Act;
'the Consequential Provisions Act' means the Companies Consolidation (Consequential Provisions) Act 1985;
'the court', in relation to a company, means the court having jurisdiction to wind up the company;
'debenture' includes debenture stock, bonds and any other securities of a company, whether constituting a charge on the assets of the company or not;
'document' includes summons, notice, order, and other legal process, and registers;
'EEA State' means a State which is a Contracting Party to the Agreement on the European Economic Area signed at Oporto on 2 May 1992 as adjusted by the protocol signed at Brussels on 17 March 1993;

'equity share capital' means, in relation to a company, its issued share capital excluding any part of that capital which, neither as respects dividends nor as respects capital, carries any right to participate beyond a specified amount in a distribution;
'expert' has the meaning given by section 62;
'floating charge' includes a floating charge within the meaning given by section 462;
'the Gazette' means, as respects companies registered in England and Wales, the London Gazette and, as respects companies registered in Scotland, the Edinburgh Gazette;
'hire-purchase agreement' has the same meaning as in the Consumer Credit Act 1974;
'the insider dealing legislation' means Part V of the Criminal Justice Act 1993 (insider dealing);
'insurance company' means the same as in the Insurance Companies Act 1982;
'joint stock company' has the meaning given by section 683;
'memorandum', in relation to a company, means its memorandum of association, as originally framed or as altered in pursuance of any enactment;
'number', in relation to shares, includes amount, where the context admits of the reference to shares being construed to include stock;
'officer', in relation to a body corporate, includes a director, manager or secretary;
'official seal', in relation to the registrar of companies, means a seal prepared under section 704(4) for the authentication of documents required for or in connection with the registration of companies;
'oversea company' means—
    (a)   a company incorporated elsewhere than in Great Britain which, after the commencement of this Act, establishes a place of business in Great Britain, and
    (b)   a company so incorporated which has, before that commencement, established a place of business and continues to have an established place of business in Great Britain at that commencement;
'place of business' includes a share transfer or share registration office;
'prescribed' means—
    (a)   as respects provisions of this Act relating to winding up, prescribed by general rules, and
    (b)   otherwise, prescribed by statutory instrument made by the Secretary of State;
'prospectus' means any prospectus, notice, circular, advertisement, or other invitation, offering to the public for subscription or purchase any shares in or debentures of a company;
'prospectus issued generally' means a prospectus issued to persons who are not existing members of the company or holders of its debentures;
'the registrar of companies' and 'the registrar' mean the registrar or other officer performing under this Act the duty of registration of companies in England and Wales or in Scotland, as the case may require;
'share' means share in the share capital of a company, and includes stock (except where a distinction between shares and stock is express or implied); and
'undistributable reserves' has the meaning given by section 264(3).
[*The definitions of 'authorised minimum', 'expert', 'floating charge', 'joint stock company' and 'undistributable reserves' would be repealed if the relevant provisions of sch. 24 to the Companies Act 1989 were brought into force.*

The definition of 'prospectus issued generally' was repealed by the Financial Services Act 1986, sch. 17, part I, but this repeal has been brought into force only in so far as is necessary to have the effect that the definition ceases to apply to a prospectus offering for subscription, or to any form of application for, units in a body corporate which is a recognised scheme (Financial Services Act 1986 (Commencement) (No. 8) Order 1988 (SI 1988/740), art. 2 and sch.).]

744A.   Index of defined expressions.

The following Table shows provisions defining or otherwise explaining expressions for the purposes of this Act generally—

accounting reference date, accounting reference period	sections 224 and 742(1)
acquisition (in relation to a non-cash asset)	section 739(2)
agent	section 744
allotment (and related expressions)	section 738
annual accounts	sections 261(2), 262(1) and 742(1)
annual general meeting	section 366
annual return	section 363
articles	section 744
authorised minimum	section 118
balance sheet and balance sheet date	sections 261(2), 262(1) and 742(1)
bank holiday	section 744
banking company	section 744
body corporate	section 740
books and papers, books or papers	section 744
called-up share capital	section 737(1)
capital redemption reserve	section 170(1)
the Companies Acts	section 744
companies charges register	section 397
company	section 735(1)
the Consequential Provisions Act	section 744
corporation	section 740
the court (in relation to a company)	section 744
current assets	sections 262(1) and 742(1)
debenture	section 744
director	section 741(1)
document	section 744
EEA State	section 744
elective resolution	section 379A
employees' share scheme	section 743
equity share capital	section 744
existing company	section 735(1)
extraordinary general meeting	section 368
extraordinary resolution	section 378(1)
financial year (of a company)	sections 223 and 742(1)
fixed assets	sections 262(1) and 742(1)
floating charge (in Scotland)	section 462
the former Companies Acts	section 735(1)
the Gazette	section 744
hire-purchase agreement	section 744
holding company	section 736
the insider dealing legislation	section 744
the Insolvency Act	section 735A(1)
insurance company	section 744
the Joint Stock Companies Acts	section 735(3)
limited company	section 1(2)
member (of a company)	section 22
memorandum (in relation to a company)	section 744
non-cash asset	section 739(1)

number (in relation to shares)	section 744
office copy (in relation to a court order in Scotland)	section 743A
officer (in relation to a body corporate)	section 744
official seal (in relation to the registrar of companies)	section 744
oversea company	section 744
overseas branch register	section 362
paid up (and related expressions)	section 738
parent company and parent undertaking	sections 258 and 742(1)
place of business	section 744
prescribed	section 744
private company	section 1(3)
profit and loss account	sections 261(2), 262(1) and 742(1)
prospectus	section 744
public company	section 1(3)
realised profits or losses	sections 262(3) and 742(2)
registered number (of a company)	section 705(1)
registered office (of a company)	section 287
registrar and registrar of companies	section 744
resolution for reducing share capital	section 135(3)
shadow director	section 741(2) and (3)
share	section 744
share premium account	section 130(1)
share warrant	section 188
special notice (in relation to a resolution)	section 379
special resolution	section 378(2)
subsidiary	section 736
subsidiary undertaking	sections 258 and 742(1)
transfer (in relation to a non-cash asset)	section 739(2)
uncalled share capital	section 737(2)
undistributable reserves	section 264(3)
unlimited company	section 1(2)
unregistered company	section 718
wholly-owned subsidiary	section 736(2)

PART XXVII
FINAL PROVISIONS

745. Northern Ireland.

(1) Except where otherwise expressly provided, nothing in this Act (except provisions relating expressly to companies registered or incorporated in Northern Ireland or outside Great Britain) applies to or in relation to companies so registered or incorporated.

(2) Subject to any such provision, and to any express provision as to extent, this Act does not extend to Northern Ireland.

746. Commencement.

This Act comes into force on 1 July 1985.

747. Citation.

This Act may be cited as the Companies Act 1985.

SCHEDULES

Section 10   SCHEDULE 1

PARTICULARS OF DIRECTORS ETC. TO BE CONTAINED IN STATEMENT UNDER SECTION 10

Directors

1. Subject as provided below, the statement under section 10(2) shall contain the following particulars with respect to each person named as director—

(a)   in the case of an individual, his present name, any former name, his usual residential address, his nationality, his business occupation (if any), particulars of any other directorships held by him, or which have been held by him and his date of birth;

(b)   in the case of a corporation or Scottish firm, its corporate or firm name and registered or principal office.

2.—(1)   It is not necessary for the statement to contain particulars of a director-ship—

(a)   which has not been held by a director at any time during the 5 years preceding the date on which the statement is delivered to the registrar,

(b)   which is held by a director in a company which—

(i)   is dormant or grouped with the company delivering the statement, and

(ii)   if he also held that directorship for any period during those 5 years, was for the whole of that period either dormant or so grouped,

(c)   which was held by a director for any period during those 5 years in a company which for the whole of that period was either dormant or grouped with the company delivering the statement.

(2)   For these purposes, 'company' includes any body corporate incorporated in Great Britain; and—

(a)   section 250(3) applies as regards whether and when a company is or has been 'dormant', and

(b)   a company is treated as being or having been at any time grouped with another company if at that time it is or was a company of which that other is or was a wholly-owned subsidiary, or if it is or was a wholly-owned subsidiary of the other or of another company of which that other is or was a wholly-owned subsidiary.

Secretaries

3.—(1)   The statement shall contain the following particulars with respect to the person named as secretary or, where there are to be joint secretaries, with respect to each person named as one of them—

(a)   in the case of an individual, his present name, any former name and his usual residential address,

(b)   in the case of a corporation or a Scottish firm, its corporate or firm name and registered or principal office.

(2)   However, if all the partners in a firm are joint secretaries, the name and principal office of the firm may be stated instead of the particulars otherwise required by this paragraph.

Interpretation

4.   In paragraphs 1(a) and 3(1)(a) above—

(a)   'name' means a person's Christian name (or other forename) and surname, except that in the case of a peer, or an individual usually known by a title, the title may be stated instead of his Christain name (or other forename) and surname or in addition to either or both of them; and

(b)   the reference to a former name does not include—

(i)   in the case of a peer, or an individual normally known by a British title, the name by which he was known previous to the adoption of or succession to the title, or

(ii)   in the case of any person, a former name which was changed or disused before he attained the age of 18 years or which has been changed or disused for 20 years or more, or

(iii)   in the case of a married woman, the name by which she was known previous to the marriage.

Section 56   SCHEDULE 3

MANDATORY CONTENTS OF PROSPECTUS

PART I

MATTERS TO BE STATED

The company's proprietorship, management and its capital requirement

2.   Where shares are offered to the public for subscription, the prospectus must give particulars as to—

(a)   the minimum amount which, in the opinion of the directors, must be raised by the issue of those shares in order to provide the sums (or, if any part of them is to be defrayed in any other manner, the balance of the sums) required to be provided in respect of each of the following—

(i)   the purchase price of any property purchased or to be purchased which is to be defrayed in whole or in part out of the proceeds of the issue,

(ii)   any preliminary expenses payable by the company, and any commission so payable to any person in consideration of his agreeing to subscribe for, or of his procuring or agreeing to procure subscriptions for, any shares in the company,

(iii)   the repayment of any money borrowed by the company in respect of any of the foregoing matters,

(iv)   working capital, and

(b)   the amounts to be provided in respect of the matters above mentioned otherwise than out of the proceeds of the issue and the sources out of which those amounts are to be provided.

[*The Financial Services Act 1986, sch. 17, part I, has repealed the Companies Act 1985, sch. 3, except for para. 2 in so far as it is necessary for the purposes of s. 83(1)(a) (Financial Services Act 1986 (Commencement) (No. 13) Order 1995 (SI 1995/1538)).*]

Section 226   SCHEDULE 4

FORM AND CONTENT OF COMPANY ACCOUNTS

PART I

GENERAL RULES AND FORMATS

SECTION A

GENERAL RULES

1.—(1)   Subject to the following provisions of this Schedule—

(a)   every balance sheet of a company shall show the items listed in either of the balance sheet formats set out below in section B of this Part; and

(b)   every profit and loss account of a company shall show the items listed in any one of the profit and loss account formats so set out;

in either case in the order and under the headings and sub-headings given in the format adopted.

(2)   Sub-paragraph (1) above is not to be read as requiring the heading or sub-heading for any item to be distinguished by any letter or number assigned to that item in the format adopted.

2.—(1) Where in accordance with paragraph 1 a company's balance sheet or profit and loss account for any financial year has been prepared by reference to one of the formats set out in section B below, the directors of the company shall adopt the same format in preparing the accounts for subsequent financial years of the company unless in their opinion there are special reasons for a change.

(2) Particulars of any change in the format adopted in preparing a company's balance sheet or profit and loss account in accordance with paragraph 1 shall be disclosed, and the reasons for the change shall be explained, in a note to the accounts in which the new format is first adopted.

3.—(1) Any item required in accordance with paragraph 1 to be shown in a company's balance sheet or profit and loss account may be shown in greater detail than required by the format adopted.

(2) A company's balance sheet or profit and loss account may include an item representing or covering the amount of any asset or liability, income or expenditure not otherwise covered by any of the items listed in the format adopted, but the following shall not be treated as assets in any company's balance sheet—

    (a)   preliminary expenses;

    (b)   expenses of and commission on any issue of shares or debentures; and

    (c)   costs of reserach.

(3) In preparing a company's balance sheet or profit and loss account the directors of the company shall adapt the arrangement and headings and sub-headings otherwise required by paragraph 1 in respect of items to which an Arabic number is assigned in the format adopted, in any case where the special nature of the company's business requires such adaptation.

(4) Items to which Arabic numbers are assigned in any of the formats set out in section B below may be combined in a company's accounts for any financial year if either—

    (a)   their individual amounts are not material to assessing the state of affairs or profit or loss of the company for that year; or

    (b)   the combination facilitates that assessment;

but in a case within paragraph (b) the individual amounts of any items so combined shall be disclosed in a note to the accounts.

(5) Subject to paragraph 4(3) below, a heading or sub-heading corresponding to an item listed in the format adopted in preparing a company's balance sheet or profit and loss account shall not be included if there is no amount to be shown for that item in respect of the financial year to which the balance sheet or profit and loss account relates.

(6) Every profit and loss account of a company shall show the amounts of the company's profit or loss on ordinary activities before taxation.

(7) Every profit and loss account of a company shall show separately as additional items—

    (a)   any amount set aside or proposed to be set aside to, or withdrawn or proposed to be withdrawn from, reserves;

    (b)   the agreement amount of any dividends paid and proposed;

    (c)   if it is not shown in the notes to the accounts, the aggregate amount of any dividends proposed.

4.—(1) In respect of every item shown in a company's balance sheet or profit and loss account the corresponding amount for the financial year immediately preceding that to which the balance sheet or profit and loss account relates shall also be shown.

(2) Where that corresponding amount is not comparable with the amount to be shown for the item in question in respect of the financial year to which the balance sheet or profit and loss account relates, the former amount shall be adjusted and particulars of the adjustment and the reasons for it shall be disclosed in a note to the accounts.

(3)   Paragraph 3(5) does not apply in any case where an amount can be shown for the item in question in respect of the financial year immediately preceding that to which the balance sheet or profit and loss account relates, and that amount shall be shown under the heading or sub-heading required by paragraph 1 for the item.

5.   Amounts in respect of items representing assets or income may not be set off against amounts in respect of items representing liabilities or expenditure (as the case may be), or vice versa.

SECTION B
THE REQUIRED FORMATS FOR ACCOUNTS

Preliminary

6.   References in this Part of this Schedule to the items listed in any of the formats set out below are to those items read together with any of the notes following the formats which apply to any of those items, and the requirement imposed by paragraph 1 to show the items listed in any such format in the order adopted in the format is subject to any provision in those notes for alternative positions for any particular items.

7.   A number in brackets following any item in any of the formats set out below is a reference to the note of that number in the notes following the formats.

8.   In the notes following the formats—

(a)   the heading of each note gives the required heading or sub-heading for the item to which it applies and a reference to any letters and numbers assigned to that item in the formats set out below (taking a reference in the case of Format 2 of the balance sheet formats to the item listed under 'Assets' or under 'Liabilities' as the case may require); and

(b)   references to a numbered format are to the balance sheet format or (as the case may require) to the profit and loss account format of that number set out below.

Balance Sheet Formats

Format 1

A.   Called-up share capital not paid *(1)*
B.   Fixed assets
   I   Intangible assets
      1.   Development costs
      2.   Concessions, patents, licences, trade marks and similar rights and assets *(2)*
      3.   Goodwill *(3)*
      4.   Payments on account
   II   Tangible assets
      1.   Land and buildings
      2.   Plant and machinery
      3.   Fixtures, fittings, tools and equipment
      4.   Payments on account and assets in course of construction
   III   Investments
      1.   Shares in group undertakings
      2.   Loans to group undertakings
      3.   Participating interests
      4.   Loans to undertakings in which the company has a participating interest
      5.   Other investments other than loans
      6.   Other loans
      7.   Own shares *(4)*

C.   Current assets
  I   Stocks
      1.   Raw materials and consumables
      2.   Work in progress
      3.   Finished goods and goods for resale
      4.   Payments on account
  II   Debtors *(5)*
      1.   Trade debtors
      2.   Amounts owed by group undertakings
      3.   Amounts owed by undertakings in which the company has a participating
         interest
      4.   Other debtors
      5.   Called-up share capital not paid *(1)*
      6.   Prepayments and accrued income *(6)*
  III Investments
      1.   Shares in group undertakings
      2.   Own shares *(4)*
      3.   Other investments
  IV Cash at bank and in hand
D.   Prepayments and accrued income *(6)*
E.   Creditors: amounts falling due within one year
      1.   Debenture loans *(7)*
      2.   Bank loans and overdrafts
      3.   Payments received on account *(8)*
      4.   Trade creditors
      5.   Bills of exchange payable
      6.   Amounts owed to group undertakings
      7.   Amounts owed to undertakings in which the company has a participating
         interest
      8.   Other creditors including taxation and social security *(9)*
      9.   Accruals and deferred income *(10)*
F.   Net current assets (liabilities) *(11)*
G.   Total assets less current liabilities
H.   Creditors: amounts falling due after more than one year
      1.   Debenture loans *(7)*
      2.   Bank loans and overdrafts
      3.   Payments received on account *(8)*
      4.   Trade creditors
      5.   Bills of exchange payable
      6.   Amounts owed to group undertakings
      7.   Amounts owed to undertakings in which the company has a participating
         interest
      8.   Other creditors including taxation and social security *(9)*
      9.   Accruals and deferred income *(10)*
I.   Provisions for liabilities and charges
      1.   Pensions and similar obligations
      2.   Taxation, including deferred taxation
      3.   Other provisions
J.   Accruals and deferred income *(10)*
K.   Capital and reserves
  I   Called-up share capital *(12)*
  II   Share premium account
  III Revaluation reserve

IV   Other reserves
     1.   Capital redemption reserve
     2.   Reserve for own shares
     3.   Reserves provided for by the articles of association
     4.   Other reserves
V   Profit and loss account

Balance Sheet Formats

Format 2

ASSETS
A.   Called-up share capital not paid *(1)*
B.   Fixed assets
   I   Intangible assets
       1.   Development costs
       2.   Concessions, patents, licences, trade marks and similar rights and assets *(2)*
       3.   Goodwill *(3)*
       4.   Payments on account
   II   Tangible assets
       1.   Land and buildings
       2.   Plant and machinery
       3.   Fixtures, fittings, tools and equipment
       4.   Payments on account and assets in course of construction
   III Investments
       1.   Shares in group undertakings
       2.   Loans to group undertakings
       3.   Participating interests
       4.   Loans to undertakings in which the company has a participating interest
       5.   Other investments other than loans
       6.   Other loans
       7.   Own shares *(4)*
C.   Current assets
   I   Stocks
       1.   Raw materials and consumables
       2.   Work in progress
       3.   Finished goods and goods for resale
       4.   Payments on account
   II   Debtors *(5)*
       1.   Trade debtors
       2.   Amounts owed by group undertakings
       3.   Amounts owed by undertakings in which the company has a participating interest
       4.   Other debtors
       5.   Called-up share capital not paid *(1)*
       6.   Prepayments and accrued income *(6)*
   III Investments
       1.   Shares in group undertakings
       2.   Own shares *(4)*
       3.   Other investments
   IV Cash at bank and in hand
D.   Prepayments and accrued income *(6)*

LIABILITIES
- A. Capital and reserves
  - I Called-up share capital (12)
  - II Share premium account
  - III Revaluation reserve
  - IV Other reserves
    1. Capital redemption reserve
    2. Reserve for own shares
    3. Reserves provided for by the articles of association
    4. Other reserves
  - V Profit and loss account
- B. Provisions for liabilities and charges
    1. Pensions and similar obligations
    2. Taxation including deferred taxation
    3. Other provisions
- C. Creditors (13)
    1. Debenture loans (7)
    2. Bank loans and overdrafts
    3. Payments received on account (8)
    4. Trade creditors
    5. Bills of exchange payable
    6. Amounts owed to group undertakings
    7. Amounts owed to undertakings in which the company has a participating interest.
    8. Other creditors including taxation and social security (9)
    9. Accruals and deferred income (10)
- D. Accruals and deferred income (10)

Notes on the balance sheet formats

(1) Called-up share capital not paid
  (Formats 1 and 2, items A and C.II.5.)
  This item may be shown in either of the two positions given in Formats 1 and 2.
(2) Concessions, patents, licences, trade marks and similar rights and assets
  (Formats 1 and 2, item B.I.2.)
  Amounts in respect of assets shall only be included in a company's balance sheet under this item if either—
       (a) the assets were acquired for valuable consideration and are not required to be shown under goodwill; or
       (b) the assets in question were created by the company itself.
(3) Goodwill
  (Formats 1 and 2, item B.I.3.)
  Amounts representing goodwill shall only be included to the extent that the goodwill was acquired for valuable consideration
(4) Own shares
  (Formats 1 and 2, items B.III.7 and C.III.2.)
  The nominal value of the shares held shall be shown separately.
(5) Debtors
  (Formats 1 and 2, items C.II.1 to 6.)
  The amount falling due after more than one year shall be shown separately for each item included under debtors.
(6) Prepayments and accrued income
  (Formats 1 and 2, items C.II.6 and D.)
  This item may be shown in either of the two positions given in Formats 1 and 2.

(7)   Debenture loans
  (Format 1, items E.1 and H.1 and Format 2, item C.1.)
  The amount of any convertible loans shall be shown separately.
(8)   Payments received on account
  (Format 1, items E.3 and H.3 and Format 2, item C.3.)
  Payments received on account of orders shall be shown for each of these items in so
  far as they are not shown as deductions from stocks.
(9)   Other creditors including taxation and social security
  (Format 1, items E. 8 and H. 8 and Format 2, item C.8.)
  The amount for creditors in respect of taxation and social security shall be shown
  separately from the amount for other creditors.
(10)   Accruals and deferred income
  (Format 1, items E.9, H.9 and J and Format 2, items C.9 and D.)
  The two positions given for this item in Format 1 at E.9 and H.9 are an alternative
  to the position at J, but if the item is not shown in a position corresponding to that
  at J it may be shown in either or both of the other two positions (as the case may
  require).
  The two positions given for this item in Format 2 are alternatives.
(11)   Net current assets (liabilities)
  (Format 1, item F.)
  In determining the amount to be shown for this item any amounts shown under
  'prepayments and accrued income' shall be taken into account wherever shown.
(12)   Called-up share capital
  (Format 1, item K.I and Format 2, item A.I.)
  The amount of allotted share capital and the amount of called-up share capital
  which has been paid up shall be shown separately.
(13)   Creditors
  (Format 2, items C.1 to 9.)
  Amounts falling due within one year and after one year shall be shown separately
  for each of these items and for the aggregate of all these items.

Profit and loss account formats

Format 1

(see note *(17)* below)

1.   Turnover
2.   Cost of sales *(14)*
3.   Gross profit or loss
4.   Distribution costs *(14)*
5.   Administrative expenses *(14)*
6.   Other operating income
7.   Income from shares in group undertakings
8.   Income from participating interests
9.   Income from other fixed asset investments *(15)*
10.   Other interest receivable and similar income *(15)*
11.   Amounts written off investments
12.   Interest payable and similar charges *(16)*
13.   Tax on profit or loss on ordinary activities
14.   Profit or loss on ordinary activities after taxation
15.   Extraordinary income
16.   Extraordinary charges
17.   Extraordinary profit or loss

18. Tax on extraordinary profit or loss
19. Other taxes not shown under the above items
20. Profit or loss for the financial year

Profit and loss account formats

Format 2

1. Turnover
2. Change in stocks of finished goods and in work in progress
3. Own work capitalised
4. Other operating income
5. (a) Raw materials and consumables
    (b) Other external charges
6. Staff costs:
    (a) wages and salaries
    (b) social security costs
    (c) other pension costs
7. (a) Depreciation and other amounts written off tangible and intangible fixed assets
    (b) Exceptional amounts written off current assets
8. Other operating charges
9. Income from shares in group undertakings
10. Income from participating interests
11. Income from other fixed asset investments *(15)*
12. Other interest receivable and similar income *(15)*
13. Amounts written off investments
14. Interest payable and similar charges *(16)*
15. Tax on profit or loss on ordinary activities
16. Profit or loss on ordinary activities after taxation
17. Extraordinary income
18. Extraordinary charges
19. Extraordinary profit or loss
20. Tax on extraordinary profit or loss
21. Other taxes not shown under the above items
22. Profit or loss for the financial year

Profit and loss account formats

Format 3

(see note *(17)* below)

A. Charges
    1. Cost of sales *(14)*
    2. Distribution costs *(14)*
    3. Administrative expenses *(14)*
    4. Amounts written off investments
    5. Interest payable and similar charges *(16)*
    6. Tax on profit or loss on ordinary activities
    7. Profit or loss on ordinary activities after taxation
    8. Extraordinary charges
    9. Tax on extraordinary profit or loss
    10. Other taxes not shown under the above items
    11. Profit or loss for the financial year

B.   Income
   1.   Turnover
   2.   Other operating income
   3.   Income from shares in group undertakings
   4.   Income from participating interests
   5.   Income from other fixed asset investments *(15)*
   6.   Other interest receivable and similar income *(15)*
   7.   Profit or loss on ordinary activities after taxation
   8.   Extraordinary income
   9.   Profit or loss for the financial year

Profit and loss account formats

Format 4

A.   Charges
   1.   Reduction in stocks of finished goods and in work in progress
   2.   (a)   Raw materials and consumables
      (b)   Other external charges
   3.   Staff costs:
      (a)   wages and salaries
      (b)   social security costs
      (c)   other pension costs
   4.   (a)   Depreciation and other amounts written off tangible and intangible fixed
         assets
      (b)   Exceptional amounts written off current assets
   5.   Other operating charges
   6.   Amounts written off investments
   7.   Interest payable and similar charges *(16)*
   8.   Tax on profit or loss on ordinary activities
   9.   Profit or loss on ordinary activities after taxation
  10.   Extraordinary income
  11.   Tax on extraordinary profit or loss
  12.   Other taxes not shown under the above items
  13.   Profit or loss for the financial year
B.   Income
   1.   Turnover
   2.   Increase in stocks of finished goods and in work in progress
   3.   Own work capitalised
   4.   Other operating income
   5.   Income from shares in group undertakings
   6.   Income from participating interests
   7.   Income from other fixed asset investments *(15)*
   8.   Other interest receivable and similar income *(15)*
   9.   Profit or loss on ordinary activities after taxation
  10.   Extraordinary income
  11.   Profit or loss for the financial year

Notes on the profit and loss account formats

(14)   Cost of sales: distribution costs: administrative expenses
   (Format 1, items 2, 4 and 5 and Format 3, items A.1, 2 and 3.)
     These items shall be stated after taking into account any necessary provisions for
depreciation or diminution in value of assets.

(15)   Income from other fixed asset investments: other interest receivable and similar income
(Format 1, items 9 and 10: Format 2, items 11 and 12: Format 3, items B.5 and 6:
Format 4, items B.7 and 8.)
  Income and interest derived from group undertakings shall be shown separately
from income and interest derived from other sources.

(16)   Interest payable and similar charges
(Format 1, item 12: Format 2, item 14: Format 3, item A.5: Format 4, item A.7.)
  The amount payable to group undertakings shall be shown separately.

(17)   Formats 1 and 3
  The amount of any provisions for depreciation and diminution in value of tangible
and intangible fixed assets falling to be shown under items 7(a) and A.4(a)
respectively in Formats 2 and 4 shall be disclosed in a note to the accounts in any case
where the profit and loss account is prepared by reference to Format 1 or Format 3.

PART II
ACCOUNTING PRINCIPLES AND RULES
SECTION A
ACCOUNTING PRINCIPLES

Preliminary

9.   Subject to paragraph 15 below, the amounts to be included in respect of all items
shown in a company's accounts shall be determined in accordance with the principles
set out in paragraphs 10 to 14.

Accounting principles

10.   The company shall be presumed to be carrying on business as a going concern.

11.   Accounting policies shall be applied consistently within the same accounts and
from one financial year to the next.

12.   The amount of any item shall be determined on a prudent basis, and in particular—
   (a)   only profits realised at the balance sheet date shall be included in the profit
and loss account; and
   (b)   all liabilities and losses which have arisen or are likely to arise in respect of the
financial year to which the accounts relate or a previous financial year shall be taken into
account, including those which only become apparent between the balance sheet date
and the date on which it is signed on behalf of the board of directors in pursuance of
section 223 of this Act.

13.   All income and charges relating to the financial year to which the accounts relate
shall be taken into account, without regard to the date of receipt or payment.

14.   In determining the aggregate amount of any item the amount of each individual
asset or liability that falls to be taken into account shall be determined separately.

Departure from the accounting principles

15.   If it appears to the directors of a company that there are special reasons for
departing from any of the principles stated above in preparing the company's accounts
in respect of any financial year they may do so, but particulars of the departure, the
reasons for it and its effect shall be given in a note to the accounts.

SECTION B
HISTORICAL COST ACCOUNTING RULES

Preliminary

16.   Subject to section C of this Part of this Schedule, the amounts to be included in
respect of all items shown in a company's accounts shall be determined in accordance
with the rules set out in paragraphs 17 to 28.

Fixed assets

General rules

17.   Subject to any provision for depreciation or diminution in value made in accordance with paragraph 18 or 19 the amount to be included in respect of any fixed asset shall be its purchase price or production cost.

18.   In the case of any fixed asset which has a limited useful economic life, the amount of—

(a)   its purchase price or production cost; or

(b)   where it is estimated that any such asset will have a residual value at the end of the period of its useful economic life, its purchase price or production cost less that estimated residual value;

shall be reduced by provisions for depreciation calculated to write off that amount systematically over the period of the asset's useful economic life.

19.—(1)   Where a fixed asset investment of a description falling to be included under item B.III of either of the balance sheet formats set out in part I of this Schedule has diminished in value provisions for diminution in value may be made in respect of it and the amount to be included in respect of it may be reduced accordingly; and any such provisions which are not shown in the profit and loss account shall be disclosed (either separately or in aggregate) in a note to the accounts.

(2)   Provisions for diminution in value shall be made in respect of any fixed asset which has diminished in value if the reduction in its value is expected to be permanent (whether its useful economic life is limited or not), and the amount to be included in respect of it shall be reduced accordingly; and any such provisions which are not shown in the profit and loss account shall be disclosed (either separately or in aggregate) in a note to the accounts.

(3)   Where the reasons for which any provision was made in accordance with sub-paragraph (1) or (2) have ceased to apply to any extent, that provision shall be written back to the extent that it is no longer necessary; and any amounts written back in accordance with this sub-paragraph which are not shown in the profit and loss account shall be disclosed (either separately or in aggregate) in a note to the accounts.

Rules for determining particular fixed asset items

20.—(1)   Notwithstanding that an item in respect of 'development costs' is included under 'fixed assets' in the balance sheet formats set out in Part I of this Schedule, an amount may only be included in a company's balance sheet in respect of development costs in special circumstances.

(2)   If any amount is included in a company's balance sheet in respect of development costs the following information shall be given in a note to the accounts—

(a)   the period over which the amount of those costs originally capitalised is being or is to be written off; and

(b)   the reasons for capitalising the development costs in question.

21.—(1)   The application of paragraphs 17 to 19 in relation to goodwill (in any case where goodwill is treated as an asset) is subject to the following provisions of this paragraph.

(2)   Subject to sub-paragraph (3) below, the amount of the consideration for any goodwill acquired by a company shall be reduced by provisions for depreciation calculated to write off that amount systematically over a period chosen by the directors of the company.

(3)   The period chosen shall not exceed the useful economic life of the goodwill in question.

(4)   In any case where any goodwill acquired by a company is shown or included as an asset in the company's balance sheet the period chosen for writing off the

consideration for that goodwill and the reasons for choosing that period shall be disclosed in a note to the accounts.

Current assets

22. Subject to paragraph 23, the amount to be included in respect of any current asset shall be its purchase price or production cost.

23.—(1) If the net realisable value of any current asset is lower than its purchase price or production cost the amount to be included in respect of that asset shall be the net realisable value.

(2) Where the reasons for which any provision for diminution in value was made in accordance with sub-paragraph (1) have ceased to apply to any extent, that provision shall be written back to the extent that it is no longer necessary.

Miscellaneous and supplementary provisions

Excess of money owed over value received as an asset item

24.—(1) Where the amount repayable on any debt owed by a company is greater than the value of the consideration received in the transaction giving rise to the debt, the amount of the difference may be treated as an asset.

(2) Where any such amount is so treated—

(a) it shall be written off by reasonable amounts each year and must be completely written off before repayment of the debt; and

(b) if the current amount is not shown as a separate item in the company's balance sheet it must be disclosed in a note to the accounts.

Assets included at a fixed amount

25.—(1) Subject to the following sub-paragraph, assets which fall to be included—

(a) amongst the fixed assets of a company under the item 'tangible assets'; or

(b) amongst the current assets of a company under the item 'raw materials and consumables';

may be included at a fixed quantity and value.

(2) Sub-paragraph (1) applies to assets of a kind which are constantly being replaced, where—

(a) their overall value is not material to assessing the company's state of affairs; and

(b) their quantity, value and composition are not subject to material variation.

Determination of purchase price or production cost

26.—(1) The purchase price of an asset shall be determined by adding to the actual price paid any expenses incidental to its acquisition.

(2) The production cost of an asset shall be determined by adding to the purchase price of the raw materials and consumables used the amount of the costs incurred by the company which are directly attributable to the production of that asset.

(3) In addition, there may be included in the production cost of an asset—

(a) a reasonable proportion of the costs incurred by the company which are only indirectly attributable to the production of that asset, but only to the extent that they relate to the period of production; and

(b) interest on capital borrowed to finance the production of that asset to the extent that it accrues in respect of the period of production;

provided, however, in a case within paragraph (b) above, that the inclusion of the interest in determining the cost of that asset and the amount of the interest so included is disclosed in a note to the accounts.

(4) In the case of current assets distribution costs may not be included in production costs.

27.—(1) Subject to the qualification mentioned below, the purchase price or production cost of—

(a) any assets which fall to be included under any item shown in a company's balance sheet under the general item 'stocks'; and

(b) any assets which are fungible assets (including investments);

may be determined by the application of any of the methods mentioned in sub-paragraph (2) below in relation to any such assets of the same class.

The method chosen must be one which appears to the directors to be appropriate in the circumstances of the company.

(2) Those methods are—

(a) the method known as 'first in, first out' (FIFO);

(b) the method known as 'last in, first out' (LIFO);

(c) a weighted average price; and

(d) any other method similar to any of the methods mentioned above.

(3) Where in the case of any company—

(a) the purchase price or production cost of assets falling to be included under any item shown in the company's balance sheet has been determined by the application of any method permitted by this paragraph; and

(b) the amount shown in respect of that item differs materially from the relevant alternative amount given below in this paragraph;

the amount of that difference shall be disclosed in a note to the accounts.

(4) Subject to sub-paragraph (5) below, for the purposes of sub-paragraph (3)(b) above, the relevant alternative amount, in relation to any item shown in a company's balance sheet, is the amount which would have been shown in respect of that item if assets of any class included under that item at an amount determined by any method permitted by this paragraph had instead been included at their replacement cost as at the balance sheet date.

(5) The relevant alternative amount may be determined by reference to the most recent actual purchase price or production cost before the balance sheet date of assets of any class included under the item in question instead of by reference to their replacement cost as at that date, but only if the former appears to the directors of the company to constitute the more appropriate standard of comparison in the case of assets of that class.

(6) For the purposes of this paragraph, assets of any description shall be regarded as fungible if assets of that description are substantially indistinguishable one from another.

Substitution of original stated amount where price or cost unknown

28. Where there is no record of the purchase price or production cost of any asset of a company or of any price, expenses or costs relevant for determining its purchase price or production cost in accordance with paragraph 26, or any such record cannot be obtained without unreasonable expense or delay, its purchase price or production cost shall be taken for the purposes of paragraphs 17 to 23 to be the value ascribed to it in the earliest available record of its value made on or after its acquisition or production by the company.

SECTION C
ALTERNATIVE ACCOUNTING RULES

Preliminary

29.—(1) The rules set out in section B are referred to below in this Schedule as the historical cost accounting rules.

(2)   Those rules, with the omission of paragraphs 16, 21 and 25 to 28, are referred to below in this Part of this Schedule as the depreciation rules; and references below in this Schedule to the historical cost accounting rules do not include the depreciation rules as they apply by virtue of paragraph 32.

30.   Subject to paragraphs 32 to 34, the amounts to be included in respect of assets of any description mentioned in paragraph 31 may be determined on any basis so mentioned.

Alternative accounting rules

31.—(1)   Intangible fixed assets, other than goodwill, may be included at their current cost.

(2)   Tangible fixed assets may be included at a market value determined as at the date of their last valuation or at their current cost.

(3)   Investments of any description falling to be included under item B.III of either of the balance sheet formats set out in Part I of this Schedule may be included either—

  (a)   at a market value determined as at the date of their last valuation; or

  (b)   at a value determined on any basis which appears to the directors to be appropriate in the circumstances of the company;

but in the latter case particulars of the method of valuation adopted and of the reasons for adopting it shall be disclosed in a note to the accounts.

(4)   Investments of any description falling to be included under item C.III of either of the balance sheet formats set out in Part I of this Schedule may be included at their current cost.

(5)   Stocks may be included at their current cost.

Application of the depreciation rules

32.—(1)   Where the value of any asset of a company is determined on any basis mentioned in paragraph 31, that value shall be, or (as the case may require) be the starting point for determining, the amount to be included in respect of that asset in the company's accounts, instead of its purchase price or production cost or any value previously so determined for that asset; and the depreciation rules shall apply accordingly in relation to any such asset with the substitution for any reference to its purchase price or production cost of a reference to the value most recently determined for that asset on any basis mentioned in paragraph 31.

(2)   The amount of any provision for depreciation required in the case of any fixed asset by paragraph 18 or 19 as it applies by virtue of sub-paragraph (1) is referred to below in this paragraph as the adjusted amount, and the amount of any provision which would be required by that paragraph in the case of that asset according to the historical cost accounting rules is referred to as the historical cost amount.

(3)   Where sub-paragraph (1) applies in the case of any fixed asset the amount of any provision for depreciation in respect of that asset—

  (a)   included in any item shown in the profit and loss account in respect of amounts written off assets of the description in question; or

  (b)   taken into account in stating any item so shown which is required by note *(14)* of the notes on the profit and loss account formats set out in Part I of this Schedule to be stated after taking into account any necessary provisions for depreciation or diminution in value of assets included under it;

may be the historical cost amount instead of the adjusted amount, provided that the amount of any difference between the two is shown separately in the profit and loss account or in a note to the accounts.

Additional information to be provided in case of departure from historical cost accounting rules

33.—(1) This paragraph applies where the amounts to be included in respect of assets covered by any items shown in a company's accounts have been determined on any basis mentioned in paragraph 31.

(2) The items affected and the basis of valuation adopted in determining the amounts of the assets in question in the case of each such item shall be disclosed in a note to the accounts.

(3) In the case of each balance sheet item affected (except stocks) either—

(a) the comparable amounts determined according to the historical cost accounting rules; or

(b) the differences between those amounts and the corresponding amounts actually shown in the balance sheet in respect of that item;

shall be shown separately in the balance sheet or in a note to the accounts.

(4) In sub-paragraph (3) above, references in relation to any item to the comparable amounts determined as there mentioned are references to—

(a) the aggregate amount which would be required to be shown in respect of that item if the amounts to be included in respect of all the assets covered by that item were determined according to the historical cost accounting rules; and

(b) the aggregate amount of the cumulative provisions for depreciation or diminution in value which would be permitted or required in determining those amounts according to those rules.

Revaluation reserve

34.—(1) With respect to any determination of the value of an asset of a company on any basis mentioned in paragraph 31, the amount of any profit or loss arising from that determination (after allowing, where appropriate, for any provisions for depreciation or diminution in value made otherwise than by reference to the value so determined and any adjustments of any such provisions made in the light of that determination) shall be credited or (as the case may be) debited to a separate reserve ('the revaluation reserve').

(2) The amount of the revaluation reserve shall be shown in the company's balance sheet under a separate sub-heading in the position given for the item 'revaluation reserve' in Format 1 or 2 of the balance sheet formats set out in Part I of this Schedule, but need not be shown under that name.

(3) An amount may be transferred—

(a) from the revaluation reserve—

(i) to the profit and loss account, if the amount was previously charged to that account or represents realised profit, or

(ii) on capitalisation,

(b) to or from the revaluation reserve in respect of the taxation relating to any profit or loss credited or debited to the reserve;

and the revaluation reserve shall be reduced to the extent that the amounts transferred to it are no longer necessary for the purposes of the valuation method used.

(3A) In sub-paragraph (3)(a)(ii) 'capitalisation', in relation to an amount standing to the credit of the revaluation reserve, means applying it in wholly or partly paying up unissued shares in the company to be allotted to members of the company as fully or partly paid shares.

(3B) The revaluation reserve shall not be reduced except as mentioned in this paragraph.

(4) The treatment for taxation purposes of amounts credited or debited to the revaluation reserve shall be disclosed in a note to the accounts.

PART VII
INTERPRETATION OF SCHEDULE

76.   The following paragraphs apply for the purposes of this Schedule and its interpretation.

Historical cost accounting rules

82.   References to the historical cost accounting rules shall be read in accordance with paragraph 29.

Leases

83.—(1)   'Long lease' means a lease in the case of which the portion of the term for which it was granted remaining unexpired at the end of the financial year is not less than 50 years.

(2)   'Short lease' means a lease which is not a long lease.

(3)   'Lease' includes an agreement for a lease.

Listed investments

84.   'Listed investment' means an investment as respects which there has been granted a listing on a recognised investment exchange other than an overseas investment exchange within the meaning of the Financial Services Act 1986 or on any stock exchange of repute outside Great Britain.

Loans

85.   A loan is treated as falling due for repayment, and an instalment of a loan is treated as falling due for payment, on the earliest date on which the lender could require repayment or (as the case may be) payment, if he exercised all options and rights available to him.

Materiality

86.   Amounts which in the particular context of any provision of this Schedule are not material may be disregarded for the purposes of that provision.

Provisions

88.—(1)   References to provisions for depreciation or diminution in value of assets are to any amount written off by way of providing for depreciation or diminution in value of assets.

(2)   Any reference in the profit and loss account formats set out in Part I of this Schedule to the depreciation of, or amounts written off, assets of any description is to any provision for depreciation or diminution in value of assets of that description.

89.   References to provisions for liabilities or charges are to any amount retained as reasonably necessary for the purpose of providing for any liability or loss which is either likely to be incurred, or certain to be incurred but uncertain as to amount or as to the date on which it will arise.

Scots land tenure

93.   In the application of this Schedule to Scotland, 'land of freehold tenure' means land in respect of which the company is the proprietor of the *dominium utile* or, in the case of land not held on feudal tenure, is the owner; 'land of leasehold tenure' means land of which the company is the tenant under a lease; and the reference to ground-rents, rates and other outgoings includes feu-duty and ground annual.

Staff costs

94.—(1) 'Social security costs' means any contributions by the company to any state social security or pension scheme, fund or arrangement.

(2) 'Pension costs' includes any costs incurred by the company in respect of any pension scheme established for the purpose of providing pensions for persons currently or formerly employed by the company, any sums set aside for the future payment of pensions directly by the company to current or former employees and any pensions paid directly to such persons without having first been set aside.

(3) Any amount stated in respect of the item 'social security costs' or in respect of the item 'wages and salaries' in the company's profit and loss account shall be determined by reference to payments made or costs incurred in respect of all persons employed by the company during the financial year who are taken into account in determining the relevant annual number for the purposes of paragraph 56(1)(a).

Section 232   SCHEDULE 6
DISCLOSURE OF INFORMATION: EMOLUMENTS AND OTHER BENEFITS
OF DIRECTORS AND OTHERS

PART I
CHAIRMAN'S AND DIRECTORS' EMOLUMENTS, PENSIONS AND
COMPENSATION FOR LOSS OF OFFICE

Aggregate amount of directors' emoluments etc.

1.—(1) Subject to sub-paragraph (2), the following shall be shown, namely—
    (a) the aggregate amount of emoluments paid to or receivable by directors in respect of qualifying services;
    (b) the aggregate of the amount of gains made by directors on the exercise of share options;
    (c) the aggregate of the following, namely—
        (i) the amount of money paid to or receivable by directors under long term incentive schemes in respect of qualifying services; and
        (ii) the net value of assets (other than money and share options) received or receivable by directors under such schemes in respect of such services;
    (d) the aggregate value of any company contributions paid, or treated as paid, to a pension scheme in respect of directors' qualifying services, being contributions by reference to which the rate or amount of any money purchase benefits that may become payable will be calculated; and
    (e) in the case of each of the following, namely—
        (i) money purchase schemes; and
        (ii) defined benefit schemes,
the number of directors (if any) to whom retirement benefits are accruing under such schemes in respect of qualifying services.

(2) In the case of a company which is not a listed company—
    (a) sub-paragraph (1) shall have effect as if paragraph (b) were omitted and, in paragraph (c)(ii), 'assets' did not include shares; and
    (b) the number of each of the following (if any) shall be shown, namely—
        (i) the directors who exercised share options; and
        (ii) the directors in respect of whose qualifying services shares were received or receivable under long term incentive schemes.

(3) In this paragraph 'emoluments' of a director—
    (a) includes salary, fees and bonuses, sums paid by way of expenses allowance (so far as they are chargeable to United Kingdom income tax) and, subject to paragraph

(b), the estimated money value of any other benefits received by him otherwise than in cash; but

(b)   does not include any of the following, namely—

(i)   the value of any share options granted to him or the amount of any gains made on the exercise of any such options;

(ii)   any company contributions paid, or treated as paid, in respect of him under any pension scheme or any benefits to which he is entitled under any such scheme; or

(iii)   any money or other assets paid to or received or receivable by him under any long term incentive scheme.

(4)   In this paragraph 'long term incentive scheme' means any agreement or arrangement under which money or other assets may become receivable by a director and which includes one or more qualifying conditions with respect to service or performance which cannot be fulfilled within a single financial year; and for this purpose the following shall be disregarded, namely—

(a)   bonuses the amount of which falls to be determined by reference to service or performance within a single financial year;

(b)   compensation for loss of office, payments for breach of contract and other termination payments; and

(c)   retirement benefits.

(5)   In this paragraph—

'amount', in relation to a gain made on the exercise of a share option, means the difference between—

(a)   the market price of the shares on the day on which the option was exercised; and

(b)   the price actually paid for the shares;

'company contributions', in relation to a pension scheme and a director, means any payments (including insurance premiums) made, or treated as made, to the scheme in respect of the director by a person other than the director;

'defined benefits' means retirement benefits payable under a pension scheme which are not money purchase benefits;

'defined benefit scheme', in relation to a director, means a pension scheme which is not a money purchase scheme;

'listed company' means a company—

(a)   whose securities have been admitted to the Official List of the Stock Exchange in accordance with the provisions of Part IV of the Financial Services Act 1986; or

(b)   dealings in whose securities are permitted on any exchange which is an approved exchange for the purposes of that Part;

'money purchase benefits', in relation to a director, means retirement benefits payable under a pension scheme the rate or amount of which is calculated by reference to payments made, or treated as made, by the director or by any other person in respect of the director and which are not average salary benefits;

'money purchase scheme', in relation to a director, means a pension scheme under which all of the benefits that may become payable to or in respect of the director are money purchase benefits;

'net value', in relation to any assets received or receivable by a director, means value after deducting any money paid or other value given by the director in respect of those assets;

'qualifying services', in relation to any person, means his services as a director of the company, and his services while director of the company—

(a)   as director of any of its subsidiary undertakings; or

(b)   otherwise in connection with the management of the affairs of the company or any of its subsidiary undertakings;

'shares' means shares (whether allotted or not) in the company, or any undertaking which is a group undertaking in relation to the company, and includes a share warrant as defined by section 188(1);

'share option' means a right to acquire shares;

'value', in relation to shares received or receivable by a director on any day, means the market price of the shares on that day.

(6)   For the purposes of this paragraph—

(a)   any information, other than the aggregate amount of gains made by directors on the exercise of share options, shall be treated as shown if it is capable of being readily ascertained from other information which is shown; and

(b)   emoluments paid or receivable or share options granted in respect of a person's accepting office as a director shall be treated as emoluments paid or receivable or share options granted in respect of his services as a director.

(7)   Where a pension scheme provides for any benefits that may become payable to or in respect of any director to be whichever are the greater of—

(a)   money purchase benefits as determined by or under the scheme; and

(b)   defined benefits as so determined,

the company may assume for the purposes of this paragraph that those benefits will be money purchase benefits, or defined benefits, according to whichever appears more likely at the end of the financial year.

(8)   For the purpose of determining whether a pension scheme is a money purchase or defined benefit scheme, any death in service benefits provided for by the scheme shall be disregarded.

Details of highest paid director's emoluments etc.

2.—(1)   Where the aggregates shown under paragraph 1(1)(a), (b) and (c) total £200,000 or more, the following shall be shown, namely—

(a)   so much of the total of those aggregates as is attributable to the highest paid director; and

(b)   so much of the aggregate mentioned in paragraph 1(1)(d) as is so attributable.

(2)   Where sub-paragraph (1) applies and the highest paid director has performed qualifying services during the financial year by reference to which the rate or amount of any defined benefits that may become payable will be calculated, there shall also be shown—

(a)   the amount at the end of the year of his accrued pension; and

(b)   where applicable, the amount at the end of the year of his accrued lump sum.

(3)   Subject to sub-paragraph (4), where sub-paragraph (1) applies in the case of a company which is not a listed company, there shall also be shown—

(a)   whether the highest paid director exercised any share options; and

(b)   whether any shares were received or receivable by that director in respect of qualifying services under a long term incentive scheme.

(4)   Where the highest paid director has not been involved in any of the transactions specified in sub-paragraph (3), that fact need not be stated.

(5)   In this paragraph—

'accrued pension' and 'accrued lump sum', in relation to any pension scheme and any director, mean respectively the amount of the annual pension, and the amount of the lump sum, which would be payable under the scheme on his attaining normal pension age if—

(a)   he had left the company's service at the end of the financial year;

(b)   there were no increase in the general level of prices in Great Britain during the period beginning with the end of that year and ending with his attaining that age;

(c)   no question arose of any commutation of the pension or inverse commutation of the lump sum; and

(d)   any amounts attributable to voluntary contributions paid by the director to the scheme, and any money purchase benefits which would be payable under the scheme, were disregarded;

'the highest paid director' means the director to whom is attributable the greatest part of the total of the aggregates shown under paragraph 1(1)(a), (b) and (c);

'normal pension age', in relation to any pension scheme and any director, means the age at which the director will first become entitled to receive a full pension on retirement of an amount determined without reduction to take account of its payment before a later age (but disregarding any entitlement to pension upon retirement in the event of illness, incapacity or redundancy).

(6)   Sub-paragraphs (4) to (8) of paragraph 1 apply for the purposes of this paragraph as they apply for the purposes of that paragraph.

Excess retirement benefits of directors and past directors

7.—(1)   Subject to sub-paragraph (2), there shall be shown the aggregate amount of—

(a)   so much of retirement benefits paid to or receivable by directors under pension schemes; and

(b)   so much of retirement benefits paid to or receivable by past directors under such schemes,

as (in each case) is in excess of the retirement benefits to which they were respectively entitled on the date on which the benefits first became payable or 31 March 1997, whichever is the later.

(2)   Amounts paid or receivable under a pension scheme need not be included in the aggregate amount if—

(a)   the funding of the scheme was such that the amounts were or, as the case may be, could have been paid without recourse to additional contributions; and

(b)   amounts were paid to or receivable by all pensioner members of the scheme on the same basis;

and in this sub-paragraph 'pensioner member', in relation to a pension scheme, means any person who is entitled to the present payment of retirement benefits under the scheme.

(3)   In this paragraph—

(a)   references to retirement benefits include benefits otherwise than in cash; and

(b)   in relation to so much of retirement benefits as consists of a benefit otherwise than in cash, references to their amount are to the estimated money value of the benefit;

and the nature of any such benefit shall also be disclosed.

Compensation to directors for loss of office

8.—(1)   There shall be shown the aggregate amount of any compensation to directors or past directors in respect of loss of office.

(2)   This amount includes compensation received or receivable by a director or past director for—

(a)   loss of office as director of the company, or

(b)   loss, while director of the company or on or in connection with his ceasing to be a director of it, of—

(i)   any other office in connection with the management of the company's affairs, or

(ii)   any office as director or otherwise in connection with the management of the affairs of any subsidiary undertaking of the company.

(3)   References to compensation include benefits otherwise than in cash; and in relation to such compensation references to its amount are to the estimated money value of the benefit.

The nature of any such compensation shall be disclosed.

(4)   In this paragraph, references to compensation for loss of office include the following, namely—

(a)   compensation in consideration for, or in connection with, a person's retirement from office; and

(b)   where such a retirement is occasioned by a breach of the person's contract with the company or with a subsidiary undertaking of the company—

(i)   payments made by way of damages for the breach; or

(ii)   payments made by way of settlement or compromise of any claim in respect of the breach.

(5)   Sub-paragraph (6)(a) of paragraph 1 applies for the purposes of this paragraph as it applies for the purposes of that paragraph.

Sums paid to third parties in respect of directors' services

9.—(1)   There shall be shown the aggregate amount of any consideration paid to or receivable by third parties for making available the services of any person—

(a)   as a director of the company, or

(b)   while director of the company—

(i)   as director of any of its subsidiary undertakings, or

(ii)   otherwise in connection with the management of the affairs of the company or any of its subsidiary undertakings.

(2)   The reference to consideration includes benefits otherwise than in cash; and in relation to such consideration the reference to its amount is to the estimated money value of the benefit.

The nature of any such consideration shall be disclosed.

(3)   The reference to third parties is to persons other than—

(a)   the director himself or a person connected with him or body corporate controlled by him, and

(b)   the company or any of its subsidiary undertakings.

Supplementary

10.—(1)   The following applies with respect to the amounts to be shown under this Part of this Schedule.

(2)   The amount in each case includes all relevant sums paid by or receivable from—

(a)   the company; and

(b)   the company's subsidiary undertakings; and

(c)   any other person,

except sums to be accounted for to the company or any of its subsidiary undertakings or, by virtue of sections 314 and 315 of this Act (duty of directors to make disclosure on company takeover; consequence of non-compliance), to past or present members of the company or any of its subsidiaries or any class of those members.

(4)   References to amounts paid to or receivable by a person include amounts paid to or receivable by a person connected with him or a body corporate controlled by him (but not so as to require an amount to be counted twice).

11.—(1)   The amounts to be shown for any financial year under this Part of this Schedule are the sums receivable in respect of that year (whenever paid) or, in the case of sums not receivable in respect of a period, the sums paid during that year.

(2)   But where—

(a)   any sums are not shown in a note to the accounts for the relevant financial year on the ground that the person receiving them is liable to account for them as mentioned in paragraph 10(2), but the liability is thereafter wholly or partly released or is not enforced within a period of 2 years; or

(b)   any sums paid by way of expenses allowance are charged to United Kingdom income tax after the end of the relevant financial year,

those sums shall, to the extent to which the liability is released or not enforced or they are charged as mentioned above (as the case may be), be shown in a note to the first accounts in which it is practicable to show them and shall be distinguished from the amounts to be shown apart from this provision.

12.   Where it is necessary to do so for the purpose of making any distinction required by the preceding paragraphs in an amount to be shown in compliance with this Part of this Schedule, the directors may apportion any payments between the matters in respect of which these have been paid or are receivable in such manner as they think appropriate.

Interpretation

13.—(1)   The following applies for the interpretation of this Part of this Schedule.

(2)   A reference to a subsidiary undertaking of the company—

(a)   in relation to a person who is or was, while a director of the company, a director also, by virtue of the company's nomination (direct or indirect) of any other undertaking, includes (subject to the following sub-paragraph) that undertaking, whether or not it is or was in fact a subsidiary undertaking of the company, and

(b)   for the purposes of paragraphs 1 to 7 is to an undertaking which is a subsidiary undertaking at the time the services were rendered, and for the purposes of paragraph 8 to a subsidiary undertaking immediately before the loss of office as director.

(3)   The following definitions apply—

(a)   'pension scheme' has the meaning assigned to 'retirement benefits scheme' by section 611 of the Income and Corporation Taxes Act 1988;

(b)   'retirement benefits' has the meaning assigned to relevant benefits by section 612(1) of that Act.

(4)   References in this Part of this Schedule to a person being 'connected' with a director, and to a director 'controlling' a body corporate, shall be construed in accordance with section 346.

Supplementary

14.   This Part of this Schedule requires information to be given only so far as it is contained in the company's books and papers or the company has the right to obtain it from the persons concerned.

Section 234   SCHEDULE 7
MATTERS TO BE DEALT WITH IN DIRECTORS' REPORT

PART I
MATTERS OF A GENERAL NATURE

Asset values

1.—(2)   If, in the case of such of the fixed assets of the company or of any of its subsidiary undertakings as consist in interests in land, their market value (as at the end of the financial year) differs substantially from the amount at which they are included in the balance sheet, and the difference is, in the directors' opinion of such significance as to require that the attention of members of the company or of holders of its debentures should be drawn to it, the report shall indicate the difference with such degree of precision as is practicable.

Directors' interests

2.—(1) The information required by paragraphs 2A and 2B shall be given in the directors' report, or by way of notes to the company's annual accounts, with respect to each person who at the end of the financial year was a director of the company.

(2) In those paragraphs—

(a) 'the register' means the register of directors' interests kept by the company under section 325; and

(b) references to a body corporate being in the same group as the company are to its being a subsidiary or holding company, or another subsidiary of a holding company, of the company.

2A.—(1) It shall be stated with respect to each director whether, according to the register, he was at the end of the financial year interested in shares in or debentures of the company or any other body corporate in the same group.

(2) If he was so interested, there shall be stated the number of shares in and amount of debentures of each body (specifying it) in which, according to the register, he was then interested.

(3) If a director was interested at the end of the financial year in shares in or debentures of the company or any other body corporate in the same group—

(a) it shall also be stated whether, according to the register, he was at the beginning of the financial year (or, if he was not then a director, when he became one) interested in shares in or debentures of the company or any other body corporate in the same group, and

(b) if he was so interested, there shall be stated the number of shares in and amount of debentures of each body (specifying it) in which, according to the register, he was then interested.

(4) In this paragraph references to an interest in shares or debentures have the same meaning as in section 324; and references to the interest of a director include any interest falling to be treated as his for the purposes of that section.

(5) The reference above to the time when a person became a director is, in the case of a person who became a director on more than one occasion, to the time when he first became a director.

2B.—(1) It shall be stated with respect to each director whether, according to the register, any right to subscribe for shares in or debentures of the company or another body corporate in the same group was during the financial year granted to, or exercised by, the director or a member of his immediate family.

(2) If any such right was granted to, or exercised by, any such person during the financial year, there shall be stated the number of shares in and amount of debentures of each body (specifying it) in respect of which, according to the register, the right was granted or exercised.

(3) A director's 'immediate family' means his or her spouse and infant children; and for this purpose 'children' includes stepchildren, and 'infant', in relation to Scotland, means pupil or minor.

(4) The reference above to a member of the director's immediate family does not include a person who is himself or herself a director of the company.

Political and charitable gifts

3.—(1) The following applies if the company (not being the wholly-owned subsidiary of a company incorporated in Great Britain) has in the financial year given money for political purposes or charitable purposes or both.

(2) If the money given exceeded £200 in amount, there shall be contained in the directors' report for the year—

(a)   in the case of each of the purposes for which money has been given, a statement of the amount of money given for that purpose, and

(b)   in the case of political purposes for which money has been given, the following particulars (so far as applicable)—

(i)   the name of each person to whom money has been given for those purposes exceeding £200 in amount and the amount of money given,

(ii)   if money exceeding £200 in amount has been given by way of donation or subscription to a political party, the identity of the party and the amount of money given.

4.—(1)   Paragraph 3 does not apply to a company which, at the end of the financial year, has subsidiaries which have, in that year, given money as mentioned above, but is not itself the wholly-owned subsidiary of a company incorporated in Great Britain.

(2)   But in such a case there shall (if the amount of money so given in that year by the company and the subsidiaries between them exceeds £200) be contained in the directors' report for the year—

(a)   In the case of each of the purposes for which money has been given by the company and the subsidiaries between them, a statement of the amount of money given for that purpose, and

(b)   in the case of political purposes for which money has been given, the like particulars (so far as applicable) as are required by paragraph 3.

5.—(1)   The following applies for the interpretation of paragraphs 3 and 4.

(2)   A company is to be treated as giving money for political purposes if, directly or indirectly—

(a)   it gives a donation or subscription to a political party of the United Kingdom or any part of it; or

(b)   it gives a donation or subscription to a person who, to the company's knowledge, is carrying on, or proposing to carry on, any activities which can, at the time at which the donation or subscription was given, reasonably be regarded as likely to affect public support for such a political party as is mentioned above.

(3)   Money given for charitable purposes to a person who, when it was given, was ordinarily resident outside the United Kingdom is to be left out of account.

(4)   'Charitable purposes' means purposes which are exclusively charitable; and, as respects Scotland, 'charitable' is to be construed as if it were contained in the Income Tax Acts.

Miscellaneous

6.   The directors' report shall contain—

(a)   particulars of any important events affecting the company or any of its subsidiary undertakings which have occurred since the end of the financial year,

(b)   an indication of likely future developments in the business of the company and of its subsidiary undertakings,

(c)   an indication of the activities (if any) of the company and its subsidiary undertakings in the field of research and development, and

(d)   (unless the company is an unlimited company) an indication of the existence of branches (as defined in section 698(2)) of the company outside the United Kingdom.

PART II
DISCLOSURE REQUIRED BY COMPANY ACQUIRING ITS OWN
SHARES, ETC.

7.   This Part of this Schedule applies where shares in a company—

(a)   are purchased by the company or are acquired by it by forfeiture or surrender in lieu of forfeiture, or in pursuance of section 143(3) of this Act (acquisition of own shares by company limited by shares), or

(b)   are acquired by another person in circumstances where paragraph (c) or (d) of section 146(1) applies (acquisition by company's nominee, or by another with company financial assistance, the company having a beneficial interest), or

(c)   are made subject to a lien or other charge taken (whether expressly or otherwise) by the company and permitted by section 150(2) or (4), or section 6(3) of the Consequential Provisions Act (exceptions from general rule against a company having a lien or charge on its own shares).

8.   The directors' report with respect to a financial year shall state—

(a)   the number and nominal value of the shares so purchased, the aggregate amount of the consideration paid by the company for such shares and the reasons for their purchase;

(b)   the number and nominal value of the shares so acquired by the company, acquired by another person in such circumstances and so charged respectively during the financial year;

(c)   the maximum number and nominal value of shares which, having been so acquired by the company, acquired by another person in such circumstances or so charged (whether or not during that year) are held at any time by the company or that other person during that year;

(d)   the number and nominal value of the shares so acquired by the company, acquired by another person in such circumstances or so charged (whether or not during that year) which are disposed of by the company or that other person or cancelled by the company during that year;

(e)   where the number and nominal value of the shares of any particular description are stated in pursuance of any of the preceding sub-paragraphs, the percentage of the called-up share capital which shares of that description represent;

(f)   where any of the shares have been so charged the amount of the charge in each case; and

(g)   where any of the shares have been disposed of by the company or the person who acquired them in such circumstances for money or money's worth the amount or value of the consideration in each case.

PART III
DISCLOSURE CONCERNING EMPLOYMENT, ETC. OF DISABLED PERSONS

9.—(1)   This Part of this Schedule applies to the directors' report where the average number of persons employed by the company in each week during the financial year exceeded 250.

(2)   That average number is the quotient derived by dividing, by the number of weeks in the financial year, the number derived by ascertaining, in relation to each of those weeks, the number of persons who, under contracts of service, were employed in the week (whether throughout it or not) by the company, and adding up the numbers ascertained.

(3)   The directors' report shall in that case contain a statement describing such policy as the company has applied during the financial year—

(a)   for giving full and fair consideration to applications for employment by the company made by disabled persons, having regard to their particular aptitudes and abilities,

(b)   for continuing the employment of, and for arranging appropriate training for, employees of the company who have become disabled persons during the period when they were employed by the company, and

(c)   otherwise for the training, career development and promotion of disabled persons employed by the company.

(4)   In this Part—

(a) 'employment' means employment other than employment to work wholly or mainly outside the United Kingdom, and 'employed' and 'employee' shall be construed accordingly; and

(b) 'disabled person' means the same as in the Disability Discrimination Act 1995.

PART V
EMPLOYEE INVOLVEMENT

11.—(1) This Part of this Schedule applies to the directors' report where the average number of persons employed by the company in each week during the financial year exceeded 250.

(2) That average number is the quotient derived by dividing by the number of weeks in the financial year the number derived by ascertaining, in relation to each of those weeks, the number of persons who, under contracts of service, were employed in the week (whether throughout it or not) by the company, and adding up the numbers ascertained.

(3) The directors' report shall in that case contain a statement describing the action that has been taken during the financial year to introduce, maintain or develop arrangements aimed at—

(a) providing employees systematically with information on matters of concern to them as employees,

(b) consulting employees or their representatives on a regular basis so that the views of employees can be taken into account in making decisions which are likely to affect their interests,

(c) encouraging the involvement of employees in the company's performance through an employees' share scheme or by some other means,

(d) achieving a common awareness on the part of all employees of the financial and economic factors affecting the performance of the company.

(4) In sub-paragraph (3) 'employee' does not include a person employed to work wholly or mainly outside the United Kingdom; and for the purposes of sub-paragraph (2) no regard is to be had to such a person.

PART VI
POLICY AND PRACTICE ON PAYMENT OF CREDITORS

12.—(1) This Part of this Schedule applies to the directors' report for a financial year if—

(a) the company was at any time within the year a public company, or

(b) the company did not qualify as small or medium-sized in relation to the year by virtue of section 247 and was at any time within the year a member of a group of which the parent company was a public company.

(2) The report shall state, with respect to the next following financial year—

(a) whether in respect of some or all of its suppliers it is the company's policy to follow any code or standard on payment practice and, if so, the name of the code or standard and the place where information about, and copies of, the code or standard can be obtained,

(b) whether in respect of some or all of its suppliers it is the company's policy—

(i) to settle the terms of payment with those suppliers when agreeing the terms of each transaction,

(ii) to ensure that those suppliers are made aware of the terms of payment, and

(iii) to abide by the terms of payment,

(c) where the company's policy is not as mentioned in paragraph (a) or (b) in respect of some or all of its suppliers, what its policy is with respect to the payment of those suppliers;

and if the company's policy is different for different suppliers or classes of suppliers, the report shall identify the suppliers to which the different policies apply.

In this sub-paragraph references to the company's suppliers are references to persons who are or may become its suppliers.

(3) The report shall also state the number of days which bears to the number of days in the financial year the same proportion as X bears to Y where—

X = the aggregate of the amounts which were owed to trade creditors at the end of the year; and

Y = the aggregate of the amounts in which the company was invoiced by suppliers during the year.

(4) For the purposes of sub-paragraphs (2) and (3) a person is a supplier of the company at any time if—

(a) at that time, he is owed an amount in respect of goods or services supplied, and

(b) that amount would be included under the heading corresponding to item E.4 (trade creditors) in Format 1 if—

(i) the company's accounts fell to be prepared as at that time,

(ii) those accounts were prepared in accordance with Schedule 4, and

(iii) that Format were adopted.

(5) For the purpose of sub-paragraph (3), the aggregate of the amounts which at the end of the financial year were owed to trade creditors shall be taken to be—

(a) where in the company's accounts Format 1 of the balance sheet formats set out in Part I of Schedule 4 is adopted, the amount shown under the heading corresponding to item E.4 (trade creditors) in that Format,

(b) where Format 2 is adopted, the amount which, under the heading corresponding to item C.4 (trade creditors) in that Format, is shown as falling due within one year, and

(c) where the company's accounts are prepared in accordance with Schedule 9 or 9A, the amount which would be shown under the heading corresponding to item E.4 (trade creditors) in Format 1 if the company's accounts were prepared in accordance with Schedule 4 and that Format were adopted.

Section 258   SCHEDULE 10A

PARENT AND SUBSIDIARY UNDERTAKINGS: SUPPLEMENTARY PROVISIONS

Introduction

1. The provisions of this Schedule explain expressions used in section 258 (parent and subsidiary undertakings) and otherwise supplement that section.

Voting rights in an undertaking

2.—(1) In section 258(2)(a) and (d) the references to the voting rights in an undertaking are to the rights conferred on shareholders in respect of their shares or, in the case of an undertaking not having a share capital, on members, to vote at general meetings of the undertaking on all, or substantially all, matters.

(2) In relation to an undertaking which does not have general meetings at which matters are decided by the exercise of voting rights, the references to holding a majority of the voting rights in the undertaking shall be construed as references to having the right under the constitution of the undertaking to direct the overall policy of the undertaking or to alter the terms of its constitution.

Right to appoint or remove a majority of the directors

3.—(1)   In section 258(2)(b) the reference to the right to appoint or remove a majority of the board of directors is to the right to appoint or remove directors holding a majority of the voting rights at meetings of the board on all, or substantially all, matters.

(2)   An undertaking shall be treated as having the right to appoint to a directorship if—

(a)   a person's appointment to it follows necessarily from his appointment as director of the undertaking, or

(b)   the directorship is held by the undertaking itself.

(3)   A right to appoint or remove which is exercisable only with the consent or concurrence of another person shall be left out of account unless no other person has a right to appoint or, as the case may be, remove in relation to that directorship.

Right to exercise dominant influence

4.—(1)   For the purposes of section 258(2)(c) an undertaking shall not be regarded as having the right to exercise a dominant influence over another undertaking unless it has a right to give directions with respect to the operating and financial policies of that other undertaking which its directors are obliged to comply with whether or not they are for the benefit of that other undertaking.

(2)   A 'control contract' means a contract in writing conferring such a right which—

(a)   is of a kind authorised by the memorandum or articles of the undertaking in relation to which the right is exercisable, and

(b)   is permitted by the law under which that undertaking is established.

(3)   This paragraph shall not be read as affecting the construction of the expression 'actually exercises a dominant influence' in section 258(4)(a).

Rights exercisable only in certain circumstances or temporarily incapable of exercise

5.—(1)   Rights which are exercisable only in certain circumstances shall be taken into account only—

(a)   when the circumstances have arisen, and for so long as they continue to obtain, or

(b)   when the circumstances are within the control of the person having the rights.

(2)   Rights which are normally exercisable but are temporarily incapable of exercise shall continue to be taken into account.

Rights held by one person on behalf of another

6.   Rights held by a person in a fiduciary capacity shall be treated as not held by him.

7.—(1)   Rights held by a person as nominee for another shall be treated as held by the other.

(2)   Rights shall be regarded as held as nominee for another if they are exercisable only on his instructions or with his consent or concurrence.

Rights attached to shares held by way of security

8.   Rights attached to shares held by way of security shall be treated as held by the person providing the security—

(a)   where apart from the right to exercise them for the purpose of preserving the value of the security, or of realising it, the rights are exercisable only in accordance with his instructions, and

(b)   where the shares are held in connection with the granting of loans as part of normal business activities and apart from the right to exercise them for the purpose of preserving the value of the security, or of realising it, the rights are exercisable only in his interests.

Rights attributed to parent undertaking

9.—(1) Rights shall be treated as held by a parent undertaking if they are held by any of its subsidiary undertakings.

(2) Nothing in paragraph 7 or 8 shall be construed as requiring rights held by a parent undertaking to be treated as held by any of its subsidiary undertakings.

(3) For the purposes of paragraph 8 rights shall be treated as being exercisable in accordance with the instructions or in the interests of an undertaking if they are exercisable in accordance with the instructions of or, as the case may be, in the interests of any group undertaking.

Disregard of certain rights

10. The voting rights in an undertaking shall be reduced by any rights held by the undertaking itself.

Supplementary

11. References in any provision of paragraphs 6 to 10 to rights held by a person include rights falling to be treated as held by him by virtue of any other provision of those paragraphs but not rights which by virtue of any such provision are to be treated as not held by him.

Section 381A   SCHEDULE 15A
WRITTEN RESOLUTIONS OF PRIVATE COMPANIES
PART I
EXCEPTIONS

1. Section 381A does not apply to—

(a) a resolution under section 303 removing a director before the expiration of his period of office, or

(b) a resolution under section 391 removing an auditor before the expiration of his term of office.

PART II
ADAPTATION OF PROCEDURAL REQUIREMENTS

Introductory

2.—(1) In this Part of this Schedule (which adapts certain requirements of this Act in relation to proceedings under section 381A)—

(a) a 'written resolution' means a resolution agreed to, or proposed to be agreed to, in accordance with that section, and

(b) a 'relevant member' means a member by whom, or on whose behalf, the resolution is required to be signed in accordance with that section.

(2) A written resolution is not effective if any of the requirements of this Part of this Schedule is not complied with.

Section 95 (disapplication of pre-emption rights)

3.—(1) The following adaptations have effect in relation to a written resolution under section 95(2) (disapplication of pre-emption rights), or renewing a resolution under that provision.

(2) So much of section 95(5) as requires the circulation of a written statement by the directors with a notice of meeting does not apply, but such a statement must be

supplied to each relevant member at or before the time at which the resolution is supplied to him for signature.

(3)   Section 95(6) (offences) applies in relation to the inclusion in any such statement of matter which is misleading, false or deceptive in a material particular.

Section 155 (financial assistance for purchase of company's own shares or those of holding company)

4.   In relation to a written resolution giving approval under section 155(4) or (5) (financial assistance for purchase of company's own shares or those of holding company), section 157(4)(a) (documents to be available at meeting) does not apply, but the documents referred to in that provision must be supplied to each relevant member at or before the time at which the resolution is supplied to him for signature.

Sections 164, 165 and 167 (authority for off-market purchase or contingent purchase contract of company's own shares)

5.—(1)   The following adaptations have effect in relation to a written resolution—
(a)   conferring authority to make an off-market purchase of the company's own shares under section 164(2),
(b)   conferring authority to vary a contract for an off-market purchase of the company's own shares under section 164(7), or
(c)   varying, revoking or renewing any such authority under section 164(3).

(2)   Section 164(5) (resolution ineffective if passed by exercise of voting rights by member holding shares to which the resolution relates) does not apply; but for the purposes of section 381A(1) a member holding shares to which the resolution relates shall not be regarded as a member who would be entitled to attend and vote.

(3)   Section 164(6) (documents to be available at company's registered office and at meeting) does not apply, but the documents referred to in that provision and, where that provision applies by virtue of section 164(7), the further documents referred to in that provision must be supplied to each relevant member at or before the time at which the resolution is supplied to him for signature.

(4)   The above adaptations also have effect in relation to a written resolution in relation to which the provisions of section 164(3) to (7) apply by virtue of—
(a)   section 165(2) (authority for contingent purchase contract), or
(b)   section 167(2) (approval of release of rights under contract approved under section 164 or 165).

Section 173 (approval for payment out of capital)

6.—(1)   The following adaptations have effect in relation to a written resolution giving approval under section 173(2) (redemption or purchase of company's own shares out of capital).

(2)   Section 174(2) (resolution ineffective if passed by exercise of voting rights by member holding shares to which the resolution relates) does not apply; but for the purposes of section 381A(1) a member holding shares to which the resolution relates shall not be regarded as a member who would be entitled to attend and vote.

(3)   Section 174(4) (documents to be available at meeting) does not apply, but the documents referred to in that provision must be supplied to each relevant member at or before the time at which the resolution is supplied to him for signature.

Section 319 (approval of director's service contract)

7.   In relation to a written resolution approving any such term as is mentioned in section 319(1) (director's contract of employment for more than five years), section 319(5) (documents to be available at company's registered office and at meeting) does not apply, but the documents referred to in that provision must be supplied to each

relevant member at or before the time at which the resolution is supplied to him for signature.

Section 337 (funding of director's expenditure in performing his duties)

8.   In relation to a written resolution giving approval under section 337(3)(a) (funding a director's expenditure in performing his duties), the requirement of that provision that certain matters be disclosed at the meeting at which the resolution is passed does not apply, but those matters must be disclosed to each relevant member at or before the time at which the resolution is supplied to him for signature.

Section 730

SCHEDULE 24

PUNISHMENT OF OFFENCES UNDER THIS ACT

Section of Act creating offence		General nature of offence	Mode of prosecution	Punishment	Daily default fine (where applicable)
6(3)	...	Company failing to deliver to registrar notice or other document, following alteration of its objects.	Summary.	One-fifth of the statutory maximum.	One-fiftieth of the statutory maximum.
18(3)	...	Company failing to register change in memorandum or articles.	Summary.	One-fifth of the statutory maximum.	One-fiftieth of the statutory maximum.
19(2)	...	Company failing to send to one of its members a copy of the memorandum or articles, when so required by the member.	Summary.	One-fifth of the statutory maximum.	
20(2)	...	Where company's memorandum altered, company issuing copy of the memorandum without the alteration.	Summary.	One-fifth of the statutory maximum for each occasion on which copies are so issued after the date of the alteration.	
28(5)	...	Company failing to change name on direction of Secretary of State.	Summary.	One-fifth of the statutory maximum.	One-fiftieth of the statutory maximum.
31(5)	...	Company altering its memorandum or articles, so ceasing to be exempt from having 'limited' as part of its name.	Summary.	The statutory maximum maximum.	One-tenth of the statutory maximum.
31(6)	...	Company failing to change name, on Secretary of State's direction, so as to have 'limited' (or Welsh equivalent) at the end.	Summary.	One-fifth of the statutory maximum.	One-fiftieth of the statutory maximum.
32(4)	...	Company failing to comply with Secretary of State's direction to change its name, on grounds that the name is misleading.	Summary.	One-fifth of the statutory maximum.	One-fiftieth of the statutory maximum.

Section of Act creating offence	General nature of offence	Mode of prosecution	Punishment	Daily default fine (where applicable)
33	Trading under misleading name (use of 'public limited company' or Welsh equivalent when not so entitled); purporting to be a private company.	Summary.	One-fifth of the statutory maximum.	One-fiftieth of the statutory maximum.
34	Trading or carrying on business with improper use of 'limited' or 'cyfyngedig'.	Summary.	One-fifth of the statutory maximum.	One-fiftieth of the statutory maximum.
54(10)	Public company failing to give notice, or copy of court order, to registrar, concerning application to re-register as private company.	Summary.	One-fifth of the statutory maximum.	One-fiftieth of the statutory maximum.
80(9)	Directors exercising company's power of allotment without the authority required by section 80(1).	1. On indictment. 2. Summary.	A fine. The statutory maximum.	
81(2)	Private limited company offering shares to the public, or allotting shares with a view to their being so offered. [See note 1 at the end of the schedule.]	1. On indictment. 2. Summary.	A fine. The statutory maximum.	
82(5)	Allotting shares or debentures before third day after issue of prospectus. [See note 1 at the end of the schedule.]	1. On indictment. 2. Summary.	A fine. The statutory maximum.	
86(6)	Company failing to keep money in separate bank accounts, where received in pursuance of prospectus stating that stock exchange listing is to be applied for. [See note 1 at the end of the schedule.]	1. On indictment. 2. Summary.	A fine. The statutory maximum.	
87(4)	Offeror of shares for sale failing to keep proceeds in separate bank account. [See note 1 at the end of the schedule.]	1. On indictment. 2. Summary.	A fine. The statutory maximum.	
88(5)	Officer of company failing to deliver return of allotments, etc., to registrar.	1. On indictment. 2. Summary.	A fine. The statutory maximum.	One-tenth of the statutory maximum.
95(6)	Knowingly or recklessly authorising or permitting misleading, false or deceptive material in statement by directors under section 95(5).	1. On indictment. 2. Summary.	2 years or a fine; or both. 6 months or the statutory maximum; or both.	

Section		Description	Mode	*One-fifth of the statutory maximum.*	
97(4)	...	*Company failing to deliver to registrar the prescribed form disclosing amount or rate of share commission*	*Summary.*		One-tenth of the statutory maximum.
110(2)	...	Making misleading, false or deceptive statement in connection with valuation under section 103 or 104.	1. On indictment. 2. Summary.	2 years or a fine; or both. 6 months or the statutory maximum; or both.	One-fiftieth of the statutory maximum.
111(3)	...	Officer of company failing to deliver copy of asset valuation report to registrar.	1. On indictment. 2. Summary.	A fine. The statutory maximum.	
111(4)	...	Company failing to deliver to registrar copy of resolution under section 104(4), with respect to transfer of an asset as consideration for allotment.	Summary.	One-fifth of the statutory maximum.	
114	...	Contravention of any of the provisions of sections 99 to 104, 106.	1. On indictment. 2. Summary.	A fine. The statutory maximum.	One-fiftieth of the statutory maximum.
117(7)	...	Company doing business or exercising borrowing powers contrary to section 117.	1. On indictment. 2. Summary.	A fine. The statutory maximum.	One-fiftieth of the statutory maximum.
122(2)	...	Company failing to give notice to registrar of reorganisation of share capital.	Summary.	One-fifth of the statutory maximum.	One-fiftieth of the statutory maximum.
123(4)	...	Company failing to give notice to registrar of increase of share capital.	Summary.	One-fifth of the statutory maximum.	One-fiftieth of the statutory maximum.
127(5)	...	Company failing to forward to registrar copy of court order, when application made to cancel resolution varying shareholders' rights.	Summary.	One-fifth of the statutory maximum.	One-fiftieth of the statutory maximum.
128(5)	...	Company failing to send to registrar statement or notice required by section 128 (particulars of shares carrying special rights).	Summary.	One-fifth of the statutory maximum.	One-fiftieth of the statutory maximum.
129(4)	...	Company failing to deliver to registrar statement or notice required by section 129 (registration of newly created class rights).	Summary.	One-fifth of the statutory maximum.	One-fiftieth of the statutory maximum.
141	...	Officer of company concealing name of creditor entitled to object to reduction of capital, or wilfully misrepresenting nature or amount of debt or claim, etc.	1. On indictment. 2. Summary.	A fine. The statutory maximum.	

Section of Act creating offence	General nature of offence	Mode of prosecution	Punishment	Daily default fine (where applicable)
142(2) ...	Director authorising or permitting non-compliance with section 142 (requirement to convene company meeting to consider serious loss of capital).	1. On indictment. 2. Summary.	A fine. The statutory maximum.	
143(2) ...	Company acquiring its own shares in breach of section 143.	1. On indictment.	In the case of the company, a fine. In the case of an officer of the company who is in default, 2 years or a fine; or both.	
		2. Summary.	In the case of the company, the statutory maximum. In the case of an officer of the company who is in default, 6 months or the statutory maximum; or both.	
149(2) ...	Company failing to cancel its own shares, acquired by itself, as required by section 146(2); or failing to apply for re-registration as private company as so required in the case there mentioned.	Summary.	One-fifth of the statutory maximum.	One-fiftieth of the statutory maximum.
151(3) ...	Company giving financial assistance towards acquisition of its own shares.	1. On indictment.	Where the company is convicted, a fine. Where an officer of the company is convicted, 2 years or a fine; or both.	
		2. Summary.	Where the company is convicted, the statutory maximum. Where an officer of the company is convicted, 6 months or the statutory maximum; or both.	

Section		Description	Mode	Punishment	Daily default fine
156(6)	...	Company failing to register statutory declaration under section 155.	Summary.	The statutory maximum.	One-fiftieth of the statutory maximum.
156(7)	...	Director making statutory declaration under section 155, without having reasonable grounds for opinion expressed in it.	1. On indictment. 2. Summary.	2 years or a fine; or both. 6 months or the statutory maximum; or both.	
169(6)	...	Default by company's officer in delivering to registrar the return required by section 169 (disclosure by company of purchase of own shares).	1. On indictment. 2. Summary.	A fine. The statutory maximum.	One-tenth of the statutory maximum.
169(7)	...	Company failing to keep copy of contract, etc., at registered office; refusal of inspection to person demanding it.	Summary.	One-fifth of the statutory maximum.	One-fiftieth of the statutory maximum.
173(6)	...	Director making statutory declaration under section 173 without having reasonable grounds for the opinion expressed in the declaration.	1. On indictment. 2. Summary.	2 years or a fine; or both. 6 months or the statutory maximum; or both.	
175(7)	...	Refusal of inspection of statutory declaration and auditors' report under section 173, etc.	Summary.	One-fifth of the statutory maximum.	One-fiftieth of the statutory maximum.
176(4)	...	Company failing to give notice to registrar of application to court under section 176, or to register court order.	Summary.	One-fifth of the statutory maximum.	One-fiftieth of the statutory maximum.
183(6)	...	Company failing to send notice of refusal to register a transfer of shares or debentures.	Summary.	One-fifth of the statutory maximum.	One-fiftieth of the statutory maximum.
185(5)	...	Company default in compliance with section 185(1) (certificates to be made ready following allotment or transfer of shares, etc.).	Summary.	One-fifth of the statutory maximum.	One-fiftieth of the statutory maximum.
191(4)	...	Refusal of inspection or copy of register of debenture-holders, etc.	Summary.	One-fifth of the statutory maximum.	One-fiftieth of the statutory maximum.
210(3)	...	Failure to discharge obligation of disclosure under Part VI; other forms of non-compliance with that Part.	1. On indictment. 2. Summary.	2 years or a fine; or both. 6 months or the statutory maximum; or both.	

Section of Act creating offence	General nature of offence	Mode of prosecution	Punishment	Daily default fine (where applicable)
211(10) ...	Company failing to keep register of interests disclosed under Part VI; other contraventions of section 211.	Summary.	One-fifth of the statutory maximum.	One-fiftieth of the statutory maximum.
214(5) ...	Company failing to exercise powers under section 212, when so required by the members.	1. On indictment. 2. Summary.	A fine. The statutory maximum.	
215(8) ...	Company default in compliance with section 215 (company report of investigation of shareholdings on members' requisition).	1. On indictment. 2. Summary.	A fine. The statutory maximum.	
216(3) ...	Failure to comply with company notice under section 212; making false statement in response, etc.	1. On indictment. 2. Summary.	2 years or a fine; or both. 6 months or the statutory maximum; or both.	
217(7) ...	Company failing to notify a person that he has been named as a shareholder; on removal of name from register, failing to alter associated index.	Summary.	One-fifth of the statutory maximum.	One-fiftieth of the statutory maximum.
218(3) ...	Improper removal of entry from register of interests disclosed; company failing to restore entry improperly removed.	Summary.	One-fifth of the statutory maximum.	For continued contravention of section 218(2) one-fiftieth of the statutory maximum.
219(3) ...	Refusal of inspection of register or report under Part VI; failure to send copy when required.	Summary.	One-fifth of the statutory maximum.	One-fiftieth of the statutory maximum.
221(5) or 222(4) ...	Company failing to keep accounting records (liability of officers).	1. On indictment. 2. Summary.	2 years or a fine; or both. 6 months or the statutory maximum; or both.	
222(6) ...	Officer of company failing to secure compliance with, or intentionally causing default under, section 222(5) (preservation of accounting records for requisite number of years).	1. On indictment. 2. Summary.	2 years or a fine; or both. 6 months or the statutory maximum; or both.	
231(6) ...	Company failing to annex to its annual return certain particulars required by Schedule 5 and not included in annual accounts.	Summary.	One-fifth of the statutory maximum.	One-fiftieth of the statutory maximum.

Section	Description	Mode of prosecution	Punishment	Daily default fine
232(4)	Default by director or officer of a company in giving notice of matters relating to himself for purposes of Schedule 6 Part I.	Summary.	One-fifth of the statutory maximum.	
233(5)	Approving defective accounts.	1. On indictment. 2. Summary.	A fine. The statutory maximum.	
233(6)	Laying or delivery of unsigned balance sheet; circulating copies of balance sheet without signatures.	Summary.	One-fifth of the statutory maximum.	
234(5)	Non-compliance with Part VII, as to directors' report and its content; directors individually liable.	1. On indictment. 2. Summary.	A fine. The statutory maximum.	
234A(4)	Laying circulating or delivering directors' report without required signature.	Summary.	One-fifth of the statutory maximum.	
236(4)	Laying, circulating or delivering auditors' report without required signature.	Summary.	One-fifth of the statutory maximum.	
238(5)	Failing to send company's annual accounts, directors' report and auditors' report to those entitled to receive them.	1. On indictment. 2. Summary.	A fine. The statutory maximum.	
239(3)	Company failing to supply copy of accounts and reports to shareholder on his demand.	Summary.	One-fifth of the statutory maximum.	One-fiftieth of the statutory maximum.
240(6)	Failure to comply with requirements in connection with publication of accounts.	Summary.	One-fifth of the statutory maximum.	
241(2) or 242(2)	Director in default as regards duty to lay and deliver company's annual accounts, directors' report and auditors' report.	Summary.	The statutory maximum.	One-tenth of the statutory maximum.
251(6)	Failure to comply with requirements in relation to summary financial statements.	Summary.	One-fifth of the statutory maximum.	
288(4)	Default in complying with section 288 (keeping register of directors and secretaries, refusal of inspection).	Summary.	The statutory maximum.	One-tenth of the statutory maximum.
291(5)	Acting as director of a company without having the requisite share qualification.	Summary.	One-fifth of the statutory maximum.	One-fiftieth of the statutory maximum.

Section of Act creating offence	General nature of offence	Mode of prosecution	Punishment	Daily default fine (where applicable)
294(3) ⋮	Director failing to give notice of his attaining retirement age; acting as director under appointment invalid due to his attaining it.	Summary.	One-fifth of the statutory maximum.	One-fiftieth of the statutory maximum.
305(3) ⋮	Company default in complying with section 305 (directors' names to appear on company correspondence, etc.).	Summary.	One-fifth of the statutory maximum.	
306(4) ⋮	Failure to state that liability of proposed director or manager is unlimited; failure to give notice of that fact to person accepting office.	1. On indictment. 2. Summary.	A fine. The statutory maximum.	
314(3) ⋮	Director failing to comply with section 314 (duty to disclose compensation payable on takeover, etc.); a person's failure to include required particulars in a notice he has to give of such matters.	Summary.	One-fifth of the statutory maximum.	
317(7) ⋮	Director failing to disclose interest in contract.	1. On indictment. 2. Summary.	A fine. The statutory maximum.	
318(8) ⋮	Company default in complying with section 318(1) or (5) (directors' service contracts to be open to inspection); 14 days' default in complying with section 318(4) (notice to registrar as to where copies of contracts and memoranda are kept); refusal of inspection required under section 318(7).	Summary.	One-fifth of the statutory maximum.	One-fiftieth of the statutory maximum.
322B(4) ⋮	Terms of unwritten contract between sole member of a private company limited by shares or by guarantee and the company not set out in a written memorandum or recorded in minutes of a directors' meeting.	Summary.	Level 5 on the standard scale.	
323(2) ⋮	Director dealing in options to buy or sell company's listed shares or debentures.	1. On indictment. 2. Summary.	2 years or a fine; or both. 6 months or the statutory maximum; or both.	

Section		Nature of offence	Mode of prosecution	Punishment	Daily default fine
324(7)	...	Director failing to notify interest in company's shares; making false statement in purported notification.	1. On indictment. 2. Summary.	2 years or a fine; or both. 6 months or the statutory maximum; or both.	
326(2), (3), (4), (5).		Various defaults in connection with company register of directors' interests.	Summary.	One-fifth of the statutory maximum.	Except in the case of section 326(5), one-fiftieth of the statutory maximum.
328(6)	...	Director failing to notify company that members of his family have, or have exercised, options to buy shares or debentures; making false statement in purported notification.	1. On indictment. 2. Summary.	2 years or a fine; or both. 6 months or the statutory maximum; or both.	
329(3)	...	Company failing to notify investment exchange of acquisition of its securities by a director.	Summary.	One-fifth of the statutory maximum.	One-fiftieth of the statutory maximum.
342(1)	...	Director of relevant company authorising or permitting company to enter into transaction or arrangement, knowing or suspecting it to contravene section 330.	1. On indictment. 2. Summary.	2 years or a fine; or both. 6 months or the statutory maximum; or both.	
342(2)	...	Relevant company entering into transaction or arrangement for a director in contravention of section 330.	1. On indictment. 2. Summary.	2 years or a fine; or both. 6 months or the statutory maximum; or both.	
342(3)	...	Procuring a relevant company to enter into transaction or arrangement known to be contrary to section 330.	1. On indictment. 2. Summary.	2 years or a fine; or both. 6 months or the statutory maximum; or both.	
343(8)	...	Company failing to maintain register of transactions, etc., made with and for directors and not disclosed in company accounts; failing to make register available at registered office or at company meeting.	1. On indictment. 2. Summary.	A fine. The statutory maximum.	
348(2)	...	Company failing to paint or affix name; failing to keep it painted or affixed.	Summary.	One-fifth of the statutory maximum.	In the case of failure to keep the name painted or affixed, one-fiftieth of the statutory maximum.
349(2)	...	Company failing to have name on business correspondence, invoices, etc.	Summary.	One-fifth of the statutory maximum.	

Section of Act creating offence	General nature of offence	Mode of prosecution	Punishment	Daily default fine (where applicable)
349(3) ...	Officer of company issuing business letter or document not bearing company's name.	Summary.	One-fifth of the statutory maximum.	
349(4) ...	Officer of company signing cheque, bill of exchange, etc. on which company's name not mentioned.	Summary.	One-fifth of the statutory maximum.	
350(1) ...	Company failing to have its name engraved on company seal.	Summary.	One-fifth of the statutory maximum.	
350(2) ...	Officer or company, etc., using company seal without name engraved on it.	Summary.	One-fifth of the statutory maximum.	
351(5)(a) ...	Company failing to comply with section 351(1) or (2) (matters to be stated on business correspondence, etc.).	Summary.	One-fifth of the statutory maximum.	
351(5)(b) ...	Officer or agent of company issuing, or authorising issue of, business document not complying with those subsections.	Summary.	One-fifth of the statutory maximum.	
351(5)(c) ...	Contravention of section 351(3) or (4) (information in English to be stated on Welsh company's business correspondence, etc.).	Summary.	One-fifth of the statutory maximum.	For contravention of section 351(3), one-fiftieth of the statutory maximum.
352(5) ...	Company default in complying with section 352 (requirement to keep register of members and their particulars).	Summary.	One-fifth of the statutory maximum.	One-fiftieth of the statutory maximum.
352A(3) ...	Company default in complying with section 352A (statement that company has only one member).	Summary.	Level 2 on the standard scale.	One-tenth of level 2 on the standard scale.
353(4) ...	Company failing to send notice to registrar as to place where register of members is kept.	Summary.	One-fifth of the statutory maximum.	One-fiftieth of the statutory maximum.
354(4) ...	Company failing to keep index of members.	Summary.	One-fifth of the statutory maximum.	One-fiftieth of the statutory maximum.
356(5) ...	Refusal of inspection of members' register; failure to send copy on requisition.	Summary.	One-fifth of the statutory maximum.	One-fiftieth of the statutory maximum.

Section		Offence	Mode of prosecution	Punishment	Daily default fine
363(3)	...	Company with share capital failing to make annual return.	Summary.	The statutory maximum.	One-tenth of the statutory maximum.
364(4)	...	Company without share capital failing to complete and register annual return in due time.	Summary.	The statutory maximum.	One-tenth of the statutory maximum.
366(4)	...	Company default in holding annual general meeting.	1. On indictment. 2. Summary.	A fine. The statutory maximum.	
367(3)	...	Company default in complying with Secretary of State's direction to hold company meeting.	1. On indictment. 2. Summary.	A fine. The statutory maximum.	
367(5)	...	Company failing to register resolution that meeting held under section 367 is to be its annual general meeting.	Summary.	One-fifth of the statutory maximum.	One-fiftieth of the statutory maximum.
372(4)	...	Failure to give notice, to member entitled to vote at company meeting, that he may do so by proxy.	Summary.	One-fifth of the statutory maximum.	
372(6)	...	Officer of company authorising or permitting issue of irregular invitation to appoint proxies.	Summary.	One-fifth of the statutory maximum.	
376(7)	...	Officer of company in default as to circulation of members' resolutions for company meeting.	1. On indictment. 2. Summary.	A fine. The statutory maximum.	
380(5)	...	Company failing to comply with section 380 (copies of certain resolutions etc. to be sent to registrar of companies).	Summary.	One-fifth of the statutory maximum.	One-fiftieth of the statutory maximum.
380(6)		Company failing to include copy of resolution to which section 380 applies in articles; failing to forward copy to member on request.	Summary.	One-fifth of the statutory maximum for each occasion on which copies are issued or, as the case may be, requested.	
381B(2)	...	Director or secretary of company failing to notify auditors of proposed written resolution.	Summary.	Level 3 on the standard scale.	
382(5)	...	Company failing to keep minutes of proceedings at company and board meetings, etc.	Summary.	One-fifth of the statutory maximum.	
382B(2)	...	Failure of sole member to provide the company with a written record of decision.	Summary.	Level 2 on the standard scale.	

Section of Act creating offence	General nature of offence	Mode of prosecution	Punishment	Daily default fine (where applicable)
383(4) ...	Refusal of inspection of minutes of general meeting; failure to send copy of minutes on member's request.	Summary.	One-fifth of the statutory maximum.	
387(2) ...	Company failing to give Secretary of State notice of non-appointment of auditors.	Summary.	One-fifth of the statutory maximum.	One-fiftieth of the statutory maximum.
389(10) ...	Person acting as company auditor knowing himself to be disqualified; failing to give notice vacating office when he becomes disqualified. [See note 2 at the end of the schedule.]	1. On indictment. 2. Summary.	A fine. The statutory maximum.	One-tenth of the statutory maximum.
389A(2) ...	Officer of company making false, misleading or deceptive statement to auditors.	1. On indictment. 2. Summary.	2 years or a fine; or both. 6 months or the statutory maximum; or both.	
389A(3) ...	Subsidiary undertaking or its auditor failing to give information to auditors of parent company.	Summary.	One-fifth of the statutory maximum.	
389A(4) ...	Parent company failing to obtain from subsidiary undertaking information for purposes of audit.	Summary.	One-fifth of the statutory maximum.	
391(2) ...	Failing to give notice to registrar of removal of auditor.	Summary.	One-fifth of the statutory maximum.	One-fiftieth of the statutory maximum.
392(3) ...	Company failing to forward notice of auditor's resignation to registrar.	1. On indictment. 2. Summary.	A fine. The statutory maximum.	One-tenth of the statutory maximum.
392A(5) ...	Directors failing to convene meeting requisitioned by resigning auditor.	1. On indictment. 2. Summary.	A fine. The statutory maximum.	
394A(1) ...	Person ceasing to hold office as auditor failing to deposit statement as to circumstances.	1. On indictment. 2. Summary.	A fine. The statutory maximum.	
394A(4) ...	Company failing to comply with requirements as to statement of person ceasing to hold office as auditor.	1. On indictment. 2. Summary.	A fine. The statutory maximum.	One-tenth of the statutory maximum.

Section		Description	Mode of prosecution	Punishment	Daily default fine
399(3)	...	Company failing to send to registrar particulars of charge created by it, or of issue of debentures which requires registration. [See note 3 at the end of the schedule.]	1. On indictment. 2. Summary.	A fine. The statutory maximum.	One-tenth of the statutory maximum.
400(4)	...	Company failing to send to registrar particulars of charge on property acquired. [See note 3 at the end of the schedule.]	1. On indictment. 2. Summary.	A fine. The statutory maximum.	One-tenth of the statutory maximum.
402(3)	...	Authorising or permitting delivery of debenture or certificate of debenture stock, without endorsement on it of certificate of registration of charge. [See note 3 at the end of the schedule.]	Summary.	One-fifth of the statutory maximum.	
405(4)	...	Failure to give notice to registrar of appointment of receiver or manager, or of his ceasing to act. [See note 3 at the end of the schedule.]	Summary.	One-fifth of the statutory maximum.	One-fiftieth of the statutory maximum.
407(3)	...	Authorising or permitting omission from company register of charges. [See note 3 at the end of the schedule.]	1. On indictment. 2. Summary.	A fine. The statutory maximum.	
408(3)	...	Officer of company refusing inspection of charging instrument, or of register of charges. [See note 3 at the end of the schedule.]	Summary.	One-fifth of the statutory maximum.	One-fiftieth of the statutory maximum.
...	...				
425(4)	...	Company failing to annex to memorandum court order sanctioning compromise or arrangement with creditors.	Summary.	One-fifth of the statutory maximum.	
426(6)	...	Company failing to comply with requirements of section 426 (information to members and creditors about compromise or arrangement).	1. On indictment. 2. Summary.	A fine. The statutory maximum.	
426(7)	...	Director or trustee for debenture holders failing to give notice to company of matters necessary for purposes of section 426.	Summary.	One-fifth of the statutory maximum.	

Section of Act creating offence	General nature of offence	Mode of prosecution	Punishment	Daily default fine (where applicable)
427(5) ...	Failure to deliver to registrar office copy of court order under section 427 (company reconstruction or amalgamation).	Summary.	One-fifth of the statutory maximum.	One-fiftieth of the statutory maximum.
429(6) ...	Offeror failing to send copy of notice or making statutory declaration knowing it to be false, etc.	1. On indictment. 2. Summary.	2 years or a fine; or both. 6 months or the statutory maximum; or both.	One-fiftieth of the statutory maximum.
430A(6) ...	Offeror failing to give notice of rights to minority shareholder.	1. On indictment. 2. Summary.	A fine. The statutory maximum.	One-fiftieth of the statutory maximum.
444(3) ...	Failing to give Secretary of State, when required to do so, information about interests in shares, etc.; giving false information.	1. On indictment. 2. Summary.	2 years or a fine; or both. 6 months or the statutory maximum; or both.	
447(6) ...	Failure to comply with requirement to produce documents imposed by Secretary of State under section 447.	1. On indictment. 2. Summary.	A fine. The statutory maximum.	
448(7) ...	Obstructing the exercise of any rights conferred by a warrant or failing to comply with a requirement imposed under subsection (3)(d).	1. On indictment. 2. Summary.	A fine. The statutory maximum.	
449(2) ...	Wrongful disclosure of information or document obtained under section 447 or 448.	1. On indictment. 2. Summary.	2 years or a fine; or both. 6 months or the statutory maximum; or both.	
450 ...	Destroying or mutilating company documents; falsifying such documents or making false entries; parting with such documents or altering them or making omissions.	1. On indictment. 2. Summary.	7 years or a fine; or both. 6 months or the statutory maximum; or both.	
451 ...	Making false statement or explanation in purported compliance with section 447.	1. On indictment. 2. Summary.	2 years or a fine; or both. 6 months or the statutory maximum; or both.	

Section		General nature of offence	Mode of prosecution	Punishment	Daily default fine
455(1)	...	Exercising a right to dispose of, or vote in respect of, shares which are subject to restrictions under Part XV; failing to give notice in respect of shares so subject; entering into agreement void under section 454(2), (3).	1. On indictment. 2. Summary.	A fine. The statutory maximum.	
455(2)	...	Issuing shares in contravention of restrictions of Part XV.	1. On indictment. 2. Summary.	A fine. The statutory maximum.	
458	...	Being a party to carrying on company's business with intent to defraud creditors, or for any fraudulent purpose.	1. On indictment. 2. Summary.	7 years or a fine; or both. 6 months or the statutory maximum; or both.	
461(5)	...	Failure to register office copy of court order under Part XVII altering, or giving leave to alter, company's memorandum.	Summary.	One-fifth of the statutory maximum.	One-fiftieth of the statutory maximum.
651(3)	...	Person obtaining court order to declare company's dissolution void, then failing to register the order.	Summary.	One-fifth of the statutory maximum.	One-fiftieth of the statutory maximum.
652E(1)	...	Person breaching or failing to perform duty imposed by section 652B or 652C.	1. On indictment. 2. Summary.	A fine. The statutory maximum.	
652E(2)	...	Person failing to perform duty imposed by section 652B(6) or 652C(2) with intent to conceal the making of application under section 652A.	1. On indictment. 2. Summary.	7 years or a fine; or both. 6 months or the statutory maximum; or both.	
652F(1)	...	Person furnishing false or misleading information in connection with application under section 652A.	1. On indictment. 2. Summary.	A fine. The statutory maximum.	
652F(2)	...	Person making false application under section 652A.	1. On indictment. 2. Summary.	A fine. The statutory maximum.	
...					

Section of Act creating offence	General nature of offence	Mode of prosecution	Punishment	Daily default fine (where applicable)
722(3) ...	Company failing to comply with section 722(2), as regards the manner of keeping registers, minute books and accounting records.	Summary.	One-fifth of the statutory maximum.	One-fiftieth of the statutory maximum.
...				

[*Note 1. The Financial Services Act 1986, sch. 17, part I, has repealed the entries relating to ss. 81(2), 82(5), 86(6), 87(4) and 97(4) to the extent to which they would apply in relation to: (a) any investment which is listed or the subject of an application for listing in accordance with part IV of the Financial Services Act 1986 (Financial Services Act 1986 (Commencement No. 3) Order 1986 (SI 1986/2246), art. 5 and sch. 4); (b) a prospectus offering for subscription, or any form of application for, units in a body corporate which is a recognised scheme (Financial Services Act 1986 (Commencement) (No. 8) Order 1988 (SI 1988/740), art. 2 and sch.).*

Note 2. The entry relating to s. 389(10) will be repealed when the relevant provision of the Companies Act 1989, sch. 14, is brought into force. Section 389 itself was repealed as from 1 October 1991 (Companies Act 1989 (Commencement No. 12 and Transitional Provision) Order 1991 (SI 1991/1996), art. 2(1)(c)(i)).

Note 3. The entries relating to ss. 399(3) to 408(3) would be replaced by new provisions if para. 2 of sch. 16 to the Companies Act 1989 were brought into force.]

BUSINESS NAMES ACT 1985
(1985, c. 7)

An Act to consolidate certain enactments relating to the names under which persons may carry on business in Great Britain.   [11 March 1985]

1. Persons subject to this Act.

(1)   This Act applies to any person who has a place of business in Great Britain and who carries on business in Great Britain under a name which—

(a)   in the case of a partnership, does not consist of the surnames of all partners who are individuals and the corporate names of all partners who are bodies corporate without any addition other than an addition permitted by this Act;

(b)   in the case of an individual, does not consist of his surname without any addition other than one so permitted;

(c)   in the case of a company, being a company which is capable of being wound up under the Companies Act 1985, does not consist of its corporate name without any addition other than one so permitted.

(2)   The following are permitted additions for the purposes of subsection (1)—

(a)   in the case of a partnership, the forenames of individual partners or the initials of those forenames or, where two or more individual partners have the same surname, the addition of 's' at the end of that surname; or

(b)   in the case of an individual, his forename or its initial;

(c)   in any case, any addition merely indicating that the business is carried on in succession to a former owner of the business.

2. Prohibition of use of certain business names.

(1)   Subject to the following subsections, a person to whom this Act applies shall not, without the written approval of the Secretary of State, carry on business in Great Britain under a name which—

(a)   would be likely to give the impression that the business is connected with Her Majesty's Government or with any local authority; or

(b)   includes any word or expression for the time being specified in regulations made under this Act.

(2)   Subsection (1) does not apply to the carrying on of a business by a person—

(a)   to whom the business has been transferred on or after 26 February 1982; and

(b)   who carries on the business under the name which was its lawful business name immediately before that transfer,

during the period of 12 months beginning with the date of that transfer.

(3)   Subsection (1) does not apply to the carrying on of a business by a person who—

(a)   carried on that business immediately before 26 February 1982; and

(b)   continues to carry it on under the name which immediately before that date was its lawful business name.

(4)   A person who contravenes subsection (1) is guilty of an offence.

3. Words and expressions requiring Secretary of State's approval.

(1)   The Secretary of State may by regulations—

(a)   specify words or expressions for the use of which as or as part of a business name his approval is required by section 2(1)(b); and

(b)   in relation to any such word or expression, specify a Government department or other body as the relevant body for purposes of the following subsection.

(2)   Where a person to whom this Act applies proposes to carry on a business under a name which is or includes any such word or expression, and a Government department or other body is specified under subsection (1)(b) in relation to that word or expression, that person shall—

(a)   request (in writing) the relevant body to indicate whether (and if so why) it has any objections to the proposal; and

(b)   submit to the Secretary of State a statement that such a request has been made and a copy of any response received from the relevant body.

4.   Disclosure required of persons using business names.

(1)   A person to whom this Act applies shall—

(a)   subject to subsection (3), state in legible characters on all business letters, written orders for goods or services to be supplied to the business, invoices and receipts issued in the course of the business and written demands for payment of debts arising in the course of the business—

    (i)   in the case of a partnership, the name of each partner,

    (ii)   in the case of an individual, his name,

    (iii)   in the case of a company, its corporate name, and

    (iv)   in relation to each person so named, an address in Greater Britain at which service of any document relating in any way to the business will be effective; and

(b)   in any premises where the business is carried on and to which the customers of the business or suppliers of any goods or services to the business have access, display in a prominent position so that it may easily be read by such customers or suppliers a notice containing such names and addresses.

(2)   A person to whom this Act applies shall secure that the names and addresses required by subsection (1)(a) to be stated on his business letters, or which would have been so required but for the subsection next following, are immediately given, by written notice to a person with whom anything is done or discussed in the course of the business and who asks for such names and addresses.

(3)   Subsection (1)(a) does not apply in relation to any document issued by a partnership of more than 20 persons which maintains at its principal place of business a list of the names of all the partners if—

(a)   none of the names of the partners appears in the document otherwise than in the text or as a signatory; and

(b)   the document states in legible characters the address of the partnership's principal place of business and that the list of the partners' names is open to inspection at that place.

(4)   Where a partnership maintains a list of the partners' names for purposes of subsection (3), any person may inspect the list during office hours.

(5)   The Secretary of State may by regulations require notices under subsection (1)(b) or (2) to be displayed or given in a specified form.

(6)   A person who without reasonable excuse contravenes subsection (1) or (2), or any regulations made under subsection (5), is guilty of an offence.

(7)   Where an inspection required by a person in accordance with subsection (4) is refused, any partner of the partnership concerned who without reasonable excuse refused that inspection, or permitted it to be refused, is guilty of an offence.

5.   Civil remedies for breach of s. 4.

(1)   Any legal proceedings brought by a person to whom this Act applies to enforce a right arising out of a contract made in the course of a business in respect of which he was, at the time the contract was made, in breach of subsection (1) or (2) of section 4 shall be dismissed if the defendant (or, in Scotland, the defender) to the proceedings shows—

(a)   that he has a claim against the plaintiff (pursuer) arising out of that contract which he has been unable to pursue by reason of the latter's breach of section 4(1) or (2), or

(b)   that he has suffered some financial loss in connection with the contract by reason of the plaintiff's (pursuer's) breach of section 4(1) or (2), unless the court before which the proceedings are brought is satisfied that it is just and equitable to permit the proceedings to continue.

(2)   This section is without prejudice to the right of any person to enforce such rights as he may have against another person in any proceedings brought by that person.

6.   Regulations.

(1)   Regulations under this Act shall be made by statutory instrument and may contain such transitional provisions and savings as the Secretary of State thinks appropriate, and may make different provision for different cases or classes of case.

(2)   In the case of regulations made under section 3, the statutory instrument containing them shall be laid before Parliament after the regulations are made and shall cease to have effect at the end of the period of 28 days beginning with the day on which they were made (but without prejudice to anything previously done by virtue of them or to the making of new regulations) unless during that period they are approved by a resolution of each House of Parliament.

In reckoning this period of 28 days, no account is to be taken of any time during which Parliament is dissolved or prorogued, or during which both Houses are adjourned for more than 4 days.

(3)   In the case of regulations made under section 4, the statutory instrument containing them is subject to annulment in pursuance of a resolution of either House of Parliament.

7.   Offences.

(1)   Offences under this Act are punishable on summary conviction.

(2)   A person guilty of an offence under this Act is liable to a fine not exceeding one-fifth of the statutory maximum.

(3)   If after a person has been convicted summarily of an offence under section 2 or 4(6) the original contravention is continued, he is liable on a second or subsequent summary conviction of the offence to a fine not exceeding one-fiftieth of the statutory maximum for each day on which the contravention is continued (instead of to the penalty which may be imposed on the first conviction of the offence).

(4)   Where an offence under section 2 or 4(6) or (7) committed by a body corporate is proved to have been committed with the consent or connivance of, or to be attributable to any neglect on the part of, any director, manager, secretary or other similar officer of the body corporate, or any person who was purporting to act in any such capacity, he as well as the body corporate is guilty of the offence and liable to be proceeded against and punished accordingly.

(5)   Where the affairs of a body corporate are managed by its members, subsection (4) applies in relation to the acts and defaults of a member in connection with his functions of management as if he were a director of the body corporate.

(6)   For purposes of the following provisions of the Companies Act 1985—

    (a)   section 731 (summary proceedings under the Companies Acts), and

    (b)   section 732(3) (legal professional privilege),

this Act is to be treated as included in those Acts.

8.   Interpretation.

(1)   The following definitions apply for purposes of this Act—

'business' includes a profession;

'initial' includes any recognised abbreviation of a name;

'lawful business name', in relation to a business, means a name under which the business was carried on without contravening section 2(1) of this Act or section 2 of the Registration of Business Names Act 1916;

'local authority' means any local authority within the meaning of the Local Government Act 1972 or the Local Government (Scotland) Act 1973, the Common Council of the City of London or the Council of the Isles of Scilly;

'partnership' includes a foreign partnership;

and 'surname', in relation to a peer or person usually known by a British title different from his surname, means the title by which he is known.

(2) Any expression used in this Act and also in the Companies Act 1985 has the same meaning in this Act as in that.

9. Northern Ireland.

This Act does not extend to Northern Ireland.

10. Commencement.

This Act comes into force on 1 July 1985.

11. Citation.

This Act may be cited as the Business Names Act 1985.

INSOLVENCY ACT 1986
(1986, c. 45)

An Act to consolidate the enactments relating to company insolvency and winding up (including the winding up of companies that are not insolvent, and of unregistered companies); enactments relating to the insolvency and bankruptcy of individuals; and other enactments bearing on those two subject matters, including the functions and qualification of insolvency practitioners, the public administration of insolvency, the penalisation and redress of malpractice and wrong-doing, and the avoidance of certain transactions at an undervalue. [25 July 1986]

THE FIRST GROUP OF PARTS
COMPANY INSOLVENCY; COMPANIES WINDING UP

PART I
COMPANY VOLUNTARY ARRANGEMENTS

The proposal

1. Those who may propose an arrangement.

(1) The directors of a company (other than one for which an administration order is in force, or which is being wound up) may make a proposal under this Part to the company and to its creditors for a composition in satisfaction of its debts or a scheme of arrangement of its affairs (from here on referred to, in either case, as a 'voluntary arrangement').

(2) A proposal under this Part is one which provides for some person ('the nominee') to act in relation to the voluntary arrangement either as trustee or otherwise for the purpose of supervising its implementation; and the nominee must be a person who is qualified to act as an insolvency practitioner in relation to the company.

(3) Such a proposal may also be made—

(a) where an administration order is in force in relation to the company, by the administrator, and

(b) where the company is being wound up, by the liquidator.

2. Procedure where nominee is not the liquidator or administrator.

(1) This section applies where the nominee under section 1 is not the liquidator or administrator of the company.

(2) The nominee shall, within 28 days (or such longer period as the court may allow) after he is given notice of the proposal for a voluntary arrangement, submit a report to the court stating—

(a) whether, in his opinion, meetings of the company and of its creditors should be summoned to consider the proposal, and

(b) if in his opinion such meetings should be summoned, the date on which, and time and place at which, he proposes the meetings should be held.

(3)   For the purposes of enabling the nominee to prepare his report, the person intending to make the proposal shall submit to the nominee—

(a)   a document setting out the terms of the proposed voluntary arrangement, and

(b)   a statement of the company's affairs containing—

(i)   such particulars of its creditors and of its debts and other liabilities and of its assets as may be prescribed, and

(ii)   such other information as may be prescribed.

(4)   The court may, on an application made by the person intending to make the proposal, in a case where the nominee has failed to submit the report required by this section, direct that the nominee be replaced as such by another person qualified to act as an insolvency practitioner in relation to the company.

3.   Summoning of meetings.

(1)   Where the nominee under section 1 is not the liquidator or administrator, and it has been reported to the court that such meetings as are mentioned in section 2(2) should be summoned, the person making the report shall (unless the court otherwise directs) summon those meetings for the time, date and place proposed in the report.

(2)   Where the nominee is the liquidator or administrator, he shall summon meetings of the company and of its creditors to consider the proposal for such a time, date and place as he thinks fit.

(3)   The persons to be summoned to a creditors' meeting under this section are every creditor of the company of whose claim and address the person summoning the meeting is aware.

Consideration and implementation of proposal

4.   Decisions of meetings.

(1)   The meetings summoned under section 3 shall decide whether to approve the proposed voluntary arrangement (with or without modifications).

(2)   The modifications may include one conferring the functions proposed to be conferred on the nominee on another person qualified to act as an insolvency practitioner in relation to the company.

But they shall not include any modification by virtue of which the proposal ceases to be a proposal such as is mentioned in section 1.

(3)   A meeting so summoned shall not approve any proposal or modification which affects the right of a secured creditor of the company to enforce his security, except with the concurrence of the creditor concerned.

(4)   Subject as follows, a meeting so summoned shall not approve any proposal or modification under which—

(a)   any preferential debt of the company is to be paid otherwise than in priority to such of its debts as are not preferential debts, or

(b)   a preferential creditor of the company is to be paid an amount in respect of a preferential debt that bears to that debt a smaller proportion than is borne to another preferential debt by the amount that is to be paid in respect of that other debt.

However, the meeting may approve such a proposal or modification with the concurrence of the preferential creditor concerned.

(5)   Subject as above, each of the meetings shall be conducted in accordance with the rules.

(6)   After the conclusion of either meeting in accordance with the rules, the chairman of the meeting shall report the result of the meeting to the court, and, immediately after reporting to the court, shall give notice of the result of the meeting to such persons as may be prescribed.

(7)   References in this section to preferential debts and preferential creditors are to be read in accordance with section 386 in Part XII of this Act.

5. Effect of approval.

(1)   This section has effect where each of the meetings summoned under section 3 approves the proposed voluntary arrangement either with the same modifications or without modifications.

(2)   The approved voluntary arrangement—

(a)   takes effect as if made by the company at the creditors' meeting, and

(b)   binds every person who in accordance with the rules had notice of, and was entitled to vote at, that meeting (whether or not he was present or represented at the meeting) as if he were a party to the voluntary arrangement.

(3)   Subject as follows, if the company is being wound up or an administration order is in force, the court may do one or both of the following, namely—

(a)   by order stay or sist all proceedings in the winding up or discharge the administration order;

(b)   give such directions with respect to the conduct of the winding up or the administration as it thinks appropriate for facilitating the implementation of the approved voluntary arrangement.

(4)   The court shall not make an order under subsection (3)(a)—

(a)   at any time before the end of the period of 28 days beginning with the first day on which each of the reports required by section 4(6) has been made to the court, or

(b)   at any time when an application under the next section or an appeal in respect of such an application is pending, or at any time in the period within which such an appeal may be brought.

6. Challenge of decisions.

(1)   Subject to this section, an application to the court may be made, by any of the persons specified below, on one or both of the following grounds, namely—

(a)   that a voluntary arrangement approved at the meetings summoned under section 3 unfairly prejudices the interests of a creditor, member or contributory of the company;

(b)   that there has been some material irregularity at or in relation to either of the meetings.

(2)   The persons who may apply under this section are—

(a)   a person entitled, in accordance with the rules, to vote at either of the meetings;

(b)   the nominee or any person who has replaced him under section 2(4) or 4(2); and

(c)   if the company is being wound up or an administration order is in force, the liquidator or administrator.

(3)   An application under this section shall not be made after the end of the period of 28 days beginning with the first day on which each of the reports required by section 4(6) has been made to the court.

(4)   Where on such an application the court is satisfied as to either of the grounds mentioned in subsection (1), it may do one or both of the following, namely—

(a)   revoke or suspend the approvals given by the meetings or, in a case falling within subsection (1)(b), any approval given by the meeting in question;

(b)   give a direction to any person for the summoning of further meetings to consider any revised proposal the person who made the original proposal may make or, in a case falling within subsection (1)(b), a further company or (as the case may be) creditors' meeting to reconsider the original proposal.

(5)   Where at any time after giving a direction under subsection (4)(b) for the summoning of meetings to consider a revised proposal the court is satisfied that the person who made the original proposal does not intend to submit a revised proposal, the court shall revoke the direction and revoke or suspend any approval given at the previous meetings.

(6)   In a case where the court, on an application under this section with respect to any meeting—
    (a)   gives a direction under subsection (4)(b), or
    (b)   revokes or suspends an approval under subsection (4)(a) or (5),
the court may give such supplemental directions as it thinks fit and, in particular, directions with respect to things done since the meeting under any voluntary arrangement approved by the meeting.

(7)   Except in pursuance of the preceding provisions of this section, an approval given at a meeting summoned under section 3 is not invalidated by any irregularity at or in relation to the meeting.

7.   Implementation of proposal.

(1)   This section applies where a voluntary arrangement approved by the meetings summoned under section 3 has taken effect.

(2)   The person who is for the time being carrying out in relation to the voluntary arrangement the functions conferred—
    (a)   by virtue of the approval on the nominee or
    (b)   by virtue of section 2(4) or 4(2) on a person other than the nominee,
shall be known as the supervisor of the voluntary arrangement.

(3)   If any of the company's creditors or any other person is dissatisfied by any act, omission or decision of the supervisor, he may apply to the court; and on the application the court may—
    (a)   confirm, reverse or modify any act or decision of the supervisor,
    (b)   give him directions, or
    (c)   make such other order as it thinks fit.

(4)   The supervisor—
    (a)   may apply to the court for directions in relation to any particular matter arising under the voluntary arrangement, and
    (b)   is included among the persons who may apply to the court for the winding up of the company or for an administration order to be made in relation to it.

(5)   The court may, whenever—
    (a)   it is expedient to appoint a person to carry out the functions of the supervisor, and
    (b)   it is inexpedient, difficult or impracticable for an appointment to be made without the assistance of the court,
make an order appointing a person who is qualified to act as an insolvency practitioner in relation to the company, either in substitution for the existing supervisor or to fill a vacancy.

(6)   The power conferred by subsection (5) is exercisable so as to increase the number of persons exercising the functions of supervisor or, where there is more than one person exercising those functions, so as to replace one or more of those persons.

PART II
ADMINISTRATION ORDERS

Making etc. of administration order

8.   Power of court to make order.

(1)   Subject to this section, if the court—
    (a)   is satisfied that a company is or is likely to become unable to pay its debts (within the meaning given to that expression by section 123 of this Act), and
    (b)   considers that the making of an order under this section would be likely to achieve one or more of the purposes mentioned below,
the court may make an administration order in relation to the company.

(2)   An administration order is an order directing that, during the period for which the order is in force, the affairs, business and property of the company shall be managed by a person ('the administrator') appointed for the purpose by the court.

(3)   The purposes for whose achievement an administration order may be made are—

(a)   the survival of the company, and the whole or any part of its undertaking, as a going concern;

(b)   the approval of a voluntary arrangement under Part I;

(c)   the sanctioning under section 425 of the Companies Act of a compromise or arrangement between the company and any such persons as are mentioned in that section; and

(d)   a more advantageous realisation of the company's assets than would be effected on a winding up;

and the order shall specify the purpose or purposes for which it is made.

(4)   An administration order shall not be made in relation to a company after it has gone into liquidation, nor where it is—

(a)   an insurance company within the meaning of the Insurance Companies Act 1982, or

(b)   an authorised institution or former authorised institution within the meaning of the Banking Act 1987.

9.   Application for order.

(1)   An application to the court for an administration order shall be by petition presented either by the company or the directors, or by a creditor or creditors (including any contingent or prospective creditor or creditors), or by the clerk of a magistrates' court in the exercise of the power conferred by section 87A of the Magistrates' Courts Act 1980 (enforcement of fines imposed on companies) or by all or any of those parties, together or separately.

(2)   Where a petition is presented to the court—

(a)   notice of the petition shall be given forthwith to any person who has appointed, or is or may be entitled to appoint, an administrative receiver of the company, and to such other persons as may be prescribed, and

(b)   the petition shall not be withdrawn except with the leave of the court.

(3)   Where the court is satisfied that there is an administrative receiver of the company, the court shall dismiss the petition unless it is also satisfied either—

(a)   that the person by whom or on whose behalf the receiver was appointed has consented to the making of the order, or

(b)   that, if an administration order were made, any security by virtue of which the receiver was appointed would—

(i)   be liable to be released or discharged under sections 238 to 240 in Part VI (transactions at an undervalue and preferences),

(ii)   be avoided under section 245 in that Part (avoidance of floating charges), or

(iii)   be challengeable under section 242 (gratuitous alienations) or 243 (unfair preferences) in that Part, or under any rule of law in Scotland.

(4)   Subject to subsection (3), on hearing a petition the court may dismiss it, or adjourn the hearing conditionally or unconditionally, or make an interim order or any other order that it thinks fit.

(5)   Without prejudice to the generality of subsection (4), an interim order under that subsection may restrict the exercise of any powers of the directors or of the company (whether by reference to the consent of the court or of a person qualified to act as an insolvency practitioner in relation to the company, or otherwise).

[*Section 9(3)(b) would be amended if para. 3(2) of sch. 16 to the Companies Act 1989 were brought into force.*]

10. Effect of application.

(1) During the period beginning with the presentation of a petition for an administration order and ending with the making of such an order or the dismissal of the petition—

(a) no resolution may be passed or order made for the winding up of the company;

(b) no steps may be taken to enforce any security over the company's property, or to repossess goods in the company's possession under any hire-purchase agreement, except with the leave of the court and subject to such terms as the court may impose; and

(c) no other proceedings and no execution or other legal process may be commenced or continued, and no distress may be levied, against the company or its property except with the leave of the court and subject to such terms as aforesaid.

(2) Nothing in subsection (1) requires the leave of the court—

(a) for the presentation of a petition for the winding up of the company,

(b) for the appointment of an administrative receiver of the company, or

(c) for the carrying out by such a receiver (whenever appointed) of any of his functions.

(3) Where—

(a) a petition for an administration order is presented at a time when there is an administrative receiver of the company, and

(b) the person by or on whose behalf the receiver was appointed has not consented to the making of the order,

the period mentioned in subsection (1) is deemed not to begin unless and until that person so consents.

(4) References in this section and the next to hire-purchase agreements include conditional sale agreements, chattel leasing agreements and retention of title agreements.

(5) In the application of this section and the next to Scotland, references to execution being commenced or continued include references to diligence being carried out or continued, and references to distress being levied shall be omitted.

11. Effect of order.

(1) On the making of an administration order—

(a) any petition for the winding up of the company shall be dismissed, and

(b) any administrative receiver of the company shall vacate office.

(2) Where an administration order has been made, any receiver of part of the company's property shall vacate office on being required to do so by the administrator.

(3) During the period for which an administration order is in force—

(a) no resolution may be passed or order made for the winding up of the company;

(b) no administrative receiver of the company may be appointed;

(c) no other steps may be taken to enforce any security over the company's property, or to repossess goods in the company's possession under any hire-purchase agreement, except with the consent of the administrator or the leave of the court and subject (where the court gives leave) to such terms as the court may impose; and

(d) no other proceedings and no execution or other legal process may be commenced or continued, and no distress may be levied, against the company or its property except with the consent of the administrator or the leave of the court and subject (where the court gives leave) to such terms as aforesaid.

(4) Where at any time an administrative receiver of the company has vacated office under subsection (1)(b), or a receiver of part of the company's property has vacated office under subsection (2)—

(a) his remuneration and any expenses properly incurred by him, and

(b)   any indemnity to which he is entitled out of the assets of the company,
shall be charged on and (subject to subsection (3) above) paid out of any property of the
company which was in his custody or under his control at that time in priority to any
security held by the person by or on whose behalf he was appointed.

(5)   Neither an administrative receiver who vacates office under subsection (1)(b)
nor a receiver who vacates office under subsection (2) is required on or after so vacating
office to take any steps for the purpose of complying with any duty imposed on him by
section 40 or 59 of this Act (duty to pay preferential creditors).

12.   Notification of order.

(1)   Every invoice, order for goods or business letter which, at a time when an
administration order is in force in relation to a company, is issued by or on behalf of the
company or the administrator, being a document on or in which the company's name
appears, shall also contain the administrator's name and a statement that the affairs,
business and property of the company are being managed by the administrator.

(2)   If default is made in complying with this section, the company and any of the
following persons who without reasonable excuse authorises or permits the default,
namely, the administrator and any officer of the company, is liable to a fine.

Administrators

13.   Appointment of administrator.

(1)   The administrator of a company shall be appointed either by the administration
order or by an order under the next subsection.

(2)   If a vacancy occurs by death, resignation or otherwise in the office of the
administrator, the court may by order fill the vacancy.

(3)   An application for an order under subsection (2) may be made—

(a)   by any continuing administrator of the company; or

(b)   where there is no such administrator, by a creditors' committee established
under section 26 below; or

(c)   where there is no such administrator and no such committee, by the company
or the directors or by any creditor or creditors of the company.

14.   General powers.

(1)   The administrator of a company—

(a)   may do all such things as may be necessary for the management of the affairs,
business and property of the company, and

(b)   without prejudice to the generality of paragraph (a), has the powers specified
in Schedule 1 to this Act;
and in the application of that Schedule to the administrator of a company the words 'he'
and 'him' refer to the administrator.

(2)   The administrator also has power—

(a)   to remove any director of the company and to appoint any person to be a
director of it, whether to fill a vacancy or otherwise, and

(b)   to call any meeting of the members or creditors of the company.

(3)   The administrator may apply to the court for directions in relation to any
particular matter arising in connection with the carrying out of his functions.

(4)   Any power conferred on the company or its officers, whether by this Act or the
Companies Act or by the memorandum or articles of association, which could be
exercised in such a way as to interfere with the exercise by the administrator of his
powers is not exercisable except with the consent of the administrator, which may be
given either generally or in relation to particular cases.

(5)   In exercising his powers the administrator is deemed to act as the company's agent.

(6)   A person dealing with the administrator in good faith and for value is not
concerned to inquire whether the administrator is acting within his powers.

15. Power to deal with charged property, etc.

(1)   The administrator of a company may dispose of or otherwise exercise his powers in relation to any property of the company which is subject to a security to which this subsection applies as if the property were not subject to the security.

(2)   Where, on an application by the administrator, the court is satisfied that the disposal (with or without other assets) of—

(a)   any property of the company subject to a security to which this subsection applies, or

(b)   any goods in the possession of the company under a hire-purchase agreement, would be likely to promote the purpose or one or more of the purposes specified in the administration order, the court may by order authorise the administrator to dispose of the property as if it were not subject to the security or to dispose of the goods as if all rights of the owner under the hire-purchase agreement were vested in the company.

(3)   Subsection (1) applies to any security which, as created, was a floating charge; and subsection (2) applies to any other security.

(4)   Where property is disposed of under subsection (1), the holder of the security has the same priority in respect of any property of the company directly or indirectly representing the property disposed of as he would have had in respect of the property subject to the security.

(5)   It shall be a condition of an order under subsection (2) that—

(a)   the net proceeds of the disposal, and

(b)   where those proceeds are less than such amount as may be determined by the court to be the net amount which would be realised on a sale of the property or goods in the open market by a willing vendor, such sums as may be required to make good the deficiency,

shall be applied towards discharging the sums secured by the security or payable under the hire-purchase agreement.

(6)   Where a condition imposed in pursuance of subsection (5) relates to two or more securities, that condition requires the net proceeds of the disposal and, where paragraph (b) of that subsection applies, the sums mentioned in that paragraph to be applied towards discharging the sums secured by those securities in the order of their priorities.

(7)   An office copy of an order under subsection (2) shall, within 14 days after the making of the order, be sent by the administrator to the registrar of companies.

(8)   If the administrator without reasonable excuse fails to comply with subsection (7), he is liable to a fine and, for continued contravention, to a daily default fine.

(9)   References in this section to hire-purchase agreements include conditional sale agreements, chattel leasing agreements and retention of title agreements.

17. General duties.

(1)   The administrator of a company shall, on his appointment, take into his custody or under his control all the property to which the company is or appears to be entitled.

(2)   The administrator shall manage the affairs, business and property of the company—

(a)   at any time before proposals have been approved (with or without modifications) under section 24 below, in accordance with any directions given by the court, and

(b)   at any time after proposals have been so approved, in accordance with those proposals as from time to time revised, whether by him or a predecessor of his.

(3)   The administrator shall summon a meeting of the company's creditors if—

(a)   he is requested, in accordance with the rules, to do so by one-tenth, in value, of the company's creditors, or

(b)   he is directed to do so by the court.

18.   Discharge or variation of administration order.

(1)   The administrator of a company may at any time apply to the court for the administration order to be discharged, or to be varied so as to specify an additional purpose.

(2)   The administrator shall make an application under this section if—

(a)   it appears to him that the purpose or each of the purposes specified in the order either has been achieved or is incapable of achievement, or

(b)   he is required to do so by a meeting of the company's creditors summoned for the purpose in accordance with the rules.

(3)   On the hearing of an application under this section, the court may by order discharge or vary the administration order and make such consequential provision as it thinks fit, or adjourn the hearing conditionally or unconditionally, or make an interim order or any other order it thinks fit.

(4)   Where the administration order is discharged or varied the administrator shall, within 14 days after the making of the order effecting the discharge or variation, send an office copy of that order to the registrar of companies.

(5)   If the administrator without reasonable excuse fails to comply with subsection (4), he is liable to a fine and, for continued contravention, to a daily default fine.

19.   Vacation of office.

(1)   The administrator of a company may at any time be removed from office by order of the court and may, in the prescribed circumstances, resign his office by giving notice of his resignation to the court.

(2)   The administrator shall vacate office if—

(a)   he ceases to be qualified to act as an insolvency practitioner in relation to the company, or

(b)   the administration order is discharged.

(3)   Where at any time a person ceases to be administrator, the following subsections apply.

(4)   His remuneration and any expenses properly incurred by him shall be charged on and paid out of any property of the company which is in his custody or under his control at that time in priority to any security to which section 15(1) then applies.

(5)   Any sums payable in respect of debts or liabilities incurred, while he was administrator, under contracts entered into by him or a predecessor of his in the carrying out of his or the predecessor's functions shall be charged on and paid out of any such property as is mentioned in subsection (4) in priority to any charge arising under that subsection.

(6)   Any sums payable in respect of liabilities incurred, while he was administrator, under contracts of employment adopted by him or a predecessor of his in the carrying out of his or the predecessor's functions shall, to the extent that the liabilities are qualifying liabilities, be charged on and paid out of any such property as is mentioned in subsection (4) and enjoy the same priority as any sums to which subsection (5) applies.

For this purpose, the administrator is not to be taken to have adopted a contract of employment by reason of anything done or omitted to be done within 14 days after his appointment.

(7)   For the purposes of subsection (6), a liability under a contract of employment is a qualifying liability if—

(a)   it is a liability to pay a sum by way of wages or salary or contribution to an occupational pension scheme, and

(b)   it is in respect of services rendered wholly or partly after the adoption of the contract.

(8)   There shall be disregarded for the purposes of subsection (6) so much of any qualifying liability as represents payment in respect of services rendered before the adoption of the contract.

(9)   For the purposes of subsections (7) and (8)—

(a)   wages or salary payable in respect of a period of holiday or absence from work through sickness or other good cause are deemed to be wages or (as the case may be) salary in respect of services rendered in that period, and

(b)   a sum payable in lieu of holiday is deemed to be wages or (as the case may be) salary in respect of services rendered in the period by reference to which the holiday entitlement arose.

(10)   In subsection (9)(a), the reference to wages or salary payable in respect of a period of holiday includes any sums which, if they had been paid, would have been treated for the purposes of the enactments relating to social security as earnings in respect of that period.

20.   Release of administrator.

(1)   A person who has ceased to be the administrator of a company has his release with effect from the following time, that is to say—

(a)   in the case of a person who has died, the time at which notice is given to the court in accordance with the rules that he has ceased to hold office;

(b)   in any other case, such time as the court may determine.

(2)   Where a person has his release under this section, he is with effect from the time specified above, discharged from all liability both in respect of acts or omissions of his in the administration and otherwise in relation to his conduct as administrator.

(3)   However, nothing in this section prevents the exercise, in relation to a person who has had his release as above, of the court's powers under section 212 in Chapter X of Part IV (summary remedy against delinquent directors, liquidators, etc.).

Ascertainment and investigation of company's affairs

21.   Information to be given by administrator.

(1)   Where an administration order has been made, the administrator shall—

(a)   forthwith send to the company and publish in the prescribed manner a notice of the order, and

(b)   within 28 days after the making of the order, unless the court otherwise directs, send such a notice to all creditors of the company (so far as he is aware of their addresses).

(2)   Where an administration order has been made, the administrator shall also, within 14 days after the making of the order, send an office copy of the order to the registrar of companies and to such other persons as may be prescribed.

(3)   If the administrator without reasonable excuse fails to comply with this section, he is liable to a fine and, for continued contravention, to a daily default fine.

22.   Statement of affairs to be submitted to administrator.

(1)   Where an administration order has been made, the administrator shall forthwith require some or all of the persons mentioned below to make out and submit to him a statement in the prescribed form as to the affairs of the company.

(2)   The statement shall be verified by affidavit by the persons required to submit it and shall show—

(a)   particulars of the company's assets, debts and liabilities;

(b)   the names and addresses of its creditors;

(c)   the securities held by them respectively;

(d)   the dates when the securities were respectively given; and

(e)   such further or other information as may be prescribed.

(3)   The persons referred to in subsection (1) are—

(a) those who are or have been officers of the company;
(b) those who have taken part in the company's formation at any time within one year before the date of the administration order;
(c) those who are in the company's employment or have been in its employment within that year, and are in the administrator's opinion capable of giving the information required;
(d) those who are or have been within that year officers of or in the employment of a company which is, or within that year was, an officer of the company.
In this subsection 'employment' includes employment under a contract for services.

(4) Where any persons are required under this section to submit a statement of affairs to the administrator, they shall do so (subject to the next subsection) before the end of the period of 21 days beginning with the day after that on which the prescribed notice of the requirement is given to them by the administrator.

(5) The administrator, if he thinks fit, may—
(a) at any time release a person from an obligation imposed on him under subsection (1) or (2), or
(b) either when giving notice under subsection (4) or subsequently, extend the period so mentioned;
and where the administrator has refused to exercise a power conferred by this subsection, the court, if it thinks fit, may exercise it.

(6) If a person without reasonable excuse fails to comply with any obligation imposed under this section, he is liable to a fine and, for continued contravention, to a daily default fine.

Administrator's proposals

23. Statement of proposals.

(1) Where an administration order has been made, the administrator shall, within 3 months (or such longer period as the court may allow) after the making of the order—
(a) send to the registrar of companies and (so far as he is aware of their addresses) to all creditors a statement of his proposals for achieving the purpose or purposes specified in the order, and
(b) lay a copy of the statement before a meeting of the company's creditors summoned for the purpose on not less than 14 days' notice.

(2) The administrator shall also, within 3 months (or such longer period as the court may allow) after the making of the order, either—
(a) send a copy of the statement (so far as he is aware of their addresses) to all members of the company, or
(b) publish in the prescribed manner a notice stating an address to which members of the company should write for copies of the statement to be sent to them free of charge.

(3) If the administrator without reasonable excuse fails to comply with this section, he is liable to a fine and, for continued contravention, to a daily default fine.

24. Consideration of proposals by creditors' meeting.

(1) A meeting of creditors summoned under section 23 shall decide whether to approve the administrator's proposals.

(2) The meeting may approve the proposals with modifications, but shall not do so unless the administrator consents to each modification.

(3) Subject as above, the meeting shall be conducted in accordance with the rules.

(4) After the conclusion of the meeting in accordance with the rules, the administrator shall report the result of the meeting to the court and shall give notice of that result to the registrar of companies and to such persons as may be prescribed.

(5) If a report is given to the court under subsection (4) that the meeting has declined to approve the administrator's proposals (with or without modifications), the court may by order discharge the administration order and make such consequential provision as it thinks fit, or adjourn the hearing conditionally or unconditionally, or make an interim order or any other order that it thinks fit.

(6) Where the administration order is discharged, the administrator shall, within 14 days after the making of the order effecting the discharge, send an office copy of that order to the registrar of companies.

(7) If the administrator without reasonable excuse fails to comply with subsection (6), he is liable to a fine and, for continued contravention, to a daily default fine.

25. Approval of substantial revisions.

(1) This section applies where—

(a) proposals have been approved (with or without modifications) under section 24, and

(b) the administrator proposes to make revisions of those proposals which appear to him substantial.

(2) The administrator shall—

(a) send to all creditors of the company (so far as he is aware of their addresses) a statement in the prescribed form of his proposed revisions, and

(b) lay a copy of the statement before a meeting of the company's creditors summoned for the purpose on not less than 14 days' notice;
and he shall not make the proposed revisions unless they are approved by the meeting.

(3) The administrator shall also either—

(a) send a copy of the statement (so far as he is aware of their addresses) to all members of the company, or

(b) publish in the prescribed manner a notice stating an address to which members of the company should write for copies of the statement to be sent to them free of charge.

(4) The meeting of creditors may approve the proposed revisions with modifications, but shall not do so unless the administrator consents to each modification.

(5) Subject as above, the meeting shall be conducted in accordance with the rules.

(6) After the conclusion of the meeting in accordance with the rules, the administrator shall give notice of the result of the meeting to the registrar of companies and to such persons as may be prescribed.

Miscellaneous

26. Creditors' committee.

(1) Where a meeting of creditors summoned under section 23 has approved the administrator's proposals (with or without modifications), the meeting may, if it thinks fit, establish a committee ('the creditors' committee') to exercise the functions conferred on it by or under this Act.

(2) If such a committee is established, the committee may, on giving not less than 7 days' notice, require the administrator to attend before it at any reasonable time and furnish it with such information relating to the carrying out of his functions as it may reasonably require.

27. Protection of interests of creditors and members.

(1) At any time when an administration order is in force, a creditor or member of the company may apply to the court by petition for an order under this section on the ground—

(a) that the company's affairs, business and property are being or have been managed by the administrator in a manner which is unfairly prejudicial to the interests of its creditors or members generally, or of some part of its creditors or members (including at least himself), or

(b)   that any actual or proposed act or omission of the administrator is or would be so prejudicial.

(2)   On an application for an order under this section the court may, subject as follows, make such order as it thinks fit for giving relief in respect of the matters complained of, or adjourn the hearing conditionally or unconditionally, or make an interim order or any other order that it thinks fit.

(3)   An order under this section shall not prejudice or prevent—

(a)   the implementation of a voluntary arrangement approved under section 4 in Part I, or any compromise or arrangement sanctioned under section 425 of the Companies Act; or

(b)   where the application for the order was made more than 28 days after the approval of any proposals or revised proposals under section 24 or 25, the implementation of those proposals or revised proposals.

(4)   Subject as above, an order under this section may in particular—

(a)   regulate the future management by the administrator of the company's affairs, business and property;

(b)   require the administrator to refrain from doing or continuing an act complained of by the petitioner, or to do an act which the petitioner has complained he has omitted to do;

(c)   require the summoning of a meeting of creditors or members for the purpose of considering such matters as the court may direct;

(d)   discharge the administration order and make such consequential provision as the court thinks fit.

(5)   Nothing in section 15 or 16 is to be taken as prejudicing applications to the court under this section.

(6)   Where the administration order is discharged, the administrator shall, within 14 days after the making of the order effecting the discharge, send an office copy of that order to the registrar of companies; and if without reasonable excuse he fails to comply with this subsection, he is liable to a fine and, for continued contravention, to a daily default fine.

PART III
RECEIVERSHIP

CHAPTER I
RECEIVERS AND MANAGERS (ENGLAND AND WALES)

Preliminary and general provisions

28.   Extent of this Chapter.
This Chapter does not apply to receivers appointed under Chapter II of this Part (Scotland).

29.   Definitions.
(1)   It is hereby declared that, except where the context otherwise requires—

(a)   any reference in the Companies Act or this Act to a receiver or manager of the property of a company, or to a receiver of it, includes a receiver or manager, or (as the case may be) a receiver of part only of that property and a receiver only of the income arising from the property or from part of it; and

(b)   any reference in the Companies Act or this Act to the appointment of a receiver or manager under powers contained in an instrument includes an appointment made under powers which, by virtue of any enactment, are implied in and have effect as if contained in an instrument.

(2)   In this Chapter 'administrative receiver' means—

(a)   a receiver or manager of the wholly (or substantially the whole) of a company's property appointed by or on behalf of the holders of any debentures of the company secured by a charge which, as created, was a floating charge, or by such a charge and one or more other securities; or

(b)   a person who would be such a receiver or manager but for the appointment of some other person as the receiver of part of the company's property.

30. Disqualification of body corporate from acting as receiver.

A body corporate is not qualified for appointment as receiver of the property of a company, and any body corporate which acts as such a receiver is liable to a fine.

31. Disqualification of undischarged bankrupt.

If a person being an undischarged bankrupt acts as receiver or manager of the property of a company on behalf of debenture holders, he is liable to imprisonment or a fine, or both.

This does not apply to a receiver or a manager acting under an appointment made by the court.

32. Power for court to appoint official receiver.

Where application is made to the court to appoint a receiver on behalf of the debenture holders or other creditors of a company which is being wound up by the court, the official receiver may be appointed.

Receivers and managers appointed out of court

33. Time from which appointment is effective.

(1)   The appointment of a person as a receiver or manager of a company's property under powers contained in an instrument—

(a)   is of no effect unless it is accepted by that person before the end of the business day next following that on which the instrument of appointment is received by him or on his behalf, and

(b)   subject to this, is deemed to be made at the time at which the instrument of appointment is so received.

(2)   This section applies to the appointment of two or more persons as joint receivers or managers of a company's property under powers contained in an instrument, subject to such modifications as may be prescribed by the rules.

34. Liability for invalid appointment.

Where the appointment of a person as the receiver or manager of a company's property under powers contained in an instrument is discovered to be invalid (whether by virtue of the invalidity of the instrument or otherwise), the court may order the person by whom or on whose behalf the appointment was made to indemnify the person appointed against any liability which arises solely by reason of the invalidity of the appointment.

35. Application to court for directions.

(1)   A receiver or manager of the property of a company appointed under powers contained in an instrument, or the persons by whom or on whose behalf a receiver or manager has been so appointed, may apply to the court for directions in relation to any particular matter arising in connection with the performance of the functions of the receiver or manager.

(2)   On such an application, the court may give such directions, or may make such order declaring the rights of persons before the court or otherwise, as it thinks just.

36. Court's power to fix remuneration.

(1)   The court may, on an application made by the liquidator of a company, by order fix the amount to be paid by way of remuneration to a person who, under powers

contained in an instrument, has been appointed receiver or manager of the company's property.

(2) The court's power under subsection (1), where no previous order has been made with respect thereto under the subsection—

(a) extends to fixing the remuneration for any period before the making of the order or the application for it,

(b) is exercisable notwithstanding that the receiver or manager has died or ceased to act before the making of the order or the application, and

(c) where the receiver or manager has been paid or has retained for his remuneration for any period before the making of the order any amount in excess of that so fixed for that period, extends to requiring him or his personal representatives to account for the excess or such part of it as may be specified in the order.

But the power conferred by paragraph (c) shall not be exercised as respects any period before the making of the application for the order under this section, unless in the court's opinion there are special circumstances making it proper for the power to be exercised.

(3) The court may from time to time on an application made either by the liquidator or by the receiver or manager, vary or amend an order made under subsection (1).

37. Liability for contracts, etc.

(1) A receiver or manager appointed under powers contained in an instrument (other than an administrative receiver) is, to the same extent as if he had been appointed by order of the court—

(a) personally liable on any contract entered into by him in the performance of his functions (except in so far as the contract otherwise provides) and on any contract of employment adopted by him in the performance of those functions, and

(b) entitled in respect of that liability to indemnity out of the assets.

(2) For the purposes of subsection (1)(a), the receiver or manager is not to be taken to have adopted a contract of employment by reason of anything done or omitted to be done within 14 days after his appointment.

(3) Subsection (1) does not limit any right to indemnity which the receiver or manager would have apart from it, nor limit his liability on contracts entered into without authority, nor confer any right to indemnity in respect of that liability.

(4) Where at any time the receiver or manager so appointed vacates office—

(a) his remuneration and any expenses properly incurred by him, and

(b) any indemnity to which he is entitled out of the assets of the company,

shall be charged on and paid out of any property of the company which is in his custody or under his control at that time in priority to any charge or other security held by the person by or on whose behalf he was appointed.

38. Receivership accounts to be delivered to registrar.

(1) Except in the case of an administrative receiver, every receiver or manager of a company's property who has been appointed under powers contained in an instrument shall deliver to the registrar of companies for registration the requisite accounts of his receipts and payments.

(2) The accounts shall be delivered within one month (or such longer period as the registrar may allow) after the expiration of 12 months from the date of his appointment and of every subsequent period of 6 months, and also within one month after he ceases to act as receiver or manager.

(3) The requisite accounts shall be an abstract in the prescribed form showing—

(a) receipts and payments during the relevant period of 12 or 6 months, or

(b) where the receiver or manager ceases to act, receipts and payments during the period from the end of the period of 12 or 6 months to which the last preceding abstract related (or, if no preceding abstract has been delivered under this section, from the date of his appointment) up to the date of his so ceasing, and the aggregate amount of receipts and payments during all preceding periods since his appointment.

(4)   In this section 'prescribed' means prescribed by regulations made by statutory instrument by the Secretary of State.

(5)   A receiver or manager who makes default in complying with this section is liable to a fine and, for continued contravention, to a daily default fine.

Provisions applicable to every receivership

39.   Notification that receiver or manager appointed.

(1)   When a receiver or manager of the property of a company has been appointed, every invoice, order for goods or business letter issued by or on behalf of the company or the receiver or manager or the liquidator of the company, being a document on or in which the company's name appears, shall contain a statement that a receiver or manager has been appointed.

(2)   If default is made in complying with this section, the company and any of the following persons, who knowingly and wilfully authorises or permits the default, namely, any officer of the company, any liquidator of the company and any receiver or manager, is liable to a fine.

40.   Payment of debts out of assets subject to floating charge.

(1)   The following applies, in the case of a company, where a receiver is appointed on behalf of the holders of any debentures of the company secured by a charge which, as created, was a floating charge.

(2)   If the company is not at the time in course of being wound up, its preferential debts (within the meaning given to that expression by section 386 in Part XII) shall be paid out of the assets coming to the hands of the receiver in priority to any claims for principal or interest in respect of the debentures.

(3)   Payments made under this section shall be recouped, as far as may be, out of the assets of the company available for payment of general creditors.

41.   Enforcement of duty to make returns.

(1)   If a receiver or manager of a company's property—

(a)   having made default in filing, delivering or making any return, account or other document, or in giving any notice, which a receiver or manager is by law required to file, deliver, make or give, fails to make good the default within 14 days after the service on him of a notice requiring him to do so, or

(b)   having been appointed under powers contained in an instrument, has, after being required at any time by the liquidator of the company to do so, failed to render proper accounts of his receipts and payments and to vouch them and pay over to the liquidator the amount properly payable to him,

the court may, on an application made for the purpose, make an order directing the receiver or manager (as the case may be) to make good the default within such time as may be specified in the order.

(2)   In the case of the default mentioned in subsection (1)(a), application to the court may be made by any member or creditor of the company or by the registrar of companies; and in the case of the default mentioned in subsection (1)(b), the application shall be made by the liquidator.

In either case the court's order may provide that all costs of and incidental to the application shall be borne by the receiver or manager, as the case may be.

(3)   Nothing in this section prejudices the operation of any enactment imposing penalties on receivers in respect of any such default as is mentioned in subsection (1).

Administrative receivers: general

42. General powers.

(1)   The powers conferred on the administrative receiver of a company by the debentures by virtue of which he was appointed are deemed to include (except in so far as they are inconsistent with any of the provisions of those debentures) the powers specified in Schedule 1 to this Act.

(2)   In the application of Schedule 1 to the administrative receiver of a company—

    (a)   the words 'he' and 'him' refer to the administrative receiver, and

    (b)   references to the property of the company are to the property of which he is or, but for the appointment of some other person as the receiver of part of the company's property, would be the receiver or manager.

(3)   A person dealing with the administrative receiver in good faith and for value is not concerned to inquire whether the receiver is acting within his powers.

43. Power to dispose of charged property, etc.

(1)   Where, on an application by the administrative receiver, the court is satisfied that the disposal (with or without other assets) of any relevant property which is subject to a security would be likely to promote a more advantageous realisation of the company's assets than would otherwise be effected, the court may by order authorise the administrative receiver to dispose of the property as if it were not subject to the security.

(2)   Subsection (1) does not apply in the case of any security held by the person by or on whose behalf the administrative receiver was appointed, or of any security to which a security so held has priority.

(3)   It shall be a condition of an order under this section that—

    (a)   the net proceeds of the disposal, and

    (b)   where those proceeds are less than such amount as may be determined by the court to be the net amount which would be realised on a sale of the property in the open market by a willing vendor, such sums as may be required to make good the deficiency,

shall be applied towards discharging the sums secured by the security.

(4)   Where a condition imposed in pursuance of subsection (3) relates to two or more securities, that condition shall require the net proceeds of the disposal and, where paragraph (b) of that subsection applies, the sums mentioned in that paragraph to be applied towards discharging the sums secured by those securities in the order of their priorities.

(5)   An office copy of an order under this section shall, within 14 days of the making of the order, be sent by the administrative receiver to the registrar of companies.

(6)   If the administrative receiver without reasonable excuse fails to comply with subsection (5), he is liable to a fine and, for continued contravention, to a daily default fine.

(7)   In this section 'relevant property', in relation to the administrative receiver, means the property of which he is or, but for the appointment of some other person as the receiver of part of the company's property, would be the receiver or manager.

44. Agency and liability for contracts.

(1)   The administrative receiver of a company—

    (a)   is deemed to be the company's agent, unless and until the company goes into liquidation;

    (b)   is personally liable on any contract entered into by him in the carrying out of his functions (except in so far as the contract otherwise provides) and, to the extent of any qualifying liability, on any contract of employment adopted by him in the carrying out of those functions; and

    (c)   is entitled in respect of that liability to an indemnity out of the assets of the company.

(2)   For the purposes of subsection (1)(b) the administrative receiver is not to be taken to have adopted a contract of employment by reason of anything done or omitted to be done within 14 days after his appointment.

(2A)   For the purposes of subsection (1)(b), a liability under a contract of employment is a qualifying liability if—

(a)   it is a liability to pay a sum by way of wages or salary or contribution to an occupational pension scheme,

(b)   it is incurred while the administrative receiver is in office, and

(c)   it is in respect of services rendered wholly or partly after the adoption of the contract.

(2B)   Where a sum payable in respect of a liability which is a qualifying liability for the purposes of subsection (1)(b) is payable in respect of services rendered partly before and partly after the adoption of the contract, liability under subsection (1)(b) shall only extend to so much of the sum as is payable in respect of services rendered after the adoption of the contract.

(2C)   For the purposes of subsections (2A) and (2B)—

(a)   wages or salary payable in respect of a period of holiday or absence from work through sickness or other good cause are deemed to be wages or (as the case may be) salary in respect of services rendered in that period, and

(b)   a sum payable in lieu of holiday is deemed to be wages or (as the case may be) salary in respect of services rendered in the period by reference to which the holiday entitlement arose.

(2D)   In subsection (2C)(a), the reference to wages or salary payable in respect of a period of holiday includes any sums which, if they had been paid, would have been treated for the purposes of the enactments relating to social security as earnings in respect of that period.

(3)   This section does not limit any right to indemnity which the administrative receiver would have apart from it, nor limit his liability on contracts entered into or adopted without authority, nor confer any right to indemnity in respect of that liability.

45.   Vacation of office.

(1)   An administrative receiver of a company may at any time be removed from office by order of the court (but not otherwise) and may resign his office by giving notice of his resignation in the prescribed manner to such persons as may be prescribed.

(2)   An administrative receiver shall vacate office if he ceases to be qualified to act as an insolvency practitioner in relation to the company.

(3)   Where at any time an administrative receiver vacates office—

(a)   his remuneration and any expenses properly incurred by him, and

(b)   any indemnity to which he is entitled out of the assets of the company,

shall be charged on and paid out of any property of the company which is in his custody or under his control at that time in priority to any security held by the person by or on whose behalf he was appointed.

(4)   Where an administrative receiver vacates office otherwise than by death, he shall, within 14 days after his vacation of office, send a notice to that effect to the registrar of companies.

(5)   If an administrative receiver without reasonable excuse fails to comply with subsection (4), he is liable to a fine *and, for continued contravention, to a daily default fine.* [*The words in italics would be repealed if para. 3(3) of sch. 16 to the Companies Act 1989 were brought into force.*]

Administrative receivers: ascertainment and investigation of company's affairs

46.   Information to be given by administrative receiver.

(1)   Where an administrative receiver is appointed, he shall—

(a)   forthwith send to the company and publish in the prescribed manner a notice of his appointment, and

(b)   within 28 days after his appointment, unless the court otherwise directs, send such a notice to all the creditors of the company (so far as he is aware of their addresses).

(2)   This section and the next do not apply in relation to the appointment of an administrative receiver to act—

(a)   with an existing administrative receiver, or

(b)   in place of an administrative receiver dying or ceasing to act,

except that, where they apply to an administrative receiver who dies or ceases to act before they have been fully complied with, the references in this section and the next to the administrative receiver include (subject to the next subsection) his successor and any continuing administrative receiver.

(3)   If the company is being wound up, this section and the next apply notwithstanding that the administrative receiver and the liquidator are the same person, but with any necessary modifications arising from that fact.

(4)   If the administrative receiver without reasonable excuse fails to comply with this section, he is liable to a fine and, for continued contravention, to a daily default fine.

47.   Statement of affairs to be submitted.

(1)   Where an administrative receiver is appointed, he shall forthwith require some or all of the persons mentioned below to make out and submit to him a statement in the prescribed form as to the affairs of the company.

(2)   A statement submitted under this section shall be verified by affidavit by the persons required to submit it and shall show—

(a)   particulars of the company's assets, debts and liabilities;

(b)   the names and addresses of its creditors;

(c)   the securities held by them respectively;

(d)   the dates when the securities were respectively given; and

(e)   such further or other information as may be prescribed.

(3)   The persons referred to in subsection (1) are—

(a)   those who are or have been officers of the company;

(b)   those who have taken part in the company's formation at any time within one year before the date of the appointment of the administrative receiver;

(c)   those who are in the company's employment, or have been in its employment within that year, and are in the administrative receiver's opinion capable of giving the information required;

(d)   those who are or have been within that year officers of or in the employment of a company which is, or within that year was, an officer of the company.

In this subsection 'employment' includes employment under a contract for services.

(4)   Where any persons are required under this section to submit a statement of affairs to the administrative receiver, they shall do so (subject to the next subsection) before the end of the period of 21 days beginning with the day after that on which the prescribed notice of the requirement is given to them by the administrative receiver.

(5)   The administrative receiver, if he thinks fit, may—

(a)   at any time release a person from an obligation imposed on him under subsection (1) or (2), or

(b)   either when giving notice under subsection (4) or subsequently, extend the period so mentioned;

and where the administrative receiver has refused to exercise a power conferred by this subsection, the court, if it thinks fit, may exercise it.

(6)   If a person without reasonable excuse fails to comply with any obligation imposed under this section, he is liable to a fine and, for continued contravention, to a daily default fine.

48. Report by administrative receiver.

(1) Where an administrative receiver is appointed, he shall, within 3 months (or such longer period as the court may allow) after his appointment, send to the registrar of companies, to any trustees for secured creditors of the company and (so far as he is aware of their addresses) to all such creditors a report as to the following matters, namely—

(a)   the events leading up to his appointment, so far as he is aware of them;

(b)   the disposal or proposed disposal by him of any property of the company and the carrying on or proposed carrying on by him of any business of the company;

(c)   the amounts of principal and interest payable to the debenture holders by whom or on whose behalf he was appointed and the amounts payable to preferential creditors; and

(d)   the amount (if any) likely to be available for the payment of other creditors.

(2)   The administrative receiver shall also, within 3 months (or such longer period as the court may allow) after his appointment, either—

(a)   send a copy of the report (so far as he is aware of their addresses) to all unsecured creditors of the company; or

(b)   publish in the prescribed manner a notice stating an address to which unsecured creditors of the company should write for copies of the report to be sent to them free of charge,

and (in either case), unless the court otherwise directs, lay a copy of the report before a meeting of the company's unsecured creditors summoned for the purpose on not less than 14 days' notice.

(3)   The court shall not give a direction under subsection (2) unless—

(a)   the report states the intention of the administrative receiver to apply for the direction, and

(b)   a copy of the report is sent to the person mentioned in paragraph (a) of that subsection, or a notice is published as mentioned in paragraph (b) of that subsection, not less than 14 days before the hearing of the application.

(4)   Where the company has gone or goes into liquidation, the administrative receiver—

(a)   shall, within 7 days after his compliance with subsection (1) or, if later, the nomination or appointment of the liquidator, send a copy of the report to the liquidator, and

(b)   where he does so within the time limited for compliance with subsection (2), is not required to comply with that subsection.

(5)   A report under this section shall include a summary of the statement of affairs made out and submitted to the administrative receiver under section 47 and of his comments (if any) upon it.

(6)   Nothing in this section is to be taken as requiring any such report to include any information the disclosure of which would seriously prejudice the carrying out by the administrative receiver of his functions.

(7)   Section 46(2) applies for the purposes of this section also.

(8)   If the administrative receiver without reasonable excuse fails to comply with this section, he is liable to a fine and, for continued contravention, to a daily default fine.

49. Committee of creditors.

(1)   Where a meeting of creditors is summoned under section 48, the meeting may, if it thinks fit, establish a committee ('the creditors' committee') to exercise the functions conferred on it by or under this Act.

(2)   If such a committee is established, the committee may, on giving not less than 7 days' notice, require the administrative receiver to attend before it at any reasonable time and furnish it with such information relating to the carrying out by him of his functions as it may reasonably require.

CHAPTER III
RECEIVERS' POWERS IN GREAT BRITAIN AS A WHOLE

72.   Cross-border operation of receivership provisions.

(1)   A receiver appointed under the law of either part of Great Britain in respect of the whole or any part of any property or undertaking of a company and in consequence of the company having created a charge which, as created, was a floating charge may exercise his powers in the other part of Great Britain so far as their exercise is not inconsistent with the law applicable there.

(2)   In subsection (1) 'receiver' includes a manager and a person who is appointed both receiver and manager.

PART IV
WINDING UP OF COMPANIES REGISTERED UNDER THE COMPANIES ACTS

CHAPTER I
PRELIMINARY

Modes of winding up

73.   Alternative modes of winding up.

(1)   The winding up of a company, within the meaning given to the expression by section 735 of the Companies Act, may be either voluntary (Chapters II, III, IV and V in this Part) or by the court (Chapter VI).

(2)   This Chapter, and Chapters VII to X, relate to winding up generally, except where otherwise stated.

Contributories

74.   Liability as contributories of present and past members.

(1)   When a company is wound up, every present and past member is liable to contribute to its assets to any amount sufficient for payment of its debts and liabilities, and the expenses of the winding up, and for the adjustment of the rights of the contributories among themselves.

(2)   This is subject as follows—

(a)   a past member is not liable to contribute if he has ceased to be a member for one year or more before the commencement of the winding up;

(b)   a past member is not liable to contribute in respect of any debt or liability of the company contracted after he ceased to be a member;

(c)   a past member is not liable to contribute, unless it appears to the court that the existing members are unable to satisfy the contributions required to be made by them in pursuance of the Companies Act and this Act;

(d)   in the case of a company limited by shares, no contribution is required from any member exceeding the amount (if any) unpaid on the shares in respect of which he is liable as a present or past member;

(e)   nothing in the Companies Act or this Act invalidates any provision contained in a policy of insurance or other contract whereby the liability of individual members on the policy or contract is restricted, or whereby the funds of the company are alone made liable in respect of the policy or contract;

(f)   a sum due to any member of the company (in his character of a member) by way of dividends, profits or otherwise is not deemed to be a debt of the company, payable to that member in a case of competition between himself and any other creditor not a member of the company, but any such sum may be taken into account for the purpose of the final adjustment of the rights of the contributories among themselves.

(3)   In the case of a company limited by guarantee, no contribution is required from any member exceeding the amount undertaken to be contributed by him to the company's assets in the event of its being wound up; but if it is a company with a share capital, every member of it is liable (in addition to the amount so undertaken to be contributed to the assets), to contribute to the extent of any sums unpaid on shares held by him.

75. Directors, etc. with unlimited liability.

(1)   In the winding up of a limited company, any director or manager (whether past or present) whose liability is under the Companies Act unlimited is liable, in addition to his liability (if any) to contribute as an ordinary member, to make a further contribution as if he were at the commencement of the winding up a member of an unlimited company.

(2)   However—

(a)   a past director or manager is not liable to make such further contribution if he has ceased to hold office for a year or more before the commencement of the winding up;

(b)   a past director or manager is not liable to make such further contribution in respect of any debt or liability of the company contracted after he ceased to hold office;

(c)   subject to the company's articles, a director or manager is not liable to make such further contribution unless the court deems it necessary to require that contribution in order to satisfy the company's debts and liabilities, and the expenses of the winding up.

76. Liability of past directors and shareholders.

(1)   This section applies where a company is being wound up and—

(a)   it has under Chapter VII of Part V of the Companies Act (redeemable shares; purchase by a company of its own shares) made a payment out of capital in respect of the redemption or purchase of any of its own shares (the payment being referred to below as 'the relevant payment'), and

(b)   the aggregate amount of the company's assets and the amounts paid by way of contribution to its assets (apart from this section) is not sufficient for payment of its debts and liabilities, and the expenses of the winding up.

(2)   If the winding up commenced within one year of the date on which the relevant payment was made, then—

(a)   the person from whom the shares were redeemed or purchased, and

(b)   the directors who signed the statutory declaration made in accordance with section 173(3) of the Companies Act for purposes of the redemption or purchase (except a director who shows that he had reasonable grounds for forming the opinion set out in the declaration),

are, so as to enable that insufficiency to be met, liable to contribute to the following extent to the company's assets.

(3)   A person from whom any of the shares were redeemed or purchased is liable to contribute an amount not exceeding so much of the relevant payment as was made by the company in respect of his shares; and the directors are jointly and severally liable with that person to contribute that amount.

(4)   A person who has contributed any amount to the assets in pursuance of this section may apply to the court for an order directing any other person jointly and severally liable in respect of that amount to pay him such amount as the court thinks just and equitable.

(5)   Sections 74 and 75 do not apply in relation to liability accruing by virtue of this section.

(6)   This section is deemed included in Chapter VII of Part V of the Companies Act for the purposes of the Secretary of State's power to make regulations under section 179 of that Act.

77. Limited company formerly unlimited.

(1) This section applies in the case of a company being wound up which was at some former time registered as unlimited but has re-registered—

    (a) as a public company under section 43 of the Companies Act (or the former corresponding provision, section 5 of the Companies Act 1980), or

    (b) as a limited company under section 51 of the Companies Act (or the former corresponding provision, section 44 of the Companies Act 1967).

(2) Notwithstanding section 74(2)(a) above, a past member of the company who was a member of it at the time of re-registration, if the winding up commences within the period of 3 years beginning with the day on which the company was re-registered, is liable to contribute to the assets of the company in respect of debts and liabilities contracted before that time.

(3) If no persons who were members of the company at that time are existing members of it, a person who at that time was a present or past member is liable to contribute as above notwithstanding that the existing members have satisfied the contributions required to be made by them under the Companies Act and this Act.

This applies subject to section 74(2)(a) above and to subsection (2) of this section, but notwithstanding section 74(2)(c).

(4) Notwithstanding section 74(2)(d) and (3), there is no limit on the amount which a person who, at that time, was a past or present member of the company is liable to contribute as above.

78. Unlimited company formerly limited.

(1) This section applies in the case of a company being wound up which was at some former time registered as limited but has been re-registered as unlimited under section 49 of the Companies Act (or the former corresponding provision, section 43 of the Companies Act 1967).

(2) A person who, at the time when the application for the company to be re-registered was lodged, was a past member of the company and did not after that again become a member of it is not liable to contribute to the assets of the company more than he would have been liable to contribute had the company not been re-registered.

79. Meaning of 'contributory'.

(1) In this Act and the Companies Act the expression 'contributory' means every person liable to contribute to the assets of a company in the event of its being wound up, and for the purposes of all proceedings for determining, and all proceedings prior to the final determination of, the persons who are to be deemed contributories, includes any person alleged to be a contributory.

(2) The reference in subsection (1) to persons liable to contribute to the assets does not include a person so liable by virtue of a declaration by the court under section 213 (imputed responsibility for company's fraudulent trading) or section 214 (wrongful trading) in Chapter X of this Part.

(3) A reference in a company's articles to a contributory does not (unless the context requires) include a person who is a contributory only by virtue of section 76.

This subsection is deemed included in Chapter VII of Part V of the Companies Act for the purposes of the Secretary of State's power to make regulations under section 179 of that Act.

80. Nature of contributory's liability.

The liability of a contributory creates a debt (in England and Wales in the nature of a specialty) accruing due from him at the time when his liability commenced, but payable at the times when calls are made for enforcing the liability.

81. Contributories in case of death of a member.

(1) If a contributory dies either before or after he has been placed on the list of contributories, his personal representatives, and the heirs and legatees of heritage of his

heritable estate in Scotland, are liable in a due course of administration to contribute to the assets of the company in discharge of his liability and are contributories accordingly.

(2) Where the personal representatives are placed on the list of contributories, the heirs or legatees of heritage need not be added, but they may be added as and when the court thinks fit.

(3) If in England and Wales the personal representatives make default in paying any money ordered to be paid by them, proceedings may be taken for administering the estate of the deceased contributory and for compelling payment out of it of the money due.

82. Effect of contributory's bankruptcy.

(1) The following applies if a contributory becomes bankrupt, either before or after he has been placed on the list of contributories.

(2) His trustee in bankruptcy represents him for all purposes of the winding up, and is a contributory accordingly.

(3) The trustee may be called on to admit to proof against the bankrupt's estate, or otherwise allow to be paid out of the bankrupt's assets in due course of law, any money due from the bankrupt in respect of his liability to contribute to the company's assets.

(4) There may be proved against the bankrupt's estate the estimated value of his liability to future calls as well as calls already made.

CHAPTER II
VOLUNTARY WINDING UP (INTRODUCTORY AND GENERAL)

Resolutions for, and commencement of, voluntary winding up

84. Circumstances in which company may be wound up voluntarily.

(1) A company may be wound up voluntarily—

(a) when the period (if any) fixed for the duration of the company by the articles expires, or the event (if any) occurs, on the occurrence of which the articles provide that the company is to be dissolved, and the company in general meeting has passed a resolution requiring it to be wound up voluntarily;

(b) if the company resolves by special resolution that it be wound up voluntarily;

(c) if the company resolves by extraordinary resolution to the effect that it cannot by reason of its liabilities continue its business, and that it is advisable to wind up.

(2) In this Act the expression 'a resolution for voluntary winding up' means a resolution passed under any of the paragraphs of subsection (1).

(3) A resolution passed under paragraph (a) of subsection (1), as well as a special resolution under paragraph (b) and an extraordinary resolution under paragraph (c), is subject to section 380 of the Companies Act (copy of resolution to be forwarded to registrar of companies within 15 days).

85. Notice of resolution to wind up.

(1) When a company has passed a resolution for voluntary winding up, it shall, within 14 days after the passing of the resolution, give notice of the resolution by advertisement in the Gazette.

(2) If default is made in complying with this section, the company and every officer of it who is in default is liable to a fine and, for continued contravention, to a daily default fine.

For purposes of this subsection the liquidator is deemed an officer of the company.

86. Commencement of winding up.

A voluntary winding up is deemed to commence at the time of the passing of the resolution for voluntary winding up.

Consequences of resolution to wind up

87. Effect of business and status of company.

(1)   In case of a voluntary winding up, the company shall from the commencement of the winding up cease to carry on its business, except so far as may be required for its beneficial winding up.

(2)   However, the corporate state and corporate powers of the company, notwithstanding anything to the contrary in its articles, continue until the company is dissolved.

88. Avoidance of share transfers, etc. after winding-up resolution.

Any transfer of shares, not being a transfer made to or with the sanction of the liquidator, and any alteration in the status of the company's members, made after the commencement of a voluntary winding up, is void.

Declaration of solvency

89. Statutory declaration of solvency.

(1)   Where it is proposed to wind up a company voluntarily, the directors (or, in the case of a company having more than two directors, the majority of them) may at a directors' meeting make a statutory declaration to the effect that they have made a full inquiry into the company's affairs and that, having done so, they have formed the opinion that the company will be able to pay its debts in full, together with interest at the official rate (as defined in section 251), within such period, not exceeding 12 months from the commencement of the winding up, as may be specified in the declaration.

(2)   Such a declaration by the directors has no effect for purposes of this Act unless—

(a)   it is made within the 5 weeks immediately preceding the date of the passing of the resolution for winding up, or on that date but before the passing of the resolution, and

(b)   it embodies a statement of the company's assets and liabilities as at the latest practicable date before the making of the declaration.

(3)   The declaration shall be delivered to the registrar of companies before the expiration of 15 days immediately following the date on which the resolution for winding up is passed.

(4)   A director making a declaration under this section without having reasonable grounds for the opinion that the company will be able to pay its debts in full, together with interest at the official rate, within the period specified is liable to imprisonment or a fine, or both.

(5)   If the company is wound up in pursuance of a resolution passed within 5 weeks after the making of the declaration, and its debts (together with interest at the official rate) are not paid or provided for in full within the period specified, it is to be presumed (unless the contrary is shown) that the director did not have reasonable grounds for his opinion.

(6)   If a declaration required by subsection (3) to be delivered to the registrar is not so delivered within the time prescribed by that subsection, the company and every officer in default is liable to a fine and, for continued contravention, to a daily default fine.

90. Distinction between 'members'' and 'creditors'' voluntary winding up.

A winding up in the case of which a directors' statutory declaration under section 89 has been made is a 'members' voluntary winding up'; and a winding up in the case of which such a declaration has not been made is a 'creditors' voluntary winding up'.

CHAPTER III
MEMBERS' VOLUNTARY WINDING UP

91. Appointment of liquidator.

(1)   In a members' voluntary winding up, the company in general meeting shall appoint one or more liquidators for the purpose of winding up the company's affairs and distributing its assets.

(2)   On the appointment of a liquidator all the powers of the directors cease, except so far as the company in general meeting or the liquidator sanctions their continuance.

92.   Power to fill vacancy in office of liquidator.

(1)   If a vacancy occurs by death, resignation or otherwise in the office of liquidator appointed by the company, the company in general meeting may, subject to any arrangement with its creditors, fill the vacancy.

(2)   For that purpose a general meeting may be convened by any contributory or, if there were more liquidators than one, by the continuing liquidators.

(3)   The meeting shall be held in manner provided by this Act or by the articles, or in such manner as may, on application by any contributory or by the continuing liquidators, be determined by the court.

93.   General company meeting at each year's end.

(1)   Subject to sections 96 and 102, in the event of the winding up continuing for more than one year, the liquidator shall summon a general meeting of the company at the end of the first year from the commencement of the winding up, and of each succeeding year, or at the first convenient date within 3 months from the end of the year or such longer period as the Secretary of State may allow.

(2)   The liquidator shall lay before the meeting an account of his acts and dealings, and of the conduct of the winding up, during the preceding year.

(3)   If the liquidator fails to comply with this section, he is liable to a fine.

94.   Final meeting prior to dissolution.

(1)   As soon as the company's affairs are fully wound up, the liquidator shall make up an account of the winding up, showing how it has been conducted and the company's property has been disposed of, and thereupon shall call a general meeting of the company for the purpose of laying before it the account, and giving an explanation of it.

(2)   The meeting shall be called by advertisement in the Gazette, specifying its time, place and object and published at least one month before the meeting.

(3)   Within one week after the meeting, the liquidator shall send to the registrar of companies a copy of the account, and shall make a return to him of the holding of the meeting and of its date.

(4)   If the copy is not sent or the return is not made in accordance with subsection (3), the liquidator is liable to a fine and, for continued contravention, to a daily default fine.

(5)   If a quorum is not present at the meeting, the liquidator shall, in lieu of the return mentioned above, make a return that the meeting was duly summoned and that no quorum was present; and upon such a return being made, the provisions of subsection (3) as to the making of the return are deemed complied with.

(6)   If the liquidator fails to call a general meeting of the company as required by subsection (1), he is liable to a fine.

95.   Effect of company's insolvency.

(1)   This section applies where the liquidator is of the opinion that the company will be unable to pay its debts in full (together with interest at the official rate) within the period stated in the directors' declaration under section 89.

(2)   The liquidator shall—

(a)   summon a meeting of creditors for a day not later than the 28th day after the day on which he formed that opinion;

(b)   send notices of the creditors' meeting to the creditors by post not less than 7 days before the day on which that meeting is to be held;

(c)   cause notice of the creditors' meeting to be advertised once in the Gazette and once at least in 2 newspapers circulating in the relevant locality (that is to say the locality in which the company's principal place of business in Great Britain was situated during the relevant period); and

(d)   during the period before the day on which the creditors' meeting is to be held, furnish creditors free of charge with such information concerning the affairs of the company as they may reasonably require;

and the notice of the creditors' meeting shall state the duty imposed by paragraph (d) above.

(3)   The liquidator shall also—

(a)   make out a statement in the prescribed form as to the affairs of the company;

(b)   lay that statement before the creditors' meeting; and

(c)   attend and preside at that meeting.

(4)   The statement as to the affairs of the company shall be verified by affidavit by the liquidator and shall show—

(a)   particulars of the company's assets, debts and liabilities;

(b)   the names and addresses of the company's creditors;

(c)   the securities held by them respectively;

(d)   the dates when the securities were respectively given; and

(e)   such further or other information as may be prescribed.

(5)   Where the company's principal place of business in Great Britain was situated in different localities at different times during the relevant period, the duty imposed by subsection (2)(c) applies separately in relation to each of those localities.

(6)   Where the company had no place of business in Great Britain during the relevant period, references in subsections (2)(c) and (5) to the company's principal place of business in Great Britain are replaced by references to its registered office.

(7)   In this section 'the relevant period' means the period of 6 months immediately preceding the day on which were sent the notices summoning the company meeting at which it was resolved that the company be wound up voluntarily.

(8)   If the liquidator without reasonable excuse fails to comply with this section, he is liable to a fine.

96.   Conversion to creditors' voluntary winding up.

As from the day on which the creditors' meeting is held under section 95, this Act has effect as if—

(a)   the directors' declaration under section 89 had not been made; and

(b)   the creditors' meeting and the company meeting at which it was resolved that the company be wound up voluntarily were the meetings mentioned in section 98 in the next Chapter;

and accordingly the winding up becomes a creditors' voluntary winding up.

CHAPTER IV
CREDITORS' VOLUNTARY WINDING UP

97.   Application of this Chapter.

(1)   Subject as follows, this Chapter applies in relation to a creditors' voluntary winding up.

(2)   Sections 98 and 99 do not apply where, under section 96 in Chapter III, a members' voluntary winding up has become a creditors' voluntary winding up.

98.   Meeting of creditors.

(1)   The company shall—

(a)   cause a meeting of its creditors to be summoned for a day not later than the 14th day after the day on which there is to be held the company meeting at which the resolution for voluntary winding up is to be proposed;

(b)   cause the notices of the creditors' meeting to be sent by post to the creditors not less than 7 days before the day on which that meeting is to be held; and

(c)   cause notice of the creditors' meeting to be advertised once in the Gazette and once at least in two newspapers circulating in the relevant locality (that is to say the locality in which the company's principal place of business in Great Britain was situated during the relevant period).

(2)   The notice of the creditors' meeting shall state either—

(a)   the name and address of a person qualified to act as an insolvency practitioner in relation to the company who, during the period before the day on which that meeting is to be held, will furnish creditors free of charge with such information concerning the company's affairs as they may reasonably require; or

(b)   a place in the relevant locality where, on the two business days falling next before the day on which that meeting is to be held, a list of the names and addresses of the company's creditors will be available for inspection free of charge.

(3)   Where the company's principal place of business in Great Britain was situated in different localities at different times during the relevant period, the duties imposed by subsections (1)(c) and (2)(b) above apply separately in relation to each of those localities.

(4)   Where the company had no place of business in Great Britain during the relevant period, references in subsections (1)(c) and (3) to the company's principal place of business in Great Britain are replaced by references to its registered office.

(5)   In this section 'the relevant period' means the period of 6 months immediately preceding the day on which were sent the notices summoning the company meeting at which it was resolved that the company be wound up voluntarily.

(6)   If the company without reasonable excuse fails to comply with subsection (1) or (2), it is guilty of an offence and liable to a fine.

99.   Directors to lay statement of affairs before creditors.

(1)   The directors of the company shall—

(a)   make out a statement in the prescribed form as to the affairs of the company;

(b)   cause that statement to be laid before the creditors' meeting under section 98; and

(c)   appoint one of their number to preside at the meeting;

and it is the duty of the director so appointed to attend the meeting and preside over it.

(2)   The statement as to the affairs of the company shall be verified by affidavit by some or all of the directors and shall show—

(a)   particulars of the company's assets, debts and liabilities;

(b)   the names and addresses of the company's creditors;

(c)   the securities held by them respectively;

(d)   the dates when the securities were respectively given; and

(e)   such further or other information as may be prescribed.

(3)   If—

(a)   the directors without reasonable excuse fail to comply with subsection (1) or (2); or

(b)   any director without reasonable excuse fails to comply with subsection (1), so far as requiring him to attend and preside at the creditors' meeting,

the directors are or (as the case may be) the director is guilty of an offence and liable to a fine.

100.   Appointment of liquidator.

(1)   The creditors and the company at their respective meetings mentioned in section 98 may nominate a person to be liquidator for the purpose of winding up the company's affairs and distributing its assets.

(2)   The liquidator shall be the person nominated by the creditors or, where no person has been so nominated, the person (if any) nominated by the company.

(3)   In the case of different persons being nominated, any director, member or creditor of the company may, within 7 days after the date on which the nomination was made by the creditors, apply to the court for an order either—

(a)   directing that the person nominated as liquidator by the company shall be liquidator instead of or jointly with the person nominated by the creditors, or

(b)   appointing some other person to be liquidator instead of the person nominated by the creditors.

101.   Appointment of liquidation committee.

(1)   The creditors at the meeting to be held under section 98 or at any subsequent meeting may, if they think fit, appoint a committee ('the liquidation committee') of not more than 5 persons to exercise the functions conferred on it by or under this Act.

(2)   If such a committee is appointed, the company may, either at the meeting at which the resolution for voluntary winding up is passed or at any time subsequently in general meeting, appoint such number of persons as they think fit to act as members of the committee, not exceeding 5.

(3)   However, the creditors may, if they think fit, resolve that all or any of the persons so appointed by the company ought not to be members of the liquidation committee; and if the creditors so resolve—

(a)   the persons mentioned in the resolution are not then, unless the court otherwise directs, qualified to act as members of the committee; and

(b)   on any application to the court under this provision the court may, if it thinks fit, appoint other persons to act as such members in place of the persons mentioned in the resolution.

(4)   In Scotland, the liquidation committee has, in addition to the powers and duties conferred and imposed on it by this Act, such of the powers and duties of commissioners on a bankrupt estate as may be conferred and imposed on liquidation committees by the rules.

102.   Creditors' meeting where winding up converted under s. 96.

Where, in the case of a winding up which was, under section 96 in Chapter III, converted to a creditors' voluntary winding up, a creditors' meeting is held in accordance with section 95, any appointment made or committee established by that meeting is deemed to have been made or established by a meeting held in accordance with section 98 in this Chapter.

103.   Cesser of directors' powers.

On the appointment of a liquidator, all the powers of the directors cease, except so far as the liquidation committee (or, if there is no such committee, the creditors) sanction their continuance.

104.   Vacancy in office of liquidator.

If a vacancy occurs, by death, resignation or otherwise, in the office of a liquidator (other than a liquidator appointed by, or by the direction of, the court), the creditors may fill the vacancy.

105.   Meetings of company and creditors at each year's end.

(1)   If the winding up continues for more than one year, the liquidator shall summon a general meeting of the company and a meeting of the creditors at the end of the first year from the commencement of the winding up, and of each succeeding year, or at the first convenient date within 3 months from the end of the year or such longer period as the Secretary of State may allow.

(2)   The liquidator shall lay before each of the meetings an account of his acts and dealings and of the conduct of the winding up during the preceding year.

(3)   If the liquidator fails to comply with this section, he is liable to a fine.

(4)   Where under section 96 a members' voluntary winding up has become a creditors' voluntary winding up, and the creditors' meeting under section 95 is held 3 months or less before the end of the first year from the commencement of the winding

up, the liquidator is not required by this section to summon a meeting of creditors at the end of that year.

106. Final meeting prior to dissolution.

(1)   As soon as the company's affairs are fully wound up, the liquidator shall make an account of the winding up, showing how it has been conducted and the company's property has been disposed of, and thereupon shall call a general meeting of the company and a meeting of the creditors for the purpose of laying the account before the meetings and giving an explanation of it.

(2)   Each such meeting shall be called by advertisement in the Gazette specifying the time, place and object of the meeting, and published at least one month before it.

(3)   Within one week after the date of the meetings (or, if they are not held on the same date, after the date of the later one) the liquidator shall send to the registrar of companies a copy of the account, and shall make a return to him of the holding of the meetings and of their dates.

(4)   If the copy is not sent or the return is not made in accordance with subsection (3), the liquidator is liable to a fine and, for continued contravention, to a daily default fine.

(5)   However, if a quorum is not present at either such meeting, the liquidator shall, in lieu of the return required by subsection (3), make a return that the meeting was duly summoned and that no quorum was present; and upon such return being made the provisions of that subsection as to the making of the return are, in respect of that meeting, deemed complied with.

(6)   If the liquidator fails to call a general meeting of the company or a meeting of the creditors as required by this section, he is liable to a fine.

CHAPTER V
PROVISIONS APPLYING TO BOTH KINDS OF VOLUNTARY WINDING UP

107. Distribution of company's property.

Subject to the provisions of this Act as to preferential payments, the company's property in a voluntary winding up shall on the winding up be applied in satisfaction of the company's liabilities *pari passu* and, subject to that application, shall (unless the articles otherwise provide) be distributed among the members according to their rights and interests in the company.

108. Appointment or removal of liquidator by the court.

(1)   If from any cause whatever there is no liquidator acting, the court may appoint a liquidator.

(2)   The court may, on cause shown, remove a liquidator and appoint another.

109. Notice by liquidator of his appointment.

(1)   The liquidator shall, within 14 days after his appointment, publish in the Gazette and deliver to the registrar of companies for registration a notice of his appointment in the form prescribed by statutory instrument made by the Secretary of State.

(2)   If the liquidator fails to comply with this section, he is liable to a fine and, for continued contravention, to a daily default fine.

110. Acceptance of shares, etc., as consideration for sale of company property.

(1)   This section applies, in the case of a company proposed to be, or being, wound up voluntarily, where the whole or part of the company's business or property is proposed to be transferred or sold to another company ('the transferee company'), whether or not the latter is a company within the meaning of the Companies Act.

(2)   With the requisite sanction, the liquidator of the company being, or proposed to be, wound up ('the transferor company') may receive, in compensation or part compensation for the transfer or sale, shares, policies or other like interests in the transferee company for distribution among the members of the transferor company.

(3)   The sanction requisite under subsection (2) is—

(a)   in the case of a members' voluntary winding up, that of a special resolution of the company, conferring either a general authority on the liquidator or an authority in respect of any particular arrangement, and

(b)   in the case of a creditors' voluntary winding up, that of either the court or the liquidation committee.

(4)   Alternatively to subsection (2), the liquidator may (with that sanction) enter into any other arrangement whereby the members of the transferor company may, in lieu of receiving cash, shares, policies or other like interests (or in addition thereto), participate in the profits of, or receive any other benefit from, the transferee company.

(5)   A sale or arrangement in pursuance of this section is binding on members of the transferor company.

(6)   A special resolution is not invalid for purposes of this section by reason that it is passed before or concurrently with a resolution for voluntary winding up or for appointing liquidators; but, if an order is made within a year for winding up the company by the court, the special resolution is not valid unless sanctioned by the court.

111.   Dissent from arrangement under s. 110.

(1)   This section applies in the case of a voluntary winding up where, for the purposes of section 110(2) or (4), there has been passed a special resolution of the transferor company providing the sanction requisite for the liquidator under that section.

(2)   If a member of the transferor company who did not vote in favour of the special resolution expresses his dissent from it in writing, addressed to the liquidator and left at the company's registered office within 7 days after the passing of the resolution, he may require the liquidator either to abstain from carrying the resolution into effect or to purchase his interest at a price to be determined by agreement or by arbitration under this section.

(3)   If the liquidator elects to purchase the member's interest, the purchase money must be paid before the company is dissolved and be raised by the liquidator in such manner as may be determined by special resolution.

(4)   For purposes of an arbitration under this section, the provisions of the Companies Clauses Consolidation Act 1845 or, in the case of a winding up in Scotland, the Companies Clauses Consolidation (Scotland) Act 1845 with respect to the settlement of disputes by arbitration are incorporated with this Act, and—

(a)   in the construction of those provisions this Act is deemed the special Act and 'the company' means the transferor company, and

(b)   any appointment by the incorporated provisions directed to be made under the hand of the secretary or any two of the directors may be made in writing by the liquidator (or, if there is more than one liquidator, then any two or more of them).

112.   Reference of questions to court.

(1)   The liquidator or any contributory or creditor may apply to the court to determine any question arising in the winding up of a company, or to exercise, as respects the enforcing of calls or any other matter, all or any of the powers which the court might exercise if the company were being wound up by the court.

(2)   The court, if satisfied that the determination of the question or the required exercise of power will be just and beneficial, may accede wholly or partially to the application on such terms and conditions as it thinks fit, or may make such other order on the application as it thinks just.

(3) A copy of an order made by virtue of this section staying the proceedings in the winding up shall forthwith be forwarded by the company, or otherwise as may be prescribed, to the registrar of companies, who shall enter it in his records relating to the company.

114. No liquidator appointed or nominated by company.

(1) This section applies where, in the case of a voluntary winding up, no liquidator has been appointed or nominated by the company.

(2) The powers of the directors shall not be exercised, except with the sanction of the court or (in the case of a creditors' voluntary winding up) so far as may be necessary to secure compliance with sections 98 (creditors' meeting) and 99 (statement of affairs), during the period before the appointment or nomination of a liquidator of the company.

(3) Subsection (2) does not apply in relation to the powers of the directors—

(a) to dispose of perishable goods and other goods the value of which is likely to diminish if they are not immediately disposed of, and

(b) to do all such other things as may be necessary for the protection of the company's assets.

(4) If the directors of the company without reasonable excuse fail to comply with this section, they are liable to a fine.

115. Expenses of voluntary winding up.

All expenses properly incurred in the winding up, including the remuneration of the liquidator, are payable out of the company's assets in priority to all other claims.

116. Saving for certain rights.

The voluntary winding up of a company does not bar the right of any creditor or contributory to have it wound up by the court; but in the case of an application by a contributory the court must be satisfied that the rights of the contributories will be prejudiced by a voluntary winding up.

CHAPTER VI
WINDING UP BY THE COURT

Jurisdiction (England and Wales)

117. High Court and county court jurisdiction.

(1) The High Court has jurisdiction to wind up any company registered in England and Wales.

(2) Where the amount of a company's share capital paid up or credited as paid up does not exceed £120,000, then (subject to this section) the county court of the district in which the company's registered office is situated has concurrent jurisdiction with the High Court to wind up the company.

(3) The money sum for the time being specified in subsection (2) is subject to increase or reduction by order under section 416 in Part XV.

(4) The Lord Chancellor may by order in a statutory instrument exclude a county court from having winding-up jurisdiction, and for the purposes of that jurisdiction may attach its district, or any part thereof, to any other county court, and may by statutory instrument revoke or vary any such order.

In exercising the powers of this section, the Lord Chancellor shall provide that a county court is not to have winding-up jurisdiction unless it has for the time being jurisdiction for the purposes of Parts VIII to XI of this Act (individual insolvency).

(5) Every court in England and Wales having winding-up jurisdiction has for the purposes of that jurisdiction all the powers of the High Court; and every prescribed officer of the court shall perform any duties which an officer of the High Court may discharge by order of a judge of that court or otherwise in relation to winding up.

(6)   For the purposes of this section, a company's 'registered office' is the place which has longest been its registered office during the 6 months immediately preceding the presentation of the petition for winding up.

118.   Proceedings taken in wrong court.

(1)   Nothing in section 117 invalidates a proceeding by reason of its being taken in the wrong court.

(2)   The winding up of a company by the court in England and Wales, or any proceedings in the winding up, may be retained in the court in which the proceedings were commenced, although it may not be the court in which they ought to have been commenced.

119.   Proceedings in county court; case stated for High Court.

(1)   If any question arises in any winding-up proceedings in a county court which all the parties to the proceedings, or which one of them and the judge of the court, desire to have determined in the first instance in the High Court, the judge shall state the facts in the form of a special case for the opinion of the High Court.

(2)   Thereupon the special case and the proceedings (or such of them as may be required) shall be transmitted to the High Court for the purposes of the determination.

Grounds and effect of winding-up petition

122.   Circumstances in which company may be wound up by the court.

(1)   A company may be wound up by the court if—

(a)   the company has by special resolution resolved that the company be wound up by the court,

(b)   being a public company which was registered as such on its original incorporation, the company has not been issued with a certificate under section 117 of the Companies Act (public company share capital requirements) and more than a year has expired since it was so registered,

(c)   it is an old public company, within the meaning of the Consequential Provisions Act,

(d)   the company does not commence its business within a year from its incorporation or suspends its business for a whole year,

(e)   except in the case of a private company limited by shares or by guarantee, the number of members is reduced below 2,

(f)   the company is unable to pay its debts,

(g)   the court is of the opinion that it is just and equitable that the company should be wound up.

(2)   In Scotland, a company which the Court of Session has jurisdiction to wind up may be wound up by the Court if there is subsisting a floating charge over property comprised in the company's property and undertaking, and the court is satisfied that the security of the creditor entitled to the benefit of the floating charge is in jeopardy.

For this purpose a creditor's security is deemed to be in jeopardy if the Court is satisfied that events have occurred or are about to occur which render it unreasonable in the creditor's interests that the company should retain power to dispose of the property which is subject to the floating charge.

123.   Definition of inability to pay debts.

(1)   A company is deemed unable to pay its debts—

(a)   if a creditor (by assignment or otherwise) to whom the company is indebted in a sum exceeding £750 then due has served on the company, by leaving it at the company's registered office, a written demand (in the prescribed form) requiring the company to pay the sum so due and the company has for 3 weeks thereafter neglected to pay the sum or to secure or compound for it to the reasonable satisfaction of the creditor, or

(b) if, in England and Wales, execution or other process issued on a judgment, decree or order of any court in favour of a creditor of the company is returned unsatisfied in whole or in part, or

(c) if, in Scotland, the induciae of a charge for payment on an extract decree, or an extract registered bond, or an extract registered protest, have expired without payment being made, or

(d) if, in Northern Ireland, a certificate of unenforceability has been granted in respect of a judgment against the company, or

(e) if it is proved to the satisfaction of the court that the company is unable to pay its debts as they fall due.

(2) A company is also deemed unable to pay its debts if it is proved to the satisfaction of the court that the value of the company's assets is less than the amount of its liabilities, taking into account its contingent and prospective liabilities.

(3) The money sum for the time being specified in subsection (1)(a) is subject to increase or reduction by order under section 416 in Part XV.

124. Application for winding up.

(1) Subject to the provisions of this section, an application to the court for the winding up of a company shall be by petition presented either by the company, or the directors, or by any creditor or creditors (including any contingent or prospective creditor or creditors), contributory or contributories or by the clerk of a magistrates' court in the exercise of the power conferred by section 87A of the Magistrates' Courts Act 1980 (enforcement of fines imposed on companies), or by all or any of those parties, together or separately.

(2) Except as mentioned below, a contributory is not entitled to present a winding-up petition unless either—

(a) the number of members is reduced below 2, or

(b) the shares in respect of which he is a contributory, or some of them, either were originally allotted to him, or have been held by him, and registered in his name, for at least 6 months during the 18 months before the commencement of the winding up, or have devolved on him through the death of a former holder.

(3) A person who is liable under section 76 to contribute to a company's assets in the event of it being wound up may petition on either of the grounds set out in section 122(1)(f) and (g), and subsection (2) above does not then apply; but unless the person is a contributory otherwise than under section 76, he may not in his character as contributory petition on any other ground.

This subsection is deemed included in Chapter VII of Part V of the Companies Act (redeemable shares; purchase by a company of its own shares) for the purposes of the Secretary of State's power to make regulations under section 179 of that Act.

(4) A winding-up petition may be presented by the Secretary of State—

(a) if the ground of the petition is that in section 122(1)(b) or (c), or

(b) in a case falling within section 124A below.

(5) Where a company is being wound up voluntarily in England and Wales, a winding-up petition may be presented by the official receiver attached to the court as well as by any other person authorised in that behalf under the other provisions of this section; but the court shall not make a winding-up order on the petition unless it is satisfied that the voluntary winding up cannot be continued with due regard to the interests of the creditors or contributories.

124A. Petition for winding up on grounds of public interest.

(1) Where it appears to the Secretary of State from—

(a) any report made or information obtained under Part XIV of the Companies Act 1985 (company investigations, &c.),

(b) any report made under section 94 or 177 of the Financial Services Act 1986 or any information obtained under section 105 of that Act,

(c) any information obtained under section 2 of the Criminal Justice Act 1987 or section 52 of the Criminal Justice (Scotland) Act 1987 (fraud investigations), or

(d) any information obtained under section 83 of the Companies Act 1989 (powers exercisable for purpose of assisting overseas regulatory authorities), that it is expedient in the public interest that a company should be wound up, he may present a petition for it to be wound up if the court thinks it just and equitable for it to be so.

(2) This section does not apply if the company is already being wound up by the court.

125. Powers of court on hearing of petition.

(1) On hearing a winding-up petition the court may dismiss it, or adjourn the hearing conditionally or unconditionally, or make an interim order, or any other order that it thinks fit; but the court shall not refuse to make a winding-up order on the ground only that the company's assets have been mortgaged to an amount equal to or in excess of those assets, or that the company has no assets.

(2) If the petition is presented by members of the company as contributories on the ground that it is just and equitable that the company should be wound up, the court, if it is of opinion—

(a) that the petitioners are entitled to relief either by winding up the company or by some other means, and

(b) that in the absence of any other remedy it would be just and equitable that the company should be wound up,
shall make a winding-up order; but this does not apply if the court is also of the opinion both that some other remedy is available to the petitioners and that they are acting unreasonably in seeking to have the company wound up instead of pursuing that other remedy.

126. Power to stay or restrain proceedings against company.

(1) At any time after the presentation of a winding-up petition, and before a winding-up order has been made, the company, or any creditor or contributory, may—

(a) where any action or proceeding against the company is pending in the High Court or Court of Appeal in England and Wales or Northern Ireland, apply to the court in which the action or proceeding is pending for a stay of proceedings therein, and

(b) where any other action or proceeding is pending against the company, apply to the court having jurisdiction to wind up the company to restrain further proceedings in the action or proceeding;
and the court to which application is so made may (as the case may be) stay, sist or restrain the proceedings accordingly on such terms as it thinks fit.

(2) In the case of a company registered under section 680 of the Companies Act (pre-1862 companies; companies formed under legislation other than the Companies Acts) or the previous corresponding legislation, where the application to stay, sist or restrain is by a creditor, this section extends to actions and proceedings against any contributory of the company.

127. Avoidance of property dispositions, etc.

In a winding up by the court, any disposition of the company's property, and any transfer of shares, or alteration in the status of the company's members, made after the commencement of the winding up is, unless the court otherwise orders, void.

128. Avoidance of attachments, etc.

(1) Where a company registered in England and Wales is being wound up by the court, any attachment, sequestration, distress or execution put in force against the estate or effects of the company after the commencement of the winding up is void.

(2)   This section, so far as relates to any estate or effects of the company situated in England and Wales, applies in the case of a company registered in Scotland as it applies in the case of a company registered in England and Wales.

Commencement of winding up

129.   Commencement of winding up by the court.

(1)   If, before the presentation of a petition for the winding up of a company by the court, a resolution has been passed by the company for voluntary winding up, the winding up of the company is deemed to have commenced at the time of the passing of the resolution; and unless the court, on proof of fraud or mistake, directs otherwise, all proceedings taken in the voluntary winding up are deemed to have been validly taken.

(2)   In any other case, the winding up of a company by the court is deemed to commence at the time of the presentation of the petition for winding up.

130.   Consequences of winding-up order.

(1)   On the making of a winding-up order, a copy of the order must forthwith be forwarded by the company (or otherwise as may be prescribed) to the registrar of companies, who shall enter it in his records relating to the company.

(2)   When a winding-up order has been made or a provisional liquidator has been appointed, no action or proceeding shall be proceeded with or commenced against the company or its property, except by leave of the court and subject to such terms as the court may impose.

(3)   When an order has been made for winding up a company registered under section 680 of the Companies Act, no action or proceeding shall be commenced or proceeded with against the company or its property or any contributory of the company, in respect of any debt of the company, except by leave of the court, and subject to such terms as the court may impose.

(4)   An order for winding up a company operates in favour of all the creditors and of all contributories of the company as if made on the joint petition of a creditor and of a contributory.

Investigation procedures

131.   Company's statement of affairs.

(1)   Where the court has made a winding-up order or appointed a provisional liquidator, the official receiver may require some or all of the persons mentioned in subsection (3) below to make out and submit to him a statement in the prescribed form as to the affairs of the company.

(2)   The statement shall be verified by affidavit by the persons required to submit it and shall show—

    (a)   particulars of the company's assets, debts and liabilities;

    (b)   the names and addresses of the company's creditors;

    (c)   the securities held by them respectively;

    (d)   the dates when the securities were respectively given; and

    (e)   such further or other information as may be prescribed or as the official receiver may require.

(3)   The persons referred to in subsection (1) are—

    (a)   those who are or have been officers of the company;

    (b)   those who have taken part in the formation of the company at any time within one year before the relevant date;

    (c)   those who are in the company's employment, or have been in its employment within that year, and are in the official receiver's opinion capable of giving the information required;

(d)   those who are or have been within that year officers of, or in the employment of, a company which is, or within that year was, an officer of the company.

(4)   Where any persons are required under this section to submit a statement of affairs to the official receiver, they shall do so (subject to the next subsection) before the end of the period of 21 days beginning with the day after that on which the prescribed notice of the requirement is given to them by the official receiver.

(5)   The official receiver, if he thinks fit, may—

(a)   at any time release a person from an obligation imposed on him under subsection (1) or (2) above; or

(b)   either when giving the notice mentioned in subsection (4) or subsequently, extend the period so mentioned;

and where the official receiver has refused to exercise a power conferred by this subsection, the court, if it thinks fit, may exercise it.

(6)   In this section—

'employment' includes employment under a contract for services; and

'the relevant date' means—

(a)   in a case where a provisional liquidator is appointed, the date of his appointment; and

(b)   in a case where no such appointment is made, the date of the winding-up order.

(7)   If a person without reasonable excuse fails to comply with any obligation imposed under this section, he is liable to a fine and, for continued contravention, to a daily default fine.

(8)   In the application of this section to Scotland references to the official receiver are to the liquidator or, in a case where a provisional liquidator is appointed, the provisional liquidator.

132.   Investigation by official receiver.

(1)   Where a winding-up order is made by the court in England and Wales, it is the duty of the official receiver to investigate—

(a)   if the company has failed, the causes of the failure; and

(b)   generally, the promotion, formation, business, dealings and affairs of the company,

and to make such report (if any) to the court as he thinks fit.

(2)   The report is, in any proceedings, prima facie evidence of the facts stated in it.

133.   Public examination of officers.

(1)   Where a company is being wound up by the court, the official receiver or, in Scotland, the liquidator may at any time before the dissolution of the company apply to the court for the public examination of any person who—

(a)   is or has been an officer of the company; or

(b)   has acted as liquidator or administrator of the company or as receiver or manager or, in Scotland, receiver of its property; or

(c)   not being a person falling within paragraph (a) or (b), is or has been concerned, or has taken part, in the promotion, formation or management of the company.

(2)   Unless the court otherwise orders, the official receiver or, in Scotland, the liquidator shall make an application under subsection (1) if he is requested in accordance with the rules to do so by—

(a)   one-half, in value, of the company's creditors; or

(b)   three-quarters, in value, of the company's contributories.

(3)   On an application under subsection (1), the court shall direct that a public examination of the person to whom the application relates shall be held on a day appointed by the court; and that person shall attend on that day and be publicly

examined as to the promotion, formation or management of the company or as to the conduct of its business and affairs, or his conduct or dealings in relation to the company.

(4)   The following may take part in the public examination of a person under this section and may question that person concerning the matters mentioned in subsection (3), namely—

(a)   the official receiver;

(b)   the liquidator of the company;

(c)   any person who has been appointed as special manager of the company's property or business;

(d)   any creditor of the company who has tendered a proof or, in Scotland, submitted a claim in the winding up;

(e)   any contributory of the company.

134.   Enforcement of s. 133.

(1)   If a person without reasonable excuse fails at any time to attend his public examination under section 133, he is guilty of a contempt of court and liable to be punished accordingly.

(2)   In a case where a person without reasonable excuse fails at any time to attend his examination under section 133 or there are reasonable grounds for believing that a person has absconded, or is about to abscond, with a view to avoiding or delaying his examination under that section, the court may cause a warrant to be issued to a constable or prescribed officer of the court—

(a)   for the arrest of that person; and

(b)   for the seizure of any books, papers, records, money or goods in that person's possession.

(3)   In such a case the court may authorise the person arrested under the warrant to be kept in custody, and anything seized under such a warrant to be held, in accordance with the rules, until such time as the court may order.

Appointment of liquidator

135.   Appointment and powers of provisional liquidator.

(1)   Subject to the provisions of this section, the court may, at any time after the presentation of a winding-up petition, appoint a liquidator provisionally.

(2)   In England and Wales, the appointment of a provisional liquidator may be made at any time before the making of a winding-up order; and either the official receiver or any other fit person may be appointed.

(3)   In Scotland, such an appointment may be made at any time before the first appointment of liquidators.

(4)   The provisional liquidator shall carry out such functions as the court may confer on him.

(5)   When a liquidator is provisionally appointed by the court, his powers may be limited by the order appointing him.

136.   Functions of official receiver in relation to office of liquidator.

(1)   The following provisions of this section have effect, subject to section 140 below, on a winding-up order being made by the court in England and Wales.

(2)   The official receiver, by virtue of his office, becomes the liquidator of the company and continues in office until another person becomes liquidator under the provisions of this Part.

(3)   The official receiver is, by virtue of his office, the liquidator during any vacancy.

(4)   At any time when he is the liquidator of the company, the official receiver may summon separate meetings of the company's creditors and contributories for the purpose of choosing a person to be liquidator of the company in place of the official receiver.

(5)   It is the duty of the official receiver—

(a)   as soon as practicable in the period of 12 weeks beginning with the day on which the winding-up order was made, to decide whether to exercise his power under subsection (4) to summon meetings, and

(b)   if in pursuance of paragraph (a) he decides not to exercise that power, to give notice of his decision, before the end of that period, to the court and to the company's creditors and contributories, and

(c)   (whether or not he has decided to exercise that power) to exercise his power to summon meetings under subsection (4) if he is at any time requested, in accordance with the rules, to do so by one-quarter, in value, of the company's creditors;

and accordingly, where the duty imposed by paragraph (c) arises before the official receiver has performed a duty imposed by paragraph (a) or (b), he is not required to perform the latter duty.

(6)   A notice given under subsection (5)(b) to the company's creditors shall contain an explanation of the creditors' power under subsection (5)(c) to require the official receiver to summon meetings of the company's creditors and contributories.

137.   Appointment by Secretary of State.

(1)   In a winding up by the court in England and Wales the official receiver may, at any time when he is the liquidator of the company, apply to the Secretary of State for the appointment of a person as liquidator in his place.

(2)   If meetings are held in pursuance of a decision under section 136(5)(a), but no person is chosen to be liquidator as a result of those meetings, it is the duty of the official receiver to decide whether to refer the need for an appointment to the Secretary of State.

(3)   On an application under subsection (1), or a reference made in pursuance of a decision under subsection (2), the Secretary of State shall either make an appointment or decline to make one.

(4)   Where a liquidator has been appointed by the Secretary of State under subsection (3), the liquidator shall give notice of his appointment to the company's creditors or, if the court so allows, shall advertise his appointment in accordance with the directions of the court.

(5)   In that notice or advertisement the liquidator shall—

(a)   state whether he proposes to summon a general meeting of the company's creditors under section 141 below for the purpose of determining (together with any meeting of contributories) whether a liquidation committee should be established under that section, and

(b)   if he does not propose to summon such a meeting, set out the power of the company's creditors under that section to require him to summon one.

139.   Choice of liquidator at meetings of creditors and contributories.

(1)   This section applies where a company is being wound up by the court and separate meetings of the company's creditors and contributories are summoned for the purpose of choosing a person to be liquidator of the company.

(2)   The creditors and the contributories at their respective meetings may nominate a person to be liquidator.

(3)   The liquidator shall be the person nominated by the creditors or, where no person has been so nominated, the person (if any) nominated by the contributories.

(4)   In the case of different persons being nominated, any contributory or creditor may, within 7 days after the date on which the nomination was made by the creditors, apply to the court for an order either—

(a)   appointing the person nominated as liquidator by the contributories to be a liquidator instead of, or jointly with, the person nominated by the creditors; or

(b)   appointing some other person to be liquidator instead of the person nominated by the creditors.

140. Appointment by the court following administration or voluntary arrangement.

(1) Where a winding-up order is made immediately upon the discharge of an administration order, the court may appoint as liquidator of the company the person who has ceased on the discharge of the administration order to be the administrator of the company.

(2) Where a winding-up order is made at a time when there is a supervisor of a voluntary arrangement approved in relation to the company under Part I, the court may appoint as liquidator of the company the person who is the supervisor at the time when the winding-up order is made.

(3) Where the court makes an appointment under this section, the official receiver does not become the liquidator as otherwise provided by section 136(2), and he has no duty under section 136(5)(a) or (b) in respect of the summoning of creditors' or contributories' meetings.

Liquidation committees

141. Liquidation committee (England and Wales).

(1) Where a winding-up order has been made by the court in England and Wales and separate meetings of creditors and contributories have been summoned for the purpose of choosing a person to be liquidator, those meetings may establish a committee ('the liquidation committee') to exercise the functions conferred on it by or under this Act.

(2) The liquidator (not being the official receiver) may at any time, if he thinks fit, summon separate general meetings of the company's creditors and contributories for the purpose of determining whether such a committee should be established and, if it is so determined, of establishing it.

The liquidator (not being the official receiver) shall summon such a meeting if he is requested, in accordance with the rules, to do so by one-tenth, in value, of the company's creditors.

(3) Where meetings are summoned under this section, or for the purpose of choosing a person to be liquidator, and either the meeting of creditors or the meeting of contributories decides that a liquidation committee should be established, but the other meeting does not so decide or decides that a committee should not be established, the committee shall be established in accordance with the rules, unless the court otherwise orders.

(4) The liquidation committee is not to be able or required to carry out its functions at any time when the official receiver is liquidator; but at any such time its functions are vested in the Secretary of State except to the extent that the rules otherwise provide.

(5) Where there is for the time being no liquidation committee, and the liquidator is a person other than the official receiver, the functions of such a committee are vested in the Secretary of State except to the extent that the rules otherwise provide.

The liquidator's functions

143. General functions in winding up by the court.

(1) The functions of the liquidator of a company which is being wound up by the court are to secure that the assets of the company are got in, realised and distributed to the company's creditors and, if there is a surplus, to the persons entitled to it.

(2) It is the duty of the liquidator of a company which is being wound up by the court in England and Wales, if he is not the official receiver—

    (a) to furnish the official receiver with such information,

    (b) to produce to the official receiver, and permit inspection by the official receiver of, such books, papers and other records, and

(c)   to give the official receiver such other assistance,
as the official receiver may reasonably require for the purposes of carrying out his functions in relation to the winding up.

144.   Custody of company's property.

(1)   When a winding-up order has been made, or where a provisional liquidator has been appointed, the liquidator or the provisional liquidator (as the case may be) shall take into his custody or under his control all the property and things in action to which the company is or appears to be entitled.

(2)   In a winding up by the court in Scotland, if and so long as there is no liquidator, all the property of the company is deemed to be in the custody of the court.

145.   Vesting of company property in liquidator.

(1)   When a company is being wound up by the court, the court may on the application of the liquidator by order direct that all or any part of the property of whatsoever description belonging to the company or held by trustees on its behalf shall vest in the liquidator by his official name; and thereupon the property to which the order relates vests accordingly.

(2)   The liquidator may, after giving such indemnity (if any) as the court may direct, bring or defend in his official name any action or other legal proceeding which relates to that property or which it is necessary to bring or defend for the purpose of effectually winding up the company and recovering its property.

146.   Duty to summon final meeting.

(1)   Subject to the next subsection, if it appears to the liquidator of a company which is being wound by the court that the winding up of the company is for practical purposes complete and the liquidator is not the official receiver, the liquidator shall summon a final general meeting of the company's creditors which—

(a)   shall receive the liquidator's report of the winding up, and

(b)   shall determine whether the liquidator should have his release under section 174 in Chapter VII of this Part.

(2)   The liquidator may, if he thinks fit, give the notice summoning the final general meeting at the same time as giving notice of any final distribution of the company's property but, if summoned for an earlier date, that meeting shall be adjourned (and, if necessary, further adjourned) until a date on which the liquidator is able to report to the meeting that the winding up of the company is for practical purposes complete.

(3)   In the carrying out of his functions in the winding up it is the duty of the liquidator to retain sufficient sums from the company's property to cover the expenses of summoning and holding the meeting required by this section.

General powers of court

147.   Power to stay or sist winding up.

(1)   The court may at any time after an order for winding up, on the application either of the liquidator or the official receiver or any creditor or contributory, and on proof to the satisfaction of the court that all proceedings in the winding up ought to be stayed or sisted, make an order staying or sisting the proceedings, either altogether or for a limited time, on such terms and conditions as the court thinks fit.

(2)   The court may, before making an order, require the official receiver to furnish to it a report with respect to any facts or matters which are in his opinion relevant to the application.

(3)   A copy of every order made under this section shall forthwith be forwarded by the company, or otherwise as may be prescribed, to the registrar of companies, who shall enter it in his records relating to the company.

148.   Settlement of list of contributories and application of assets.

(1)   As soon as may be after making a winding-up order, the court shall settle a list of contributories, with power to rectify the register of members in all cases where rectification is required in pursuance of the Companies Act or this Act, and shall cause the company's assets to be collected, and applied in discharge of its liabilities.

(2)   If it appears to the court that it will not be necessary to make calls on or adjust the rights of contributories, the court may dispense with the settlement of a list of contributories.

(3)   In settling the list, the court shall distinguish between persons who are contributories in their own right and persons who are contributories as being representatives of or liable for the debts of others.

149.   Debts due from contributory to company.

(1)   The court may, at any time after making a winding-up order, make an order on any contributory for the time being on the list of contributories to pay, in manner directed by the order, any money due from him (or from the estate of the person who he represents) to the company, exclusive of any money payable by him or the estate by virtue of any call in pursuance of the Companies Act or this Act.

(2)   The court in making such an order may—

(a)   in the case of an unlimited company, allow to the contributory by way of set-off any money due to him or the estate which he represents from the company on any independent dealing or contract with the company, but not any money due to him as a member of the company in respect of any dividend or profit, and

(b)   in the case of a limited company, make to any director or manager whose liability is unlimited or to his estate the like allowance.

(3)   In the case of any company, whether limited or unlimited, when all the creditors are paid in full (together with interest at the official rate), any money due on any account whatever to a contributory from the company may be allowed to him by way of set-off against any subsequent call.

150.   Power to make calls.

(1)   The court may, at any time after making a winding-up order, and either before or after it has ascertained the sufficiency of the company's assets, make calls on all or any of the contributories for the time being settled on the list of the contributories to the extent of their liability, for payment of any money which the court considers necessary to satisfy the company's debts and liabilities, and the expenses of winding up, and for the adjustment of the rights of the contributories among themselves, and make an order for payment of any calls so made.

(2)   In making a call the court may take into consideration the probability that some of the contributories may partly or wholly fail to pay it.

151.   Payment into bank of money due to company.

(1)   The court may order any contributory, purchaser or other person from whom money is due to the company to pay the amount due into the Bank of England (or any branch of it) to the account of the liquidator instead of to the liquidator, and such an order may be enforced in the same manner as if it had directed payment to the liquidator.

(2)   All money and securities paid or delivered into the Bank of England (or branch) in the event of a winding up by the court are subject in all respects to the orders of the court.

152.   Order on contributory to be conclusive evidence.

(1)   An order made by the court on a contributory is conclusive evidence that the money (if any) thereby appearing to be due or ordered to be paid is due, but subject to any right of appeal.

(2) All other pertinent matters stated in the order are to be taken as truly stated as against all persons and in all proceedings except proceedings in Scotland against the heritable estate of a deceased contributory; and in that case the order is only prima facie evidence for the purpose of charging his heritable estate, unless his heirs or legatees of heritage were on the list of contributories at the time of the order being made.

153. Power to exclude creditors not proving in time.

The court may fix a time or times within which creditors are to prove their debts or claims or to be excluded from the benefit of any distribution made before those debts are proved.

154. Adjustment of rights of contributories.

The court shall adjust the rights of the contributories among themselves and distribute any surplus among the persons entitled to it.

155. Inspection of books by creditors, etc.

(1) The court may, at any time after making a winding-up order, make such order for inspection of the company's books and papers by creditors and contributories as the court thinks just; and any books and papers in the company's possession may be inspected by creditors and contributories accordingly, but not further or otherwise.

(2) Nothing in this section excludes or restricts any statutory rights of a government department or person acting under the authority of a government department.

156. Payment of expenses of winding up.

The court may, in the event of the assets being insufficient to satisfy the liabilities, make an order as to the payment out of the assets of the expenses incurred in the winding up in such order of priority as the court thinks just.

158. Power to arrest absconding contributory.

The court, at any time either before or after making a winding-up order, on proof of probable cause for believing that a contributory is about to quit the United Kingdom or otherwise to abscond or to remove or conceal any of his property for the purpose of evading payment of calls, may cause the contributory to be arrested and his books and papers and movable personal property to be seized and him and them to be kept safely until such time as the court may order.

159. Powers of court to be cumulative.

Powers conferred by this Act and the Companies Act on the court are in addition to, and not in restriction of, any existing powers of instituting proceedings against a contributory or debtor of the company, or the estate of any contributory or debtor, for the recovery of any call or other sums.

160. Delegation of powers to liquidator (England and Wales).

(1) Provision may be made by rules for enabling or requiring all or any of the powers and duties conferred and imposed on the court in England and Wales by the Companies Act and this Act in respect of the following matters—

(a) the holding and conducting of meetings to ascertain the wishes of creditors and contributories,

(b) the settling of lists of contributories and the rectifying of the register of members where required, and the collection and application of the assets,

(c) the payment, delivery, conveyance, surrender or transfer of money, property, books or papers to the liquidator,

(d) the making of calls,

(e) the fixing of a time within which debts and claims must be proved,

to be exercised or performed by the liquidator as an officer of the court, and subject to the court's control.

(2)   But the liquidator shall not, without the special leave of the court, rectify the register of members, and shall not make any call without either that special leave or the sanction of the liquidation committee.

CHAPTER VII
LIQUIDATORS

Preliminary

163.   Style and title of liquidators.
The liquidator of a company shall be described—
  (a)   where a person other than the official receiver is liquidator, by the style of 'the liquidator' of the particular company, or
  (b)   where the official receiver is liquidator, by the style of 'the official receiver and liquidator' of the particular company;
and in neither case shall he be described by an individual name.

164.   Corrupt inducement affecting appointment.
A person who gives, or agrees or offers to give, to any member or creditor of a company any valuable consideration with a view to securing his own appointment or nomination, or to securing or preventing the appointment or nomination of some person other than himself, as the company's liquidator is liable to a fine.

Liquidator's powers and duties

165.   Voluntary winding up.
  (1)   This section has effect where a company is being wound up voluntarily, but subject to section 166 below in the case of a creditors' voluntary winding up.
  (2)   The liquidator may—
  (a)   in the case of a members' voluntary winding up, with the sanction of an extraordinary resolution of the company, and
  (b)   in the case of a creditors' voluntary winding up, with the sanction of the court or the liquidation committee (or, if there is no such committee, a meeting of the company's creditors),
exercise any of the powers specified in Part I of Schedule 4 to this Act (payment of debts, compromise of claims, etc.).
  (3)   The liquidator may, without sanction, exercise either of the powers specified in Part II of the Schedule (institution and defence of proceedings; carrying on the business of the company) and any of the general powers specified in Part III of that Schedule.
  (4)   The liquidator may—
  (a)   exercise the court's power of settling a list of contributories (which list is prima facie evidence of the liability of the persons named in it to be contributories),
  (b)   exercise the court's power of making calls,
  (c)   summon general meetings of the company for the purpose of obtaining its sanction by special or extraordinary resolution or for any other purpose he may think fit.
  (5)   The liquidator shall pay the company's debts and adjust the rights of the contributories among themselves.
  (6)   Where the liquidator in exercise of the powers conferred on him by this Act disposes of any property of the company to a person who is connected with the company (within the meaning of section 249 in Part VII), he shall, if there is for the time being a liquidation committee, give notice to the committee of that exercise of his powers.

166.   Creditors' voluntary winding up.
  (1)   This section applies where, in the case of a creditors' voluntary winding up, a liquidator has been nominated by the company.

(2) The powers conferred on the liquidator by section 165 shall not be exercised, except with the sanction of the court, during the period before the holding of the creditors' meeting under section 98 in Chapter IV.

(3) Subsection (2) does not apply in relation to the power of the liquidator—

(a) to take into his custody or under his control all the property to which the company is or appears to be entitled;

(b) to dispose of perishable goods and other goods the value of which is likely to diminish if they are not immediately disposed of; and

(c) to do all such other things as may be necessary for the protection of the company's assets.

(4) The liquidator shall attend the creditors' meeting held under section 98 and shall report to the meeting on any exercise by him of his powers (whether or not under this section or under section 112 or 165).

(5) If default is made—

(a) by the company in complying with subsection (1) or (2) of section 98, or

(b) by the directors in complying with subsection (1) or (2) of section 99,

the liquidator shall, within 7 days of the relevant day, apply to the court for directions as to the manner in which that default is to be remedied.

(6) 'The relevant day' means the day on which the liquidator was nominated by the company or the day on which he first became aware of the default, whichever is the later.

(7) If the liquidator without reasonable excuse fails to comply with this section, he is liable to a fine.

167. Winding up by the court.

(1) Where a company is being wound up by the court, the liquidator may—

(a) with the sanction of the court or the liquidation committee, exercise any of the powers specified in Parts I and II of Schedule 4 to this Act (payment of debts; compromise of claims, etc.; institution and defence of proceedings; carrying on of the business of the company), and

(b) with or without that sanction, exercise any of the general powers specified in Part III of that Schedule.

(2) Where the liquidator (not being the official receiver), in exercise of the powers conferred on him by this Act—

(a) disposes of any property of the company to a person who is connected with the company (within the meaning of section 249 in Part VII), or

(b) employs a solicitor to assist him in the carrying out of his functions,

he shall, if there is for the time being a liquidation committee, give notice to the committee of that exercise of his powers.

(3) The exercise by the liquidator in a winding up by the court of the powers conferred by this section is subject to the control of the court, and any creditor or contributory may apply to the court with respect to any exercise or proposed exercise of any of those powers.

168. Supplementary powers (England and Wales).

(1) This section applies in the case of a company which is being wound up by the court in England and Wales.

(2) The liquidator may summon general meetings of the creditors or contributories for the purpose of ascertaining their wishes; and it is his duty to summon meetings at such times as the creditors or contributories by resolution (either at the meeting appointing the liquidator or otherwise) may direct, or whenever requested in writing to do so by one-tenth in value of the creditors or contributories (as the case may be).

(3) The liquidator may apply to the court (in the prescribed manner) for directions in relation to any particular matter arising in the winding up.

(4) Subject to the provisions of this Act, the liquidator shall use his own discretion in the management of the assets and their distribution among the creditors.

(5) If any person is aggrieved by an act or decision of the liquidator, that person may apply to the court; and the court may confirm, reverse or modify the act or decision complained of, and make such order in the case as it thinks just.

. . .

170. Enforcement of liquidator's duty to make returns, etc.

(1) If a liquidator who has made any default—

    (a) in filing, delivering or making any return, account or other document, or

    (b) in giving any notice which he is by law required to file, deliver, make or give,

fails to make good the default within 14 days after the service on him of a notice requiring him to do so, the court has the following powers.

(2) On an application made by any creditor or contributory of the company, or by the registrar of companies, the court may make an order directing the liquidator to make good the default within such time as may be specified in the order.

(3) The court's order may provide that all costs of and incidental to the application shall be borne by the liquidator.

(4) Nothing in this section prejudices the operation of any enactment imposing penalties on a liquidator in respect of any such default as is mentioned above.

Removal; vacation of office

171. Removal, etc. (voluntary winding up).

(1) This section applies with respect to the removal from office and vacation of office of the liquidator of a company which is being wound up voluntarily.

(2) Subject to the next subsection, the liquidator may be removed from office only by an order of the court or—

    (a) in the case of a members' voluntary winding up, by a general meeting of the company summoned specially for that purpose, or

    (b) in the case of a creditors' voluntary winding up, by a general meeting of the company's creditors summoned specially for that purpose in accordance with the rules.

(3) Where the liquidator was appointed by the court under section 108 in Chapter V, a meeting such as is mentioned in subsection (2) above shall be summoned for the purpose of replacing him only if he thinks fit or the court so directs or the meeting is requested, in accordance with the rules—

    (a) in the case of a members' voluntary winding up, by members representing not less than one-half of the total voting rights of all the members having at the date of the request a right to vote at the meeting, or

    (b) in the case of a creditors' voluntary winding up, by not less than one-half, in value, of the company's creditors.

(4) A liquidator shall vacate office if he ceases to be a person who is qualified to act as an insolvency practitioner in relation to the company.

(5) A liquidator may, in the prescribed circumstances, resign his office by giving notice of his resignation to the registrar of companies.

(6) Where—

    (a) in the case of a members' voluntary winding up, a final meeting of the company has been held under section 94 in Chapter III, or

    (b) in the case of a creditors' voluntary winding up, final meetings of the company and of the creditors have been held under section 106 in Chapter IV,

the liquidator whose report was considered at the meeting or meetings shall vacate office as soon as he has complied with subsection (3) of that section and has given notice to the registrar of companies that the meeting or meetings have been held and of the decisions (if any) of the meeting or meetings.

172. Removal, etc. (winding up by the court).

(1) This section applies with respect to the removal from office and vacation of office of the liquidator of a company which is being wound up by the court, or of a provisional liquidator.

(2) Subject as follows, the liquidator may be removed from office only by an order of the court or by a general meeting of the company's creditors summoned specially for that purpose in accordance with the rules; and a provisional liquidator may be removed from office only by an order of the court.

(3) Where—

(a) the official receiver is liquidator otherwise than in succession under section 136(3) to a person who held office as a result of a nomination by a meeting of the company's creditors or contributories, or

(b) the liquidator was appointed by the court otherwise than under section 139(4)(a) or 140(1), or was appointed by the Secretary of State,

a general meeting of the company's creditors shall be summoned for the purpose of replacing him only if he thinks fit, or the court so directs, or the meeting is requested, in accordance with the rules, by not less than one-quarter, in value, of the creditors.

(4) If appointed by the Secretary of State, the liquidator may be removed from office by a direction of the Secretary of State.

(5) A liquidator or provisional liquidator, not being the official receiver, shall vacate office if he ceases to be a person who is qualified to act as an insolvency practitioner in relation to the company.

(6) A liquidator may, in the prescribed circumstances, resign his office by giving notice of his resignation to the court.

(7) Where an order is made under section 204 (early dissolution in Scotland) for the dissolution of the company, the liquidator shall vacate office when the dissolution of the company takes effect in accordance with that section.

(8) Where a final meeting has been held under section 146 (liquidator's report on completion of winding up), the liquidator whose report was considered at the meeting shall vacate office as soon as he has given notice to the court and the registrar of companies that the meeting has been held and of the decisions (if any) of the meeting.

Release of liquidator

173. Release (voluntary winding up).

(1) This section applies with respect to the release of the liquidator of a company which is being wound up voluntarily.

(2) A person who has ceased to be a liquidator shall have his release with effect from the following time, that is to say—

(a) in the case of a person who has been removed from office by a general meeting of the company or by a general meeting of the company's creditors that has not resolved against his release or who has died, the time at which notice is given to the registrar of companies in accordance with the rules that that person has ceased to hold office;

(b) in the case of a person who has been removed from office by a general meeting of the company's creditors that has resolved against his release, or by the court, or who has vacated office under section 171(4) above, such time as the Secretary of State may, on the application of that person, determine;

(c) in the case of a person who has resigned, such time as may be prescribed;

(d) in the case of a person who has vacated office under subsection (6)(a) of section 171, the time at which he vacated office;

(e) in the case of a person who has vacated office under subsection (6)(b) of that section—

(i)   if the final meeting of the creditors referred to in that subsection has resolved against that person's release, such time as the Secretary of State may, on an application by that person, determine, and

(ii)   if that meeting has not resolved against that person's release, the time at which he vacated office.

(3)   In the application of subsection (2) to the winding up of a company registered in Scotland, the references to a determination by the Secretary of State as to the time from which a person who has ceased to be liquidator shall have his release are to be read as references to such a determination by the Accountant of Court.

(4)   Where a liquidator has his release under subsection (2), he is, with effect from the time specified in that subsection, discharged from all liability both in respect of acts or omissions of his in the winding up and otherwise in relation to his conduct as liquidator.

But nothing in this section prevents the exercise, in relation to a person who has had his release under subsection (2), of the court's powers under section 212 of this Act (summary remedy against delinquent directors, liquidators, etc.).

174.   Release (winding up by the court).

(1)   This section applies with respect to the release of the liquidator of a company which is being wound up by the court, or of a provisional liquidator.

(2)   Where the official receiver has ceased to be liquidator and a person becomes liquidator in his stead, the official receiver has his release with effect from the following time, that is to say—

(a)   in a case where that person was nominated by a general meeting of creditors or contributories, or was appointed by the Secretary of State, the time at which the official receiver gives notice to the court that he has been replaced;

(b)   in a case where that person is appointed by the court, such time as the court may determine.

(3)   If the official receiver while he is a liquidator gives notice to the Secretary of State that the winding up is for practical purposes complete, he has his release with effect from such time as the Secretary of State may determine.

(4)   A person other than the official receiver who has ceased to be a liquidator has his release with effect from the following time, that is to say—

(a)   in the case of a person who has been removed from office by a general meeting of creditors that has not resolved against his release or who has died, the time at which notice is given to the court in accordance with the rules that that person has ceased to hold office;

(b)   in the case of a person who has been removed from office by a general meeting of creditors that has resolved against his release, or by the court or the Secretary of State, or who has vacated office under section 172(5) or (7), such time as the Secretary of State may, on an application by that person, determine;

(c)   in the case of a person who has resigned, such time as may be prescribed;

(d)   in the case of a person who has vacated office under section 172(8)—

(i)   if the final meeting referred to in that subsection has resolved against that person's release, such time as the Secretary of State may, on an application by that person, determine, and

(ii)   if that meeting has not so resolved, the time at which that person vacated office.

(5)   A person who has ceased to hold office as a provisional liquidator has his release with effect from such time as the court may, on an application by him, determine.

(6)   Where the official receiver or a liquidator or provisional liquidator has his release under this section, he is, with effect from the time specified in the preceding provisions of this section, discharged from all liability both in respect of acts or omissions of his in

the winding up and otherwise in relation to his conduct as liquidator or provisional liquidator.

But nothing in this section prevents the exercise, in relation to a person who has had his release under this section, of the court's powers under section 212 (summary remedy against delinquent directors, liquidators, etc.).

(7)   In the application of this section to a case where the order for winding up has been made by the court in Scotland, the references to a determination by the Secretary of State as to the time from which a person who has ceased to be liquidator has his release are to such a determination by the Accountant of Court.

CHAPTER VIII
PROVISIONS OF GENERAL APPLICATION IN WINDING UP

Preferential debts

175.   Preferential debts (general provision).

(1)   In a winding up the company's preferential debts (within the meaning given by section 386 in Part XII) shall be paid in priority to all other debts.

(2)   Preferential debts—

(a)   rank equally among themselves after the expenses of the winding up and shall be paid in full, unless the assets are insufficient to meet them, in which case they abate in equal proportions; and

(b)   so far as the assets of the company available for payment of general creditors are insufficient to meet them, have priority over the claims of holders of debentures secured by, or holders of, any floating charge created by the company, and shall be paid accordingly out of any property comprised in or subject to that charge.

176.   Preferential charge on goods distrained.

(1)   This section applies where a company is being wound up by the court in England and Wales, and is without prejudice to section 128 (avoidance of attachments, etc.).

(2)   Where any person (whether or not a landlord or person entitled to rent) has distrained upon the goods or effects of the company in the period of 3 months ending with the date of the winding-up order, those goods or effects, or the proceeds of their sale, shall be charged for the benefit of the company with the preferential debts of the company to the extent that the company's property is for the time being insufficient for meeting them.

(3)   Where by virtue of a charge under subsection (2) any person surrenders any goods or effects to a company or makes a payment to a company, that person ranks, in respect of the amount of the proceeds of sale of those goods or effects by the liquidator or (as the case may be) the amount of the payment, as a preferential creditor of the company, except as against so much of the company's property as is available for the payment of preferential creditors by virtue of the surrender or payment.

Special managers

177.   Power to appoint special manager.

(1)   Where a company has gone into liquidation or a provisional liquidator has been appointed, the court may, on an application under this section, appoint any person to be the special manager of the business or property of the company.

(2)   The application may be made by the liquidator or provisional liquidator in any case where it appears to him that the nature of the business or property of the company, or the interests of the company's creditors or contributories or members generally, require the appointment of another person to manage the company's business or property.

(3)   The special manager has such powers as may be entrusted to him by the court.

(4) The court's power to entrust powers to the special manager includes power to direct that any provision of this Act that has effect in relation to the provisional liquidator or liquidator of a company shall have the like effect in relation to the special manager for the purposes of the carrying out by him of any of the functions of the provisional liquidator or liquidator.

(5) The special manager shall—

    (a) give such security or, in Scotland, caution as may be prescribed;

    (b) prepare and keep such accounts as may be prescribed; and

    (c) produce those accounts in accordance with the rules to the Secretary of State or to such other persons as may be prescribed.

Disclaimer (England and Wales only)

178. Power to disclaim onerous property.

(1) This and the next two sections apply to a company that is being wound up in England and Wales.

(2) Subject as follows, the liquidator may, by the giving of the prescribed notice, disclaim any onerous property and may do so notwithstanding that he has taken possession of it, endeavoured to sell it, or otherwise exercised rights of ownership in relation to it.

(3) The following is onerous property for the purposes of this section—

    (a) any unprofitable contract, and

    (b) any other property of the company which is unsaleable or not readily saleable or is such that it may give rise to a liability to pay money or perform any other onerous act.

(4) A disclaimer under this section—

    (a) operates so as to determine, as from the date of the disclaimer, the rights, interests and liabilities of the company in or in respect of the property disclaimed; but

    (b) does not, except so far as is necessary for the purpose of releasing the company from any liability, affect the rights or liabilities of any other person.

(5) A notice of disclaimer shall not be given under this section in respect of any property if—

    (a) a person interested in the property has applied in writing to the liquidator or one of his predecessors as liquidator requiring the liquidator or that predecessor to decide whether he will disclaim or not, and

    (b) the period of 28 days beginning with the day on which that application was made, or such longer period as the court may allow, has expired without a notice of disclaimer having been given under this section in respect of that property.

(6) Any person sustaining loss or damage in consequence of the operation of a disclaimer under this section is deemed a creditor of the company to the extent of the loss or damage and accordingly may prove for the loss or damage in the winding up.

179. Disclaimer of leaseholds.

(1) The disclaimer under section 178 of any property of a leasehold nature does not take effect unless a copy of the disclaimer has been served (so far as the liquidator is aware of their addresses) on every person claiming under the company as underlessee or mortgagee and either—

    (a) no application under section 181 below is made with respect to that property before the end of the period of 14 days beginning with the day on which the last notice served under this subsection was served; or

    (b) where such an application has been made, the court directs that the disclaimer shall take effect.

(2) Where the court gives a direction under subsection (1)(b) it may also, instead of or in addition to any order it makes under section 181, make such orders with respect

to fixtures, tenant's improvements and other matters arising out of the lease as it thinks fit.

180. Land subject to rentcharge.

(1)   The following applies where, in consequence of the disclaimer under section 178 of any land subject to a rentcharge, that land vests by operation of law in the Crown or any other person (referred to in the next subsection as 'the proprietor').

(2)   The proprietor and the successors in title of the proprietor are not subject to any personal liability in respect of any sums becoming due under the rentcharge except sums becoming due after the proprietor, or some person claiming under or through the proprietor, has taken possession or control of the land or has entered into occupation of it.

181. Powers of court (general).

(1)   This section and the next apply where the liquidator has disclaimed property under section 178.

(2)   An application under this section may be made to the court by—
    (a)   any person who claims an interest in the disclaimed property, or
    (b)   any person who is under any liability in respect of the disclaimed property, not being a liability discharged by the disclaimer.

(3)   Subject as follows, the court may on the application make an order, on such terms as it thinks fit, for the vesting of the disclaimed property in, or for its delivery to—
    (a)   a person entitled to it or a trustee for such a person, or
    (b)   a person subject to such a liability as is mentioned in subsection (2)(b) or a trustee for such a person.

(4)   The court shall not make an order under subsection (3)(b) except where it appears to the court that it would be just to do so for the purpose of compensating the person subject to the liability in respect of the disclaimer.

(5)   The effect of any order under this section shall be taken into account in assessing for the purpose of section 178(6) the extent of any loss or damage sustained by any person in consequence of the disclaimer.

(6)   An order under this section vesting property in any person need not be completed by conveyance, assignment or transfer.

182. Powers of court (leaseholds).

(1)   The court shall not make an order under section 181 vesting property of a leasehold nature in any person claiming under the company as underlessee or mortgagee except on terms making that person—
    (a)   subject to the same liabilities and obligations as the company was subject to under the lease at the commencement of the winding up, or
    (b)   if the court thinks fit, subject to the same liabilities and obligations as that person would be subject to if the lease had been assigned to him at the commencement of the winding up.

(2)   For the purposes of an order under section 181 relating to only part of any property comprised in a lease, the requirements of subsection (1) apply as if the lease comprised only the property to which the order relates.

(3)   Where subsection (1) applies and no person claiming under the company as underlessee or mortgagee is willing to accept an order under section 181 on the terms required by virtue of that subsection, the court may, by order under that section, vest the company's estate or interest in the property in any person who is liable (whether personally or in a representative capacity, and whether alone or jointly with the company) to perform the lessee's covenants in the lease.

The court may vest that estate and interest in such a person freed and discharged from all estates, encumbrances and interests created by the company.

(4)   Where subsection (1) applies and a person claiming under the company as underlessee or mortgagee declines to accept an order under section 181, that person is excluded from all interest in the property.

Execution, attachment and the Scottish equivalents

183.   Effect of execution or attachment (England and Wales).

(1)   Where a creditor has issued execution against the goods or land of a company or has attached any debt due to it, and the company is subsequently wound up, he is not entitled to retain the benefit of the execution or attachment against the liquidator unless he has completed the execution or attachment before the commencement of the winding up.

(2)   However—

(a)   if a creditor has had notice of a meeting having been called at which a resolution for voluntary winding up is to be proposed, the date on which he had notice is substituted, for the purpose of subsection (1), for the date of commencement of the winding up;

(b)   a person who purchases in good faith under a sale by the sheriff any goods of a company on which execution has been levied in all cases acquires a good title to them against the liquidator; and

(c)   the rights conferred by subsection (1) on the liquidator may be set aside by the court in favour of the creditor to such extent and subject to such terms as the court thinks fit.

(3)   For purposes of this Act—

(a)   an execution against goods is completed by seizure and sale, or by the making of a charging order under section 1 of the Charging Orders Act 1979;

(b)   an attachment of a debt is completed by receipt of the debt; and

(c)   an execution against land is completed by seizure, by the appointment of a receiver, or by the making of a charging order under section 1 of the Act above-mentioned.

(4)   In this section, 'goods' includes all chattels personal; and 'the sheriff' includes any officer charged with the execution of a writ or other process.

(5)   This section does not apply in the case of a winding up in Scotland.

184.   Duties of sheriff (England and Wales).

(1)   The following applies where a company's goods are taken in execution and, before their sale or the completion of the execution (by the receipt or recovery of the full amount of the levy), notice is served on the sheriff that a provisional liquidator has been appointed or that a winding-up order has been made, or that a resolution for voluntary winding up has been passed.

(2)   The sheriff shall, on being so required, deliver the goods and any money seized or received in part satisfaction of the execution to the liquidator; but the costs of execution are a first charge on the goods or money so delivered, and the liquidator may sell the goods, or a sufficient part of them, for the purpose of satisfying the charge.

(3)   If under an execution in respect of a judgment for a sum exceeding £500 a company's goods are sold or money is paid in order to avoid sale, the sheriff shall deduct the costs of the execution from the proceeds of sale or the money paid and retain the balance for 14 days.

(4)   If within that time notice is served on the sheriff of a petition for the winding up of the company having been presented, or of a meeting having been called at which there is to be proposed a resolution for voluntary winding up, and an order is made or a resolution passed (as the case may be), the sheriff shall pay the balance to the liquidator, who is entitled to retain it as against the execution creditor.

(5)   The rights conferred by this section on the liquidator may be set aside by the court in favour of the creditor to such extent and subject to such terms as the court thinks fit.

(6)   In this section, 'goods' includes all chattels personal; and 'the sheriff' includes any officer charged with the execution of a writ or other process.

(7)   The money sum for the time being specified in subsection (3) is subject to increase or reduction by order under section 416 in Part XV.

(8)   This section does not apply in the case of a winding up in Scotland.

185.   Effect of diligence (Scotland).

(1)   In the winding up of a company registered in Scotland, the following provisions of the Bankruptcy (Scotland) Act 1985—

  (a)   subsections (1) to (6) of section 37 (effect of sequestration on diligence); and

  (b)   subsections (3), (4), (7) and (8) of section 39 (realisation of estate),

apply, so far as consistent with this Act, in like manner as they apply in the sequestration of a debtor's estate, with the substitutions specified below and with any other necessary modifications.

(2)   The substitutions to be made in those sections of the Act of 1985 are as follows—

  (a)   for references to the debtor, substitute references to the company;

  (b)   for references to the sequestration, substitute references to the winding up;

  (c)   for references to the date of sequestration, substitute references to the commencement of the winding up of the company; and

  (d)   for references to the permanent trustee, substitute references to the liquidator.

(3)   In this section, 'the commencement of the winding up of the company' means, where it is being wound up by the court, the day on which the winding-up order is made.

(4)   This section, so far as relating to any estate or effects of the company situated in Scotland, applies in the case of a company registered in England and Wales as in the case of one registered in Scotland.

Miscellaneous matters

186.   Rescission of contracts by the court.

(1)   The court may, on the application of a person who is, as against the liquidator, entitled to the benefit or subject to the burden of a contract made with the company, make an order rescinding the contract on such terms as to payment by or to either party of damages for the non-performance of the contract, or otherwise as the court thinks just.

(2)   Any damages payable under the order to such a person may be proved by him as a debt in the winding up.

187.   Power to make over assets to employees.

(1)   On the winding up of a company (whether by the court or voluntarily), the liquidator may, subject to the following provisions of this section, make any payment which the company has, before the commencement of the winding up, decided to make under section 719 of the Companies Act (power to provide for employees or former employees on cessation or transfer of business).

(2)   The power which a company may exercise by virtue only of that section may be exercised by the liquidator after the winding up has commenced if, after the company's liabilities have been fully satisfied and provision has been made for the expenses of the winding up, the exercise of that power has been sanctioned by such a resolution of the company as would be required of the company itself by section 719(3) before that commencement, if paragraph (b) of that subsection were omitted and any other requirement applicable to its exercise by the company had been met.

(3)   Any payment which may be made by a company under this section (that is, a payment after the commencement of its winding up) may be made out of the company's assets which are available to the members on the winding up.

(4)   On a winding up by the court, the exercise by the liquidator of his powers under this section is subject to the court's control, and any creditor or contributory may apply to the court with respect to any exercise or proposed exercise of the power.

(5)   Subsections (1) and (2) above have effect notwithstanding anything in any rule of law or in section 107 of this Act (property of company after satisfaction of liabilities to be distributed among members).

188.   Notification that company is in liquidation.

(1)   When a company is being wound up, whether by the court or voluntarily, every invoice, order for goods or business letter issued by or on behalf of the company, or a liquidator of the company, or a receiver or manager of the company's property, being a document on or in which the name of the company appears, shall contain a statement that the company is being wound up.

(2)   If default is made in complying with this section, the company and any of the following persons who knowingly and wilfully authorises or permits the default, namely, any officer of the company, any liquidator of the company and any receiver or manager, is liable to a fine.

189.   Interest on debts.

(1)   In a winding up interest is payable in accordance with this section on any debt proved in the winding up, including so much of any such debt as represents interest on the remainder.

(2)   Any surplus remaining after the payment of the debts proved in a winding up shall, before being applied for any other purpose, be applied in paying interest on those debts in respect of the periods during which they have been outstanding since the company went into liquidation.

(3)   All interest under this section ranks equally, whether or not the debts on which it is payable rank equally.

(4)   The rate of interest payable under this section in respect of any debt ('the official rate' for the purposes of any provision of this Act in which that expression is used) is whichever is the greater of—

   (a)   the rate specified in section 17 of the Judgments Act 1838 on the day on which the company went into liquidation, and

   (b)   the rate applicable to that debt apart from the winding up.

(5)   In the application of this section to Scotland—

   (a)   references to a debt proved in a winding up have effect as references to a claim accepted in a winding up, and

   (b)   the reference to section 17 of the Judgments Act 1838 has effect as a reference to the rules.

192.   Information as to pending liquidations.

(1)   If the winding up of a company is not concluded within one year after its commencement, the liquidator shall, at such intervals as may be prescribed, until the winding up is concluded, send to the registrar of companies a statement in the prescribed form and containing the prescribed particulars with respect to the proceedings in, and position of, the liquidation.

(2)   If a liquidator fails to comply with this section, he is liable to a fine and, for continued contravention, to a daily default fine.

194.   Resolutions passed at adjourned meetings.

Where a resolution is passed at an adjourned meeting of a company's creditors or contributories, the resolution is treated for all purposes as having been passed on the date on which it was in fact passed, and not as having been passed on any earlier date.

195. Meetings to ascertain wishes of creditors or contributories.

(1) The court may—

(a) as to all matters relating to the winding up of a company, have regard to the wishes of the creditors or contributories (as proved to it by any sufficient evidence), and

(b) if it thinks fit, for the purpose of ascertaining those wishes, direct meetings of the creditors or contributories to be called, held and conducted in such manner as the court directs, and appoint a person to act as chairman of any such meeting and report the result of it to the court.

(2) In the case of creditors, regard shall be had to the value of each creditor's debt.

(3) In the case of contributories, regard shall be had to the number of votes conferred on each contributory by the Companies Act or the articles.

CHAPTER IX
DISSOLUTION OF COMPANIES AFTER WINDING UP

201. Dissolution (voluntary winding up).

(1) This section applies, in the case of a company wound up voluntarily, where the liquidator has sent to the registrar of companies his final account and return under section 94 (members' voluntary) or section 106 (creditors' voluntary).

(2) The registrar on receiving the account and return shall forthwith register them; and on the expiration of 3 months from the registration of the return the company is deemed to be dissolved.

(3) However, the court may, on the application of the liquidator or any other person who appears to the court to be interested, make an order deferring the date at which the dissolution of the company is to take effect for such time as the court thinks fit.

(4) It is the duty of the person on whose application an order of the court under this section is made within 7 days after the making of the order to deliver to the registrar an office copy of the order for registration; and if that person fails to do so he is liable to a fine and, for continued contravention, to a daily default fine.

202. Early dissolution (England and Wales).

(1) This section applies where an order for the winding up of a company has been made by the court in England and Wales.

(2) The official receiver, if—

(a) he is the liquidator of the company, and

(b) it appears to him—

(i) that the realisable assets of the company are insufficient to cover the expenses of the winding up, and

(ii) that the affairs of the company do not require any further investigation,

may at any time apply to the registrar of companies for the early dissolution of the company.

(3) Before making that application, the official receiver shall give not less than 28 days' notice of his intention to do so to the company's creditors and contributories and, if there is an administrative receiver of the company, to that receiver.

(4) With the giving of that notice the official receiver ceases (subject to any directions under the next section) to be required to perform any duties imposed on him in relation to the compay, its creditors or contributories by virtue of any provision of this Act, apart from a duty to make an application under subsection (2) of this section.

(5) On the receipt of the official receiver's application under subsection (2) the registrar shall forthwith register it and, at the end of the period of 3 months

beginning with the day of the registration of the application, the company shall be dissolved.

However, the Secretary of State may, on the application of the official receiver or any other person who appears to the Secretary of State to be interested, give directions under section 203 at any time before the end of that period.

203. Consequence of notice under s. 202.

(1) Where a notice has been given under section 202(3), the official receiver or any creditor or contributory of the company, or the administrative receiver of the company (if there is one) may apply to the Secretary of State for directions under this section.

(2) The grounds on which that application may be made are—

(a) that the realisable assets of the company are sufficient to cover the expenses of the winding up;

(b) that the affairs of the company do require further investigation; or

(c) that for any other reason the early dissolution of the company is inappropriate.

(3) Directions under this section—

(a) are directions making such provision as the Secretary of State thinks fit for enabling the winding up of the company to proceed as if no notice had been given under section 202(3), and

(b) may, in the case of an application under section 202(5), include a direction deferring the date at which the dissolution of the company is to take effect for such period as the Secretary of State thinks fit.

(4) An appeal to the court lies from any decision of the Secretary of State on an application for directions under this section.

(5) It is the duty of the person on whose application any directions are given under this section, or in whose favour an appeal with respect to an application for such directions is determined, within 7 days after the giving of the directions or the determination of the appeal, to deliver to the registrar of companies for registration such a copy of the directions or determination as is prescribed.

(6) If a person without reasonable excuse fails to deliver a copy as required by subsection (5), he is liable to a fine and, for continued contravention, to a daily default fine.

205. Dissolution otherwise than under ss. 202–204.

(1) This section applies where the registrar of companies receives—

(a) a notice served for the purposes of section 172(8) (final meeting of creditors and vacation of office by liquidator), or

(b) a notice from the official receiver that the winding up of a company by the court is complete.

(2) The registrar shall, on receipt of the notice, forthwith register it; and, subject as follows, at the end of the period of 3 months beginning with the day of the registration of the notice, the company shall be dissolved.

(3) The Secretary of State may, on the application of the official receiver or any other person who appears to the Secretary of State to be interested, give a direction deferring the date at which the dissolution of the company is to take effect for such period as the Secretary of State thinks fit.

(4) An appeal to the court lies from any decision of the Secretary of State on an application for a direction under subsection (3).

(5) Subsection (3) does not apply in a case where the winding-up order was made by the court in Scotland, but in such a case the court may, on an application by any person appearing to the court to have an interest, order that the date at which the dissolution of the company is to take effect shall be deferred for such period as the court thinks fit.

(6)   It is the duty of the person—

(a)   on whose application a direction is given under subsection (3);

(b)   in whose favour an appeal with respect to an application for such a direction is determined; or

(c)   on whose application an order is made under subsection (5),

within 7 days after the giving of the direction, the determination of the appeal or the making of the order, to deliver to the registrar for registration such a copy of the direction, determination or order as is prescribed.

(7)   If a person without reasonable excuse fails to deliver a copy as required by subsection (6), he is liable to a fine and, for continued contravention, to a daily default fine.

CHAPTER X
MALPRACTICE BEFORE AND DURING LIQUIDATION; PENALISATION OF COMPANIES AND COMPANY OFFICERS; INVESTIGATIONS AND PROSECUTIONS

Offences of fraud, deception, etc.

206.   Fraud, etc. in anticipation of winding up.

(1)   When a company is ordered to be wound up by the court, or passes a resolution for voluntary winding up, any person, being a past or present officer of the company, is deemed to have committed an offence if, within the 12 months immediately preceding the commencement of the winding up, he has—

(a)   concealed any part of the company's property to the value of £500 or more, or concealed any debt due to or from the company, or

(b)   fraudulently removed any part of the company's property to the value of £500 or more, or

(c)   concealed, destroyed, mutilated or falsified any book or paper affecting or relating to the company's property or affairs, or

(d)   made any false entry in any book or paper affecting or relating to the company's property or affairs, or

(e)   fraudulently parted with, altered or made any omission in any document affecting or relating to the company's property or affairs, or

(f)   pawned, pledged or disposed of any property of the company which has been obtained on credit and has not been paid for (unless the pawning, pledging or disposal was in the ordinary way of the company's business).

(2)   Such a person is deemed to have committed an offence if within the period above-mentioned he has been privy to the doing by others of any of the things mentioned in paragraphs (c), (d) and (e) of subsection (1); and he commits an offence if, at any time after the commencement of the winding up, he does any of the things mentioned in paragraphs (a) to (f) of that subsection, or is privy to the doing by others of any of the things mentioned in paragraphs (c) to (e) of it.

(3)   For purposes of this section, 'officer' includes a shadow director.

(4)   It is a defence—

(a)   for a person charged under paragraph (a) or (f) of subsection (1) (or under subsection (2) in respect of the things mentioned in either of those two paragraphs) to prove that he had no intent to defraud, and

(b)   for a person charged under paragraph (c) or (d) of subsection (1) (or under subsection (2) in respect of the things mentioned in either of those two paragraphs) to prove that he had no intent to conceal the state of affairs of the company or to defeat the law.

(5)   Where a person pawns, pledges or disposes of any property in circumstances which amount to an offence under subsection (1)(f), every person who takes in pawn or

pledge, or otherwise receives, the property knowing it to be pawned, pledged or disposed of in such circumstances, is guilty of an offence.

(6) A person guilty of an offence under this section is liable to imprisonment or a fine, or both.

(7) The money sums specified in paragraphs (a) and (b) of subsection (1) are subject to increase or reduction by order under section 416 in Part XV.

207. Transactions in fraud of creditors.

(1) When a company is ordered to be wound up by the court or passes a resolution for voluntary winding up, a person is deemed to have committed an offence if he, being at the time an officer of the company—

(a) has made or caused to be made any gift or transfer of, or charge on, or has caused or connived at the levying of any execution against, the company's property, or

(b) has concealed or removed any part of the company's property since, or within 2 months before, the date of any unsatisfied judgment or order for the payment of money obtained against the company.

(2) A person is not guilty of an offence under this section—

(a) by reason of conduct constituting an offence under subsection (1)(a) which occurred more than 5 years before the commencement of the winding up, or

(b) if he proves that, at the time of the conduct constituting the offence, he had no intent to defraud the company's creditors.

(3) A person guilty of an offence under this section is liable to imprisonment or a fine, or both.

208. Misconduct in course of winding up.

(1) When a company is being wound up, whether by the court or voluntarily, any person, being a past or present officer of the company, commits an offence if he—

(a) does not to the best of his knowledge and belief fully and truly discover to the liquidator all the company's property, and how and to whom and for what consideration and when the company disposed of any part of that property (except such part as has been disposed of in the ordinary way of the company's business), or

(b) does not deliver up to the liquidator (or as he directs) all such part of the company's property as is in his custody or under his control, and which he is required by law to deliver up, or

(c) does not deliver up to the liquidator (or as he directs) all books and papers in his custody or under his control belonging to the company and which he is required by law to deliver up, or

(d) knowing or believing that a false debt has been proved by any person in the winding up, fails to inform the liquidator as soon as practicable, or

(e) after the commencement of the winding up, prevents the production of any book or paper affecting or relating to the company's property or affairs.

(2) Such a person commits an offence if after the commencement of the winding up he attempts to account for any part of the company's property by fictitious losses or expenses; and he is deemed to have committed that offence if he has so attempted at any meeting of the company's creditors within the 12 months immediately preceding the commencement of the winding up.

(3) For purposes of this section, 'officer' includes a shadow director.

(4) It is a defence—

(a) for a person charged under paragraph (a), (b) or (c) of subsection (1) to prove that he had no intent to defraud, and

(b) for a person charged under paragraph (e) of that subsection to prove that he had no intent to conceal the state of affairs of the company or to defeat the law.

(5) A person guilty of an offence under this section is liable to imprisonment or a fine, or both.

209. Falsification of company's books.

(1)   When a company is being wound up, an officer or contributory of the company commits an offence if he destroys, mutilates, alter or falsifies any books, papers or securities, or makes or is privy to the making of any false or fraudulent entry in any register, book of account or document belonging to the company with intent to defraud or deceive any person.

(2)   A person guilty of an offence under this section is liable to imprisonment or a fine, or both.

210. Material omissions from statement relating to company's affairs.

(1)   When a company is being wound up, whether by the court or voluntarily, any person, being a past or present officer of the company, commits an offence if he makes any material omission in any statement relating to the company's affairs.

(2)   When a company has been ordered to be wound up by the court, or has passed a resolution for voluntary winding up, any such person is deemed to have committed that offence if, prior to the winding up, he has made any material omission in any such statement.

(3)   For purposes of this section, 'officer' includes a shadow director.

(4)   It is a defence for a person charged under this section to prove that he had no intent to defraud.

(5)   A person guilty of an offence under this section is liable to imprisonment or a fine, or both.

211. False representations to creditors.

(1)   When a company is being wound up, whether by the court or voluntarily, any person, being a past or present officer of the company—

(a)   commits an offence if he makes any false representation or commits any other fraud for the purpose of obtaining the consent of the company's creditors or any of them to an agreement with reference to the company's affairs or to the winding up, and

(b)   is deemed to have committed that offence if, prior to the winding up, he has made any false representation, or committed any other fraud, for that purpose.

(2)   For purposes of this section, 'officer' includes a shadow director.

(3)   A person guilty of an offence under this section is liable to imprisonment or a fine, or both.

Penalisation of directors and officers

212. Summary remedy against delinquent directors, liquidators, etc.

(1)   This section applies if in the course of the winding up of a company it appears that a person who—

(a)   is or has been an officer of the company,

(b)   has acted as liquidator, administrator or administrative receiver of the company, or

(c)   not being a person falling within paragraph (a) or (b), is or has been concerned, or has taken part, in the promotion, formation or management of the company,

has misapplied or retained, or become accountable for, any money or other property of the company, or been guilty of any misfeasance or breach of any fiduciary or other duty in relation to the company.

(2)   The reference in subsection (1) to any misfeasance or breach of any fiduciary or other duty in relation to the company includes, in the case of a person who has acted as liquidator or administrator of the company, any misfeasance or breach of any fiduciary or other duty in connection with the carrying out of his functions as liquidator or administrator of the company.

(3)   The court may, on the application of the official receiver or the liquidator, or of any creditor or contributory, examine into the conduct of the person falling within subsection (1) and compel him—

(a)   to repay, restore or account for the money or property or any part of it, with interest at such rate as the court thinks just, or

(b)   to contribute such sum to the company's assets by way of compensation in respect of the misfeasance or breach of fiduciary or other duty as the court thinks just.

(4)   The power to make an application under subsection (3) in relation to a person who has acted as liquidator or administrator of the company is not exercisable, except with the leave of the court, after that person has had his release.

(5)   The power of a contributory to make an application under subsection (3) is not exercisable except with the leave of the court, but is exercisable notwithstanding that he will not benefit from any order the court may make on the application.

213.   Fraudulent trading.

(1)   If in the course of the winding up of a company it appears that any business of the company has been carried on with intent to defraud creditors of the company or creditors of any other person, or for any fraudulent purpose, the following has effect.

(2)   The court, on the application of the liquidator may declare that any persons who were knowingly parties to the carrying on of the business in the manner abovementioned are to be liable to make such contributions (if any) to the company's assets as the court thinks proper.

214.   Wrongful trading.

(1)   Subject to subsection (3) below, if in the course of the winding up of a company it appears that subsection (2) of this section applies in relation to a person who is or has been a director of the company, the court, on the application of the liquidator, may declare that that person is to be liable to make such contribution (if any) to the company's assets as the court thinks proper.

(2)   This subsection applies in relation to a person if—

(a)   the company has gone into insolvent liquidation,

(b)   at some time before the commencement of the winding up of the company, that person knew or ought to have concluded that there was no reasonable prospect that the company would avoid going into insolvent liquidation, and

(c)   that person was a director of the company at that time;

but the court shall not make a declaration under this section in any case where the time mentioned in paragraph (b) above was before 28 April 1986.

(3)   The court shall not make a declaration under this section with respect to any person if it is satisfied that after the condition specified in subsection (2)(b) was first satisfied in relation to him that person took every step with a view to minimising the potential loss to the company's creditors as (assuming him to have known that there was no reasonable prospect that the company would avoid going into insolvent liquidation) he ought to have taken.

(4)   For the purposes of subsections (2) and (3), the facts which a director of a company ought to know or ascertain, the conclusions which he ought to reach and the steps which he ought to take are those which would be known or ascertained, or reached or taken, by a reasonably diligent person having both—

(a)   the general knowledge, skill and experience that may reasonably be expected of a person carrying out the same functions as are carried out by that director in relation to the company, and

(b)   the general knowledge, skill and experience that that director has.

(5)   The reference in subsection (4) to the functions carried out in relation to a company by a director of the company includes any functions which he does not carry out but which have been entrusted to him.

(6)   For the purposes of this section a company goes into insolvent liquidation if it goes into liquidation at a time when its assets are insufficient for the payment of its debts and other liabilities and the expenses of the winding up.

(7)   In this section 'director' includes a shadow director.

(8)   This section is without prejudice to section 213.

215.   Proceedings under ss. 213, 214.

(1)   On the hearing of an application under section 213 or 214, the liquidator may himself give evidence or call witnesses.

(2)   Where under either section the court makes a declaration, it may give such further directions as it thinks proper for giving effect to the declaration; and in particular, the court may—

(a)   provide for the liability of any person under the declaration to be a charge on any debt or obligation due from the company to him, or on any mortgage or charge or any interest in a mortgage or charge on assets of the company held by or vested in him, or any person on his behalf, or any person claiming as assignee from or through the person liable or any person acting on his behalf, and

(b)   from time to time make such further order as may be necessary for enforcing any charge imposed under this subsection.

(3)   For the purposes of subsection (2), 'assignee'—

(a)   includes a person to whom or in whose favour, by the directions of the person made liable, the debt, obligation, mortgage or charge was created, issued or transferred or the interest created, but

(b)   does not include an assignee for valuable consideration (not including consideration by way of marriage) given in good faith and without notice of any of the matters on the grounds of which the declaration is made.

(4)   Where the court makes a declaration under either section in relation to a person who is a creditor of the company, it may direct that the whole or any part of any debt owed by the company to that person and any interest thereon shall rank in priority after all other debts owed by the company and after any interest on those debts.

(5)   Sections 213 and 214 have effect notwithstanding that the person concerned may be criminally liable in respect of matters on the ground of which the declaration under the section is to be made.

216.   Restriction on reuse of company names.

(1)   This section applies to a person where a company ('the liquidating company') has gone into insolvent liquidation on or after the appointed day and he was a director or shadow director of the company at any time in the period of 12 months ending with the day before it went into liquidation.

(2)   For the purposes of this section, a name is a prohibited name in relation to such a person if—

(a)   it is a name by which the liquidating company was known at any time in that period of 12 months, or

(b)   it is a name which is so similar to a name falling within paragraph (a) as to suggest an association with that company.

(3)   Except with leave of the court or in such circumstances as may be prescribed, a person to whom this section applies shall not at any time in the period of 5 years beginning with the day on which the liquidating company went into liquidation—

(a)   be a director of any other company that is known by a prohibited name, or

(b)   in any way, whether directly or indirectly, be concerned or take part in the promotion, formation or management of any such company, or

(c)   in any way, whether directly or indirectly, be concerned or take part in the carrying on of a business carried on (otherwise than by a company) under a prohibited name.

(4)   If a person acts in contravention of this section, he is liable to imprisonment or a fine, or both.

(5)   In subsection (3) 'the court' means any court having jurisdiction to wind up companies; and on an application for leave under that subsection, the Secretary of State or the official receiver may appear and call the attention of the court to any matters which seem to him to be relevant.

(6)   References in this section, in relation to any time, to a name by which a company is known are to the name of the company at that time or to any name under which the company carries on business at that time.

(7)   For the purposes of this section a company goes into insolvent liquidation if it goes into liquidation at a time when its assets are insufficient for the payment of its debts and other liabilities and the expenses of the winding up.

(8)   In this section 'company' includes a company which may be wound up under Part V of this Act.

217.   Personal liability for debts, following contravention of s. 216.

(1)   A person is personally responsible for all the relevant debts of a company if at any time—

(a)   in contravention of section 216, he is involved in the management of the company, or

(b)   as a person who is involved in the management of the company, he acts or is willing to act on instructions given (without the leave of the court) by a person whom he knows at that time to be in contravention in relation to the company of section 216.

(2)   Where a person is personally responsible under this section for the relevant debts of a company, he is jointly and severally liable in respect of those debts with the company and any other person who, whether under this section or otherwise, is so liable.

(3)   For the purposes of this section the relevant debts of a company are—

(a)   in relation to a person who is personally responsible under paragraph (a) of subsection (1), such debts and other liabilities of the company as are incurred at a time when that person was involved in the management of the company, and

(b)   in relation to a person who is personally responsible under paragraph (b) of the subsection, such debts and other liabilities of the company as are incurred at a time when that person was acting or was willing to act on instructions given as mentioned in that paragraph.

(4)   For the purposes of this section, a person is involved in the management of a company if he is a director of the company or if he is concerned, whether directly or indirectly, or takes part, in the management of the company.

(5)   For the purposes of this section a person who, as a person involved in the management of a company, has at any time acted on instructions given (without the leave of the court) by a person whom he knew at that time to be in contravention in relation to the company of section 216 is presumed, unless the contrary is shown, to have been willing at any time thereafter to act on any instructions given by that person.

(6)   In this section 'company' includes a company which may be wound up under Part V.

Investigation and prosecution of malpractice

218.   Prosecution of delinquent officers and members of company.

(1)   If it appears to the court in the course of a winding up by the court that any past or present officer, or any member, of the company has been guilty of any offence in

relation to the company for which he is criminally liable, the court may (either on the application of a person interested in the winding up or of its own motion) direct the liquidator to refer the matter to the prosecuting authority.

(2) 'The prosecuting authority' means—

(a) in the case of a winding up in England and Wales, the Director of Public Prosecutions, and

(b) in the case of a winding up in Scotland, the Lord Advocate.

(3) If in the case of a winding up by the court in England and Wales it appears to the liquidator, not being the official receiver, that any past or present officer of the company, or any member of it, has been guilty of an offence in relation to the company for which he is criminally liable, the liquidator shall report the matter to the official receiver.

(4) If it appears to the liquidator in the course of a voluntary winding up that any past or present officer of the company, or any member of it, has been guilty of an offence in relation to the company for which he is criminally liable, he shall—

(a) forthwith report the matter to the prosecuting authority, and

(b) furnish to that authority such information and give to him such access to and facilities for inspecting and taking copies of documents (being information or documents in the possession or under the control of the liquidator and relating to the matter in question) as the authority requires.

(5) Where a report is made to him under subsection (4), the prosecuting authority may, if he thinks fit, refer the matter to the Secretary of State for further enquiry; and the Secretary of State—

(a) shall thereupon investigate the matter reported to him and such other matters relating to the affairs of the company as appear to him to require investigation, and

(b) for the purpose of his investigation may exercise any of the powers which are exercisable by inspectors appointed under section 431 or 432 of the Companies Act to investigate a company's affairs.

(6) If it appears to the court in the course of a voluntary winding up that—

(a) any past or present officer of the company, or any member of it, has been guilty as above-mentioned, and

(b) no report with respect to the matter has been made by the liquidator to the prosecuting authority under subsection (4),

the court may (on the application of any person interested in the winding up or of its own motion) direct the liquidator to make such a report.

On a report being made accordingly, this section has effect as though the report had been made in pursuance of subsection (4).

219. Obligations arising under s. 218.

(1) For the purpose of an investigation by the Secretary of State under section 218(5), any obligation imposed on a person by any provision of the Companies Act to produce documents or give information to, or otherwise to assist, inspectors appointed as mentioned in that subsection is to be regarded as an obligation similarly to assist the Secretary of State in his investigation.

(2) An answer given by a person to a question put to him in exercise of the powers conferred by section 218(5) may be used in evidence against him.

(3) Where criminal proceedings are instituted by the prosecuting authority or the Secretary of State following any report or reference under section 218, it is the duty of the liquidator and every officer and agent of the company past and present (other than the defendant or defender) to give to that authority or the Secretary of State (as the case may be) all assistance in connection with the prosecution which he is reasonably able to give.

For this purpose 'agent' includes any banker or solicitor of the company and any person employed by the company as auditor, whether that person is or is not an officer of the company.

(4) If a person fails or neglects to give assistance in the manner required by subsection (3), the court may, on the application of the prosecuting authority or the Secretary of State (as the case may be) direct the person to comply with that subsection; and if the application is made with respect to a liquidator, the court may (unless it appears that the failure or neglect to comply was due to the liquidator not having in his hands sufficient assets of the company to enable him to do so) direct that the costs shall be borne by the liquidator personally.

PART VI
MISCELLANEOUS PROVISIONS APPLYING TO COMPANIES WHICH ARE INSOLVENT OR IN LIQUIDATION

Office-holders

230. Holders of office to be qualified insolvency practitioners.

(1) Where an administration order is made in relation to a company, the administrator must be a person who is qualified to act as an insolvency practitioner in relation to the company.

(2) Where an administrative receiver of a company is appointed, he must be a person who is so qualified.

(3) Where a company goes into liquidation, the liquidator must be a person who is so qualified.

(4) Where a provisional liquidator is appointed, he must be a person who is so qualified.

(5) Subsections (3) and (4) are without prejudice to any enactment under which the official receiver is to be, or may be liquidator or provisional liquidator.

231. Appointment to office of two or more persons.

(1) This section applies if an appointment or nomination of any person to the office of administrator, administrative receiver, liquidator or provisional liquidator—
  (a) relates to more than one person, or
  (b) has the effect that the office is to be held by more than one person.

(2) The appointment or nomination shall declare whether any act required or authorised under any enactment to be done by the administrator, administrative receiver, liquidator or provisional liquidator is to be done by all or any one or more of the persons for the time being holding the office in question.

232. Validity of office-holder's acts.

The acts of an individual as administrator, administrative receiver, liquidator or provisonal liquidator of a company are valid notwithstanding any defect in his appointment, nomination or qualifications.

Management by administrators, liquidators, etc.

233. Supplies of gas, water, electricity, etc.

(1) This section applies in the case of a company where—
  (a) an administration order is made in relation to the company, or
  (b) an administrative receiver is appointed, or
  (c) a voluntary arrangement under Part I, approved by meetings summoned under section 3, has taken effect, or
  (d) the company goes into liquidation, or
  (e) a provisional liquidator is appointed;

and 'the office-holder' means the administrator, the administrative receiver, the supervisor of the voluntary arrangement, the liquidator or the provisional liquidator, as the case may be.

(2)   If the request is made by or with the concurrence of the office-holder for the giving, after the effective date, of any of the supplies mentioned in the next subsection, the supplier—

(a)   may make it a condition of the giving of the supply that the office-holder personally guarantees the payment of any charges in respect of the supply, but

(b)   shall not make it a condition of the giving of the supply, or do anything which has the effect of making it a condition of the giving of the supply, that any outstanding charges in respect of a supply given to the company before the effective date are paid.

(3)   The supplies referred to in subsection (2) are—

(a)   a public supply of gas,

(b)   a public supply of electricity,

(c)   a supply of water by a water undertaker or, in Scotland, a water authority,

(d)   a supply of telecommunication services by a public telecommunications operator.

(4)   'The effective date' for the purposes of this section is whichever is applicable of the following dates—

(a)   the date on which the administration order was made,

(b)   the date on which the administrative receiver was appointed (or, if he was appointed in succession to another administrative receiver, the date on which the first of his predecessors was appointed),

(c)   the date on which the voluntary arrangement was approved by the meetings summoned under section 3,

(d)   the date on which the company went into liquidation,

(e)   the date on which the provisional liquidator was appointed.

(5)   The following applies to expressions used in subsection (3)—

(a)   'public supply of gas' means a supply of gas by the British Gas Corporation or a public gas supplier within the meaning of Part I of the Gas Act 1986,

(b)   'public supply of electricity' means a supply of electricity by a public electricity supplier within the meaning of Part I of the Electricity Act 1989,

(c)   'water authority' means the same as in the Water (Scotland) Act 1980, and

(d)   'telecommunication services' and 'public telecommunications operator' mean the same as in the Telecommunications Act 1984, except that the former does not include local delivery services within the meaning of Part II of the Broadcasting Act 1990.

234.   Getting in the company's property.

(1)   This section applies in the case of a company where—

(a)   an administration order is made in relation to the company, or

(b)   an administrative receiver is appointed, or

(c)   the company goes into liquidation, or

(d)   a provisional liquidator is appointed;

and 'the office-holder' means the administrator, the administrative receiver, the liquidator or the provisional liquidator, as the case may be.

(2)   Where any person has in his possession or control any property, books, papers or records to which the company appears to be entitled, the court may require that person forthwith (or within such period as the court may direct) to pay, deliver, convey, surrender or transfer the property, books, papers or records to the office-holder.

(3)   Where the office-holder—

(a)   seizes or disposes of any property which is not property of the company, and

(b)   at the time of seizure or disposal believes, and has reasonable grounds for believing, that he is entitled (whether in pursuance of an order of the court or otherwise) to seize or dispose of that property,
the next subsection has effect.

(4)   In that case the office-holder—

(a)   is not liable to any person in respect of any loss or damage resulting from the seizure or disposal except in so far as that loss or damage is caused by the office-holder's own negligence, and

(b)   has a lien on the property, or the proceeds of its sale, for such expenses as were incurred in connection with the seizure of disposal.

235.   Duty to cooperate with office-holder.

(1)   This section applies as does section 234; and it also applies, in the case of a company in respect of which a winding-up order has been made by the court in England and Wales, as if references to the office-holder included the official receiver, whether or not he is the liquidator.

(2)   Each of the persons mentioned in the next subsection shall—

(a)   give to the office-holder such information concerning the company and its promotion, formation, business, dealings, affairs or property as the office-holder may at any time after the effective date reasonably require, and

(b)   attend on the office-holder at such times as the latter may reasonably require.

(3)   The persons referred to above are—

(a)   those who are or have at any time been officers of the company,

(b)   those who have taken part in the formation of the company at any time within one year before the effective date,

(c)   those who are in the employment of the company, or have been in its employment (including employment under a contract for services) within that year, and are in the office-holder's opinion capable of giving information which he requires,

(d)   those who are, or have within the year been, officers of, or in the employment (including employment under a contract for services) of, another company which is, or within that year was, an officer of the company in question, and

(e)   in the case of a company being wound up by the court, any person who has acted as administrator, administrative receiver or liquidator of the company.

(4)   For the purposes of subsections (2) and (3), 'the effective date' is whichever is applicable of the following dates—

(a)   the date on which the administration order was made,

(b)   the date on which the administrative receiver was appointed or, if he was appointed in succession to another administrative receiver, the date on which the first of his predecessors was appointed,

(c)   the date on which the provisional liquidator was appointed, and

(d)   the date on which the company went into liquidation.

(5)   If a person without reasonable excuse fails to comply with any obligation imposed by this section, he is liable to a fine and, for continued contravention, to a daily default fine.

236.   Inquiry into company's dealings, etc.

(1)   This section applies as does section 234; and it also applies in the case of a company in respect of which a winding-up order has been made by the court in England and Wales as if references to the office-holder included the official receiver, whether or not he is the liquidator.

(2)   The court may, on the application of the office-holder, summon to appear before it—

(a)   any officer of the company,

(b)   any person known or suspected to have in his possession any property of the company or supposed to be indebted to the company, or

(c)   any person whom the court thinks capable of giving information concerning the promotion, formation, business, dealings, affairs or property of the company.

(3)   The court may require any such person as is mentioned in subsection (2)(a) to (c) to submit an affidavit to the court containing an account of his dealings with the company or to produce any books, papers or other records in his possession or under his control relating to the company or the matters mentioned in paragraph (c) of the subsection.

(4)   The following applies in a case where—

(a)   a person without reasonable excuse fails to appear before the court when he is summoned to do so under this section, or

(b)   there are reasonable grounds for believing that a person has absconded, or is about to abscond, with a view to avoiding his appearance before the court under this section.

(5)   The court may, for the purpose of bringing that person and anything in his possession before the court, cause a warrant to be issued to a constable or prescribed officer of the court—

(a)   for the arrest of that person, and

(b)   for the seizure of any books, papers, records, money or goods in that person's possession.

(6)   The court may authorise a person arrested under such a warrant to be kept in custody, and anything seized under such a warrant to be held, in accordance with the rules, until that person is brought before the court under the warrant or until such other time as the court may order.

237.   Court's enforcement powers under s. 236.

(1)   If it appears to the court, on consideration of any evidence obtained under section 236 or this section, that any person has in his possession any property of the company, the court may, on the application of the office-holder, order that person to deliver the whole or any part of the property to the office-holder at such time, in such manner and on such terms as the court thinks fit.

(2)   If it appears to the court, on consideration of any evidence so obtained, that any person is indebted to the company, the court may, on the application of the office-holder, order that person to pay to the office-holder, at such time and in such manner as the court may direct, the whole or any part of the amount due, whether in full discharge of the debt or otherwise, as the court thinks fit.

(3)   The court may, if it thinks fit, order that any person who is within the jurisdiction of the court would be liable to be summoned to appear before it under section 236 or this section shall be examined in any part of the United Kingdom where he may for the time being be, or in a place outside the United Kingdom.

(4)   Any person who appears or is brought before the court under section 236 or this section may be examined on oath, either orally or (except in Scotland) by interrogatories, concerning the company or the matters mentioned in section 236(2)(c).

Adjustment of prior transactions (administration and liquidation)

238.   Transactions at an undervalue (England and Wales).

(1)   This section applies in the case of a company where—

(a)   an administration order is made in relation to the company, or

(b)   the company goes into liquidation;

and 'the office-holder' means the administrator or the liquidator, as the case may be.

(2)   Where the company has at a relevant time (defined in section 240) entered into a transaction with any person at an undervalue, the office-holder may apply to the court for an order under this section

(3)   Subject as follows, the court shall, on such an application, make such order as it thinks fit for restoring the position to what it would have been if the company had not entered into that transaction.

(4)   For the purposes of this section and section 241, a company enters into a transaction with a person at an undervalue if—

(a)   the company makes a gift to that person or otherwise enters into a transaction with that person on terms that provide for the company to receive no consideration, or

(b)   the company enters into a transaction with that person for a consideration the value of which, in money or money's worth, is significantly less than the value, in money or money's worth, of the consideration provided by the company.

(5)   The court shall not make an order under this section in respect of a transaction at an undervalue if it is satisfied—

(a)   that the company which entered into the transaction did so in good faith and for the purpose of carrying on its business, and

(b)   that at the time it did so there were reasonable grounds for believing that the transaction would benefit the company.

239.   Preferences (England and Wales).

(1)   This section applies as does section 238.

(2)   Where the company has at a relevant time (defined in the next section) given a preference to any person, the office-holder may apply to the court for an order under this section.

(3)   Subject as follows, the court shall, on such an application, make such order as it thinks fit for restoring the position to what it would have been if the company had not given that preference.

(4)   For the purposes of this section and section 241, a company gives a preference to a person if—

(a)   that person is one of the company's creditors or a surety or guarantor for any of the company's debts or other liabilities, and

(b)   the company does anything or suffers anything to be done which (in either case) has the effect of putting that person into a position which, in the event of the company going into insolvent liquidation, will be better than the position he would have been in if that thing had not been done.

(5)   The court shall not make an order under this section in respect of a preference given to any person unless the company which gave the preference was influenced in deciding to give it by a desire to produce in relation to that person the effect mentioned in subsection (4)(b).

(6)   A company which has given a preference to a person connected with the company (otherwise than by reason only of being its employee) at the time the preference was given is presumed, unless the contrary is shown, to have been influenced in deciding to give it by such a desire as is mentioned in subsection (5).

(7)   The fact that something has been done in pursuance of the order of a court does not, without more, prevent the doing or suffering of that thing from constituting the giving of a preference.

240.   'Relevant time' under ss. 238, 239.

(1)   Subject to the next subsection, the time at which a company enters into a transaction at an undervalue or gives a preference is a relevant time if the transaction is entered into, or the preference given—

(a)   in the case of a transaction at an undervalue or of a preference which is given to a person who is connected with the company (otherwise than by reason only of being its employee), at a time in the period of 2 years ending with the onset of insolvency (which expression is defined below),

(b)   in the case of a preference which is not such a transaction and is not so given, at a time in the period of 6 months ending with the onset of insolvency, and

(c)   in either case, at a time between the presentation of a petition for the making of an administration order in relation to the company and the making of such an order on that petition.

(2)   Where a company enters into a transaction at an undervalue or gives a preference at a time mentioned in subsection (1)(a) or (b), that time is not a relevant time for the purposes of section 238 or 239 unless the company—

(a)   is at that time unable to pay its debts within the meaning of section 123 in Chapter VI of Part IV, or

(b)   becomes unable to pay its debts within the meaning of that section in consequence of the transaction or preference;

but the requirements of this subsection are presumed to be satisfied, unless the contrary is shown, in relation to any transaction at an undervalue which is entered into by a company with a person who is connected with the company.

(3)   For the purposes of subsection (1), the onset of insolvency is—

(a)   in a case where section 238 or 239 applies by reason of the making of an administration order or of a company going into liquidation immediately upon the discharge of an administration order, the date of the presentation of the petition on which the administration order was made, and

(b)   in a case where the section applies by reason of a company going into liquidation at any other time, the date of the commencement of the winding up.

241.   Orders under ss. 238, 239.

(1)   Without prejudice to the generality of sections 238(3) and 239(3), an order under either of those sections with respect to a transaction or preference entered into or given by a company may (subject to the next subsection)—

(a)   require any property transferred as part of the transaction, or in connection with the giving of the preference, to be vested in the company,

(b)   require any property to be so vested if it represents in any person's hands the application either of the proceeds of sale of property so transferred or of money so transferred,

(c)   release or discharge (in whole or in part) any security given by the company,

(d)   require any person to pay, in respect of benefits received by him from the company, such sums to the office-holder as the court may direct,

(e)   provide for any surety or guarantor whose obligations to any person were released or discharged (in whole or in part) under the transaction, or by the giving of the preference, to be under such new or revived obligations to that person as the court thinks appropriate,

(f)   provide for security to be provided for the discharge of any obligation imposed by or arising under the order, for such an obligation to be charged on any property and for the security or charge to have the same priority as a security or charge released or discharged (in whole or in part) under the transaction or by the giving of the preference, and

(g)   provide for the extent to which any person whose property is vested by the order in the company, or on whom obligations are imposed by the order, is to be able to prove in the winding up of the company for debts or other liabilities which arose from, or were released or discharged (in whole or in part) under or by, the transaction or the giving of the preference.

(2)   An order under section 238 or 239 may affect the property of, or impose any obligation on, any person whether or not he is the person with whom the company in question entered into the transaction or (as the case may be) the person to whom the preference was given; but such an order—

(a) shall not prejudice any interest in property which was acquired from a person other than the compay and was acquired in good faith and for value, or prejudice any interest deriving from such an interest, and

(b) shall not require a person who received a benefit from the transaction or preference in good faith and for value to pay a sum to the office-holder, except where that person was a party to thè transaction or the payment is to be in respect of a preference given to that person at a time when he was a creditor of the company.

(2A) Where a person has acquired an interest in property from a person other than the company in question, or has received a benefit from the transaction or preference, and at the time of that acquisition or receipt—

(a) he had notice of the relevant surrounding circumstances and of the relevant proceedings, or

(b) he was connected with, or was an associate of, either the company in question or the person with whom that company entered into the transaction or to whom that company gave the preference,

then, unless the contrary is shown, it shall be presumed for the purposes of paragraph (a) or (as the case may be) paragraph (b) of subsection (2) that the interest was acquired or the benefit was received otherwise than in good faith.

(3) For the purposes of subsection (2A)(a), the relevant surrounding circumstances are (as the case may require)—

(a) the fact that the company in question entered into the transaction at an undervalue; or

(b) the circumstances which amounted to the giving of the preference by the company in question;

and subsections (3A) to (3C) have effect to determine whether, for those purposes, a person has notice of the relevant proceedings.

(3A) In a case where section 238 or 239 applies by reason of the making of an administration order, a person has notice of the relevant proceedings if he has notice—

(a) of the fact that the petition on which the administration order is made has been presented; or

(b) of the fact that the administration order has been made.

(3B) In a case where section 238 or 239 applies by reason of the company in question going into liquidation immediately upon the discharge of an administration order, a person has notice of the relevant proceedings if he has notice—

(a) of the fact that the petition on which the administration order is made has been presented;

(b) of the fact that the administration order has been made; or

(c) of the fact that the company has gone into liquidation.

(3C) In a case where section 238 or 239 applies by reason of the company in question going into liquidation at any other time, a person has notice of the relevant proceedings if he has notice—

(a) where the company goes into liquidation on the making of a winding-up order, of the fact that the petition on which the winding-up order is made has been presented or of the fact that the company has gone into liquidation;

(b) in any other case, of the fact that the company has gone into liquidation.

(4) The provisions of section 238 to 241 apply without prejudice to the availability of any other remedy, even in relation to a transaction or preference which the company had no power to enter into or give.

244. Extortionate credit transactions.

(1) This section applies as does section 238, and where the company is, or has been, a party to a transaction for, or involving, the provision of credit to the company.

(2)   The court may, on the application of the office-holder, make an order with respect to the transaction if the transaction is or was extortionate and was entered into in the period of 3 years ending with the day on which the administration order was made or (as the case may be) the company went into liquidation.

(3)   For the purposes of this section a transaction is extortionate if, having regard to the risk accepted by the person providing the credit—

(a)   the terms of it are or were such as to require grossly exorbitant payments to be made (whether unconditionally or in certain contingencies) in respect of the provision of the credit, or

(b)   it otherwise grossly contravened ordinary principles of fair dealing;
and it shall be presumed, unless the contrary is proved, that a transaction with respect to which an application is made under this section is or, as the case may be, was extortionate.

(4)   An order under this section with respect to any transaction may contain such one or more of the following as the court thinks fit, that is to say—

(a)   provision setting aside the whole or part of any obligation created by the transaction,

(b)   provision otherwise varying the terms of the transaction or varying the terms on which any security for the purposes of the transaction is held,

(c)   provision requiring any person who is or was a party to the transaction to pay to the office-holder any sums paid to that person, by virtue of the transaction, by the company,

(d)   provision requiring any person to surrender to the office-holder any property held by him as security for the purposes of the transaction,

(e)   provision directing accounts to be taken between any persons.

(5)   The powers conferred by this section are exercisable in relation to any transaction concurrently with any powers exercisable in relation to that transaction as a transaction at an undervalue or under section 242 (gratuitous alienations in Scotland).

245.   Avoidance of certain floating charges.

(1)   This section applies as does section 238, but applies to Scotland as well as to England and Wales.

(2)   Subject as follows, a floating charge on the company's undertaking or property created at a relevant time is invalid except to the extent of the aggregate of—

(a)   the value of so much of the consideration for the creation of the charge as consists of money paid, or goods or services supplied, to the company at the same time as, or after, the creation of the charge,

(b)   the value of so much of that consideration as consists of the discharge or reduction, at the same time as, or after, the creation of the charge, of any debt of the company, and

(c)   the amount of such interest (if any) as is payable on the amount falling within paragraph (a) or (b) in pursuance of any agreement under which the money was so paid, the goods or services were so supplied or the debt was so discharged or reduced.

(3)   Subject to the next subsection, the time at which a floating charge is created by the company is a relevant time for the purposes of this section if the charge is created—

(a)   in the case of a charge which is created in favour of a person who is connected with the company, at a time in the period of 2 years ending with the onset of insolvency,

(b)   in the case of a charge which is created in favour of any other person, at a time in the period of 12 months ending with the onset of insolvency, or

(c)   in either case, at a time between the presentation of a petition for the making of an administration order in relation to the company and the making of such an order on that petition.

(4)   Where a company creates a floating charge at a time mentioned in subsection (3)(b) and the person in favour of whom the charge is created is not connected with the company, that time is not a relevant time for the purposes of this section unless the company—

(a) is at that time unable to pay its debts within the meaning of section 123 in Chapter VI of Part IV, or

(b) becomes unable to pay its debts within the meaning of that section in consequence of the transaction under which the charge is created.

(5)   For the purposes of subsection (3), the onset of insolvency is—

(a) in a case where this section applies by reason of the making of an administration order, the date of the presentation of the petition on which the order was made, and

(b) in a case where this section applies by reason of a company going into liquidation, the date of the commencement of the winding up.

(6)   For the purposes of subsection (2)(a) the value of any goods or services supplied by way of consideration for a floating charge is the amount in money which at the time they were supplied could reasonably have been expected to be obtained for supplying the goods or services in the ordinary course of business and on the same terms (apart from the consideration) as those on which they were supplied to the company.

246. Unenforceability of liens on books, etc.

(1)   This section applies in the case of a company where—

(a) an administration order is made in relation to the company, or

(b) the company goes into liquidation, or

(c) a provisional liquidator is appointed;

and 'the office-holder' means the administrator, the liquidator or the provisional liquidator, as the case may be.

(2)   Subject as follows, a lien or other right to retain possession of any of the books, papers or other records of the company is unenforceable to the extent that its enforcement would deny possession of any books, papers or other records to the office-holder.

(3)   This does not apply to a lien on documents which give a title to property and are held as such.

PART VII
INTERPRETATION FOR FIRST GROUP OF PARTS

247. 'Insolvency' and 'go into liquidation'.

(1)   In this Group of Parts, except in so far as the context otherwise requires, 'insolvency', in relation to a company, includes the approval of a voluntary arrangement under Part I, the making of an administration order or the appointment of an administrative receiver.

(2)   For the purposes of any provision in this Group of Parts, a company goes into liquidation if it passes a resolution for voluntary winding up or an order for its winding up is made by the court at a time when it has not already gone into liquidation by passing such a resolution.

248. 'Secured creditor', etc.

In this Group of Parts, except in so far as the context otherwise requires—

(a) 'secured creditor', in relation to a company, means a creditor of the company who holds in respect of his debt a security over property of the company, and 'unsecured creditor' is to be read accordingly; and

(b) 'security' means—

(i) in relation to England and Wales, any mortgage, charge, lien or other security, and

(ii) in relation to Scotland, any security (whether heritable or movable), any floating charge and any right of lien or preference and any right of retention (other than a right of compensation or set-off).

249. 'Connected' with a company.

For the purposes of any provision in this Group of Parts, a person is connected with a company if—

    (a) he is a director or shadow director of the company or an associate of such a director or shadow director, or

    (b) he is an associate of the company;

and 'associate' has the meaning given by section 435 in Part XVIII of this Act.

250. 'Member' of a company.

For the purposes of any provision in this Group of Parts, a person who is not a member of a company but to whom shares in the company have been transferred, or transmitted by operation of law, is to be regarded as a member of the company, and references to a member or members are to be read accordingly.

251. Expressions used generally.

In this Group of Parts, except in so far as the context otherwise requires—

'administrative receiver' means—

    (a) an administrative receiver as defined by section 29(2) in Chapter I of Part III, or

    (b) a receiver appointed under section 51 in Chapter II of that Part in a case where the whole (or substantially the whole) of the company's property is attached by the floating charge;

'business day' means any day other than a Saturday, a Sunday, Christmas Day, Good Friday or a day which is a bank holiday in any part of Great Britain;

'chattel leasing agreement' means an agreement for the bailment or, in Scotland, the hiring of goods which is capable of subsisting for more than 3 months;

'contributory' has the meaning given by section 79;

'director' includes any person occupying the position of director, by whatever name called;

'floating charge' means a charge which, as created, was a floating charge and includes a floating charge within section 462 of the Companies Act (Scottish floating charges);

'office copy', in relation to Scotland, means a copy certified by the clerk of court;

'the official rate', in relation to interest, means the rate payable under section 189(4);

'prescribed' means prescribed by the rules;

'receiver', in the expression 'receiver or manager', does not include a receiver appointed under section 51 in Chapter II of Part III;

'retention of title agreement' means an agreement for the sale of goods to a company, being an agreement—

    (a) which does not constitute a charge on the goods, but

    (b) under which, if the seller is not paid and the company is wound up, the seller will have priority over all other creditors of the company as respects the goods or any property representing the goods;

'the rules' means rules under section 411 in Part XV; and

'shadow director', in relation to a company, means a person in accordance with whose directions or instructions the directors of the company are accustomed to act (but so that a person is not deemed a shadow director by reason only that the directors act on advice given by him in a professional capacity);

and any expression for whose interpretation provision is made by Part XXVI of the Companies Act, other than an expression defined above in this section, is to be construed in accordance with that provision.

THE THIRD GROUP OF PARTS
MISCELLANEOUS MATTERS BEARING ON BOTH COMPANY AND INDIVIDUAL INSOLVENCY; GENERAL INTERPRETATION; FINAL PROVISIONS
PART XII
PREFERENTIAL DEBTS IN COMPANY AND INDIVIDUAL INSOLVENCY

386. Categories of preferential debts.

(1) A reference in this Act to the preferential debts of a company or an individual is to the debts listed in Schedule 6 to this Act (money owed to the Inland Revenue for income tax deducted at source; VAT, insurance premium tax, landfill tax, car tax, betting and gaming duties, beer duty, lottery duty; social security and pension scheme contributions; remuneration etc. of employees; levies on coal and steel production); and references to preferential creditors are to be read accordingly.

(2) In that Schedule 'the debtor' means the company or the individual concerned.

(3) Schedule 6 is to be read with Schedule 4 to the Pension Schemes Act 1993 (occupational pension scheme contributions).

387. 'The relevant date'.

(1) This section explains references in Schedule 6 to the relevant date (being the date which determines the existence and amount of a preferential debt).

(2) For the purposes of section 4 in part I (meetings to consider company voluntary arrangement), the relevant date in relation to a company which is not being wound up is—

(a) where an administration order is in force in relation to the company, the date of the making of that order, and

(b) where no such order has been made, the date of the approval of the voluntary arrangement.

(3) In relation to a company which is being wound up, the following applies—

(a) if the winding up is by the court, and the winding-up order was made immediately upon the discharge of an administration order, the relevant date is the date of the making of the administration order;

(b) if the case does not fall within paragraph (a) and the company—

(i) is being wound up by the court, and

(ii) had not commenced to be wound up voluntarily before the date of the making of the winding-up order,

the relevant date is the date of the appointment (or first appointment) of a provisional liquidator or, if no such appointment has been made, the date of the winding-up order;

(c) if the case does not fall within either paragraph (a) or (b), the relevant date is the date of the passing of the resolution for the winding up of the company.

(4) In relation to a company in receivership (where section 40 or, as the case may be, section 59 applies), the relevant date is—

(a) in England and Wales, the date of the appointment of the receiver by debenture-holders, and

(b) in Scotland, the date of the appointment of the receiver under section 53(6) or (as the case may be) 54(5).

...

PART XVI
PROVISIONS AGAINST DEBT AVOIDANCE (ENGLAND AND WALES ONLY)

423. Transactions defrauding creditors.

(1) This section relates to transactions entered into at an undervalue; and a person enters into such a transaction with another person if—

(a) he makes a gift to the other person or he otherwise enters into a transaction with the other on terms that provide for him to receive no consideration;

(b)   he enters into a transaction with the other in consideration of marriage; or

(c)   he enters into a transaction with the other for a consideration the value of which, in money or money's worth, is significantly less than the value, in money or money's worth, of the consideration provided by himself.

(2)   Where a person has entered into such a transaction, the court may, if satisfied under the next subsection, make such order as it thinks fit for—

(a)   restoring the position to what it would have been if the transaction had not been entered into, and

(b)   protecting the interests of persons who are victims of the transaction.

(3)   In the case of a person entering into such a transaction, an order shall only be made if the court is satisfied that it was entered into by him for the purpose—

(a)   of putting assets beyond the reach of a person who is making, or may at some time make, a claim against him, or

(b)   of otherwise prejudicing the interests of such a person in relation to the claim which he is making or may make.

(4)   In this section 'the court' means the High Court or—

(a)   if the person entering into the transaction is an individual, any other court which would have jurisdiction in relation to a bankruptcy petition relating to him;

(b)   if that person is a body capable of being wound up under Part IV or V of this Act, any other court having jurisdiction to wind it up.

(5)   In relation to a transaction at an undervalue, references here and below to a victim of the transaction are to a person who is, or is capable of being, prejudiced by it; and in the following two sections the person entering into the transaction is referred to as 'the debtor'.

424.   Those who may apply for an order under s. 423.

(1)   An application for an order under section 423 shall not be made in relation to a transaction except—

(a)   in a case where the debtor has been adjudged bankrupt or is a body corporate which is being wound up or in relation to which an administration order is in force, by the official receiver, by the trustee of the bankrupt's estate or the liquidator or administrator of the body corporate or (with the leave of the court) by a victim of the transaction;

(b)   in a case where a victim of the transaction is bound by a voluntary arrangement approved under Part I or Part VIII of this Act, by the supervisor of the voluntary arrangement or by any person who (whether or not so bound) is such a victim; or

(c)   in any other case, by a victim of the transaction.

(2)   An application made under any of the paragraphs of subsection (1) is to be treated as made on behalf of every victim of the transaction.

425.   Provision which may be made by order under s. 423.

(1)   Without prejudice to the generality of section 423, an order made under that section with respect to a transaction may (subject as follows)—

(a)   require any property transferred as part of the transaction to be vested in any person, either absolutely or for the benefit of all the persons on whose behalf the application for the order is treated as made;

(b)   require any property to be so vested if it represents, in any person's hands, the application either of the proceeds of sale of property so transferred or of money so transferred;

(c)   release or discharge (in whole or in part) any security given by the debtor;

(d)   require any person to pay to any other person in respect of benefits received from the debtor such sums as the court may direct;

(e)   provide for any surety or guarantor whose obligations to any person were released or discharged (in whole or in part) under the transaction to be under such new or revived obligations as the court thinks appropriate;

(f)   provide for security to be provided for the discharge of any obligation imposed by or arising under the order, for such an obligation to be charged on any property and for such security or charge to have the same priority as a security or charge released or discharged (in whole or in part) under the transaction.

(2)   An order under section 423 may affect the property of, or impose any obligation on, any person whether or not he is the person with whom the debtor entered into the transaction; but such an order—

(a)   shall not prejudice any interest in property which was acquired from a person other than the debtor and was acquired in good faith, for value and without notice of the relevant circumstances, or prejudice any interest deriving from such an interest, and

(b)   shall not require a person who received a benefit from the transaction in good faith, for value and without notice of the relevant circumstances to pay any sum unless he was a party to the transaction.

(3)   For the purposes of this section the relevant circumstances in relation to a transaction are the circumstances by virtue of which an order under section 423 may be made in respect of the transaction.

(4)   In this section 'security' means any mortgage, charge, lien or other security.

PART XVII
MISCELLANEOUS AND GENERAL

430.   Provision introducing Schedule of punishments.

(1)   Schedule 10 to this Act has effect with respect to the way in which offences under this Act are punishable on conviction.

(2)   In relation to an offence under a provision of this Act specified in the first column of the Schedule (the general nature of the offence being described in the second column), the third column shows whether the offence is punishable on conviction on indictment, or on summary conviction, or either in the one way or the other.

(3)   The fourth column of the Schedule shows, in relation to an offence, the maximum punishment by way of fine or imprisonment under this Act which may be imposed on a person convicted of the offence in the way specified in relation to it in the third column (that is to say, on indictment or summarily) a reference to a period of years or months being to a term of imprisonment of that duration.

(4)   The fifth column shows (in relation to an offence for which there is an entry in that column) that a person convicted of the offence after continued contravention is liable to a daily default fine; that is to say, he is liable on a second or subsequent conviction of the offence to the fine specified in that column for each day on which the contravention is continued (instead of the penalty specified for the offence in the fourth column of the Schedule).

(5)   For the purpose of any enactment in this Act whereby an officer of a company who is in default is liable to a fine or penalty, the expression 'officer who is in default' means any officer of the company who knowingly and wilfully authorises or permits the default, refusal or contravention mentioned in the enactment.

431.   Summary proceedings.

(1)   Summary proceedings for any offence under any of Parts I to VII of this Act may (without prejudice to any jurisdiction exercisable apart from the subsection) be taken against a body corporate at any place at which the body has a place of business, and against any other person at any place at which he is for the time being.

(2)   Notwithstanding anything in section 127(1) of the Magistrates' Courts Act 1980, an information relating to such an offence which is triable by a magistrates' court

in England and Wales may be so tried if it is laid at any time within 3 years after the commission of the offence and within 12 months after the date on which evidence sufficient in the opinion of the Director of Public Prosecutions or the Secretary of State (as the case may be) to justify the proceedings comes to his knowledge.

(3) Summary proceedings in Scotland for such an offence shall not be commenced after the expiration of 3 years from the commission of the offence.

Subject to this (and notwithstanding anything in section 136 of the Criminal Procedure (Scotland) Act 1995), such proceedings may (in Scotland) be commenced at any time within 12 months after the date on which evidence sufficient in the Lord Advocate's opinion to justify the proceedings came to his knowledge or, where such evidence was reported to him by the Secretary of State, within 12 months after the date on which it came to the knowledge of the latter; and subsection (3) of that section applies for the purpose of this subsection as it applies for the purpose of that section.

(4) For purposes of this section, a certificate of the Director of Public Prosecutions, the Lord Advocate or the Secretary of State (as the case may be) as to the date on which such evidence as is referred to above came to his knowledge is conclusive evidence.

432. Offences by bodies corporate.

(1) This section applies to offences under this Act other than those excepted by subsection (4).

(2) Where a body corporate is guilty of an offence to which this section applies and the offence is proved to have been committed with the consent or connivance of, or to be attributable to any neglect on the part of, any director, manager, secretary or other similar officer of the body corporate or any person who was purporting to act in any such capacity he, as well as the body corporate, is guilty of the offence and liable to be proceeded against and punished accordingly.

(3) Where the affairs of a body corporate are managed by its members, subsection (2) applies in relation to the acts and defaults of a member in connection with his functions of management as if he were a director of the body corporate.

(4) The offences excepted from this section are those under sections 30, 39, 51, 53, 54, 62, 64, 66, 85, 89, 164, 188, 201, 206, 207, 208, 209, 210 and 211.

433. Admissibility in evidence of statements of affairs, etc.

In any proceedings (whether or not under this Act)—

(a) a statement of affairs prepared for the purposes of any provision of this Act which is derived from the Insolvency Act 1985, and

(b) any other statement made in pursuance of a requirement imposed by or under any such provision or by or under rules made under this Act,

may be used in evidence against any person making or concurring in making the statement.

434. Crown application.

For the avoidance of doubt it is hereby declared that provisions of this Act which derive from the Insolvency Act 1985 bind the Crown so far as affecting or relating to the following matters, namely—

(a) remedies against, or against the property of, companies or individuals;

(b) priorities of debts;

(c) transactions at an undervalue or preferences;

(d) voluntary arrangements approved under Part I or Part VIII, and

(e) discharge from bankruptcy.

PART XVIII
INTERPRETATION

435. Meaning of 'associate'.

(1) For the purposes of this Act any question whether a person is an associate of another person is to be determined in accordance with the following provisions of this

section (any provision that a person is an associate of another person being taken to mean that they are associates of each other).

(2)   A person is an associate of an individual if that person is the individual's husband or wife, or is a relative, or the husband or wife of a relative, of the individual or of the individual's husband or wife.

(3)   A person is an associate of any person with whom he is in partnership, and of the husband or wife or a relative of any individual with whom he is in partnership; and a Scottish firm is an associate of any person who is a member of the firm.

(4)   A person is an associate of any person whom he employs or by whom he is employed.

(5)   A person in his capacity as trustee of a trust other than—

(a)   a trust arising under any of the second Group of Parts or the Bankruptcy (Scotland) Act 1985, or

(b)   a pension scheme or an employees' share scheme (within the meaning of the Companies Act),

is an associate of another person if the beneficiaries of the trust include, or the terms of the trust confer a power that may be exercised for the benefit of, that other person or an associate of that other person.

(6)   A company is an associate of another company—

(a)   if the same person has control of both, or a person has control of one and persons who are his associates, or he and persons who are his associates, have control of the other, or

(b)   if a group of two or more persons has control of each company, and the groups either consist of the same persons or could be regarded as consisting of the same persons by treating (in one or more cases) a member of either group as replaced by a person of whom he is an associate.

(7)   A company is an associate of another person if that person has control of it or if that person and persons who are his associates together have control of it.

(8)   For the purposes of this section a person is a relative of an individual if he is that individual's brother, sister, uncle, aunt, nephew, niece, lineal ancestor or lineal descendant, treating—

(a)   any relationship of the half blood as a relationship of the whole blood and the stepchild or adopted child of any person as his child, and

(b)   an illegitimate child as the legitimate child of his mother and reputed father; and references in this section to a husand or wife include a former husband or wife and a reputed husband or wife.

(9)   For the purposes of this section any director or other officer of a company is to be treated as employed by that company.

(10)   For the purposes of this section a person is to be taken as having control of a company if—

(a)   the directors of the company or of another company which has control of it (or any of them) are accustomed to act in accordance with his directions or instructions, or

(b)   he is entitled to exercise, or control the exercise of, one third or more of the voting power at any general meeting of the company or of another company which has control of it; and where two or more persons together satisfy either of the above conditions, they are to be taken as having control of the company.

(11)   In this section 'company' includes any body corporate (whether incorporated in Great Britain or elsewhere); and references to directors and other officers of a company and to voting power at any general meeting of a company have effect with any necessary modifications.

436.   Expressions used generally.

In this Act, except in so far as the context otherwise requires (and subject to Parts VII and XI)—

...

'the appointed day' means the day on which this Act comes into force under section 443;

'associate' has the meaning given by section 435;

'business' includes a trade or profession;

'the Companies Act' means the Companies Act 1985;

'conditional sale agreement' and 'hire-purchase agreement' have the same meanings as in the Consumer Credit Act 1974;

...

'modifications' includes additions, alterations and omissions and cognate expressions shall be construed accordingly;

...

'property' includes money, goods, things in action, land and every description of property wherever situated and also obligations and every description of interest, whether present or future or vested or contingent, arising out of, or incidental to, property;

'records' includes computer records and other non-documentary records;

...

'subordinate legislation' has the same meaning as in the Interpretation Act 1978; and 'transaction' includes a gift, agreement or arrangement, and references to entering into a transaction shall be construed accordingly.

...

PART XIX
FINAL PROVISIONS

443. Commencement.

This Act comes into force on the day appointed under section 236(2) of the Insolvency Act 1985 for the coming into force of Part III of that Act (individual insolvency and bankruptcy), immediately after that Part of that Act comes into force for England and Wales.

[*The day appointed for the coming into force of part III of the Insolvency Act 1985 was 29 December 1986 (Insolvency Act 1985 (Commencement No. 5) Order 1986 (SI 1986/1924), art. 3).*]

444. Citation.

This Act may be cited as the Insolvency Act 1986.

SCHEDULES

Sections 14, 42   SCHEDULE 1

POWERS OF ADMINISTRATOR OR ADMINISTRATIVE RECEIVER

1.   Power to take possession of, collect and get in the property of the company and, for that purpose, to take such proceedings as may seem to him expedient.

2.   Power to sell or otherwise dispose of the property of the company by public auction or private contract or, in Scotland, to sell, feu, hire out or otherwise dispose of the property of the company by public roup or private bargain.

3.   Power to raise or borrow money and grant security therefor over the property of the company.

4.   Power to appoint a solicitor or accountant or other professionally qualified person to assist him in the performance of his functions.

5.   Power to bring or defend any action or other legal proceedings in the name and on behalf of the company.

6.   Power to refer to arbitration any question affecting the company.

7. Power to effect and maintain insurances in respect of the business and property of the company.

8. Power to use the company's seal.

9. Power to do all acts and to execute in the name and on behalf of the company any deed, receipt or other document.

10. Power to draw, accept, make and endorse any bill of exchange or promissory note in the name and on behalf of the company.

11. Power to appoint any agent to do any business which he is unable to do himself or which can more conveniently be done by an agent and power to employ and dismiss employees.

12. Power to do all such things (including the carrying out of works) as may be necessary for the realisation of the property of the company.

13. Power to make any payment which is necessary or incidental to the performance of his functions.

14. Power to carry on the business of the company.

15. Power to establish subsidiaries of the company.

16. Power to transfer to subsidiaries of the company the whole or any part of the business and property of the company.

17. Power to grant or accept a surrender of a lease or tenancy of any of the property of the company, and to take a lease or tenancy of any property required or convenient for the business of the company.

18. Power to make any arrangement or compromise on behalf of the company.

19. Power to call up any uncalled capital of the company.

20. Power to rank and claim in the bankruptcy, insolvency, sequestration or liquidation of any person indebted to the company and to receive dividends, and to accede to trust deeds for the creditors of any such person.

21. Power to present or defend a petition for the winding up of the company.

22. Power to change the situation of the company's registered office.

23. Power to do all other things incidental to the exercise of the foregoing powers.

Sections 165, 167   SCHEDULE 4

POWERS OF LIQUIDATOR IN A WINDING UP

PART I
POWERS EXERCISABLE WITH SANCTION

1. Power to pay any class of creditors in full.

2. Power to make any compromise or arrangement with creditors or persons claiming to be creditors, or having or alleging themselves to have any claim (present or future, certain or contingent, ascertained or sounding only in damages) against the company, or whereby the company may be rendered liable.

3. Power to compromise, on such terms as may be agreed—

(a)   all calls and liabilities to calls, all debts and liabilities capable of resulting in debts, and all claims (present or future, certain or contingent, ascertained or sounding only in damages) subsisting or supposed to subsist between the company and a contributory or alleged contributory or other debtor or person apprehending liability to the company, and

(b)   all questions in any way relating to or affecting the assets or the winding up of the company,

and take any security for the discharge of any such call, debt, liability or claim and give a complete discharge in respect of it.

PART II
POWERS EXERCISABLE WITHOUT SANCTION IN VOLUNTARY WINDING UP, WITH SANCTION IN WINDING UP BY THE COURT

4.   Power to bring or defend any action or other legal proceeding in the name and on behalf of the company.

5.   Power to carry on the business of the company so far as may be necessary for its beneficial winding up.

PART III
POWERS EXERCISABLE WITHOUT SANCTION IN ANY WINDING UP

6.   Power to sell any of the company's property by public auction or private contract with power to transfer the whole of it to any person or to sell the same in parcels.

7.   Power to do all acts and execute, in the name and on behalf of the company, all deeds, receipts and other documents and for that purpose to use, when necessary, the company's seal.

8.   Power to prove, rank and claim in the bankruptcy, insolvency or sequestration of any contributory for any balance against his estate, and to receive dividends in the bankruptcy, insolvency or sequestration in respect of that balance, as a separate debt due from the bankrupt or insolvent, and rateably with the other separate creditors.

9.   Power to draw, accept, make and endorse any bill of exchange or promissory note in the name and on behalf of the company, with the same effect with respect to the company's liability as if the bill or note had been drawn, accepted, made or endorsed by or on behalf of the company in the course of its business.

10.   Power to raise on the security of the assets of the company any money requisite.

11.   Power to take out in his official name letters of administration to any deceased contributory, and to do in his official name any other act necessary for obtaining payment of any money due from a contributory or his estate which cannot conveniently be done in the name of the company.

In all such cases the money due is deemed, for the purpose of enabling the liquidator to take out the letters of administration or recover the money, to be due to the liquidator himself.

12.   Power to appoint an agent to do any business which the liquidator is unable to do himself.

13.   Power to do all such other things as may be necessary for winding up the company's affairs and distributing its assets.

Section 386   SCHEDULE 6

THE CATEGORIES OF PREFERENTIAL DEBTS

Category 1: Debts due to Inland Revenue

1.   Sums due at the relevant date from the debtor on account of deductions of income tax from emoluments paid during the period of 12 months next before that date.

The deductions here referred to are those which the debtor was liable to make under section 203 of the Income and Corporation Taxes Act 1988 (pay as you earn), less the amount of the repayments of income tax which the debtor was liable to make during that period.

2.   Sums due at the relevant date from the debtor in respect of such deductions as are required to be made by the debtor for that period under section 559 of the Income and Corporation Taxes Act 1988 (sub-contractors in the construction industry).

Category 2: Debts due to Customs and Excise

3.   Any value added tax which is referable to the period of 6 months next before the relevant date (which period is referred to below as 'the 6-month period').

For the purposes of this paragraph—

(a)   where the whole of the prescribed accounting period to which any value added tax is attributable falls within the 6-month period, the whole amount of that tax is referable to that period; and

(b)   in any other case the amount of any value added tax which is referable to the 6-month period is the proportion of the tax which is equal to such proportion (if any) of the accounting reference period in question as falls within the 6-month period;

and in sub-paragraph (a) 'prescribed' means prescribed by regulations under the Value Added Tax Act 1994.

3A.   Any insurance premium tax which is referable to the period of 6 months next before the relevant date (which period is referred to below as 'the 6-month period').

For the purposes of this paragraph—

(a)   where the whole of the accounting period to which any insurance premium tax is attributable falls within the 6-month period, the whole amount of that tax is referable to that period; and

(b)   in any other case the amount of any insurance premium tax which is referable to the 6-month period is the proportion of the tax which is equal to such proportion (if any) of the accounting period in question as falls within the 6-month period;

and references here to accounting periods shall be construed in accordance with Part III of the Finance Act 1994.

3B.   Any landfill tax which is referable to the period of 6 months next before the relevant date (which period is referred to below as 'the 6-month period').

For the purposes of this paragraph—

(a)   where the whole of the accounting period to which any landfill tax is attributable falls within the 6-month period, the whole amount of that tax is referable to that period; and

(b)   in any other case the amount of any landfill tax which is referable to the 6-month period is the proportion of the tax which is equal to such proportion (if any) of the accounting period in question as falls within the 6-month period;

and references here to accounting periods shall be construed in accordance with Part III of the Finance Act 1996.

4.   The amount of any car tax which is due at the relevant date from the debtor and which became due within a period of 12 months next before that date.

5.   Any amount which is due—

(a)   by way of general betting duty, bingo duty or gaming duty, or

(b)   under section 12(1) of the Betting and Gaming Duties Act 1981 (general betting duty and pool betting duty recoverable from agent collecting stakes),

from the debtor at the relevant date and which became due within the period of 12 months next before that date.

5A.   The amount of any excise duty on beer which is due at the relevant date from the debtor and which became due within a period of 6 months next before that date.

5B.   Any amount which is due by way of lottery duty from the debtor at the relevant date and which became due within the period of 12 months next before that date.

5C.   Any amount which is due by way of air passenger duty from the debtor at the relevant date and which became due within the period of six months next before that date.

Category 3: Social security contributions

6.   All sums which on the relevant date are due from the debtor on account of Class 1 or Class 2 contributions under the Social Security Contributions and Benefits Act 1992 or the Social Security (Northern Ireland) Act 1975 and which became due from the debtor in the 12 months next before the relevant date.

[*Before an amendment was made by the Social Security (Consequential Provisions) Act 1992, sch. 2, para. 73, this paragraph referred to the Social Security Act 1975 instead of the Social Security Contributions and Benefits Act 1992. The reference in paragraph 7 to 'either of those Acts of 1975' was not amended to reflect the amendment made in this paragraph. The reference to the Social Security (Northern Ireland) Act 1975 is to be construed as including a reference to the Social Security Contributions and Benefits (Northern Ireland) Act 1992 (Social Security (Consequential Provisions) (Northern Ireland) Act 1992, s. 2(4)).*]

7.   All sums which on the relevant date have been assessed on and are due from the debtor on account of Class 4 contributions under either of those Acts of 1975, being sums which—

(a)   are due to the Commissioners of Inland Revenue (rather than to the Secretary of State or a Northern Ireland department), and

(b)   are assessed on the debtor up to 5 April next before the relevant date,

but not exceeding, in the whole, any one year's assessment.

Category 4: Contributions to occupational pension schemes, etc.

8.   Any sum which is owed by the debtor and is a sum to which Schedule 4 to the Pension Schemes Act 1993 applies (contributions to occupational pension schemes and state scheme premiums).

Category 5: Remuneration, etc., of employees

9.   So much of any amount which—

(a)   is owed by the debtor to a person who is or has been an employee of the debtor, and

(b)   is payable by way of remuneration in respect of the whole or any part of the period of 4 months next before the relevant date,

as does not exceed so much as may be prescribed by order made by the Secretary of State.

10.   An amount owed by way of accrued holiday remuneration, in respect of any period of employment before the relevant date, to a person whose employment by the debtor has been terminated, whether before, on or after that date.

11.   So much of any sum owed in respect of money advanced for the purpose as has been applied for the payment of a debt which, if it had not been paid, would have been a debt falling within paragraph 9 or 10.

12.   So much of any amount which—

(a)   is ordered (whether before or after the relevant date) to be paid by the debtor under the Reserve Forces (Safeguard of Employment) Act 1985, and

(b)   is so ordered in respect of a default made by the debtor before that date in the discharge of his obligations under that Act,

as does not exceed such amount as may be prescribed by order made by the Secretary of State.

Interpretation for Category 5

13.—(1)   For the purposes of paragraphs 9 to 12, a sum is payable by the debtor to a person by way of remuneration in respect of any period if—

(a)   it is paid as wages or salary (whether payable for time or for piece work or earned wholly or partly by way of commission) in respect of services rendered to the debtor in that period, or

(b)   it is an amount falling within the following sub-paragraph and is payable by the debtor in respect of that period.

(2)   An amount falls within this sub-paragraph if it is—

(a)   a guarantee payment under Part III of the Employment Rights Act 1996 (employee without work to do);

(b) any payment for time off under section 53 (time off to look for work or arrange training) or section 56 (time off for ante-natal care) of that Act or under section 169 of the Trade Union and Labour Relations (Consolidation) Act 1992 (time off for carrying out trade union duties etc.);

(c) remuneration on suspension on medical grounds, or on maternity grounds, under Part VII of the Employment Rights Act 1996; or

(d) remuneration under a protective award under section 189 of the Trade Union and Labour Relations (Consolidation) Act 1992 (redundancy dismissal with compensation).

14.—(1) This paragraph relates to a case in which a person's employment has been terminated by or in consequence of his employer going into liquidation or being adjudged bankrupt or (his employer being a company not in liquidation) by or in consequence of—

(a) a receiver being appointed as mentioned in section 40 of this Act (debenture-holders secured by floating charge), or

(b) the appointment of a receiver under section 53(6) or 54(5) of this Act (Scottish company with property subject to floating charge), or

(c) the taking of possession by debenture-holders (so secured), as mentioned in section 196 of the Companies Act.

(2) For the purposes of paragraphs 9 to 12, holiday remuneration is deemed to have accrued to that person in respect of any period of employment if, by virtue of his contract of employment or of any enactment that remuneration would have accrued in respect of that period if his employment had continued until he became entitled to be allowed the holiday.

(3) The reference in sub-paragraph (2) to any enactment includes an order or direction made under an enactment.

15. Without prejudice to paragraphs 13 and 14—

(a) any remuneration payable by the debtor to a person in respect of a period of holiday or of absence from work through sickness or other good cause is deemed to be wages or (as the case may be) salary in respect of services rendered to the debtor in that period, and

(b) references here and in those paragraphs to remuneration in respect of a period of holiday include any sums which, if they had been paid, would have been treated for the purposes of the enactments relating to social security as earnings in respect of that period.

Category 6: Levies on coal and steel production

15A. Any sums due at the relevant date from the debtor in respect of—

(a) the levies on the production of coal and steel referred to in Articles 49 and 50 of the E.C.S.C. Treaty, or

(b) any surcharge for delay provided for in Article 50(3) of that Treaty and Article 6 of Decision 3/52 of the High Authority of the Coal and Steel Community.

Orders

16. An order under paragraph 9 or 12—

(a) may contain such transitional provisions as may appear to the Secretary of State necessary or expedient;

(b) shall be made by statutory instrument subject to annulment in pursuance of a resolution of either House of Parliament.

Section 430

SCHEDULE 10

PUNISHMENT OF OFFENCES UNDER THIS ACT

Section of Act creating offence	General nature of offence	Mode of prosecution	Punishment	Daily default fine (where applicable)
12(2)	Company and others failing to state in correspondence etc. that administrator appointed.	Summary.	One-fifth of the statutory maximum.	One-fiftieth of the statutory maximum.
15(8)	Failure of administrator to register office copy of court order permitting disposal of charged property.	Summary.	One-fifth of the statutory maximum.	One-fiftieth of the statutory maximum.
18(5)	Failure of administrator to register office copy of court order varying or discharging administration order.	Summary.	One-fifth of the statutory maximum.	One-fiftieth of the statutory maximum.
21(3)	Administrator failing to register administration order and give notice of appointment.	Summary.	One-fifth of the statutory maximum.	One-fiftieth of the statutory maximum.
22(6)	Failure to comply with provisions relating to statement of affairs, where administrator appointed.	1. On indictment. 2. Summary.	A fine. The statutory maximum.	One-tenth of the statutory maximum.
23(3)	Administrator failing to send out, register and lay before creditors statement of his proposals.	Summary.	One-fifth of the statutory maximum.	One-fiftieth of the statutory maximum.
24(7)	Administrator failing to file court order discharging administration order under s. 24.	Summary.	One-fifth of the statutory maximum.	One-fiftieth of the statutory maximum.
27(6)	Administrator failing to file court order discharging administration order under s. 27.	Summary.	One-fifth of the statutory maximum.	One-fiftieth of the statutory maximum.
30	Body corporate acting as receiver.	1. On indictment. 2. Summary.	A fine. The statutory maximum.	
31	Undischarged bankrupt acting as receiver or manager.	1. On indictment. 2. Summary.	2 years or a fine; or both. 6 months or the statutory maximum, or both.	

Section		General nature of offence	Mode of prosecution	Punishment	Daily default fine (where applicable)
38(5)	...	Receiver failing to deliver accounts to registrar.	Summary.	One-fifth of the statutory maximum.	One-fiftieth of the statutory maximum.
39(2)	...	Company and others failing to state in correspondence that receiver appointed.	Summary.	One-fifth of the statutory maximum.	One-fiftieth of the statutory maximum.
43(6)	...	Administrative receiver failing to file office copy of order permitting disposal of charged property.	Summary.	One-fifth of the statutory maximum.	One-fiftieth of the statutory maximum.
45(5)	...	Administrative receiver failing to file notice of vacation of office.	Summary.	One-fifth of the statutory maximum.	*One-fiftieth of the statutory maximum.*
46(4)	...	Administrative receiver failing to give notice of his appointment.	Summary.	One-fifth of the statutory maximum.	One-fiftieth of the statutory maximum.
47(6)	...	Failure to comply with provisions relating to statement of affairs, where administrative receiver appointed.	1. On indictment. 2. Summary.	A fine. The statutory maximum.	One-tenth of the statutory maximum.
48(8)	...	Administrative receiver failing to comply with requirements as to his report.	Summary.	One-fifth of the statutory maximum.	One-fiftieth of the statutory maximum.
...					
85(2)	...	Company failing to give notice in Gazette of resolution for voluntary winding up.	Summary.	One-fifth of the statutory maximum.	One-fiftieth of the statutory maximum.
89(4)	...	Director making statutory declaration of company's solvency without reasonable grounds for his opinion.	1. On indictment. 2. Summary.	2 years or a fine; or both. 6 months or the statutory maximum, or both.	One-fiftieth of the statutory maximum.
89(6)	...	Declaration under section 89 not delivered to registrar within prescribed time.	Summary.	One-fifth of the statutory maximum.	One-fiftieth of the statutory maximum.
93(3)	...	Liquidator failing to summon general meeting of company at each year's end.	Summary.	One-fifth of the statutory maximum.	One-fiftieth of the statutory maximum.
94(4)	...	Liquidator failing to send to registrar a copy of account of winding up and return of final meeting.	Summary.	One-fifth of the statutory maximum.	One-fiftieth of the statutory maximum.
94(6)	...	Liquidator failing to call final meeting.	Summary.	One-fifth of the statutory maximum.	One-fiftieth of the statutory maximum.

Section of Act creating offence	General nature of offence	Mode of prosecution	Punishment	Daily default fine (where applicable)
95(8) ...	Liquidator failing to comply with s. 95, where company insolvent.	Summary.	The statutory maximum.	
98(6) ...	Company failing to comply with s. 98 in respect of summoning and giving notice of creditors' meeting.	1. On indictment. 2. Summary.	A fine. The statutory maximum.	
99(3) ...	Directors failing to attend and lay statement in prescribed form before creditors' meeting.	1. On indictment. 2. Summary.	A fine. The statutory maximum.	
105(3) ...	Liquidator failing to summon company general meeting and creditors' meeting at each year's end.	Summary.	One-fifth of the statutory maximum.	
106(4) ...	Liquidator failing to send to registrar account of winding up and return of final meetings.	Summary.	One-fifth of the statutory maximum.	One-fiftieth of the statutory maximum.
106(6) ...	Liquidator failing to call final meeting of company or creditors.	Summary.	One-fifth of the statutory maximum.	
109(2) ...	Liquidator failing to publish notice of his appointment.	Summary.	One-fifth of the statutory maximum.	One-fiftieth of the statutory maximum.
114(4) ...	Directors exercising powers in breach of s. 114, where no liquidator.	Summary.	The statutory maximum.	
131(7) ...	Failing to comply with requirements as to statement of affairs, where liquidator appointed.	1. On indictment. 2. Summary.	A fine. The statutory maximum.	One-tenth of the statutory maximum.
164 ...	Giving, offering etc. corrupt inducement affecting appointment of liquidator.	1. On indictment. 2. Summary.	A fine. The statutory maximum.	
166(7) ...	Liquidator failing to comply with requirements of s. 166 in creditors' voluntary winding up.	Summary.	The statutory maximum.	
188(2) ...	Default in compliance with s. 188 as to notification that company being wound up.	Summary.	One-fifth of the statutory maximum.	

Section		Description	Mode of prosecution	Punishment	Daily default fine
192(2)	...	Liquidator failing to notify registrar as to progress of winding up.	Summary.	One-fifth of the statutory maximum.	One-fiftieth of the statutory maximum.
201(4)	...	Failing to deliver to registrar office copy of court order deferring dissolution.	Summary.	One-fifth of the statutory maximum.	One-fiftieth of the statutory maximum.
203(6)	...	Failing to deliver to registrar copy of directions or result of appeal under s. 203.	Summary.	One-fifth of the statutory maximum.	One-fiftieth of the statutory maximum.
204(7)	...	Liquidator failing to deliver to registrar copy of court order for early dissolution.	Summary.	One-fifth of the statutory maximum.	One-fiftieth of the statutory maximum.
204(8)	...	Failing to deliver to registrar copy of court order deferring early dissolution.	Summary.	One-fifth of the statutory maximum.	One-fiftieth of the statutory maximum.
205(7)	...	Failing to deliver to registrar copy of Secretary of State's directions or court order deferring dissolution.	Summary.	One-fifth of the statutory maximum.	One-fiftieth of the statutory maximum.
206(1)	...	Fraud etc. in anticipation of winding up.	1. On indictment. 2. Summary.	7 years or a fine, or both. 6 months or the statutory maximum, or both.	
206(2)	...	Privity to fraud in anticipation of winding up; fraud, or privity to fraud, after commencement of winding up.	1. On indictment. 2. Summary.	7 years or a fine, or both. 6 months or the statutory maximum, or both.	
206(5)	...	Knowingly taking in pawn or pledge, or otherwise receiving, company property.	1. On indictment. 2. Summary.	7 years or a fine, or both. 6 months or the statutory maximum, or both.	
207	...	Officer of company entering into transaction in fraud of company's creditors.	1. On indictment. 2. Summary.	2 years or a fine, or both. 6 months or the statutory maximum, or both.	
208	...	Officer of company misconducting himself in course of winding up.	1. On indictment. 2. Summary.	7 years or a fine, or both. 6 months or the statutory maximum, or both.	
209	...	Officer or contributory destroying, falsifying, etc. company's books.	1. On indictment. 2. Summary.	7 years or a fine, or both. 6 months or the statutory maximum, or both.	

Section of Act creating offence	General nature of offence	Mode of prosecution	Punishment	Daily default fine (where applicable)
210 ...	Officer of company making material omission from statement relating to company's affairs.	1. On indictment. 2. Summary.	7 years or a fine, or both. 6 months or the statutory maximum, or both.	
211 ...	False representation or fraud for purpose of obtaining creditors' consent to an agreement in connection with winding up.	1. On indictment. 2. Summary.	7 years or a fine, or both. 6 months or the statutory maximum, or both.	
216(4) ...	Contravening restrictions on reuse of name of company in insolvent liquidation.	1. On indictment. 2. Summary.	2 years or a fine, or both. 6 months or the statutory maximum, or both.	
235(5) ...	Failing to cooperate with office-holder.	1. On indictment. 2. Summary.	A fine. The statutory maximum.	One-tenth of the statutory maximum.
...				

[The entry in column 5 (daily default fine) relating to s. 45(5) would be repealed if the relevant provision of sch. 24 to the Companies Act 1989 were brought into force.]

COMPANY DIRECTORS DISQUALIFICATION ACT 1986
(1986, c. 46)

An Act to consolidate certain enactments relating to the disqualification of persons from being directors of companies, and from being otherwise concerned with a company's affairs.

[25 July 1986]

Preliminary

1. Disqualification orders: general.

(1)   In the circumstances specified below in this Act a court may, and under section 6 shall, make against a person a disqualification order, that is to say an order that he shall not, without leave of the court—

(a)   be a director of a company, or

(b)   be a liquidator or administrator of a company, or

(c)   be a receiver or manager of a company's property, or

(d)   in any way, whether directly or indirectly, be concerned or take part in the promotion, formation or management of a company,

for a specified period beginning with the date of the order.

(2)   In each section of this Act which gives to a court power or, as the case may be, imposes on it the duty to make a disqualification order there is specified the maximum (and, in section 6, the minimum) period of disqualification which may or (as the case may be) must be imposed by means of the order.

(3)   Where a disqualification order is made against a person who is already subject to such an order, the periods specified in those orders shall run concurrently.

(4)   A disqualification order may be made on grounds which are or include matters other than criminal convictions, notwithstanding that the person in respect of whom it is to be made may be criminally liable in respect of those matters.

Disqualification for general misconduct in connection with companies

2. Disqualification on conviction of indictable offence.

(1)   The court may make a disqualification order against a person where he is convicted of an indictable offence (whether on indictment or summarily) in connection with the promotion, formation, management, liquidation or striking off of a company, or with the receivership or management of a company's property.

(2)   'The court' for this purpose means—

(a)   any court having jurisdiction to wind up the company in relation to which the offence was committed, or

(b)   the court by or before which the person is convicted of the offence, or

(c)   in the case of a summary conviction in England and Wales, any other magistrates' court acting for the same petty sessions area;

and for the purposes of this section the definition of 'indictable offence' in Schedule 1 to the Interpretation Act 1978 applies for Scotland as it does for England and Wales.

(3)   The maximum period of disqualification under this section is—

(a)   where the disqualification order is made by a court of summary jurisdiction, 5 years, and

(b)   in any other case, 15 years.

3. Disqualification for persistent breaches of companies legislation.

(1)   The court may make a disqualification order against a person where it appears to it that he has been persistently in default in relation to provisions of the companies legislation requiring any return, account or other document to be filed with, delivered or sent, or notice of any matter to be given, to the registrar of companies.

(2)   On an application to the court for an order to be made under this section, the fact that a person has been persistently in default in relation to such provisions as are mentioned above may (without prejudice to its proof in any other manner) be conclusively proved by showing that in the 5 years ending with the date of the application he has been adjudged guilty (whether or not on the same occasion) of three or more defaults in relation to those provisions.

(3)   A person is to be treated under subsection (2) as being adjudged guilty of a default in relation to any provision of that legislation if—

(a)   he is convicted (whether on indictment or summarily) of an offence consisting in a contravention of or failure to comply with that provision (whether on his own part or on the part of any company), or

(b)   a default order is made against him, that is to say an order under any of the following provisions—

(i)   section 242(4) of the Companies Act (order requiring delivery of company accounts),

(ia)   section 245B of that Act (order requiring preparation of revised accounts),

(ii)   section 713 of that Act (enforcement of company's duty to make returns),

(iii)   section 41 of the Insolvency Act (enforcement of receiver's or manager's duty to make returns), or

(iv)   section 170 of that Act (corresponding provision for liquidator in winding up),

in respect of any such contravention of or failure to comply with that provision (whether on his own part or on the part of any company).

(4)   In this section 'the court' means any court having jurisdiction to wind up any of the companies in relation to which the offence or other default has been or is alleged to have been committed.

(5)   The maximum period of disqualification under this section is 5 years.

4.   Disqualification for fraud, etc., in winding up.

(1)   The court may make a disqualification order against a person if, in the course of the winding up of a company, it appears that he—

(a)   has been guilty of an offence for which he is liable (whether he has been convicted or not) under section 458 of the Companies Act (fraudulent trading), or

(b)   has otherwise been guilty, while an officer or liquidator of the company or receiver or manager of its property, of any fraud in relation to the company or of any breach of his duty as such officer, liquidator, receiver or manager.

(2)   In this section 'the court' means any court having jurisdiction to wind up any of the companies in relation to which the offence or other default has been or is alleged to have been committed; and 'officer' includes a shadow director.

(3)   The maximum period of disqualification under this section is 15 years.

5.   Disqualification on summary conviction.

(1)   An offence counting for the purposes of this section is one of which a person is convicted (either on indictment or summarily) in consequence of a contravention of, or failure to comply with, any provision of the companies legislation requiring a return, account or other document to be filed with, delivered or sent, or notice of any matter to be given, to the registrar of companies (whether the contravention or failure is on the person's own part or on the part of any company).

(2)   Where a person is convicted of a summary offence counting for those purposes, the court by which he is convicted (or, in England and Wales, any other magistrates' court acting for the same petty sessions area) may make a disqualification order against him if the circumstances specified in the next subsection are present.

(3)   Those circumstances are that, during the 5 years ending with the date of the conviction, the person has had made against him, or has been convicted of, in total not

less than 3 default orders and offences counting for the purposes of this section; and those offences may include that of which he is convicted as mentioned in subsection (2) and any other offence of which he is convicted on the same occasion.

(4) For the purposes of this section—

(a) the definition of 'summary offence' in Schedule 1 to the Interpretation Act 1978 applies for Scotland as for England and Wales, and

(b) 'default order' means the same as in section 3(3)(b).

(5) The maximum period of disqualification under this section is 5 years.

Disqualification for unfitness

6. Duty of court to disqualify unfit directors of insolvent companies.

(1) The court shall make a disqualification order against a person in any case where, on an application under this section, it is satisfied—

(a) that he is or has been a director of a company which has at any time become insolvent (whether while he was a director or subsequently), and

(b) that his conduct as a director of that company (either taken alone or taken together with his conduct as a director of any other company or companies) makes him unfit to be concerned in the management of a company.

(2) For the purposes of this section and the next, a company becomes insolvent if—

(a) the company goes into liquidation at a time when its assets are insufficient for the payment of its debts and other liabilities and the expenses of the winding up,

(b) an administration order is made in relation to the company, or

(c) an administrative receiver of the company is appointed;

and references to a person's conduct as a director of any company or companies include, where that company or any of those companies has become insolvent, that person's conduct in relation to any matter connected with or arising out of the insolvency of that company.

(3) In this section and the next 'the court' means—

(a) in the case of a person who is or has been a director of a company which is being wound up by the court, the court by which the company is being wound up,

(b) in the case of a person who is or has been a director of a company which is being wound up voluntarily, any court having jurisdiction to wind up the company,

(c) in the case of a person who is or has been a director of a company in relation to which an administration order is in force, the court by which that order was made, and

(d) in any other case, the High Court or, in Scotland, the Court of Session;

and in both sections 'director' includes a shadow director.

(4) Under this section the minimum period of disqualification is 2 years, and the maximum period is 15 years.

7. Applications to court under s. 6; reporting provisions.

(1) If it appears to the Secretary of State that it is expedient in the public interest that a disqualification order under section 6 should be made against any person, an application for the making of such an order against that person may be made—

(a) by the Secretary of State, or

(b) if the Secretary of State so directs in the case of a person who is or has been a director of a company which is being wound up by the court in England and Wales, by the official receiver.

(2) Except with the leave of the court, an application for the making under that section of a disqualification order against any person shall not be made after the end of the period of 2 years beginning with the day on which the company of which that person is or has been a director became insolvent.

(3)   If it appears to the office-holder responsible under this section, that is to say—

(a)   in the case of a company which is being wound up by the court in England and Wales, the official receiver,

(b)   in the case of a company which is being wound up otherwise, the liquidator,

(c)   in the case of a company in relation to which an administration order is in force, the administrator, or

(d)   in the case of a company of which there is an administrative receiver, that receiver,

that the conditions mentioned in section 6(1) are satisfied as respects a person who is or has been a director of that company, the office-holder shall forthwith report the matter to the Secretary of State.

(4)   The Secretary of State or the official receiver may require the liquidator, administrator or administrative receiver of a company, or the former liquidator, administrator or administrative receiver of a company—

(a)   to furnish him with such information with respect to any person's conduct as a director of the company, and

(b)   to produce and permit inspection of such books, papers and other records relevant to that person's conduct as such a director,

as the Secretary of State or the official receiver may reasonably require for the purpose of determining whether to exercise, or of exercising, any function of his under this section.

8.   Disqualification after investigation of company.

(1)   If it appears to the Secretary of State from a report made by inspectors under section 437 of the Companies Act or section 94 or 177 of the Financial Services Act 1986, or from information or documents obtaind under section 447 or 448 of the Companies Act or section 105 of the Financial Services Act 1986 or section 2 of the Criminal Justice Act 1987 or section 28 of the Criminal Law (Consolidation) (Scotland) Act 1995 or section 83 of the Companies Act 1989, that it is expedient in the public interest that a disqualification order should be made against any person who is or has been a director or shadow director of any company, he may apply to the court for such an order to be made against that person.

(2)   The court may make a disqualification order against a person where, on an application under this section, it is satisfied that his conduct in relation to the company makes him unfit to be concerned in the management of a company.

(3)   In this section 'the court' means the High Court or, in Scotland, the Court of Session.

(4)   The maximum period of disqualification under this section is 15 years.

9.   Matters for determining unfitness of directors.

(1)   Where it falls to a court to determine whether a person's conduct as a director or shadow diretor of any particular company or companies makes him unfit to be concerned in the management of a company, the court shall, as respects his conduct as a director of that company or, as the case may be, each of those companies, have regard in particular—

(a)   to the matters mentioned in Part I of Schedule 1 to this Act, and

(b)   where the company has become insolvent, to the matters mentioned in Part II of that Schedule;

and references in that Schedule to the director and the company are to be read accordingly.

(2)   Section 6(2) applies for the purposes of this section and Schedule 1 as it applies for the purposes of sections 6 and 7.

(3)   Subject to the next subsection, any reference in Schedule 1 to an enactment contained in the Companies Act or the Insolvency Act includes, in relation to any time

before the coming into force of that enactment, the corresponding enactment in force at that time.

(4)   The Secretary of State may by order modify any of the provisions of Schedule 1; and such an order may contain such transitional provisions as may appear to the Secretary of State necessary or expedient.

(5)   The power to make orders under this section is exercisable by statutory instrument subject to annulment in pursuance of a resolution of either House of Parliament.

Other cases of disqualification

10.   Participation in wrongful trading.

(1)   Where the court makes a declaration under section 213 or 214 of the Insolvency Act that a person is liable to make a contribution to a company's assets, then, whether or not an application for such an order is made by any person, the court may, if it thinks fit, also make a disqualification order against the person to whom the declaration relates.

(2)   The maximum period of disqualification under this section is 15 years.

11.   Undischarged bankrupts.

(1)   It is an offence for a person who is an undischarged bankrupt to act as director of, or directly or indirectly to take part in or be concerned in the promotion, formation or management of, a company, except with the leave of the court.

(2)   'The court' for this purpose is the court by which the person was adjudged bankrupt or, in Scotland, sequestration of his estates was awarded.

(3)   In England and Wales, the leave of the court shall not be given unless notice of intention to apply for it has been served on the official receiver; and it is the latter's duty, if he is of opinion that it is contrary to the public interest that the application should be granted, to attend on the hearing of the application and oppose it.

12.   Failure to pay under county court administration order.

(1)   The following has effect where a court under section 429 of the Insolvency Act revokes an administration order under Part VI of the County Courts Act 1984.

(2)   A person to whom that section applies by virtue of the order under section 429(2)(b) shall not, except with the leave of the court which made the order, act as director or liquidator of, or directly or indirectly take part or be concerned in the promotion, formation or management of, a company.

Consequences of contravention

13.   Criminal penalties.

If a person acts in contravention of a disqualification order or of section 12(2), or is guilty of an offence under section 11, he is liable—

(a)   on conviction on indictment, to imprisonment for not more than 2 years or a fine, or both; and

(b)   on summary conviction, to imprisonment for not more than 6 months or a fine not exceeding the statutory maximum, or both.

14.   Offences by body corporate.

(1)   Where a body corporate is guilty of an offence of acting in contravention of a disqualification order, and it is proved that the offence occurred with the consent or connivance of, or was attributable to any neglect on the part of any director, manager, secretary or other similar officer of the body corporate, or any person who was purporting to act in any such capacity he, as well as the body corporate, is guilty of the offence and liable to be proceeded against and punished accordingly.

(2)   Where the affairs of a body corporate are managed by its members, subsection (1) applies in relation to the acts and defaults of a member in connection with his functions of management as if he were a director of the body corporate.

15. Personal liability for company's debts where person acts while disqualified.

(1)   A person is personally responsible for all the relevant debts of a company if at any time—

(a)   in contravention of a disqualification order or of section 11 of this Act he is involved in the management of the company, or

(b)   as a person who is involved in the management of the company, he acts or is willing to act on instructions given without the leave of the court by a person whom he knows at that time to be the subject of a disqualification order or to be an undischarged bankrupt.

(2)   Where a person is personally responsible under this section for the relevant debts of a company, he is jointly and severally liable in respect of those debts with the company and any other person who, whether under this section or otherwise, is so liable.

(3)   For the purposes of this section the relevant debts of a company are—

(a)   in relation to a person who is personally responsible under paragraph (a) of subsection (1), such debts and other liabilities of the company as are incurred at a time when that person was involved in the management of the company, and

(b)   in relation to a person who is personally responsible under paragraph (b) of that subsection, such debts and other liabilities of the company as are incurred at a time when that person was acting or was willing to act on instructions given as mentioned in that paragraph.

(4)   For the purposes of this section, a person is involved in the management of a company if he is a director of the company or if he is concerned, whether directly or indirectly, or takes part, in the management of the company.

(5)   For the purposes of this section a person who, as a person involved in the management of a company, has at any time acted on instructions given without the leave of the court by a person whom he knew at that time to be the subject of a disqualification order or to be an undischarged bankrupt is presumed, unless the contrary is shown, to have been willing at any time thereafter to act on any instructions given by that person.

Supplementary provisions

16. Application for disqualification order.

(1)   A person intending to apply for the making of a disqualification order by the court having jurisdiction to wind up a company shall give not less than 10 days' notice of his intention to the person against whom the order is sought; and on the hearing of the application the last-mentioned person may appear and himself give evidence or call witnesses.

(2)   An application to a court with jurisdiction to wind up companies for the making against any person of a disqualification order under any of sections 2 to 5 may be made by the Secretary of State or the official receiver, or by the liquidator or any past or present member or creditor of any company in relation to which that person has committed or is alleged to have committed an offence or other default.

(3)   On the hearing of any application under this Act made by the Secretary of State or the official receiver or the liquidator, the applicant shall appear and call the attention of the court to any matters which seem to him to be relevant, and may himself give evidence or call witnesses.

17. Application for leave under an order.

(1)   As regards the court to which application must be made for leave under a disqualification order, the following applies—

(a)   where the application is for leave to promote or form a company, it is any court with jurisdiction to wind up companies, and

(b)   where the application is for leave to be a liquidator, administrator or director of, or otherwise to take part in the management of a company, or to be a receiver or manager of a company's property, it is any court having jurisdiction to wind up that company.

(2)   On the hearing of an application for leave made by a person against whom a disqualification order has been made on the application of the Secretary of State, the official receiver or the liquidator, the Secretary of State, official receiver or liquidator shall appear and call the attention of the court to any matters which seem to him to be relevant, and may himself give evidence or call witnesses.

18.   Register of disqualification orders.

(1)   The Secretary of State may make regulations requiring officers of courts to furnish him with such particulars as the regulations may specify of cases in which—

(a)   a disqualification order is made, or

(b)   any action is taken by a court in consequence of which such an order is varied or ceases to be in force, or

(c)   leave is granted by a court for a person subject to such an order to do anything which otherwise the order prohibits him from doing;

and the regulations may specify the time within which, and the form and manner in which, such particulars are to be furnished.

(2)   The Secretary of State shall, from the particulars so furnished, continue to maintain the register of orders, and of cases in which leave has been granted as mentioned in subsection (1)(c), which was set up by him under section 29 of the Companies Act 1976 and continued under section 301 of the Companies Act 1985.

(3)   When an order of which entry is made in the register ceases to be in force, the Secretary of State shall delete the entry from the register and all particulars relating to it which have been furnished to him under this section or any previous corresponding provision.

(4)   The register shall be open to inspection on payment of such fee as may be specified by the Secretary of State in regulations.

(5)   Regulations under this section shall be made by statutory instrument subject to annulment in pursuance of a resolution of either House of Parliament.

Miscellaneous and general

20.   Admissibility in evidence of statements.

In any proceedings (whether or not under this Act), any statement made in pursuance of a requirement imposed by or under sections 6 to 10, 15 or 19(c) of, or Schedule 1 to, this Act, or by or under rules made for the purposes of this Act under the Insolvency Act, may be used in evidence against any person making or concurring in making the statement.

21.   Interaction with Insolvency Act.

(1)   References in this Act to the official receiver, in relation to the winding up of a company or the bankruptcy of an individual, are to any person who, by virtue of section 399 of the Insolvency Act, is authorised to act as the official receiver in relation to that winding up or bankruptcy; and, in accordance with section 401(2) of that Act, references in this Act to an official receiver includes a person appointed as his deputy.

(2)   Sections 6 to 10, 15, 19(c) and 20 of, and Schedule 1 to, this Act are deemed included in Parts I to VII of the Insolvency Act for the purposes of the following sections of that Act—

section 411 (power to make insolvency rules);

section 414 (fees orders);

section 420 (orders extending provisions about insolvent companies to insolvent partnerships);

section 422 (modification of such provisions in their application to recognised banks).

(3)   Section 434 of that Act (Crown application) applies to sections 6 to 10, 15, 19(c) and 20 of, and Schedule 1 to, this Act as it does to the provisions of that Act which are there mentioned. . . .

22.   Interpretation.

(1)   This section has effect with respect to the meaning of expressions used in this Act, and applies unless the context otherwise requires.

(2)   The expression 'company'—

(a)   in section 11, includes an unregistered company and a company incorporated outside Great Britain which has an established place of buisness in Great Britain, and

(b)   elsewhere, includes any company which may be wound up under Part V of the Insolvency Act.

(3)   Section 247 in Part VII of the Insolvency Act (interpretation for the first Group of parts of that Act) applies as regards references to a company's insolvency and to its going into liquidation; and 'administrative receiver' has the meaning given by section 251 of that Act.

(4)   'Director' includes any person occupying the position of director, by whatever name called, and in sections 6 to 9 includes a shadow director.

(5)   'Shadow director', in relation to a company, means a person in accordance with whose directions or instructions the directors of the company are accustomed to act (but so that a person is not deemed a shadow director by reason only that the directors act on advice given by him in a professional capacity).

(6)   Section 740 of the Companies Act applies as regards the meaning of 'body corporate'; and 'officer' has the meaning given by section 744 of that Act.

(7)   In references to legislation other than this Act—

'the Companies Act' means the Companies Act 1985;

'the Companies Acts' has the meaning given by section 744 of that Act; and

'the Insolvency Act' means the Insolvency Act 1986;

and in sections 3(1) and 5(1) of this Act 'the companies legislation' means the Companies Acts (except the Insider Dealing Act), Parts I to VII of the Insolvency Act and, in Part XV of that Act, sections 411, 413, 414, 416 and 417.

[*Before an amendment was made by the Criminal Justice Act 1993, sch. 5, para. 4, the Companies Act 1985, s. 744, provided: '"the Insider Dealing Act" means the Company Securities (Insider Dealing) Act 1985'.*]

(8)   Any reference to provisions, or a particular provision, of the Companies Acts or the Insolvency Act includes the corresponding provisions or provision of the former Companies Acts (as defined by section 735(1)(c) of the Companies Act, but including also that Act itself) or, as the case may be, the Insolvency Act 1985.

(9)   Any expression for whose interpretation provision is made by Part XXVI of the Companies Act (and not by subsections (3) to (8) above) is to be construed in accordance with that provision.

24.   Extent.

(1)   This Act extends to England and Wales and to Scotland.

(2)   Nothing in this Act extends to Northern Ireland.

25.   Commencement.

This Act comes into force simultaneously with the Insolvency Act 1986.

26.   Citation.

This Act may be cited as the Company Directors Disqualification Act 1986.

SCHEDULES

Section 9   SCHEDULE 1

MATTERS FOR DETERMINING UNFITNESS OF DIRECTORS

PART I
MATTERS APPLICABLE IN ALL CASES

1.   Any misfeasance or breach of any fiduciary or other duty by the director in relation to the company.

2.   Any misapplication or retention by the director of, or any conduct by the director giving rise to an obligation to account for, any money or other property of the company.

3.   The extent of the director's responsibility for the company entering into any transaction liable to be set aside under Part XVI of the Insolvency Act (provisions against debt avoidance).

4.   The extent of the director's responsibility for any failure by the company to comply with any of the following provisions of the Companies Act, namely—

    (a)   section 221 (companies to keep accounting records);

    (b)   section 222 (where and for how long records to be kept);

    (c)   section 288 (register of directors and secretaries);

    (d)   section 352 (obligation to keep and enter up register of members);

    (e)   section 353 (location of register of members);

    (f)   section 363 (duty of company to make annual returns);

    (h)   sections 399 and 415 (company's duty to register charges it creates).

[*A new subpara. (h) would be substituted if para. 4 of sch. 16 to the Companies Act 1989 were brought into force.*]

5.   The extent of the director's responsibility for any failure by the directors of the company to comply with—

    (a)   section 226 or 227 of the Companies Act (duty to prepare annual accounts), or

    (b)   section 233 of that Act (approval and signature of accounts).

PART II
MATTERS APPLICABLE WHERE COMPANY HAS BECOME INSOLVENT

6.   The extent of the director's responsibility for the causes of the company becoming insolvent.

7.   The extent of the director's responsibility for any failure by the company to supply any goods or services which have been paid for (in whole or in part).

8.   The extent of the director's responsibility for the company entering into any transaction or giving any preference, being a transaction or preference—

    (a)   liable to be set aside under section 127 or sections 238 to 240 of the Insolvency Act, or

    (b)   challengeable under section 242 or 243 of that Act or under any rule of law in Scotland.

9.   The extent of the director's responsibility for any failure by the directors of the company to comply with section 98 of the Insolvency Act (duty to call creditors' meeting in creditors' voluntary winding up).

10.   Any failure by the director to comply with any obligation imposed on him by or under any of the following provisions of the Insolvency Act—

    (a)   section 22 (company's statement of affairs in administration);

    (b)   section 47 (statement of affairs to administrative receiver);

    (c)   section 66 (statement of affairs in Scottish receivership);

    (d)   section 99 (directors' duty to attend meeting; statement of affairs in creditors' voluntary winding up);

(e)   section 131 (statement of affairs in winding up by the court);
(f)   section 234 (duty of any one with company property to deliver it up);
(g)   section 235 (duty to cooperate with liquidator, etc.).

FINANCIAL SERVICES ACT 1986
(1986, c. 60)

An Act to regulate the carrying on of investment business; ... to make new provision with respect to the official listing of securities, ... takeover offers and insider dealing; ... and for connected purposes.   [7 November 1986]

PART I
REGULATION OF INVESTMENT BUSINESS

CHAPTER I
PRELIMINARY

1.   Investments and investment business.

(1)   In this Act, unless the context otherwise requires, 'investment' means any asset, right or interest falling within any paragraph in Part I of Schedule 1 to this Act.

(2)   In this Act 'investment business' means the business of engaging in one or more of the activities which fall within the paragraphs in Part II of that Schedule and are not excluded by Part III of that Schedule.

(3)   For the purposes of this Act a person carries on investment business in the United Kingdom if he—

(a)   carries on investment business from a permanent place of business maintained by him in the United Kingdom; or

(b)   engages in the United Kingdom in one or more of the activities which fall within the paragraphs in Part II of that Schedule and are not excluded by Part III or IV of that Schedule and his doing so constitutes the carrying on by him of a business in the United Kingdom.

(4)   Parts I to IV of that Schedule shall be construed in accordance with Part V.

2.   Power to extend or restrict scope of Act.

(1)   The Secretary of State may by order amend Schedule 1 to this Act so as—

(a)   to extend or restrict the meaning of investment for the purposes of all or any provisions of this Act; or

(b)   to extend or restrict for the purposes of all or any of those provisions the activities that are to constitute the carrying on of investment business or the carrying on of such business in the United Kingdom.

(2)   The amendments that may be made for the purposes of subsection (1)(b) above include amendments conferring powers on the Secretary of State, whether by extending or modifying any provision of that Schedule which confers such powers or by adding further such provisions.

(3)   An order under this section which extends the meaning of investment or extends the activities that are to constitute the carrying on of investment business or the carrying on of such business in the United Kingdom shall be laid before Parliament after being made and shall cease to have effect at the end of the period of twenty-eight days beginning with the day on which it is made (but without prejudice to anything done under the order or to the making of a new order) unless before the end of that period the order is approved by a resolution of each House of Parliament.

(4)   In reckoning the period mentioned in subsection (3) above no account shall be taken of any time during which Parliament is dissolved or prorogued or during which both Houses are adjourned for more than four days.

(5) Any order under this section to which subsection (3) above does not apply shall be subject to annulment in pursuance of a resolution of either House of Parliament.

(6) An order under this section may contain such transitional provisions as the Secretary of State thinks necessary or expedient.

CHAPTER II
RESTRICTION ON CARRYING ON BUSINESS

3. Persons entitled to carry on investment business.

No person shall carry on, or purport to carry on, investment business in the United Kingdom unless he is an authorised person under Chapter III or an exempted person under Chapter IV of this Part of this Act.

4. Offences.

(1) Any person who carries on, or purports to carry on, investment business in contravention of section 3 above shall be guilty of an offence and liable—

(a) on conviction on indictment, to imprisonment for a term not exceeding two years or to a fine or to both;

(b) on summary conviction, to imprisonment for a term not exceeding six months or to a fine not exceeding the statutory maximum or to both.

(2) In proceedings brought against any person for an offence under this section it shall be a defence for him to prove that he took all reasonable precautions and exercised all due diligence to avoid the commission of the offence.

CHAPTER V
CONDUCT OF INVESTMENT BUSINESS

57. Restrictions on advertising.

(1) Subject to section 58 below, no person other than an authorised person shall issue or cause to be issued an investment advertisement in the United Kingdom unless its contents have been approved by an authorised person.

(2) In this Act 'an investment advertisement' means any advertisement inviting persons to enter or offer to enter into an investment agreement or to exercise any rights conferred by an investment to acquire, dispose of, underwrite or convert an investment or containing information calculated to lead directly or indirectly to persons doing so.

(3) Subject to subsection (4) below, any person who contravenes this section shall be guilty of an offence and liable—

(a) on conviction on indictment, to imprisonment for a term not exceeding two years or to a fine or to both;

(b) on summary conviction, to imprisonment for a term not exceeding six months or to a fine not exceeding the statutory maximum or to both.

(4) A person who in the ordinary course of a business other than investment business issues an advertisement to the order of another person shall not be guilty of an offence under this section if he proves that he believed on reasonable grounds that the person to whose order the advertisement was issued was an authorised person, that the contents of the advertisement were approved by an authorised person or that the advertisement was permitted by or under section 58 below.

(5) If in contravention of this section a person issues or causes to be issued an advertisement inviting persons to enter or offer to enter into an investment agreement or containing information calculated to lead directly or indirectly to persons doing so, then, subject to subsection (8) below—

(a) he shall not be entitled to enforce any agreement to which the advertisement related and which was entered into after the issue of the advertisement; and

(b)   the other party shall be entitled to recover any money or other property paid or transferred by him under the agreement, together with compensation for any loss sustained by him as a result of having parted with it.

(6)   If in contravention of this section a person issues or causes to be issued an advertisement inviting persons to exercise any rights conferred by an investment or containing information calculated to lead directly or indirectly to persons doing so, then, subject to subsection (8) below—

(a)   he shall not be entitled to enforce any obligation to which a person is subject as a result of any exercise by him after the issue of the advertisement of any rights to which the advertisement related; and

(b)   that person shall be entitled to recover any money or other property paid or transferred by him under any such obligation, together with compensation for any loss sustained by him as a result of having parted with it.

(7)   The compensation recoverable under subsection (5) or (6) above shall be such as the parties may agree or as a court may, on the application of either party, determine.

(8)   A court may allow any such agreement or obligation as is mentioned in subsection (5) or (6) above to be enforced or money or property paid or transferred under it to be retained if it is satisfied—

(a)   that the person against whom enforcement is sought or who is seeking to recover the money or property was not influenced, or not influenced to any material extent, by the advertisement in making his decision to enter into the agreement or as to the exercise of the rights in question; or

(b)   that the advertisement was not misleading as to the nature of the investment, the terms of the agreement or, as the case may be, the consequences of exercising the rights in question and fairly stated any risks involved in those matters.

(9)   Where a person elects not to perform an agreement or an obligation which by virtue of subsection (5) or (6) above is unenforceable against him or by virtue of either of those subsections recovers money paid or other property transferred by him under an agreement or obligation he shall repay any money and return any other property received by him under the agreement or, as the case may be, as a result of exercising the rights in question.

(10)   Where any property transferred under an agreement or obligation to which subsection (5) or (6) above applies has passed to a third party the references to that property in this section shall be construed as references to its value at the time of its transfer under the agreement or obligation.

58.   Exceptions from restrictions on advertising.

(1)   Section 57 above does not apply to—

(a)   any advertisement issued or caused to be issued by, and relating only to investments issued by—

(i)   the government of the United Kingdom, of Northern Ireland or of any country or territory outside the United Kingdom;

(ii)   a local authority in the United Kingdom or elsewhere;

(iii)   the Bank of England or the central bank of any country or territory outside the United Kingdom; or

(iv)   any international organisation the members of which include the United Kingdom or another member State;

(b)   any advertisement issued or caused to be issued by a person who is exempt under section 36, 38, 42, 43, 44 or 45 above, or by virtue of an order under section 46 above, if the advertisement relates to a matter in respect of which he is exempt.

(c)   any advertisement which is issued or caused to be issued by a national of a member State other than the United Kingdom in the course of investment business lawfully carried on by him in such a State and which conforms with any rules made under section 48(2)(e) above;

(d) any advertisement which—
    (i) is subject to section 154 below; or
    (ii) consists of or any part of listing particulars, supplementary listing particulars, a prospectus approved in accordance with listing rules made under section 144(2) or 156A(1) below, a supplementary prospectus approved in accordance with listing rules made for the purposes of section 147(1) below as applied by section 154A or 156A(3) below or any other document required or permitted to be published by listing rules under Part IV of this Act.

[Subsection (2) has been repealed.]

(3) Section 57 above does not apply to an advertisement issued in such circumstances as may be specified in an order made by the Secretary of State for the purpose of exempting from that section—

    (a) advertisements appearing to him to have a private character, whether by reason of a connection between the person issuing them and those to whom they are issued or otherwise;

    (b) advertisements appearing to him to deal with investment only incidentally;

    (c) advertisements issued to persons appearing to him to be sufficiently expert to understand any risks involved; or

    (d) such other classes of advertisement as he thinks fit.

(4) An order under subsection (3) above may require any person who by virtue of the order is authorised to issue an advertisement to comply with such requirements as are specified in the order.

(5) An order made by virtue of paragraph (a), (b) or (c) of subsection (3) above shall be subject to annulment in pursuance of a resolution of either House of Parliament; and no order shall be made by virtue of paragraph (d) of that subsection unless a draft of it has been laid before and approved by a resolution of each House of Parliament.

(6) Subsection (1)(c) above does not apply to any advertisement relating to an investment falling within paragraph 5 of Schedule 1 to this Act.

CHAPTER VIII
COLLECTIVE INVESTMENT SCHEMES

Preliminary

75. Interpretation.

(1) In this Act 'a collective investment scheme' means, subject to the provisions of this section, any arrangements with respect to property of any description, including money, the purpose or effect of which is to enable persons taking part in the arrangements (whether by becoming owners of the property or any part of it or otherwise) to participate in or receive profits or income arising from the acquisition, holding, management or disposal of the property or sums paid out of such profits or income.

(2) The arrangements must be such that the persons who are to participate as mentioned in subsection (1) above (in this Act referred to as 'participants') do not have any day to day control over the management of the property in question, whether or not they have the right to be consulted or to give directions; and the arrangements must also have either or both of the characteristics mentioned in subsection (3) below.

(3) Those characteristics are—

    (a) that the contributions of the participants and the profits or income out of which payments are to be made to them are pooled;

    (b) that the property in question is managed as a whole by or on behalf of the operator of the scheme.

. . .

(7)   No body incorporated under the law of, or of any part of, the United Kingdom relating to building societies or industrial and provident societies or registered under any such law relating to friendly societies, and no other body corporate other than an open-ended investment company, shall be regarded as constituting a collective investment scheme.

(8)   In this Act—

'a unit trust scheme' means a collective investment scheme under which the property in question is held on trust for the participants;

'an open-ended investment company' means a collective investment scheme under which—

  (a)   the property in question belongs beneficially to, and is managed by or on behalf of, a body corporate having as its purpose the investment of its funds with the aim of spreading investment risk and giving its members the benefit of the results of the management of those funds by or on behalf of that body; and

  (b)   the rights of the participants are represented by shares in or securities of that body which—

  (i)   the participants are entitled to have redeemed or repurchased, or which (otherwise than under Chapter VII of Part V of the Companies Act 1985 or the corresponding Northern Ireland provision) are redeemed or repurchased from them by, or out of funds provided by, that body; or

  (ii)   the body ensures can be sold by the participants on an investment exchange at a price related to the value of the property to which they relate;

'trustee', in relation to a unit trust scheme, means the person holding the property in question on trust for the participants and, in relation to a collective investment scheme constituted under the law of a country or territory outside the United Kingdom, means any person who (whether or not under a trust) is entrusted with the custody of the property in question;

'units' means the rights or interests (however described) of the participants in a collective investment scheme;

'the operator', in relation to a unit trust scheme with a separate trustee, means the manager and, in relation to an open-ended investment company, means that company.

. . .

CHAPTER XIII
TRANSFER OF FUNCTIONS TO DESIGNATED AGENCY

114.   Power to transfer functions to designated agency.

(1)   If it appears to the Secretary of State—

  (a)   that a body corporate has been established which is able and willing to discharge all or any of the functions to which this section applies; and

  (b)   that the requirements of Schedule 7 to this Act are satisfied in the case of that body,

he may, subject to the provisions of this section and Chapter XIV of this Part of this Act, make an order transferring all or any of those functions to that body.

(2)   The body to which functions are transferred by the first order made under subsection (1) above shall be the body known as The Securities and Investments Board Limited if it appears to the Secretary of State that it is able and willing to discharge them, that the requirements mentioned in paragraph (b) of that subsection are satisfied in the case of that body and that he is not precluded from making the order by the subsequent provisions of this section or Chapter XIV of this Part of this Act.

(3)   An order under subsection (1) above is in this Act referred to as 'a delegation order' and a body to which functions are transferred by a delegation order is in this Act referred to as 'a designated agency'.

. . .

PART IV
OFFICIAL LISTING OF SECURITIES

142. Official listing.

(1)   No investment to which this section applies shall be admitted to the Official List except in accordance with the provisions of this Part of this Act.

(2)   Subject to subsections (3) and (4) below, this section applies to any investment falling within paragraph 1, 2, 4 or 5 of Schedule 1 to this Act.

(3)   In the application of those paragraphs for the purposes of subsection (2) above—

(a)   paragraphs 1, 4, and 5 shall have effect as if paragraph 1 did not contain the exclusion relating to building societies, industrial and provident societies or credit unions;

(b)   paragraph 2 shall have effect as if it included any instrument falling within paragraph 3 issued otherwise than by the government of a member State or a local authority in a member State; and

(c)   paragraphs 4 and 5 shall have effect as if they referred only to investments falling within paragraph 1.

(4)   The Secretary of State may by order direct that this section shall apply also to investments falling within paragraph 6 of Schedule 1 to this Act or to such investments of any class or description.

(5)   An order under subsection (4) above shall be subject to annulment in pursuance of a resolution of either House of Parliament.

(6)   In this Part of this Act 'the competent authority' means, subject to section 157 below, The International Stock Exchange of the United Kingdom and the Republic of Ireland Ltd; and that authority may make rules (in this Act referred to as 'listing rules') for the purposes of any of the following provisions.

(7)   In this Part of this Act—

'approved exchange' means, in relation to dealings in securities, a recognised investment exchange approved by the Treasury for the purposes of the Public Offers of Securities Regulations 1995 either generally or in relation to such dealings;

'issuer', in relation to any securities, means the person by whom they have been or are to be issued except that in relation to a certificate or other instrument falling within paragraph 5 of Schedule 1 to this Act it means the person who issued or is to issue the securities to which the certificate or instrument relates;

'the Official List' means the list maintained by the competent authority for the purposes of this Part of this Act;

'securities' means investments to which this section applies;

and references to listing are references to inclusion in the Official List in pursuance of this Part of this Act.

(7A)   For the purposes of this Part of this Act—

(a)   a person offers securities if, as principal—

(i)   he makes an offer which, if accepted, would give rise to a contract for their issue or sale (which for this purpose includes any disposal for valuable consideration) by him or by another person with whom he has made arrangements for their issue or sale; or

(ii)   he invites a person to make such an offer,

but not otherwise; and, except where the context otherwise requires, 'offer' and 'offeror' shall be construed accordingly; and

(b)   whether a person offers securities to the public in the United Kingdom shall be determined in accordance with Schedule 11A to this Act.

(8)   Any functions of the competent authority under this Part of this Act may be exercised by its governing body or by any committee or sub-committee of that body or by any officer or servant of the authority except that listing rules—

(a)   shall be made only by the governing body of the authority or by a committee or sub-committee of that body; and

(b)   if made by a committee or sub-committee, shall cease to have effect at the end of the period of twenty-eight days beginning with the day on which they are made (but without prejudice to anything done under them) unless before the end of that period they are confirmed by the governing body of the authority.

(9)   Nothing in this Part of this Act affects the powers of the competent authority in respect of investments to which this section does not apply and such investments may be admitted to the Official List otherwise than in accordance with this Part of this Act.

143.   Applications for listing.

(1)   An application for listing shall be made to the competent authority in such manner as the listing rules may require.

(2)   No application for the listing of any securities shall be made except by or with the consent of the issuer of the securities.

(3)   No application for listing shall be made in respect of securities to be issued by a private company or by an old public company within the meaning of section 1 of the Companies Consolidation (Consequential Provisions) Act 1985 or the corresponding Northern Ireland provision.

144.   Admission to list.

(1)   The competent authority shall not admit any securities to the Official List except on an application duly made in accordance with section 143 above and unless satisfied that—

(a)   the requirements of the listing rules made by the authority for the purposes of this section and in force when the application is made; and

(b)   any other requirements imposed by the authority in relation to that application, are complied with.

(2)   Listing rules shall require as a condition of the admission to the Official List of any securities for which application for admission has been made and which are to be offered to the public in the United Kingdom for the first time before admission—

(a)   the submission to, and approval by, the authority of a prospectus in such form and containing such information as may be specified in the rules; and

(b)   the publication of that prospectus.

(2A)   Listing rules may require as a condition of the admission to the Official List of any other securities—

(a)   the submission to, and approval by, the authority of a document (in this Act referred to as 'listing particulars') in such form and containing such information as may be specified in the rules; and

(b)   the publication of that document;

or, in such cases as may be specified by the rules, the publication of a document other than listing particulars or a prospectus.

(2B)   Subsections (2) and (2A) have effect without prejudice to the generality of the power of the competent authority to make listing rules for the purposes of this section.

(3)   The competent authority may refuse an application—

(a)   if it considers that by reason of any matter relating to the issuer the admission of the securities would be detrimental to the interests of investors; or

(b)   in the case of securities already officially listed in another member State, if the issuer has failed to comply with any obligations to which he is subject by virtue of that listing.

(4)   The competent authority shall notify the applicant of its decision on the application within six months from the date on which the application is received or, if

within that period the authority has required the applicant to furnish further information in connection with the application, from the date on which that information is furnished.

(5) If the competent authority does not notify the applicant of its decision within the time required by subsection (4) above it shall be taken to have refused the application.

(6) When any securities have been admitted to the Official List their admission shall not be called in question on the ground that any requirement or condition for their admission has not been complied with.

145. Discontinuance and suspension of listing.

(1) The competent authority may, in accordance with the listing rules, discontinue the listing of any securities if satisfied that there are special circumstances which preclude normal regular dealings in the securities.

(2) The competent authority may in accordance with the listing rules suspend the listing of any securities.

(3) Securities the listing of which is suspended under subsection (2) above shall nevertheless be regarded as listed for the purposes of sections 153 and 155 below.

(4) This section applies to securities included in the Official List at the coming into force of this Part of this Act as it applies to securities included by virtue of this Part.

146. General duty of disclosure in listing particulars.

(1) In addition to the information specified by listing rules or required by the competent authority as a condition of the admission of any securities to the Official List any listing particulars submitted to the competent authority under section 144 above shall contain all such information as investors and their professional advisers would reasonably require, and reasonably expect to find there, for the purpose of making an informed assessment of—

(a) the assets and liabilities, financial position, profits and losses, and prospects of the issuer of the securities; and

(b) the rights attaching to those securities.

(2) The information to be included by virtue of this section shall be such information as is mentioned in subsection (1) above which is within the knowledge of any person responsible for the listing particulars or which it would be reasonable for him to obtain by making enquiries.

(3) In determining what information is required to be included in listing particulars by virtue of this section regard shall be had—

(a) to the nature of the securities and of the issuer of the securities;

(b) to the nature of the persons likely to consider their acquisition;

(c) to the fact that certain matters may reasonably be expected to be within the knowledge of professional advisers of any kind which those persons may reasonably be expected to consult; and

(d) to any information available to investors or their professional advisers by virtue of requirements imposed under section 153 below or by or under any other enactment or by virtue of requirements imposed by a recognised investment exchange for the purpose of complying with paragraph 2(2)(b) of Schedule 4 to this Act.

147. Supplementary listing particulars.

(1) If at any time after the preparation of listing particulars for submission to the competent authority under section 144 above and before the commencement of dealings in the securities following their admission to the Official List—

(a) there is a significant change affecting any matter contained in those particulars whose inclusion was required by section 146 above or by listing rules or by the competent authority; or

(b)   a significant new matter arises the inclusion of information in respect of which would have been so required if it had arisen when the particulars were prepared,
the issuer of the securities shall, in accordance with listing rules made for the purposes of this section, submit to the competent authority for its approval and, if approved, publish supplementary listing particulars of the change or new matter.

(2)   In subsection (1) above 'significant' means significant for the purpose of making an informed assessment of the matters mentioned in section 146(1) above.

(3)   Where the issuer of the securities is not aware of the change or new matter in question he shall not be under any duty to comply with subsection (1) above unless he is notified of it by a person responsible for the listing particulars; but it shall be the duty of any person responsible for those particulars who is aware of such a matter to give notice of it to the issuer.

(4)   Subsection (1) above applies also as respects matters contained in any supplementary listing particulars previously published under this section in respect of the securities in question.

148.   Exemptions from disclosure.

(1)   The competent authority may authorise the omission from listing particulars or supplementary listing particulars of any information the inclusion of which would otherwise be required by section 146 above—

(a)   on the ground that its disclosure would be contrary to the public interest;

(b)   subject to subsection (2) below, on the ground that its disclosure would be seriously detrimental to the issuer of the securities; or

(c)   in the case of securities which fall within paragraph 2 of Schedule 1 to this Act as modified by section 142(3)(b) above and are of any class specified by listing rules, on the ground that its disclosure is unnecessary for persons of the kind who may be expected normally to buy or deal in the securities.

(2)   No authority shall be granted under subsection (1)(b) above in respect of, and no such authority shall be regarded as extending to, information the non-disclosure of which would be likely to mislead a person considering the acquisition of the securities as to any facts the knowledge of which it is essential for him to have in order to make an informed assessment.

(3)   The Secretary of State or the Treasury may issue a certificate to the effect that the disclosure of any information (including information that would otherwise have to be included in particulars for which they are themselves responsible) would be contrary to the public interest and the competent authority shall be entitled to act on any such certificate in exercising its powers under subsection (1)(a) above.

(4)   This section is without prejudice to any powers of the competent authority under rules made by virtue of section 156(2) below.

149.   Registration of listing particulars.

(1)   On or before the date on which listing particulars or supplementary listing particulars are published as required by listing rules a copy of the particulars shall be delivered for registration to the registrar of companies and a statement that a copy has been delivered to him shall be included in the particulars.

(2)   In subsection (1) above 'the registrar of companies' means—

(a)   if the securities in question are or are to be issued by a company incorporated in Great Britain, the registrar of companies in England and Wales or the registrar of companies in Scotland according to whether the company's registered office is in England and Wales or in Scotland;

(b)   if the securities in question are or are to be issued by a company incorporated in Northern Ireland, the registrar of companies for Northern Ireland;

(c)   in any other case, any of those registrars.

(3)   If any particulars are published without a copy of them having been delivered as required by this section the issuer of the securities in question and any person who is knowingly a party to the publication shall be guilty of an offence and liable—

    (a)   on conviction on indictment, to a fine;

    (b)   on summary conviction, to a fine not exceeding the statutory maximum.

150.   Compensation for false or misleading particulars.

(1)   Subject to section 151 below, the person or persons responsible for any listing particulars or supplementary listing particulars shall be liable to pay compensation to any person who has acquired any of the securities in question and suffered loss in respect of them as a result of any untrue or misleading statement in the particulars or the omission from them of any matter required to be included by section 146 or 147 above.

(2)   Where listing rules require listing particulars to include information as to any particular matter on the basis that the particulars must include a statement either as to that matter or, if such is the case, that there is no such matter, the omission from the particulars of the information shall be treated for the purposes of subsection (1) above as a statement that there is no such matter.

(3)   Subject to section 151 below, a person who fails to comply with section 147 above shall be liable to pay compensation to any person who has acquired any of the securities in question and suffered loss in respect of them as a result of the failure.

(4)   This section does not affect any liability which any person may incur apart from this section.

(5)   References in this section to the acquisition by any person of securities include references to his contracting to acquire them or an interest in them.

(6)   No person shall by reason of being a promoter of a company or otherwise incur any liability for failing to disclose any information which he would not be required to disclose in listing particulars in respect of a company's securities if he were responsible for those particulars or, if he is responsible for them, which he is entitled to omit by virtue of section 148 above.

The reference above to a person incurring liability includes a reference to any other person being entitled as against that person to be granted any civil remedy or to rescind or repudiate any agreement.

151.   Exemption from liability to pay compensation.

(1)   A person shall not incur any liability under section 150(1) above for any loss in respect of securities caused by any such statement or omission as is there mentioned if he satisfies the court that at the time when the particulars were submitted to the competent authority he reasonably believed, having made such enquiries (if any) as were reasonable, that the statement was true and not misleading or that the matter whose omission caused the loss was properly omitted and—

    (a)   that he continued in that belief until the time when the securities were acquired; or

    (b)   that they were acquired before it was reasonably practicable to bring a correction to the attention of persons likely to acquire the securities in question; or

    (c)   that before the securities were acquired he had taken all such steps as it was reasonable for him to have taken to secure that a correction was brought to the attention of those persons; or

    (d)   that he continued in that belief until after the commencement of dealings in the securities following their admission to the Official List and that the securities were acquired after such a lapse of time that he ought in the circumstances to be reasonably excused.

(2)   A person shall not incur any liability under section 150(1) above for any loss in respect of securities caused by a statement purporting to be made by or on the authority of another person as an expert which is, and is stated to be, included in the particulars with that other person's consent if he satisfies the court that at the time when the particulars were submitted to the competent authority he believed on reasonable grounds that the other person was competent to make or authorise the statement and had consented to its inclusion in the form and context in which it was included and—

   (a)   that he continued in that belief until the time when the securities were acquired; or

   (b)   that they were acquired before it was reasonably practicable to bring the fact that the expert was not competent or had not consented to the attention of persons likely to acquire the securities in question; or

   (c)   that before the securities were acquired he had taken all such steps as it was reasonable for him to have taken to secure that that fact was brought to the attention of those persons; or

   (d)   that he continued in that belief until after the commencement of dealings in the securities following their admission to the Official List and that the securities were acquired after such a lapse of time that he ought in the circumstances to be reasonably excused.

(3)   Without prejudice to subsections (1) and (2) above, a person shall not incur any liability under section 150(1) above for any loss in respect of any securities caused by any such statement or omission as is there mentioned if he satisfies the court—

   (a)   that before the securities were acquired a correction, or where the statement was such as is mentioned in subsection (2), the fact that the expert was not competent or had not consented had been published in a manner calculated to bring it to the attention of persons likely to acquire the securities in question; or

   (b)   that he took all such steps as it was reasonable for him to take to secure such publication and reasonably believed that it had taken place before the securities were acquired.

(4)   A person shall not incur any liability under section 150(1) above for any loss resulting from a statement made by an official person or contained in a public official document which is included in the particulars if he satisfies the court that the statement is accurately and fairly reproduced.

(5)   A person shall not incur any liability under section 150(1) or (3) above if he satisfies the court that the person suffering the loss acquired the securities in question with knowledge that the statement was false or misleading, of the omitted matter or of the change or new matter, as the case may be.

(6)   A person shall not incur any liability under section 150(3) above if he satisfies the court that he reasonably believed that the change or new matter in question was not such as to call for supplementary listing particulars.

(7)   In this section 'expert' includes any engineer, valuer, accountant or other person whose profession, qualifications or experience give authority to a statement made by him; and references to the acquisition of securities include references to contracting to acquire them or an interest in them.

152.   Persons responsible for particulars.

(1)   For the purposes of this Part of this Act the persons responsible for listing particulars or supplementary listing particulars are—

   (a)   the issuer of the securities to which the particulars relate;

   (b)   where the issuer is a body corporate, each person who is a director of that body at the time when the particulars are submitted to the competent authority;

(c) where the issuer is a body corporate, each person who has authorised himself to be named, and is named, in the particulars as a director or as having agreed to become a director of that body either immediately or at a future time;

(d) each person who accepts, and is stated in the particulars as accepting, responsibility for, or for any part of, the particulars;

(e) each person not falling within any of the foregoing paragraphs who has authorised the contents of, or any part of, the particulars.

(2) A person is not responsible for any particulars by virtue of subsection (1)(b) above if they are published without his knowledge or consent and on becoming aware of their publication he forthwith gives reasonable public notice that they were published without his knowledge or consent.

(3) Where a person has accepted responsibility for, or authorised, only part of the contents of any particulars, he is responsible under subsection (1)(d) or (e) above for only that part and only if it is included in (or substantially in) the form and context to which he has agreed.

(4) Where the particulars relate to securities which are to be issued in connection with an offer by (or by a wholly-owned subsidiary of), the issuer for, or an agreement for the acquisition by (or by a wholly-owned subsidiary of) the issuer of, securities issued by another person or in connection with any arrangement whereby the whole of the undertaking of another person is to become the undertaking of the issuer (of a wholly-owned subsidiary of the issuer or of a body corporate which will become such a subsidiary by virtue of the arrangement) then if—

(a) that other person; and

(b) where that other person is a body corporate, each person who is a director of that body at the time when the particulars are submitted to the competent authority and each other person who has authorised himself to be named, and is named, in the particulars as a director of that body,

is responsible by virtue of paragraph (d) of subsection (1) above for any part of the particulars relating to that other person or to the securities or undertaking to which the offer, agreement or arrangement relates, no person shall be responsible for that part under paragraph (a), (b) or (c) of that subsection but without prejudice to his being responsible under paragraph (d).

...

(5) Neither paragraph (b) nor paragraph (c) of subsection (1) above applies in the case of an issuer of international securities of a class specified by listing rules for the purposes of section 148(1)(c) above; and neither of those paragraphs nor paragraph (b) of subsection (4) above applies in the case of any director certified by the competent authority as a person to whom that paragraph should not apply by reason of his having an interest, or of any other circumstances, making it inappropriate for him to be responsible by virtue of that paragraph.

(6) In subsection (5) above 'international securities' means any investment falling within paragraph 2 of Schedule 1 to this Act as modified by section 142(3)(b) above which is of a kind likely to be dealt in by bodies incorporated in or persons resident in a country or territory outside the United Kingdom, is denominated in a currency other than sterling or is otherwise connected with such a country or territory.

(7) In this section 'wholly-owned subsidiary', in relation to a person other than a body corporate, means any body corporate that would be his wholly-owned subsidiary if he were a body corporate.

(8) Nothing in this section shall be construed as making a person responsible for any particulars by reason of giving advice as to their contents in a professional capacity.

(9) Where by virtue of this section the issuer of any shares pays or is liable to pay compensation under section 150 above for loss suffered in respect of shares for which a person has subscribed no account shall be taken of that liability or payment in

determining any question as to the amount paid on subscription for those shares or as to the amount paid up or deemed to be paid up on them.

153. Obligations of issuers of listed securities.

(1) Listing rules may specify requirements to be complied with by issuers of listed securities and make provision with respect to the action that may be taken by the competent authority in the event of non-compliance, including provision—

(a) authorising the authority to publish the fact that an issuer has contravened any provision of the rules; and

(b) if the rules require an issuer to publish any information, authorising the authority to publish it in the event of his failure to do so.

(2) This section applies to the issuer of securities included in the Official List at the coming into force of this Part of this Act as it applies to the issuer of securities included by virtue of this Part.

154. Advertisements etc. in connection with listing applications.

(1) Where listing particulars are or are to be published in connection with an application for the listing of any securities no advertisement or other information of a kind specified by listing rules shall be issued in the United Kingdom unless the contents of the advertisement or other information have been submitted to the competent authority and that authority has either—

(a) approved those contents; or

(b) authorised the issue of the advertisement or information without such approval.

(2) An authorised person who contravenes this section shall be treated as having contravened rules made under Chapter V of Part I of this Act or, in the case of a person who is an authorised person by virtue of his membership of a recognised self-regulating organisation or certification by a recognised professional body, the rules of that organisation or body.

(3) Subject to subsection (4) below, a person other than an authorised person, who contravenes this section shall be guilty of an offence and liable—

(a) on conviction on indictment, to imprisonment for a term not exceeding two years or to a fine or to both;

(b) on summary conviction, to a fine not exceeding the statutory maximum.

(4) A person who in the ordinary course of a business other than investment business issues an advertisement or other information to the order of another person shall not be guilty of an offence under this section if he proves that he believed on reasonable grounds that the advertisement or information had been approved or its issue authorised by the competent authority.

(5) Where information has been approved, or its issue has been authorised, under this section neither the person issuing it nor any person responsible for, or for any part of, the listing particulars shall incur any civil liability by reason of any statement in or omission from the information if that information and the listing particulars, taken together, would not be likely to mislead persons of the kind likely to consider the acquisition of the securities in question.

The reference above to a person incurring civil liability includes a reference to any other person being entitled as against that person to be granted any civil remedy or to rescind or repudiate any agreement.

154A. Application of Part IV to prospectuses.

Sections 146 to 152 and 154 above shall apply in relation to a prospectus required by listing rules in accordance with section 144(2) above as they apply in relation to listing particulars, but as if—

(a)   any reference to listing particulars were a reference to a prospectus and any reference to supplementary listing particulars were a reference to a supplementary prospectus; and

(b)   notwithstanding section 142(7) above, any reference in section 152 above (other than in subsection (1)(b) of that section) to the issuer of securities included a reference to the person offering or proposing to offer them.

155.   Fees.

Listing rules may require the payment of fees to the competent authority in respect of applications for listing and the retention of securities in the Official List.

156.   Listing rules: general provisions.

(1)   Listing rules may make different provision for different cases.

(2)   Listing rules may authorise the competent authority to dispense with or modify the application of the rules in particular cases and by reference to any circumstances.

(3)   Listing rules shall be made by an instrument in writing.

(4)   Immediately after an instrument containing listing rules is made it shall be printed and made available to the public with or without payment.

(5)   A person shall not be taken to have contravened any listing rule if he shows that at the time of the alleged contravention the instrument containing the rule had not been made available as required by subsection (4) above.

(6)   The production of a printed copy of an instrument purporting to be made by the competent authority on which is endorsed a certificate signed by an officer of the authority authorised by it for that purpose and stating—

(a)   that the instrument was made by the authority;

(b)   that the copy is a true copy of the instrument; and

(c)   that on a specified date the instrument was made available to the public as required by subsection (4) above,

shall be prima facie evidence or, in Scotland, sufficient evidence of the facts stated in the certificate.

(7)   Any certificate purporting to be signed as mentioned in subsection (6) above shall be deemed to have been duly signed unless the contrary is shown.

(8)   Any person wishing in any legal proceedings to cite an instrument made by the competent authority may require the authority to cause a copy of it to be endorsed with such a certificate as is mentioned in subsection (6) above.

156A.   Approval of prospectus where no application for listing.

(1)   Listing rules may also provide for a prospectus to be submitted to and approved by the competent authority where—

(a)   securities are to be offered to the public in the United Kingdom for the first time;

(b)   no application for listing of the securities has been made under this Part of this Act; and

(c)   the prospectus is submitted by or with the consent of the issuer of the securities.

(2)   Listing rules made under subsection (1) above may make provision—

(a)   as to the information to be contained in, and the form of, a prospectus submitted under any such rules; and

(b)   subject to the provisions of the Public Offers of Securities Regulations 1995, as to the timing and manner of publication of such a prospectus.

(3)   Sections 146 to 152 and 154 above shall apply in relation to such a prospectus as they apply in relation to listing particulars but as if—

(a)   any reference to listing particulars were a reference to a prospectus and any reference to supplementary listing particulars were a reference to a supplementary prospectus;

(b)   in section 146(1) above—

(i)   the words 'as a condition of the admission of any securities to the Official List' were omitted; and

(ii)   for the words 'section 144 above' there were substituted 'section 156A(1) below';

(c)   in section 147(1) above, for the words 'under section 144 above and before the commencement of dealings in the securities following their admission to the Official List' there were substituted 'under section 156A(1) below and before the end of the period during which the offer to which the prospectus relates remains open';

(d)   in subsections (1)(d) and (2)(d) of section 151 above—

(i)   the words 'that he continued in that belief until after the commencement of dealings in the securities following their admission to the Official List and' were omitted; and

(ii)   the words 'and, if the securities are dealt in on an approved exchange, that he continued in that belief until after the commencement of dealings in the securities on that exchange' were added at the end;

(e)   notwithstanding section 142(7) above, any reference in section 152 above (other than in subsection (1)(b) of that section) to the issuer of securities included a reference to the person offering or proposing to offer them; and

(f)   in section 154(1) above, for the words 'Where listing particulars are or are to be published in connection with an application for the listing of any securities' there were substituted 'Where a prospectus is or is to be published in connection with an appliction for approval, then, until the end of the period during which the offer to which the prospectus relates remains open,'.

(4)   Listing rules made under this section may require the payment of fees to the competent authority in respect of a prospectus submitted for approval under the rules.

156B.   Publication of prospectus.

(1)   Where listing rules made under section 144(2) above require the publication of a prospectus, it shall not be lawful, before the time of publication of the prospectus, to offer the securities in question to the public in the United Kingdom.

(2)   An authorised person who contravenes subsection (1) above shall be treated as contravening rules made under Chapter V of Part I of this Act or, in the case of a person who is an authorised person by virtue of his membership of a recognised self-regulating organisation or certification by a recognised professional body, the rules of that organisation or body.

(3)   A person, other than an authorised person, who contravenes subsection (1) above shall be guilty of an offence and liable—

(a)   on conviction on indictment, to imprisonment for a term not exceeding two years or to a fine or to both;

(b)   on summary conviction, to imprisonment for a term not exceeding three months or a fine not exceeding level 5 on the standard scale.

(4)   Without prejudice to any liability under section 150 above, a person shall not be regarded as contravening subsection (1) above by reason only of a prospectus not having fully complied with the requirements of listing rules as to its form or content.

(5)   Any contravention of subsection (1) above shall be actionable at the suit of a person who suffers loss as a result of the contravention subject to the defences and other incidents applying to actions for breach of statutory duty.

PART VII
INSIDER DEALING

177.   Investigations into insider dealing.

(1)   If it appears to the Secretary of State that there are circumstances suggesting that an offence under Part V of the Criminal Justice Act 1993 (insider dealing) may have

been committed, he may appoint one or more competent inspectors to carry out such investigations as are requisite to establish whether or not any such offence has been committed and to report the results of their investigations to him.

(2) The appointment under this section of an inspector may limit the period during which he is to continue his investigation or confine it to particular matters.

(2A) At any time during the investigation the Secretary of State may vary the appointment by limiting or extending the period during which the inspector is to continue his investigation or by confining the investigation to particular matters.

(3) If the inspectors consider that any person is or may be able to give information concerning any such offence they may require that person—

(a) to produce to them any documents in his possession or under his control which appear to them to be relevant to the investigation;

(b) to attend before them; and

(c) otherwise to give them all assistance in connection with the investigation which he is reasonably able to give;

and it shall be the duty of that person to comply with that requirement.

(4) An inspector may examine on oath any person who he considers is or may be able to give information concerning any such offence, and may administer an oath accordingly.

(5) The inspectors shall make such interim reports to the Secretary of State as they think fit or he may direct and on the conclusion of the investigation they shall make a final report to him.

(5A) If the Secretary of State thinks fit, he may direct the inspector to take no further steps in the investigation or to take only such further steps as are specified in the direction; and where an investigation is the subject of such a direction, the inspectors shall make a final report to the Secretary of State only where the Secretary of State directs them to do so.

(6) A statement made by a person in compliance with a requirement imposed by virtue of this section may be used in evidence against him.

(7) A person shall not under this section be required to disclose any information or produce any document which he would be entitled to refuse to disclose or produce on grounds of legal professional privilege in proceedings in the High Court or on grounds of confidentiality as between client and professional legal adviser in proceedings in the Court of Session.

(8) A person shall not under this section be required to disclose any information or produce any document in respect of which he owes an obligation of confidence by virtue of carrying on the business of banking unless—

(a) the person to whom the obligation of confidence is owed consents to the disclosure or production, or

(b) the making of the requirement was authorised by the Secretary of State.

(9) Where a person claims a lien on a document its production under this section shall be without prejudice to his lien.

(10) In this section 'document' includes information recorded in any form; and in relation to information recorded otherwise than in legible form the power to require its production includes power to require the production of a copy of the information in legible form.

(11) A person who is convicted on a prosecution instituted as a result of an investigation under this section may in the same proceedings be ordered to pay the expenses of the investigation to such extent as may be specified in the order.

There shall be treated as expenses of the investigation, in particular, such reasonable sums as the Secretary of State may determine in respect of general staff costs and overheads.

178.   Penalties for failure to cooperate with s. 177 investigations.

(1)   If any person—

(a)   refuses to comply with any request under subsection (3) of section 177 above; or

(b)   refuses to answer any question put to him by the inspectors appointed under that section with respect to any matter relevant for establishing whether or not any suspected offence has been committed,

the inspectors may certify that fact in writing to the court and the court may inquire into the case.

(2)   If, after hearing any witness who may be produced against or on behalf of the alleged offender and any statement which may be offered in defence, the court is satisfied that he did without reasonable excuse refuse to comply with such a request or answer any such question, the court may—

(a)   punish him in like manner as if he had been guilty of contempt of the court; or

(b)   direct that the Secretary of State may exercise his powers under this section in respect of him;

and the court may give a direction under paragraph (b) above notwithstanding that the offender is not within the jurisdiction of the court if the court is satisfied that he was notified of his right to appear before the court and of the powers available under this section.

(3)   Where the court gives a direction under subsection (2)(b) above in respect of an authorised person the Secretary of State may serve a notice on him—

(a)   cancelling any authorisation of his to carry on investment business after the expiry of a specified period after the service of the notice;

(b)   disqualifying him from becoming authorised to carry on investment business after the expiry of a specified period;

(c)   restricting any authorisation of his in respect of investment business during a specified period to the performance of contracts entered into before the notice comes into force;

(d)   prohibiting him from entering into transactions of a specified kind or entering into them except in specified circumstances or to a specified extent;

(e)   prohibiting him from soliciting business from persons of a specified kind or otherwise than from such persons; or

(f)   prohibiting him from carrying on business in a specified manner or otherwise than in a specified manner.

(4)   The period mentioned in paragraphs (a) and (c) of subsection (3) above shall be such period as appears to the Secretary of State reasonable to enable the person on whom the notice is served to complete the performance of any contracts entered into before the notice comes into force and to terminate such of them as are of a continuing nature.

(5)   Where the court gives a direction under subsection (2)(b) above in the case of an unauthorised person the Secretary of State may direct that any authorised person who knowingly transacts investment business of a specified kind, or in specified circumstances or to a specified extent, with or on behalf of that unauthorised person shall be treated as having contravened rules made under Chapter V of Part I of this Act or, in the case of a person who is an authorised person by virtue of his membership of a recognised self-regulating organisation or certification by a recognised professional body, the rules of that organisation or body.

(6)   A person shall not be treated for the purposes of subsection (2) above as having a reasonable excuse for refusing to comply with a request or answer a question in a case where the offence or suspected offence being investigated relates to dealing by

him on the instructions or for the account of another person, by reason that at the time of the refusal—

(a)   he did not know the identity of that other person; or

(b)   he was subject to the law of a country or territory outside the United Kingdom which prohibited him from disclosing information relating to the dealing without the consent of that other person, if he might have obtained that consent or obtained exemption from that law.

(7)   A notice served on a person under subsection (3) above may be revoked at any time by the Secretary of State by serving a revocation notice on him; and the Secretary of State shall revoke such a notice if it appears to him that he has agreed to comply with the relevant request or answer the relevant question.

(8)   The revocation of such a notice as is mentioned in subsection (3)(a) above shall not have the effect of reviving the authorisation cancelled by the notice except where the person would (apart from the notice) at the time of the revocation be an authorised person by virtue of his membership of a recognised self-regulating organisation or certification by a recognised professional body; but nothing in this subsection shall be construed as preventing any person who has been subject to such a notice from again becoming authorised after the revocation of the notice.

(9)   If it appears to the Secretary of State—

(a)   that a person on whom he serves a notice under subsection (3) above is an authorised person by virtue of an authorisation granted by a designated agency or by virtue of membership of a recognised self-regulating organisation or certification by a recognised professional body; or

(b)   that a person on whom he serves a revocation notice under subsection (7) above was such an authorised person at the time that the notice which is being revoked was served,

he shall serve a copy of the notice on that agency, organisation or body.

(10)   The functions to which section 114 above applies shall include the functions of the Secretary of State under this section but any transfer of those functions shall be subject to a reservation that they are to be exercisable by him concurrently with the designated agency and so as to be exercisable by the agency subject to such conditions or restrictions as the Treasury may from time to time impose.

PART X
MISCELLANEOUS AND SUPPLEMENTARY

199.   Powers of entry.

(1)   A justice of the peace may issue a warrant under this section if satisfied on information on oath given by or on behalf of the Secretary of State that there are reasonable grounds for believing that an offence has been committed—

(a)   under section 4, 47, 57, 130 or 133 above, or

(b)   under Part V of the Criminal Justice Act 1993 (insider dealing),

and that there are on any premises documents relevant to the question whether that offence has been committed.

. . .

(3)   A warrant under this section shall authorise a constable, together with any other person named in it and any other constables—

(a)   to enter the premises specified in the information, using such force as is reasonably necessary for the purpose;

(b)   to search the premises and take possession of any documents appearing to be such documents as are mentioned in subsection (1) or, as the case may be, in subsection (2) above or to take, in relation to any such documents, any other steps which may appear to be necessary for preserving them or preventing interference with them;

(c)   to take copies of any such documents; and

(d)   to require any person named in the warrant to provide an explanation of them or to state where they may be found.

(4)   A warrant under this section shall continue in force until the end of the period of one month beginning with the day on which it is issued.

(5)   Any documents of which possession is taken under this section may be retained—

(a)   for a period of three months; or

(b)   if within that period proceedings to which the documents are relevant are commenced against any person for any criminal offence, until the conclusion of those proceedings.

(6)   Any person who intentionally obstructs the exercise of any rights conferred by a warrant issued under this section or fails without reasonable excuse to comply with any requirement imposed in accordance with subsection (3)(d) above shall be guilty of an offence and liable—

(a)   on conviction on indictment, to a fine;

(b)   on summary conviction, to a fine not exceeding the statutory maximum.

(7)   The functions to which section 114 above applies shall include the functions of the Secretary of State under this section; but if any of those functions are transferred under that section the transfer may be subject to a reservation that they are to be exercisable by the Secretary of State concurrently with the designated agency and, in the case of functions exercisable by virtue of subsection (1) above, so as to be exercisable by the agency subject to such conditions or restrictions as the Treasury may from time to time impose.

. . .

(9)   In this section 'documents' includes information recorded in any form.

207.   Interpretation.

(1)   In this Act, except where the context otherwise requires—

. . .

'authorised person' means a person authorised under Chapter III of Part I of this Act;

'authorised unit trust scheme' means a unit trust scheme declared by an order of the Secretary of State for the time being in force to be an authorised unit trust scheme for the purposes of this Act;

'body corporate' includes a body corporate constituted under the law of a country or territory outside the United Kingdom;

'certified' and 'certification' mean certified or certification by a recognised professional body for the purposes of Part I of this Act;

. . .

'competent authority' means the competent authority for the purposes of Part IV of this Act;

'collective investment scheme' has the meaning given in section 75 above;

'delegation order' and 'designated agency' have the meaning given in section 114(3) above;

'director', in relation to a body corporate, includes a person occupying in relation to it the position of a director (by whatever name called) and any person in accordance with whose directions or instructions (not being advice given in a professional capacity) the directors of that body are accustomed to act;

'exempted person' means a person exempted under Chapter IV of Part I of this Act;

'group', in relation to a body corporate, means that body corporate, any other body corporate which is its holding company or subsidiary and any other body corporate which is a subsidiary of that holding company;

. . .

'investment advertisement' has the meaning given in section 57(2) above;

...

'listing particulars' has the meaning given in section 144(2A) above;

'member', in relation to a self-regulating organisation or professional body, has the meaning given in section 8(2) or 16(2) above;

...

'open-ended investment company' has the meaning given in section 75(8) above;

'overseas investment exchange' and 'overseas clearing house' mean a recognised investment exchange or recognised clearing house in the case of which the recognition order was made by virtue of section 40 above;

...

'private company' has the meaning given in section 1(3) of the Companies Act 1985 or the corresponding Northern Ireland provision;

'recognised clearing house' means a body declared by an order of the Secretary of State for the time being in force to be a recognised clearing house for the purposes of this Act;

'recognised investment exchange' means a body declared by an order of the Secretary of State for the time being in force to be a recognised investment exchange for the purposes of this Act;

'recognised professional body' means a body declared by an order of the Secretary of State for the time being in force to be a recognised professional body for the purposes of this Act;

'recognised scheme' means a scheme recognised under section 86, 87 or 88 above;

'recognised self-regulating organisation' means a body declared by an order of the Secretary of State for the time being in force to be a recognised self-regulating organisation for the purposes of this Act;

...

'recognition order' means an order declaring a body to be a recognised self-regulating organisation, self-regulating organisation for friendly societies, professional body, investment exchange or clearing house;

...

'rules', in relation to a self-regulating organisation, professional body, investment exchange or clearing house, has the meaning given in section 8(3), 16(3), 36(2) or 38(2) above;

...

'unit trust scheme' and 'units' have the meaning given in section 75(8) above.

(2)   In this Act 'advertisement' includes every form of advertising, whether in a publication, by the display of notices, signs, labels or showcards, by means of circulars, catalogues, price lists or other documents, by an exhibition of pictures or photographic or cinematographic films, by way of sound broadcasting or television or by inclusion in any programme service (within the meaning of the Broadcasting Act 1990) other than a sound or television broadcasting service, by the distribution of recordings, or in any other manner; and references to the issue of an advertisement shall be construed accordingly.

(3)   For the purposes of this Act an advertisement or other information issued outside the United Kingdom shall be treated as issued in the United Kingdom if it is directed to persons in the United Kingdom or is made available to them otherwise than in a newspaper, journal, magazine or other periodical publication published and circulating principally outside the United Kingdom or in a sound or television broadcast transmitted principally for reception outside the United Kingdom.

...

(8)   Section 736 of the Companies Act 1985 (meaning of subsidiary and holding company) shall apply for the purposes of this Act.

...

(10)   For the purposes of any provision of this Act authorising or requiring a person to do anything within a specified number of days no account shall be taken of any day which is a public holiday in any part of the United Kingdom.

...

SCHEDULES

Sections 1 and 2   SCHEDULE 1

INVESTMENTS AND INVESTMENT BUSINESS

PART I
INVESTMENTS

Shares etc.

1.   Shares and stock in the share capital of a company.

Note.   In this paragraph 'company' includes any body corporate and also any unincorporated body constituted under the law of a country or territory outside the United Kingdom but does not, except in relation to any shares of a class defined as deferred shares for the purposes of section 119 of the Building Societies Act 1986, include a building society incorporated under the law of, or of any part of, the United Kingdom, nor does it include an open-ended investment company or any body incorporated under the law of, or of any part of, the United Kingdom relating to industrial and provident societies or credit unions.

Debentures

2.   Debentures, including debenture stock, loan stock, bonds, certificates of deposit and other instruments creating or acknowledging indebtedness, not being instruments falling within paragraph 3 below.

Note.   This paragraph shall not be construed as applying—

(a)   to any instrument acknowledging or creating indebtedness for, or for money borrowed to defray, the consideration payable under a contract for the supply of goods or services;

(b)   to a cheque or other bill of exchange, a banker's draft or a letter of credit; or

(c)   to a banknote, a statement showing a balance in a current, deposit or savings account or (by reason of any financial obligation contained in it) to a lease or other disposition of property, a heritable security or an insurance policy.

Instruments entitling to shares or securities

4.   Warrants or other instruments entitling the holder to subscribe for investments falling within paragraph 1, 2 or 3 above.

Notes

(1)   It is immaterial whether the investments are for the time being in existence or identifiable.

(2)   An investment falling within this paragraph shall not be regarded as falling within paragraph 7, 8 or 9 below.

Certificates representing securities

5.   Certificates or other instruments which confer—

(a)   property rights in respect of any investment falling within paragraph 1, 2, 3 or 4 above;

(b)   any right to acquire, dispose of, underwrite or convert an investment, being a right to which the holder would be entitled if he held any such investment to which the certificate or instrument relates; or

(c)   a contractual right (other than an option) to acquire any such investment otherwise than by subscription.

Note. This paragraph does not apply to any instrument which confers rights in respect of two or more investments issued by different persons or in respect of two or more different investments falling within paragraph 3 above and issued by the same person.

Units in collective investment scheme

6.   Units in a collective investment scheme, including shares in or securities of an open-ended investment company.

Options

7.   Options to acquire or dispose of—
   (a)   an investment falling within any other paragraph of this Part of this Schedule;
   (b)   currency of the United Kingdom or of any other country or territory;
   (c)   gold, palladium, platinum or silver; or
   (d)   an option to acquire or dispose of an investment falling within this paragraph by virtue of (a), (b) or (c) above.

Futures

8.   Rights under a contract for the sale of a commodity or property of any other description under which delivery is to be made at a future date and at a price agreed upon when the contract is made.

Notes

(1)   This paragraph does not apply if the contract is made for commercial and not investment purposes.

(2)   A contract shall be regarded as made for investment purposes if it is made or traded on a recognised investment exchange or made otherwise than on a recognised investment exchange but expressed to be as traded on such an exchange or on the same terms as those on which an equivalent contract would be made on such an exchange.

(3)   A contract not falling within Note (2) above shall be regarded as made for commercial purposes if under the terms of the contract delivery is to be made within seven days.

(4)   The following are indications that any other contract is made for a commercial purpose and the absence of any of them is an indication that it is made for investment purposes—
   (a)   either or each of the parties is a producer of the commodity or other property or uses it in his business;
   (b)   the seller delivers or intends to deliver the property or the purchaser takes or intends to take delivery of it.

(5)   It is an indication that a contract is made for commercial purposes that the price, the lot, the delivery date or the other terms are determined by the parties for the purposes of the particular contract and not by reference to regularly published prices, to standard lots or delivery dates or to standard terms.

(6)   The following are also indications that a contract is made for investment purposes—
   (a)   it is expressed to be as traded on a market or on an exchange;
   (b)   performance of the contract is ensured by an investment exchange or a clearing house;
   (c)   there are arrangements for the payment or provision of margin.

(7)   A price shall be taken to have been agreed upon when a contract is made—
   (a)   notwithstanding that it is left to be determined by reference to the price at which a contract is to be entered into on a market or exchange or could be entered into at a time and place specified in the contract; or

(b)   in a case where the contract is expressed to be by reference to a standard lot and quality, notwithstanding that provision is made for a variation in the price to take account of any variation in quantity or quality on delivery.

Contracts for differences etc.

9.   Rights under a contract for differences or under any other contract the purpose or pretended purpose of which is to secure a profit or avoid a loss by reference to fluctuations in the value or price of property of any description or in an index or other factor designated for that purpose in the contract.

Notes.   (1)   This paragraph does not apply where the parties intend that the profit is to be obtained or the loss avoided by taking delivery of any property to which the contract relates.

(2)   This paragraph does not apply to rights under any contract under which money is received by the Director of Savings as deposits or otherwise in connection with the business of the National Savings Bank or raised under the National Loans Act 1968 under the auspices of the Director of Savings or under which money raised is treated as having been so raised by virtue of section 11(3) of the National Debt Act 1972.

Rights and interests in investments

11.   Rights to and interests in anything which is an investment falling within any other paragraph of this Part of this Schedule.

Notes.   (1)   This paragraph does not apply to interests under the trusts of an occupational pension scheme.

(2)   This paragraph does not apply to rights or interests which are investments by virtue of any other paragraph of this Part of this Schedule.

PART II
ACTIVITIES CONSTITUTING INVESTMENT BUSINESS

Dealing in investments

12.   Buying, selling, subscribing for or underwriting investments or offering or agreeing to do so, either as principal or as an agent.

Notes.   (1)   This paragraph does not apply to a person by reason of his accepting, or offering or agreeing to accept, whether as principal or as agent, an instrument creating or acknowledging indebtedness in respect of any loan, credit, guarantee or other similar financial accommodation or assurance which he or his principal has made, granted or provided or which he or his principal has offered or agreed to make, grant or provide.

(2)   The references in (1) above to a person accepting, or offering or agreeing to accept, an instrument include references to a person becoming, or offering or agreeing to become, a party to an instrument otherwise than as a debtor or a surety.

Arranging deals in investments

13.   Making, or offering or agreeing to make—

(a)   arrangements with a view to another person buying, selling, subscribing for or underwriting a particular investment; or

(b)   arrangements with a view to a person who participates in the arrangements buying, selling, subscribing for or underwriting investments.

Notes.   (1)   This paragraph does not apply to a person by reason of his making, or offering or agreeing to make, arrangements with a view to a transaction to which he will himself be a party as principal or which will be entered into by him as agent for one of the parties.

(2)   The arrangements in (a) above are arrangements which bring about or would bring about the transaction in question.

. . .

(4) This paragraph does not apply to a person by reason of his making, or offering or agreeing to make, arrangements with a view to a person accepting, whether as principal or as agent, an instrument creating or acknowledging indebtedness in respect of any loan, credit, guarantee or other similar financial accommodation or assurance which he or his principal has made, granted or provided or which he or his principal has offered or agreed to make, grant or provide.

(5) Arrangements do not fall within (b) above by reason of their having as their purpose the provision of finance to enable a person to buy, sell, subscribe for or underwrite investments.

(6) This paragraph does not apply to arrangements for the introduction of persons to another person if—

(a) the person to whom the introduction is made is an authorised or exempted person or is a person whose ordinary business involves him in engaging in activities which fall within this Part of this Schedule or would do apart from the provisions of Part III or Part IV and who is not unlawfully carrying on investment business in the United Kingdom; and

(b) the introduction is made with a view to the provision of independent advice or the independent exercise of discretion either—

(i) in relation to investments generally; or

(ii) in relation to any class of investments if the transaction or advice is or is to be with respect to an investment within that class.

(7) The references in (4) above to a person accepting an instrument include references to a person becoming a party to an instrument otherwise than as a debtor or a surety.

Custody of investments

13A.—(1) Safeguarding and administering or arranging for the safeguarding and administration of assets belonging to another where—

(a) those assets consist of or include investments; or

(b) the arrangements for their safeguarding and administration are such that those assets may consist of or include investments and the arrangements have at any time been held out as being arrangements under which investments would be safeguarded and administered.

(2) Offering or agreeing to safeguard and administer, or to arrange for the safeguarding and administration of, assets belonging to another where the circumstances fall within sub-pargraph (1)(a) or (b) above.

Notes. (1) This paragraph does not apply to a person by reason of his safeguarding and administering assets, or offering or agreeing to do so, under arrangements—

(a) under which another person ('the primary custodian'), who is permitted to provide a service falling within this paragraph, undertakes to the person to whom the assets belong a responsibility in respect of the assets which is no less onerous than the responsibility which the primary custodian would undertake to that person if the primary custodian were safeguarding and administering the assets himself, and

(b) which are operated by the primary custodian in the course of carrying on in the United Kingdom investment business falling within this paragraph.

(2) None of the following activities constitutes the administration of assets—

(a) providing information as to the number of units or the value of any assets safeguarded;

(b) converting currency; and

(c) receiving documents relating to an investment solely for the purpose of onward transmission to, from or at the direction of the person to whom the investment belongs.

428 Financial Services Act 1986

(3) For the purposes of this paragraph it is immaterial that the assets safeguarded and administered—

(a) constitute units of a security, title to which is recorded on the relevant register of securities as being held in uncertificated form; or

(b) may be transferred to another person, subject to a commitment by the person safeguarding and administering them, or arranging for their safeguarding and administration, that they will be replaced by equivalent assets at some future date or when so requested by the person to whom they belong.

(4) This paragraph does not apply to arrangements for the introduction of persons to another person if—

(a) the person to whom the introduction is made is permitted to provide a service falling within this paragraph; and

(b) the introduction is made with a view to the provision in the United Kingdom of a service falling within this paragraph or the making of arrangements operated in the United Kingdom for the provision of a service falling within this paragraph by a person who is not connected with the person by whom the introduction is made.

For the purposes of this Note, the person making the introduction shall be regarded as connected with the other person if he is either a body corporate in the same group as that other person or remunerated by that other person.

(5) For the purposes of Notes (1) and (4) above, a person is permitted to provide a service falling within this paragraph if—

(a) he is an authorised person who may provide that service—

(i) without contravening any rules that apply to him under section 48 of this Act; or

(ii) by virtue of his membership of a recognised self-regulating organisation or his certification by a recognised professional body; or

(b) he is an exempted person as respects any investment business which consists of or includes that service; or

(c) he is entitled to carry on investment business in the United Kingdom which consists of or includes that service pursuant either to regulation 5 of the Banking Coordination (Second Council Directive) Regulations 1992 or to regulation 5 of the Investment Services Regulations 1995.

Managing investments

14. Managing, or offering or agreeing to manage, assets belonging to another person if—

(a) those assets consist of or include investments; or

(b) the arrangements for their management are such that those assets may consist of or include investments at the discretion of the person managing or offering or agreeing to manage them and either they have at any time since the date of the coming into force of section 3 of this Act done so or the arrangements have at any time (whether before or after that date) been held out as arrangements under which they would do so.

Investment advice

15. Giving, or offering or agreeing to give, to persons in their capacity as investors or potential investors advice on the merits of their purchasing, selling, subscribing for or underwriting an investment, or exercising any right conferred by an investment to acquire, dispose of, underwrite or convert on investment.

Establishing etc. collective investment schemes

16. Establishing, operating or winding up a collective investment scheme, including acting as trustee of an authorised unit trust scheme or as depositary or sole director of an investment company with variable capital.

Sending dematerialised instructions etc.

16A.   Sending on behalf of another person dematerialised instructions relating to an investment by means of—

(a)   a relevant system in respect of which an Operator is approved under the Uncertificated Securities Regulations 1995; or

(b)   a computer-based system, established by the Bank of England and the London Stock Exchange, through the medium of which specified securities may be transferred or allotted without the need for an instrument in writing,

or offering or agreeing to do so, or causing on behalf of another person such instructions to be sent by such means or offering or agreeing to do so.

Notes.   (1)   This paragraph does not apply to a person by reason of his sending, or causing the sending of, instructions by means of a system falling within (a) above on behalf of—

(a)   a participating issuer or settlement bank acting in its capacity as such; or

(b)   an offeror making a takeover offer,

or by reason of his offering or agreeing to do so.

(1A)   This paragraph does not apply to a person—

(a)   by reason of his sending, or causing the sending of, instructions by means of a system falling within (b) above on behalf of a settlement bank acting in its capacity as such, or by reason of his offering or agreeing to do so; or

(b)   by reason of any activity in which he engages, or in which he offers or agrees to engage, at a time when he is accredited by the Bank of England as a provider of a network for the purposes of a system falling within (b) above and which is a necessary part of the provision of such a network.

(2)   For the purposes of this paragraph a person shall be taken to cause, or to offer or agree to cause, the sending of a dematerialised instruction only if—

(a)   in the case of a system falling within (a) above, he is a system-participant; and

(b)   in the case of a system falling within (b) above, he is a person who, under an agreement with the Bank of England, is responsible for the operation of, and the maintenance of security over, a gateway.

(3)   In this paragraph—

'dematerialised instruction'—

(a)   in relation to a system falling within (a) above, has the meaning given by regulation 3 of the Uncertificated Securities Regulations 1995, and

(b)   in relation to a system falling within (b) above, means an instruction sent by means of a gateway;

'gateway', in relation to a system falling within (b) above, means computer hardware and software by means of which instructions are authenticated and encrypted for processing by the system;

'offeror' has the meaning given by section 428 of the Companies Act 1985;

'Operator', 'participating issuer' and 'relevant system' have the meaning given by regulation 3 of the Uncertificated Securities Regulations 1995;

'settlement bank'—

(a)   in relation to a system falling within (a) above, has the meaning given by regulation 3 of the Uncertificated Securities Regulations 1995, and

(b)   in relation to a system falling within (b) above, means a person who has agreed to make payments in connection with the discharge of debts or liabilities arising from the transfer or allotment of specified securities made through the medium of that system;

'specified securities' has the meaning given by the Stock Transfer Act 1982;

'system-participant' has the meaning given by regulation 3 of the Uncertificated Securities Regulations 1995;

'takeover offer' has the meaning given by section 428 of the Companies Act 1985.

PART V
INTERPRETATION

28.—(1)   In this Schedule—

(a)   'property' includes currency of the United Kingdom or any other country or territory;

(b)   references to an instrument include references to any record whether or not in the form of a document;

(c)   references to an offer include references to an invitation to treat;

(d)   references to buying and selling include references to any acquisition or disposal for valuable consideration.

(2)   In sub-paragraph (1)(d) above 'disposal' includes—

(a)   in the case of an investment consisting of rights under a contract or other arrangements, assuming the corresponding liabilities under the contract or arrangements;

(b)   in the case of any other investment, issuing or creating the investment or granting the rights or interests of which it consists;

(c)   in the case of an investment consisting of rights under a contract, surrendering, assigning or converting those rights.

(3)   A company shall not by reason of issuing its own shares or share warrants, and a person shall not by reason of issuing his own debentures or debenture warrants, be regarded for the puposes of this Schedule as disposing of them or, by reason of anything done for the purpose of issuing them, be regarded as making arrangements with a view to a person subscribing for or otherwise acquiring them or underwriting them.

(4)   In sub-paragraph (3) above 'company' has the same meaning as in paragraph 1 above, 'shares' and 'debentures' include any investments falling within paragraph 1 or 2 above and 'share warrants' and 'debenture warrants' means any investment which falls within paragraph 4 above and relates to shares in the company concerned or, as the case may be, to debentures issued by the person concerned.

Section 142   SCHEDULE 11A

OFFERS OF SECURITIES TO THE PUBLIC IN THE UNITED KINGDOM

1.   A person offers securities to the public in the United Kingdom if—

(a)   to the extent that the offer is made to persons in the United Kingdom, it is made to the public; and

(b)   paragraph 2 below does not apply in relation to the offer;
and, for this purpose, an offer which is made to any section of the public, whether selected as members or debenture holders of a body corporate, or as clients of the person making the offer, or in any other manner, is to be regarded as made to the public.

2.   This paragraph applies in relation to an offer of securities where, to the extent that the offer is made to persons in the United Kingdom—

(a)   the condition specified in any one of the paragraphs of sub-paragraph (1) of paragraph 3 below is satisfied in relation to the offer; or

(b)   paragraph 4 below applies in relation to the offer.

3.—(1)   The following are the conditions specified in this sub-paragraph—

(a)   the securities are offered to persons—

(i)   whose ordinary activities involve them in acquiring, holding, managing or disposing of investments (as principal or agent) for the purposes of their businesses; or

(ii)   who it is reasonable to expect will acquire, hold, manage or dispose of investments (as principal or agent) for the purposes of their businesses;
or are otherwise offered to persons in the context of their trades, professions or occupations;

(b)   the securities are offered to no more than fifty persons;

(c)   the securities are offered to the members of a club or association (whether or not incorporated) and the members can reasonably be regarded as having a common interest with each other and with the club or association in the affairs of the club or association and in what is to be done with the proceeds of the offer;

(d)   the securities are offered to a restricted circle of persons whom the offeror reasonably believes to be sufficiently knowledgeable to understand the risks involved in accepting the offer;

(e)   the securities are offered in connection with a bona fide invitation to enter into an underwriting agreement with respect to them;

(f)   the securities are offered to a government, local authority or public authority, as defined in paragraph 3 of Schedule 1 to this Act;

(g)   the total consideration payable for the securities cannot exceed ecu 40,000 (or an equivalent amount);

(h)   the minimum consideration which may be paid for securities acquired pursuant to the offer is at least ecu 40,000 (or an equivalent amount);

(i)   the securities are denominated in amounts of at least ecu 40,000 (or an equivalent amount);

(j)   the securities are offered in connection with a takeover offer;

(k)   the securities are offered in connection with a merger within the meaning of Council Directive No. 78/855/EEC;

(l)   the securities are shares and are offered free of charge to any or all of the holders of shares in the issuer;

(m)   the securities are shares, or investments falling within paragraph 4 or 5 of Schedule 1 to this Act relating to shares, in a body corporate and are offered in exchange for shares in the same body corporate, and the offer cannot result in any increase in the issued share capital of the body corporate;

(n)   the securities are issued by a body corporate and offered—

    (i)   by the issuer;

    (ii)   only to qualifying persons; and

    (iii)   on terms that a contract to acquire any such securities may be entered into only by the qualifying person to whom they were offered or, if the terms of the offer so permit, any qualifying person;

(o)   the securities result from the conversion of convertible securities and listing particulars or a prospectus relating to the convertible securities were or was published in the United Kingdom under or by virtue of Part IV of this Act, Part III of the Companies Act 1985 or the Public Offers of Securities Regulations 1995;

(p)   the securities are issued by—

    (i)   a charity within the meaning of section 96(1) of the Charities Act 1993;

    (ii)   a housing association within the meaning of section 5(1) of the Housing Act 1985;

    (iii)   an industrial or provident society registered in accordance with section 1(2)(b) of the Industrial and Provident Societies Act 1965; or

    (iv)   a non-profit making association or body, recognised by the country or territory in which it is established, with objectives similar to those of a body falling within any of sub-paragraphs (i) to (iii) above;

and the proceeds of the offer will be used for the purposes of the issuer's objectives;

(q)   the securities offered are shares which are issued by, or ownership of which entitles the holder to membership of or to obtain the benefit of services provided by,—

    (i)   a building society incorporated under the law of, or of any part of, the United Kingdom;

    (ii)   any body incorporated under the law of, or of any part of, the United Kingdom relating to industrial and provident societies or credit unions; or

 (iii) a body of a similar nature established in a member State;

 (r) the securities offered are Euro-securities and are not the subject of advertising likely to come to the attention of persons who are not professionally experienced in matters relating to investment;

 (s) the securities are of the same class, and were issued at the same time, as securities in respect of which a prospectus has been published under or by virtue of Part IV of this Act, Part III of the Companies Act 1985 or the Public Offers of Securities Regulations 1995;

 (t) the securities are investments falling within paragraph 2 of Schedule 1 to this Act with a maturity of less than one year from their date of issue;

 (u) the securities are investments falling within paragraph 3 of Schedule 1 to this Act;

 (v) the securities are not transferable.

(2) For the purposes of this paragraph—

'convertible securities' means—

 (a) securities falling within paragraph 2 of Schedule 1 to this Act which can be converted into, or exchanged for, or which confer rights to acquire, securities; or

 (b) securities falling within paragraph 4 or 5 of that Schedule (as applied for the purposes of section 142(2) of this Act);

and 'conversion' in relation to convertible securities means their conversion into or exchange for, or the exercise of rights conferred by them to acquire, other securities;

'credit institution' means a credit institution as defined in Article 1 of Council Directive No. 77/780/EEC;

'ecu' means the European currency unit as defined in Article 1 of Council Regulation No. 3320/94/EC or any Council regulation replacing the same, in either case as amended from time to time;

'Euro-securities' means investments which—

 (a) are to be underwritten and distributed by a syndicate at least two of the members of which have their registered offices in different countries or territories;

 (b) are to be offered on a significant scale in one or more countries or territories other than the country or territory in which the issuer has its registered office; and

 (c) may be acquired pursuant to the offer only through a credit institution or other financial institution;

'financial institution' means a financial institution as defined in Article 1 of Council Directive No. 89/646/EEC; and

'shares', except in relation to a takeover offer, means investments which are securities by virtue of falling within paragraph 1 of Schedule 1 to this Act (as applied for the purposes of section 142(3) of this Act).

(3) For the purposes of determining whether the condition specified in paragraph (b) or (g) of sub-paragraph (1) above is satisfied in relation to an offer, the offer shall be taken together with any other offer of the same securities which was—

 (a) made by the same person;

 (b) open at any time within the period of 12 months ending with the date on which the offer is first made; and

 (c) not an offer to the public in the United Kingdom by virtue of that condition being satisfied.

(4) In determining for the purposes of paragraph (d) of sub-paragraph (1) above whether a person is sufficiently knowledgeable to understand the risks involved in accepting an offer of securities, any information supplied by the person making the offer shall be disregarded, apart from information about—

 (a) the issuer of the securities; or

 (b) if the securities confer the right to acquire other securities, the issuer of those other securities.

(5)   For the purposes of determining whether the condition specified in paragraph (g), (h) or (i) of sub-paragraph (1) above is satisfied in relation to an offer, an amount, in relation to an amount denominated in ecu, is an 'equivalent amount' if it is an amount of equal value, calculated at the latest practicable date before (but in any event not more than 3 days before) the date on which the offer is first made, denominated wholly or partly in another currency or unit of account.

(6)   For the purposes of paragraph (j) of sub-paragraph (1) above, 'takeover offer' means—

(a)   an offer which is a takeover offer within the meaning of Part XIIIA of the Companies Act 1985 (or would be such an offer if that Part of that Act applied in relation to any body corporate); or

(b)   an offer made to all the holders of shares, or of shares of a particular class, in a body corporate to acquire a specified proportion of those shares ('holders' and 'shares' being construed in accordance with that Part);

but in determining for the purposes of paragraph (b) above whether an offer is made to all the holders of shares, or of shares of any class, the offeror, any associate of his (within the meaning of section 430E of that Act) and any person whose shares the offeror or any such associate has contracted to acquire shall not be regarded as holders of the shares.

(7)   For the purposes of paragraph (l) of sub-paragraph (1) above, 'holders of shares' means the persons who, at the close of business on a date specified in the offer and falling within the period of 28 days ending with the date on which the offer is first made, were the holders of such shares.

(8)   For the purposes of paragraph (n) of sub-paragraph (1) above—

(a)   a person is a 'qualifying person', in relation to an issuer, if he is a bona fide employee or former employee of the issuer or of another body corporate in the same group or the wife, husband, widow, widower or child or stepchild under the age of eighteen of such an employee or former employee; and

(b)   the definition of 'issuer' in section 142(7) applies with the omission of the words from 'except that' to the end of the definition.

4.—(1)   This paragraph applies in relation to an offer where the condition specified in one relevant paragraph is satisfied in relation to part, but not the whole, of the offer and, in relation to each other part of the offer, the condition specified in a different relevant paragraph is satisfied.

(2)   For the purposes of this paragraph, 'relevant paragraph' means any of paragraphs (a) to (f), (j) to (m), (o), (p) and (s) of paragraph 3(1) above.

COMPANIES ACT 1989
(1989, c. 40)

An Act ... to make new provision with respect to the registration of company charges and otherwise to amend the law relating to companies; ... and for connected purposes.

[16 November 1989]

[*The Department of Trade and Industry has indicated that the provisions of the Companies Act 1989 which are printed here in italics will not be brought into force.*]

PART IV
REGISTRATION OF COMPANY CHARGES

Introduction

92.   Introduction.
The provisions of this Part amend the provisions of the Companies Act 1985 relating to the registration of company charges—

(a)   by inserting in Part XII of that Act (in place of sections 395 to 408 and 410 to 423) new provisions with respect to companies registered in Great Britain, and

(b)   by inserting as Chapter III of Part XXIII of that Act (in place of sections 409 and 424) new provisions with respect to oversea companies.

Registration in the companies charges register

93.   Charges requiring registration.

The following sections are inserted in Part XII of the Companies Act 1985—

'*Registration in the company charges register*

395.   Introductory provisions.

(1)   The purpose of this Part is to secure the registration of charges on a company's property.

(2)   In this Part—

'*charge*' means any form of security interest (fixed or floating) over property, other than an interest arising by operation of law; and

'*property*', in the context of what is the subject of a charge, includes future property.

(3)   It is immaterial for the purposes of this Part where the property subject to a charge is situated.

(4)   References in this Part to '*the registrar*' are—

(a)   in relation to a company registered in England and Wales, to the registrar of companies for England and Wales, and

(b)   in relation to a company registered in Scotland, to the registrar of companies for Scotland;

and references to registration, in relation to a charge, are to registration in the register kept by him under this Part.

396.   Charges requiring registration.

(1)   The charges requiring registration under this Part are—

(a)   a charge on land or any interest in land, other than—

(i)   in England and Wales, a charge for rent or any other periodical sum issuing out of the land,

(ii)   in Scotland, a charge for any rent, ground annual or other periodical sum payable in respect of the land;

(b)   a charge on goods or any interest in goods, other than a charge under which the chargee is entitled to possession either of the goods or of a document of title to them;

(c)   a charge on intangible movable property (in Scotland, incorporeal movable property) of any of the following descriptions—

(i)   goodwill,

(ii)   intellectual property,

(iii)   book debts (whether book debts of the company or assigned to the company),

(iv)   uncalled share capital of the company or calls made but not paid;

(d)   a charge for securing an issue of debentures; or

(e)   a floating charge on the whole or part of the company's property.

(2)   The descriptions of charge mentioned in subsection (1) shall be construed as follows—

(a)   a charge on a debenture forming part of an issue or series shall not be treated as falling within paragraph (a) or (b) by reason of the fact that the debenture is secured by a charge on land or goods (or on an interest in land or goods);

(b)   in paragraph (b) 'goods' means any tangible movable property (in Scotland, corporeal movable property) other than money;

(c)   a charge is not excluded from paragraph (b) because the chargee is entitled to take possession in case of default or on the occurrence of some other event;

    (d)   in paragraph (c) (ii) 'intellectual property' means—

        (i)   any patent, trade mark, registered design, copyright or design right, or

        (ii)   any licence under or in respect of any such right;

    (e)   a debenture which is part of an issue or series shall not be treated as a book debt for the purposes of paragraph (c) (iii);

    (f)   the deposit by way of security of a negotiable instrument given to secure the payment of book debts shall not be treated for the purposes of paragraph (c) (iii) as a charge on book debts;

    (g)   a shipowner's lien on subfreights shall not be treated as a charge on book debts for the purposes of paragraph (c) (iii) or as a floating charge for the purposes of paragraph (e).

    (3)   Whether a charge is one requiring registration under this Part shall be determined—

    (a)   in the case of a charge created by a company, as at the date the charge is created, and

    (b)   in the case of a charge over property acquired by a company, as at the date of the acquisition.

    (4)   The Secretary of State may by regulations amend subsections (1) and (2) so as to add any description of charge to, or remove any description of charge from, the charges requiring registration under this Part.

    (5)   Regulations under this section shall be made by statutory instrument which shall be subject to annulment in pursuance of a resolution of either House of Parliament.

    (6)   In the following provisions of this Part references to a charge are, unless the context otherwise requires, to a charge requiring registration under this Part.

    Where a charge not otherwise requiring registration relates to property by virtue of which it requires to be registered and to other property, the references are to the charge so far as it relates to property of the former description.'.

94.   *The companies charges register.*

The following section is inserted in Part XII of the Companies Act 1985—

'397.   *The companies charges register.*

    (1)   The registrar shall keep for each company a register, in such form as he thinks fit, of charges on property of the company.

    (2)   The register shall consist of a file containing with respect to each charge the particulars and other information delivered to the registrar under the provisions of this Part.

    (3)   Any person may require the registrar to provide a certificate stating the date on which any specified particulars of, or other information relating to, a charge were delivered to him.

    (4)   The certificate shall be signed by the registrar or authenticated by his official seal.

    (5)   The certificate shall be conclusive evidence that the specified particulars or other information were delivered to the registrar no later than the date stated in the certificate; and it shall be presumed unless the contrary is proved that they were not delivered earlier than that date.'.

95.   *Delivery of particulars for registration.*

The following sections are inserted in Part XII of the Companies Act 1985—

'398.   *Company's duty to deliver particulars of charge for registration.*

    (1)   It is the duty of a company which creates a charge, or acquires property subject to a charge—

    (a)   to deliver the prescribed particulars of the charge, in the prescribed form, to the registrar for registration, and

    (b)   to do so within 21 days after the date of the charge's creation or, as the case may be, the date of the acquisition;

but particulars of a charge may be delivered for registration by any person interested in the charge.

(2)   Where the particulars are delivered for registration by a person other than the company concerned, that person is entitled to recover from the company the amount of any fees paid by him to the registrar in connection with the registration.

(3)   If a company fails to comply with subsection (1), then, unless particulars of the charge have been delivered for registration by another person, the company and every officer of it who is in default is liable to a fine.

(4)   Where prescribed particulars in the prescribed form are delivered to the registrar for registration, he shall file the particulars in the register and shall note, in such form as he thinks fit, the date on which they were delivered to him.

(5)   The registrar shall send to the company and any person appearing from the particulars to be the chargee, and if the particulars were delivered by another person interested in the charge to that person, a copy of the particulars filed by him and of the note made by him as to the date on which they were delivered.

399.   Effect of failure to deliver particulars for registration.

(1)   Where a charge is created by a company and no prescribed particulars in the prescribed form are delivered for registration within the period of 21 days after the date of the charge's creation, the charge is void against—

(a)   an administrator or liquidator of the company, and

(b)   any person who for value acquires an interest in or right over property subject to the charge,

where the relevant event occurs after the creation of the charge, whether before or after the end of the 21 day period.

This is subject to section 400 (late delivery of particulars).

(2)   In this Part 'the relevant event' means—

(a)   in relation to the voidness of a charge as against an administrator or liquidator, the beginning of the insolvency proceedings, and

(b)   in relation to the voidness of a charge as against a person acquiring an interest in or right over property subject to a charge, the acquisition of that interest or right;

and references to 'a relevant event' shall be construed accordingly.

(3)   Where a relevant event occurs on the same day as the charge is created, it shall be presumed to have occurred after the charge is created unless the contrary is proved.

400.   Late delivery of particulars.

(1)   Where prescribed particulars of a charge created by a company, in the prescribed form, are delivered for registration more than 21 days after the date of the charge's creation, section 399(1) does not apply in relation to relevant events occurring after the particulars are delivered.

(2)   However, where in such a case—

(a)   the company is at the date of delivery of the particulars unable to pay its debts, or subsequently becomes unable to pay its debts in consequence of the transaction under which the charge is created, and

(b)   insolvency proceedings begin before the end of the relevant period beginning with the date of delivery of the particulars,

the charge is void as against the administrator or liquidator.

(3)   For this purpose—

(a)   the company is 'unable to pay its debts' in the circumstances specified in section 123 of the Insolvency Act 1986; and

(b)   the 'relevant period' is—

(i)   two years in the case of a floating charge created in favour of a person connected with the company (within the meaning of section 249 of that Act),

(ii)   one year in the case of a floating charge created in favour of a person not so connected, and

(iii)   six months in any other case.

(4)   Where a relevant event occurs on the same day as the particulars are delivered, it shall be presumed to have occurred before the particulars are delivered unless the contrary is proved.'.

96.   Delivery of further particulars.
The following section is inserted in Part XII of the Companies Act 1985—

'401.   Delivery of further particulars.

(1)   Further particulars of a charge, supplementing or varying the registered particulars, may be delivered to the registrar for registration at any time.

(2)   Further particulars must be in the prescribed form signed by or on behalf of both the company and the chargee.

(3)   Where further particulars are delivered to the registrar for registration and appear to him to be duly signed, he shall file the particulars in the register and shall note, in such form as he thinks fit, the date on which they were delivered to him.

(4)   The registrar shall send to the company and any person appearing from the particulars to be the chargee, and if the particulars were delivered by another person interested in the charge to that other person, a copy of the further particulars filed by him and of the note made by him as to the date on which they were delivered.'.

97.   Effect of omissions and errors in registered particulars.
The following section is inserted in Part XII of the Companies Act 1985—

'402.   Effect of omissions and errors in registered particulars.

(1)   Where the registered particulars of a charge created by a company are not complete and accurate, the charge is void, as mentioned below, to the extent that rights are not disclosed by the registered particulars which would be disclosed if they were complete and accurate.

(2)   The charge is void to that extent, unless the court on the application of the chargee orders otherwise, as against—

(a)   an administrator or liquidator of the company, and

(b)   any person who for value acquires an interest in or right over property subject to the charge,

where the relevant event occurs at a time when the particulars are incomplete or inaccurate in a relevant respect.

(3)   Where a relevant event occurs on the same day as particulars or further particulars are delivered, it shall be presumed to have occurred before those particulars are delivered unless the contrary is proved.

(4)   The court may order that the charge is effective as against an administrator or liquidator of the company if it is satisfied—

(a)   that the omission or error is not likely to have misled materially to his prejudice any unsecured creditor of the company, or

(b)   that no person became an unsecured creditor of the company at a time when the registered particulars of the charge were incomplete or inaccurate in a relevant respect.

(5)   The court may order that the charge is effective as against a person acquiring an interest in or right over proprty subject to the charge if it is satisfied that he did not rely, in connection with the acquisition, on registered particulars which were incomplete or inaccurate in a relevant respect.

(6)   For the purposes of this section an omission or inaccuracy with respect to the name of the chargee shall not be regarded as a failure to disclose the rights of the chargee.'.

98.   Memorandum of charge ceasing to affect company's property.
The following section is inserted in Part XII of the Companies Act 1985—

'403.   Memorandum of charge ceasing to affect company's property.

(1)   Where a charge of which particulars have been delivered ceases to affect the company's property, a memorandum to that effect may be delivered to the registrar for registration.

(2)   The memorandum must be in the prescribed form signed by or on behalf of both the company and the chargee.

(3)   Where a memorandum is delivered to the registrar for registration and appears to him to be duly signed, he shall file it in the register, and shall note, in such form as he thinks fit, the date on which it was delivered to him.

(4)   The registrar shall send to the company and any person appearing from the memorandum to be the chargee, and if the memorandum was delivered by another person interested in the charge to that person, a copy of the memorandum filed by him and of the note made by him as to the date on which it was delivered.

(5)   If a duly signed memorandum is delivered in a case where the charge in fact continues to affect the company's property, the charge is void as against—

(a)   an administrator or liquidator of the company, and

(b)   any person who for value acquires an interest in or right over property subject to the charge,

where the relevant event occurs after the delivery of the memorandum.

(6)   Where a relevant event occurs on the same day as the memorandum is delivered, it shall be presumed to have occurred before the memorandum is delivered unless the contrary is proved.'.

99.   Further provisions with respect to voidness of charges.

The following sections are inserted in Part XII of the Companies Act 1985—

'Further provisions with respect to voidness of charges

404.   Exclusion of voidness as against unregistered charges.

(1)   A charge is not void by virtue of this Part as against a subsequent charge unless some or all of the relevant particulars of that charge are duly delivered for registration—

(a)   within 21 days after the date of its creation, or

(b)   before complete and accurate relevant particulars of the earlier charge are duly delivered for registration.

(2)   Where relevant particulars of the subsequent charge so delivered are incomplete or inaccurate, the earlier charge is void as against that charge only to the extent that rights are disclosed by registered particulars of the subsequent charge duly delivered for registration before the corresponding relevant particulars of the earlier charge.

(3)   The relevant particulars of a charge for the purposes of this section are those prescribed particulars relating to rights inconsistent with those conferred by or in relation to the other charge.

405.   Restrictions on voidness by virtue of this Part.

(1)   A charge is not void by virtue of this Part as against a person acquiring an interest in or right over property where the acquisition is expressly subject to the charge.

(2)   Nor is a charge void by virtue of this Part in relation to any property by reason of a relevant event occurring after the company which created the charge has disposed of the whole of its interest in that property.

406.   Effect of exercise of power of sale.

(1)   A chargee exercising a power of sale may dispose of property to a purchaser freed from any interest or right arising from the charge having become void to any extent by virtue of this Part—

(a)   against an administrator or liquidator of the company, or

(b)   against a person acquiring a security interest over property subject to the charge;

and a purchaser is not concerned to see or inquire whether the charge has become so void.

(2)   The proceeds of the sale shall be held by the chargee in trust to be applied—

First, in discharge of any sum effectively secured by prior encumbrances to which the sale is not made subject;

Second, in payment of all costs, charges and expenses properly incurred by him in connection with the sale, or any previous attempted sale, of the property;

Third, in discharge of any sum effectively secured by the charge and encumbrances ranking pari passu with the charge;

Fourth, in discharge of any sum effectively secured by encumbrances ranking after the charge; and any residue is payable to the company or to a person authorised to give a receipt for the proceeds of the sale of the property.

(3)   For the purposes of subsection (2)—

(a)   prior encumbrances include any encumbrance to the extent that the charge is void as against it by virtue of this Part; and

(b)   no sum is effectively secured by a charge to the extent that it is void as against an administrator or liquidator of the company.

(4)   In this section—

(a)   references to things done by a chargee include things done by a receiver appointed by him, whether or not the receiver acts as his agent;

(b)   'power of sale' includes any power to dispose of, or grant on interest out of, property for the purpose of enforcing a charge (but in relation to Scotland does not include the power to grant a lease), and references to 'sale' shall be construed accordingly; and

(c)   'purchaser' means a person who in good faith and for valuable consideration acquires an interest in property.

(5)   The provisions of this section as to the order of application of the proceeds of sale have effect subject to any other statutory provision (in Scotland, any other statutory provision or rule of law) applicable in any case.

(6)   Where a chargee exercising a power of sale purports to dispose of property freed from any such interest or right as is mentioned in subsection (1) to a person other than a purchaser, the above provisions apply, with any necessary modifications, in relation to a disposition to a purchaser by that person or any successor in title of his.

(7)   In Scotland, subsections (2) and (7) of section 27 of the Conveyancing and Feudal Reform (Scotland) Act 1970 apply to a chargee unable to obtain a discharge for any payment which he is required to make under subsection (2) above as they apply to a creditor in the circumstances mentioned in those subsections.

407.   Effect of voidness on obligation secured.

(1)   Where a charge becomes void to any extent by virtue of this Part, the whole of the sum secured by the charge is payable forthwith on demand; and this applies notwithstanding that the sum secured by the charge is also the subject of other security.

(2)   Where the charge is to secure the repayment of money, the references in subsection (1) to the sum secured include any interest payable.'.

100.   Additional information to be registered.
The following sections are inserted in Part XII of the Companies Act 1985—

'Additional information to be registered

408.   Particulars of taking up of issue of debentures.

(1)   Where particulars of a charge for securing an issue of debentures have been delivered for registration, it is the duty of the company—

(a)   to deliver to the registrar for registration particulars in the prescribed form of the date on which any debentures of the issue are taken up, and of the amount taken up, and

(b)   to do so before the end of the period of 21 days after the date on which they are taken up.

(2)   Where particulars in the prescribed form are delivered to the registrar for registration under this section, he shall file them in the register.

(3)   If a company fails to comply with subsection (1), the company and every officer of it who is in default is liable to a fine.

409.   Notice of appointment of receiver or manager, &c.

(1)   If a person obtains an order for the appointment of a receiver or manager of a company's property, or appoints such a receiver or manager under powers contained in an instrument, he shall within seven days of the order or of the appointment under those powers, give notice of that fact in the prescribed form to the registrar for registration.

(2)   Where a person appointed receiver or manager of a company's property under powers contained in an instrument ceases to act as such receiver or manager, he shall, on so ceasing, give notice of that fact in the prescribed form to the registrar for registration.

(3)   Where a notice under this section in the prescribed form is delivered to the registrar for registration, he shall file it in the register.

(4)   If a person makes default in complying with the requirements of subsection (1) or (2), he is liable to a fine.

(5)   This section does not apply in relation to companies registered in Scotland (for which corresponding provision is made by sections 53, 54 and 62 of the Insolvency Act 1986).

410.   Notice of crystallisation of floating charge, &c.

(1)   The Secretary of State may by regulations require notice in the prescribed form to be given to the registrar of—

   (a)   the occurrence of such events as may be prescribed affecting the nature of the security under a floating charge of which particulars have been delivered for registration, and

   (b)   the taking of such action in exercise of powers conferred by a fixed or floating charge of which particulars have been delivered for registration, or conferred in relation to such a charge by an order of the court, as may be prescribed.

(2)   The regulations may make provision as to—

   (a)   the persons by whom notice is required to be, or may be, given, and the period within which notice is required to be given;

   (b)   the filing in the register of the particulars contained in the notice and the noting of the date on which the notice was given; and

   (c)   the consequences of failure to give notice.

(3)   As regards the consequences of failure to give notice of an event causing a floating charge to crystallise, the regulations may include provision to the effect that the crystallisation—

   (a)   shall be treated as ineffective until the prescribed particulars are delivered, and

   (b)   if the prescribed particulars are delivered after the expiry of the prescribed period, shall continue to be ineffective against such persons as may be prescribed,
subject to the exercise of such powers as may be conferred by the regulations on the court.

(4)   The regulations may provide that if there is a failure to comply with such of the requirements of the regulations as may be prescribed, such persons as may be prescribed are liable to a fine.

(5)   Regulations under this section shall be made by statutory instrument which shall be subject to annulment in pursuance of a resolution of either House of Parliament.

(6)   Regulations under this section shall not apply in relation to a floating charge created under the law of Scotland by a company registered in Scotland.'.

Copies of instruments and register to be kept by company

101.   Copies of instruments and register to be kept by company.

The following sections are inserted in Part XII of the Companies Act 1985—

'Copies of instruments and register to be kept by company

411.   Duty to keep copies of instruments and register.

(1)   Every company shall keep at its registered office a copy of every instrument creating or evidencing a charge over the company's property.

In the case of a series of uniform debentures, a copy of one debenture of the series is sufficient.

(2)   *Every company shall also keep at its registered office a register of all such charges, containing entries for each charge giving a short description of the property charged, the amount of the charge and (except in the case of securities to bearer) the names of the persons entitled to it.*

(3)   *This section applies to any charge, whether or not particulars are required to be delivered to the registrar for registration.*

(4)   *If a company fails to comply with any requirement of this section, the company and every officer of it who is in default is liable to a fine.*

412.   Inspection of copies and register.

(1)   *The copies and the register referred to in section 411 shall be open to the inspection of any creditor or member of the company without fee; and to the inspection of any other person on payment of such fee as may be prescribed.*

(2)   *Any person may request the company to provide him with a copy of—*

(a)   *any instrument creating or evidencing a charge over the company's property, or*

(b)   *any entry in the register of charges kept by the company, on payment of such fee as may be prescribed.*

This subsection applies to any charge, whether or not particulars are required to be delivered to the registrar for registration.

(3)   *The company shall send the copy to him not later than ten days after the day on which the request is received or, if later, on which payment is received.*

(4)   *If inspection of the copies or register is refused, or a copy requested is not sent within the time specified above—*

(a)   *the company and every officer of it who is in default is liable to a fine, and*

(b)   *the court may by order compel an immediate inspection of the copies or register or, as the case may be, direct that the copy be sent immediately.'.*

Supplementary provisions

102.   Power to make further provision by regulations.
The following section is inserted in Part XII of the Companies Act 1985—

'Supplementary provisions

413.   Power to make further provision by regulations.

(1)   *The Secretary of State may by regulations make further provision as to the application of the provisions of this Part in relation to charges of any description specified in the regulations.*

Nothing in the following provisions shall be construed as restricting the generality of that power.

(2)   *The regulations may require that where the charge is contained in or evidenced or varied by a written instrument there shall be delivered to the registrar for registration, instead of particulars or further particulars of the charge, the instrument itself or a certified copy of it together with such particulars as may be prescribed.*

(3)   *The regulations may provide that a memorandum of a charge ceasing to affect property of the company shall not be accepted by the registrar unless supported by such evidence as may be prescribed, and that a memorandum not so supported shall be treated as not having been delivered.*

(4)   *The regulations may also provide that where the instrument creating the charge is delivered to the registrar in support of such a memorandum, the registrar may mark the instrument as cancelled before returning it and shall send copies of the instrument cancelled to such persons as may be prescribed.*

(5)   *The regulations may exclude or modify, in such circumstances and to such extent as may be prescribed, the operation of the provisions of this Part relating to the voidness of a charge.*

(6) The regulations may require, in connection with the delivery of particulars, further particulars or a memorandum of the charge's ceasing to affect property of the company, the delivery of such supplementary information as may be prescribed, and may—

(a) apply in relation to such supplementary information any provisions of this Part relating to particulars, further particulars or such a memorandum, and

(b) provide that the particulars, further particulars or memorandum shall be treated as not having been delivered until the required supplementary information is delivered.

(7) Regulations under this section shall be made by statutory instrument which shall be subject to annulment in pursuance of a resolution of either House of Parliament.'.

103. Other supplementary provisions.

The following sections are inserted in Part XII of the Companies Act 1985—

'414. Date of creation of charge.

(1) References in this Part to the date of creation of a charge by a company shall be construed as follows.

(2) A charge created under the law of England and Wales shall be taken to be created—

(a) in the case of a charge created by an instrument in writing, when the instrument is executed by the company or, if its execution by the company is conditional, upon the conditions being fulfilled, and

(b) in any other case, when an enforceable agreement is entered into by the company conferring a security interest intended to take effect forthwith or upon the company acquiring an interest in property subject to the charge.

(3) A charge created under the law of Scotland shall be taken to be created—

(a) in the case of a floating charge, when the instrument creating the floating charge is executed by the company, and

(b) in any other case, when the right of the person entitled to the benefit of the charge is constituted as a real right.

(4) Where a charge is created in the United Kingdom but comprises property outside the United Kingdom, any further proceedings necessary to make the charge valid or effectual under the law of the country where the property is situated shall be disregarded in ascertaining the date on which the charge is to be taken to be created.

415. Prescribed particulars and related expressions.

(1) References in this Part to the prescribed particulars of a charge are to such particulars of, or relating to, the charge as may be prescribed.

(2) The prescribed particulars may, without prejudice to the generality of subsection (1), include—

(a) whether the company has undertaken not to create other charges ranking in priority to or pari passu with the charge, and

(b) whether the charge is a market charge within the meaning of Part VII of the Companies Act 1989 or a charge to which the provisions of that Part apply as they apply to a market charge.

(3) References in this Part to the registered particulars of a charge at any time are to such particulars and further particulars of the charge as have at that time been duly delivered for registration.

(4) References in this Part to the registered particulars of a charge being complete and accurate at any time are to their including all the prescribed particulars which would be required to be delivered if the charge were then newly created.

416. Notice of matters disclosed on register.

(1) A person taking a charge over a company's property shall be taken to have notice of any matter requiring registration and disclosed on the register at the time the charge is created.

(2)   Otherwise, a person shall not be taken to have notice of any matter by reason of its being disclosed on the register or by reason of his having failed to search the register in the course of making such inquiries as ought reasonably to be made.

(3)   The above provisions have effect subject to any other statutory provision as to whether a person is to be taken to have notice of any matter disclosed on the register.

417.   Power of court to dispense with signature.

(1)   Where it is proposed to deliver further particulars of a charge, or to deliver a memorandum of a charge ceasing to affect the company's property, and—

(a)   the chargee refuses to sign or authorise a person to sign on his behalf, or cannot be found, or

(b)   the company refuses to authorise a person to sign on its behalf,

the court may on the application of the company or the chargee, or of any other person having a sufficient interest in the matter, authorise the delivery of the particulars or memorandum without that signature.

(2)   The order may be made on such terms as appear to the court to be appropriate.

(3)   Where particulars or a memorandum are delivered to the registrar for registration in reliance on an order under this section, they must be accompanied by an office copy of the order.

In such a case the references in sections 401 and 403 to the particulars or memorandum being duly signed are to their being otherwise duly signed.

(4)   The registrar shall file the office copy of the court order along with the particulars or memorandum.'.

104.   Interpretation, &c.

The following sections are inserted in Part XII of the Companies Act 1985—

'418.   Regulations.

Regulations under any provision of this Part, or prescribing anything for the purposes of any such provision—

(a)   may make different provision for different cases, and

(b)   may contain such supplementary, incidental and transitional provisions as appear to the Secretary of State to be appropriate.

419.   Minor definitions.

(1)   In this Part—

'chargee' means the person for the time being entitled to exercise the security rights conferred by the charge;

'issue of debentures' means a group of debentures, or an amount of debenture stock, secured by the same charge; and

'series of debentures' means a group of debentures each containing or giving by reference to another instrument a charge to the benefit of which the holders of debentures of the series are entitled pari passu.

(2)   References in this Part to the creation of a charge include the variation of a charge which is not registrable so as to include property by virtue of which it becomes registrable.

The provisions of section 414 (construction of references to date of creation of charge) apply in such a case with any necessary modifications.

(3)   References in this Part to the date of acquisition of property by a company are—

(a)   in England and Wales, to the date on which the acquisition is completed, and

(b)   in Scotland, to the date on which the transaction is settled.

(4)   In the application of this Part to a floating charge created under the law of Scotland, references to crystallisation shall be construed as references to the attachment of the charge.

(5)   References in this Part to the beginning of insolvency proceedings are to—

(a)   the presentation of a petition on which an administration order or winding-up order is made, or

(b)   the passing of a resolution for voluntary winding up.

420. Index of defined expressions.

The following Table shows the provisions of this Part defining or otherwise explaining expressions used in this Part (other than expressions used only in the same section)—

charge	sections 395(2) and 396(6)
charge requiring registration	section 396
chargee	section 419(1)
complete and accurate (in relation to registered particulars)	section 415(4)
creation of charge	section 419(2)
crystallisation (in relation to Scottish floating charge)	section 419(4)
date of acquisition (of property by a company)	section 419(3)
date of creation of charge	section 414
further particulars	section 401
insolvency proceedings, beginning of	section 419(5)
issue of debentures	section 419(1)
memorandum of charge ceasing to affect company's property	section 403
prescribed particulars	section 415(1) and (2)
property	section 395(2)
registered particulars	section 415(3)
registrar and registration in relation to a charge	section 395(4)
relevant event	section 399(2)
series of debentures	section 419(1).'.

107. Consequential amendments.

The enactments specified in Schedule 16 have effect with the amendments specified there, which are consequential on the amendments made by the preceding provisions of this Part.

PART V
OTHER AMENDMENTS OF COMPANY LAW

Deregulation of private companies

117. Power to make further provision by regulations.

(1)   The Secretary of State may by regulations make provision enabling private companies to elect, by elective resolution in accordance with section 379A of the Companies Act 1985, to dispense with compliance with such requirements of that Act as may be specified in the regulations, being requirements which appear to the Secretary of State to relate primarily to the internal administration and procedure of companies.

(2)   The regulations may add to, amend or repeal provisions of that Act; and may provide for any such provision to have effect, where an election is made, subject to such adaptations and modifications as appear to the Secretary of State to be appropriate.

(3)   The regulations may make different provision for different cases and may contain such supplementary, incidental and transitional provisions as appear to the Secretary of State to be appropriate.

(4)   Regulations under this section shall be made by statutory instrument.

(5)   No regulations under this section shall be made unless a draft of the instrument containing the regulations has been laid before Parliament and approved by a resolution of each House.

Miscellaneous

133. Issue of redeemable shares.

(1)   In Part V of the Companies Act 1985 (share capital, its increase, maintenance and reduction), Chapter III (redeemable shares, purchase by a company of its own shares) is amended as follows.

(2)   After section 159 (power to issue redeemable shares) insert—

'159A.   Terms and manner of redemption.

(1)   Redeemable shares may not be issued unless the following conditions are satisfied as regards the terms and manner of redemption.

(2)   The date on or by which, or dates between which, the shares are to be or may be redeemed must be specified in the company's articles or, if the articles so provide, fixed by the directors, and in the latter case the date or dates must be fixed before the shares are issued.

(3)   Any other circumstances in which the shares are to be or may be redeemed must be specified in the company's articles.

(4)   The amount payable on redemption must be specified in, or determined in accordance with, the company's articles, and in the latter case the articles must not provide for the amount to be determined by reference to any person's discretion or opinion.

(5)   Any other terms and conditions of redemption shall be specified in the company's articles.

(6)   Nothing in this section shall be construed as requiring a company to provide in its articles for any matter for which provision is made by this Act.'.

(3)   In section 160 (financing, &c. of redemption)—

(a)   omit subsection (3) (which is superseded by the new section 159A), and

(b)   in subsection (4) (cancellation of shares on redemption) for 'redeemed under this section' substitute 'redeemed under this Chapter'.

(4)   In section 162 (power of company to purchase own shares), for subsection (2) (application of provisions relating to redeemable shares) substitute—

'(2)   Sections 159, 160 and 161 apply to the purchase by a company under this section of its own shares as they apply to the redemption of redeemable shares.'.

142.   Abolition of doctrine of deemed notice.

(1)   In Part XXIV of the Companies Act 1985 (the registrar of companies, his functions and offices), after section 711 insert—

'711A.   Exclusion of deemed notice.

(1)   A person shall not be taken to have notice of any matter merely because of its being disclosed in any document kept by the registrar of companies (and thus available for inspection) or made available by the company for inspection.

(2)   This does not affect the question whether a person is affected by notice of any matter by reason of a failure to make such inquiries as ought reasonably to be made.

(3)   In this section 'document' includes any material which contains information.

(4)   Nothing in this section affects the operation of—

(a)   section 416 of this Act (under which a person taking a charge over a company's property is deemed to have notice of matters disclosed on the companies charges register), or

(b)   section 198 of the Law of Property Act 1925 as it applies by virtue of section 3(7) of the Land Charges Act 1972 (under which the registration of certain land charges under Part XII, or Chapter III of Part XXIII, of this Act is deemed to constitute actual notice for all purposes connected with the land affected).'.

. . .

PART X
MISCELLANEOUS AND GENERAL PROVISIONS
General

215.   Commencement and transitional provisions.

(1)   The following provisions of this Act come into force on Royal Assent—

(a)   in Part V (amendments of company law), section 141 (application to declare dissolution of company void);

(b)   in Part VI (mergers)—
  (i)   sections 147 to 150, and
  (ii)   paragraphs 2 to 12, 14 to 16, 18 to 20, 22 to 25 of Schedule 20, and section 153 so far as relating to those paragraphs;
(c)   in Part VIII (amendments of the Financial Services Act 1986), section 202 (offers of short-dated debentures);
(d)   in Part X (miscellaneous and general provisions), the repeals made by Schedule 24 in sections 71, 74, 88 and 89 of, and Schedule 9 to, the Fair Trading Act 1973, and section 212 so far as relating to those repeals.

(2)   The other provisions of this Act come into force on such day as the Secretary of State may appoint by order made by statutory instrument; and different days may be appointed for different provisions and different purposes.

(3)   An order bringing into force any provision may contain such transitional provisions and savings as appear to the Secretary of State to be necessary or expedient.

(4)   The Secretary of State may also by order under this section amend any enactment which refers to the commencement of a provision brought into force by the order so as to substitute a reference to the actual date on which it comes into force.

216.   Short title.

This Act may be cited as the Companies Act 1989.

Section 107   **SCHEDULE 16**
AMENDMENTS CONSEQUENTIAL ON PART IV
Companies Act 1985 (c. 6)

1A.   Section 695A(1) is amended by the insertion of the words 'or Chapter III of this Part' after 'Schedule 21C'.

2.—(1)   Schedule 24 to the Companies Act 1985 (punishment of offences) is amended as follows.

(2)   For the entries relating to sections 399(3) to 423(3) (offences under Part XII: registration of charges) substitute—

'398(3)	Company failing to deliver particulars of charge to registrar.	1. On indictment. 2. Summary.	A fine. The statutory maximum.
408(3)	Company failing to deliver particulars of taking up of issue of debentures.	Summary.	One-fifth of the statutory maximum.
409(4)	Failure to give notice to registrar of appointment of receiver or manager, or of his ceasing to act.	Summary.	One-fifth of the statutory maximum.
410(4)	Failure to comply with requirements of regulations under s. 410.	Summary.	One-fifth of the statutory maximum.
411(4)	Failure to keep copies of charging instruments or register at registered office.	1. On indictment. 2. Summary.	A fine. The statutory maximum.
412(4)	Refusing inspection of charging instrument or register or failing to supply copies.	Summary.	One-fifth of the statutory maximum. '.

(3)   After the entry relating to section 703(1) insert—

'703D(5)	Oversea company failing to deliver particulars of charge to registrar.	1. On indictment. 2. Summary.	A fine. The statutory maximum. '.

Insolvency Act 1986 (c. 45)

3.—*(1)   The Insolvency Act 1986 is amended as follows.*

(2)   In section 9(3)   (restrictions on making administration order where administrative receiver has been appointed), in paragraph (b) (exceptions) insert—

'*(i)   be void against the administrator to any extent by virtue of the provisions of Part XII of the Companies Act 1985 (registration of company charges),';*
and renumber the existing sub-paragraphs as (ii) to (iv).

(3)   In sections 45(5), 53(2), 54(3) and 62(5)   (offences of failing to deliver documents relating to appointment or cessation of appointment of receiver) omit the words 'and, for continued contravention, to a daily default fine'.

Company Directors Disqualification Act 1986 (c. 46)

4.   *In Schedule 1 to the Company Directors Disqualification Act 1986 (matters relevant to determining unfitness of directors), in paragraph 4 (failure of company to comply with certain provisions), for sub-paragraph (h) substitute—*

'*(h)   sections 398 and 703D (duty of company to deliver particulars of charge on its property).'.*

Section 212   SCHEDULE 24

                                              REPEALS

Chapter	Short title	Extent of repeal
... 1986 c. 45. ...	Insolvency Act 1986.	In sections 45(5), 53(2), 54(3) and 62(5), the words 'and, for continued contravention, to a daily default fine'. In Schedule 10, the entries in column 5 relating to sections 45(5), 53(2), 54(3) and 62(5).

CRIMINAL JUSTICE ACT 1993
(1993, c. 36)

An Act . . . to implement provisions of the Community Council Directive No. 89/592/EEC and to amend and restate the law about insider dealing in securities; . . . and for connected purposes.
                                                                        [27 July 1993]

PART V
INSIDER DEALING

The offence of insider dealing

52.   The offence.
   (1)   An individual who has information as an insider is guilty of insider dealing if, in the circumstances mentioned in subsection (3), he deals in securities that are price-affected securities in relation to the information.
   (2)   An individual who has information as an insider is also guilty of insider dealing if—
      (a)   he encourages another person to deal in securities that are (whether or not that other knows it) price-affected securities in relation to the information, knowing or

having reasonable cause to believe that the dealing would take place in the circumstances mentioned in subsection (3); or

(b)   he discloses the information, otherwise than in the proper performance of the functions of his employment, office or profession, to another person.

(3)   The circumstances referred to above are that the acquisition or disposal in question occurs on a regulated market, or that the person dealing relies on a professional intermediary or is himself acting as a professional intermediary.

(4)   This section has effect subject to section 53.

53. Defences.

(1)   An individual is not guilty of insider dealing by virtue of dealing in securities if he shows—

(a)   that he did not at the time expect the dealing to result in a profit attributable to the fact that the information in question was price-sensitive information in relation to the securities, or

(b)   that at the time he believed on reasonable grounds that the information had been disclosed widely enough to ensure that none of those taking part in the dealing would be prejudiced by not having the information, or

(c)   that he would have done what he did even if he had not had the information.

(2)   An individual is not guilty of insider dealing by virtue of encouraging another person to deal in securities if he shows—

(a)   that he did not at the time expect the dealing to result in a profit attributable to the fact that the information in question was price-sensitive information in relation to the securities, or

(b)   that at the time he believed on reasonable grounds that the information had been or would be disclosed widely enough to ensure that none of those taking part in the dealing would be prejudiced by not having the information, or

(c)   that he would have done what he did even if he had not had the information.

(3)   An individual is not guilty of insider dealing by virtue of a disclosure of information if he shows—

(a)   that he did not at the time expect any person, because of the disclosure, to deal in securities in the circumstances mentioned in subsection (3) of section 52; or

(b)   that, although he had such an expectation at the time, he did not expect the dealing to result in a profit attributable to the fact that the information was price-sensitive information in relation to the securities.

(4)   Schedule 1 (special defences) shall have effect.

(5)   The Treasury may by order amend Schedule 1.

(6)   In this section references to a profit include references to the avoidance of a loss.

Interpretation

54. Securities to which Part V applies.

(1)   This Part applies to any security which—

(a)   falls within any paragraph of Schedule 2; and

(b)   satisfies any conditions applying to it under an order made by the Treasury for the purposes of this subsection;

and in the provisions of this Part (other than that Schedule) any reference to a security is a reference to a security to which this Part applies.

(2)   The Treasury may by order amend Schedule 2.

55. 'Dealing' in securities.

(1)   For the purposes of this Part, a person deals in securities if—

(a)   he acquires or disposes of the securities (whether as principal or agent); or

(b)   he procures, directly or indirectly, an acquisition or disposal of the securities by any other person.

(2)   For the purposes of this Part, 'acquire', in relation to a security, includes—
  (a)   agreeing to acquire the security; and
  (b)   entering into a contract which creates the security.
(3)   For the purposes of this Part, 'dispose', in relation to a security, includes—
  (a)   agreeing to dispose of the security; and
  (b)   bringing to an end a contract which created the security.
(4)   For the purposes of subsection (1), a person procures an acquisition or disposal of a security if the security is acquired or disposed of by a person who is—
  (a)   his agent,
  (b)   his nominee, or
  (c)   a person who is acting at his direction,
in relation to the acquisition or disposal.
(5)   Subsection (4) is not exhaustive as to the circumstances in which one person may be regarded as procuring an acquisition or disposal of securities by another.

56.   'Inside information', etc.

(1)   For the purposes of this section and section 57, 'inside information' means information which—
  (a)   relates to particular securities or to a particular issuer of securities or to particular issuers of securities and not to securities generally or to issuers of securities generally;
  (b)   is specific or precise;
  (c)   has not been made public; and
  (d)   if it were made public would be likely to have a significant effect on the price of any securities.
(2)   For the purposes of this Part, securities are 'price-affected securities' in relation to inside information, and inside information is 'price-sensitive information' in relation to securities, if and only if the information would, if made public, be likely to have a significant effect on the price of the securities.
(3)   For the purposes of this section 'price' includes value.

57.   'Insiders'.

(1)   For the purposes of this Part, a person has information as an insider if and only if—
  (a)   it is, and he knows that it is, inside information, and
  (b)   he has it, and knows that he has it, from an inside source.
(2)   For the purposes of subsection (1), a person has information from an inside source if and only if—
  (a)   he has it through—
    (i)   being a director, employee or shareholder of an issuer of securities; or
    (ii)   having access to the information by virtue of his employment, office or profession; or
  (b)   the direct or indirect source of his information is a person within paragraph (a).

58.   Information 'made public'.

(1)   For the purposes of section 56, 'made public', in relation to information, shall be construed in accordance with the following provisions of this section; but those provisions are not exhaustive as to the meaning of that expression.
(2)   Information is made public if—
  (a)   it is published in accordance with the rules of a regulated market for the purpose of informing investors and their professional advisers;
  (b)   it is contained in records which by virtue of any enactment are open to inspection by the public;

    (c) it can be readily acquired by those likely to deal in any securities—
       (i)   to which the information relates, or
      (ii)   of an issuer to which the information relates; or
    (d) it is derived from information which has been made public.
  (3) Information may be treated as made public even though—
    (a) it can be acquired only by persons exercising diligence or expertise;
    (b) it is communicated to a section of the public and not to the public at large;
    (c) it can be acquired only by observation;
    (d) it is communicated only on payment of a fee; or
    (e) it is published only outside the United Kingdom.

59. 'Professional intermediary'.

  (1) For the purposes of this Part, a 'professional intermediary' is a person—
    (a) who carries on a business consisting of an activity mentioned in sub-section (2) and who holds himself out to the public or any section of the public (including a section of the public constituted by persons such as himself) as willing to engage in any such business; or
    (b) who is employed by a person falling within paragraph (a) to carry out any such activity.
  (2) The activities referred to in subsection (1) are—
    (a) acquiring or disposing of securities (whether as principal or agent); or
    (b) acting as an intermediary between persons taking part in any dealing in securities.
  (3) A person is not to be treated as carrying on a business consisting of an activity mentioned in subsection (2)—
    (a) if the activity in question is merely incidental to some other activity not falling within subsection (2); or
    (b) merely because he occasionally conducts one of those activities.
  (4) For the purposes of section 52, a person dealing in securities relies on a professional intermediary if and only if a person who is acting as a professional intermediary carries out an activity mentioned in subsection (2) in relation to that dealing.

60. Other interpretation provisions.

  (1) For the purposes of this Part, 'regulated market' means any market, however operated, which, by an order made by the Treasury, is identified (whether by name or by reference to criteria prescribed by the order) as a regulated market for the purposes of this Part.
  (2) For the purposes of this Part an 'issuer', in relation to any securities, means any company, public sector body or individual by which or by whom the securities have been or are to be issued.
  (3) For the purposes of this Part—
    (a) 'company' means any body (whether or not incorporated and wherever incorporated or constituted) which is not a public sector body; and
    (b) 'public sector body' means—
       (i)   the government of the United Kingdom, of Northern Ireland or of any country or territory outside the United Kingdom;
      (ii)   a local authority in the United Kingdom or elsewhere;
     (iii)   any international organisation the members of which include the United Kingdom or another member state;
     (iv)   the Bank of England; or
     (v)   the central bank of any sovereign State.

(4)   For the purposes of this Part, information shall be treated as relating to an issuer of securities which is a company not only where it is about the company but also where it may affect the company's business prospects.

Miscellaneous

61.   Penalties and prosecution.

(1)   An inividual guilty of insider dealing shall be liable—

(a)   on summary conviction, to a fine not exceeding the statutory maximum or imprisonment for a term not exceeding six months or to both; or

(b)   on conviction on indictment, to a fine or imprisonment for a term not exceeding seven years or to both.

(2)   Proceedings for offences under this Part shall not be instituted in England and Wales except by or with the consent of—

(a)   the Secretary of State; or

(b)   the Director of Public Prosecutions.

(3)   In relation to proceedings in Northern Ireland for offences under this Part, subsection (2) shall have effect as if the reference to the Director of Public Prosecutions were a reference to the Director of Public Prosecutions for Northern Ireland.

62.   Territorial scope of offence of insider dealing.

(1)   An individual is not guilty of an offence falling within subsection (1) of section 52 unless—

(a)   he was within the United Kingdom at the time when he is alleged to have done any act constituting or forming part of the alleged dealing;

(b)   the regulated market on which the dealing is alleged to have occurred is one which, by an order made by the Treasury, is identified (whether by name or by reference to criteria prescribed by the order) as being, for the purposes of this Part, regulated in the United Kingdom; or

(c)   the professional intermediary was within the United Kingdom at the time when he is alleged to have done anything by means of which the offence is alleged to have been committed.

(2)   An individual is not guilty of an offence falling within subsection (2) of section 52 unless—

(a)   he was within the United Kingdom at the time when he is alleged to have disclosed the information or encouraged the dealing; or

(b)   the alleged recipient of the information or encouragement was within the United Kingdom at the time when he is alleged to have received the information or encouragement.

63.   Limits on section 52.

(1)   Section 52 does not apply to anything done by an individual acting on behalf of a public sector body in pursuit of monetary policies or policies with respect to exchange rates or the management of public debt or foreign exchange reserves.

(2)   No contract shall be void or unenforceable by reason only of section 52.

64.   Orders.

(1)   Any power under this Part to make an order shall be exercisable by statutory instrument.

(2)   No order shall be made under this Part unless a draft of it has been laid before and approved by a resolution of each House of Parliament.

(3)   An order under this Part—

(a)   may make different provision for different cases; and

(b)   may contain such incidental, supplemental and transitional provisions as the Treasury consider expedient.

SCHEDULES

SCHEDULE 1

SPECIAL DEFENCES

Market makers

1.—(1)   An individual is not guilty of insider dealing by virtue of dealing in securities or encouraging another person to deal if he shows that he acted in good faith in the course of—

(a)   his business as a market maker, or

(b)   his employment in the business of a market maker.

(2)   A market maker is a person who—

(a)   holds himself out at all normal times in compliance with the rules of a regulated market or an approved organisation as willing to acquire or dispose of securities; and

(b)   is recognised as doing so under those rules.

(3)   In this paragraph 'approved organisation' means an international securities self-regulating organisation approved under paragraph 25B of Schedule 1 to the Financial Services Act 1986.

Market information

2.—(1)   An individual is not guilty of insider dealing by virtue of dealing in securities or encouraging another person to deal if he shows that—

(a)   the information which he had as an insider was market information; and

(b)   it was reasonable for an individual in his position to have acted as he did despite having that information as an insider at the time.

(2)   In determining whether it is reasonable for an individual to do any act despite having market information at the time, there shall, in particular, be taken into account—

(a)   the content of the information;

(b)   the circumstances in which he first had the information and in what capacity; and

(c)   the capacity in which he now acts.

3.   An individual is not guilty of insider dealing by virtue of dealing in securities or encouraging another person to deal if he shows—

(a)   that he acted—

(i)   in connection with an acquisition or disposal which was under consideration or the subject of negotiation, or in the course of a series of such acquisitions or disposals; and

(ii)   with a view to facilitating the accomplishment of the acquisition or disposal or the series of acquisitions or disposals; and

(b)   that the information which he had as an insider was market information arising directly out of his involvement in the acquisition or disposal or series of acquisitions or disposals.

4.   For the purposes of paragraphs 2 and 3 market information is information consisting of one or more of the following facts—

(a)   that securities of a particular kind have been or are to be acquired or disposed of, or that their acquisition or disposal is under consideration or the subject of negotiation;

(b)   that securities of a particular kind have not been or are not to be acquired or disposed of;

(c)   the number of securities acquired or disposed of or to be acquired or disposed of or whose acquisition or disposal is under consideration or the subject of negotiation;

(d)   the price (or range of prices) at which securities have been or are to be acquired or disposed of or the price (or range of prices) at which securities whose acquisition or disposal is under consideration or the subject of negotiation may be acquired or disposed of;

(e)   the identity of the persons involved or likely to be involved in any capacity in an acquisition or disposal.

Price stabilisation

5.—(1)   An individual is not guilty of insider dealing by virtue of dealing in securities or encouraging another person to deal if he shows that he acted in conformity with the price stabilisation rules.

(2)   In this paragraph 'the price stabilisation rules' means rules which—

(a)   are made under section 48 of the Financial Services Act 1986 (conduct of business rules); and

(b)   make provision of a description mentioned in paragraph (i) of subsection (2) of that section (price stabilisation rules).

Section 54   SCHEDULE 2

                                    SECURITIES

Shares

1.   Shares and stock in the share capital of a company ('shares').

Debt securities

2.   Any instrument creating or acknowledging indebtedness which is issued by a company or public sector body, including, in particular, debentures, debenture stock, loan stock, bonds and certificates of deposit ('debt securities').

Warrants

3.   Any right (whether conferred by warrant or otherwise) to subscribe for shares or debt securities ('warrants').

Depositary receipts

4.—(1)   The rights under any depositary receipt.

(2)   For the purposes of sub-paragraph (1) a 'depositary receipt' means a certificate or other record (whether or not in the form of a document)—

(a)   which is issued by or on behalf of a person who holds any relevant securities of a particular issuer; and

(b)   which acknowledges that another person is entitled to rights in relation to the relevant securities or relevant securities of the same kind.

(3)   In sub-paragraph (2) 'relevant securities' means shares, debt securities and warrants.

Options

5.   Any option to acquire or dispose of any security falling within any other paragraph of this Schedule.

Futures

6.—(1)   Rights under a contract for the acquisition or disposal of relevant securities under which delivery is to be made at a future date and at a price agreed when the contract is made.

(2)   In sub-paragraph (1)—

(a)   the references to a future date and to a price agreed when the contract is made include references to a date and a price determined in accordance with terms of the contract; and

(b)   'relevant securities' means any security falling within any other paragraph of this Schedule.

Contracts for differences

7.—(1)   Rights under a contract which does not provide for the delivery of securities but whose purpose or pretended purpose is to secure a profit or avoid a loss by reference to fluctuations in—

(a)   a share index or other similar factor connected with relevant securities;

(b)   the price of particular relevant securities; or

(c)   the interest rate offered on money placed on deposit.

(2)   In sub-paragraph (1) 'relevant securities' means any security falling within any other paragraph of this Schedule.

PART II   STATUTORY INSTRUMENTS

COMPANY AND BUSINESS NAMES REGULATIONS 1981
(1981 No. 1685)

The Secretary of State, in exercise of his powers under sections 31 and 32 of the Companies Act 1981 hereby makes the following regulations—

1. These Regulations may be cited as the Company and Business Names Regulations 1981 and shall come into operation on 26 February 1982.

2. In these Regulations, unless the context otherwise requires, 'the Act' means the Companies Act 1981.

3. The words and expressions stated in column (1) of the Schedule hereto (together with the plural and the possessive forms of those words and expressions) are hereby specified as words and expressions for the registration of which as or as part of a company's corporate name the approval of the Secretary of State is required by section 22(2)(b) of the Act or for the use of which as or as part of a business name his approval is required by section 28(2)(b) of the Act.

4. Subject to Regulation 5, each Government department or other body stated in column (2) of the Schedule hereto is hereby specified as the relevant body for the purposes of section 31(2) and (3) of the Act in relation to the word or expression (and the plural and the possesive forms of that word or expression) opposite to it in column (1).

5. Where two Government departments or other bodies are specified in the alternative in Column (2) of the Schedule hereto the second alternative is to be treated as specified,

  (a)   in the case of the corporate name of a company,

    (i)   if the company has not yet been registered and its principal or only place of business in Great Britain is to be in Scotland or, if it will have no place of busines in Great Britain, its proposed registered office is in Scotland, and

    (ii)   if the company is already registered and its principal or only place of business in Great Britain is in Scotland or, if it has no place of business in Great Britain, its registered office is in Scotland, and

  (b)   in the case of a business name, if the principal or only place of the business carried on or to be carried on in Great Britain is or is to be in Scotland,

and the first alternative is to be treated as specified in any other case.

Regulations 3, 4 and 5   SCHEDULE

SPECIFICATION OF WORDS, EXPRESSIONS AND RELEVANT BODIES

Column (1)	Column (2)
Word or expression	Relevant body
Abortion	Department of Health and Social Security
Apothecary	Worshipful Society of Apothecaries of London or Pharmaceutical Society of Great Britain
Association	
Assurance	
Assurer	
Authority	
Benevolent	
Board	
British	
Chamber of Commerce	
Chamber of Commerce, Training and Enterprise	
Chamber of Industry	
Chamber of Trade	
Charitable	} Charity Commission or Scottish Home and
Charity	} Health Department
Charter	
Chartered	
Chemist	
Chemistry	
Contact Lens	General Optical Council
Co-operative	
Council	
Dental	} General Dental Council
Dentistry	}
District Nurse	Panel of Assessors in District Nurse Training
Duke	Home Office or Scottish Home and Health Department
England	
English	
European	
Federation	
Friendly Society	
Foundation	
Fund	
Giro	
Great Britain	
Group	
Health Centre	} Department of Health and Social Security
Health Service	}
Health Visitor	Council for the Education and Training of Health Visitors
Her Majesty	} Home Office or Scottish Home and
His Majesty	} Health Department
Holding	
Industrial and Provident Society	
Institute	
Institution	
Insurance	
Insurer	

Column (1)	Column (2)
Word or expression	Relevant body
International	
Ireland	
Irish	
King	Home Office or Scottish Home and Health Department
Midwife	} Central Midwives Board or Central
Midwifery	} Midwives Board for Scotland
National	
Nurse	} General Nursing Council for England
Nursing	} and Wales or General Nursing Council for Scotland
Patent	
Patentee	
Police	Home Office or Scottish Home and Health Department
Polytechnic	Department for Education and Employment
Post Office	
Pregnancy Termination	Department of Health and Social Security
Prince	} Home Office or Scottish Home and
Princess	} Health Department
Queen	
Reassurance	
Reassurer	
Register	
Registered	
Reinsurance	
Reinsurer	
Royal	} Home Office or Scottish Home and
Royale	} Health Department
Royalty	
Scotland	
Scottish	
Sheffield	
Society	
Special School	Department for Education and Employment
Stock Exchange	
Trade Union	
Trust	
United Kingdom	
University	The Privy Council
Wales	
Welsh	
Windsor	Home Office or Scottish Home and Health Department

COMPANIES (REGISTERS AND OTHER RECORDS) REGULATIONS 1985
(1985 No. 724)

The Secretary of State, in exercise of his powers under section 723(4) of the Companies Act 1985, and of all other powers enabling him in that behalf, hereby makes the following Regulations—

Citation, commencement, revocation and interpretation

1.—(1)   These Regulations may be cited as the Companies (Registers and other Records) Regulations 1985 and shall come into operation on 1 July 1985.

(2)   In these Regulations, unless the context otherwise requires—

'the Act' means the Companies Act 1985;

'the place for inspection' means, in relation to a register, or a register of holders of debentures of a company, which is kept by recording the matters in question otherwise than in a legible form, the place where the duty to allow inspection of the register is for the time being performed in accordance with these Regulations;

'register' means a register or other record as is mentioned in section 722(1) of the Act;

'the register of directors' interests' means the register required to be kept under section 325(1) of the Act.

(3)   Any reference in these Regulations to the duty to allow inspection of a register, or of the register of holders of debentures, is a reference to the duty provided for in section 723(3) of the Act to allow inspection of, or to furnish, a reproduction of the recording of the register, or of the relevant part of the recording in a legible form.

(4)   Any reference in these Regulations to the register of interests in voting shares shall be construed as including a reference to the separate part of that register referred to in section 213(1) of the Act.

(5)   The Companies (Registers and other Records) Regulations 1979 are hereby revoked.

Requirements with respect to registers kept otherwise than in a legible form

2.—(1)   This Regulation applies with repect to any register specified in Schedule 1 to these Regulations which is kept by a company by recording the matters in question otherwise than in a legible form.

(2)   The company shall perform the duty to allow inspection of any register to which this Regulation applies at a place specified in the said Schedule 1 in relation to that register.

(3)   In the case of any register to which this Regulation applies, the company shall not be required—

(a)   to keep the register in any place where it is required to be kept under the Act,

(b)   to give any notice to the registrar of companies required to be given under the Act of the place where the register is kept, or of any change in that place, or

(c)   to include in its annual return any statement required to be given under the Act of the address of the place where the register is kept.

(4)   Where provision is made in the Act with respect to default in complying with any requirement of that Act regarding the place where a register specified in Schedule 1 to these Regulations is to be kept, the provision shall have effect in relation to any such register to which this Regulation applies as if there were substituted for the reference therein to such default, a reference to default in complying with the requirements of paragraph (2) above.

Notification of place for inspection of registers

3.—(1)   Subject to the provisions of paragraph (3) below, where a company keeps any register specified in paragraph (2) below by recording the matters in question otherwise than in a legible form, the company shall send to the registrar of companies notice, in the form indicated in Part I of Schedule 2 to these Regulations, of the place' for inspection of that register and of any change in that place.

(2)   The registers referred to in paragraph (1) above are

(a)   the register of members,

(b)   an overseas branch register, and

(c) the register of directors' interests.

(3) The company shall not be obliged to give notice under paragraph (1) above—

(a) where the company changes from keeping a register in a legible form to keeping it otherwise than in a legible form and the place for inspection of the register immediately following the change is the same as the place where the register was kept in a legible form immediately prior to the change, or

(b) in the case of a register specified in paragraph 2(a) or (c) above, where since the register first came into existence—

(i) it has been kept by recording the matters in question otherwise than in a legible form, and

(ii) the place for inspection has been the registered office of the company.

(4) Where the register of members of a company is kept by recording the matters in question otherwise than in a legible form and the place for inspection of that register is elsewhere than at the registered office, the company shall include in its annual return a statement of the address of the place for inspection of that register.

(5) Subsection (4) of section 353 of the Act shall apply with respect to any default in complying with paragraph (1) above as it applies in relation to a default in complying with subsection (2) of that section; and subsection (7) of section 363 of the Act shall apply with respect to any failure to comply with paragraph (4) above as it applies in relation to a failure to comply with that section.

Requirements with respect to a register of debenture holders kept otherwise than in a legible form

4.—(1) This Regulation applies to any register of holders of debentures of a company which is kept by a company by recording the matters in question otherwise than in a legible form.

(2) A company registered in England and Wales shall not perform the duty to allow inspection of a register to which this Regulation applies in Scotland and a company registered in Scotland shall not perform such duty in England and Wales.

(3) A company shall not perform the duty to allow inspection of a register to which this Regulation applies in England and Wales, in the case of a company registered in England and Wales, or in Scotland, in the case of a company registered in Scotland, elsewhere than at—

(a) the registered office of the company,

(b) any other office of the company at which the work of ensuring that the register is duly made up is done, or

(c) if the company arranges with some other person for the carrying out of the work referred to in (b) above to be undertaken on behalf of the company by that other person, the office of that other person at which the work is done.

(4) The requirements of section 190 of the Act (provisions as to registers of debenture holders) and sections 363 and 364 of and Schedule 15 to that Act (annual returns) shall not apply to a register to which this Regulation applies in so far as they relate to any of the following matters—

(a) the place where the register is permitted to be kept,

(b) the giving of notice to the registrar of companies of the place where the register is kept, or of any change in that place, and

(c) the inclusion in the annual return of a statement of the address of the place where the register is kept.

Notification of the place for inspection of registers of debenture holders

5.—(1) Subject to paragraph (2) below, where the place for inspection of a register to which Regulation 4 above applies is in England and Wales or Scotland, the company shall send to the registrar of companies, notice in the form indicated in Part II of Schedule 2 to these Regulations of the place for inspection of that register and of any change in that place.

(2)   The company shall not be obliged to give notice under paragraph (1) above—

(a)   where a company changes from keeping the register in a legible form to keeping it otherwise than in a legible form and the place for inspection of the register immediately following the change is the same as the place where the register was kept in a legible form immediately prior to the change, or

(b)   where since the register first came into existence—

(i)   it has been kept by recording the matters in question otherwise than in a legible form, and

(ii)   the place for inspection has been the registered office of the company.

(3)   Where the place for inspection of a register to which Regulation 4 above applies is situated in England and Wales, in the case of a company registered in England and Wales, or in Scotland, in the case of a company registered in Scotland, elsewhere than at the registered office of the company, the company shall include in its annual return a statement of the address of that place.

(4)   Subsection (7) of section 363 of the Act shall apply with respect to any failure to comply with paragraph (3) above as it applies in relation to a failure to comply with that section.

Other provisions relating to registers kept otherwise than in a legible form

6.—(1)   Where a register or a register of holders of debentures is kept by recording the matters in question otherwise than in a legible form, any reference to such register in any provision of the Act relating to the place where a duplicate of such register, another register or duplicate of another register is required to be kept, shall be construed as a reference to the place for inspection of the first mentioned register.

(2)   Where the place for inspection of the register of members is the office of some person other than the company and by reason of any default of that person the company fails to comply with—

(a)   the provisions of Regulation 2 above relating to the duty to allow inspection of the index of the register of members, or

(b)   the provisions of Regulation 3 above relating to the register of members, section 357 of the Act (consequences of failure to comply with requirements as to register owing to agent's default) shall apply with respect to such failure as it applies in relation to a failure to comply with the provisions specified in that section by reason of any default of the person other than the company, at whose office the register of members is kept.

(3)   Where an overseas branch register is kept by a company by recording the matters in question otherwise than in a legible form, paragraphs 2(2) and 3(1) of Schedule 14 to the Act shall have effect as if, for the references to the country or territory where that register is kept, there were substituted references to the country or territory where the place for inspection of the register is situated.

(4)   Where the register of directors' interests is kept by a company by recording the matters in question otherwise than in a legible form, paragraph 29 of Schedule 13 to the Act shall have effect as if, for the reference to that register, there were substituted a reference to a reproduction of the recording of that register in a legible form.

(5)   Where the accounting records of a company are kept otherwise than in a legible form and the place for inspection of such records is outside Great Britain, section 222(2) of the Act shall have effect as if, for the references to the accounting records being kept at a place outside Great Britain, there were substituted references to the place for inspection of such records being at a place outside Great Britain.

Regulation 2   SCHEDULE 1

PLACES FOR PERFORMANCE OF DUTY TO ALLOW INSPECTION OF
REGISTERS KEPT OTHERWISE THAN IN A LEGIBLE FORM

Statutory Provision	Register	Place
COMPANIES ACT 1985		
Section 211(8)	Register and any associated index of interests in voting shares	(a) Where the register of directors' interests is kept otherwise than in a legible form, the place for inspection of that register. (b) Where the register of directors' interests is kept in a legible form, the place where it is so kept.
Section 222(1)	Accounting records	The registered office of the company or such other place as the directors of the company think fit.
Section 288(1)	Register of directors and secretaries	The registered office of the company.
Section 353(1)	Register of members	The registered office of the company provided that— (a) if the work of ensuring that the requirements of the Act with regard to entries in the register are complied with is done at another office of the company, the place for inspection may be that other office and (b) if the company arranges with some other person for the carrying out of the work referred to in (a) above to be undertaken on behalf of the company by that other person, the place for inspection may be the office of that other person at which the work is done; so however that the place for inspection shall not, in the case of a company registered in England and Wales, be at a place outside England and Wales and, in the case of a company registered in Scotland, be at a place outside Scotland.
Section 354(3)	Index of the register of members	(a) Where the register of members is kept otherwise than in a legible form, the place for inspection of that register. (b) Where the register of members is kept in a legible form, the place where it is so kept.
Section 362(1)	Overseas branch register	Any place where, but for these Regulations, the register would be permitted to be kept under section 362(1) of the Act.
Sections 407(1) and 422(1)	Register of charges	The registered office of the company.

Statutory Provision	Register	Place
Schedule 13, paragraph 25	Register of directors' interests	(a) Where the register of members is kept otherwise than in a legible form: 　　(i)　if the place for inspection of that register is the registered office of the company, that office, and 　　(ii)　if not, the place for inspection of that register or the registered office of the company. (b) Where the register of members is kept in a legible form: 　　(i)　if that register is kept at the registered office of the company, that office, and 　　(ii)　if that register is not so kept, the place where that register is kept or the registered office of the company.
Schedule 13, paragraph 28	Index of the register of directors' interests	(a) Where the register of directors' interests is kept otherwise than in a legible form, the place for inspection of that register. (b) Where the register of directors' interests is kept in a legible form, the place where it is so kept.
Schedule 14, paragraph 4(1)	Duplicate of overseas branch register	(a) Where the register of members is kept otherwise than in a legible form, the place for inspection of that register. (b) Where the register of members is kept in a legible form, the place where it is so kept.

COMPANIES (TABLES A TO F) REGULATIONS 1985
(1985 No. 805)

The Secretary of State, in exercise of the powers conferred by section 454(2) of the Companies Act 1948 and now vested in him, of the powers conferred by sections 3 and 8 of the Companies Act 1985 and of all other powers enabling him in that behalf, hereby makes the following Regulations—

1. These Regulations may be cited as the Companies (Tables A to F) Regulations 1985 and shall come into operation on 1 July 1985.

2. The regulations in Table A and the forms in Tables B, C, D, E and F in the Schedule to these Regulations shall be the regulations and forms of memorandum and articles of association for the purposes of sections 3 and 8 of the Companies Act 1985.

3. The Companies (Alteration of Table A etc.) Regulations 1984 are hereby revoked.

SCHEDULE

TABLE A
REGULATIONS FOR MANAGEMENT OF A COMPANY LIMITED
BY SHARES

INTERPRETATION

1. In these regulations—
'the Act' means the Companies Act 1985 including any statutory modification or re-enactment thereof for the time being in force.

'the articles' means the articles of the company.

'clear days' in relation to the period of a notice means that period excluding the day when the notice is given or deemed to be given and the day for which it is given or on which it is to take effect.

'executed' includes any mode of execution.

'office' means the registered office of the company.

'the holder' in relation to shares means the member whose name is entered in the register of members as the holder of the shares.

'the seal' means the common seal of the company.

'secretary' means the secretary of the company or any other person appointed to perform the duties of the secretary of the company, including a joint, assistant or deputy secretary.

'the United Kingdom' means Great Britain and Northern Ireland.

Unless the context otherwise requires, words or expressions contained in these regulations bear the same meaning as in the Act but excluding any statutory modification thereof not in force when these regulations become binding on the company.

SHARE CAPITAL

2. Subject to the provisions of the Act and without prejudice to any rights attached to any existing shares, any share may be issued with such rights or restrictions as the company may by ordinary resolution determine.

3. Subject to the provisions of the Act, shares may be issued which are to be redeemed or are to be liable to be redeemed at the option of the company or the holder on such terms and in such manner as may be provided by the articles.

4. The company may exercise the powers of paying commissions conferred by the Act. Subject to the provisions of the Act, any such commission may be satisfied by the payment of cash or by the allotment of fully or partly paid shares or partly in one way and partly in the other.

5. Except as required by law, no person shall be recognised by the company as holding any share upon any trust and (except as otherwise provided by the articles or by law) the company shall not be bound by or recognise any interest in any share except an absolute right to the entirety thereof in the holder.

SHARE CERTIFICATES

6. Every member, upon becoming the holder of any shares, shall be entitled without payment to one certificate for all the shares of each class held by him (and, upon transferring a part of his holding of shares of any class, to a certificate for the balance of such holding) or several certificates each for one or more of his shares upon payment for every certificate after the first of such reasonable sum as the directors may determine. Every certificate shall be sealed with the seal and shall specify the number, class and distinguishing numbers (if any) of the shares to which it relates and the amount or respective amounts paid up thereon. The company shall not be bound to issue more than one certificate for shares held jointly by several persons and delivery of a certificate to one joint holder shall be a sufficient delivery to all of them.

7. If a share certificate is defaced, worn-out, lost or destroyed, it may be renewed on such terms (if any) as to evidence and indemnity and payment of the expenses reasonably incurred by the company in investigating evidence as the directors may determine but otherwise free of charge, and (in the case of defacement or wearing-out) on delivery up of the old certificate.

LIEN

8. The company shall have a first and paramount lien on every share (not being a fully paid share) for all moneys (whether presently payable or not) payable at a fixed time or called in respect of that share. The directors may at any time declare any share to be wholly or in part exempt from the provisions of this regulation. The company's lien on a share shall extend to any amount payable in respect of it.

9.   The company may sell in such manner as the directors determine any shares on which the company has a lien if a sum in respect of which the lien exists is presently payable and is not paid within fourteen clear days after notice has been given to the holder of the share or to the person entitled to it in consequence of the death or bankruptcy of the holder, demanding payment and stating that if the notice is not complied with the shares may be sold.

10.   To give effect to a sale the directors may authorise some person to execute an instrument of transfer of the shares sold to, or in accordance with the directions of, the purchaser. The title of the transferee to the shares shall not be affected by any irregularity in or invalidity of the proceedings in reference to the sale.

11.   The net proceeds of the sale, after payment of the costs, shall be applied in payment of so much of the sum for which the lien exists as is presently payable, and any residue shall (upon surrender to the company for cancellation of the certificate for the shares sold and subject to a like lien for any moneys not presently payable as existed upon the shares before the sale) be paid to the person entitled to the shares at the date of the sale.

CALLS ON SHARES AND FORFEITURE

12.   Subject to the terms of allotment, the directors may make calls upon the members in respect of any moneys unpaid on their shares (whether in respect of nominal value or premium) and each member shall (subject to receiving at least fourteen clear days' notice specifying when and where payment is to be made) pay to the company as required by the notice the amount called on his shares. A call may be required to be paid by instalments. A call may, before receipt by the company of any sum due thereunder, be revoked in whole or part and payment of a call may be postponed in whole or part. A person upon whom a call is made shall remain liable for calls made upon him notwithstanding the subsequent transfer of the shares in respect whereof the call was made.

13.   A call shall be deemed to have been made at the time when the resolution of the directors authorising the call was passed.

14.   The joint holders of a share shall be jointly and severally liable to pay all calls in respect thereof.

15.   If a call remains unpaid after it has become due and payable the person from whom it is due and payable shall pay interest on the amount unpaid from the day it became due and payable until it is paid at the rate fixed by the terms of allotment of the share or in the notice of the call or, if no rate is fixed, at the appropriate rate (as defined by the Act) but the directors may waive payment of the interest wholly or in part.

16.   An amount payable in respect of a share on allotment or at any fixed date, whether in respect of nominal value or premium or as an instalment of a call, shall be deemed to be a call and if it is not paid the provisions of the articles shall apply as if that amount had become due and payable by virtue of a call.

17.   Subject to the terms of allotment, the directors may make arrangements on the issue of shares for a difference between the holders in the amounts and times of payment of calls on their shares.

18.   If a call remains unpaid after it has become due and payable the directors may give to the person from whom it is due not less than fourteen clear days' notice requiring payment of the amount unpaid together with any interest which may have accrued. The notice shall name the place where payment is to be made and shall state that if the notice is not complied with the shares in respect of which the call was made will be liable to be forfeited.

19. If the notice is not complied with any share in respect of which it was given may, before the payment required by the notice has been made, be forfeited by a resolution of the directors and the forfeiture shall include all dividends or other moneys payable in respect of the forfeited shares and not paid before the forfeiture.

20. Subject to the provisions of the Act, a forfeited share may be sold, re-alloted or otherwise disposed of on such terms and in such manner as the directors determine either to the person who was before the forfeiture the holder or to any other person and at any time before sale, re-allotment or other disposition, the forfeiture may be cancelled on such terms as the directors think fit. Where for the purposes of its disposal a forfeited share is to be transferred to any person the directors may authorise some person to execute an instrument of transfer of the share to that person.

21. A person any of whose shares have been forfeited shall cease to be a member in respect of them and shall surrender to the company for cancellation the certificate for the shares forfeited but shall remain liable to the company for all moneys which at the date of forfeiture were presently payable by him to the company in respect of those shares with interest at the rate at which interest was payable on those moneys before the forfeiture or, if no interest was so payable, at the appropriate rate (as defined in the Act) from the date of forfeiture until payment but the directors may waive payment wholly or in part or enforce payment without any allowance for the value of the shares at the time of forfeiture or for any consideration received on their disposal.

22. A statutory declaration by a director or the secretary that a share has been forfeited on a specified date shall be conclusive evidence of the facts stated in it as against all persons claiming to be entitled to the share and the declaration shall (subject to the execution of an instrument of transfer if necessary) constitute a good title to the share and the person to whom the share is disposed of shall not be bound to see to the application of the consideration, if any, nor shall his title to the share be affected by any irregularity in or invalidity of the proceedings in reference to the forfeiture or disposal of the share.

TRANSFER OF SHARES

23. The instrument of transfer of a share may be in any usual form or in any other form which the directors may approve and shall be executed by or on behalf of the transferor and, unless the share is fully paid, by or on behalf of the transferee.

24. The directors may refuse to register the transfer of a share which is not fully paid to a person of whom they do not approve and they may refuse to register the transfer of a share on which the company has a lien. They may also refuse to register a transfer unless—

(a) it is lodged at the office or at such other place as the directors may appoint and is accompanied by the certificate for the shares to which it relates and such other evidence as the directors may reasonably require to show the right of the transferor to make the transfer;

(b) it is in respect of only one class of shares; and

(c) it is in favour of not more than four transferees.

25. If the directors refuse to register a transfer of a share, they shall within two months after the date on which the transfer was lodged with the company send to the transferee notice of the refusal.

26. The registration of transfers of shares or of transfers of any class of shares may be suspended at such times and for such periods (not exceeding thirty days in any year) as the directors may determine.

27. No fee shall be charged for the registration of any instrument of transfer or other document relating to or affecting the title to any share.

28. The company shall be entitled to retain any instrument of transfer which is registered, but any instrument of transfer which the directors refuse to register shall be returned to the person lodging it when notice of the refusal is given.

TRANSMISSION OF SHARES

29. If a member dies the survivor of survivors where he was a joint holder, and his personal representatives where he was a sole holder or the only survivor of joint holders, shall be the only persons recognised by the company as having any title to his interest; but nothing herein contained shall release the estate of a deceased member from any liability in respect of any share which had been jointly held by him.

30. A person becoming entitled to a share in consequence of the death or bankruptcy of a member may, upon such evidence being produced as the directors may properly require, elect either to become the holder of the share or to have some person nominated by him registered as the transferee. If he elects to become the holder he shall give notice to the company to that effect. If he elects to have another person registered he shall execute an instrument of transfer of the share to that person. All the articles relating to the transfer of shares shall apply to the notice or instrument of transfer as if it were an instrument of transfer executed by the member and the death or bankruptcy of the member had not occurred.

31. A person becoming entitled to a share in consequence of the death or bankruptcy of a member shall have the rights to which he would be entitled if he were the holder of the share, except that he shall not, before being registered as the holder of the share, be entitled in respect of it to attend or vote at any meeting of the company or at any separate meeting of the holders of any class of shares in the company.

ALTERATION OF SHARE CAPITAL

32. The company may by ordinary resolution—

(a) increase its share capital by new shares of such amount as the resolution prescribes;

(b) consolidate and divide all or any of its share capital into shares of larger amount than its existing shares;

(c) subject to the provisions of the Act, subdivide its shares, or any of them, into shares of smaller amount and the resolution may determine that, as between the shares resulting from the subdivision, any of them may have any preference or advantage as compared with the others; and

(d) cancel shares which, at the date of the passing of the resolution, have not been taken or agreed to be taken by any person and diminish the amount of its share capital by the amount of the shares so cancelled.

33. Whenever as a result of a consolidation of shares any members would become entitled to fractions of a share, the directors may, on behalf of those members, sell the shares representing the fractions for the best price reasonably obtainable to any person (including, subject to the provisions of the Act, the company) and distribute the net proceeds of sale in due proportion among those members, and the directors may authorise some person to execute an instrument of transfer of the shares to, or in accordance with the directions of, the purchaser. The transferee shall not be bound to see to the application of the purchase money nor shall his title to the shares be affected by any irregularity in or invalidity of the proceedings in reference to the sale.

34. Subject to the provisions of the Act, the company may by special resolution reduce its share capital, any capital redemption reserve and any share premium account in any way.

PURCHASE OF OWN SHARES

35. Subject to the provisions of the Act, the company may purchase its own shares (including any redeemable shares) and, if it is a private company, make a payment in respect of the redemption or purchase of its own shares otherwise than out of distributable profits of the company or the proceeds of a fresh issue of shares.

GENERAL MEETINGS

36. All general meetings other than annual general meetings shall be called extraordinary general meetings.

37. The directors may call general meetings and, on the requisition of members pursuant to the provisions of the Act, shall forthwith proceed to convene an extraordinary general meeting for a date not later than eight weeks after receipt of the requisition. If there are not within the United Kingdom sufficient directors to call a general meeting, any director or any member of the company may call a general meeting.

NOTICE OF GENERAL MEETINGS

38. An annual general meeting and an extraordinary general meeting called for the passing of a special resolution or a resolution appointing a person as a director shall be called by at least twenty-one clear days' notice. All other extraordinary general meetings shall be called by at least fourteen clear days' notice but a general meeting may be called by shorter notice if it is so agreed—

(a)   in the case of an annual general meeting, by all the members entitled to attend and vote thereat; and

(b)   in the case of any other meeting by a majority in number of the members having a right to attend and vote being a majority together holding not less than ninety-five per cent in nominal value of the shares giving that right.

The notice shall specify the time and place of the meeting and the general nature of the business to be transacted and, in the case of an annual general meeting, shall specify the meeting as such.

Subject to the provisions of the articles and to any restrictions imposed on any shares, the notice shall be given to all the members, to all persons entitled to a share in consequence of the death or bankruptcy of a member and to the directors and auditors.

39. The accidental omission to give notice of a meeting to, or the non-receipt of notice of a meeting by, any person entitled to receive notice shall not invalidate the proceedings at that meeting.

PROCEEDINGS AT GENERAL MEETINGS

40. No business shall be transacted at any meeting unless a quorum is present. Two persons entitled to vote upon the business to be transacted, each being a member or a proxy for a member or a duly authorised representative of a corporation, shall be a quorum.

41. If such a quorum is not present within half an hour from the time appointed for the meeting, or if during a meeting such a quorum ceases to be present, the meeting shall stand adjourned to the same day in the next week at the same time and place or to such time and place as the directors may determine.

42. The chairman, if any, of the board of directors or in his absence some other director nominated by the directors shall preside as chariman of the meeting, but if neither the chairman nor such other director (if any) be present within fifteen minutes after the time appointed for holding the meeting and willing to act, the directors present shall elect one of their number to be chairman and, if there is only one director present and willing to act, he shall be chairman.

43. If no director is willing to act as chairman, or if no director is present within fifteen minutes after the time appointed for holding the meeting, the members present and entitled to vote shall choose one of their number to be chairman.

44. A director shall, notwithstanding that he is not a member, be entitled to attend and speak at any general meeting and at any separate meeting of the holders of any class of shares in the company.

45. The chairman may, with the consent of a meeting at which a quorum is present (and shall if so directed by the meeting), adjourn the meeting from time to time and from place to place, but no business shall be transacted at an adjourned meeting other than business which might properly have been transacted at the meeting had the adjournment not taken place. When a meeting is adjourned for fourteen days or more, at least seven clear days' notice shall be given specifying the time and place of the adjourned meeting and the general nature of the business to be transacted. Otherwise it shall not be necessary to give any such notice.

46. A resolution put to the vote of a meeting shall be decided on a show of hands unless before, or on the declaration of the result of, the show of hands a poll is duly demanded. Subject to the provisions of the Act, a poll may be demanded—

    (a)   by the chairman; or

    (b)   by at least two members having the right to vote at the meeting; or

    (c)   by a member or members representing not less than one-tenth of the total voting rights of all the members having the right to vote at the meeting; or

    (d)   by a member or members holding shares conferring a right to vote at the meeting being shares on which an aggregate sum has been paid up equal to not less than one-tenth of the total sum paid up on all the shares conferring that right;

and a demand by a person as proxy for a member shall be the same as a demand by the member.

47. Unless a poll is duly demanded a declaration by the chairman that a resolution has been carried or carried unanimously, or by a particular majority, or lost, or not carried by a particular majority and an entry to that effect in the minutes of the meeting shall be conclusive evidence of the fact without proof of the number or proportion of the votes recorded in favour of or against the resolution.

48. The demand for a poll may, before the poll is taken, be withdrawn but only with the consent of the chairman and a demand so withdrawn shall not be taken to have invalidated the result of a show of hands declared before the demand was made.

49. A poll shall be taken as the chairman directs and he may appoint scrutineers (who need not be members) and fix a time and place for declaring the result of the poll. The result of the poll shall be deemed to be the resolution of the meeting at which the poll was demanded.

50. In the case of an equality of votes, whether on a show of hands or on a poll, the chairman shall be entitled to a casting vote in addition to any other vote he may have.

51. A poll demanded on the election of a chairman or on a question of adjournment shall be taken forthwith. A poll demanded on any other question shall be taken either forthwith or at such time and place as the chairman directs not being more than thirty days after the poll is demanded. The demand for a poll shall not prevent the continuance of a meeting for the transaction of any business other than the question on which the poll was demanded. If a poll is demanded before the declaration of the result of a show of hands and the demand is duly withdrawn, the meeting shall continue as if the demand had not been made.

52. No notice need be given of a poll not taken forthwith if the time and place at which it is to be taken are announced at the meeting at which it is demanded. In any other case at least seven clear days' notice shall be given specifying the time and place at which the poll is to be taken.

53. A resolution in writing executed by or on behalf of each member who would have been entitled to vote upon it if it had been proposed at a general meeting at which he was present shall be as effectual as if it had been passed at a general meeting duly convened and held and may consist of several instruments in the like form each executed by or on behalf of one or more members.

VOTES OF MEMBERS

54. Subject to any rights or restrictions attached to any shares, on a show of hands every member who (being an individual) is present in person or (being a corporation) is present by a duly authorised representative, not being himself a member entitled to vote, shall have one vote and on a poll every member shall have one vote for every share of which he is the holder.

55. In the case of joint holders the vote of the senior who tenders a vote, whether in person or by proxy, shall be accepted to the exclusion of the votes of the other joint holders; and seniority shall be determined by the order in which the names of the holders stand in the register of members

56. A member in respect of whom an order has been made by any court having jurisdiction (whether in the United Kingdom or elsewhere) in matters concerning mental disorder may vote, whether on a show of hands or on a poll, by his receiver, curator bonis or other person authorised in that behalf appointed by the court, and any such receiver, curator bonis or other person may, on a poll, vote by proxy. Evidence to the satisfaction of the directors of the authority of the person claiming to exercise the right to vote shall be deposited at the office, or at such other place as is specified in accordance with the articles for the deposit of instruments of proxy, not less than 48 hours before the time appointed for holding the meeting or adjourned meeting at which the right to vote is to be exercised and in default the right to vote shall not be exercisable.

57. No member shall vote at any general meeting or at any separate meeting of the holders of any class of shares in the company, either in person or by proxy, in respect of any share held by him unless all moneys presently payable by him in respect of that share have been paid.

58. No objection shall be raised to the qualification of any voter except at the meeting or adjourned meeting at which the vote objected to is tendered, and every vote not disallowed at the meeting shall be valid. Any objection made in due time shall be referred to the chairman whose decision shall be final and conclusive.

59. On a poll votes may be given either personally or by proxy. A member may appoint more than one proxy to attend on the same occasion.

60. An instrument appointing a proxy shall be in writing, executed by or on behalf of the appointor and shall be in the following form (or in a form as near thereto as circumstances allow or in any other form which is usual or which the directors may approve)—

PLC/Limited

I/We,   , of

, being a

member/members of the above-named company, hereby appoint

of
, or failing him

of   , as my/our proxy to vote in my/our name[s] and on my/our behalf at the annual/extraordinary general meeting of the company to be held on   19   , and at any adjournment thereof.

Signed on   19

61. Where it is desired to afford members an opportunity of instructing the proxy how he shall act the instrument appointing a proxy shall be in the following form (or in a form as near thereto as circumstances allow or in any other form which is usual or which the directors may approve)—

PLC/Limited

I/We,   , of

, being a

member/members of the above-named company, hereby appoint
of
, or failing him
of   , as my/our proxy to vote in my/our name[s] and on
my/our behalf at the annual/extraordinary general meeting of the company to be
held on   19   , and at any adjournment
thereof.
This form is to be used in respect of the resolutions mentioned below as follows:
  Resolution No. 1 *for *against
  Resolution No. 2 *for *against
*Strike out whichever is not desired.
Unless otherwise instructed, the proxy may vote as he thinks fit or abstain from
voting.
Signed this   day of   19

62. The instrument appointing a proxy and any authority under which it is executed
or a copy of such authority certified notarially or in some other way approved by the
dirctors may—
  (a) be deposited at the office or at such other place within the United Kingdom as
is specified in the notice convening the meeting or in any instrument of proxy sent out
by the company in relation to the meeting not less than 48 hours before the time for
holding the meeting or adjourned meeting at which the person named in the instrument
proposes to vote; or
  (b) in the case of a poll taken more than 48 hours after it is demanded, be
deposited as aforesaid after the poll has been demanded and not less than 24 hours
before the time appointed for the taking of the poll; or
  (c) where the poll is not taken forthwith but is taken not more than 48 hours after
it was demanded, be delivered at the meeting at which the poll was demanded to the
chairman or to the secretary or to any director;
and an instrument of proxy which is not deposited or delivered in a manner so permitted
shall be invalid.
  63. A vote given or poll demanded by proxy or by the duly authorised representative
of a corporation shall be valid notwithstanding the previous determination of the
authority of the person voting or demanding a poll unless notice of the determination
was received by the company at the office or at such other place at which the instrument
of proxy was duly deposited before the commencement of the meeting or adjourned
meeting at which the vote is given or the poll demanded or (in the case of a poll taken
otherwise than on the same day as the meeting or adjourned meeting) the time
appointed for taking the poll.

NUMBER OF DIRECTORS

64. Unless otherwise determined by ordinary resolution, the number of directors
(other than alternate directors) shall not be subject to any maximum but shall be not less
than two.

ALTERNATE DIRECTORS

65. Any director (other than an alternate director) may appoint any other director,
or any other person approved by resolution of the directors and willing to act, to be an
alternate director and may remove from office an alternate director so appointed by him.
  66. An alternate director shall be entitled to receive notice of all meetings of
directors and of all meetings of committees of directors of which his appointor is a
member, to attend and vote at any such meeting at which the director appointing him is
not personally present, and generally to perform all the functions of his appointor as a

director in his absence but shall not be entitled to receive any remuneration from the company for his services as an alternate director. But it shall not be necessary to give notice of such a meeting to an alternate director who is absent from the United Kingdom.

67. An alternate director shall cease to be an alternate director if his appointor ceases to be a director; but, if a director retires by rotation or otherwise but is reappointed or deemed to have been reappointed at the meeting at which he retires, any appointment of an alternate director made by him which was in force immediately prior to his retirement shall continue after his reappointment.

68. Any appointment or removal of an alternate director shall be by notice to the company signed by the director making or revoking the appointment or in any other manner approved by the directors.

69. Save as otherwise provided in the articles, an alternate director shall be deemed for all purposes to be a director and shall alone be responsible for his own acts and defaults and he shall not be deemed to be the agent of the director appointing him.

POWERS OF DIRECTORS

70. Subject to the provisions of the Act, the memorandum and the articles and to any directions given by special resolution, the business of the company shall be managed by the directors who may exercise all the powers of the company. No alteration of the memorandum or articles and no such direction shall invalidate any prior act of the directors which would have been valid if that alteration had not been made or that direction had not been given. The powers given by this regulation shall not be limited by any special power given to the directors by the articles and a meeting of directors at which a quorum is present may exercise all powers exercisable by the directors.

71. The directors may, by power of attorney or otherwise, appoint any person to be the agent of the company for such purposes and on such conditions as they determine, including authority for the agent to delegate all or any of his powers.

DELEGATION OF DIRECTORS' POWERS

72. The directors may delegate any of their powers to any committee consisting of one or more directors. They may also delegate to any managing director or any director holding any other executive office such of their powers as they consider desirable to be exercised by him. Any such delegation may be made subject to any conditions the directors may impose, and either collaterally with or to the exclusion of their own powers and may be revoked or altered. Subject to any such conditions, the proceedings of a committee with two or more members shall be governed by the articles regulating the proceedings of directors so far as they are capable of applying.

APPOINTMENT AND RETIREMENT OF DIRECTORS

73. At the first annual general meeting all the directors shall retire from office, and at every subsequent annual general meeting one-third of the directors who are subject to retirement by rotation or, if their number is not three or a multiple of three, the number nearest to one-third shall retire from office; but, if there is only one director who is subject to retirement by rotation, he shall retire.

74. Subject to the provisions of the Act, the directors to retire by rotation shall be those who have been longest in office since their last appointment or reappointment, but as between persons who became or were last reappointed directors on the same day those to retire shall (unless they otherwise agree among themselves) be determined by lot.

75. If the company, at the meeting at which a director retires by rotation, does not fill the vacancy the retiring director shall, if willing to act, be deemed to have been reappointed unless at the meeting it is resolved not to fill the vacancy or unless a resolution for the reappointment of the director is put to the meeting and lost.

76. No person other than a director retiring by rotation shall be appointed or reappointed a director at any general meeting unless—

(a) he is recommended by the directors; or

(b) not less than fourteen nor more than thirty-five clear days before the date appointed for the meeting, notice executed by a member qualified to vote at the meeting has been given to the company of the intention to propose that person for appointment or reappointment stating the particulars which would, if he were so appointed or reappointed, be required to be included in the company's register of directors together with notice executed by that person of his willingness to be appointed or reappointed.

77. Not less than seven nor more than twenty-eight clear days before the date appointed for holding a general meeting notice shall be given to all who are entitled to receive notice of the meeting of any person (other than a director retiring by rotation at the meeting) who is recommended by the directors for appointment or reappointment as a director at the meeting or in respect of whom notice has been duly given to the company of the intention to propose him at the meeting for appointment or reappointment as a director. The notice shall give the particulars of that person which would, if he were so appointed or reappointed, be required to be included in the company's register of directors.

78. Subject as aforesaid, the company may by ordinary resolution appoint a person who is willing to act to be a director either to fill a vacancy or as an additional director and may also determine the rotation in which any additional directors are to retire.

79. The directors may appoint a person who is willing to act to be a director, either to fill a vacancy or as an additional director, provided that the appointment does not cause the number of directors to exceed any number fixed by or in accordance with the articles as the maximum number of directors. A director so appointed shall hold office only until the next following annual general meeting and shall not be taken into account in determining the directors who are to retire by rotation at the meeting. If not reappointed at such annual general meeting, he shall vacate office at the conclusion thereof.

80. Subject as aforesaid, a director who retires at an annual general meeting may, if willing to act, be reappointed. If he is not reappointed, he shall retain office until the meeting appoints someone in his place, or if it does not do so, until the end of the meeting.

DISQUALIFICATION AND REMOVAL OF DIRECTORS

81. The office of a director shall be vacated if—

(a) he ceases to be a director by virtue of any provision of the Act or he becomes prohibited by law from being a director; or

(b) he becomes bankrupt or makes any arrangement or composition with his creditors generally; or

(c) he is, or may be, suffering from mental disorder and either—

(i) he is admitted to hospital in pursuance of an application for admission for treatment under the Mental Health Act 1983 or, in Scotland, an application for admission under the Mental Health (Scotland) Act 1960, or

(ii) an order is made by a court having jurisdiction (whether in the United Kingdom or elsewhere) in matters concerning mental disorder for his detention or for the appointment of a receiver, curator bonis or other person to exercise powers with respect to his property or affairs; or

(d) he resigns his office by notice to the company; or

(e) he shall for more than six consecutive months have been absent without permission of the directors from meetings of directors held during that period and the directors resolve that his office be vacated.

REMUNERATION OF DIRECTORS

82. The directors shall be entitled to such remuneration as the company may by ordinary resolution determine and, unless the resolution provides otherwise, the remuneration shall be deemed to accrue from day to day.

DIRECTORS' EXPENSES

83. The directors may be paid all travelling, hotel, and other expenses properly incurred by them in connection with their attendance at meetings of directors or committees of directors or general meetings or separate meetings of the holders of any class of shares or of debentures of the company or otherwise in connection with the discharge of their duties.

DIRECTORS' APPOINTMENTS AND INTERESTS

84. Subject to the provisions of the Act, the directors may appoint one or more of their number to the office of managing director or to any other executive office under the company and may enter into an agreement or arrangement with any director for his employment by the company or for the provision by him of any services outside the scope of the ordinary duties of a director. Any such appointment, agreement or arrangement may be made upon such terms as the directors determine and they may remunerate any such director for his services as they think fit. Any appointment of a director to an executive office shall terminate if he ceases to be a director but without prejudice to any claim to damages for breach of the contract of service between the director and the company. A managing director and a director holding any other executive office shall not be subject to retirement by rotation.

85. Subject to the provisions of the Act, and provided that he has disclosed to the directors the nature and extent of any material interest of his, a director notwithstanding his office—

(a)　may be a party to, or otherwise interested in, any transaction or arrangement with the company or in which the company is otherwise interested;

(b)　may be a director or other officer of, or employed by, or a party to any transaction or arrangement with, or otherwise interested in, any body corporate promoted by the company or in which the company is otherwise interested; and

(c)　shall not, by reason of his office, be accountable to the company for any benefit which he derives from any such office or employment or from any such transaction or arrangement or from any interest in any such body corporate and no such transaction or arrangement shall be liable to be avoided on the ground of any such interest or benefit.

86. For the purposes of regulation 85—

(a)　a general notice given to the directors that a director is to be regarded as having an interest of the nature and extent specified in the notice in any transaction or arrangement in which a specified person or class of persons is interested shall be deemed to be a disclosure that the director has an interest in any such transaction of the nature and extent so specified; and

(b)　an interest of which a director has no knowledge and of which it is unreasonable to expect him to have knowledge shall not be treated as an interest of his.

DIRECTORS' GRATUITIES AND PENSIONS

87. The directors may provide benefits, whether by the payment of gratuities or pensions or by insurance or otherwise, for any director who has held but no longer holds any executive office or employment with the company or with any body corporate which is or has been a subsidiary of the company or a predecessor in business of the company or of any such subsidiary, and for any member of his family (including a spouse and a former spouse) or any person who is or was dependent on him, and may (as well before as after he ceases to hold such office or employment) contribute to any fund and pay premiums for the purchase or provision of any such benefit.

PROCEEDINGS OF DIRECTORS

88. Subject to the provisions of the articles, the directors may regulate their proceedings as they think fit. A director may, and the secretary at the request of a director shall, call a meeting of the directors. It shall not be necessary to give notice of a meeting to a director who is absent from the United Kingdom. Questions arising at a meeting shall be decided by a majority of votes. In the case of an equality of votes, the chairman shall have a second or casting vote. A director who is also an alternate director shall be entitled in the absence of his appointor to a separate vote on behalf of his appointor in addition to his own vote.

89. The quorum for the transaction of the business of the directors may be fixed by the directors and unless so fixed at any other number shall be two. A person who holds office only as an alternate director shall, if his appointor is not present, be counted in the quorum.

90. The continuing directors or a sole continuing director may act notwithstanding any vacancies in their number, but, if the number of directors is less than the number fixed as the quorum, the continuing directors or director may act only for the purpose of filling vacancies or of calling a general meeting.

91. The directors may appoint one of their number to be the chairman of the board of directors and may at any time remove him from that office. Unless he is unwilling to do so, the director so appointed shall preside at every meeting of directors at which he is present. But if there is no director holding that office, or if the director holding it is unwilling to preside or is not present within five minutes after the time appointed for the meeting, the directors present may appoint one of their number to be chairman of the meeting.

92. All acts done by a meeting of directors, or of a committee of directors, or by a person acting as a director shall, notwithstanding that it be afterwards discovered that there was a defect in the appointment of any director or that any of them were disqualified from holding office, or had vacated office, or were not entitled to vote, be as valid as if every such person had been duly appointed and was qualified and had continued to be a director and had been entitled to vote.

93. A resolution in writing signed by all the directors entitled to receive notice of a meeting of directors or of a committee of directors shall be as valid and effectual as if it had been passed at a meeting of directors or (as the case may be) a committee of directors duly convened and held and may consist of several documents in the like form each signed by one or more directors; but a resolution signed by an alternate director need not also be signed by his appointor and, if it is signed by a director who has appointed an alternate director, it need not be signed by the alternate director in that capacity.

94. Save as otherwise provided by the articles, a director shall not vote at a meeting of directors or of a committee of directors on any resolution concerning a matter in which he has, directly or indirectly, an interest or duty which is material and which conflicts or may conflict with the interests of the company unless his interest or duty arises only because the case falls within one or more of the following paragraphs—

(a) the resolution relates to the giving to him of a guarantee, security, or indemnity in respect of money lent to, or an obligation incurred by him for the benefit of, the company or any of its subsidiaries;

(b) the resolution relates to the giving to a third party of a guarantee, security, or indemnity in respect of an obligation of the company or any of its subsidiaries for which the director has assumed responsibility in whole or part and whether alone or jointly with others under a guarantee or indemnity or by the giving of security;

    (c) his interest arises by virtue of his subscribing or agreeing to subscribe for any shares, debentures or other securities of the company or any of its subsidiaries, or by virtue of his being, or intending to become, a participant in the underwriting or sub-underwriting of an offer of any such shares, debentures, or other securities by the company or any of its subsidiaries for subscription, purchase or exchange;

    (d) the resolution relates in any way to a retirement benefits scheme which has been approved, or is conditional upon approval, by the Board of Inland Revenue for taxation purposes.

For the purposes of this regulation, an interest of a person who is, for any purpose of the Act (excluding any statutory modification thereof not in force when this regulation becomes binding on the company), connected with a director shall be treated as an interest of the director and, in relation to an alternate director, an interest of his appointor shall be treated as an interest of the alternate director without prejudice to any interest which the alternate director has otherwise.

95. A director shall not be counted in the quorum present at a meeting in relation to a resolution on which he is not entitled to vote.

96. The company may by ordinary resolution suspend or relax to any extent, either generally or in respect of any particular matter, any provision of the articles prohibiting a director from voting at a meeting of directors or of a committee of directors.

97. Where proposals are under consideration concerning the appointment of two or more directors to offices or employments with the company or any body corporate in which the company is interested the proposals may be divided and considered in relation to each director separately and (provided he is not for another reason precluded from voting) each of the directors concerned shall be entitled to vote and be counted in the quorum in respect of each resolution except that concerning his own appointment.

98. If a question arises at a meeting of directors or of a committee of directors as to the right of a director to vote, the question may, before the conclusion of the meeting, be referred to the chairman of the meeting and his ruling in relation to any director other than himself shall be final and conclusive.

SECRETARY

99. Subject to the provisions of the Act, the secretary shall be appointed by the directors for such term, at such remuneration and upon such conditions as they may think fit; and any secretary so appointed may be removed by them.

MINUTES

100. The directors shall cause minutes to be made in books kept for the purpose—

    (a) of all appointments of officers made by the directors; and

    (b) of all proceedings at meetings of the company, of the holders of any class of shares in the company, and of the directors, and of committees of directors, including the names of the directors present at each such meeting.

THE SEAL

101. The seal shall only be used by the authority of the directors or of a committee of directors authorised by the directors. The directors may determine who shall sign any instrument to which the seal is affixed and unless otherwise so determined it shall be signed by a director and by the secretary or by a second director.

DIVIDENDS

102. Subject to the provisions of the Act, the company may by ordinary resolution declare dividends in accordance with the respective rights of the members, but no dividend shall exceed the amount recommended by the directors.

103. Subject to the provisions of the Act, the directors may pay interim dividends if it appears to them that they are justified by the profits of the company available for distribution. If the share capital is divided into different classes, the directors may pay interim dividends on shares which confer deferred or non-preferred rights with regard to dividend as well as on shares which confer preferential rights with regard to dividend, but no interim dividend shall be paid on shares carrying deferred or non-preferred rights if, at the time of payment, any preferential dividend is in arrear. The directors may also pay at intervals settled by them any dividend payable at a fixed rate if it appears to them that the profits available for distribution justify the payment. Provided the directors act in good faith they shall not incur any liability to the holders of shares conferring preferred rights for any loss they may suffer by the lawful payment of an interim dividend on any shares having deferred or non-preferred rights.

104. Except as otherwise provided by the rights attached to shares, all dividends shall be declared and paid according to the amounts paid up on the shares on which the dividend is paid. All dividends shall be apportioned and paid proportionately to the amounts paid up on the shares during any portion or portions of the period in respect of which the dividend is paid; but, if any share is issued on terms providing that it shall rank for dividend as from a particular date, that share shall rank for dividend accordingly.

105. A general meeting declaring a dividend may, upon the recommendation of the directors, direct that it shall be satisfied wholly or partly by the distribution of assets and, where any difficulty arises in regard to the distribution, the directors may settle the same and in particular may issue fractional certificates and fix the value for distribution of any assets and may determine that cash shall be paid to any member upon the footing of the value so fixed in order to adjust the rights of members and may vest any assets in trustees.

106. Any dividend or other moneys payable in respect of a share may be paid by cheque sent by post to the registered address of the person entitled or, if two or more persons are the holders of the share or are jointly entitled to it by reason of the death or bankruptcy of the holder, to the registered address of that one of those persons who is first named in the register of members or to such person and to such address as the person or persons entitled may in writing direct. Every cheque shall be made payable to the order of the person or persons entitled or to such other person as the person or persons entitled may in writing direct and payment of the cheque shall be a good discharge to the company. Any joint holder or other person jointly entitled to a share as aforesaid may give receipts for any dividend or other moneys payable in respect of the share.

107. No dividend or other moneys payable in respect of a share shall bear interest against the company unless otherwise provided by the rights attached to the share.

108. Any dividend which has remained unclaimed for twelve years from the date when it became due for payment shall, if the directors so resolve, be forfeited and cease to remain owing by the company.

ACCOUNTS

109. No member shall (as such) have any right of inspecting any accounting records or other book or document of the company except as conferred by statute or authorised by the directors or by ordinary resolution of the company.

CAPITALISATION OF PROFITS

110. The directors may with the authority of an ordinary resolution of the company—

(a) subject as hereinafter provided, resolve to capitalise any undivided profits of the company not required for paying any preferential dividend (whether or not they are available for distribution) or any sum standing to the credit of the company's share premium account or capital redemption reserve;

(b) appropriate the sum resolved to be capitalised to the members who would have been entitled to it if it were distributed by way of dividend and in the same proportions and apply such sum on their behalf either in or towards paying up the amounts, if any, for the time being unpaid on any shares held by them respectively, or in paying up in full unissued shares or debentures of the company of a nominal amount equal to that sum, and allot the shares or debentures credited as fully paid to those members, or as they may direct, in those proportions, or partly in one way and partly in the other: but the share premium account, the capital redemption reserve, and any profits which are not available for distribution may, for the purposes of this regulation, only be applied in paying up unissued shares to be allotted to members credited as fully paid;

(c) make such provision by the issue of fractional certificates or by payment in cash or otherwise as they determine in the case of shares or debentures becoming distributable under this regulation in fractions; and

(d) authorise any person to enter on behalf of all the members concerned into an agreement with the company providing for the allotment to them respectively, credited as fully paid, of any shares or debentures to which they are entitled upon such capitalisation, any agreement made under such authority being binding on all such members.

NOTICES

111. Any notice to be given to or by any person pursuant to the articles shall be in writing except that a notice calling a meeting of the directors need not be in writing.

112. The company may give any notice to a member either personally or by sending it by post in a prepaid envelope addressed to the member at his registered address or by leaving it at that address. In the case of joint holders of a share, all notices shall be given to the joint holder whose name stands first in the register of members in respect of the joint holding and notice so given shall be sufficient notice to all the joint holders. A member whose registered address is not within the United Kingdom and who gives to the company an address within the United Kingdom at which notices may be given to him shall be entitled to have notices given to him at that address, but otherwise no such member shall be entitled to receive any notice from the company.

113. A member present, either in person or by proxy, at any meeting of the company or of the holders of any class of shares in the company shall be deemed to have received notice of the meeting and, where requisite, of the purposes for which it was called.

114. Every person who becomes entitled to a share shall be bound by any notice in respect of that share which, before his name is entered in the register of members, has been duly given to a person from whom he derives his title.

115. Proof that an envelope containing a notice was properly addressed, prepaid and posted shall be conclusive evidence that the notice was given. A notice shall be deemed to be given at the expiration of 48 hours after the envelope containing it was posted.

116. A notice may be given by the company to the persons entitled to a share in consequence of the death or bankruptcy of a member by sending or delivering it, in any manner authorised by the articles for the giving of notice to a member, addressed to them by name, or by the title of representatives of the deceased, or trustee of the bankrupt or by any like description at the address, if any, within the United Kingdom supplied for that purpose by the persons claiming to be so entitled. Until such an address has been supplied, a notice may be given in any manner in which it might have been given if the death or bankruptcy had not occurred.

WINDING UP

117. If the company is wound up, the liquidator may, with the sanction of an extraordinary resolution of the company and any other sanction required by the Act, divide among the members in specie the whole or any part of the assets of the company and may, for that purpose, value any assets and determine how the division shall be carried out as between the members or different classes of members. The liquidator may, with the like sanction, vest the whole or any part of the assets in trustees upon such trusts for the benefit of the members as he with the like sanction determines, but no member shall be compelled to accept any assets upon which there is a liability.

INDEMNITY

118. Subject to the provisions of the Act but without prejudice to any indemnity to which a director may otherwise be entitled, every director or other officer or auditor of the company shall be indemnified out of the assets of the company against any liability incurred by him in defending any proceedings, whether civil or criminal, in which judgment is given in his favour or in which he is acquitted or in connection with any application in which relief is granted to him by the court from liability for negligence, default, breach of duty or breach of trust in relation to the affairs of the company.

TABLE B
A PRIVATE COMPANY LIMITED BY SHARES
MEMORANDUM OF ASSOCIATION

1. The company's name is 'The South Wales Motor Transport Company cyfyngedig'.

2. The company's registered office is to be situated in Wales.

3. The company's objects are the carriage of passengers and goods in motor vehicles between such places as the company may from time to time determine and the doing of all such other things as are incidental or conducive to the attainment of that object.

4. The liability of the members is limited.

5. The company's share capital is £50,000 divided into 50,000 shares of £1 each.

We, the subscribers to this memorandum of association, wish to be formed into a company pursuant to this memorandum; and we agree to take the number of shares shown opposite our respective names.

Names and Addresses of Subscribers	Number of shares taken by each Subscriber
1. Thomas Jones, 138 Mountfield Street, Tredegar.	1
2. Mary Evans, 19 Merthyr Road, Aberystwyth.	1
Total shares taken	2

Dated   19

Witness to the above signatures,
Anne Brown, 'Woodlands', Fieldside Road, Bryn Mawr.
. . .

TABLE F
A PUBLIC COMPANY LIMITED BY SHARES
MEMORANDUM OF ASSOCIATION

1. The company's name is 'Western Electronics Public Limited Company'.

2. The company is to be a public company.

3. The company's registered office is to be situated in England and Wales.
4. The company's objects are the manufacture and development of such descriptions of electronic equipment, instruments and appliances as the company may from time to time determine, and the doing of all such other things as are incidental or conducive to the attainment of that object.
5. The liability of the members is limited.
6. The company's share capital is £5,000,000 divided into 5,000,000 shares of £1 each.
We, the subscribers to this memorandum of association, wish to be formed into a company pursuant to this memorandum; and we agree to take the number of shares shown opposite our respective names.

Names and Addresses of Subscribers	Number of shares taken by each Subscriber
1. James White, 12 Broadmead, Birmingham.	1
2. Patrick Smith, 145A Huntley House, London Wall, London EC2.	1
Total shares taken	2

Dated   19

Witness to the above signatures,
Anne Brown, 13 Hute Street, London WC2.

ACCOUNTING STANDARDS (PRESCRIBED BODY) REGULATIONS 1990
(1990 No. 1667)

The Secretary of State, in exercise of the powers conferred on him by section 256 of the Companies Act 1985, hereby makes the following Regulations:
1. These Regulations may be cited as the Accounting Standards (Prescribed Body) Regulations 1990 and shall come into force on 20 August 1990.
2. The Accounting Standards Board Limited is hereby prescribed for the purposes of section 256(1) of the Companies Act 1985.

COMPANIES (DEFECTIVE ACCOUNTS) (AUTHORISED PERSON) ORDER 1991
(1991 No. 13)

Whereas it appears to the Secretary of State that the Financial Reporting Review Panel Limited is a person:
(a)   having an interest in, and to have satisfactory procedures directed to securing, compliance by companies with the accounting requirements of the Companies Act 1985;
(b)   having satisfactory procedures for receiving and investigating complaints about the annual accounts of companies; and
(c)   otherwise to be a fit and proper person to be authorised.
The Secretary of State, in exercise of the powers conferred on him by section 245C of the Companies Act 1985 and of all other powers enabling him in that behalf, hereby makes the following Order:
1. This Order may be cited as the Companies (Defective Accounts) (Authorised Person) Order 1991 and shall come into force on 1 February 1991.
2. The Financial Reporting Review Panel Limited is hereby authorised for the purposes of section 245B of the Companies Act 1985.

COMPANIES (INSPECTION AND COPYING OF REGISTERS, INDICES AND DOCUMENTS) REGULATIONS 1991
(1991 No. 1998)

The Secretary of State, in exercise of the powers conferred on him by section 723A of the Companies Act 1985, the provisions of the Companies Act 1985 listed in Schedule 1 to these Regulations and of all other powers enabling him in that behalf, hereby makes the following Regulations:

Citation and commencement

1.   These Regulations may be cited as the Companies (Inspection and Copying of Registers, Indices and Documents) Regulations 1991 and shall come into force on 1 November 1991.

Interpretation

2.   In these Regulations:
'the Act' means the Companies Act 1985;
'business day' means, in relation to a company subject to any provision of these Regulations, any day except a Saturday or Sunday, Christmas Day, Good Friday and any other day which is a bank holiday in the part of Great Britain where that company is registered (or in the case of a company that is a body corporate to which section 723A of the Act is applied by section 718 thereof, the part of Great Britain where its principal office was situated on 5 January 1976 or if it was incorporated after that date, the part of Great Britain where its principal office was situated immediately after incorporation); and
'company' includes a body corporate to which section 723A of the Act is applied by any enactment.

Inspection

3.—(1)   This Regulation applies to an obligation to make a register, index or document available for inspection imposed on a company by sections 169(5) (contract for purchase by company of its own shares), 175(6) (statutory declaration and auditors' report relating to payment out of capital), 191(1) (register of debenture holders), 219(1) (register of interests in shares &c), 288(3) (register of directors and secretaries), 318(7) (directors' service contracts), 356(1) (register and index of members) and 383(1) (minute books) of the Act, as well as to section 325 of, and paragraph 25 of Part IV of Schedule 13 to, the Act (register of directors' interests).

(2)   The company shall:

(a)   make the register, index or document available for such inspection for not less than two hours during the period between 9 a.m. and 5 p.m. on each business day; and

(b)   permit a person inspecting the register, index or document to copy any information made available for inspection by means of the taking of notes or the transcription of the information.

(3)   Paragraph (2)(b) shall not be construed as obliging a company to provide any facilities additional to those provided for the purposes of facilitating inspection.

Registers of members and debenture holders: presentation and extraction of entries

4.—(1)   This Regulation applies to a company's register of members maintained under section 352 of the Act, to an index of the names of the company's members maintained under section 354 thereof and to a register of debenture holders maintained under section 190 thereof.

(2)   A company is not obliged:

(a)   by virtue of section 356(1) of the Act to present for inspection its register of members or an index of members' names; or

(b)   by virtue of section 191(1) of the Act to present for inspection a register of debenture holders maintained by it,
in a manner which groups together entries by reference to whether a member or (as the case may be) a debenture holder has given an address in a particular geographical location, is of a particular nationality, has a holding of a certain size, is a natural person or not or is of a particular gender.

(3)   Nor is a company obliged:

(a)   by virtue of section 356(3) of the Act, in providing a copy of a part of its register of members; or

(b)   by virtue of section 191(2) of the Act, in providing a copy of a part of a register of debenture holders,
to extract entries from the register by reference to whether a member or (as the case may be) a debenture holder has given an address in a particular geographical location, is of a particular nationality, has a holding of a certain size, is a natural person or not or is of a particular gender.

Fees

5.   Schedule 2 to these Regulations prescribes the fees payable for the purposes of the provisions of the Act listed therein.

SCHEDULE 1

Sections 191(1), 191(2), 191(3), 219(2), 288(3), 325(5) (together with paragraphs 25 and 26(1) of Part VI of Schedule 13), 356(1), 356(3) and 383(3).

Regulation 5   SCHEDULE 2

Fees in respect of inspections of registers by non-members

1.   The fee prescribed for the purposes of the following provisions of the Act:

(a)   section 191(1) (Fee for inspection of register of debenture holders);

(b)   section 288(3) (Fee for inspection of register of directors and secretaries);

(c)   section 325(5) and paragraph 25 of Part IV of Schedule 13 (Fee for inspection of register of directors' interests in shares or debentures); and

(d)   section 356(1) (Fee for inspection of register of members and index);
is £2.50 for each hour or part thereof during which the right of inspection is exercised.

Fees for provision of copies and entries in registers and copies of reports

2.   The fee prescribed for the purposes of the following provisions of the Act:

(a)   section 191(2) (Fee for copies of entries in the register of debentures);

(b)   section 219(2) (Fees for copies of entries in the register of interests in shares or copies of reports or part of reports made pursuant to section 215(7));

(c)   section 325(5) and paragraph 26(1) of Part IV of Schedule 13 (Fee for copies of entries in the register of directors' interests in shares or debentures); and

(d)   section 356(3) (Fee for copies of entries in the register of members);
is:

(i)   for the first 100 entries,
       or part thereof copied, ... £2.50;

(ii)   for the next 1000 entries,
       or part thereof copied, ... £20.00;
       and

(iii) for every subsequent 1000 entries,
       or part thereof copied, ... £15.00.

Fees for copies of other documents

3. The fee prescribed for the purposes of the following provisions of the Act—
   (a) section 191(3) (Fee for copies of trust deeds); and
   (b) section 383(3) (Fee for copies of minutes)
is 10 pence per hundred words, or part thereof, copied.

COMPANIES (SINGLE MEMBER PRIVATE LIMITED COMPANIES) REGULATIONS 1992
(1992 No. 1699)

Whereas a draft of these Regulations has been approved by resolution of each House of Parliament in pursuance of paragraph 2(2) of Schedule 2 to the European Communities Act 1972.

Now, therefore, the Secretary of State, being a Minister designated for the purposes of section 2(2) of that Act in relation to measures relating to single member private companies limited by shares or by guarantee, in exercise of the powers conferred by that section hereby makes the following Regulations:

Citation and commencement

1. These Regulations may be cited as the Companies (Single Member Private Limited Companies) Regulations 1992 and shall come into force on the day after the day on which they were made.

[*The Regulations were made on 14 July 1992.*]

Single member private companies limited by shares or by guarantee

2.—(1) Notwithstanding any enactment or rule of law to the contrary, a private company limited by shares or by guarantee within the meaning of section 1 of the Companies Act 1985 may be formed by one person (in so far as permitted by that section as amended by these Regulations) and may have one member; and accordingly—
   (a) any enactment or rule of law which applies in relation to a private company limited by shares or by guarantee shall, in the absence of any express provision to the contrary, apply with such modification as may be necessary in relation to such a company which is formed by one person or which has only one person as a member as it does in relation to such a company which is formed by two or more persons or which has two or more persons as members....

(2) In this regulation 'enactment' shall include an enactment comprised in subordinate legislation and 'subordinate legislation' shall have the same meaning as in section 21(1) of the Interpretation Act 1978.

Transitional provision

3. A person who, before the coming into force of these Regulations, is liable by virtue of section 24 of the Companies Act 1985 for the payment of the debts of a private company limited by shares or by guarantee, shall not be so liable for the payment of the company's debts contracted on or after the day on which these Regulations come into force.

INSIDER DEALING (SECURITIES AND REGULATED MARKETS) ORDER 1994
(1994 No. 187)

Whereas a draft of this Order has been approved by a resolution of each House of Parliament pursuant to section 64(2) of the Criminal Justice Act 1993;

Now, therefore, the Treasury, in exercise of the powers conferred on them by sections 54(1), 60(1), 62(1) and 64(3) of that Act and of all other powers enabling them in that behalf, hereby make the following Order:

Title, commencement and interpretation

1. This Order may be cited as the Insider Dealing (Securities and Regulated Markets) Order 1994 and shall come into force on the twenty eighth day after the day on which it is made.
[*The Order was made on 1 February 1994.*]

2. In this Order a 'State within the European Economic Area' means a State which is a member of the European Communities and the Republics of Austria, Finland and Iceland, the Kingdoms of Norway and Sweden and the Principality of Liechtenstein.

Securities

3. Articles 4 to 8 set out conditions for the purposes of section 54(1) of the Criminal Justice Act 1993 (securities to which Part V of the Act of 1993 applies).

4. The following condition applies in relation to any security which falls within any paragraph of Schedule 2 to the Act of 1993, that is, that it is officially listed in a State within the European Economic Area or that it is admitted to dealing on, or has its price quoted on or under the rules of, a regulated market.

5. The following alternative condition applies in relation to a warrant, that is, that the right under it is a right to subscribe for any share or debt security of the same class as a share or debt security which satisfies the condition in article 4.

6. The following alternative condition applies in relation to a depositary receipt, that is, that the rights under it are in respect of any share or debt security which satisfies the condition in article 4.

7. The following alternative conditions apply in relation to an option or a future, that is, that the option or rights under the future are in respect of—

    (a)   any share or debt security which satisfies the condition in article 4, or

    (b)   any depositary receipt which satisfies the condition in article 4 or article 6.

8. The following alternative condition applies in relation to a contract for differences, that is, that the purpose or pretended purpose of the contract is to secure a profit or avoid a loss by reference to fluctuations in—

    (a)   the price of any shares or debt securities which satisfy the condition in article 4, or

    (b)   an index of the price of such shares or debt securities.

Regulated markets

9. The following markets are regulated markets for the purposes of Part V of the Act of 1993—
any market which is established under the rules of an investment exchange specified in the Schedule to this Order.

United Kingdom regulated markets

10. The regulated markets which are regulated in the United Kingdom for the purposes of Part V of the Act of 1993 are any market which is established under the rules of—

    (a)   the London Stock Exchange Limited;

    (b)   LIFFE Administration & Management;

    (c)   OMLX, the London Securities and Derivatives Exchange Limited; and

    (d)   Tradepoint Financial Networks plc.

Article 9   SCHEDULE

REGULATED MARKETS

Any market which is established under the rules of one of the following investment exchanges:

Amsterdam Stock Exchange.
Antwerp Stock Exchange.
Athens Stock Exchange.
Barcelona Stock Exchange.
Bavarian Stock Exchange.
Berlin Stock Exchange.
Bilbao Stock Exchange.
Bologna Stock Exchange.
Bremen Stock Exchange.
Brussels Stock Exchange.
Copenhagen Stock Exchange.
Dusseldorf Stock Exchange.
Florence Stock Exchange.
Frankfurt Stock Exchange.
Genoa Stock Exchange.
Hamburg Stock Exchange.
Hanover Stock Exchange.
Helsinki Stock Exchange.
Iceland Stock Exchange.
The Irish Stock Exchange Limited.
Lisbon Stock Exchange.
LIFFE Administration & Management.
The London Stock Exchange Limited.
Luxembourg Stock Exchange.
Lyon Stock Exchange.
Madrid Stock Exchange.
Milan Stock Exchange.
Naples Stock Exchange.
The exchange known as NASDAQ.
The exchange known as the Nouveau Marché.
OMLX, the London Securities and Derivatives Exchange Limited.
Oporto Stock Exchange.
Oslo Stock Exchange.
Palermo Stock Exchange.
Paris Stock Exchange.
Rome Stock Exchange.
Securities Exchange of Iceland.
Stockholm Stock Exchange.
Stuttgart Stock Exchange.
Tradepoint Financial Networks plc.
Trieste Stock Exchange.
Turin Stock Exchange.
Valencia Stock Exchange.
Venice Stock Exchange.
Vienna Stock Exchange.

SOURCES OF AMENDMENTS

The text of the legislation set out in this book is the text in force on 29 July 1998. Where this differs from the text as originally enacted, the following list identifies the legislation which made the amendment or repeal which has been taken into account. The list does not include amendments made before a repeal, unless necessary to identify what has been repealed. The following abbreviations are used: CA89 = Companies Act 1989; CDDA86 = Company Directors Disqualification Act 1986; FSA86 = Financial Services Act 1986; IA85 = Insolvency Act 1985; IA86 = Insolvency Act 1986. A reference in the form 1992/1699 is to a statutory instrument number (or, before 1948, statutory rules and orders number).

Partnership Act 1890
S. 3: Decimal Currency Act 1969, s. 10(1). **S. 9:** 1923/405, art. 2. **S. 22:** repealed by Trusts of Land and Appointment of Trustees Act 1996, sch. 4. **S. 23(1):** Statute Law Revision Act 1908. **S. 23(2):** Courts Act 1971, sch. 11, part II. **S. 35(a):** repealed by Mental Health Act 1959, sch. 8. **S. 36(2):** 1921/1804, art. 7; 1923/405, art. 2. **S. 47:** omitted (applies to Scotland only). **Ss. 48, 49 and sch.:** repealed by Statute Law Revision Act 1908.

Stock Transfer Act 1963
S. 1(4)(b)–(e): omitted. **S. 2(2) and (3):** Companies Consolidation (Consequential Provisions) Act 1985, sch. 2; see note at end of section. **S. 2(4):** omitted (applies to Scotland only and has been repealed there by Requirements of Writing (Scotland) Act 1995, sch. 5). **S. 3(5):** Stock Exchange (Completion of Bargains) Act 1976, s. 6. **S. 4(1):** definitions of terms not used in provisions printed in this book omitted. **S. 5:** omitted (applies to Northern Ireland only). **S. 6(2):** omitted.

Companies Act 1985
S. 1(3A): 1992/1699, sch., para. 1. **S. 2(6):** omitted words apply to Scotland only and have been repealed there by Requirements of Writing (Scotland) Act 1995, sch. 5. **S. 3A:** CA89, s. 110(1). **S. 4:** CA89, s. 110(2). **S. 7(3):** omitted words apply to Scotland only and have been repealed there by Requirements of Writing (Scotland) Act 1995, sch. 5. **S. 8A:** CA89, s. 128. **S. 13(4):** IA86, sch. 13, part I. **S. 21:** repealed by Welsh Language Act 1993, s. 30(2) and sch. 2. **S. 23:** CA89, s. 129(1); 1990/1392, art. 8; 1990/1707, art. 8(2); 1997/2306, regs 2 and 3. **S. 24:** 1990/1699, sch., para. 2. **S. 26:** 1996/2827, sch. 8, para. 4. **Ss. 35, 35A, 35B:** CA89, s. 108(1); Charities Act 1993, sch. 6, para. 20. **S. 36:** CA89, s. 130(1). **S. 36A:** CA89, s. 130(2). **S. 36B:** omitted (applies to Scotland only; inserted by CA89, s. 130(3), and substituted by Law Reform (Miscellaneous Provisions) (Scotland) Act 1990, s. 72(1); differently worded in Scotland because of Requirements of Writing (Scotland) Act 1995, sch. 4, para. 51). **S. 36C:** CA89, s. 130(4). **S. 38(1):** words inserted by CA89, sch. 17, para. 1, were repealed by Law Reform (Miscellaneous Provisions) Scotland Act 1990, sch. 8, para. 33(2) and sch. 9. **S. 38(2):** CA89, sch. 17, para. 1. **S. 38(3):** omitted (extends to Scotland only). **S. 39(1) and (2):** CA89, sch. 17, para. 2. **S. 39(2A):** omitted (extends

to Scotland only). **S. 39(3):** words inserted by CA89, sch. 17, para. 2(4), were repealed by Law Reform (Miscellaneous Provisions) Scotland Act 1990, sch. 8, para. 33(3) and sch. 9; differently worded in Scotland because of Requirements of Writing (Scotland) Act 1995, sch. 4, para. 53(b). **S. 40:** CA89, sch. 17, para. 3; differently worded in Scotland because of Requirements of Writing (Scotland) Act 1995, sch. 4, para. 54. **S. 41:** CA89, sch. 17, para. 4. **S. 44(7):** IA86, sch. 13, part I. **S. 46:** CA89, sch. 10, para. 1. **Ss. 56–79:** repealed by FSA86, sch. 17; see notes after ss. 58 and 62. **S. 60(8):** 1991/2000, reg. 5(1). **S. 80:** CA89, s. 115(1). **S. 80A:** CA89, s. 115(1). **Ss. 81–7:** see note after s. 81. **S. 97:** see note after s. 81; amendments made by FSA86, sch. 16, para. 16, were never brought into force and were repealed by 1995/1537, sch. 2, para. 5(e). **S. 103(7):** IA86, sch. 13, part I. **S. 111A:** CA89, s. 131(1). **S. 131(1):** CA89, sch. 19, para. 1. **S. 131(7):** IA86, sch. 13, part I. **S. 140(2):** IA86, sch. 13, part I. **S. 153(3)(f):** IA86, sch. 13, part I. **S. 153(3)(g):** IA85, sch. 6, para. 8; IA86, sch. 13, part I. **S. 153(4)(b):** CA89, s. 132. **S. 153(4)(bb):** FSA86, s. 196(2). **S. 153(5):** FSA86, s. 196(3); CA89, sch. 18, para. 33(3). **S. 156(3):** IA86, sch. 13, part I. **S. 159A:** CA89, s. 133(2). **S. 160:** CA89, s. 133(3). **S. 161:** repealed by Finance Act 1988, sch. 14, part XI. **S. 162:** CA89, s. 133(4). **S. 163:** FSA86, sch. 16, para. 17. **S. 169(5):** CA89, s. 143(2) and sch. 24. **S. 171(5):** 1997/220, reg. 7(1). **S. 173(4):** IA86, sch. 13, part I. **S. 175(6):** IA86, sch. 13, part I. **S. 178(7):** repealed by IA85, sch. 10, part II. **S. 182(1):** 1995/3272, reg. 40(1). **S. 183:** 1995/3272, reg. 40(2). **S. 185(4):** FSA86, s. 194(5). **S. 186:** CA89, sch. 17, para. 5; Law Reform (Miscellaneous Provisions) (Scotland) Act 1990, sch. 8, para. 33(4) and sch. 9; differently worded in Scotland because of Requirements of Writing (Scotland) Act 1995, sch. 4, para. 55. **S. 188:** CA89, sch. 17, para. 6; Law Reform (Miscellaneous Provisions) (Scotland) Act 1990, sch. 8, para. 33(5) and sch. 9; differently worded in Scotland because of Requirements of Writing (Scotland) Act 1995, sch. 4, para. 56. **S. 191:** CA89, s. 143(4) and sch. 24. **S. 196:** IA86, sch. 13, part I. **S. 197:** omitted (applies to Scotland only). **S. 198:** 1993/1819, reg. 3. **S. 199:** 1993/1819, reg. 4; 1996/2827, sch. 8, para. 5. **S. 200:** 1993/1819, reg. 5. **S. 201:** repealed by CA89, sch. 24. **S. 202(1):** CA89, s. 134(3) and sch. 24. **S. 202(2):** 1993/1819, reg. 6(1). **S. 202(2A) and (2B):** 1993/1819, reg. 6(2). **S. 202(4):** CA89, s. 134(3). **S. 203(1):** In Scotland the words 'pupil or minor' are replaced by 'person under the age of 18 years' by Age of Legal Capacity (Scotland) Act 1991, sch. 1, para. 39. **S. 206(3), (3A) and (3B):** 1993/1819, reg. 7. **S. 206(8):** CA89, s. 134(3). **S. 209:** 1993/1819, reg. 8. **S. 209(1):** 1996/2827, sch. 8, para. 6. **S. 209(2):** 1993/2689. **S. 209(9A) and (9B):** 1996/1560, reg. 2. **S. 209(10)(b):** Church of Scotland (Properties and Investments) Order Confirmation Act 1994, sch., para. 42(1). **S. 209(10)(d):** repealed by Law of Property (Miscellaneous Provisions) Act 1994, sch. 2. **S. 210(5A):** 1991/1646, reg. 3. **S. 210A:** CA89, s. 134(5). **S. 211(9):** CA89, sch. 10, para. 3. **S. 215(4):** CA89, sch. 10, para. 3. **S. 216:** 1991/1646, reg. 4. **S. 219:** CA89, s. 143(5) and sch. 24. **S. 220(1):** 1993/1819, reg. 9; 1996/2827, sch. 8, para. 7. **Ss. 221–62A:** CA89, s. 1. **Ss. 221–2:** CA89, s. 2. **Ss. 223–5:** CA89, s. 3. **S. 224:** 1990/355, art. 15; 1996/189, reg. 2. **S. 225:** 1996/189, reg. 3. **S. 226:** CA89, s. 4(1). **S. 227:** CA89, s. 5(1). **Ss. 228–9:** CA89, s. 5(3). **S. 228(2)(b):** 1992/3178, reg. 4; 1993/3246, sch. 2, para. 1. **S. 228(2)(d):** repealed by 1996/189, reg. 4. **S. 228(2)(f):** Welsh Language Act 1993, s. 30(3). **S. 230:** CA89, s. 5(4). **S. 231:** CA89, s. 6(1); 1993/1820, reg. 11(1); 1996/189, reg. 15(1). **S. 232:** CA89, s. 6(3). **S. 233:** CA89, s. 7. **Ss. 234 and 234A:** CA89, s. 8(1). **S. 234:** 1996/189, reg. 5; 1997/571, reg. 2(1). **Ss. 235–7:** CA89, s. 9. **S. 237(4A):** 1996/189, reg. 6. **Ss. 238–40:** CA89, s. 10. **S. 240:** 1994/1935, sch. 1, para. 1. **Ss. 241–4:** CA89, s. 11. **S. 242(1):** Welsh Language Act 1993, s. 30(4); words inserted by 1992/1083, reg. 2(2), were repealed by Welsh Language Act 1993, sch. 2. **S. 242B:** 1992/2452, reg. 3. **S. 243(4):** Welsh Language Act 1993, s. 30(4); words inserted by 1992/1083, reg. 2(3), were repealed by Welsh Language Act 1993, sch. 2. **Ss. 245, 245A, 245B and 245C:** CA89, s. 12. **S. 245:**

1994/1935, sch. 1, para. 1(2). **Ss. 246 and 247:** CA89, s. 13(1). **S. 246:** 1997/220, reg. 2(1); 1997/570, reg. 6(1). **S. 246A:** 1997/220, reg. 3. **S. 247(2) and (3):** 1992/2452, reg. 5. **S. 247(5):** 1997/220, reg. 7(2). **S. 247(6):** 1996/189, reg. 8. **S. 247A:** 1997/220, reg. 4. **S. 247B:** 1997/220, reg. 5. **Ss. 248 and 249:** CA89, s. 13(3). **S. 248(3) and (4):** repealed by 1996/189, reg. 9. **S. 248A:** 1997/220, reg. 6. **S. 249:** 1992/2452, reg. 6. **S. 249A:** 1994/1935, reg. 2; 1997/936, reg. 2. **S. 249B:** 1994/1935, reg. 2; 1996/189, reg. 10; 1997/936, reg. 3. **Ss. 249C and 249D:** omitted. **S. 249E:** 1994/1935, reg. 2. **S. 249E(2):** omitted. **S. 250:** CA89, s. 14; 1992/3003, reg. 2; 1996/189, reg. 11(2); 1997/220, reg. 7(4). **S. 251:** CA89, s. 15; 1992/3003, reg. 3. **Ss. 252–3:** CA89, s. 16. **S. 254:** CA89, s. 17; 1991/2705, sch. 2, para. 1; 1993/1820, reg. 10; 1993/3246, sch. 2, para. 2. **Ss. 255, 255A and 255B:** omitted. **S. 255C:** repealed by 1993/3246, sch. 2, para. 3. **S. 255D:** omitted. **S. 255E:** repealed by Welsh Language Act 1993, s. 35(2). **S. 256:** CA89, s. 19. **S. 257:** CA89, s. 20. **S. 258:** CA89, s. 21. **Ss. 259–62A:** CA89, s. 22. **S. 260(6):** 1991/2705, reg. 2; 1993/3246, sch. 2, para. 4; 1997/220, reg. 4(5). **S. 262(1):** 1992/3178, reg. 7; words inserted by 1996/189, reg. 12(1), were repealed by 1997/2306, reg. 4(2). **S. 262A:** 1991/2705, sch. 2, para. 3; 1994/233, reg. 4(2); 1993/3246, sch. 2, para. 5; 1994/1935, sch. 1, para. 3; 1997/220, reg. 7(6); words inserted by 1996/189, reg. 12(2), were repealed by 1997/2306, reg. 4(4). **S. 265:** FSA86, sch. 16, para. 19. **S. 266(4):** Finance Act 1988, s. 117(3). **S. 268:** omitted. **S. 269(2):** 1997/220, reg. 7(7). **S. 271:** CA89, sch. 10, para. 4. **S. 272(3):** CA89, sch. 10, para. 5. **S. 272(5):** CA89, sch. 10, para. 6; Welsh Language Act 1993, s. 30(4). **S. 273(7):** CA89, sch. 10, para. 6; Welsh Language Act 1993, s. 30(4). **S. 276:** CA89, sch. 10, para. 7; 1997/220, reg. 7(8). **S. 279:** omitted. **S. 287:** CA89, s. 136. **S. 288(3):** CA89, s. 143(6) and sch. 24. **S. 289(1) and (2):** CA89, sch. 19, para. 2. **S. 289(4):** CA89, sch. 10, para. 9. **S. 290:** CA89, sch. 19, para. 3. **Ss. 295–9:** repealed by CDDA86, sch. 4. **S. 300:** repealed by IA85, sch. 10, part II. **Ss. 301–2:** repealed by CDDA86, sch. 4. **S. 305:** CA89, sch. 19, para. 4. **S. 310(3):** CA89, s. 137(1). **S. 318(7):** CA89, s. 143(7) and sch. 24. **S. 320(2):** 1990/1393. **S. 321(4):** CA89, sch. 19, para. 8. **S. 322A:** CA89, s. 109(1). **S. 322B:** 1992/1699, sch., para. 3(1). **S. 327(2)(b):** In Scotland the words 'pupil or minor' are replaced by 'person under the age of 18 years' by Age of Legal Capacity (Scotland) Act 1991, sch. 1, para. 39. **S. 328(8):** In Scotland the words 'pupil or minor' are replaced by 'person under the age of 18 years' by Age of Legal Capacity (Scotland) Act 1991, sch. 1, para. 39. **S. 329(1):** FSA86, sch. 16, para. 20. **S. 331(5):** repealed by Banking Act 1987, sch. 7, part 1. **S. 332(1)(b):** CA89, s. 138(a). **S. 334:** CA89, s. 138(b). **S. 335(1):** 1990/1393. **S. 337(3):** 1990/1393. **S. 338(4):** Banking Act 1987, sch. 6, para. 18(6); CA89, sch. 10, para. 10; CA89, s. 138(c). **S. 338(6):** CA89, s. 138(c). **S. 339(4):** Banking Act 1987, sch. 6, para. 18(6); CA89, sch. 10, para. 10. **S. 340(7):** 1990/1393. **Ss. 343 and 344:** omitted. **S. 350(1):** CA89, sch. 17, para. 7. **S. 351(3), (4) and (5)(c):** repealed by Welsh Language Act 1993, s. 31 and sch. 2. **S. 352A:** 1992/1699, sch., para. 4(1). **S. 356:** CA89, sch. 24 and s. 143(8). **S. 362:** omitted. **Ss. 363–5:** CA89, s. 139(1). **S. 363(5):** 1990/1707, art 7. **S. 366A:** CA89, s. 115(2). **S. 368(8):** CA89, sch. 19, para. 9. **S. 369(4):** CA89, s. 115(3). **S. 370A:** 1992/1699, sch., para. 5. **S. 378(3):** CA89, s. 115(3). **S. 379A:** CA89, s. 116(2). **S. 379A(2A):** 1996/1471, art. 2. **S. 380(4)(bb):** CA89, s. 116(3). **S. 380(4)(j):** IA86, sch. 13, part I. **S. 380(4)(l) and (m):** 1995/3272, reg. 40(3). **Ss. 381A–C:** CA89, s. 113(2). **S. 381A(5):** 1996/1471, art. 3(2)(a). **S. 381B:** 1996/1471, art. 3. **S. 381C(1):** 1996/1471, art. 4. **S. 382A:** CA89, s. 113(3). **S. 382B:** 1992/1699, sch., para. 6(1). **S. 383:** CA89, s. 143(9) and sch. 24. **Ss. 384–8A:** CA89, s. 119(1). **S. 384(1):** 1994/1935, sch. 1, para. 4. **S. 388A:** 1994/1935, reg. 3. **S. 389:** repealed by CA89, sch. 24. **Ss. 389A and 390:** CA89, s. 120(1). **S. 390(2):** 1996/1471, art. 3(2). **Ss. 390A and 390B:** CA89, s. 121. **Ss. 391–3:** CA89, s. 122(1). **Ss. 394 and 394A:** CA89, s. 123(1). **S. 395(1):** IA85, sch. 6, para. 10. **S. 396:** Copyright, Designs and Patents Act 1988, sch. 7, para. 31(2); Trade Marks Act 1994, sch. 5. **Ss. 409–24:** omitted (ss. 410–24 apply to Scotland only). **S. 425(1):** IA85, sch. 6, para. 11. **S. 425(5):** omitted (applies to Scotland only; differently worded in Scotland because of Court of Session Act 1988, sch. 2). **S. 426(6):** IA85, sch. 6, para. 12. **S. 427A:** omitted. **Ss. 428–30F:** FSA86, s. 172 and sch. 12. **S. 432(2A):** CA89, s. 55. **S. 433(2):** repealed by FSA86, sch. 13, para. 7. **S. 434:** CA89, s. 56(2)–(5). **S. 435:** repealed by CA89, sch. 24. **S. 436(1):** CA89, s. 56(6). **S. 437(1A):** FSA86, sch. 13, para. 7. **S. 437(1B) and (1C):** CA89, s. 57. **S. 438(1):** CA89, s. 58. **S. 439:** CA89, s. 59. **S. 440:** repealed by CA89, s. 60(1) and sch. 24. **S. 441(1):** CA89, s. 61; IA85, sch. 6, para. 3; IA86, sch. 13, part I. **S. 442(3)–(3C):** CA89, s. 62. **S. 443(4):** repealed by CA89, sch. 24. **S. 445:** 1991/1646, reg. 5. **S. 446(3):** FSA86, sch. 13, para. 8(a); CA 89, sch. 24. **S. 446(4):** FSA86, sch. 16, para. 21. **S. 446(5) and (6):** repealed by FSA86, sch. 17, part I. **S. 446(7):** repealed by CA89, sch. 24. **S. 447(1):** repealed by CA89, s. 63 and sch. 24. **S. 448:** CA89, s. 64(1). **S. 449(1):** CA89, s. 65(2) and sch. 24; FSA86, sch. 13, para. 9(1); IA85, sch. 6, para. 4; IA86, sch. 13, part I; 1994/1696, sch. 8, para. 9(2); 1992/1315, sch. 4, para. 1; Criminal Justice Act 1993, sch. 5, para. 4(2); FSA86, sch. 17, part I; Friendly Societies Act 1992, sch. 21, para. 7(1); Pensions Act 1995, sch. 3, para. 12; Banking Act 1987, sch. 6, para. 18(7); Bank of England Act 1998, sch. 5, para. 62. **S. 449(1A)–(1D):** FSA86, sch. 13, para. 9(2). **S. 449(1A):** CA89, s. 65(3). **S. 449(1B):** CA89, s. 65(4). **S. 449(2):** CA89, s. 65(5). **S. 449(3) and (3A):** CA89, s. 65(6); Friendly Societies Act 1992, sch. 21, para. 7(2) and sch. 22; Bank of England Act 1998, sch. 5, para. 62. **S. 449(4):** FSA86, sch. 13, para. 9(3); CA89, s. 65(7). **S. 450:** CA89, s. 66. **S. 451:** CA89, s. 67. **S. 451A:** CA89, s. 68; 1994/1696, sch. 8, para. 9(3). **S. 452:** CA89, s. 69; 1994/1696, sch. 8, para. 9(4). **S. 453:** CA89, s. 70. **S. 454:** 1991/1646, reg. 6; CA89, sch. 19, para. 10(2). **S. 455:** 1991/1646, reg. 7. **S. 456:** 1991/1646, reg. 8; CA89, sch. 19, para. 10(1). **S. 459(1):** CA89, sch. 19, para. 11. **S. 459(3):** Water Act 1989, sch. 25, para. 71(3); Water Consolidation (Consequential Provisions) Act 1991, sch. 1, para. 40(2); s. 459(3) extends to England and Wales only. **S. 460:** 1994/1696, sch. 8, para. 9(5); CA89, sch. 19, para. 11 and sch. 24. **S. 461(6):** IA85, sch. 6, para. 24; IA86, sch. 13, part I. **Ss. 462–6:** omitted (extend to Scotland only). **Ss. 467–85:** repealed by IA86, sch. 12. **Ss. 486–7:** omitted (extend to Scotland only). **Ss. 488–94:** repealed by IA86, sch. 12. **Ss. 495–7:** repealed by IA85, sch. 10, part II. **Ss. 498–525:** repealed by IA86, sch. 12. **Ss. 526–31:** repealed by IA85, sch. 10, part II. **S. 532:** repealed by IA86, sch. 12. **Ss. 533–4:** repealed by IA85, sch. 10, part II. **S. 535:** repealed by IA86, sch. 12. **S. 536:** repealed by IA85, sch. 10, part II. **Ss. 537–40:** repealed by IA86, sch. 12. **Ss. 541–3:** repealed by IA85, sch. 10, part II. **S. 544:** repealed by IA85, sch. 10, part I. **Ss. 545–8:** repealed by IA85, sch. 10, part II. **Ss. 549–50:** repealed by IA86, sch. 12. **S. 551:** repealed by IA85, sch. 10, part II. **Ss. 552–5:** repealed by IA86, sch. 12. **S. 556:** repealed by IA85, sch. 10, part II. **Ss. 557–60:** repealed by IA86, sch. 12. **S. 561:** repealed by IA85, sch. 10, part II. **S. 562:** repealed by IA86, sch. 12. **Ss. 563–4:** repealed by IA85, sch. 10, part II. **Ss. 565–7:** repealed by IA86, sch. 12. **S. 568:** repealed by IA85, sch. 10, part II. **S. 569:** repealed by IA86, sch. 12. **S. 570:** repealed by IA85, sch. 10, part IV. **Ss. 571–82:** repealed by IA86, sch. 12. **S. 583:** repealed by IA85, sch. 10, part II. **Ss. 584–5:** repealed by IA86, sch. 12. **S. 586:** repealed by IA85, sch. 10, part II. **S. 587:** repealed by IA86, sch. 12. **S. 588:** repealed by IA85, sch. 10, part II. **Ss. 589–600:** repealed by IA86, sch. 12. **S. 601:** repealed by IA85, sch. 10, part II. **Ss. 602–5:** repealed by IA86, sch. 12. **Ss. 606–15:** repealed by IA85, sch. 10, part II. **S. 615A and 615B:** repealed by IA86, sch. 12. **Ss. 616–18:** repealed by IA85, sch. 10, part II. **S. 619:** repealed by IA86, sch. 12. **S. 620:** repealed by IA85, sch. 10, part II. **Ss. 621–30:** repealed by IA86, sch. 12. **S. 631:** repealed by IA85, sch. 10, part II. **Ss. 632–3:** repealed by IA86, sch. 12. **S. 634:** repealed by IA85, sch. 10, part II. **Ss. 635–9:** repealed by IA86, sch. 12. **S. 640:** repealed by IA85, sch. 10, part II. **S. 641:** repealed by IA86, sch. 12. **S. 642:** repealed by IA85, sch. 10, part II. **Ss. 643–50:** repealed by IA86, sch. 12. **S. 651(1):** CA89, sch. 24. **S. 651(4)–(7):** CA89, s. 141(3). **Ss. 652A–F:** Deregulation and Contracting Out Act 1994, sch. 5, para. 2. **S. 653:** Deregulation and Contracting Out Act 1994, sch. 5, para. 3. **S. 657(2):** IA85, sch. 6, para. 46; IA86, sch. 13, part I. **S. 658(1):** IA85, sch. 6, para. 47; IA86, sch. 13, part I. **Ss. 659–74:** repealed by IA86, sch. 12. **Ss. 676–8:** omitted. **Ss. 680–97:** omitted. **S. 698:** 1992/3179, sch. 2, para. 13; definitions of terms not used in provisions printed in this book omitted. **Ss. 699–703R:** omitted. **S. 704(7) and (8):** Deregulation and Contracting Out Act 1994, sch. 16, para. 8. **S. 705:** CA89, sch. 19, para. 14; 1992/3179, sch. 3, para. 5. **S. 705A:** omitted. **S. 706:** CA89, s. 125(1); 1992/3179, sch. 3, para. 6. **S. 707:** CA89, s. 125(2); 1992/3179, sch. 3, para. 6. **S. 707A:** CA89, s. 126(1). **S. 708:** CA89, s. 127(2) and sch. 24. **Ss. 709, 710, 710A:** CA89, s. 126(2). **S. 709(3):** Civil Evidence Act 1995, sch. 1, para. 10. **S. 710B:** Welsh Language Act 1993, s. 30(6). **S. 711(1):** CA89, sch. 10, para. 14; 1987/1991, reg. 2(b); 1992/3179, sch. 3, para. 7. **S. 711(2):** IA86, sch. 13, part I. **S. 712:** repealed by CA89, s. 127(3) and sch. 24. **S. 713:** CA89, s. 127(4). **S. 714:** 1992/3179, sch. 3, para. 8. **S. 715:** repealed by CA89, s. 127(3) and sch. 24. **S. 715A:** CA89, s. 127(1). **S. 716(2):** 1991/1997, sch., para. 53; CA89, sch. 19, para. 15(2); 1996/2827, sch. 8, para. 8; amendment made by FSA86, sch. 16, para. 22 repealed by CA89, sch. 19, para. 15(2) and sch. 24. **S. 716(3) and (4):** CA89, sch. 19, para. 15(3). **Ss. 717 and 718:** omitted. **Ss. 720 and 721:** omitted. **S. 723A:** CA89, s. 143(1). **S. 724:** repealed by IA86, sch. 12. **S. 730(5):** CA89, sch. 19, para. 17. **S. 731(3):** Criminal Procedure (Consequential Provisions) (Scotland) Act 1995, sch. 4, para. 56(3). **S. 733:** IA85, sch. 6, para. 7; IA86, sch. 13, part I; CA89, s. 123(3) and sch. 24. **S. 734(1):** CA89, s. 120(2) and s. 123(4). **S. 734(4):** Criminal Procedure (Consequential Provisions) (Scotland) Act 1995, sch. 4, para. 56(4). **S. 734(5) and (6):** CA89, sch. 19, para. 18. **S. 735A:** IA86, sch. 13, part II; CA89, s. 127(5) and sch. 24; Deregulation and Contracting Out Act 1994, sch. 16, para. 9. **S. 735B:** CA89, s. 127(6); Deregulation and Contracting Out Act 1994, sch. 16, para. 10. **Ss. 736 and 736A:** CA89, s. 144(1). **S. 736B:** CA89, s. 144(3). **S. 741(3):** 1992/1699, sch., para. 3(2). **S. 742:** CA89, sch. 10, para. 15. **S. 743A:** omitted (applies to Scotland only). **S. 744:** CA89, sch. 10, para. 16 and sch. 24; Criminal Justice Act 1993, sch. 5, para. 4(1) and (2); IA85, sch. 10, part II; Banking Act 1987, sch. 7, part I; FSA86, sch. 17, part I; 1997/2306, reg. 4(1). **S. 744A:** CA89, sch. 19, para. 20; Criminal Justice Act 1993, sch. 5, para. 4(2); 1997/2306, reg. 4(3). **S. 746:** CA89, sch. 24. **Sch. 1:** CA89, sch. 10, para. 17 and sch. 19, para. 7. **Sch. 2:** omitted. **Sch. 3:** see note in text. **Sch. 4, para. 3(7):** 1996/189, sch. 1, para. 2. **Sch. 4, part I, section B:** CA89, sch. 1, paras 2–4; 1996/189, sch. 1, para. 3. **Sch. 4, para. 11:** CA89, sch. 1, para. 5. **Sch. 4, para. 12:** CA89, sch. 10, para. 20. **Sch. 4, para. 34:** CA89, sch. 1, para. 6; 1996/189, sch. 1, para. 4. **Sch. 4, paras 35–59A:** omitted. **Sch. 4, paras 60–9:** repealed by CA89, sch. 24. **Sch. 4, paras 71–3:** omitted. **Sch. 4, paras 74, 75 and 77–81:** repealed by CA89, sch. 24. **Sch. 4, para. 84:** FSA86, sch. 16, para. 23(b). **Sch. 4, paras 87 and 90–2:** repealed by CA89, sch. 24. **Sch. 4, para. 94:** 1996/189, sch. 1, para. 16. **Sch. 4, para. 95:** repealed by CA89, sch. 24. **Schedules 4A and 5:** omitted. **Sch. 6 title:** CA89, sch. 4, para. 2. **Sch. 6, paras 1–14:** CA89, sch. 4, para. 3; 1997/570. **Sch. 6, paras 15–30:** omitted. **Sch. 7, para. 1:** 1996/189, regs 14(4)(a) and 15(3). **Sch. 7, paras 2, 2A and 2B:** CA89, sch. 5, para. 3. **Sch. 7, para. 5A:** inserted by CA89, s. 137(2), repealed by 1996/189, reg. 14(4)(b). **Sch. 7, para. 6:** CA89, sch. 5, para. 2(2); 1992/3178, reg. 3. **Sch. 7, para. 9:** Disability Discrimination Act 1995, sch. 6, para. 4. **Sch. 7, para. 10:** repealed by 1996/189, reg. 14(4)(c). **Sch. 7, para. 12:** 1996/189, reg. 14(5); 1997/571, reg. 2(2). **Schedules 8, 9 and 9A:** omitted. **Sch. 10:** repealed by 1993/3246, sch. 2, para. 7. **Sch. 10A:** CA89, s. 21(2) and sch. 9. **Sch. 11:** omitted. **Sch. 12:** repealed by CDDA86, sch. 4. **Schedules 13 and 14:** omitted. **Sch. 15:** repealed by CA89, sch. 24. **Sch. 15A:** CA89, s. 114(1). **Sch. 15B:** omitted.

Sch. 16: repealed by IA86, sch. 12. **Schedules 17, 18, 19 and 20, part I:** repealed by IA85, sch. 10, part II. **Sch. 20, part II:** omitted (applies to Scotland only). **Schedules 21, 21A, 21B, 21C, 21D, 22 and 23:** omitted. **Sch. 24:** Statute Law (Repeals) Act 1993, sch. 1, part XIV, group 2; FSA86, sch. 16, para. 27 and sch. 17; CA89, ss. 63(8), 64(2), 119(2), 120(3), 122(2), 123(2) and 139(3), sch. 10, para. 24 and sch. 24; CDDA86, sch. 4; 1992/1699, sch., paras 3(3), 4(2) and 6(2); 1996/1471, art. 3(2)(c); IA85, sch. 10, parts I and II; IA86, sch. 12; Deregulation and Contracting Out Act 1994, sch. 5, para. 4; omitted entries relate to sections of Act not printed in this book; see also note at end of schedule. **Sch. 25:** omitted.

Business Names Act 1985

S. 8(1): Statute Law (Repeals) Act 1993, sch. 1, part XIV, group 2.

Insolvency Act 1986

S. 8(4): Banking Act 1987, sch. 6, para. 25(1). **S. 9(1):** Criminal Justice Act 1988, s. 62(2). **S. 16:** omitted (applies only to Scotland). **S. 19:** Insolvency Act 1994, s. 1. **S. 44:** Insolvency Act 1994, s. 2. **Ss. 50–71:** omitted (extend to Scotland only). **S. 113:** omitted (applies to Scotland only). **Ss. 120–1:** omitted (apply to Scotland only). **S. 122(1):** 1992/1699, sch., para. 8. **S. 124(1):** Criminal Justice Act 1988, s. 62(2). **S. 124(4):** CA89, s. 60(2). **S. 124A:** CA89, s. 60(3). **Ss. 138, 142, 157 and 161–2:** omitted (apply to Scotland only). **S. 168(5A)–(5C):** omitted. **S. 169:** omitted (applies to Scotland only). **S. 184(3):** 1986/1996, art. 2 and sch. part I. **Ss. 190–1:** omitted. **S. 193:** omitted (applies to Scotland only). **Ss. 196–200:** omitted. **S. 204:** omitted (applies to Scotland only). **S. 206(1):** 1986/1996, art. 2 and sch. part I. **S. 218(5):** CA89, s. 78. **Ss. 220–9:** omitted. **S. 233(3):** Electricity Act 1989, sch. 16, para. 35(2)(a); Water Act 1989, sch. 25, para. 78(1). **S. 233(5):** Electricity Act 1989, sch. 16, para. 35(2)(b); Broadcasting Act 1990, sch. 20, para. 43. **S. 241:** Insolvency (No. 2) Act 1994, s. 1. **Ss. 242–3:** omitted (apply to Scotland only). **Ss. 252–385:** omitted. **S. 386(1):** Finance Act 1994, sch. 7, para. 7(2); Finance Act 1996, sch. 5, para. 12; Finance Act 1991, sch. 2, para 21A (inserted by Finance (No. 2) Act 1992, s. 9(2)); Finance Act 1993, s. 36(1); 1987/2093, reg. 2(2). **S. 386(3):** Pension Schemes Act 1993, sch. 8, para. 18. **S. 387(5) and (6) and ss. 388–422:** omitted. **Ss. 426–9:** omitted. **S. 431(3):** Criminal Procedure (Consequential Provisions) (Scotland) Act 1995, sch. 4, para. 61. **S. 436:** definitions (added by 1994/2421, art. 2(1) and (2)) not relevant to provisions printed in this book are omitted. **Ss. 437–42:** omitted. **Schedules 2, 3 and 5:** omitted. **Sch. 6, paras 1 and 2:** Income and Corporation Taxes Act 1988, sch. 29, para. 32. **Sch. 6, para. 3:** Value Added Tax Act 1994, sch. 14, para. 8. **Sch. 6, para. 3A:** Finance Act 1994, sch. 7, para. 7(2). **Sch. 6, para. 3B:** Finance Act 1996, sch. 5, para. 12. **Sch. 6, para. 5:** Finance Act 1997, sch. 2, para. 6 and sch. 18, part II. **Sch. 6, para. 5A:** Finance Act 1991, sch. 2, para. 22. **Sch. 6, para. 5B:** Finance Act 1993, s. 36(2). **Sch. 6, para. 5C:** Finance Act 1994, sch. 6, para. 13(1). **Sch. 6, para. 6:** Social Security (Consequential Provisions) Act 1992, sch. 2, para. 73. **Sch. 6, para. 8:** Pension Schemes Act 1993, sch. 8, para. 18. **Sch. 6, para. 13(2):** Employment Rights Act 1996, sch. 1, para. 29. **Sch. 6, para. 15A:** 1987/2093, reg. 2(1). **Schedules 7, 8 and 9:** omitted. **Sch. 10:** Statute Law (Repeals) Act 1993, sch. 1, part XIV, group 2; entries relating to sections not printed in this book omitted; see also note at end of schedule. **Schedules 11–14:** omitted.

Company Directors Disqualification Act 1986

S. 2(1): Deregulation and Contracting Out Act 1994, sch. 11, para. 6. **S. 3(3):** CA89, sch. 10, para. 35. **S. 8(1):** FSA86, s. 198(2); Criminal Justice Act 1988, s. 145(b); Criminal Justice (Scotland) Act 1987, s. 55(b); Criminal Procedure (Consequential Provisions) (Scotland) Act 1995, sch. 4, para. 62; CA89, s. 79. **S. 19:** omitted. **S. 21(4):** omitted (applies to Scotland only). **Ss. 22A, 22B and 23:** omitted. **Sch. 1, para. 4:**

CA89, s. 139(4); see note at end of paragraph. **Sch. 1, para. 5:** CA89, sch. 10, para. 35(3). **Sch. 1, para. 5A:** omitted. **Schedules 2, 3 and 4:** omitted.

Financial Services Act 1986

Only extracts from this Act are included in this book. The omissions and repeals noted here are only those from the sections or schedules printed. **S. 58:** 1995/1537, sch. 2, para. 6. **S. 75(4)–(6) and (9):** omitted. **S. 114(4)–(12):** omitted. **S. 142:** 1991/2000, reg. 3(1); 1995/1537, sch. 2, para. 1(2). **S. 144(2), (2A) and (2B):** 1995/1537, sch. 2, para. 2(1). **S. 150(6):** CA89, s. 197(1). **S. 152(4A):** omitted. **S. 154(5):** CA89, s. 197(2). **S. 154A:** 1995/1537, sch. 2, para. 2(3). **Ss. 156A and 156B:** 1995/1537, sch. 2, para. 2(4). **S. 157:** repealed by 1991/2000, reg. 3(2). **S. 177:** Criminal Justice Act 1993, sch. 5, para. 9; CA89, s. 74. **S. 178(1) and (6):** Criminal Justice Act 1993, sch. 5, para. 10. **S. 178(10):** 1992/1315, sch. 4, para. 3. **S. 199:** CA89, s. 76; 1995/1537, sch. 2, para. 7; Criminal Justice Act 1993, sch. 5, para. 12; 1992/1315, sch. 4, para. 3. **S. 199(8):** omitted (applies to Scotland only). **S. 199(8A):** omitted (applies to Northern Ireland only). **S. 207(1):** 1995/1537, sch. 2, para. 8; definitions of terms not used in provisions printed in this book omitted. **S. 207(2):** Broadcasting Act 1990, sch. 20, para. 45(1)(a). **S. 207(4):** repealed by Broadcasting Act 1990, sch. 20, para. 45(1)(b). **S. 207(5)–(7), (9) and (11):** omitted ((9) applies to Scotland only). **Sch. 1, para. 1:** 1991/1104, art. 2. **Sch. 1, para. 3:** omitted. **Sch. 1, para. 7:** 1988/496, art. 2. **Sch. 1, para. 9:** 1990/349, art. 2(2). **Sch. 1, para. 10:** omitted. **Sch. 1, para. 12:** 1988/803, art. 2. **Sch. 1, para. 13:** 1988/803, art. 3. Note (3) omitted. **Sch. 1, para. 13A:** 1996/2958, art. 3. **Sch. 1, para. 16:** 1996/2958, art. 2. **Sch. 1, para. 16A:** 1996/1322, art. 2(1); 1997/2543, art. 2. **Sch. 1, paras 17–27 and 29–37:** omitted. **Sch. 11A:** 1995/1537, sch. 2, para. 2(2) and sch. 3.

Companies Act 1989

Only extracts from this Act are included in this book. The omissions and repeals noted here are only those from the sections or schedules printed. Much of the Companies Act 1989 makes amendments to other Acts printed in this book. Where those amendments have been brought into force they have been incorporated in the text of those Acts printed in this book. Amendments which had not been brought into force when this edition went to press and which are not expected to be abandoned are noted at appropriate places in the text of the Companies Act 1985 in this book. **S. 93:** Trade Marks Act 1994, sch. 5. **S. 142(2):** omitted. **Sch. 16, para. 1:** omitted. **Sch. 16, para. 1A:** 1992/3179, sch. 3, para. 16. **Sch. 24:** only entries which have not been brought into force and which relate to provisions printed in this book are included.

SI 1981/1685

Under the Companies Consolidation (Consequential Provisions) Act 1985, s. 31(2), these Regulations are to be treated as made and having effect under the Companies Act 1985, s. 29, and the Business Names Act 1985, s. 3. **Reg. 3:** 1992/1196, reg. 2(2). **Reg. 4:** 1992/1196, reg. 2(3). **Sch.:** 1982/1653, reg. 3; 1992/1196, reg. 2(4) and (5); 1995/3022, reg. 3.

SI 1985/805

Regs 4, 41 and 115: 1985/1052. **Sch., Tables C, D and E:** omitted.

SI 1992/1699

Reg. 2(1)(b) and sch.: omitted (amendments to Companies Act 1985 and Insolvency Act 1986 which have been incorporated in the text of the Acts in this book).

SI 1994/187

Art. 10: 1996/1561, art. 3. **Sch.:** 1996/1561, art. 4.

INDEX

BLACKSTONE'S STATUTES

TITLES IN THE SERIES